PUBLISHING

EXCITING EXTRA ONLINE RESOURCES INCLUDED

Kaplan Publishing are constantly finding new ways to make a difference to your studies and our exciting online resources really do offer something different to ACCA students looking for exam success.

THIS COMPLETE TEXT COMES WITH FREE EN-gage ONLINE RESOURCES SO THAT YOU CAN STUDY ANYTIME, ANYWHERE

Having purchased this Complete Text, you have access to the following online study materials:

- An online version of the Text which allows you to click in and out of the expandable content and view the answers to the Test Your Understanding exercises
- Fixed Online Tests with instant answers
- Test History and Results to allow you to track your performance
- Interim Assessments including Questions and Answers

How to access your online resources

- **Kaplan Financial students** will already have a Kaplan EN-gage account and these extra resources will be available to you online. You do not need to register again, as this process was completed when you enrolled. If you are having problems accessing online materials, please ask your course administrator.
- **If you purchased through Kaplan Flexible Learning or via the Kaplan Publishing website** you will automatically receive an e-mail invitation to Kaplan EN-gage online. Please register your details using this e-mail to gain access to your content. If you do not receive the e-mail or book content, please contact Kaplan Flexible Learning.
- **If you are already a registered Kaplan EN-gage user** go to www.EN-gage.co.uk and log in. Select the 'add a book' feature and enter the ISBN number of this book and the unique pass key at the bottom of this card. Then click 'finished' or 'add another book'. You may add as many books as you have purchased from this screen.
- **If you are a new Kaplan EN-gage user** register at www.EN-gage.co.uk and click on the link contained in the e-mail we sent you to activate your account. Then select the 'add a book' feature, enter the ISBN number of this book and the unique pass key at the bottom of this card. Then click 'finished' or 'add another book'.

<u>Your Code and Information</u>
This code can only be used once for the registration of one book online. This registration will expire when the final sittings for the examinations covered by this book have taken place. Please allow one hour from the time you submitted your book details for us to process your request.

jVGI-AEfy-kn

D1342946

Please be aware that this code is case-s............ ,ou will need to include the dashes within the passcode, but not when entering the ISBN. For further technical support, please visit www.EN-gage.co.uk

ACCA

Paper P2 UK/INT

Corporate Reporting

Complete Text

British library cataloguing-in-publication data

A catalogue record for this book is available from the British Library.

Published by:
Kaplan Publishing UK
Unit 2 The Business Centre
Molly Millars Lane
Wokingham
Berkshire
RG41 2QZ

ISBN: 978-0-85732-143-5

© Kaplan Financial Limited, 2010

Printed in the UK by CPI William Clowes Beccles NR34 7TL.

Acknowledgements

We are grateful to the Association of Chartered Certified Accountants and the Chartered Institute of Management Accountants for permission to reproduce past examination questions. The answers have been prepared by Kaplan Publishing.

Contents

Home

Paper Introduction

How to Use the Materials

The nature of the P2 **Corporate Reporting** exam, is that of a 'pillar topic'. This means that students will need a good understanding of the basics of accounting as covered initially in F3 and then in F7.

The ACCA website www.accaglobal.com includes a useful FAQ section. Within this section the examiner recommends:

> *'It is important that students have done some pre-course work such as attempting as homework a past F7 exam as appropriate revision before starting work on P2. This message applies equally to students who have attempted and passed F7 and to those who have gained an exemption from F7'.*
>
> *P2 examiner – ACCA website*

In light of this Chapter 25 of this text includes 2 pre-tuition questions. They are both past F7 questions.

Pre-tuition test 1: Hanford and Stopple

Pre-tuition test 2: Hepburn and Salter

You must attempt these questions in full (no answers appear in this text) and then log-on to en-gage. www.en-gage.co.uk and answer pre-tuition tests 1 and 2 from your own long-form answer.

A pdf of the full answer is then available to download. If you are not achieving the 50% pass mark at F7 standard, you will find it beneficial to spend time studying chapter 1 of this text in detail.

These Kaplan Publishing learning materials have been carefully designed to make your learning experience as easy as possible and to give you the best chances of success in your examinations.

The product range contains a number of features to help you in the study process. They include:

(1) Detailed study guide and syllabus objectives

(2) Description of the examination

(3) Study skills and revision guidance

(4) Complete text or essential text

(5) Question practice

The sections on the study guide, the syllabus objectives, the examination and study skills should all be read before you commence your studies. They are designed to familiarise you with the nature and content of the examination and give you tips on how to best to approach your learning.

The **complete text or essential text** comprises the main learning materials and gives guidance as to the importance of topics and where other related resources can be found. Each chapter includes:

- The **learning objectives** contained in each chapter, which have been carefully mapped to the examining body's own syllabus learning objectives or outcomes. You should use these to check you have a clear understanding of all the topics on which you might be assessed in the examination.

- The **chapter diagram** provides a visual reference for the content in the chapter, giving an overview of the topics and how they link together.

- The **content** for each topic area commences with a brief explanation or definition to put the topic into context before covering the topic in detail. You should follow your studying of the content with a review of the illustration/s. These are worked examples which will help you to understand better how to apply the content for the topic.

- **Test your understanding** sections provide an opportunity to assess your understanding of the key topics by applying what you have learned to short questions. Answers can be found at the back of each chapter.

- **Summary diagrams** complete each chapter to show the important links between topics and the overall content of the paper. These diagrams should be used to check that you have covered and understood the core topics before moving on.

- **Question practice** is provided through this text.

Icon Explanations

Definition - these sections explain important areas of Knowledge which must be understood and reproduced in an exam environment.

Key Point - identifies topics which are key to success and are often examined.

New - identifies topics that are brand new in papers that build on, and therefore also contain, learning covered in earlier papers.

Expandable Text - within the online version of the work book is a more detailed explanation of key terms, these sections will help to provide a deeper understanding of core areas. Reference to this text is vital when self studying.

Test Your Understanding - following key points and definitions are exercises which give the opportunity to assess the understanding of these core areas. Within the work book the answers to these sections are left blank, explanations to the questions can be found within the online version which can be hidden or shown on screen to enable repetition of activities.

 Illustration - to help develop an understanding of topics and the test your understanding exercises the illustrative examples can be used.

 Exclamation Mark - this symbol signifies a topic which can be more difficult to understand, when reviewing these areas care should be taken.

 Tutorial note - included to explain some of the technical points in more detail.

 Footsteps - helpful tutor tips.

On-line subscribers

Our on-line resources are designed to increase the flexibility of your learning materials and provide you with immediate feedback on how your studies are progressing.

If you are subscribed to our on-line resources you will find:

(1) On-line referenceware: reproduces your Complete or Essential Text on-line, giving you anytime, anywhere access.

(2) On-line testing: provides you with additional on-line objective testing so you can practice what you have learned further.

(3) On-line performance management: immediate access to your on-line testing results. Review your performance by key topics and chart your achievement through the course relative to your peer group.

Ask your local customer services staff if you are not already a subscriber and wish to join.

Paper introduction
Paper background

The aim of ACCA Paper P2 (INT), **Corporate reporting**, is to apply knowledge and skills and to exercise professional judgement in the application and evaluation of financial reporting principles and practices in a range of business contexts and situations.

Objectives of the syllabus

- Discuss the professional and ethical duties of the accountant.

- Evaluate the financial reporting framework.

- Advise on and report the financial performance of entities.

- Prepare the financial statements of groups of entities in accordance with relevant accounting standards.

- Explain reporting issues relating to specialised entities.

- Discuss the implications of changes in accounting regulation on financial reporting.

- Appraise the financial performance and position of entities.

- Evaluate current developments.

Core areas of the syllabus

- The professional and ethical duty of the accountant.

- The financial reporting framework.

- Reporting the financial performance of entities.

- Financial statements of groups of entities.

- Specialised entities and specialised transactions.

- Implications of changes in accounting regulation on financial reporting.

- The appraisal of financial performance and position of entities.

- Current developments.

Approach to INT and UK syllabus elements

Due to the alignment of the UK and INT syllabus elements one text has been produced to address both variants. Both streams apply the principles of International Financial Reporting Standards (IFRS).

The international variant has been used as the basis of the text. Any variances relevant only to the UK syllabus (such as the Companies Act 2006) have been included at the end of the relevant chapter in expandable text boxes headed "UK syllabus focus". All test your understandings (where appropriate) have also been appended to reflect any UK-specific variations.

In principle, the variances consist of the additional requirement to discuss and apply the key differences between UK GAAP and IFRS.

Syllabus objectives

We have reproduced the ACCA's syllabus below, showing where the objectives are explored within this book. Within the chapters, we have broken down the extensive information found in the syllabus into easily digestible and relevant sections, called Content Objectives. These correspond to the objectives at the beginning of each chapter.

Syllabus learning objective / Chapter

A THE PROFESSIONAL AND ETHICAL DUTIES OF THE ACCOUNTANT

1 Professional behaviour and compliance with technical accounting standards

(a) Appraise and discuss the ethical and professional issues in advising on corporate reporting.[3] **Ch. 7**

(b) Assess the relevance and importance of ethical and professional issues in complying with accounting standards.[3] **Ch. 7**

2 Ethical requirements of corporate reporting and the consequences of unethical behaviour

(a) Appraise the potential ethical implications of professional and managerial decisions in the preparation of corporate reports.[3] **Ch. 7**

(b) Assess the consequences of not upholding ethical principles in the preparation of corporate reports.[3] **Ch. 7**

3 Social responsibility

(a) Discuss the increased demand for transparency in corporate reports, and the emergence of non-financial reporting standards.[3] **Ch. 19**

(b) Discuss the progress towards a framework for environmental and sustainability reporting.[3] **Ch. `19**

B THE FINANCIAL REPORTING FRAMEWORK

1 The applications, strengths and weaknesses of an accounting framework

(a) Evaluate the valuation models adopted by standard setters.[3] **Ch. 8**

(b) Discuss the use of an accounting framework in underpinning the production of accounting standards.[3] **Ch. 8**

(c) Assess the success of such a framework in introducing rigorous and consistent accounting standards.[3] **Ch. 8**

2 Critical evaluation of principles and practices

(a) Identify the relationship between accounting theory and practice.[2] **Ch. 8**

(b) Critically evaluate accounting principles and practices used in corporate reporting.[3] **Ch. 8**

C REPORTING THE FINANCIAL PERFORMANCE OF ENTITIES

1 Performance reporting

(a) Prepare reports relating to corporate performance for external stakeholders.[3] **Ch. 9**

(b) Discuss the issues relating to the recognition of revenue.[3] **Ch. 9**

(c) Evaluate proposed changes to reporting financial performance.[3] **Ch. 9**

2 Non-current assets

(a) Apply and discuss the timing of the recognition of non-current assets and the determination of their carrying amounts including impairment and revaluations.[3] **Ch. 14**

(b) Apply and discuss the treatment of non-current assets held for sale.[3] **Ch. 14**

(c) Apply and discuss the accounting treatment of investment properties including classification, recognition and measurement issues.[3] **Ch. 14**

(d) Apply and discuss the accounting treatment of intangible assets including the criteria for recognition and measurement subsequent to acquisition and classification.[3] **Ch. 14**

3 Financial instruments

(a) Apply and discuss the recognition and derecognition of financial assets and financial liabilities.[2] **Ch. 16**

(b) Apply and discuss the classification of financial assets and financial liabilities and their measurement.[2] **Ch. 16**

(c) Apply and discuss the treatment of gains and losses arising on financial assets and financial liabilities.[2] **Ch. 16**

(d) Apply and discuss the treatment of impairment of financial assets.[2] **Ch. 16**

(e) Account for derivative financial instruments, and simple embedded derivatives.[2] **Ch. 16**

(f) Outline the principle of hedge accounting and account for fair value hedges and cash flow hedges including hedge effectiveness.[2] **Ch. 16**

4 Leases

(a) Apply and discuss the classification of leases and accounting for leases by lessors and lessees.[3] **Ch. 15**

(b) Account for and discuss sale and leaseback transactions.[3] **Ch. 15**

5 Segment reporting

(a) Determine the nature and extent of reportable segments.[3] **Ch. 12**

(b) Specify and discuss the nature of segment information to be disclosed. [3] **Ch. 12**

6 Employee benefits

(a) Apply and discuss the accounting treatment of short term benefits.[3] **Ch. 10**

(b) Apply and discuss the accounting treatment of defined contribution and defined benefit plans.[3] **Ch. 10**

(c) Account for gains and losses on settlements and curtailments.[2] **Ch. 10**

(d) Account for the 'Asset Ceiling' test and the reporting of actuarial gains and losses.[2] **Ch. 10**

7 Income taxes

(a) Apply and discuss the recognition and measurement of deferred tax liabilities and deferred tax assets.[3] **Ch. 18**

(b) Determine the recognition of tax expense or income and its inclusion in the financial statements.[3] **Ch. 18**

8 Provisions, contingencies, events after the reporting date

(a) Apply and discuss the recognition, derecognition and measurement of provisions, contingent liabilities and contingent assets including environmental provisions.[3] **Ch. 17**

(b) calculate and discuss restructuring provisions.[3] **Ch. 17**

(c) Apply and discuss the accounting for events after the reporting date.[3] **Ch. 17**

(d) Determine and report going concern issues arising after the reporting date.[3] **Ch. 17**

KAPLAN PUBLISHING

9 Related parties

(a) Determine the parties considered to be related to an entity.[3] **Ch. 13**

(b) Identify the implications of related party relationships and the need for disclosure.[3] **Ch. 13**

10 Share-based payment

(a) Apply and discuss the recognition and measurement criteria for share-based payment transactions.[3] **Ch. 11**

(b) Account for modifications, cancellations and settlements of share-based payment transactions.[2] **Ch. 11**

11 Reporting requirements of small and medium-sized entities (SMEs)

(a) Outline the principal considerations in developing a set of accounting standards for SMEs.[3] **Ch. 20**

(b) Discuss solutions to the problem of differential financial reporting.[3] **Ch. 20**

(c) Discuss the reasons why the IFRS for SME's does not address certain topics.[3] **Ch. 20**

(d) Discuss the accounting treatments not allowable under the IFRS for SME's including the revaluation model for certain assets and proportionate consolidation.[3] **Ch. 20**

(e) Discuss and apply the simplifications introduced by the IFRS for SMEs including accounting for goodwill and intangible assets, financial instruments, defined benefit schemes, exchange differences and associates and joint ventures.[3] **Ch. 20**

D FINANCIAL STATEMENTS OF GROUPS OF ENTITIES

1 Group accounting including statements of cash flow

(a) Apply the method of accounting for business combinations, including complex group structures.[3] **Ch. 1, 2 and 3**

(b) Apply the principles in determining the cost of a business combination.[3] **Ch. 1, 2 and 3**

(c) Apply the recognition and measurement criteria for identifiable acquired assets and liabilities and goodwill including step acquisitions.[3] **Ch. 1, 2 and 3**

(d) Apply and discuss the criteria used to identify a subsidiary and an associate.[3] **Ch. 1**

(e) Determine and apply appropriate procedures to be used in preparing group financial statements.[3] **Ch. 1, 2 and 3**

(f) Identify and outline the circumstances in which a group is required to prepare consolidated financial statements; the circumstances when a group may claim an exemption from the preparation of group financial statements, and why directors may not wish to consolidate a subsidiary and where this is permitted.[2] **Ch. 1**

(g) Apply the equity method of accounting for associates[3] **Ch. 1**

(h) Outline and apply the key definitions and accounting methods which relate to interests in joint ventures.[3] **Ch. 1**

(i) Prepare and discuss group statements of cash flows.[3] **Ch. 6**

2 Continuing and discontinued interests

(a) Prepare group financial statements where activities have been classified as discontinued, or have been acquired or disposed in the period.[3] **Ch. 3**

(b) Apply and discuss the treatment of a subsidiary which has been acquired exclusively with a view to subsequent disposal.[3] **Ch. 3**

3 Changes in group structures

(a) Discuss the reasons behind a group reorganisation.[3] **Ch. 4**

(b) Evaluate and assess the principal terms of a proposed group reorganisation.[3] **Ch. 4**

4 Foreign transactions and entities

(a) Outline and apply the translation of foreign currency amounts and transactions into the functional currency and the presentational currency. [3] **Ch. 5**

(b) Account for the consolidation of foreign operations and their disposal.[2] **Ch. 5**

E REPORTING FOR SPECIALISED ENTITIES

1 Financial reporting in specialised, not-for-profit and public sector entities

(a) Apply knowledge from the syllabus to straightforward transactions and events arising in specialised, not-for-profit, and public sector entities.[3] **Ch. 20**

2 Entity reconstructions

(a) Identify when an entity may no longer be viewed as a going concern or uncertainty exists surrounding the going concern status.[2] **Ch. 20**

(b) Identify and outline the circumstances in which a reconstruction would be an appropriate alternative to a company liquidation.[2] **Ch. 20**

(c) Outline the appropriate accounting treatment required relating to reconstructions.[2] **Ch. 20**

F IMPLICATIONS OF CHANGES IN ACCOUNTING REGULATION ON FINANCIAL REPORTING

1 The effect of changes in accounting standards on accounting systems

(a) Apply and discuss the accounting implications of the first time adoption of a body of new accounting standards.[3] **Ch. 21**

2 Proposed changes to accounting standards

(a) Identify the issues and deficiencies which have led to a proposed change to an accounting standard.[2] **Ch. 22**

G THE APPRAISAL OF FINANCIAL PERFORMANCE AND POSITION OF ENTITIES

1 The creation of suitable accounting policies

(a) Develop accounting policies for an entity which meets the entity's reporting requirements.[3] **Ch. 23**

(b) Identify accounting treatments adopted in financial statements and assess their suitability and acceptability.[3] **Ch. 23**

2 Analysis and interpretation of financial information and measurement of performance

(a) Select and calculate relevant indicators of financial and non-financial performance.[3] **Ch. 23**

(b) Identify and evaluate significant features and issues in financial statements.[3] **Ch. 23**

(c) Highlight inconsistencies in financial information through analysis and application of knowledge.[3] **Ch. 23**

(d) Make inferences from the analysis of information taking into account the limitation of the information, the analytical methods used and the business environment in which the entity operates.[3] **Ch. 23**

H CURRENT DEVELOPMENTS

1 Environmental and social reporting

(a) Appraise the impact of environmental, social, and ethical factors on performance measurement.[3] **Ch. 19**

(b) Evaluate current reporting requirements in the area.[3] **Ch. 19**

(c) Discuss why entities might include disclosures relating to the environment and society.[3] **Ch. 19**

2 Convergence between national and international reporting standards

(a) Evaluate the implications of worldwide convergence with International Financial Reporting Standards.[3] **Ch. 21**

(b) Discuss the influence of national regulators on international financial reporting.[2] **Ch. 21**

3 Current reporting issues

(a) Discuss current issues in corporate reporting.[3] **Ch. 22**

The superscript numbers in square brackets indicate the intellectual depth at which the subject area could be assessed within the examination. Level 1 (knowledge and comprehension) broadly equates with the Knowledge module, Level 2 (application and analysis) with the Skills module and Level 3 (synthesis and evaluation) to the Professional level. However, lower level skills can continue to be assessed as you progress through each module and level.

The examination

Examination format

The syllabus is assessed by a three-hour paper-based examination. It examines professional competences within the corporate reporting environment.

Students will be examined on concepts, theories and principles and on their ability to question and comment on proposed accounting treatments.

Students should be capable of relating professional issues to relevant concepts and practical situations. The evaluation of alternative accounting practices and the identification and prioritisation of issues will be a key element of the paper. Professional and ethical judgement will need to be exercised, together with the integration of technical knowledge when addressing corporate reporting issues in a business context.

Global issues will be addressed via the current issues questions on the paper. Students will be required to adopt either a stakeholder or an external focus in answering questions and to demonstrate personal skills such as problem solving, dealing with information and decision making.

The paper also deals with specific professional knowledge appropriate to the preparation and presentation of consolidated and other financial statements from accounting data, to conform with accounting standards.

Section A will consist of one scenario based question worth 50 marks. It will deal with the preparation of consolidated financial statements including group statements of cash flows and with issues in financial reporting.

Students will be required to answer two out of three questions in Section B, which will normally comprise two questions which will be scenario or case-study based and one essay question which may have some computational element. Section B could deal with any aspects of the syllabus.

	Number of marks
Section A	
Compulsory question	50
Section B	
Two from three 25-mark questions	50
	———
Total time allowed: 3 hours	100

Study skills and revision guidance

This section aims to give guidance on how to study for your ACCA exams and to give ideas on how to improve your existing study techniques.

Preparing to study

Set your objectives

Before starting to study decide what you want to achieve - the type of pass you wish to obtain. This will decide the level of commitment and time you need to dedicate to your studies.

Devise a study plan

Determine which times of the week you will study.

Split these times into sessions of at least one hour for study of new material. Any shorter periods could be used for revision or practice.

Put the times you plan to study onto a study plan for the weeks from now until the exam and set yourself targets for each period of study – in your sessions make sure you cover the course, course assignments and revision.

If you are studying for more than one paper at a time, try to vary your subjects as this can help you to keep interested and see subjects as part of wider knowledge.

When working through your course, compare your progress with your plan and, if necessary, re-plan your work (perhaps including extra sessions) or, if you are ahead, do some extra revision/practice questions.

Effective studying

Active reading

You are not expected to learn the text by rote, rather, you must understand what you are reading and be able to use it to pass the exam and develop good practice. A good technique to use is SQ3Rs – Survey, Question, Read, Recall, Review:

(1) **Survey the chapter** – look at the headings and read the introduction, summary and objectives, so as to get an overview of what the chapter deals with.

(2) **Question** – whilst undertaking the survey, ask yourself the questions that you hope the chapter will answer for you.

(3) **Read** through the chapter thoroughly, answering the questions and making sure you can meet the objectives. Attempt the exercises and activities in the text, and work through all the examples.

(4) **Recall** – at the end of each section and at the end of the chapter, try to recall the main ideas of the section/chapter without referring to the text. This is best done after a short break of a couple of minutes after the reading stage.

(5) **Review** – check that your recall notes are correct.

KAPLAN PUBLISHING

You may also find it helpful to re-read the chapter to try to see the topic(s) it deals with as a whole.

Note-taking

Taking notes is a useful way of learning, but do not simply copy out the text. The notes must:

- be in your own words
- be concise
- cover the key points
- be well-organised
- be modified as you study further chapters in this text or in related ones.

Trying to summarise a chapter without referring to the text can be a useful way of determining which areas you know and which you don't.

Three ways of taking notes:

Summarise the key points of a chapter.

Make linear notes – a list of headings, divided up with subheadings listing the key points. If you use linear notes, you can use different colours to highlight key points and keep topic areas together. Use plenty of space to make your notes easy to use.

Try a diagrammatic form – the most common of which is a mind-map. To make a mind-map, put the main heading in the centre of the paper and put a circle around it. Then draw short lines radiating from this to the main sub-headings, which again have circles around them. Then continue the process from the sub-headings to sub-sub-headings, advantages, disadvantages, etc.

Highlighting and underlining

You may find it useful to underline or highlight key points in your study text – but do be selective. You may also wish to make notes in the margins.

Revision

The best approach to revision is to revise the course as you work through it. Also try to leave four to six weeks before the exam for final revision. Make sure you cover the whole syllabus and pay special attention to those areas where your knowledge is weak. Here are some recommendations:

Read through the text and your notes again and condense your notes into key phrases. It may help to put key revision points onto index cards to look at when you have a few minutes to spare.

Review any assignments you have completed and look at where you lost marks – put more work into those areas where you were weak.

Practise exam standard questions under timed conditions. If you are short of time, list the points that you would cover in your answer and then read the model answer, but do try to complete at least a few questions under exam conditions.

Also practise producing answer plans and comparing them to the model answer.

If you are stuck on a topic find somebody (a tutor) to explain it to you.

Read good newspapers and professional journals, especially ACCA's Student Accountant – this can give you an advantage in the exam.

Ensure you know the structure of the exam – how many questions and of what type you will be expected to answer. During your revision attempt all the different styles of questions you may be asked.

Further reading

'A student's guide to International Financial Reporting Standards', 2nd edition by Clare Finch.

'A student's guide to Group Accounts' by Tom Clendon.

You can find further reading and technical articles under the student section of ACCA's website.

Technical update

This text has been updated to reflect Examinable Documents 2011 issued by ACCA. Specifically, this includes the most recently issued reporting standards, IFRS 9 Financial instruments and IFRS for SME, together with recently revised reporting standards.

Current developments are included throughout the text in the relevant chapters. For example, chapter 16 includes information regarding continuing developments in the reporting of financial instruments and chapter 21 deals with the convergence process between IFRS and US GAAP.

Group accounting – basic groups

Chapter learning objectives

Upon completion of this chapter you will be able to:

- apply the method of accounting for business combinations
- apply the principles relating to the cost of a business combination
- apply the recognition and measurement criteria for identifiable acquired assets and liabilities and goodwill
- apply and discuss the criteria used to identify a subsidiary and an associate
- determine appropriate procedures to be used in preparing group financial statements
- apply the equity method of accounting for associates
- outline and apply the key definitions and accounting methods that relate to interests in joint ventures
- understand and discuss current issues in group accounting.

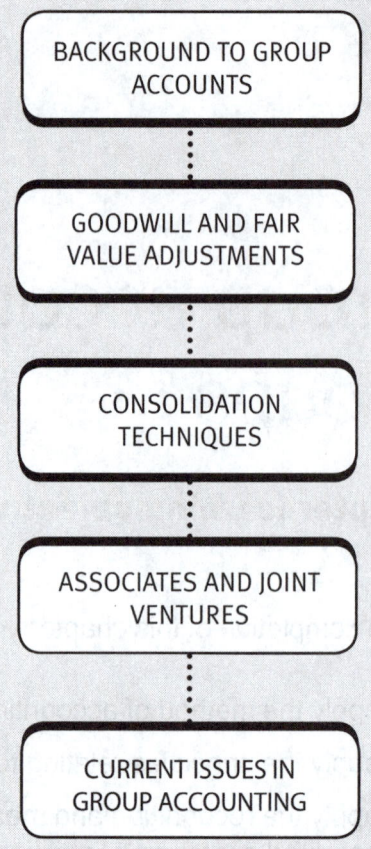

BACKGROUND TO GROUP ACCOUNTS

GOODWILL AND FAIR VALUE ADJUSTMENTS

CONSOLIDATION TECHNIQUES

ASSOCIATES AND JOINT VENTURES

CURRENT ISSUES IN GROUP ACCOUNTING

Expandable text - Background to group accounts

This chapter revises the basic principles of group accounting seen at F7, and introduces the new and amended requirements of IFRS 3 and IAS 27, as revised in 2008.

In particular, the revision of IFRS 3 has meant significant changes to

- new restrictions on what expenses can form part of the acquisition costs

- revisions of the treatment of contingent consideration.

- measurement of non-controlling interests (NCI) (the new name for minority interests) and the knock on effect that this has on consolidated goodwill

- considerable guidance on recognising and measuring the identifiable assets and liabilities of the acquired subsidiary, in particular the illustrative examples discuss several intangibles, such as market-related, customer-related, artistic-related and technology-related assets

- accounting for step acquisitions (covered in chapter 2)

- clarifies that an entity must classify and designate all contractual arrangement at acquisition date, subject to two exceptions: leases and insurance contracts.

Expandable text - Definitions and key points

Definitions

A **parent** is an entity that has one or more subsidiaries.

A **subsidiary** is an entity, including an unincorporated entity, such as a partnership, that is controlled by another entity (known as the parent).

Control is the power to govern the financial and operating policies of an entity so as to obtain benefits from its activities.

The **non-controlling interest** is the equity in a subsidiary not attributable to a parent. This was previously known as the minority interest.

Key points

- As the parent and its subsidiaries are acting as a single unit (the group), the users of the accounts will only be able to make informed economic decisions if they have access to a set of financial statements that combines the results, assets and liabilities of all entities in the group.

- Consolidated accounts must exclude transactions between group members as their inclusion could inflate the assets and profits of individual entities.

- For the purposes of consolidated accounts all group members must use the same accounting policies and currencies.

- All group members should have the same financial reporting date as the parent. If this is not practical, there are two possible solutions to this problem:
  - prepare interim financial statements up to the group reporting date
  - use the most recent set of the subsidiary's own accounts. The date for these must be within three months before the group reporting date.

- There are a number of exemptions from consolidation and special rules.

Expandable text - Exemptions for intermediate parent companies

An intermediate parent entity is an entity which has a subsidiary but is also itself a subsidiary of another entity. For example:

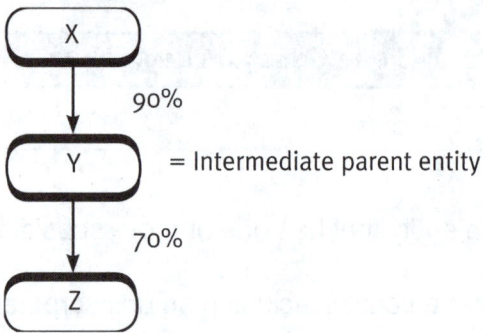

An intermediate parent entity is exempt from the requirement to prepare group accounts if:

*   it is a wholly owned subsidiary
*   it is partially owned, and the owners of the non-controlling interest do not object to the non-preparation.

Such a parent should disclose:

*   the fact that consolidated financial statements have not been presented
*   a list of significant investments (subsidiaries, associates, etc.) including percentage shareholdings
*   the bases on which the investments listed above have been accounted for in its separate financial statements.

Special rules

IAS 27 Consolidated and separate financial statements states that all subsidiaries should be consolidated, subject to special rules.

(a) Severe long-term restrictions

Consolidation is based on the concept of control, i.e. an entity is a subsidiary because the parent controls it. If there are severe restrictions on the ability of the parent to manage a subsidiary so that control is lost, then it should no longer be classified as a subsidiary and therefore cannot be consolidated.

KAPLAN PUBLISHING

(b) Acquired for resale

A subsidiary acquired exclusively with a view to disposal within 12 months will probably meet the conditions in IFRS 5 **Non-current assets held for sale and discontinued activities** for classification as held for sale. If it does, it is not accounted for under IAS 27 but under IFRS 5; the effect is that all its assets are presented as a single line item below current assets and all its liabilities are presented as a single line item below current liabilities. So it is still consolidated, but in a different way.

(c) Different activities

In the past, some subsidiaries were excluded on the grounds of dissimilar activities. For example, a supermarket chain might also own a bank. IAS 27 states that exclusion is not justified in these situations. If a group does contain diverse business activities, then this will be explained by the segment information required by IFRS 8 Segment reporting.

(d) Materiality

Accounting standards do not apply to immaterial items. Therefore an immaterial subsidiary need not be consolidated.

Summary

Reason	IAS 27	Treatment
Severe long-term restrictions meaning loss of control	Mandatory exclusion	Non-current asset investment per IAS 39
Acquired for resale	Mandatory inclusion	Single line items under IFRS 5
Different activities	Mandatory inclusion	Consolidate. Prepare IFRS 8 segment information
Immaterial	Not applicable	Optional

Expandable text - Purchase consideration

- This includes the acquisition date fair value of all consideration.
- It includes contingent consideration, even if it is not deemed to be probable of payment at the date of acquisition.
- It does not include costs of acquisition, which must be expensed as incurred, or in the case of debt or equity issue costs, dealt with according to IAS 39 / IAS 32.

Acquisition costs

In the previous IFRS 3 directly related acquisition costs such as professional fees (legal, accounting, valuation etc) could be included as part of the cost of the acquisition. This has now been stopped and such costs must be expensed. The costs of issuing debt or equity are to be accounted for under the rules of IAS 39 Financial Instruments: Recognition and Measurement (generally charged to share premium).

Contingent consideration

IFRS 3 defines contingent consideration as:

Usually, an obligation of the acquirer to transfer additional assets or equity interests to the former owners of an acquiree as part of the exchange for control of the acquiree if specified future events occur or conditions are met. However, contingent consideration also may give the acquirer the right to the return of previously transferred consideration if specified conditions are met.

The previous version of IFRS 3 required contingent consideration to be accounted for only if it was probable that it would become payable.

The revised Standard requires the acquirer to recognise the acquisition-date fair value of contingent consideration as part of the consideration for the acquiree. This 'fair value' approach is consistent with how other forms of consideration are valued and fair value is defined as:

The amount for which an asset could be exchanged, **or a liability settled**, between knowledgeable, willing parties in an arm's length transaction.

Expandable text - Contingent consideration

Applying the definition to contingent consideration is not easy as the definition is largely hypothetical i.e. it is highly unlikely that the acquisition date liability for contingent consideration could be or would be settled by 'willing parties in an arm's length transaction'. In an examination question the acquisition date fair value (or how to calculate it) of any contingent consideration would be given.

The payment of contingent consideration may be in the form of equity or a liability (issuing a debt instrument or cash) and should be recorded as such under the rules of IAS 32 Financial Instruments: Presentation (or other applicable standard).

KAPLAN PUBLISHING

Changes in the fair value of any contingent consideration after the acquisition date are also discussed in the Standard. If the change is due to additional information obtained after the acquisition date that affects the facts or circumstances as they existed at the acquisition date this is treated as a 'measurement period adjustment' and the liability (and goodwill) are remeasured. This is effectively a retrospective adjustment and is rather similar to an adjusting event under IAS 10 Events after the Reporting Period. However changes due to events after the acquisition date (for example, meeting an earnings target which triggers a higher payment than was provided for at acquisition) are treated as follows:

(a) Contingent consideration classified as equity shall not be remeasured and its subsequent settlement shall be accounted for within equity (e.g. Cr share capital/share premium Dr retained earnings).

(b) Contingent consideration classified as an asset or a liability that:

   (i) is a financial instrument and is within the scope of IAS 39 shall be measured at fair value, with any resulting gain or loss recognised either in profit or loss or in other comprehensive income in accordance with that IFRS.

   (ii) is not within the scope of IAS 39 shall be accounted for in accordance with IAS 37 Provisions, contingent liabilities and contingent assets or other IFRSs as appropriate.

ED 2009/11 Improvements to IFRS clarifies that IAS 32 and IAS 39, together with IFRS 7, do not apply to contingent consideration which arose prior to the implementation of IFRS 3 Revised

Note: although contingent consideration is usually a liability, it may be an asset if the acquirer has the right to a return of some of the consideration transferred if certain conditions are met.

1 Non-controlling interest (NCI) and its impact on goodwill

IFRS 3 revised provides a choice in valuing the non-controlling interest at acquisition:

Either

Method 1 – 'the old method'	Method 2 – 'the new method'
NCI % x Fair value of the Net assets of the subsidiary at the acquisition date	Fair value of NCI at date of acquisition

- **Method 1** is essentially the same as the calculation of the minority interest under the previous version of IFRS 3.

- Where an exam question requires the use of this method, it will state that 'it is group policy to value the non-controlling interest at its proportionate share of the fair value of the subsidiary's identifiable net assets'.

- **Method 2** requires that where shares are publicly traded, the fair value of the NCI is measured according to market prices. Where this is not the case other valuation techniques must be used.

- This method is known as the 'full goodwill' method, since 100% of goodwill is reflected in the group financial statements as an asset (with the NCI line then effectively including the proportion of goodwill relating to them).

- Where an exam question requires the use of this method, it will state that 'it is group policy to value the non-controlling interest using the full (fair value) method'.

Note that, for any subsidiary, there should be a consistent accounting treatment of goodwill and non-controlling interest; they should both be accounted for either on a full basis or a proportionate basis.

Note also that IFRS 3 permits the goodwill accounting policy to be selected and applied on an acquisition-by-acquisition basis. This means that, within the same group, some subsidiaries may be accounted for applying the full goodwill policy, whilst other subsidiaries may be accounted for applying the proportion of net assets basis.

Expandable text – Non-controlling interest

Choice of method

The standard indicates that the method used should be decided on a transaction by transaction basis.

The upside of recognising full goodwill (method 2) is that assets on the statement of financial position will be increased.

The potential downside is that any future impairment of goodwill will be greater. However, goodwill impairment testing may be easier in that there is no need to gross up goodwill for partially owned subsidiaries.

Full goodwill method – valuation

Where the full goodwill method is chosen, the fair value of the NCI may differ from that of the controlling interest on a per-share basis. This is likely to be due to the inclusion of a control premium in the per-share fair value of the parent's controlling interest.

KAPLAN PUBLISHING

Subsequent measurement of the NCI

In subsequent years the NCI is increased by the proportion of post-acquisition retained earnings and any other reserves (e.g. revaluation reserve) due to the NCI. This is true regardless of which method is initially used to value the NCI.

Unlike the existing standard, the revisions to IAS 27 require that an entity must attribute their share of total comprehensive income to the NCI even if this results in a deficit balance.

ED 2009/11 Improvements to IFRS issued in August 2009 clarifies that NCI measurement is based upon only those instruments which are entitled to share in the net assets of the acquired entity. Any other instruments which meet the definition of NCI in the entity should be measured at fair value or in accordance with the applicable IFRS.

Expandable text - Illustration Rosa

Rosa acquires 80% of the Parks's equity capital in a share-for-share exchange. Parks has issued equity capital comprising 100 shares, each of $1 nominal value.

The consideration that Rosa gives to acquire Parks is by making a two for one share issue when the share price of each Rosa share is $5.

At the date of acquisition the fair value of the net assets of the Parks is $600 and the market value of a Parks share is $8.

Required:

(i) **Calculate the goodwill arising valuing the NCI using the proportion of the net assets method.**

(ii) **Calculate the goodwill arising valuing the NCI using the full goodwill method**

Expandable text - Solution Rosa

(i) Goodwill calculation using the proportion of net assets method:

	$
Purchase consideration (2/1 x (80% x 100) = 160 x $5)	800
NCI value at acquisition** 20% x 600	120
	920
Less: fair value of all identifiable net assets at acquisition (per net assets working)	(600)
Prop goodwill at acquisition	320
Less: impairment to date	(X)
Goodwill to consolidated statement of financial position	X

**if fair value method adopted, NCI value = FV of NCI at date of acquisition; this will normally be given in a question.

**if proportionate basis adopted, NCI value = NCI% of net assets at acquisition (per net assets working).

(i) Goodwill calculation using the full fair value method:

	$
Purchase consideration (2/1 x (80% x 100) = 160 x $5)	800
NCI value at acquisition**(20% x 100 x $8)	160
	960
Less: fair value of all identifiable net assets at acquisition (per net assets working)	(600)
Goodwill at acquisition	360
Less: impairment to date	(X)
Goodwill to consolidated statement of financial position	360

**if fair value method adopted, NCI value = FV of NCI at date of acquisition; this will normally be given in a question.

KAPLAN PUBLISHING

**if proportionate basis adopted, NCI value = NCI% of net assets at acquisition (per net assets working).

The cost of the investment that the Rosa, the parent has made in the Parks, the subsidiary, is the fair value of the consideration given. This is the fair value of the shares that Rosa has issued.

Expandable text - Illustration Malawi

Malawi has made an acquisition of 100% of the equity shares in Blantyre when the net assets of Blantyre were $80,000. The consideration that Malawi gave for the investment in the subsidiary Blantyre comprised:

(1) Cash paid $25,454

(2) Shares – Malawi issued 10,000 shares to the shareholders of Blantyre, each with a nominal value of $1 and a market value of $4.

(3) Deferred consideration – $20,000 is to be paid one year after the date of acquisition. The relevant discount rate is 10%.

(4) Contingent consideration – $100,000 may be paid one year after the date of acquisition. It is judged that there is only a 40% chance that this will occur. The fair value of this consideration can be measured as the present value of the expected value.

(5) Legal fees associated with the acquisition amounted to $15,000.

Required:
Calculate the goodwill arising on the acquisition of Blantyre.

Expandable text - Solution Malawi

The goodwill on acquisition of Blantyre is as follows:

Fair value of consideration paid:		$
Cash		25,454
Shares at fair value	10,000 × $4	40,000
Deferred consideration	$20,000 × 1/1.1	18,182
Contingent consideration	$100,000 × 40% × 1/1.1	36,364
		120,000
Less: Fair value of net assets at acquisition		80,000
		40,000

Note – legal fees are expensed and not capitalised.

Expandable text – Fair value of net assets of acquiree

- In line with the original standard, IFRS 3 revised requires that the identifiable net assets of the subsidiary should be measured at their fair values at the date of acquisition.

- There are certain exceptions to this rule such as deferred tax and pension obligations, which are valued according to the relevant standard.

- Contingent liabilities that are present obligations arising from past events and can be measured reliably are recognised at fair value at the acquisition date. This is true even where an economic outflow is not probable.

- A provision for future operating losses cannot be created as this is a post-acquisition item. Similarly, restructuring costs are only recognised to the extent that a liability actually exists at the date of acquisition.

- The fair value exercise affects both the values given to the assets and liabilities acquired in the group statement of financial position and the value of goodwill.

Recognition of identifiable assets acquired and liabilities assumed

An asset is identifiable if:

- It is capable of disposal separately from the business owning it, or

- It arises from contractual or other legal rights, regardless of whether those rights can be sold separately.

The identifiable assets and liabilities of the acquiree (subsidiary) should be recognised at fair value where:

- They meet the definitions of assets and liabilities in the Framework

- And they are exchanged as part of the business combination rather than a separate transaction.

Items that are not identifiable or do not meet the definitions of assets or liabilities are subsumed into the calculation of purchased goodwill.

KAPLAN PUBLISHING

Fair value – exceptions.

There are certain exceptions to the requirement to measure the subsidiary's net assets at fair value when accounting for business combinations:

- The assets and liabilities falling within the scope of IAS 12 Income Taxes, IAS 19 Employee benefits, IFRS 2 Share-based Payment and IFRS 5 Non-current assets held for sale and Discontinued Operations are required to be valued according to those standards;

- Leases are required to be classified on the basis of factors at the inception date rather than factors at the acquisition date of the subsidiary.

Intangible assets

Acquired intangible assets must always be recognised and measured; unlike the previous IFRS 3 there is no exception where reliable measurement cannot be ascertained.

Expandable text - Illustration Brussels

Brussels acquired 82% of Madrid

- At acquisition, the statement of financial position of Madrid showed issued equity capital of $3,000,000 and retained earnings of $3,255,000. Included in this total is freehold land with a book value of $400,000 (market value $958,000), a brand with a nil book value (market value $500,000), plant and machinery with a book value of $1,120,000 and a market value of $890,000. The fair value of all other assets and liabilities is approximately equal to book value.

- The directors of Brussels intend to close down one of the divisions of Madrid and wish to provide for operating losses up to the date of closure, which are forecast as $729,000.

- An investment in plant and machinery will be required to bring the remaining production line of Madrid up to date. This will amount to $405,000 in the next 12 months.

- The consideration comprised cash of $4,000,000, 1,500,000 shares with a nominal value of $1.00 and fair value of $1.50 each as well as further cash consideration of $400,000 to be paid one year after acquisition.

The discount rate is 10%.

Required:

Calculate the goodwill arising on consolidation using the proportionate share of the fair value of net assets method to value the NCI.

Expandable text - Solution Brussels

Goodwill on acquisition - proportionate basis:

	$	$
Consideration paid by parent		
Cash	4,000,000	
Shares at FV 1,500,000 × $1.50	2,250,000	
Deferred consideration 400,000 × 1/1.1	363,636	
		6,613,636
NCI value at acquisition	18% x 7083,000 (W1)	1,274,940
		7,888,576
Less: 100% of net assets at acquisition (W1)		(7,083,000)
Goodwill		805,576

(W1) Net assets at acquisition	$
Issued equity capital	3,000,000
Retained earnings	3,255,000
Freehold land (958 – 400)	558,000
Brand	500,000
Plant and machinery (890 – 1,120)	(230,000)
	7,083,000

- The goodwill must be calculated on the basis of assets and liabilities that exist on the date of acquisition which means the provision for operating losses and investment in plant cannot be recognised.

> • Deferred consideration is discounted to its present value at the date of acquisition.

Expandable text - Bargain purchases

Bargain purchases

- If the share of net assets acquired exceeds the consideration given, then 'negative goodwill' arises on acquisition.

- IFRS 3 revised requires that the fair values of the consideration and the net assets acquired are checked carefully to ensure that no errors have been made.

- After the checking exercise is complete, if there is still negative goodwill it should credited to profits for the year immediately

2 Consolidation techniques

- To produce consolidated statements of financial position and comprehensive income you should follow the standard workings step by step.

- The five workings below show you how to calculate amounts for goodwill, non-controlling interest and group reserves to be shown in the statement of financial position.

Consolidated statement of financial position

W1 Group structure

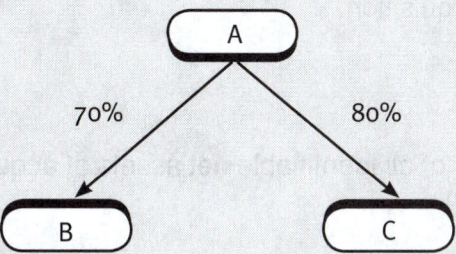

This working is useful to sort out the structure of the group and show whether you are dealing with subsidiaries or associates. It is particularly helpful when dealing with complex groups. You may also want to include the date of acquisition for each subsidiary or associate, together with non-controlling interest percentages as appropriate.

W2 Net assets of each subsidiary and associate

	At acquisition	At reporting date
	$000	$000
Equity capital	X	X
Share premium	X	X
Retained earnings	X	X
Other components of equity	X	X
Fair value adjustments	X	X
	X (to W3)	X (to W4)

This working sets out the net assets at acquisition and at the reporting date, which are used in the goodwill, non-controlling interest and retained earnings calculations.

W3 Goodwill

IFRS 3 Revised introduced an accounting policy choice when accounting for goodwill on acquisition. It can either be calculated on a full ("fair value") basis or a proportionate ("net") basis. One template can be used to calculate goodwill based the accounting policy choice made as follows:

	$000
Purchase consideration (i.e fair value paid by parent)	X
NCI value at acquisition**	X
	X
Less: fair value of all identifiable net assets at acquisition (per net assets working)	(X)
Goodwill at acquisition	**X**
Less: impairment to date	(X)
Goodwill to consolidated statement of financial position	X

**if fair value method adopted, NCI value = FV of NCI at date of acquisition; this will normally be given in a question.

**if proportionate basis adopted, NCI value = NCI% of net assets at acquisition (per net assets working).

Alternatively, the following template will arrive at the same answer for goodwill. This template may be useful when dealing with foreign subsidiaries to help allocate exchange differences relating to goodwill between the group and NCI respectively. Foreign subsidiaries are dealt with in chapter 5 of this text.

Alternative template		$
Purchase consideration paid by parent (i.e fair value paid by parent)		X
Fair value of net assets at acquisition x group share		(X)
		——
Goodwill – Parent share		X
NCI value at acquisition (**as above)	X	
Fair value of net assets an acquisition x NCI share	(X)	
		——
NCI share of goodwill		X
		——
Goodwill		**X**
Less: impairment to date		(X)
		——
Goodwill to consolidated statement of financial position		X
		——

Accounting policy for goodwill

IFRS 3 requires that goodwill is accounted for as a permanent intangible non-current asset, subject to an annual impairment review.
If there is impairment to recognise under the full goodwill method, the impairment is charged as an expense in the group statement of comprehensive income. The practical consequence of this is that impairment is allocated between the group and non-controlling interest based upon their respective shareholdings.

This point may be relevant in questions if you are required to prepare the group statement of financial position where impairment of goodwill has been identified or determined; you may need to allocate impairment between the group and non-controlling interests respectively.

Impairment of goodwill is dealt with in detail within chapter 14 of this publication.

W4 Non-controlling interest

As with calculation of goodwill on a full or proportionate basis, there is an accounting policy choice for calculating the value of non-controlling interest, which can be calculated on a fair value or proportionate basis. Note that the choice of accounting policy for goodwill and non-controlling interest must be on a consistent basis for each subsidiary.

The following template accomodates the calculation of NCI for either accounting policy choice as follows:

	$000
NCI value at acquisition (per W3)	X
NCI % of post-acquisition retained earnings	X
Less: NCI % of unrealised profit in inventory/non-current assets	(X)
Less: NCI% of goodwill impairment (full basis only)	(X)
NCI to consolidated statement of financial position	X

The NCI must be adjusted for any unrealised profit from sales made by the subsidiary to the parent or other members of the group. (unless retained earnings are adjusted within W2)

W5 Group retained earnings

	$000
Parent entity (100%)	X
For each subsidiary: group share of post-acquisition retained earnings (W2)	X
Less goodwill impairment (W3)	(X)
Less group share of unrealised profits (if any)	(X)
Total group retained earnings	X

The group reserves include the group's share of the post-acquisition retained earnings of each subsidiary. Pre-acquisition earnings cannot be included in group reserves as they have already been dealt with in the net assets working which leads to the calculation of goodwill.

KAPLAN PUBLISHING

W6 Investment in associate (for reference - as required)

	$000
Cost of investment in associate	X
For each associate: group share of post-acquisition retained earnings (W2)	X
Less impairment	(X)
	___
To group SOFP	X
	___

Consolidated income statement

As with the statement of financial position, we need a set of workings to produce a consolidated income statement. Some of these are the same as those we have already seen in the statement of financial position.

Note: At this stage we are not considering other comprehensive income.

W1 Group structure (as before)

W2 Net assets at acquisition to be able to calculate goodwill (as before)

W3 Goodwill – so you can calculate the impairment charge (as before)

W4 Consolidation schedule

- If the subsidiary has been acquired part way through the year, you will have to time apportion income and expenses. All items from revenue down to profit after tax must be time apportioned.

- Don't forget to remove intercompany trading from revenue and cost of sales. If there is any unrealised profit, this must be removed from cost of sales and inventory in the statement of financial position.

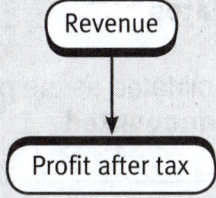

W5 Non-controlling interest

NCI share of subsidiary profit after tax (must be time apportioned if a mid year acquisition)

W6 Group retained earnings brought forward

	$000
Parent (100% of reserves at beginning of year)	X
Subsidiary: group share of post-acquisition reserves at beginning of year	X
Less goodwill impairment at beginning of year	(X)
	X

If the subsidiary has been acquired during the year, then there will be no post-acquisition reserves brought forward as the subsidiary did not belong to the group at the start of the year.

Expandable text - Associates and joint ventures

IAS 28 Investments in associates

Definition:

- An **Associate** is an entity over which the investor has **significant influence** and which is neither a subsidiary nor a joint venture of the investor.

- **Significant influence** is the power to participate in, but not control, the financial and operating policy decisions of an entity. It is usually evidenced by representation on the board of directors, which allows the investing entity to participate in policy decisions. A holding between 20% and 50% of the voting power is presumed to give significant influence, unless it can be clearly demonstrated that this is not the case. Conversely, it is presumed that a holding of less than 20% does not give significant influence, unless such influence can be clearly demonstrated.

Accounting for associates

Associates are not consolidated as the parent does not have control. Instead they are **equity accounted.**

KAPLAN PUBLISHING

IAS 28 requires that the carrying value of the associate is determined as follows:

Investment in Associate	$000
Cost	X
Add: share of increase in net assets	X
Less: impairment losses	(X)
	X

This is shown in the non-current assets section of the statement of financial position.

Note that IFRS 3 Revised does not apply to associates as they are not under the control of the investing entity.

You will need to produce W2 (net assets) to calculate the share of the increase in net assets (post-acquisition retained earnings).

Include in W5 (group retained earnings) the **group's share of A's post acquisition retained earnings.**

Income statement

Include the group's share of the associate's (**profit after tax** less any impairment losses).

Inter-company transactions

Remember that you do **not** eliminate inter-company sales and purchases, receivables or payables between the group and the associate as the associate is outside of the group. The only exception to this is any unrealised profit on transactions, of which the **group's share only** must be eliminated.

Fair value adjustments

Fair value adjustments relating to an associate are included in the net assets working (W2) as normal. However, you do **not** include any fair value adjustments relating to an associate within the various net assets on the group SOFP. As seen already, there is one amount for the carrying value of the interest in the associate on the group SOFP.

Expandable text - Equity accounting

Accounting for associates

An investment in an associate is accounted for using the equity method. The equity method is not used when:

- the investment is classified as held for sale in accordance with IFRS 5 **Non-current assets held for sale and discontinued operations**

- the investor is itself a subsidiary, its owners do not object to the equity method not being applied and its debt and equity securities are not publicly traded. In this case, the investor's parent must present consolidated financial statements that do use the equity method.

The equity method

The associate is initially recorded at cost in the statement of financial position. Thereafter it is stated at cost plus the investor's share of the increase in the associate's net assets.

The investor's share of the associate's post-tax result for the year is recognised in the income statement.

Applying the equity method of accounting

Statement of financial position

(a) The associate is disclosed separately as a non-current asset.

(b) The associate is initially recognised at cost. Thereafter it is recognised at cost plus the investor's share of the increase in the associate's net assets.

(c) There may well be premium arising on the acquisition, but this does not need to be calculated. The reason is that under IFRS 3 Revised and IAS 28 it is the total carrying amount for the associate that is subject to impairment testing, and premium in relation to the associate is not separately identified.

Income statement

The associate is not under the control of the investor and it is not part of the group. In the income statement the group share of the associate's profit after tax is included in the profit for the period. This is disclosed separately on the face of the income statement.

General points and disclosures

(a) Inter-company transactions and balances cannot be cancelled, because the associate's side of any balance is only shown as a share of a net amount. Loans from the investor to the associate will be presented alongside the investment in the associate. Other significant transactions and balances should be disclosed.

(b) Allowances for unrealised profit. Only the group share of any allowance for unrealised profit will be accounted for. (Unrealised profit in subsidiaries is eliminated in full.) The allowance will be recognised in the statement of financial position as follows:

   (i) Inventory held by the investor: reduce the value of the inventories.

   (ii) Inventory held by the associate: reduce the value of the investment in the associate.

(c) Reporting date. The financial statements used to consolidate the associate should be drawn up to the investor's reporting date. Because the investor does not control the associate it may not be possible to change the year-end, and so interim accounts would have to be used. If this is not possible, then the most recent accounts are used, as long as the difference in reporting dates is no more than three months.

(d) Accounting policies. These should be harmonised.

(e) Contingencies. The investor should disclose its share of contingencies. It should also disclose any of the associate's liabilities that it is contingently liable for (e.g. by guaranteeing an overdraft).

(f) Descriptions. A list and description of significant associates should be disclosed. This will note the ownership interests, voting interests, and consolidation method for each associate.

Illustration 1 - Pauline

On 1 April 2007 Pauline acquired the following non-current investments:

- 6 million equity shares in Sonia by an exchange of two shares in Pauline for every four shares in Sonia plus $1.25 per acquired Sonia share in cash. The market price of each Pauline share at the date of acquisition was $6 and the market price of each Sonia share at the date of acquisition was $3.25.

- 30% of the equity shares of Arthur at a cost of $7.50 per share in cash.

Only the cash consideration of the above investments has been recorded by Pauline. In addition $1,000,000 of professional costs relating to the acquisition of Sonia is also included in the cost of the investment.

The summarised draft statements of financial position of the three companies at 31 March 2008 are:

	Pauline	Sonia	Arthur
	$000	$000	$000
Assets			
Non-current assets			
Property, plant and equipment	36,800	20,800	36,000
Investments in Sonia and Arthur	26,500	Nil	Nil
Held for trading investments	13,000	Nil	Nil
	76,300	20,800	36,000
Current assets			
Inventory	13,800	12,400	7,200
Trade receivables	6,400	3,000	4,800
Total assets	96,500	36,200	48,000

Equity and liabilities

Equity shares of $1 each	20,000	8,000	8,000
Retained earnings			
– at 31 March 2007	32,000	12,000	22,000
– for year ended 31 March 2008	18,500	5,800	10,000
	70,500	25,800	40,000
Non-current liabilities			
7% Loan notes	10,000	2,000	2,000
Current liabilities	16,000	8,400	6,000
	96,500	36,200	48,000

The following information is relevant:

(i) At the date of acquisition Sonia had an internally generated brand name. The directors of Pauline estimate that the value of this brand name has a fair value of $2 million, an indefinite life and has not suffered any impairment.

(ii) On 1 April 2007, Pauline sold an item of plant to Sonia at its agreed fair value of $5 million. Its carrying amount prior to the sale was $4 million. The estimated remaining life of the plant at the date of sale was five years (straight-line depreciation).

(iii) During the year ended 31 March 2008 Sonia sold goods to Pauline for $5.4 million. Sonia had marked up these goods by 50% on cost. Pauline had a third of the goods still in its inventory at 31 March 2008. There were no intra-group payables/receivables at 31 March 2008.

(iv) Pauline has a policy of valuing non-controlling interests at fair value at the date of acquisition. For this purpose the share price of Sonia at this date should be used. Impairment tests on 31 March 2008 concluded that neither consolidated goodwill or the value of the investment in Arthur have been impaired.

(v) The held for trading investments are included in Pauline's statement of financial position (above) at their fair value on 1 April 2007, but they have a fair value of $18 million at 31 March 2008.

(vi) No dividends were paid during the year by any of the companies.

Required:

Prepare the consolidated statement of financial position for Pauline as at 31 March 2008.

(25 marks)

Expandable text - Solution Pauline

Consolidated statement of financial position of Pauline as at 31 March 2008

	$000	$000
Assets		
Non-current assets:		
Property, plant and equipment (36,800 + 20,800 – 800 (W8))		56,800
Goodwill (W3)		10,000
Brand name		2,000
Investments – associate (W6)		21,000
– held for trading		18,000
		107,800
Current assets		
Inventory (13,800 + 12,400 – 600 URP (W7))	25,600	
Trade receivables	9,400	35,000
Total assets		142,800
Equity and liabilities		
Equity attributable to equity holders of the parent		
Equity shares of $1 each (W3)		23,000
Share premium (W3)	15,000	
Retained earnings (W5)	60,600	75,600
		98,600
Non-controlling interest (W4)		7,800
Total equity		106,400
Non-current liabilities		
7% Loan notes (10,000 + 2,000)		12,000
Current liabilities (16,000 + 8,400)		24,400
Total equity and liabilities		142,800

Workings

(W1) Group structure

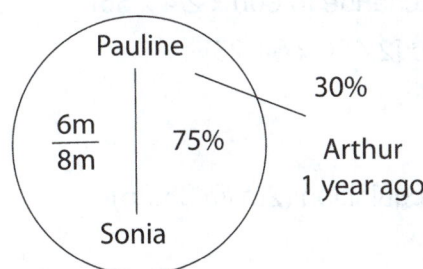

(W2)   Net assets – Sonia

	At reporting date	At acquisition date
	$000	$000
Equity capital	8,000	8,000
Retained earnings	17,800	12,000
Fair value adj:		
Brand	2,000	2,000
PURP (W7)	(600)	
	27,200	22,000

Arthur

	At reporting date	At acquisition date
	$000	$000
Equity capital	8,000	8,000
Retained earnings	32,000	22,000
	40,000	30,000

(W3) Goodwill

	Sonia
	$000
Pauline - cost of investment	
– Share exchange [6,000 x 2/4 x $6]	18,000
– cash paid [2,400 x $1.25]	7,500
	25,500
FV of NCI at acquisition (2m @ $3.25)	6,500
	32,000
Less: 100% of NA @ Acq: 75% (22,000 W2)	(22,000)
Total goodwill	10,000

Tutorial note:

The consideration given by Pauline for the shares of Sonia works out at $4.25 per share i.e. consideration of $25.50 million for 6 million shares. This is considerably higher than the market price of Sonia's shares ($3.25) before the acquisition. This probably reflects the cost of gaining control of Sonia. This is also why it is probably appropriate to value the NCI in Sonia at $3.25 each, because (by definition) the NCI does not have any control. This also explains why Pauline's share of Sonia's goodwill at 90% (i.e. 9,000/10,000) is much higher than its proportionate shareholding in Sonia (which is 75%).

The 3 million shares issued by Pauline in the share exchange at a value of $6 each would be recorded as $1 per share as equity capital and $5 per share as premium giving an increase in equity capital of $3 million and a share premium of $15 million.

(W4) NCI

	$000
Fair value of NCI at acquisition (as above)	6,500
NCI share of post-acquisition profit (25% x (27,200 - 22,000)) (W2)	1,300
	7,800

KAPLAN PUBLISHING

	$000
(W5) Group retained earnings	
100% Parent (32,000 + 18,500)	50,500
Professional costs written off	(1,000)
Gain on held for trading financial asset	5,000
75% Sonia post-acquisition reserves (75% x (27,200 - 22,000)) (W2))	3,900
30% Arthur post-acquisition reserves (30% x (40,000 - 30,000)) (W2))	3,000
Less PURP in plant(W8)	(800)
	_____
	60,600
	_____

(W6) Investment in associate

	$000
Cost (8,000 x 30% x $7.50)	18,000
Share post-acquisition profit (10,000 x 30%)	3,000
	_____
	21,000
	_____

(W7) PURP in inventory

The unrealised profit (PURP) in inventory is calculated as:

Intra-group sales are $5.4 million on which Sonia made a profit of $1,800,000 (5,400 x 50/150). One third of these are still in inventory of Pauline, thus there is an unrealised profit of $600,000.

(W8) PURP in PPE

The transfer of the plant creates an initial unrealised profit (PURP) of $1,000,000. This is reduced by $200,000 for each year (straight-line depreciation over 5 years) of depreciation in the post-acquisition period. Thus at 31 March 2008 the net unrealised profit is $800,000. This should be eliminated from Pauline's retained profits and from the carrying amount of the plant.

(W9) Held for trading financial asset

The gain on held for trading financial assets are classified as fair value through profit or loss and will be recognised in income for the year.

Test your understanding 1 - Borough High Street

Borough High Street

	Date of acquisi-tion	FV of the NCI at acquisi-tion	Retained earnings at acquisi-tion	Total of the fair value of net assets at acquisition	Cost of invest-ment	Equity shares acquired
		$	$	$	$	$
High	1 July 20X7	55,000	30,000	120,000	100,000	45,000
Street	1 July 20X7	N/R	25,000	70,000	21,000	10,500

Summarised accounts of three entities for the year ended 30 June 20X8 are as follows:

Statements of financial position:

	Borough	High	Street
Assets:	$	$	$
Tangible Non Current Assets	100,000	80,000	60,000
Investments	121,000		
Inventory	22,000	30,000	15,000
Receivables	70,000	10,000	2,000
Cash at Bank	37,000	20,000	3,000
	350,000	140,000	80,000
Equity and liabilities			
Equity capital ($1 shares)	100,000	75,000	35,000
Retained earnings	200,000	50,000	40,000
Liabilities	50,000	15,000	5,000
	350,000	140,000	80,000

Income statements:	$	$	$
Revenue	500,000	200,000	100,000
Cost of sales	(300,000)	(140,000)	(60,000)
Gross profit	200,000	60,000	40,000
Administration costs	(50,000)	(10,000)	(10,000)
Operating profit	150,000	50,000	30,000
Interest	10,000	(10,000)	
Profit before tax	160,000	40,000	30,000
Tax	(60,000)	(20,000)	(15,000)
Profit after tax	100,000	20,000	15,000

The fair value adjustment in respect of High relates to tangible assets with a five-year life. The fair value adjustment in respect of Street relates to land. The fair values have not been incorporated. It is group policy to value the non-controlling interest using the full goodwill method. Goodwill has been subject to an impairment review and there is impairment to the extent of $7,000.

During the year Borough sold goods to High for $10,000 at a margin of 50%. At the year end the group had sold only 80% of these goods.

During the year Borough gave High substantial short-term loans – most of which was repaid shortly before the year-end. The final balance of $5,000 was paid on 10 July 20X8. The interest charged in High's income statement and the interest receivable in Borough's income statement represents interest on this loan.

Required:

Prepare the consolidated income statement for the year ended 30 June 20X8 and consolidated statement of financial position as at 30 June 20X8.

Illustration 2 H, S & A

The following are the summarised accounts of H, S, and A for the year ended 30 June 20X8.

During the year H paid a dividend of $25,000.

The shares in S and A were acquired on 1 July 20X5 when the retained earnings of S were $15,000 and the retained earnings of A were $10,000.

At the date of acquisition, the fair value of S's non-current assets, which at that time had a remaining useful life of ten years, exceeded the book value by $10,000.

During the year S sold goods to H for $10,000 at a margin of 50%. At the year-end H had sold 80% of the goods.

The group accounting policy is to measure the non-controlling interest of the subsidiary using the proportion of net assets method. At 30 June 20X8 the goodwill in respect of S had been impaired by 30% of its original amount, of which the current year loss was $1,200.

At 30 June 20X8 the investment in A had been impaired by $450, of which the current year loss was $150.

Statements of financial position	**H**	**S**	**A**
	$	$	$
Tangible non-current assets	87,000	88,000	62,000
Shares in: S (80%)	92,000		
A (30%)	15,000		
Current assets	97,000	40,000	9,000
	291,000	128,000	71,000
Equity capital ($1 shares)	200,000	75,000	35,000
Retained earnings	89,000	51,000	34,000
Liabilities	2,000	2,000	2,000
	291,000	128,000	71,000

Income statements

	$	$	S
Revenue	500,000	200,000	100,000
Operating costs	(400,000)	(140,000)	(60,000)
Profit from operations	100,000	60,000	40,000
Tax	(23,000)	(21,000)	(14,000)
Profit after tax	77,000	39,000	26,000

Required:

Prepare the consolidated income statement for the year ended 30 June 20X8 and consolidated statement of financial position as at 30 June 20X8.

Expandable text - Solution - H, S & A

Group income statement for the year ended 30 June 20X8

	$
Revenue (500,000 + 200,000 -10,000 intra-group)	690,000
Operating costs (400,000 + 140,000 + 1,200 goodwill impairment −10,000 intra-group + 1,000 20X8 depreciation on FV adj + 1,000 PURP)	(533,200)
Profit from operations	156,800
Income from associate ((30% × 26,000) – goodwill impairment 150)	7,650
Profit before tax	164,450
Tax (23,000 + 21,000)	(44,000)
Profit for the period	120,450
Attributable to:	
Equity holders of the parent	113,050
Non-controlling interest (20% × (39,000 – 1,000 20X8 depreciation on FV adj – 1,000 PURP)	7,400
Profit for the financial year	120,450

Consolidated statement of financial position as at 30 June 20X8

	$
Goodwill (W3)	8,400
Investment in associate (W6)	21,750
Tangible non-current assets	
(87,000 + 88,000 + 10,000 FV – 3,000 FV	
depreciation (W2))	182,000
Current assets (97,000 + 40,000 – 1,000 PURP (W2))	136,000
	348,150

	$
Retained earnings (W5)	117,750
Non-controlling interest (W4)	26,400
Liabilities (2,000 + 2,000)	4,000
	348,150

Workings

(W1) Group structure

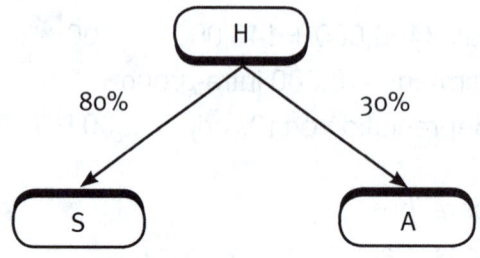

(W2) Net assets

	S		A	
	Acq	**Rep date**	**Acq**	**Rep date**
	$	$	$	$
Equity share capital	75,000	75,000	35,000	35,000
Retained earnings	15,000	51,000	10,000	34,000
Fair value adj	10,000	10,000		
Depreciation (3/10 × FV adj)	–	(3,000)		
URPS inventory (W7)		(1,000)		
	100,000	132,000	45,000	69,000

(W3) Goodwill – Proportionate share method

	$
Consideration paid by parent	92,000
NCI value at acquisition (20% x 100,000)(W2)	20,000
	————
Share of Net assets of S (80% 100,000)	112,000
Less: 100% of net assets at acquisition (W2)	(100,000)
	————
	12,000
Less: impairment loss – 30% thereof	(3,600)
	————
	8,400
	————

(W4) Non-controlling interest on proportionate basis

	$
NCI value at acquisition (W3)	20,000
NII share of post-acquisition profit (20% × 32,000) (W2)	6,400
	————
	26,400
	————

(W5) Retained earnings

	$
Parent	89,000
Less: impairment:	
S (W3)	(3,600)
A (W6)	(450)
Group share post-acq retained earnings:	
S 80% × 32,000 (W2)	25,600
A 30% × 24,000 (W2)	7,200
	————
	117,750
	————

(W6) Investment in associate

	$
Cost	15,000
Share of increase in net assets	
30% × 24,000 (W2)	7,200
	22,200
Less: impairment	(450)
	21,750

(W7) Inter company trading

Subsidiary made sales to parent
80% Group
20% NCI

	$
Unrealised profit	
10,000 × 20% × 50%	1,000
Dr group retained earnings	
80% × 1000	800
Dr NCI	
20% × 1000	200
Cr Inventory	1000

Note that as the unrealised profit on inventory has been earned by S. the consolidation adjustment required can be made in the net assets working at the reporting date.

Expandable text - Types of joint venture

IAS 31 Interests in joint ventures

A **joint venture** is a contractual arrangement whereby two or more parties undertake an economic activity that is subject to joint control.

In practice, joint control means that none of the parties alone can control the activity. To be classified as a joint venture, the contract must specify that all important decisions on financial and operating policy require each venturer's consent.

IAS 31 identifies three basic types of joint venture.

- **Jointly controlled operations**– involves the use of assets and resources of the venturers rather than establishing a separate entity.

- **Jointly controlled assets** – the venturers jointly control an asset dedicated to the use within the joint venture rather than establishing a separate entity.
- **Jointly controlled entities**– this involves the establishment of a separate entity in which each venturer has an interest.

Expandable text - Accounting for joint ventures

Jointly controlled operations

It is rare for a jointly controlled operation to have its own financial statements (although it is possible).

The individual financial statements of each individual venturer will recognise:

- the assets that it controls and the liabilities that it incurs
- the expenses that it incurs and its share of the revenue that it earns from the sale of goods or services by the joint venture.

As the income, expenses, assets and liabilities of the joint venture are included in the individual financial statements they will automatically flow through to the consolidated financial statements.

Jointly controlled assets

It is unlikely that there is a full set of accounts for this type of joint venture so the individual venturers will set up a joint venture account in their own records for the income and expenses incurred in respect of the joint venture and a memorandum income statement is prepared periodically to calculate the amount payable or receivable from the other venturers.

Jointly controlled entities

A jointly controlled entity keeps its own accounting records.

In the individual financial statements of the venturers, the investment in the joint venture is recorded at cost.

In the consolidated financial statements, IAS 31 gives a choice of treatment.

- **Proportionate consolidation** – the venturer includes its share of the assets, liabilities, income and expenses of the jointly controlled entity. This is the preferred method of accounting per IAS 31.
- **Equity method** – as used for associates (IAS 28).

Expandable text - Joint ventures: further detail

(a) Jointly controlled operations

A jointly controlled operation is a joint venture that involves the use of the assets and other resources of the venturers rather than the establishment of an entity that is separate from the venturers themselves. Each venturer uses its own assets and incurs its own expenses and liabilities. Profits are shared among the venturers in accordance with the contractual agreement.

Example

A and B decide to enter into a joint venture agreement to produce a new product. A undertakes one manufacturing process and B undertakes the other. A and B each bear their own expenses and take an agreed share of the sales revenue from the product.

(b) Jointly controlled assets

A jointly controlled asset is a joint venture in which the venturers control jointly (and often own jointly) an asset contributed to or acquired for the purpose of the joint venture. The venturers each take a share of the profit or income from the asset and each bears a share of the expenses involved.

Example

C and D together buy a house, which they let to tenants. C is responsible for the initial refurbishment and maintenance of the house and D finds the tenants and collects the rents. C and D each take an agreed share of the rental income from the house.

(c) Jointly controlled entities

A jointly controlled entity is a joint venture that involves the establishment of a corporation, partnership or other entity in which each venturer has an interest. The agreement between the venturers provides for their joint control over the entity. Otherwise, a jointly controlled entity operates in the same way as any other entity. Each venturer is entitled to a share of the entity's results.

Example

E and F enter into a joint venture agreement to manufacture and sell a new product. They set up an entity that carries out these activities. E and F each own 50% of the equity share capital of the entity and are its only directors. They share equally in major policy decisions and are each entitled to 50% of the profits of the entity.

(d) Accounting implications of joint ventures

There are three different aspects to the accounting for joint ventures:

- the financial statements of the joint venture
- the individual financial statements of each individual venturer
- the consolidated (group) financial statements of each individual venturer.

(1) Jointly controlled operations

The financial statements of the joint venture

Separate records

In theory it is possible for a jointly controlled operation to have a full set of records, but this is rare in practice.

A full set of separate accounting records would be kept for the joint venture so that the venturers can assess the performance of the venture (e.g. through regular management accounts).

Where the venture maintains a full set of accounting records, the transactions are recorded in exactly the same way as for an ordinary business. A separate income statement can be extracted, from which each venturer will be credited or debited with their agreed share of the profit or loss.

No separate records

Often (and certainly in examination questions), due to the short lifetime or size of the joint venture, it is not considered worthwhile opening a new set of records for what may only be a few transactions. In this case each venturer will record transactions on behalf of the venture in their own records, alongside their other business dealings.The individual and consolidated financial statements of the venturers

In its separate financial statements each individual venturer recognises:

- the assets that it controls and the liabilities that it incurs
- the expenses that it incurs and its share of the revenue that it earns from the sale of goods or services by the joint venture.

Because the assets, liabilities, income and expenses are recognised in the separate financial statements of a venturer, they will automatically be included in the venturer's consolidated financial statements, and no particular consolidation adjustments will be required.

(2) Jointly controlled assets

The accounts of the joint venture

As with jointly controlled operations, it is unlikely that a full set of separate accounting records will be kept for this type of joint venture. In practice, the accounting treatment of a jointly controlled asset is very similar to that of a jointly controlled operation:

- each individual venturer may set up a joint venture account in its own records for income and expenses directly incurred as part of the venture (the balance on the account represents the amount receivable from or payable to the other venturers)
- a memorandum income statement is prepared periodically in order to calculate the shares of income and expenses due to/from the individual venturers (this may also be used to assess the performance of the venture).

The extent of the accounting records kept will normally depend upon the exact terms of the agreement. In some cases, all that is necessary is an annual statement of joint expenses.

The individual and consolidated financial statements of the venturers

A jointly controlled asset may have a considerable impact on the financial statements of the individual venturers.

In its separate financial statements, and consequently in its consolidated financial statements, each venturer should recognise the following:

- its share of the jointly controlled assets, classified according to their nature (e.g. plant and equipment)
- any liabilities that it has incurred
- its share of any liabilities incurred jointly with the other venturers in relation to the joint venture
- any income from the sale or use of its share of the output of the joint venture
- any expenses that it has incurred in respect of its interest in the joint venture.

(3) Jointly controlled entities

The accounts of the joint venture

A jointly controlled entity keeps its own accounting records and prepares and presents financial statements in the same way as any other entity.

The individual accounts of the venturers

Each venturer usually contributes cash or other resources to the jointly controlled entity. For example, if the entity is a limited liability company a venturer normally exchanges cash or other assets for equity shares.

SIC 13 Jointly controlled entities – non-monetary contributions by venturers considers the circumstances in which a venturer can recognise a gain or loss in his or her income statement from contributing a non-monetary asset to the jointly controlled entity in exchange for an equity interest. SIC 13 states that recognition is appropriate unless:

- the risks and rewards relating to the non-monetary asset are not transferred to the jointly controlled entity
- the gain or loss cannot be measured reliably.

The venturers' interests in the joint venture are interests in the entity as a whole, not in its individual assets and liabilities. Therefore a venturer's interest in a jointly controlled entity is recognised in its own financial statements either at cost, or in accordance with IAS 39.

Consolidated financial statements of the venturers

IAS 31 contains a choice of accounting treatments. One possible treatment is proportionate consolidation (also called proportional consolidation in the UK). The venturer includes in its consolidated statements its share of each of the assets, liabilities, income and expenses of the jointly controlled entity, either combined on a line-by-line basis with similar items in the venturer's financial statements, or reported as separate line items.

Some academics argue that the proportionate consolidation method is most appropriate, since it best reflects the consideration of substance over form. The consolidated statement of financial position will include the venturer's share of the assets that it controls jointly and its shares of the liabilities for which it is jointly responsible.

The allowed alternative accounting treatment is the **equity method**, described earlier in the context of IAS 28 and associates. The argument for the equity method is that it is inappropriate to combine controlled items with jointly controlled items on the face of the consolidated statement of financial position.

Exception to the two treatments specified

If an interest in a jointly controlled entity is classified as held for sale under IFRS 5 it should be accounted for as per IFRS 5.

Transactions between a venturer and the joint venture

When a venturer buys assets from, or sells assets to, a joint venture, the question of unrealised profits arises. IAS 31 requires that when a venturer has sold an asset that is retained by the joint venture, the venturer should only recognise that portion of the gain which is attributable to the interests of the other venturers – no entity can make a profit by selling goods to itself.

The venturer should recognise the full amount of any loss arising, when the sale provides evidence of a reduction in the net realisable value of current assets or an impairment in the value of a non-current asset.

When a venturer purchases an asset from a joint venture, it cannot recognise its share of the profit on the sale until it resells the asset to an independent third party.

Losses on such transactions should be recognised immediately if they represent a reduction in the net realisable value of current assets or an impairment in the value of a non-current asset.

Disclosure requirements

A venturer should disclose a listing and description of interests in significant joint ventures, and the proportion of ownership interest held in jointly controlled entities.

A venturer should also disclose any contingencies and capital commitments associated with its interests in joint ventures.

A venturer should disclose the method used to account for jointly controlled entities – either proportionate consolidation or the equity method.

Expandable text - Current issues in group accounting

Consolidation and disclosures

As part of the US GAAP convergence process, the IASB and FASB aims to replace IAS 27 Business combinations and SIC 12 dealing with Special Purpose Entities, and the US equivalent, with a single new standard applicable to all entities.

The project addresses the following:

- a revised definition of control and related application guidance so that a single control model can be applied to all entities.

- enhanced disclosures about consolidated and unconsolidated entities to be published in a separate comprehensive disclosure standard related to involvement with other entities.

In April 2008, in response to the global financial crisis and the recommendation of the Financial Stability Forum, the Board decided to accelerate the consolidation project and proceed directly to the publication of an exposure draft. The Board published the exposure draft in December 2008 (ED10). In October 2009, the IASB and the FASB agreed to conduct their respective consolidation projects jointly, though with different time lines.

The IASB expects to issue the final consolidation and disclosure requirements by the end of 2010.

The following paragraphs summarise the main decisions made relating to the development of the proposed new standard:

Definition of control

A reporting entity controls another entity when the reporting entity has the power to direct the activities of that other entity to generate returns for the reporting entity. A reporting entity has the power to direct the activities of another entity when it has the ability to enforce its will in making decisions about the activities of an entity that significantly affect the returns at the time that decisions need to be taken. For this purpose, returns have a wide meaning and include, for example, dividends, interest, valuation gains or losses, service fees and other forms of remuneration as well as synergies.

Power with less than a majority of the voting rights

A reporting entity can have power to direct the activities of another entity by different means. A reporting entity generally has that power when it holds the majority of the voting rights in another entity. A reporting entity can also have that power, even though it holds less than a majority of the voting rights, because of agreements with other vote holders, other contractual agreements, options and convertible instruments, its voting rights or a combination thereof. To assess whether a reporting entity has the power to direct the activities of another entity because of its voting rights, even though it holds less than a majority of the voting rights in that entity, the reporting entity considers all available evidence. The evidence to be considered includes the size of the reporting entity's holding of voting rights relative to the size and dispersion of holdings of the other vote holders, voting patterns at previous shareholders meetings, options and convertible instruments and other contractual arrangements.

Options and convertible instruments

A reporting entity should consider options and convertible instruments when assessing whether it has the power to direct the activities of an entity that significantly affect the returns. Therefore, the assessment of whether a reporting entity has the power to direct the activities of another other entity includes not only a reporting entity's voting rights in another entity, but also consideration of all the facts and circumstances associated with options and convertible instruments.

Principal-agency relationships

An agent is a party engaged to act on behalf of another party or parties (the principal) that delegate some decision-making authority to the agent. When assessing its power to direct the activities of another entity, the principal considers the decision-making authority that it has delegated to agents. The agent does not have power over another entity only because decision-making authority has been delegated to it. When assessing whether a party acts as an agent or a principal, the reporting entity considers all facts and circumstances, including the overall relationship between that party, the entity being managed and the other interest holders.

Disclosures

A reporting entity should disclose information that helps users of financial statements to understand:

- the significant judgements and assumptions (and changes to those judgements and assumptions) made by the reporting entity in determining whether it controls (or does not control) another entity and/or the reporting entity's involvement with structured entities;

- the interest that the non-controlling interests have in the group's activities;

- the effect of restrictions on the reporting entity's ability to access and use assets or settle liabilities of consolidated entities, as a result of where the assets or liabilities are held in the group;

- the nature of, and changes in, the risks associated with the reporting entity's control of consolidated structured entities or involvement with unconsolidated structured entities.

The disclosure requirements for subsidiaries, joint arrangements and associates will be combined within a comprehensive disclosure standard that addresses a reporting entity's involvement with other entities. The disclosure standard will also contain disclosure requirements for unconsolidated structured entities (special purpose entities).

As a separate project, whilst still part of developing a new reporting standard for consolidation, particular consideration is being given to the circumstances of investment entities. IAS 27 Consolidated and Separate Financial Statements requires an investment entity to consolidate all investments in entities that it controls. ED 10 Consolidated Financial Statements did not propose to change the scope of the consolidation requirements. However, many respondents to ED 10 asked the IASB to consider whether investment entities should be exempt from consolidating investments in entities that are controlled.

In response to those requests, the IASB initiated a project to define an investment entities for the purpose of such an exemption (February 2010). The IASB conducts the project jointly with the FASB, though with different time lines. The boards completed their initial deliberations in June 2010. The IASB will issue an exposure draft early in Q4 2010. The FASB will decide early in Q4 2010 whether to issue a comprehensive exposure draft on consolidation. That exposure draft would include a proposal to amend the definition of an investment entity (or investment company) for US GAAP.

Joint ventures

The objective of the project is to develop an IFRS that enhances the accounting for, and the quality of information being reported about, joint arrangements by establishing a principle-based approach to the accounting for joint arrangements and by improving the disclosure requirements to allow investors to gain a better understanding of the nature, extent and financial effects of the activities that an entity carries out through joint arrangements.

The principle-based approach developed in the project requires an entity to recognise its contractual rights and obligations arising from its joint arrangements. Such a principle-based approach will provide investors with greater clarity about an entity's involvement in its joint arrangements by increasing the consistency, transparency and comparability of the reporting of these arrangements and it will do so by addressing principally two aspects of IAS 31 Interests in Joint Ventures:

* the structure of an arrangement will no longer be the most significant factor in determining the accounting, and

* accounting options will be eliminated.

In group accounts, IAS 31 permits accounting for joint ventures using either equity accounting or proportionate consolidation. Under the proposed new standard, proportionate consolidation will no longer ber permitted. This should have the effect of improving comparability of financial statements which include accounting for joint ventures.

The the main decisions made by the Board during its redeliberations on the exposure draft ED 9 include:

Scope

The IFRS on Joint Arrangements will be applied by all entities that have an interest in a joint arrangement. The scope exclusion in the exposure draft for venture capital organisations, mutual funds, unit trusts and similar entities, including investment-linked insurance funds, has been eliminated, and will be characterised in the final IFRS as a measurement exemption.

Joint Control

The final IFRS will maintain the term 'joint control' as one of the features that, along with the existence of an agreement, defines 'joint arrangements'.

Types of joint arrangement

Joint arrangements will be classified in two types, 'joint operations' and 'joint ventures', instead of the three types proposed in the exposure draft (which were 'joint operations', 'joint assets' and 'joint ventures'). Each type of joint arrangement is aligned with a specific accounting requirement (ie accounting for assets, liabilities, revenues and expenses in the case of a joint operation, and accounting for an investment using the equity method in the case of a joint venture).

When joint arrangements are established in a separate entity, it will be necessary to consider all relevant facts and circumstances to assess whether the arrangement is a joint operation or a joint venture, including the structure and form of the arrangement and the contractual terms agreed by the parties.

Investors in a joint arrangement

The final IFRS will introduce the term 'investors in a joint arrangement' to designate a party to a joint arrangement that does not have joint control over the activity of that joint arrangement.

Consensus of SIC-13

The consensus of SIC-13 Jointly Controlled Entities—Non-Monetary Contributions by Venturers will be incorporated as an amendment to IAS 28 Investments in Associates.

Loss of joint control

The proposals in ED 9 for the accounting for the loss of joint control when significant influence is retained will be carried forward into the final IFRS. All descriptions that associate 'loss of joint control' and 'loss of significant influence' in existing IFRSs with the term 'significant economic event' will be removed. This term will be retained only for the event of 'loss of control'. As such, IAS 21 The Effects of Changes in Foreign Exchange Rates will therefore be amended so that the accounting for the loss of joint control over a joint venture that includes a foreign operation, but in which the investor retains significant influence, is treated as a partial disposal instead of as an entire disposal.

The final IFRS will additionally require that when an entity partially disposes of an interest in a joint venture or in an associate, it should reclassify as held for sale only the interest disposed of if such a partial disposal fulfils the criteria for classification as held for sale set out in IFRS 5. The retained interest should continue to be accounted for using the equity method until the disposal takes place.

Disclosures

The disclosure requirements for joint arrangements will be placed in a separate IFRS that will include disclosure requirements for involvement with entities that are not within the scope of IFRS 9 Financial Instruments, such as subsidiaries, associates and unconsolidated structured entities. The main disclosure requirements affecting both joint arrangements and associates will be:

- a list and description of interests in individually-material joint arrangements and associates;

- disclosure of commitments in relation to an entity's interests in joint ventures and contingent liabilities in relation to an entity's interests in joint ventures and associates; and

- summarised financial information will be provided for individually-material joint ventures and associates.

Transition

The final IFRS will not require an entity to adjust the differences between the proportionate consolidation method and the equity method retrospectively, when an entity transitions from accounting for its joint arrangements from proportionate consolidation to the equity method. Instead, it will require an entity to aggregate the previously proportionate consolidated balances into a single investment line at the opening balance of the earliest period presented. An entity will be required to apply paragraphs 31-34 of IAS 28 with regard to impairment losses to the opening balance of the investment, and to recognise any related impairment in retained earnings at the opening balance of the earliest period presented. An entity will be required to disclose a breakdown of the assets and liabilities that have been aggregated into the single line investment balance at the opening balance of the earliest period presented

At August 2010, the intention would appear to be that a new reporting standard will be issued before the end of 2010.

Expandable text - UK syllabus focus

The ACCA UK syllabus contains a requirement that UK variant candidates should be able to discuss and apply the key differences between UK GAAP and IFRS GAAP. The accounting requirements of UK GAAP and IFRS GAAP are very similar in this area, but there are one or two differences.

You should approach questions using the standard approach of completing the five standard workings identified within chapter 1. However, there are some key similarities and differences:

- Both UK GAAP and IFRS GAAP require consolidation when one entity acquires control of another; the basic mechanics of how this is achieved is similar under both sets of regulation. For example, UK FRS 7 and IFRS 3 both require that the fair value of the net assets at the date of acquisition to be determined as a basis for calculation of goodwill.

- Under UK GAAP, goodwill, and therefore minority interest (non-controlling interest under IFRS GAAP) is calculated only on the cost of acquisition incurred by the parent entity; i.e. the 'proportionate basis' referred to within this publication. Therefore any group accounts questions using the proportionate basis for calculation of goodwill and non-controlling interest are appropriate for compliance with UK GAAP.

- Under UK GAAP, goodwill is normally amortised over its expected useful life in accordance with FRS 10. On occasion, examination questions have stated that goodwill is to be regarded as a permanent asset, subject to annual impairment review. This would bring the accounting treatment for goodwill into alignment with IFRS GAAP. Therefore, there will also be some value in working questions where the goodwill accounting policy is to regard it as a permanent asset, subject to an annual impairment review.

- Under UK GAAP, costs of acquisition (e.g. legal and professional fees incurred) are capitalised as part of the cost of the acquistion. This is not the case under IFRS GAAP.

- If negative goodwill arises on consolidation, it is capitalised within fixed assets as a 'negative asset' and released to profit or loss based upon the nature of what has given rise to that negative goodwill. For monetary assets and liabilities (e.g debtors, creditors etc), negative goodwill is released immediately to profit and loss. For non-monetary assets (e.g. fixed assets and stocks) it is released to profit and loss over the expected life of those assets.

- UK FRS 9 deals with accounting for associates and joint ventures. There are no major differences between UK FRS 9 and IAS 28 and IAS 31 dealing with associates and joint ventures respectively. One minor detail is that in the group income statement, the share of associates operating profit, interest and tax are separately accounted for, rather than simply taking the share of associate profit after tax for the year. The end result is the same, but UK FRS 9 discloses additional detail. UK FRS 9 does not permit one of the two accounting treatments allowed by IAS 31 when accounting for joint ventures; essentially, equity accounting is used and proportional consolidation is not allowed.

- The Companies Act and FRS 2 identify reasons for the possible exclusion of a subsidiary from consolidation which can be summarised as follows:

Reason	FRS 2	Treatment
Immaterial	Not applicable	Exclude from consolidation as reporting standards do not apply to immaterial items, and such items are not required to be fairly stated in order for the financial statements to show a true and fair view.
Severe long-term restrictions in exercising control.	Mandatory exclusion	If restrictions in force at date of acquisition, initially recognise at cost. If restrictions come into force at a later date, equity account from date restrictions came into force. Consider the possible recognition of an impairment of the investment.
Interest held solely with a view to sale.	Mandatory exclusion	Recognise as a current asset at the lower of cost and NRV
Consolidation would only be possible following undue expense or delay in obtaining or preparing information.	Mandatory inclusion	Consolidate as normal
Dissimilar activities	Mandatory inclusion	Consolidate as normal. Additional disclosures would normally be provided per SSAP 25.

KAPLAN PUBLISHING

Expandable text - UK GAAP question

Crash, Bang and Wallop

	Date of acquisition	Reserves at acquisition	Total of the fair value of net assets at acquisition	Cost of investment	Ordinary shares acquired
		$	$	$	$
Bang	1 July 20X7	30,000	90,000	100,000	45,000
Wallop	1 July 20X7	25,000	70,000	30,000	10,500

Summarised accounts of three entities for the year ended 30 June 20X8 are as follows:

Balance sheets:

	Crash £	Bang £	Wallop £
Fixed assets:			
Tangible fixed assets	100,000	80,000	60,000
Investments	130,000		
Current assets:			
Stock	10,000	30,000	15,000
Debtors	70,000	10,000	2,000
Cash at Bank	40,000	20,000	3,000
Liabilities	(50,000)	(15,000)	(50,000)
	300,000	125,000	75,000
Share capital and reserves:			
Ordinary share capital (£1 shares)	100,000	75,000	35,000
Retained earnings	200,000	50,000	40,000
	300,000	125,000	75,000

Profit and loss accounts:	£	£	£
Turnover	500,000	200,000	100,000
Cost of sales	(300,000)	(140,000)	(60,000)
Gross profit	200,000	60,000	40,000
Administration costs	(50,000)	(10,000)	(10,000)
Operating profit	150,000	50,000	30,000
Interest	10,000	(10,000)	
Profit before tax	160,000	40,000	30,000
Tax	(60,000)	(20,000)	(15,000)
Profit after tax	100,000	20,000	15,000

The fair value adjustment in respect of Bang relates to tangible assets with a five-year life. The fair value adjustment in respect of Wallop relates to land. The fair values have not been incorporated.

During the year Crash sold goods to High for $10,000 at a margin of 50%. At the year end the group had sold only 80% of these goods.

During the year Crash gave Bang substantial short-term loans – most of which was repaid shortly before the year-end. The final balance of $5,000 was paid on 10 July 20X8. The interest charged in Bang's profit and loss account and the interest receivable in Crash's profit and loss account represents interest on this loan.

It is group accounting policy to amortise goodwill over five years.

Required:

Prepare the consolidated balance sheet at 30 June 20X8, together with the consolidated profit and loss account for the year ended 30 June 20X8.

Crash Group profit and loss account for the year ended 30 June 20X8

			£
Turnover	500,000 + 200,000	Less inter coy (10,000)	690,000
Cost of Sales	300,000 + 140,000	Less inter coy (10,000)	(437,200)
	Plus the PURP 1,000	Less: dep'n on the neg FVA 3,000	
	Less:g'will amort (9,200) (W3)		
Gross profit			252,800
Administration exps	50,000 + 10,000		(60,000)
Operating profit			192,800
Interest	All intercompany		nil
Income from Assoc.	(W8)		7,200
Profit before tax			200,000
Tax	60,000 + 20,000 + (30% x 15,000)		(84,500)
Profit after tax			115,500
Attributable to group	Bal fig		106,300
Attributable to MI	(W9)		92,000
			115,500

Crash Group statement of financial position as at 30 June 20X8

Fixed Assets				£
Intangible	(W3)			36,800
Tangible	100,000 + 80,000	**Less** FVA (15,000) **plus** dep'n 3,000 (W2)		168,000
Investment in Associate	(W7)			32,700
				237,500
Current Assets				
Stock	10,000 + 30,000	Less PURP (w5) (1,000)	39,000	
Debtors	70,000 + 10,000	Less intercompany (5,000)	75,000	
Cash at bank	40,000 + 20,000		60,000	
			174,000	
Creditors	50,000 + 15,000	Less intercompany (5,000)	(60,000)	114,000
				351,500

Share capital and reserves		£
Ordinary share capital		100,000
Group reserves	(W5)	206,300
Minority interest	(W4)	45,200
		351,500

(W1) Group structure

Crash is the parent
Bang is a 60% subsidiary (45/75)
Wallop is a 30% associate (10.5/35)
Both acquisitions took place a year ago

(W2) Net assets

	Bang		Wallop	
	Acq	**Y/e**	**Acq**	**Y/e**
	$	$	$	$
Equity capital	75,000	75,000	35,000	35,000
Retained earnings	30,000	50,000	25,000	40,000
FVA	*(15,0000)	(15,000)	10,000	10,000
Dep'n on FVA		3,000		
	90,000	113,000	70,000	85,000

*bal fig - it is unusual to have a negative fair value adjustment - this means that, instead of writing this off as a depreciation charge, there will, in fact, be a write-back over the estimated useful life of the assets.

(W3) Goodwill

	Bang	Wallop
	£	£
Consideration paid	100,000	30,000
Less: 60% x 90,000 re Bang (W2)	(54,000)	
Less: 30% x 70,000 re Wallop (W2)		(21,000)
Goodwill at acquisition	35,000	9,000
Amortisation 1/5	(9,200)	(1,800)
	36,800	7,200

(W4) Minority interest re Bang

	£
40% x 113,000	45,200

(W5) Group reserves

		£
Crash		200,000
Less PURP (W6)	Parent is the seller	(1,000)
Share of post-acquisition retained earnings:	(change in net assets)	
High 60% x (137,000 – 120,000) (W2)		10,200
Street 30% x (85,000 – 70,000) (W2)		4,500
Goodwill amortised - Bang (W3)		(9,200)
Goodwill amortised - Wallop (W3)		(1,800)
		206,300

(W6) Provision for unrealised profit

The parent is the seller so the parent's retained earnings are adjusted
20% x 10,000 = 2,000 (unsold goods) x 50% margin = 1,000

(W7) Investment in the associate - Wallop

EITHER:

	£
Cost	30,000
Share of increase in net assets (30% x (85–70) (W2))	4,500
Less: amortisation of premium on acquisition	(1,800)
	32,700

OR:

	£
Group share of net assets: 30% x 85,000 (W2)	25,500
Plus: unamortised premium on acquisition (W3)	7,200
	32,700

(W8) Income from the associate	£
Group % of operating profit	9,000
Less: amortisation of premium (1/5 x 9,000) (W3)	(1,800)
	7,200

	$
40% x (20,000 + *3,000)	9,200

*the depreciation write back on the negative fair value adjustment

3 Chapter summary

Background to group accounts

- Consolidated accounts show the results of the group
- Intercompany transactions and balances must be eliminated
- All companies in the group should use the same accounting policies and have the same reporting sheet date

---

Goodwill and fair value adjustments

- Goodwill is calculated as the excess of consideration + the NCI over the fair value of the net assets of the subsidiary

- The NCI is valued as either:
  - the NCI% × NAs of the subsidiary at reporting date OR
  - FV of the NCI at acquisition + NCI% × post acquisition movement in reserves

- All assets, liabilities and contingent liabilities at the acquisition date (including those not recognised in the subsidiary's financial statements) must be recognised at fair value

---

Consolidation techniques

- A methodical approach is the best way to complete a group accounting question
- The following workings should be used:
  - group structure
  - net assets
  - goodwill
  - non-controlling interest
  - group retained earnings

Associates and joint ventures

- Associates are accounted for using the equity method
- Joint ventures are accounted for according to the type of venture
- Joint ventures that are separate entities may be accounted for using the equity method in the same way as associates

---

Current issues in group accounting

- Consolidation
- Joint arrangements

Test your understanding answers

Test your understanding 1 - Borough High Street

Borough Group Income statement for the year ended 30 June 20X8

			$
Revenue	500,000 + 200,000	Less inter coy (10,000)	690,000
Cost of Sales	300,000 + 140,000	Less inter coy (10,000)	(441000)
	Plus the PURP 1,000	Add dep'n on the FVA 3,000	
	G'will impaired 7,000		
Gross profit			249,000
Administration exps	50,000 + 10,000		(60,000)
Operating profit			189,000
Interest	All intercompany		nil
Income from Ass.	(W8)		4,500
Profit before tax			193,500
Tax	60,000 + 20,000		(80,000)
Profit after tax			113,500
Attributable to owners of parent	Bal fig		109,500
Attributable to NCI	(W9)		4,000
			113,500

Borough Group statement of financial position as at 30 June 20X8

Non Current Assets			$
Intangible	(W3)		28,000
Tangible	100,000 + 80,000	Add: FVA 15,000 less dep'n 3,000 (W2)	192,000
Investment in Associate	(W7)		25,500
Current Assets			
Inventory	22,000 + 30,000	Less PURP (W5) (1,000)	51,000
Receivables	70,000 + 10,000	Less intercompany (5,000)	75,000
Cash at bank	37,000 + 20,000		57,000
			428,500
Equity capital			100,000
Retained earnings	(W5)		209,500
Non-controlling interest	(W4)		59,000
Total equity			368500
Liabilities	50,000 + 15,000	Less inter coy (5,000)	60,000
			428,500

(W1) Group structure

Borough is the parent
High is a 60% subsidiary (45/75)
Street is a 30% associate (10.5/35)
Both acquisitions took place a year ago

KAPLAN PUBLISHING

(W2) Net assets

	High		Street	
	Acq	**Y/e**	**Acq**	**Y/e**
	$	$	$	$
Equity capital	75,000	75,000	35,000	35,000
Retained earnings	30,000	50,000	25,000	40,000
FVA	15,000*	15,000	10,000	10,000
Dep'n on FVA		(3,000)		
	120,000	137,000	70,000	85,000

*bal fig

(W3) Goodwill – Full goodwill (fair value) method

			High
			$
Consideration paid			100,000
FV of NCI at acq			55,000
			155,000
Less: 100% of net assets at acquisition (W2)			(120,000)
Total goodwill at acquisition			35,000
Impairment	Group 60%	(4,200)	
	NCI 40%	(2,800)	
			(7,000)
Unimpaired goodwill			28,000

(W4) Non-controlling interest (full fair value basis)

	$
Fair value of NCI at acquisition (given)	55,000
NCI % of post-acquisition retained earnings (40% x 17,000)	6,800
NCI share of goodwill impairment (W3)	(2,800)
Total unimpaired goodwill	59,000

(W5) Group retained earnings

		$
Parent		200,000
Less PURP (W5)	Parent is the seller	(1,000)
Share of post-acquisition retained earnings:	(change in net assets)	
High 60% x (137,000 – 120,000) (W2)		10,200
Street 30% x (85,000 – 70,000) (W2)		4,500
Group share of goodwill impairment (W3)		(4,200)
		209,500

(W6) Provision for unrealised profit

The parent is the seller so the parent's retained earnings are adjusted 20% x 10,000 = 2,000 (unsold goods) x 50% margin = 1,000

(W7) Investment in the associate

	$
Cost	21,000
Share of increase in net assets (30% x (85–70) (W2))	4,500
	25,500

(W8) Income from the associate

	$
Group % of the profit after tax (30% x 15,000)	4,500

(W9) Non-controlling interest in the profit after tax

	$
40% x (20,000 - *3,000)	6,800
Less: NCI share of goodwill impairment (W3)	(2,800)
	4,000

*the depreciation charge for the year on the fair value adjustment

Complex groups

Chapter learning objectives

Upon completion of this chapter you will be able to:

Determine appropriate procedures to be used in preparing group financial statements:

- apply the method of accounting for business combinations, including complex group structures (vertical and D-shaped/mixed groups)

- apply the recognition and measurement criteria for identifiable acquired assets and liabilities and goodwill including step acquisitions

- determine the appropriate procedures to be used in preparing group financial statements.

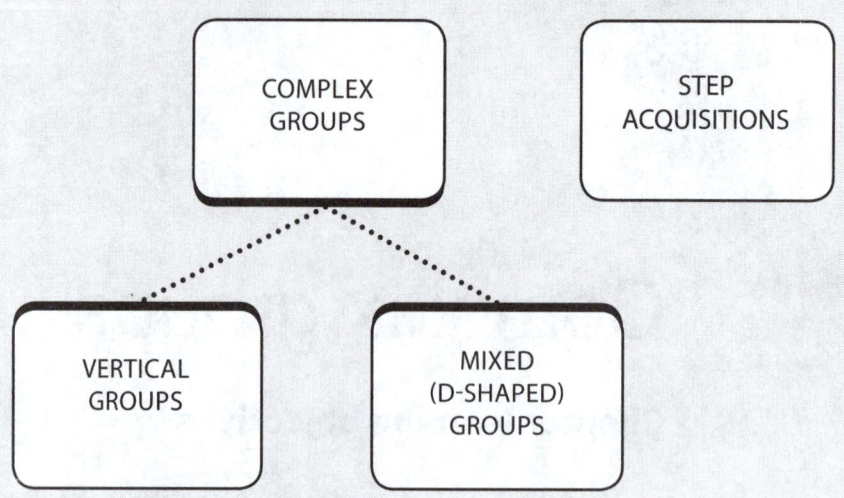

1 Complex group structures

Complex group structures exist where a subsidiary of a parent entity owns a majority shareholding in another entity which makes that other entity also a subsidiary of the parent entity.

Complex structures can be classified under two headings:

*   vertical groups
*   mixed groups.

2 Vertical groups

Definition

A **vertical group** arises where a subsidiary of the parent entity holds shares in a further entity such that control is achieved. The parent entity therefore controls both the subsidiary entity and, in turn, its subsidiary (often referred to as a sub-subsidiary entity). Look at the two situations:

Situation 1:	**Situation 2:**
H	H
owns 90% of	owns 70% of
S	S
who, in turn, owns 80% of	who, in turn, owns 60% of
T	T

In both situations, H controls both S and also T - there is a vertical group comprising three entities. H has a controlling interest in entity S. S has a controlling interest in entity T. H is therefore able to exert control over T by virtue of its ability to control S.

The normal consolidation principles and workings will be applied to consolidate a vertical group. Goodwill must be calculated and non-controlling interests recognised for each subsidiary in the group. Particular care will be needed to apply the holding entity (H in the two situations above) effective interest in the sub-subsidiary (T in the two situations above) in the workings.

The narrative which follows explains and illustrates how the group effective interest and non-controlling effective interest in a sub-subsidiary is determined, together with workings to calculate goodwill, NCI and group retained earnings as required. There is also explanation to determine when the sub-subsidiary becomes a member of the group for consolidation.

Consolidation

Where a parent entity owns a controlling interest in a subsidiary, which in turn owns a controlling interest in a sub-subsidiary, then the group accounts of the ultimate parent entity must include the underlying net assets and earnings of both the subsidiary and the sub-subsidiary companies.

Thus, both entities that are controlled by the parent are consolidated.

The basic techniques of consolidation are the same as seen previously, although calculations of goodwill and the non-controlling interest become slightly more complicated.

Effective shareholding and non-controlling interest

In the two situations identified opposite, H has a **direct** interest in S and an **indirect** interest in T (exercised via S's holding in T).

In situation 1, H has an **effective** interest of only 72% (90% × 80%) in T. Nevertheless, T is a sub-subsidiary of H because H has a controlling interest in S and S has a controlling interest in T. As H has an effective interest in T of 72%, it follows that the non-controlling interest in T is 28%. This can be analysed as follows:

	%
Owned by outside shareholders in T	20
Owned by outside shareholders in H (100% – 90%) × 80%	8
	—
Effective non-controlling interest in T	28
	—

Similarly, in situation 2, H has an **effective** interest of just 42% (70% × 60%) in T. Nevertheless, T is a sub-subsidiary of H because H has a controlling interest in S and S has a controlling interest in T. As H has an effective interest in T of 42%, it follows that the non-controlling interest in T is 58%. This can be analysed as follows:

	%
Owned by outside shareholders in T	40
Owned by outside shareholders in H (100% – 70%) × 60%)	18
	—
Effective non-controlling interest in T	58
	—

In situation 2, do not be put off by the fact that the effective group interest in T is less than 50%, and that the effective non-controlling interest in T is more than 50%. The effective interest calculations are the result of a two-stage acquisition and are used to simplify the consolidation workings.

Group reserves

Only the group or effective percentage of each of the reserves of the sub-subsidiary are included within group reserves. Often the only reserve will be retained earnings, but there could be others, such as revaluation reserve.

Date of acquisition

The date of acquisition of each subsidiary is the date on which H gains control. If S already held T when H acquired S, treat S and T as being acquired on the same day. Consider the following situations to determine when the sub-subsidiary company, T, becomes a member of the H group::

(1) H acquired control of S on 1 January 2004; S subsequently acquired control of another entity, T, on 1 July 2006.

(2) H acquired control of S on 1 July 2006; S had already acquired control of another entity, T, on 1 January 2004.

In the first situation, T does not come under the control of H until S acquires shares in T - i.e on 1 July 2006. In the second situation, H cannot gain control of T until S acquires shares in T on 1 July 2006.

To identify the date that the sub-subsidiary becomes a member of the group, include the dates of share purchases within your group structure when answering questions: the key date will be the later of the two possible dates of acquisition.

The following examples consider situations where:

(1) the subsidiary is acquired by the parent first; the subsidiary later acquires the sub-subsidiary, and

(2) the parent acquires the subsidiary that already holds the sub-subsidiary.

Illustration 1 - Vertical group

The draft statements of financial position of David, Colin and John, as at 31 December 20X4, are as follows:

	D	C	J		D	C	J
	$000	$000	$000		$000	$000	$000
Sundry assets	280	180	130	Equity capital	200	100	50
				Retained earnings	100	60	30
Shares in subsidiary	120	80		Liabilities	100	100	50
	400	260	130		400	260	130

You ascertain the following:

• David acquired 75,000 $1 shares in Colin on 1 January 20X4 when the retained earnings of Colin amounted to $40,000. At that date, the fair value attributable to the non-controlling interest in Colin was valued at $38,000.

• Colin acquired 40,000 $1 shares in John on 30 June 20X4 when the retained earnings of John amounted to $25,000; they had been $20,000 on the date of David's acquisition of Colin. At that date, the fair value of the non-controlling interest in John (both direct and indirect), based upon effective shareholdings, was valued at $31,000.

• Goodwill has suffered no impairment.

Produce the consolidated statement of financial position of the David group at 31 December 20X4. It is group policy to value the non-controlling interest at fair value.

Expandable text - Solution

Step 1

Draw a diagram of the group structure and set out the respective interests of the parent entity and the non-controlling interests, distinguishing between direct (D) and indirect (I) interests. You may find it useful to include on the diagram the dates of acquisition of the subsidiary and the sub-subsidiary.

```
David
  |        75% acquired 1 Jan X4
Colin
  |        80% acquired 30 June X4
John
```

Group and Non Controlling interests

	Colin	John
Group interest	75%	60% (75% × 80%)
Non Controlling interest	25%	40% (25% × 80%)
	100%	100%

Step 2

Start with the net assets consolidation working as normal.

Care must be taken in determining the date for the split between post-acquisition and pre-acquisition retained earnings. The relevant date will be that on which David (the parent company) acquired control of each entity:

• Colin: 1 January 20X4

• John: 30 June 20X4

Therefore, the information given regarding John's retained earnings at 1 January 20X4 is irrelevant in this context.

Net assets of subsidiaries

| | Colin | | John | |
	At acq'n	At rep date	At acq'n	At rep date
	$	$	$	$
Equity capital	100,000	100,000	50,000	50,000
Reserves	40,000	60,000	25,000	30,000
	140,000	160,000	75,000	80,000

Step 3

Goodwill

- A separate calculation is required to determine goodwill for each subsidiary.

- For the sub-subsidiary, goodwill is calculated from the perspective of the ultimate parent entity (David) rather than the immediate parent (Colin). Therefore, the effective cost of John is only David's share of the amount that Colin paid for John, i.e. $80,000 × 75% = $60,000.

	Colin	John	
	$000	$000	
Cost of investment in subsidiary	120	60	(i.e 75% of 80,000)
Fair value of NCI	38	31	
	158	91	
FV of net assets (W2)	(140)	(75)	
	18	16	

Step 4

Non-controlling interest

When taking the non-controlling share of Colin's net assets, an adjustment must be made to take out the cost of investment in John that is included in the net assets of Colin.

In the group statement of financial position, the cost of investment is replaced by including all the net assets of John, so no investment must remain.

The non-controlling interest in Colin are entitled to their (indirect) share of the net assets of John, but they receive these by virtue of the effective interest that will be used to calculate the non-controlling interest in John.

	$000
Colin: NCI FV at acquisition	38
Colin NCI share of post-acq'n retained earnings (25% x 20,000)	5
Less: NCI share of cost of investment in John (25% × 80,000)	(20)
	23
John: NCI FV at acquisition	31
John NCI share of post acq'n retained earnings (40% x 5)	2
	56

Step 5

Group retained earnings

	$000
David	100
Colin 75% × 20,000 (post-acquisition retained earnings)	15
John 60% × 5,000 (post-acquisition retained earnings)	3
	118

Note that again, only the group or effective interest of 60% is taken of the post-acquisition retained earnings of John.

Step 6

Summarised consolidated statement of financial position of David its subsidiary entities as at 31 December 20X4

	$
Goodwill (18,000 + 16,000)	34,000
Sundry assets (280,000 + 180,000 + 130,000)	590,000
	624,000

Equity and liabilities:	
Equity capital	200,000
Retained earnings (Step 5)	118,000
	318,000
Non-controlling interest (Step 4)	56,000
Total equity	374,000
Liabilities (100,000 + 100.000 +50,000)	250,000
	624,000

Expandable text - Vertical groups - further Illustration

The draft statements of financial position of Daniel, Craig and James as at 31 December 20X4 are as follows:

	D	C	J		D	C	J
	$000	$000	$000		$000	$000	$000
Sundry assets	180	80	80	Equity capital	200	100	50
Shares in subsidiary	120	80		Retained earnings	100	60	30
	300	160	80		300	160	80

- Craig acquired 40,000 $1 shares in James on 1 January 20X4 when the retained earnings of James amounted to $25,000.

- Daniel acquired 75,000 $1 shares in Craig on 30 June 20X4 when the retained earnings of Craig amounted to $40,000 and those of James amounted to $30,000.

Calculate goodwill arising on consolidation, together with the group reserves and non-controlling interest figures. It is group policy to value the non-controlling interest using the proportion of net assets method.

Solution

This illustration differs from Illustration 1 only in that Craig acquires James in the first place and then on 30 June 20X4, Daniel acquires its shares in Craig (and so achieves control over both Craig and James).

The relevant acquisition date for both entities is therefore the date that they both joined the Daniel group, i.e. 30 June 20X4.

Step 1

Group structure and group NCI percentages are exactly as detailed in Illustration 2.

Step 2

Net assets of subsidiaries

	Craig		James	
	At acquisition	At reporting date	At acquisition	At reporting date
	$	$	$	$
Share capital	100,000	100,000	50,000	50,000
Reserves	40,000	60,000	30,000	30,000
	140,000	160,000	80,000	80,000

Step 3

Goodwill

	Craig	James
	$000	$000
Cost of investment	120	60
For		
75% (140,000)	(105)	
60% (80,000)		(48)
Goodwill	15	12

Step 4

Non-controlling interest is as detailed in Illustration 2.

Step 5

Group retained earnings	$000
Daniel	100
Craig 75% × 20 (post-acquisition retained earnings)	15
James (no post-acquisition retained earnings)	–
	115

Test your understanding 1 - H, S & T

The following are the statements of financial position at 31 December 20X7 for H group companies:

	H	S	T
	$	$	$
45,000 shares in S	65,000		
30,000 shares in T		55,000	
Sundry assets	280,000	133,000	100,000
	345,000	188,000	100,000
Equity share capital ($1 shares)	100,000	60,000	50,000
Retained earnings	45,000	28,000	25,000
Liabilities	200,000	100,000	25,000
	345,000	188,000	100,000

The inter-company shareholdings were acquired on 1 January 20X1 when the retained earnings of S were $10,000 and those of T were $8,000. At that date, the fair value of the non-controlling interest in S was $20,000. The fair value of the total non-controlling interest (direct and indirect) in T was $50,000. It is group policy to value the non-controlling interest using the full goodwill method. At the reporting date, goodwill is fully impaired and had been written off in an earlier year.

Required:

Prepare the consolidated statement of financial position for the H group at 31 December 20X7.

Test your understanding 2 - Grape, Vine and Wine

Grape purchased 40,000 of the 50,000 $1 shares in Vine on 1 July 20X5, when the retained earnings of that entity were $80,000. At that time, Vine held 7,500 of the 10,000 $1 shares in Wine. These had been purchased on 1 January 20X5 when Wine's retained earnings were $65,000. On 1 July 20X5, Wine's retained earnings were $67,000.

At 1 July 20X5, the fair value of the non-controlling interest in Vine was $27,000, and that of Wine (both direct and indirect) was $31,500.

Statements of financial position of the three entities at 30 June 20X6 were as follows:

	Grape	Vine	Wine
	$000	$000	$000
Investment	110	60	
Sundry assets	350	200	120
Net assets	460	260	120
Equity share capital	100	50	10
Retained earnings	210	110	70
Liabilities	150	100	40
	460	260	120

Required:

Prepare the consolidated statement of financial position for Grape group at 30 June 20X6. It is group policy to value the non-controlling interest using the full goodwill method.

3 Mixed (D-shaped) groups

Definition

In a mixed group situation the parent entity has a direct controlling interest in at least one subsidiary. In addition, the parent entity and the subsidiary together hold a controlling interest in a further entity.

e.g.

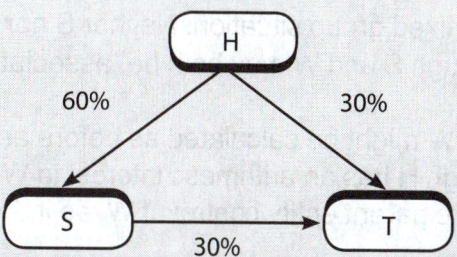

- H controls 60% of S; S is therefore a subsidiary of H.

- H controls 30% of T directly and another 30% indirectly via its interest in S. T is therefore a sub-subsidiary of the H group. H has control of 60%, either directly or indirectly, of the shares in T and is therefore able to control it.

Date of acquisition

As with the vertical group structure considered earlier in this chapter, identify the dates of the respective share purchases to help determine the date when the entity at the bottom of the group (often, but not always a sub-subsidiary) becomes a member of the group. Using the example of H, S & T above, if dates of share purchases are added as follows:

Suppose H acquired a 60% interest in S on 1 January 2004, and acquired its 30% interest on the same date. S subsequently acquired its 30% interest in T on 1 July 2006.

Initially, from 1 January 2004, H exercises significant influence over T as an associate entity. It is only from 1 July 2006 that H has access to more than 50% of the voting power in T; T is therefore consolidated into the H group accounts as a subsidiary from 1 July 2006.

Alternatively, suppose H acquired a 60% interest in S on 1 January 2006, and acquired its 30% interest on the same date. S acquired its 30% interest in T on 1 July 2004.

Initially, from 1 January 2004, S exercises significant influence over T as an associate entity. It is only from 1 July 2006 that H has access to more than 50% of the voting power in T; T is therefore consolidated into the H group accounts from 1 July 2006.

Note that the definition of a mixed group does not include the situation where the parent and an associate together hold a controlling interest in a further entity.

E.g.

H owns 35% of S, S owns 40% of W and H owns 40% of W.

This is **not** a mixed group situation. Neither S nor W is a member of the H group, although S and W may both be 'associates' of H.

H's interest in W might be calculated as before as (35% × 40%) + 40% = 54%. Although H has an arithmetic interest in W that is more than 50%, it does not have parent entity control of W, as it does not control S's 40% stake in W.

Consolidation

All three entities in the above mixed group are consolidated.

The approach is similar to dealing with sub-subsidiaries, i.e. an effective interest is computed and used to allocate share capital and retained earnings.

From the example above:

S	Group share	60%	
	NCI		40%
T	Group share		
	Direct	30%	
	Indirect 60% of 30%	18%	
		———	
	Total	48%	
	NCI		52%

All consolidation workings are the same as those used in vertical group situations, with the exception of goodwill.

The **goodwill** calculation for the sub-subsidiary differs in that two elements to cost must be considered, namely:

- the cost of the parent's direct holding
- the parent's percentage of the cost of the subsidiary's holding (the indirect holding).

Illustration 2- Mixed (D-shaped) groups

The statements of financial position of H, S and M as at 31 December 20X5 were as follows:

	H	S	M
	$	$	$
45,000 shares in S	72,000		
16,000 shares in M	25,000		
12,000 shares in M		20,000	
Sundry assets	125,000	120,000	78,000
	222,000	140,000	78,000
Equity share capital ($1 shares)	120,000	60,000	40,000
Retained earnings	95,000	75,000	35,000
Liabilities	7,000	5,000	3,000
	222,000	140,000	78,000

All shares were acquired on 31 December 20X2 when the retained earnings of S amounted to $30,000 and those of M amounted to $10,000.

It is group accounting policy to value non-controlling interest on a proportionate basis.

Required:

Prepare the statement of financial position for the H group at 31 December 20X5.

Expandable text - Solution

Group statement of financial position - H group

at 31 December 20X5

	$
Intangible - goodwill (4,500 + 8.750)(W3)	13,250
Sundry assets (125,000 + 120,000 + 78,000)	323,000
	336,250

	$
Equity and liabilities:	
Equity share capital	120,000
Retained earnings (W5)	144,375
Non-controlling interest (W4)	56,875
Total equity	321,250
Liabilities (7,000 + 5,000 + 3,000)	15,000
	336,250

Step 1 - Determine group structure:

In S: 45,000 / 60,000 × 100% =		75%

In M		
Direct	16,000 / 40,000 × 100% =	40.0%
Indirect	75% × 12,000 / 40,000 × 100% =	22.5%
		62.5%

Step 2 - Net assets - S

	At acq'n	At rep date
	$	$
Equity capital	60,000	60,000
Retained earnings	30,000	75,000
	90,000	135,000

Step 2 - Net assets - M:

	At acq'n	At rep date
	$	$
Equity capital	40,000	40,000
Retained earnings	10,000	35,000
	50,000	75,000

Step 3 - Goodwill arising on S

	$
Cost of investment	72,000
For 75% (90,000)	(67,500)
	4,500

Step 3 - Goodwill arising on M:

	$
Cost of investment	
Direct cost to H	25,000
Indirect cost via S	
75% × $20,000	15,000
	40,000
For 62.5% (50,000)	(31,250)
	8,750

Step 4 - Non-controlling interest

		$
S - 25% x $135,000 (W2)		33,750
M - 37.5% x $75,000 (W2)		28,125
Less: NCI share of S cost of investment in M	(25% x $20,000)	(5,000)
		56,875

Step 5 - Retained earnings

	$
H	95,000
S - 75% x $45,000 (W2)	33,750
M - 62.5% x $25,000 (W2)	15,625
	144,375

Test your understanding 3 - T, S & R

The following are the summarised statements of financial position of T, S and R as at 31 December 20X4.

	T	S	R
	$	$	$
Non-current assets	140,000	61,000	170,000
Investments	200,000	65,000	–
Current assets	20,000	20,000	15,000
	360,000	146,000	185,000
Equity shares of $1 each	200,000	80,000	100,000
Retained earnings	150,000	60,000	80,000
Liabilities	10,000	6,000	5,000
	360,000	146,000	185,000

On 1 January 20X3 S acquired 35,000 ordinary shares in R at a cost of $65,000 when the retained earnings of R amounted to $40,000.

On 1 January 20X4 T acquired 64,000 shares in S at a cost of $120,000 and 40,000 shares in R at a cost of $80,000. The retained earnings of S and R amounted to $50,000 and $60,000 respectively on 1 January 20X4. The fair value of the NCI in S at that date was $27,000. The fair value of the whole (direct and indirect) NCI in R was $56,000. The non-controlling interest is measured using the full goodwill method. At the reporting date, goodwill has not been impaired.

Required:

Prepare the consolidated statement of financial position of the T group as at 31 December 20X4.

4 Step acquisitions

Step acquisitions

- A step acquisition occurs when the parent entity acquires control over the subsidiary in stages. This is achieved by buying blocks of shares at different times.

- Amendments to IFRS 3 and IAS 27 mean that acquisition accounting (accounting for recognition of goodwill and non-controlling interests) is only applied at the date when control is achieved.

- Any pre-existing equity interest in an entity is accounted for according to:

  - IAS 39 in the case of simple investments

  - IAS 28 in the case of associates

  - IAS 31 in the case of joint ventures

- At the date when equity interest is increased and control achieved:

  (1) re-measure the previously held equity interest to fair value

  (2) recognise any resulting gain or loss in profit or loss

  (3) calculate goodwill and non-controlling interest on either a partial (i.e. proportionate) or full (i.e. fair value) basis in accordance with IFRS 3 Revised. The cost of acquiring control will be the fair value of the previously held equity interest plus the cost of the most recent purchase of shares at acquisition date.

- If there has been re-measurement of any previously held equity interest that was recognised in other comprehensive income, any changes in value recognised in earlier years are now reclassified from equity to profit or loss.

- The situation of a further purchase of shares in a subsidiary after control has been acquired (for example taking the group interest from 60% to 75%) is regarded as a transaction between equity holders; goodwill is not recalculated. This situation is dealt with separately within chapter 3.

Illustration 3 – Goodwill in step acquisitions

Ayre holds a 10% investment in Byrne at $24,000 in accordance with IAS 39. On 1 June 20X7, it acquires a further 50% of Byrne's equity shares at a cost of $160,000.

On this date fair values are as follows:

- Byrne's net assets – $200,000
- The non-controlling interest – $100,000
- The 10% investment – $26,000

How do you calculate the goodwill arising in Byrne

Note: the non-controlling interest is to be valued using the full method.

Expandable text - Solution

W1 Group Structure

Ayre

|
    60% (10% + 50%)
|

Byrne

Note – due to step acquisition – revalue the investment – take gain or loss to income statement – i.e. an increase in carrying value from $24,000 to $26,000.

Dr investment	2,000
Cr profit on remeasurement	2,000

(W2) Net assets

	At date of acquisition 1 June 20X7
Net assets	200,000

(W3) Goodwill – fair value (full goodwill) method

	$
Purchase consideration (26,000 + 160,000)	186,000
FV of NCI at acquisition date	100,000
	286,000
Total Goodwill	**86,000**

Test your understanding 4 - Major and Tom

The statements of financial position of two entities, Major and Tom as at 31 December 20X6 are as follows:

	Major	Tom
	$'000	$'000
Investment	160	
Sundry assets	350	250
	510	250
Equity share capital	200	100
Retained earnings	250	122
Liabilities	60	28
	510	250

Major acquired 40% of Tom on 31 December 20X1 for $90,000. At this time the retained earnings of Tom stood at $76,000. A further 20% of shares in Tom was acquired by Major three years later for $70,000. On this date, the fair value of the existing holding in Tom was $105,000. Tom's retained earnings were $100,000 on the second acquisition date, at which date the fair value of the non-controlling interest was $90,000. It is group policy to value the non-controlling interest on a full fair value basis.

Required:

Prepare the consolidated statement of financial position for the Major group as at 31 December 20X6.

Illustration 4 - Exotic

The Exotic Group carries on business as a distributor of warehouse equipment and importer of fruit. Exotic is a listed entity and was incorporated over 20 years ago to distribute warehouse equipment. Since then the group has diversified its activities to include the import and distribution of fruit, and it expanded its operations by the acquisition of shares in Melon in 20X1 and in Kiwi in 20X3, both listed entities.

Accounts for all entities are prepared up to 31 December.

The draft statements of comprehensive income for Exotic, Melon and Kiwi for the year ended 31 December 20X6 are as follows:

	Exotic	Melon	Kiwi
	$000	$000	$000
Revenue	45,600	24,700	22,800
Cost of sales	(18,050)	(5,463)	(5,320)
Gross profit	27,550	19,237	17,480
Distribution costs	(3,325)	(2,137)	(1,900)
Administrative expenses	(3,475)	(950)	(1,900)
Profit from operations	20,750	16,150	13,680
Finance costs	(325)	–	–
Profit before tax	20,425	16,150	13,680
Tax	(8,300)	(5,390)	(4,241)
Profit for the period	12,125	10,760	9,439

KAPLAN PUBLISHING

Notes

	Exotic	Melon	Kiwi
Dividends paid in the year	9,500		
Retained earnings brought forward	20,013	13,315	

The draft statements of financial position as at 31 December 20X6 are as follows:

	Exotic $000	Melon $000	Kiwi $000
Assets:			
Non-current assets (NBV)	35,483	24,273	13,063
Investments:			
Shares in Melon	6,650	–	–
Shares in Kiwi	–	3,800	–
Current assets	1,568	9,025	8,883
Total assets	43,701	37,098	21,946
Equity and liabilities:			
Equity shares ($1)	8,000	3,000	2,000
Retained earnings	22,638	24,075	19,898
Total equity	30,638	27,075	21,898
Sundry liabilities	13,063	10,023	48
Total equity and liabilities	43,701	37,098	21,946

The following information is available relating to Exotic, Melon and Kiwi:

(1) On 1 January 20X1 Exotic acquired 2,700,000 $1 equity shares in Melon for $6,650,000 at which date there was a credit balance on the retained earnings of Melon of $1,425,000. No shares have been issued by Melon since Exotic acquired its interest.

(2) On 1 January 20X3 Melon acquired 1,600,000 $1 equity shares in Kiwi for $3,800,000 at which date there was a credit balance on the retained earnings of Kiwi of $950,000. No shares have been issued by Kiwi since Melon acquired its interest.

(3) During 20X6, Kiwi had made inter-company sales to Melon of $480,000 making a profit of 25% on cost and $75,000 of these goods were in inventory at 31 December 20X6.

(4) During 20X6, Melon had made inter-company sales to Exotic of $260,000 making a profit of 33⅓% on cost and $60,000 of these goods were in inventory at 31 December 20X6.

(5) On 1 November 20X6 Exotic sold warehouse equipment to Melon for $240,000 from inventory. Melon has included this equipment in its non-current assets. The equipment had been purchased on credit by Exotic for $200,000 in October 20X6 and this amount is included in its liabilities as at 31 December 20X6.

(6) Melon charges depreciation on its warehouse equipment at 20% on cost. It is company policy to charge a full year's depreciation in the year of acquisition to be included in the cost of sales.

(7) It is group policy to account for non-controlling interest on a proportionate basis. Since acquisition, the goodwill of Melon has been fully written off as a result of an impairment review which took place two years ago. The goodwill of Kiwi has been impaired 60% by 31 December 20X5 and a further 50% of the remaining balance of goodwill was impaired in the year ended 31 December 20X6.

Required:

(a) **Prepare a consolidated statement of comprehensive income for the Exotic Group for the year ended 31 December 20X6 including a reconciliation of retained earnings for the year.**

(12 marks)

(b) **Prepare a consolidated statement of financial position as at that date.**

(13 marks)

(Total: 25 marks)

Expandable text - Solution

Key answer tips:

This is not a past exam question, but it is a great question to revise complex groups. If you can work your way through this, then you should be feeling comfortable with this topic and can attempt some of the more difficult questions.

(a) Consolidated statement of comprehensive income for the year ended 31 December 20X6

	$000
Revenue (45,600 + 24,700 + 22,800 − 480 − 260 − 240)	92,120
Cost of sales (18,050 + 5,463 + 5,320 − 480 − 260 − 200 +15 +15 (W5) − 8 (W6))	(27,915)
Gross profit (27,550 + 19,237 + 17,480 − 15 − 15 (W5) − 32 (W6))	64,205
Distribution costs (3,325 + 2,137 + 1,900)	(7,362)
Administration expenses (3,475 + 950 + 1,900 + 259 (W3))	(6,584)
Profit from operations	50,259
Finance cost	(325)
Profit before tax	49,934
Tax (8,300 + 5,390 + 4,241)	(17,931)
Profit for the period	32,003

Attributable to:	
Equity holders of the parent	28,289
Non-controlling interests (W8)	3,714
Net profit for the period	32,003

Reconciliation of retained earnings:

Retained earnings brought forward (W9)	34,115
Profit for the period	28,289
Dividends paid	(9,500)
Retained earnings carried forward	52,904

(b) Consolidated statement of financial position as at 31 December 20X6

	$000
Assets:	
Non-current assets (35,483 + 24,273 + 13,063 − 32 (W6))	72,787
Goodwill (W3)	259
Current assets (1,568 + 9,025 + 8,883 − 30)	19,446
Total assets	92,492

Equity and liabilities:

$1 equity shares	8,000
Group retained earnings (W7)	52,904
	60,904
Non-controlling interest (W4)	8,454
Total equity	69,358
Sundry liabilities:(13,063 + 10,023 + 48)	23,134
Total equity and liabilities	92,492

Workings

(W1) Group structure

$\underline{2,700} = 90\%$ Exotic
3,000

        90%

Melon

        80%

$\underline{1,600} = 80\%$ Kiwi
2,000

(W2) Net assets

	At date of acquisition		At reporting date	
	$000	$000	$000	$000
Melon				
Equity capital		3,000		3,000
Retained earnings	1,425		24,075	
Excess depreciation (W6)			8	
Unrealised profit (W5)			(15)	
		1,425		24,068
		4,425		27,068

	At date of acquisition		At reporting date	
	$000	$000	$000	$000
Kiwi				
Equity capital		2,000		2,000
Retained earnings	950		19,898	
Unrealised profit (W5)			(15)	
	————		———	
		950		19,883
		———		———
		2,950		21,883
		———		———

(W3) Goodwill

	In Melon	In Kiwi
	$000	$000
Cost of investment	6,650	
90% x 3,800		3,420
Share of net assets:		
90% x 4,425 (W2)	(3,983)	
72% x 2,950 (W2)		(2,124)
	———	———
	2,667	1,296
Impairment – in previous years (100%) / 60%	(2,667)	(778)
	———	———
	–	518
Impairment current year (50% x 518) (I/S)	–	(259)
	———	———
Statement of financial position	–	259
	———	———
Charged against retained earnings	2,667	1,037

(W4) Non Controlling Interest

Melon

10% x 27,068 (W2)	2,707
Less 10% Melon's investment in Kiwi (3,800)	(308)

Kiwi (use effective interest %)

28% x 21,883 (W2)	6,127
	8,454

(W5) Unrealised profit in inventory

KIwi – Melon	75,000 x 25 ÷ 125	= 15,000
Melon – Exotic	60,000 x $\frac{33\ 1/3}{133 1/3}$	= 15,000

(W6) Inter-company transfers of non-current assets

Exotic – Melon	240,000

Therefore Exotic has made an unrealised profit.

Debit group statement of comprehensive income	40,000
Credit group non-current assets	40,000

Depreciation is charged on $240,000 at 20% on cost (i.e. $48,000 each year). This should be charged in the group accounts at 20% on $200,000 (i.e. $40,000).

Therefore $8,000 extra depreciation has been charged each year and must be added back.

Debit depreciation group	8,000
Credit statement of comprehensive income group	8,000
Therefore net impact $40,000 – $8,000 =	32,000
Net non-current assets credit	32,000
Statement of comprehensive income debit	32,000

(W7) Consolidated retained earnings carried forward

	$000
All of Exotic	
Per the question	22,638
Unrealised profit (W6)	(40)

	22,598
Share of Melon	
90% (24,068 x 1,425) (W2)	20,378
Share of Kiwi	
72% (19,883 x 950) (W2)	13,632
Goodwill impairment (2,667 + 1,037) (W3)	(3,704)

	52,904

(W8) Non-controlling interest in profit

Melon (10,760 x 10%)	1076
Kiwi's profit (9,439 x 28%)	2,643
Less unrealised profit in inventory (28% x 15,000 + 10% x15,000)	(5)

	3,714

(W9) Consolidated retained earnings brought forward

	$000
All of Exotic	20,013
Share of Melon	
90% (13,315 x 1,425) (W2)	10,701
Share of Kiwi	
72% (10,459 x 950) (W2)	6,846
Goodwill impairment (2,667 + 778) (W3)	(3,445)

	34,115

Expandable text - UK syllabus focus

The ACCA UK syllabus contains a requirement that UK variant candidates should be able to discuss and apply the key differences between UK GAAP and IFRS GAAP. The accounting requirements of UK GAAP and IFRS GAAP are very similar in this area, but there are one or two differences.

You should approach questions using the approach of completing the five standard workings identified within chapter 1. Rather than step acquisition as detailed within this chapter, UK GAAP students should, instead, think in terms of piecemeal acquisitions. Each time an additional share purchase is made, there should be incremental adjustments to goodwill and group reserves. This means that a net assets working is required at the date of each additional share purchase as illustrated in the following question. Any subsequent remeasurement of a fair value adjustment will be treated as a revaluation.

Expandable text - UK GAAP question

On 1 January 20X2, Drew acquired 25,000 shares in Karin for £80,000, and obtained significant influence at that date. At that date, the fair value of Land owned by Karin exceeded its book value at that date by £10,000 and the balance on profit and loss reerve was ££45,000.

On 1 January 20X4, Drew acquired a further 40,000 shares in Karin for £150,000 abd obtained control at that date. The fair value of the land had increaseed to £40,000 and the balance on profit and loss reserve was £60,000.

None of the fair value increases had been reflected in the books of Karin.

Goodwill is amortised over five years.

The balance sheets of both companies at 31 December 20X8 are as follows:

	Drew	Karin
	£m	£m
Investment in Karin	230,000	
Fixed assets	275,500	100,000
Net current assets	210,100	100,000
	715,600	200,000

Share capital and reserves:	£m	£m
£1 ordinary shares	100,000	100,000
Share premium	200,000	
P&L reserve	415,600	100,000
	715,600	200,000

Required:

Prepare the group balance sheet as at 31 December 20X8.

Expandable text - UK GAAP answer

The Drew group balance sheet as at 31 December 20X8:

	£m
Fixed assets (275,000 + 100,000 + 40,000 FVA)	415,500
Net current assets (210,100 + 100,000)	310,100
	725,600

Share capital and reserves:	£m
£1 ordinary shares	100,000
Share premium	200,000
Revaluation reserve (W6)	7,500
P&L reserve (W5)	334.100
Minority interest (W5)	84,000
	725,600

(W1) Group structure

Drew
| 25% at 1 Jan X2 - associate
| 40% at 1 Jan X4
Karin   65% from 1 Jan X4 - consolidate

(W2) Net assets

	Net assets 1 Jan X2 £m	Net assets 1 Jan X4 £m	Net assets 31 Dec X8 £m
Share capital	100,000	100,000	100,000
P&L reserve	45,000	60,000	100,000
Fair value adjustment - land	10,000	40,000	40,000
	155,000	200,000	240,000

(W3) Goodwill

	1 Jan X2 £m	1 Jan X4 £m
Cost of investment	80,000	150,000
share of net assets acquired:		
1 Jan X2: 25% x 155,000 (W2)	(38,750)	
1 Jan X4: 40% x 200,000 (W2)		(80,000)
Goodwill fully amortised by balance sheet date	41,250	70,000

Note that goodwill has been calculated on an incremental basis for the purchase made on 1 January 20X4, as the investment in Karin changes from being an associate to a subsidiary.

(W4) Minority interest at balance sheet date

	£m
35% x 240,000 (W2)	84,000

Note that minority interest is is based upon the MI% at the balance sheet date.

(W5) Group profit and loss reserve

	£m
Drew	415,800
Karin: (25% x (100,000 - 45,000))	13,750
Karin: (40% x (100,000 - 60,000))	16,000
Less: goodwill amortisation (41,250 + 70,000) (W3)	(111,250)
	334,100

Note that the group share of post-acquisition reserves is calculated for each separate acquisition.

(W6) Revaluation reserve

	£m
25% x 40,000 - 10,000 (W2)	7,500

Note that this arises ar there has been a remeasurement of the fair value of land at the date of the second purchase of shares.

5 Chapter summary

Complex Groups:
where a subsidiary of a parent entity owns all or part of a shareholding, which makes another entity also a subsidiary of the parent entity

Step acquisitions:
where the parent acquires control over the subsidiary in stages

Vertical groups:
where a subsidiary of the parent company holds shares in a further company such that control is achieved:
- consolidate all companies from date P achieved control
- use effective group interest in subsidiary for goodwill, reserves and non-controlling interest calculatons

Mixed (D-shaped) groups:
where the parent entity has a direct controlling interest in at least one subsidiary. In addition, the parent entity and the subsidiary together hold a controlling interest in a further entity:
- consolidate all companies
- use effective group interest in subsidiary for goodwill, reserves and non-controlling interest calculations
- two elements to cost of subsidiary in goodwill calculation

At the date the parent acquires control, revalue the existing equity holding to FV and recognise any gain or loss in equity. Goodwill is calculated as the excess of calculated as the excess of consideration + NCI + FV of existing holding over the fair values of net assets in the acqquiree.

Acquisitions of further shares in an existing subsidiary are accounted for in equity. Goodwill is not recalculated.

Test your understanding answers

Test your understanding 1 - H, S & T

Consolidated statement of financial position as at 31 December 20X7

	$
Sundry net assets (280,000 + 133,000 + 100,000)	513,000

Equity and liabilities

Equity share capital	100,000
Retained earnings (W5)	39,938
NCI (W4)	48,062
Liabilities (200,000 + 100,000 + 25,000)	325,000
	513,000

(W1) Group structure

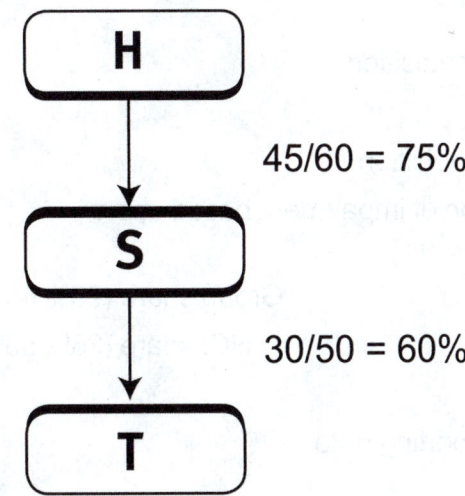

Consolidation	%	
S: Group share	75%	
NCI	25%	
T: Group share 75% of 60%	45%	
NCI	55%	(40% directly plus (25% × 60% =) 15% indirectly)

(W2) Net assets

	S		T	
	At acq'n	At rep date	At acq'n	At rep date
	$	$	$	$
Equity capital	60,000	60,000	50,000	50,000
Retained earnings	10,000	28,000	8,000	25,000
	70,000	88,000	58,000	75,000

(W3) Goodwill

	S	T
	$	$
Consideration paid	65,000	55,000
FV of NCI	20,000	50,000
Indirect Holding Adjustment (25% x $55,000)		(13,750)
	85,000	91,250
FV of NA at acquisition	(70,000)	(58,000)
Goodwill at acquisition	15,000	33,250
Less: allocation of impairment based upon shareholdings		
Group share (75%:45%)	(11,250)	(14,962)
NCI share (25%:55%)	(3,750)	(18,288)
Goodwill at reporting date	Nil	Nil

KAPLAN PUBLISHING

(W4) Non-controlling interest

	$
S - FV at date of acquisition	20,000
S - NCI share of post-acq'n retained earnings (25% x 18,000)	4,500
T - FV at date of acquisition	50,000
T - NCI share of post-acq'n retained earnings (55% x 17,000)	9,350
Indirect Holding Adjustment (25% × 55,000)	(13,750)
	70,100
Less NCI share of goodwill impairment re S & T (3,750+18,288)(W3)	(22,038)
Total for CSFP	48,062

(W5) Consolidated retained earnings

	$
Retained earnings of H	45,000
Group share of post-acquisition retained earnings or change in net assets	
S 75% of 18,000	13,500
T 45% of 17,000	7,650
Goodwill impaired (11,250+14,962)(W3)	(26,212)
	39,938

Test your understanding 2 - Grape, Vine and Wine

Consolidated statement of financial position as at 30 June 20X6

	$
Goodwill (7,000 + 2,500 (W3))	9,500
Sundry assets (350,000 + 200,000 + 120,000)	670,000
	679,500

Equity and liabilities	$
Equity share capital	100,000
Retained earnings (W5)	235,800
Non-controlling interest (W4)	53,700
Liabilities (150,000 + 100,000 + 40,000)	290,000
	679,500

(W1) Group structure

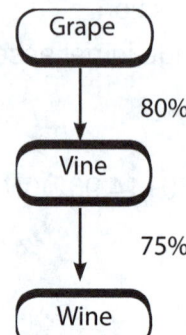

Consolidation

		%
Vine	Group share	80%
	NCI	20%
Wine	Group share 80% of 75%	60%
	NCI	40% (25% directly plus (20% × 75% =) 15% indirectly)

(W2) Net assets

	Vine		Wine	
	At acq'n	At reporting date	At acq'n	At reporting date
	$	$	$	$
Equity capital	50,000	50,000	10,000	10,000
Retained earnings	80,000	110,000	67,000	70,000
	130,000	160,000	77,000	80,000

The acquisition date for both entities is the date they joined the Grape group, i.e. 1 July 20X5.

(W3) Goodwill – full basis

	Vine	Wine
	$	$
Consideration paid	110,000	60,000
FV of NCI	27,000	31,500
Indirect holding adjustment (20% x $60,000)		(12,000)
	137,000	79,500
FV of net assets at acquisition (W2)	(130,000)	(77,000)
Goodwill – full basis	7,000	2,500

(W4) Non-controlling interest

	$
V - FV of NCI at date of acquisition	27,000
V - NCI share of post acq'n retained earnings (20% x 30,000)	6,000
W - FV of NCI at date of acquisition	31,500
W - NCI share of post acq'n retained earnings (40% x 3,000)	1,200
Indirect Holding Adjustment (20% of 60,000)	(12,000)
	53,700

(W5) Consolidated retained earnings

	$
Retained earnings of Grape	210,000
Group share of post-acquisition retained earnings	
V 80% of $30,000	24,000
W 60% of $3,000	1,800
	235,800

Test your understanding 3 - T, S & R

T consolidated statement of financial position as at 31 December 20X4

	$
Intangible fixed assets: goodwill (17,000 + 28,000(W3))	45,000
Non-current assets (140,000 + 61,000 + 170,000)	371,000
Current assets (20,000 + 20,000 + 15,000)	55,000
	471,000

	$
Equity share capital	200,000
Group retained earnings (W5)	171,600
	371,600
Non-controlling (W4)	78,400
Liabilities (10,000 + 6,000 + 5,000)	21,000
	471,000

(W1) Group structure

T has a controlling interest in both S and R as follows:

Interest in S			**Interest in R**	
T	80%	T - direct	40%	
		T - indirect (80% x 35%)	28%	68%
NCI	20%	NCI		32%
	─────			─────
	100%			100%
	─────			─────

(W2) Net assets of S and R

	S		R	
	At acq'n	At rep date	At acq'n	At rep date
	$	$	$	$
Equity share capital	80,000	80,000	100,000	100,000
Retained earnings	50,000	60,000	60,000	80,000
	─────	─────	─────	─────
	130,000	140,000	160,000	180,000
	─────	─────	─────	─────

T's acquisition date for both entities is 1 January 20X4.

(W3) Goodwill – S Fair value (full goodwill) method

	$
Consideration paid	120,000
FV of NCI	27,000
	─────
	147,000
FV of net assets at acquisition (W2)	(130,000)
	─────
Total Goodwill	17,000
	─────

Goodwill – R

	$
Direct purchase consideration	80,000
Indirect purchase consideration (80% × 65,000)	52,000
Fair value of NCI at acquisition	56,000
	188,000
FV of net assets at acquisition (W2)	(160,000)
Full goodwill	28,000

(W4) Non-controlling interest

	$
S - FV of NCI at acquisition	27,000
S - NCI share of post-acquisition retained earnings (20% x 10,000)	2,000
Less NCI share of S cost of investment in R (20% x 65,000)	(13,000)
R - FV of NCI at acquisition	56,000
R - NCI share of post-acquisition retained earnings (32% x 20,000)	6,400
Total NCI to SOFP	78,400

(W5) Group retained earnings

	$
T	150,000
S (share of post-acquisition retained earnings) 80% × $10,000	8,000
R (share of post-acquisition retained earnings) 68% × $20,000	13,600
	171,600

Test your understanding 4 - Major and Tom

Consolidated statement of financial position for Major as at 31 December 20X6

	$
Goodwill (W3)	65,000
Sundry assets (350,000 + 250,000)	600,000
	665,000

Equity and liabilities	$
Equity share capital	200,000
Retained earnings (W5)	278,200
Non-controlling interest (W4)	98,800
Liabilities (60,000 + 28,000)	88,000
	665,000

(W1) Group structure

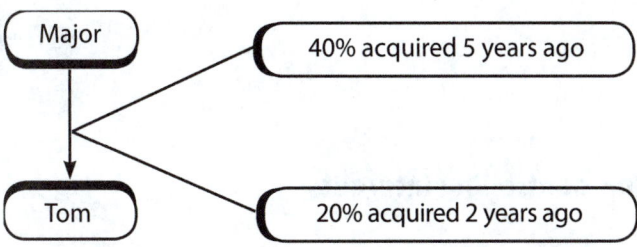

Therefore, Tom becomes a subsidiary of Major from December 20X4.

The investment will need to be revalued

Dr Investment 15,000
(105,000 – 90,000)
Cr Profit   15,000

(W2) Net assets

	At Acquisition 20X4	At Reporting date
	$	$
Share capital	100,000	100,000
Retained earnings	100,000	122,000
	200,000	222,000

(W3) Goodwill

	$
Consideration paid by parent	175,000
(105,000 + 70,000)	
FV of NCI (given)	90,000
	265,000
Less: FV of NA at acquisition (W2)	(200,000)
	65,000

(W4) Non-controlling interest

	$
FV at acquisition date	90,000
NCI % of post-acquisition retained earnings (40% x $22,000)	8,800
	98,800

(W5) Group Retained earnings

	$
Major	250,000
Gain on remeasurement	15,000
Tom 60% (222,000 – 200,000)	13,200
	278,200

Change in a group structure

Chapter learning objectives

Upon completion of this chapter you will be able to:

- prepare group financial statements where activities have been acquired, discontinued or have been disposed of in the period

- discuss and apply the treatment of a subsidiary that has been acquired exclusively with a view to subsequent disposal.

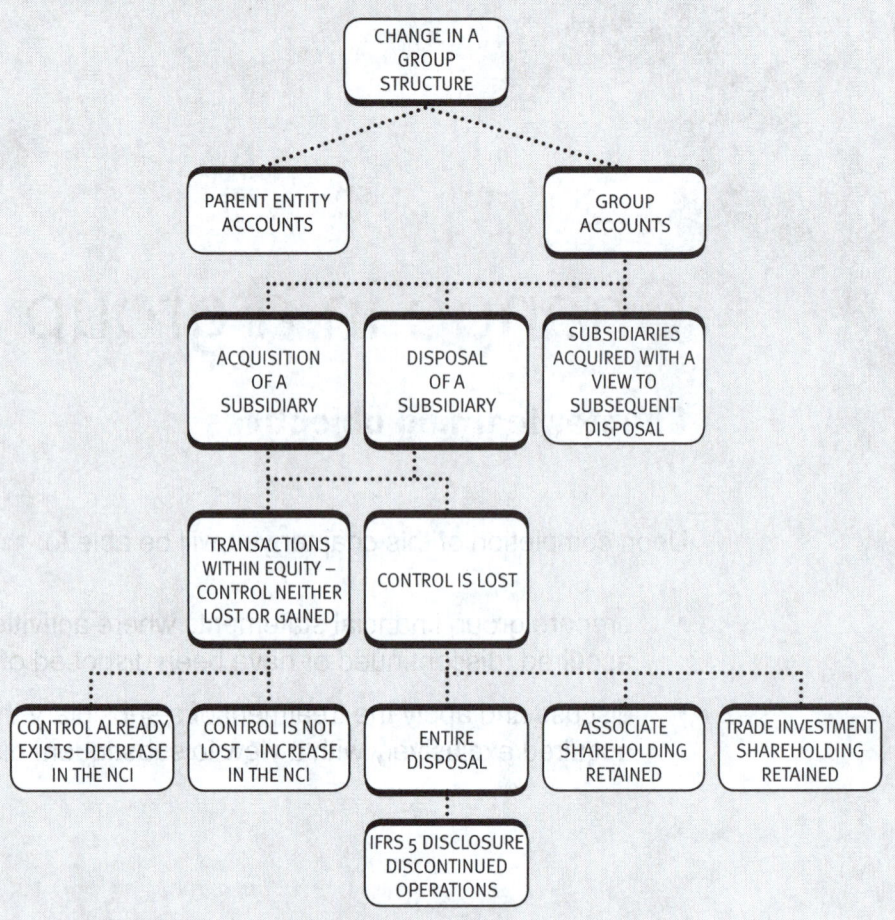

1 Acquisition of a subsidiary

Remember that a parent entity acquires control of a subsidiary from the date that it obtains a majority shareholding. If this happens mid-year, then it will be necessary to pro-rata the results of the subsidiary for the year to identify the net assets at the date of acquisition.

Illustration 1 - Tudor - mid-year acquisition of a subsidiary

On 1 July 2004 Tudor purchased 1,600,000 of 2,000,000 equity shares of $1 each in Windsor for $10,280,000. On the same date it also acquired 1,000,000 of Windsor's 10% loan notes. At the date of acquisition the retained earnings of Windsor were $6,150,000. The summarised draft statement of comprehensive income for each company for the year ended 31 March 2005 was as follows:

	Tudor	Windsor
	$000	$000
Revenue	60,000	24,000
Cost of sales	(42,000)	(20,000)
Gross profit	18,000	4,000
Distribution costs	(2,500)	(50)
Administration expenses	(3,500)	(150)
Profit from operations	12,000	3,800
Interest received/(paid)	75	(200)
Profit before tax	12,075	3,600
Tax	(3,000)	(600)
Profit for the year	9,075	3,000
Retained earnings b'fwd	16,525	5,400

The following information is relevant:

(1) The fair values of Windsor's assets at the date of acquisition were mostly equal to their book values with the exception of plant, which was stated in the books at $2,000,000 but had a fair value of $5,200,000. The remaining useful life of the plant in question was four years at the date of acquisition. Depreciation is charged to cost of sales and is time apportioned on a monthly basis.

(2) During the post-acquisition period Tudor sold Windsor some goods for $12 million. The goods had originally cost $9 million. During the remaining months of the year Windsor sold $10 million (at cost to Windsor) of these goods to third parties for $13 million.

(3) Revenues and expenses should be deemed to accrue evenly throughout the year.

(4) Tudor has a policy of valuing non-controlling interests using the full goodwill method. The fair value of non-controlling interest at the date of acquisition was $2,520,000.

(5) The fair value of goodwill was impaired by $300,000 at the reporting date.

Required:

Prepare a consolidated income statement for Tudor group for the year to 31 March 2005.

Expandable text - Solution

Answer

Tudor group statement of comprehensive income for the year ended 31 March 2005:

	Tudor	Windsor	Adjusts (9/12)	Group SOCI
	$000	$000	$000	$000
Revenue	60,000	18,000	(12,000)	66,000
Cost of sales	(42,000)	(15,000)	12,000	
URPS (W4)	(500)			(46,100)
FVA adjust dep'n (W2)		(600)		
Gross profit				19.900
Distribution costs	(2,500)	(38)		(2,538)
Administration expenses	(3,500)	(112)		
Goodwill impairment (W3)			(300)	(3,912)
Profit from operations				13,450
Interest received	75		(75)	–
Interest paid		(150)	75	(75)
Profit before tax				13,375
Tax	(3,000)	(450)		(3,450)
Profit after tax for the year		1,650		9,925
NCI – take 20% of 1,650		330		
Less: NCI goodwill impairment (300×20%)		(60)		
				270
Group share of profit after tax – bal fig				9,655
				9,925

(W1) Group structure – Tudor owns 80% of Windsor

– the acquisition took place three months into the year

– nine months is post-acquisition

(W2) Net assets

	Acq'n date	Rep date
	$000	$000
Equity capital	2,000	2,000
Retained earnings	6,150	8,400
	———	———
	8,150	10,400
FVA – PPE	3,200	3,200
FVA – dep'n adjust 3,200/48 × 9		(600)
	———	———
	11,350	13,000
	———	———

(W3) Goodwill

	Windsor
	$000
Cost of investment	10,280
FV of NCI at acquisition	2,520
	———
	12,800
FV of net assets at acquisition (W2)	(11,350)
	———
Total goodwill at acquisition	1,450
Impaired during year	(300)
	———
Unimpaired goodwill	1,150
	———

(W4) URPS of parent company

$2,000 × (33.33/133.33 = $500)

2 Disposal scenarios

During the year, one entity may sell some or all of its shares in another entity.

Possible situations include:

(1) the disposal of all the shares held in the subsidiary

(2) the disposal of part of the shareholding, leaving a controlling interest after the sale

(3) the disposal of part of the shareholding, leaving a residual holding after the sale, which is regarded as an associate

(4) the disposal of part of the shareholding, leaving a residual holding after the sale, which is regarded as a trade investment.

When a group disposes of all or part of its interest in a subsidiary undertaking, this must be reflected both in the investing entity's individual accounts and in the group accounts.

3 Investing entity's accounts

Gain to investing entity

In all of the above scenarios, the gain on disposal in the investing entity's accounts is calculated as follows:

	$
Sales proceeds	X
Carrying amount (usually cost) of shares sold	(X)
	X
Tax – amount or rate given in question	(X)
Net gain to parent	X

The gain would often be reported as an exceptional item; if so, it must be disclosed separately on the face of the parent's statement of comprehensive income/income statement after operating profit.

Tax on gain on disposal

The tax arising as a result of the disposal is always calculated based on the gain in the investing entity's accounts, as identified above.

The tax calculated forms part of the investing (parent) entity's total tax charge. As such this additional tax forms part of the group tax charge.

4 Group accounts

In the group accounts the accounting for the sale of shares in a subsidiary will depend on whether or not the transaction causes control to be lost, or whether after the sale control is still maintained.

Where control is lost, there will be a gain or loss to the group which must be included in the group income statement for the year. Additionally, there will be derecognition of the assets and liabilities of the subsidiary disposed of, together with elimination of goodwill and non-controlling interest from the group accounts. The income statement of the subsidiary will be consolidated upto the date of disposal.

Where control is of the subsidiary is retained, there is no gain or loss to be recorded in the group accounts. Instead, the transaction is regarded as one between equity holders, with the end result being an increase in non-controlling interest. The group continues to recognise the goodwill, assets and liabilities of the subsidiary at the year end, and consolidates the income statement of the subsidiary for the year.

Accounting for a disposal where control is lost

- Where control **is lost** (i.e. the subsidiary is completely disposed of or becomes an associate or investment), the parent:
  - Recognises
    - the consideration received
    - any investment retained in the former subsidiary at fair value on the date of disposal
  - Derecognises
    - the assets and liabilities of the subsidiary at the date of disposal
    - unimpaired goodwill in the subsidiary
    - the non-controlling interest at the date of disposal (including any components of other comprehensive income attributable to them)
  - Any difference between these amounts is recognised as an exceptional gain or loss on disposal in the group accounts.
  - In the group income statement, it will also be necessary to pro-rata the results of the subsidiary for the year into pre-disposal for consolidation, and post-disposal for accounting as an associate or simple investment as appropriate.

Proceeds		X
FV of retained interest		X
		X
Less interest in subsidiary disposed of:		
Net assets of subsidiary at disposal date	X	
Unimpaired goodwill at disposal date	X	
Less: carrying value of NCI	(X)	
		(X)
Pre-tax gain/loss to the group		X

Presentation in the group income statement when control is lost:

Exceptional Gain

The gain to the group would often be reported as an exceptional item, i.e. presented as an exceptional item on the face of the income statement after operating profit.

There are two ways of presenting the results of the disposed subsidiary:

(i) **Time-apportionment line-by-line**

In the group income statement, where the sale of the subsidiary has occurred during the year, basic consolidation principles will only allow the income and expenses of the subsidiary to be consolidated up to the date of disposal. The traditional way is to time apportion each line of the disposed subsidiary's results in the same way that a subsidiary's results that had been acquired part way through the year would be consolidated.

(ii) **Time-apportioned and a discontinued operation**

If however the subsidiary that has been disposed qualifies as a discontinued operation in accordance with "IFRS 5 Accounting for Non-current Assets held for sale and discontinued operations", then the pre-disposal results of the subsidiary are aggregated and presented in a single line on the face of the income statement immediately after profit after tax from continuing operations.

A discontinued operation is a component of an entity that either has been disposed of or is classified as held for sale, and:

- represents a separate major line of business or geographical area of operations,

- is part of a single co-ordinated plan to dispose of a separate major line of business or geographical area of operations, or

- is a subsidiary acquired exclusively with a view to resale and the disposal involves loss of control.

Associate time-apportioned

Further if the disposal means control is lost but it leaves a residual interest that gives that the parent significant influence, this will mean that in the group income statement there will be an associate to account for, for example if a parent sells half of its 80% holding to leave it owning a 40% associate. Associates are accounted for using equity accounting and as the associate relationship will only be relevant from the date of disposal it will be time apportioned in the group income statement.

5 Group accounts – entire disposal

Entire disposal

Illustration 2 - Rock - entire disposal

Rock has held a 70% investment in Dog for two years. Rock is disposing of this investment. Goodwill has been calculated using the full goodwill method. No goodwill has been impaired. Details are:

	$
Cost of investment	2,000
Dog – Fair value of net assets at acquisition	1,900
Dog – Fair value of the non-controlling interest at acquisition	800
Sales proceeds	3,000
Dog – Net assets at disposal	2,400

Required:

Calculate the profit/loss on disposal.

(a) In Rock's individual accounts

(b) In the consolidated accounts

Rock is subject to tax at the rate of 25%.

Expandable text - Solution Rock

(a) Gain to Rock plc

	$
Sales proceeds	3,000
Cost of shares sold	(2,000)
Gain on disposal	1,000
Tax charge against Rock at 25%	250

(b) Consolidated accounts

	$	$
Sales proceeds		3000
Net assets at disposal	2,400	
Unimpaired goodwill (W1)	900	
Less: carrying value of NCI (2,400x30%)	(950)	
		(2,350)
Gain to group before tax		650
Tax charge on gain made by Rock (as above)		250

(W1) Goodwill

	$
Cost of investment	2,000
FV of NCI at acquisition	800
	2,800
FV of net assets at acquisition	(1,900)
Total Goodwill	900

Test your understanding 1 – Snooker

Snooker purchased 80% of the shares in Billiards for $100,000 when the net assets of Billiards had a fair value of $50,000. Goodwill was calculated using the proportion of net assets method amounting to $60,000 and has not suffered any impairment to date. Snooker has just disposed of its entire shareholding in Billiards for $300,000, when the net assets were stated at $110,000. Tax is payable by Snooker at 30% on any gain on disposal of shares.

Required:

- **Calculate the gain or loss arising to the parent entity on disposal of shares in Billiards.**

- **Calculate the gain or loss arising to the group on disposal of the controlling interest in Billiards.**

Test your understanding 2 - Bridge

The following information relates to the acquisition by Bridge of a 60% subsidiary, Pontoon, where goodwill and non-controlling interests are measured on a full fair value basis. At disposal, no goodwill had been impaired and tax is payable at 30%

Net assets at acquisition	Net assets at disposal date	Fair value of NCI at acquisition	Cost of investment	Sale proceeds
$m	$m	$m	$m	$m
500	750	300	900	3,000

Required:

- **Calculate the gain arising to the parent entity on disposal.**
- **Calculate the gain arising to the group on disposal.**

Test your understanding 3 – Padstow

Padstow purchased 80% of the shares in St Merryn four years ago for $100,000. On 30 June it sold all of these shares for $250,000. The net assets of St Merryn at acquisition were $69,000 and at disposal, $88,000. Fifty per cent of the goodwill arising on acquisition had been written off in an earlier year. The fair value of the non-controlling interest in St Merryn at the date of acquisition was $15,000. It is group policy to value the non-controlling interest using the full goodwill method.

Tax is charged at 30%.

Required:

What profits/losses on disposal are reported in Padstow's income statement and in the consolidated income statement?

Expandable Text - IFRS 5 Discontinued operations

Where an entity has disposed of its entire holding in a subsidiary that represents a separate major line of business or geographical area of operations, that subsidiary will meet the IFRS 5 definition of a discontinued operation.

The examiner may therefore require you to present the group accounts in accordance with this standard.

IFRS 5 is dealt with within chapter 13 of this workbook.

---

6 Group accounts disposal – subsidiary to associate

This situation is where the disposal results in the subsidiary becoming an associate, e.g. 90% holding is reduced to a 40% holding.

After the disposal the income, expenses, assets and liabilities of the ex-subsidiary can no longer be consolidated on a line by line basis; instead they must be accounted for under the equity method, with a single amount in the statement of comprehensive income/income statement for the share of the post tax profits for the period after disposal and a single amount in the statement of financial position for the fair value of the investment retained plus the share of post-acquisition retained profits.

Consolidated statement of comprehensive income/income statement

*   Pro rate the subsidiary's results up to the date of disposal and :
    *   consolidate the results up to the date of disposal
    *   equity account for the results after the date of disposal.

*   Include the group gain on part disposal.

Consolidated statement of financial position

*   Equity account by reference to the yearend holding, based on the fair value of the associate holding at disposal date.

Illustration 3 – Disposal – subsidiary to associate

Thomas disposed of a 25% holding in Percy on 30 June 20X6 for $125,000. A 70% holding in Percy had been acquired five years prior to this. Thomas uses the full goodwill method in accordance with IFRS 3 revised. Goodwill was impaired and written off in full prior to the year of disposal.

Details of Percy are as follows:

	$
Net assets at 31 December 20X5	290,000
Profit for year ended 31 December 20X6	100,000
(assumed to accrue evenly)	
Fair value of a 45% holding at 30 June 20X6	245,000

If the carrying value of NCI is $80,000 at the date of the share disposal, what gain on disposal is reported in the Thomas Group accounts for the year ended 31 December 20X6?

Ignore tax.

Expandable text – Solution

Thomas Group - answer

(W1) Group Structure

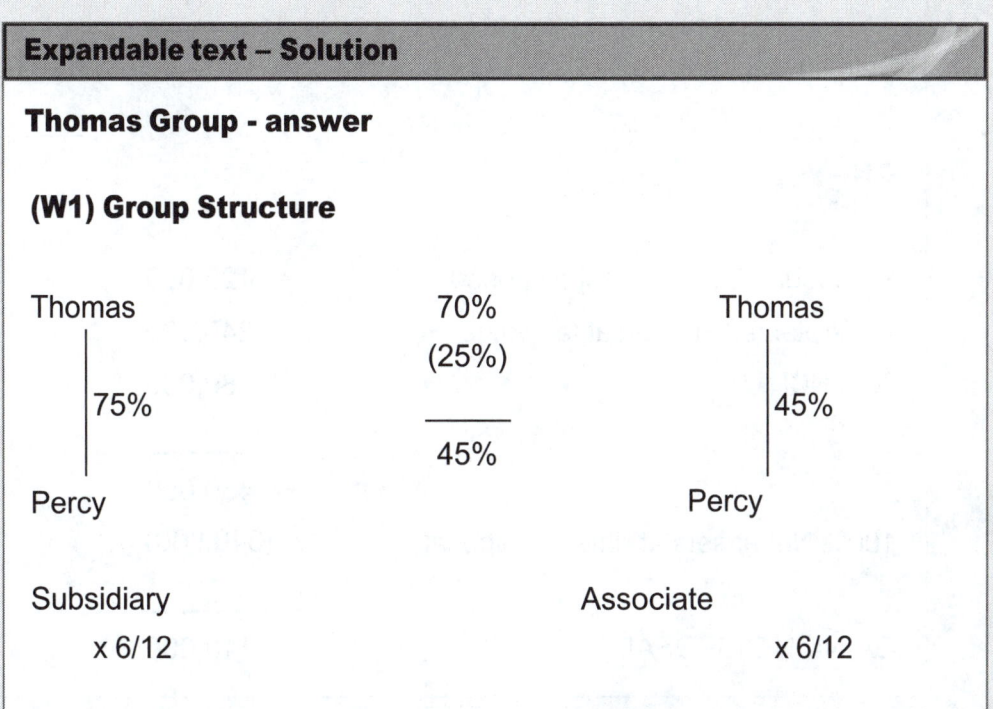

(W2) Net assets

	Date of disposal 30 June X6 $
Per question at 31 Dec X5	290,000
In yr 100,000 X 6/12	50,000
	_____
	340,000

Gain or loss to the group on disposal

		$
Proceeds		125,000
FV of retained int		245,000
		_____
		370,000
Net assets recognised at disposal	340,000	
NCI	(80,000)	(260,000)
	_____	_____
Gain on disposal		110,000
		_____

OR

	$
Proceeds - 25% interest disposed	125,000
45% retained interest at fair value	245,000
30% NCI	80,000
	_____
	450,000
100% Net assets at date of disposal	(340,000)
	_____
GAIN ON DISPOSAL	110,000

KAPLAN PUBLISHING

Test your understanding 4 - Hague

Hague has held a 60% investment in Maude for several years, using the full goodwill method to value the non-controlling interest. Half of the goodwill has been impaired prior to the date of disposal of shares by Hague. Details are as follows:

	$000
Cost of investment	6,000
Maude – Fair value of net assets at acquisition	2,000
Maude – Fair value of a 40% investment at acquisition date	1,000
Maude – Net assets at disposal	3,000
Maude – FV of a 30% investment at disposal date	3,500

Required:

(a) **Assuming a full disposal of the holding and proceeds of $10 million, calculate the profit/loss arising:**

   (i)   **in Hague's individual accounts**

   (ii) **in the consolidated accounts.**

   Tax is 25%.

(b) **Assuming a disposal of half the holding and proceeds of $5 million:**

   (i)   **calculate the profit/loss arising in the consolidated accounts**

   (ii) **explain how the residual holding will be accounted for.**

   Ignore tax.

Test your understanding 5 - Kathmandu

The income statements for the year ended 31 December 20X9 are as follows:

	Kathmandu group $	Nepal $
Revenue	553,000	450,000
Operating costs	(450,000)	(400,000)
Operating profits	103,000	50,000
Dividends receivable	8,000	–
Profit before tax	111,000	50,000
Tax	(40,000)	(14,000)
Profit after tax	71,000	36,000
Retained earnings b/f	100,000	80,000
Profit after tax	71,000	36,000
Dividend paid	(25,000)	(10,000)
Retained earnings c/f	146,000	106,000

Additional information

- The accounts of the Kathmandu group do not include the results of Nepal.

- On 1 January 20X5 Kathmandu acquired 70% of the shares of Nepal for $100,000 when the fair value of Nepal's net assets were $120,000. Nepal has equity capital of $50,000. At that date, the fair value of the the non-controlling interest was $38,000.

- Nepal paid its 20X9 dividend in cash on 31 March 20X9.

- Goodwill is to be accounted for based upon the fair value of non-controlling interest. No goodwill has been impaired.

- Kathmandu has other subsidiaries participating in the same activities as Nepal, and therefore the disposal of Nepal shares does not represent a discontinued operation per IFRS 5.

Required:

(a) (i) Prepare the consolidated income statement for the year ended 31 December 20X9 for the Kathmandu group on the basis that Kathmandu plc sold its holding in Nepal on 1 July 20X9 for $200,000. This disposal is not yet recognised in any way in Kathmandu group's income statement.

(ii) Compute the group retained earnings at 31 December 20X9.

(iii) Explain and illustrate how the results of Nepal are presented in the group income statement in the event that Nepal represented a discontinued activity per IFRS 5.

Ignore tax on the disposal.

(b) (i) Prepare the consolidated income statement for the year ended 31 December 20X9 for the Kathmandu group on the basis that Kathmandu sold half of its holding in Nepal on 1 July 20X9 for $100,000 This disposal is not yet recognised in any way in Kathmandu group's income statement. The residual holding of 35% has a fair value of $100,000 and leaves the Kathmandu group with significant influence.

(ii) Compute the group retained earnings at 31 December 20X9.

Ignore tax on the disposal.

7 Group accounts – Disposal with trade investment retained

This situation is where the subsidiary becomes a trade investment, e.g. 90% holding is reduced to a 10% holding.

Consolidated statement of comprehensive income/income statement

- Pro rate the subsidiary's results up to the date of disposal and then:
    - consolidate the results up to the date of disposal
    - only include dividend income after the date of disposal.

- Include the group gain on part disposal.

Consolidated statement of financial position

- Recognise the holding retained as an investment, measured at fair value at the date of disposal.

8 Accounting for a disposal where control is not lost

From the perspective of the group accounts, where there is a sale of shares but the parent still retains control then, in essence, this is an increase in the non-controlling interest.

For example if the parent holds 80% of the shares in a subsidiary and sells 5%, the relationship remains one of a parent and subsidiary and as such will remain consolidated in the group accounts in the normal way, but the NCI has risen from 20% to 25%.

Where there is such an increase in the non-controlling interest:

- No gain or loss on disposal is calculated
- No adjustment is made to the carrying value of goodwill
- The difference between the proceeds received and change in the non-controlling interest is accounted for in shareholders' equity as follows:

		$
Cash proceeds received		X
NCI in subsidiary pre-disposal	X	
NCI in subsidiary post-disposal	X	
Increase in NCI		X
Difference to equity		X

Illustration 4 – No loss of control

Until 30 September 20X7, Juno held 90% of Hera. On that date it sold 15% For $100,000. Prior to the disposal, the non-controlling interest was valued (using the full goodwill method) at $65,000. After the disposal, the non-controlling interest is valued at $180,000.

How should the disposal transaction be accounted for in the Juno Group accounts?

Expandable text - Solution

Dr Cash	$100,000
Dr Shareholders' equity	$15,000
Cr Non-controlling interest (180,000 – 65,000)	$115,000

Expandable text - Disposal with no loss of control

In this situation, the subsidiary remains a subsidiary, albeit the shareholding is reduced, e.g. 90% holding is reduced to a 60% holding.

Consolidated statement of comprehensive income / income statement

- Consolidate the subsidiary's results for the whole year.
- Calculate the non-controlling interest relating to the periods before and after the disposal separately and then add together:
- e.g. (X / 12 × profit × 10%) + (Y / 12 × profit × 40%)

Consolidated statement of financial position

- Consolidate as normal, with the non-controlling interest valued by reference to the year-end holding
- take the difference between proceeds and the change in the NCI to shareholders' equity as previously discussed.

Test your understanding 6 - David and Goliath

David has owned 90% of Goliath for many years.
David is considering selling part of its holding, whilst retaining control of Goliath.
At the date of considering disposal of part of the shareholding in Goliath, the NCI has a fair value of $50,000, and the net assets and goodwill have a carrying value of $70,000 and $20,000 respectively.

(i) David could sell 5% of the Goliath shares for $10,000 leaving it holding 85% and increasing the NCI to 15%, or
(ii) David could sell 25% of the Goliath shares for $20,000 leaving it holding 65% and increasing the NCI to 35%.

Required:

Calculate the difference arising that will be taken to equity for each situation

Test your understanding 7 - Cagney & Lacey

The draft financial statements of two entities at 31 March 20X1 were as follows.

Statements of Financial Position	Cagney Group	Lacey
	$000	$000
Investment in Lacey at cost	3,440	–
Sundry assets	41,950	9,500
	45,390	9,500
Equity capital ($1 shares)	20,000	3,000
Retained earnings	11,000	3,500
Sundry liabilities	5,500	3,000
Sales proceeds of disposal (Suspense account)	8,890	–
	45,390	9,500

Statements of Comprehensive Income	Cagney Group	Lacey
	$000	$000
Revenue	31,590	11,870
Cost of sales	(15,290)	(5,820)
Gross profit	16,300	6,050
Distribution costs	(3,000)	(2,000)
Administrative expenses	(350)	(250)
Profit before tax	12,950	3,800
Tax	(5,400)	(2,150)
Profit after tax for the year	7,550	1,650

The entities had retained earnings on 1 April 20X0 as follows

	$	$
Retained earnings	3,450	1,850

Cagney had acquired 90 per cent of Lacey when the retained earnings of Lacey were $700,000. Goodwill of $110,000 calculated on a proportionate basis, has been fully impaired. The Cagney group includes other 100 per cent owned subsidiaries.

On 31 December 20X0, Cagney disposed of a 15% interest in the equity capital of Lacey.

Required:

Prepare extracts from the Cagney Group statement of financial position and statement of comprehensive income on the basis that Cagney sold a 15% holding in Lacey. Include a statement of changes in equity within your answer.

9 Subsidiaries acquired exclusively with a view to subsequent disposal

IFRS 5: non-current assets held for sale and discontinued operations

- A subsidiary acquired exclusively with a view to resale is not exempt from consolidation.

- But if it meets the criteria in IFRS 5:
  - it is presented in the financial statements as a disposal group classified as held for sale. This is achieved by amalgamating all its assets into one line item and all its liabilities into another

  - it is measured, both on acquisition and at subsequent reporting dates, at fair value less costs to sell. (IFRS 5 sets down a special rule for such subsidiaries, requiring the deduction of costs to sell. Normally, it requires acquired assets and liabilities to be measured at fair value).

- The criteria include the requirements that:
  - the subsidiary is available for immediate sale

  - it is likely to be disposed of within one year of the date of its acquisition.

  - the sale is highly probable.

- A newly acquired subsidiary which meets these held for sale criteria automatically meets the criteria for being presented as a discontinued operation.

Expandable Text - Illustration: IFRS 5

David acquires Rose on 1 March 20X7. Rose is a holding entity with two wholly-owned subsidiaries, Mickey and Jackie. Jackie is acquired exclusively with a view to resale and meets the criteria for classification as held for sale. David's year-end is 30 September.

On 1 March 20X7 the following information is relevant:

- the identifiable liabilities of Jackie have a fair value of $40m
- the acquired assets of Jackie have a fair value of $180m
- the expected costs of selling Jackie are $5m.

On 30 September 20X7, the assets of Jackie have a fair value of $170.

The liabilities have a fair value of $35m and the selling costs remain at $5m.

Discuss how Jackie will be treated in the David Group financial statements on acquisition and at 30 September 20X7.

Expandable Text - Solution

On acquisition the assets and liabilities of Jackie are measured at fair value less costs to sell in accordance with IFRS 5's special rule.

	$m
Assets	180
Less selling costs	(5)
	175
Liabilities	(40)
Fair value less costs to sell	135

At the reporting date, the assets and liabilities of Jackie are remeasured to update the fair value less costs to sell.

	$m
Assets	170
Less selling costs	(5)
	165
Liabilities	(35)
Fair value less costs to sell	130

The fair value less costs to sell has decreased from $135m on 1 March to $130m on 30 September. This $5m reduction in fair value must be presented in the consolidated income statement as part of the single line item entitled 'discontinued operations'. Also included in this line items is the post-tax profit or loss earned/incurred by Jackie in the March – September 20X7 period.

The assets and liabilities of Jackie must be disclosed separately on the face of the statement of financial position. Below the subtotal for the David group's current assets Jackie's assets will be presented as follows:

	$m
Non-current assets classified as held for sale	165

Below the subtotal for the David group's current liabilities Jackie's liabilities will be presented as follows:

	$m
Liabilities directly associated with non-current assets classified as held for sale	35

No other disclosure is required.

10 Increase in group holding where control already obtained

From the perspective of the group accounts where there is a purchase of more shares in a subsidiary then, in essence, this is not an acquisition rather a decrease in the non-controlling interest.

For example if the parent holds 80% of the shares in a subsidiary and buys 5% more the relationship remains one of a parent and subsidiary and as such will be remain consolidated in the group accounts in the normal way, but the NCI has decreased from 20% to 15%.

Where there is such a decrease in the NCI:

- There is no change in the goodwill asset

- No gain or loss arises as this is a transaction within equity i.e. with the NCI

- A difference will arise that will be taken to equity and is determined in the following proforma.

	$
Cash paid	X
NCI in subsidiary pre-purchase of shares	X
NCI in subsidiary post-purchase of shares	X
Decrease in NCI	X
Difference to equity	X

Test your understanding 8 - Gordon and Mandy

Gordon has owned 80% of Mandy for many years.

Gordon is considering acquiring more shares in Mandy, which will decrease the NCI. The NCI of Mandy currently has a carrying value of $20,000, with the net assets and goodwill having a value of $125,000 and $25,000 respectively.

Gordon is considering the following two scenarios:

(i) Gordon could buy 20% of the Mandy shares leaving no NCI for $25,000, or

(ii) Gordon could buy 5% of the Mandy shares for $9,000 leaving a 15% NCI.

Required:

Calculate the difference arising that will be taken to equity for each situation

---

Expandable text - UK syllabus focus

The ACCA UK syllabus contains a requirement that UK variant candidates should be able to discuss and apply the key differences between UK GAAP and IFRS GAAP. As with other areas of group accounts, the accounting requirements of UK GAAP and IFRS GAAP are very similar in this area, but there are one or two differences.

You should approach questions using the approach of completing the five standard workings identified within chapter 1 as far as they are required. Normally a net assets working is required at the date of any disposal, together with identification of any unamortised goodwill at that date. This information helps to calculate the gain or loss on disposal for inclusion in the financial statements.

Expandable text - UK GAAP question 1

Parker purchased 80% of the shares in Tramp four years ago for £100,000. On 30 June it sold all of these shares for £250,000. The net assets of Tramp at acquisition were £69,000 and at disposal, £88,000. Half of the goodwill arising on acquisition had been amortised by the date of the share disposal.

Tax is charged at 30%.

Required:

What profits/losses on disposal are reported in Parker's profit and loss account and in the group profit and loss account?

Expandable text - UK GAAP answer 1

(a) Gain to Parker

	£000
Sales proceeds	250
Cost of shares sold	(100)
Gain on disposal	150
Tax at 30%	(45)
Net gain on disposal	105

(b) Consolidated accounts

	£000
Sales proceeds	250.0
Share of net assets sold (88,000 x 80%)	(70.4)
Goodwill disposed of (W1)	(22.4)
Gain on disposal	157.2
Tax (per parent)	(45.0)
Net gain on disposal	112.2

(W1) Goodwill

	£000
Cost of investment	100.0
Group share of FV of net assets at acquisition (80% x 69)	(55.2)
	44.8
Impaired to extent of 50%	(22.4)
Unamortised goodwill at disposal date	22.4

Normally the parent entity profit is greater than the group profit, by the share of the post-acquisition retained earnings now disposed of. In this case the reverse is true, because the $22,400 amortisation of goodwill already recognised exceeds the $15,200 ((88,000 – 69,000) × 80%) share of post acquisition profits.

The income statements for the year ended 31 December 20X9 are as follows:

	Kathmandu group	Doha
	£	£
Turnover	553,000	450,000
Operating costs	(450,000)	(400,000)
Operating profits	103,000	50,000
Dividends receivable	8,000	–
Profit before tax	111,000	50,000
Tax	(40,000)	(14,000)
Profit after tax	71,000	36,000
P&L reserve b/f	100,000	80,000
Profit after tax	71,000	36,000
Dividend paid	(25,000)	(10,000)
P&L reserve c/f	146,000	106,000

Additional information

- The accounts of the Kathmandu group do not include the results of Doha.

- On 1 January 20X5 Kathmandu acquired 70% of the shares of Doha for £100,000 when the fair value of Nepal's net assets were £120,000. Doha has ordinary share capital of $50,000.

- Doha paid its 20X9 dividend in cash on 31 March 20X9.

- Goodwill has an indefinite life, and has suffered no impairment to date.

- Kathmandu has other subsidiaries participating in the same activities as Nepal, and therefore the disposal of Nepal shares does not represent a discontinued operation per FRED 32.

Required:

(a) (i) Prepare the consolidated profit and loss account for the year ended 31 December 20X9 for the Kathmandu group on the basis that Kathmandu plc sold its holding in Doha on 1 July 20X9 for £200,000. This disposal is not yet recognised in any way in Kathmandu group's profit and loss acount.

(ii) Compute the group profit and loss reserve at 31 December 20X9.

(iii) Explain and illustrate how the results of Nepal are presented in the group income statement in the event that Nepal represented a discontinued activity per FRED 32 (equivalent of IFRS 5).

Ignore tax on the disposal.

(b) (i) Prepare the consolidated profit and loss account for the year ended 31 December 20X9 for the Kathmandu group on the basis that Kathmandu sold half of its holding in Doha on 1 July 20X9 for £200,000 This disposal is not yet recognised in any way in Kathmandu group's profit and loss account. The residual holding of 35% leaves the Kathmandu group with significant influence.

(ii) Compute the group profit and loss reserve at 31 December 20X9.

Ignore tax on the disposal.

Expandable text - UK GAAP answer 2

(a) (i) **Consolidated income statement – full disposal**

	Kathmandu group	Doha	Group
	£		£
Turnover	553,000	(6/12 x 450,000)	778,000
Operating costs	450,000	(6/12 x 400,000)	(650,000)
Operating profit			128,000
Dividend	8,000 less inter-co (70% × 10,000)		1,000
Profit on disposal **(W3)**			87,400
Profit before tax			216,400
Tax	40,000	(6/12 × 14,000)	(47,000)
Profit after tax			169,400
Attributable to:			
Equity holders of Kathmandu (β)			164,000
Minority interest		(30% × 36,000 × 6/12)	5,400
			169,400

(ii) **Group P&L reserve at 31 December 20X9 – full disposal**

	£
Brought forward:	
Kathmandu	100,000
Group % of Doha's post acquisition retained profits b/f	
(70% × (130,000 **(W1)** – 120,000) (per Q))	7,000
	107,000
Profit for year per consolidated income statement	164,000
Less Dividend paid	(25,000)
Retained profits carried forward	246,000

Notice that the post-tax results of the subsidiary upto the date of disposal are presented as a one-line entry in the group income statement. There is no line-by-line consolidation of results when this method of presentation is adopted.

(b) (i) **group profit and loss account – part disposal with residual interest**

	Kathmandu group	Nepal	Group
	£		£
Revenue	553,000	(6 / 12 × 450,000)	778,000
Operating costs	450,000	(6 / 12 × 400,000)	(650,000)
Operating profit			128,000
Dividend	8,000 less inter-co (70% × 10,000)		1,000
Income from associate	(35% × 50,000 × 6 / 12)		8,750
Profit on disposal **(W3)**			143,700
Profit before tax			281,450
Tax	40,000	(6 / 12 × 14,000)	(47,000)
- re associate		(35% x 14,000 x 6/12)	(2,450)
Profit after tax			232,000

Attributable to:

Kathmandu (β)		226,600
Minority interest	(30% × 36,000	
	× 6/12)	5,400
		232,000

(ii) Group P&L reserve at 31 December 20X9 – part disposal

	£
Brought forward	
Kathmandu	100,000
Group % of Nepal's post acquisition retained profits b/f	
(70% × (130,000 **(W1)** – 120,000) (per Q))	7,000
	107,000
Group income per consolidated income statement	226,600
Less Dividend paid	(25,000)
	308,600

Workings

(W1) Net assets - Doha

	Net assets at disposal	Net assets b/f
	£	£
Share capital	50,000	50,000
P&L reserve b/f	80,000	80,000
P&L for year: 6/12 × 36,000	18,000	
Less Dividend	(10,000)	–
	138,000	130,000

(W2) Goodwill

Cost to parent	100,000
Group share of FV of net assets at date of acquisition (70% x 120,000)	(84,000)
Unimpaired goodwill	16,000

(W3) Profit on disposal

Full disposal (a)(i)	£
Proceeds	200,000
Less: Net assets at disposal (W1)	138,000
Less: goodwill disposed of (70/70 x 16,000) (W1)	16,000
Profit on disposal	87,400

Part disposal (b)(i)		£
Proceeds		200,000
Less: net assets disposed of:	(35% x 138,000) (W1)	((48,300)
Less: goodwill disposed of:	(35/70 x 16,000) (W2)	(8,000)
		143,700

11 Chapter summary

DISPOSALS

Parent entity accounts
Gain:

Proceeds	X
Cost	(X)
Tax	(X)
	X

Group accounts gain
- No gain or loss where no loss of control
- If control is lost, calculate gain as:

proceeds		X
FV of any interest retained		X
Net assets of sub at disposal	X	
Goodwill	X	
NCI at disposal	(X)	
		(X)
		(X)

Whole shareholding disposal of SCI/IS: consolidate to disposal and show group gain
B/S: subsidiary's net assets not included

IFRSs Disclosure discontinued operations

No loss of control
SCI/IS: consolidate for full year, calculate NCI pre and post disposal
SFP: consolidate as normal with NCI based on year end holding, account for gain or loss to NCI in equity

Associate shareholding retained
SCI/IS: consolidate to date of disposal, then equity account, show gain
SFP: equity account at year end based on FV of associate shareholding at disposal

Trade investment shareholding retained
SCI/IS: consolidate to date of disposal, then include dividend income, show gain
SFP: Record retained investment at fair value at disposal date

Subsidiaries acquired with a view to subsequent disposal must consolidate present as disposal group; measure at lower of CV and FV - selling costs

Test your understanding answers

Test your understanding 1 – Snooker

(a) Gain to Snooker

	$000
Sales proceeds	300
Cost of shares sold	(100)
Gain on disposal	200
Tax at 30%	(60)
Net gain on disposal	140

(b) Consolidated accounts

		$000
Proceeds		300
FV of retained interest		NIL
		300

Less interest in subsidiary disposed of:		
Net assets of subsidiary at disposal date	110	
Unimpaired goodwill at disposal date	60	
Less: NCI share of net assets at disposal (20% × 110)	(22)	
Less: NCI share of goodwill at disposal (if applicable)	(NIL)	
		(148)
		152
Tax on gain as per Snooker (part (a))		(60)
Post-tax gain to group		92

KAPLAN PUBLISHING

Test your understanding 2 - Bridge

(a) Gain to parent entity

	$000
Sales proceeds	3,000
Cost of shares sold	(900)
Gain on disposal	2,100
Tax at 30%	(630)
Net gain on disposal	1,470

(b) Consolidated accounts

		$
Proceeds		3,000
FV of retained interest		NIL
		3,000
Less interest in subsidiary disposed of:		
Net assets of subsidiary at disposal date	750	
Unimpaired goodwill at disposal date (W1)	700	
Less: NCI at disposal date (W2)	(400)	
		(1,050)
		1,950
Tax on gain as per parent entity		(630)
Post-tax gain to group		1,320

(W1) Goodwill calculation

	$m
Cost of investment	900
FV of NCI at acquisition (given)	300
	1,200
FV of net assets acquisition	(500)
Fair value of goodwill at acquisition	
	700

(W2) NCI at disposal date

	$m
FV of NCI at acquisition (given)	300
NCI share of post-acquisition retained earnings (40% x (750 - 500))	100
	400

Test your understanding 3 – Padstow

(a) Gain to Padstow

	$000
Sales proceeds	250
Cost of shares sold	(100)
Gain on disposal	150
Tax at 30%	(45)
Net gain on disposal	105

(b) Consolidated accounts

	$000	$000
Sales proceeds		250.0
Carrying value of subsidiary at disposal date:		
Net assets at disposal date - given	88.0	
Unimpaired goodwill at disposal date (W1)	23.0	
	111.0	
Less: CV of NCI at disposal (W2)	(18.8)	
Tax (per parent)		(92.2)
Net gain on disposal		157.8
Tax (per parent in part (a)		(45.0)
		112.8

(W1) Goodwill

	$000
Cost of investment	100.0
FV of NCI at acquisition	15.0
	115.0
FV of net assets at acquisition	(69.0
	46.0
Impaired to extent of 50%	(23.0)
Unimpaired goodwill at disposal date	23.0

(W2) NCI at disposal date

	$000
FV at date of acquisition	15.0
NCI share of post-acquisition retained earnings (20% x (88.0 - 69.0))	3.8
Goodwill	18.8

Normally the parent entity profit is greater than the group profit, by the share of the post-acquisition retained earnings now disposed of. In this case the reverse is true, because the $23,000 impairment loss already recognised exceeds the $15,200 ((88,000 – 69,000) × 80%) share of post acquisition retained earnings.

KAPLAN PUBLISHING

Test your understanding 4 - Hague

(W1) Goodwill		$000
Cost of investment		6,000
FV of the NCI at date of acquisition		1,000
		7,000
FV of net assets at the date of acquisition (given)		(2000)
Total goodwill		5,000
Impaired (50%)		(2,500)
Unimpaired goodwill		2,500

(W2) NCI at disposal date		$000
FV at date of acquisition		1,000
NCI share of post-acquisition retained earnings (40% x (3,000 - 2,000))		400
Less: NCI share of goodwill impairment	(40% x 2500)	(1,000)
		400

Full disposal of shares

Gain in Hague's individual accounts

	$000
(a) (i) Sale proceeds	10,000
Less Cost of shares sold	(6,000)
Gain to parent	4,000
Tax at 25% × 4,000	(1,000)
	3,000

Full disposal of shares - gain in Hague Group accounts

		$000
Sale proceeds		10,000
FV of retained interest		nil
CV of subsidiary at disposal:		
Net Assets	3,000	
Unimpaired goodwill (W1)	2,500	
	5,500	
Less: NCI at disposal date (W2)	(400)	
		(5,100)
Gain before tax		4,900
Tax per part (a)(i)		(1,000)
		3,900

(b) (i) Disposal of half of the holding to leave a residual shareholding:

	$000	$000
Disposal proceeds		5,000
FV of retained interest		3,500
		8,500
CV of subsidiary at disposal date:		
Net assets	3,000	
Unimpaired goodwill (W1)	2,500	
	5,500	
Less: FV of NCI at disposal date (W2)	(400)	
		(5,100
		3,400

(ii) After the date of disposal, the residual holding will be equity accounted, with a single amount in the income statement for the share of the post-tax retained earnings for the period after disposal and a single amount in the statement of financial position for the fair value at disposal date of the investment retained plus the group share of post-acquisition retained earnings.

Test your understanding 5 - Kathmandu

(a) (i) **Consolidated income statement – full disposal**

	Kathmandu group	Nepal	Group
	$		$
Revenue	553,000	(6 / 12 x 450,000)	778,000
Operating costs	450,000	(6 / 12 x 400,000)	(650,000)
Operating profit			128,000
Dividend	8,000 less inter-co (70% × 10,000)		1,000
Profit on disposal **(W4)**			87,400
Profit before tax			216,400
Tax	40,000	(6 / 12 × 14,000)	(47,000)
Profit after tax			169,400
Attributable to:			
Equity holders of Kathmandu (β)			164,000
Non-controlling interest		(30% × 36,000 × 6/12)	5,400
			169,400

(ii) **Group retained earnings at 31 December 20X9 – full disposal**

	$
Brought forward	
Kathmandu	100,000
Group % of Nepal's post acquisition retained earnings b/f	
(70% × (130,000 **(W1)** – 120,000) (per Q))	7,000
	107,000
Profit for year per consolidated income statement	164,000
Less Dividend paid	(25,000)
Retained earnings carried forward	246,000

(iii) **Group income statement – discontinued operations presentation**

	Kathmandu group	Group
	$	$
Revenue	553,000	553,000
Operating costs	450,000	(450,000)
Operating profit		103,000
Dividend	8,000 less inter-co (70% × 10,000)	1,000
Profit on disposal (W4)		87,400
Profit before tax		191,400
Tax		(40,000)
Profit after tax – continuing operations		151,400
Discontinued operations ($36,000 × 6/12)		18,000
		169,400

Attributable to:

Equity holders of Kathmandu (β)		164,000
Non-controlling interest	(30% × 36,000 × 6/12)	5,400
		169,400

Notice that the post-tax results of the subsidiary upto the date of disposal are presented as a one-line entry in the group income statement. There is no line-by-line consolidation of results when this method of presentation is adopted.

(b) (i) Consolidated income statement – part disposal with residual interest

	Kathmandu group $	Nepal	Group $
Revenue	553,000	(6 / 12 × 450,000)	778,000
Operating costs	450,000	(6 / 12 × 400,000)	(650,000)
Operating profit			128,000
Dividend	8,000 less inter-co (70% × 10,000)		1,000
Income from associate	(35% × 36,000 × 6 / 12)		6,300
Profit on disposal (W4)			87,400
Profit before tax			222,700
Tax	40,000	(6 / 12 × 14,000)	(47,000)
Profit after tax			175,700

Attributable to:

Equity holders of Kathmandu (β)	170,300
Non-controlling interest (30% × 36,000 × 6 / 12)	5,400
	175,700

(ii) Group retained earnings at 31 December 20X9 – part disposal

	$
Brought forward	
Kathmandu	100,000
Group % of Nepal's post acquisition retained earnings b/f (70% × (130,000 **(W1)** – 120,000) (per Q))	7,000
	107,000
Group income per consolidated income statement	170,300
Less Dividend paid	(25,000)
	252,300

Workings

(W1) Net assets - Nepal	Net assets at disposal	Net assets b/f
	$	$
Share capital	50,000	50,000
Retained earnings		
B/f	80,000	80,000
6 / 12 × 36,000	18,000	
Less Dividend	(10,000)	–
	138,000	130,000

(W2) Goodwill

Cost to parent	100,000
FV of NCI at date of acquisition	38,000
	138,000
FV of net assets at date of acquisition (per question)	120,000
Unimpaired goodwill	18,000

(W3) NCI at disposal date

FV of NCI at date of acquisition	38,000
NCI share of post-acquisition retained earnings	
(30% x (138,000 - 120,000)	5,400
	43,400

(W4) Profit on disposal

	$	$
Full disposal (a)(i)		
Proceeds		200,000
Net assets recorded prior to disposal		
Net assets	138,000	
Full goodwill - unimpaired	18,000	
	156,000	
NCI at date of disposal (W3)	(43,400)	
		(112,600)
Profit on disposal		87,400

Part disposal (b)(i)

Proceeds		100,000
FV of retained interest (per question)		100,000
		———
		200,000
Net assets recorded prior to disposal		
Net assets	138,000	
Unimpaired goodwill at disposal date	18,000	
	———	
	156,000	
NCI at date of disposal (W3)	(43,400)	
	———	
		(112,600)
		———
		87,400
		———

Test your understanding 6 - David and Goliath

(i)   Sale of 5% of Goliath shares

	$
Cash proceeds	10,000
Increase in NCI (5% x (70,000 + 20,000)	4,500

Difference to equity (i.e. increase in equity)	5,500

(ii) Sale of 25% of Goliath shares

	$
Cash proceeds	20,000
Increase in NCI (25% x (70,000 + 20,000)	22,500

Difference to equity (i.e. decrease in equity)	2,500

Note that in both situations, Goliath remains a subsidiary of David after the sale of shares. There is no gain or loss to the group - the difference arising is taken to equity. Goliath would continue to be consolidated within the David Group like any other subsidiary; there is no change to the carrying value of goodwill. The only impact will be the calculation of NCI share of retained earnings for the year - this would need to be time-apportioned based upon the NCI percentage pre- and post-disposal during the year.

Test your understanding 7 - Cagney & Lacey

(W1) Group structure

Cagney	Cagney
90%	75%
Lacey	Lacey
Subsidiary 9/12	Subsidiary 3/12

(W2) Net assets at disposal 31 December 19X0

	$000
Equity capital	3,000
Retained earnings bought forward	1,850
Earnings for the year (pro rata – $1,650 x 9/12)	1,238
	6,088
Proportion disposed of (15%)	913

(W3) Disposal transaction

		$000
Dr Cash	Proceeds	8,890
Cr Non Controlling Interest	Net assets disposed of W2	913
Cr Shareholder Equity	Disposal adjustment	7,977

(W4) Non – Controlling Interest

	$000
Lacey's profit after tax	
($1,650 x 9/12 x 10%)	124
($1,650 x 3/12 x 25%)	103
	227

Statement of Comprehensive Income for the year ended 31 March XI

	$000
Revenue (31,590 + 11,870)	43,460
Cost of sales (15,290 + 5,820)	(21,110)
Gross profit	22,350
Distribution costs (3,000 + 2,000)	(5,000)
Admin expenses (350 + 250)	(600)
Profit before tax (12,950 + 3,800)	16,750
Tax (5,400 + 2,150)	(7,550)
Profit after tax for the year	9,200
Attributable to	
Non – controlling interest (W4)	(227)
Profit for the year	8,973

You can now reconcile the reserves

Retained earnings reconciliation

	$000
Bal b/fwd (W1)	4,375
Profit for the year	8,973
Disposal adj [8,890 – 913]	7,977
Bal c/fwd (W2)	21,325

	$000
NCI b/fwd: working	
Equity capital	3,000
Retained earnings	1,850
	4,850
Take NCI % (10% x 4,850)	485

Workings

(W1) Retained earnings bal b/fwd

	$000
100% Cagney	3,450
Lacey (1,850 – 700) x 90%	1,035
Less goodwill fully impaired	(110)
	4,375

(W2) Retained earnings bal c/fwd

100% Cagey	11,000
Profit on disposal [8,890 – 3,440 x 15/90]	8,317
Less goodwill [110 – 110 x 15/90]	(92)
Lacey (3,500 – 700) x 75%	2,100
	21,325

Now prepare the Statement of Financial Position

	$000
Sundry assets [41,950 + 9,500]	51,450
	51,450

	$000
Equity Capital	20,000
Retained earnings (W2)	21,325
Non-controlling interest [6,500 x 25%]	1,625
	42,950
Sundry liabilities (5,500 + 3,000)	8,500
	51,450

Statement of Changes in Equity

	Equity capital	Retained earnings	Non-controlling interest	Total
	$000	$000	$000	$000
31 March 20X0	20,000	4,375	485	24,860
Profit for the year		8,973	227	9,200
Disposal adjustment		7,977	913	8,890
31 March 20X1	20,000	21,325	1,625	42,950

Test your understanding 8 - Gordon and Mandy

(i) Purchase of 20% of Mandy shares

	$
Cash paid	25,000
Decrease in NCI (20% x (125,000 + 25,000))	30,000
Difference to equity (i.e. increase in equity)	5.000

(ii) Purchase of 5% of Mandy shares

	$
Cash paid	9,000
Decrease in NCI (5% x (125,000 + 25,000))	7,500
Difference to equity (i.e. decrease in equity)	1,500

Group reorganisations

Chapter learning objectives

Upon completion of this chapter you will be able to:

- discuss the reasons behind a group reorganisation
- evaluate and assess the principal terms of a proposed group reorganisation.

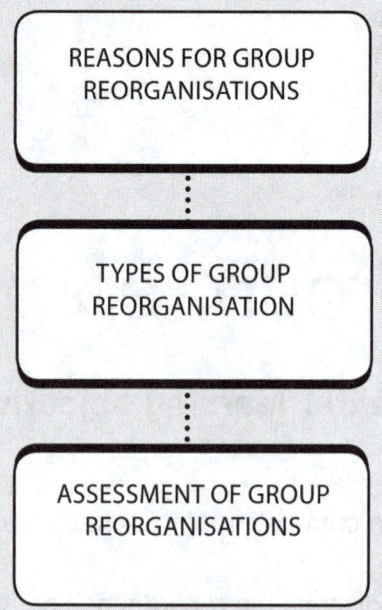

Expandable text - Definition of a group reorganisation

A group reorganisation (or restructuring) is any of the following:

(a) the transfer of shares in a subsidiary from one group entity to another

(b) the addition of a new parent entity to a group

(c) the transfer of shares in one or more subsidiaries of a group to a new entity that is not a group entity but whose shareholders are the same as those of the group's parent

(d) the combination into a group of two or more companies that before the combination had the same shareholders

(e) the acquisition of the shares of another entity that itself then issues sufficient shares so that the acquired entity has control of the combined entity.

Expandable text - Reasons for a reorganisation

There are a number of reasons why a group may wish to reorganise. These include the following.

- A group may wish to list on a public stock exchange. This is usually facilitated by creating a new holding company and keeping the business of the group in subsidiary entities.

- The ownership of subsidiaries may be transferred from one group company to another. This is often the case if the group wishes to sell a subsidiary, but retain its trade.

- The group may decide to transfer the assets and trades of a number of subsidiaries into one entity. This is called divisionalisation and is undertaken in order to simplify the group structure and save costs. The details of divisionalisation are not examinable at P2.

- The group may split into two or more parts; each part is still owned by the same shareholders but is not related to the other parts. This is a demerger and is often done to enhance shareholder value. By splitting the group, the value of each part is realised whereas previously the stock market may have undervalued the group as a whole. The details of demergers are not examinable at P2.

- An unlisted entity may purchase a listed entity with the aim of achieving a stock exchange listing itself. This is called a reverse acquisition.

Expandable text - Types of group reorganisation

There are a number of ways of effecting a group reorganisation. The type of reorganisation will depend on what the group is trying to achieve.

New holding company

A group might set up a new holding entity for an existing group in order to improve co-ordination within the group or as a vehicle for flotation.

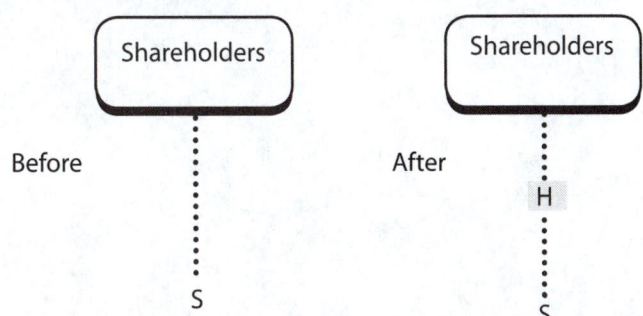

- H becomes the new holding entity of S.

- Usually, H issues shares to the shareholders of S in exchange for shares of S, but occasionally the shareholders of S may subscribe for shares in H and H may pay cash for S.

IFRS 3 excludes from its scope any business combination involving entities or businesses under 'common control', which is where the same parties control all of the combining entities/businesses both before and after the business combination.

As there is no mandatory guidance in accounting for these items, the acquisition method should certainly be used in examination questions.

Expandable text - IASB's common control project

You may be aware that the IASB is approaching the topic of business combinations in two phases. Phase I resulted in the issue of IFRS 3 revised, which states that:

- 'standard' business combinations must be accounted for using the acquisition method

- goodwill arising on consolidation is capitalised, not amortised, but subject to an annual impairment review.

Phase II is considering non-standard business combinations, e.g. combinations involving entities under common control, or combinations involving two or more mutual entities (such as mutual insurance companies). The project will examine the definition of common control and the methods of accounting for business combinations under common control in the consolidated and acquirer's individual financial statements. No firm decisions have yet been taken, but the IASB hopes to develop a standard in due course.

At April 2009. the progress of this project had still to be clarified by the IASB.

Expandable text - Change of ownership of an entity within a

Change of ownership of an entity within a group

This occurs when the internal structure of the group changes, for example, a parent may transfer the ownership of a subsidiary to another of its subsidiaries.

The key thing to remember is that the reorganisation of the entities within the group should not affect the group accounts, as shareholdings are transferred from one company to another and no assets will leave the group.

The individual accounts of the group companies will need to be adjusted for the effect of the transfer.

The following are types of reorganisation:

(a) **Subsidiary moved up**

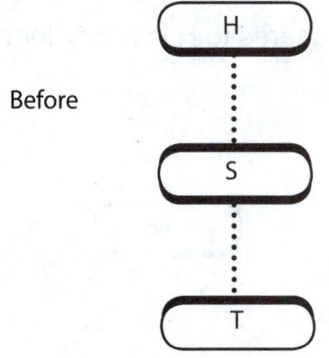
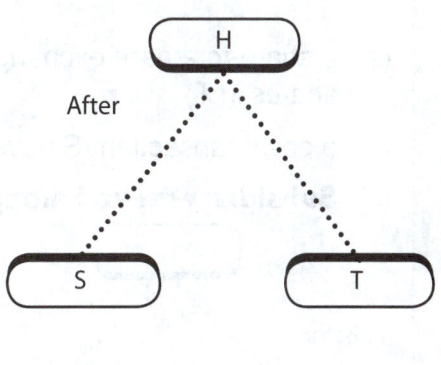

Before

After

This can be achieved in one of two ways.

(a) S transfers its investment in T to H as a dividend in specie. If this is done then S must have sufficient distributable profits to pay the dividend.

(b) H purchases the investment in T from S for cash. In practice the purchase price often equals the fair value of the net assets acquired, so that no gain or loss arises on the transaction.

Usually, it will be the carrying value of T that is used as the basis for the transfer of the investment, but there are no legal rules confirming this.

A share-for-share exchange cannot be used as in many jurisdictions it is illegal for a subsidiary to hold shares in the parent company.

(b) Subsidiary moved down

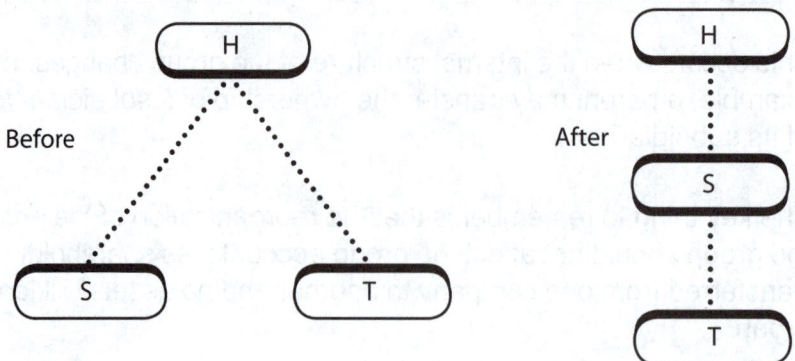

This reorganisation may be carried out where there are tax advantages in establishing a 'sub-group', or where two or more subsidiaries are linked geographically.

This can be carried out either by:

(a) a share-for-share exchange (S issues shares to H in return for the shares in T)

(b) a cash transaction (S pays cash to H).

(c) Subsidiary moved along

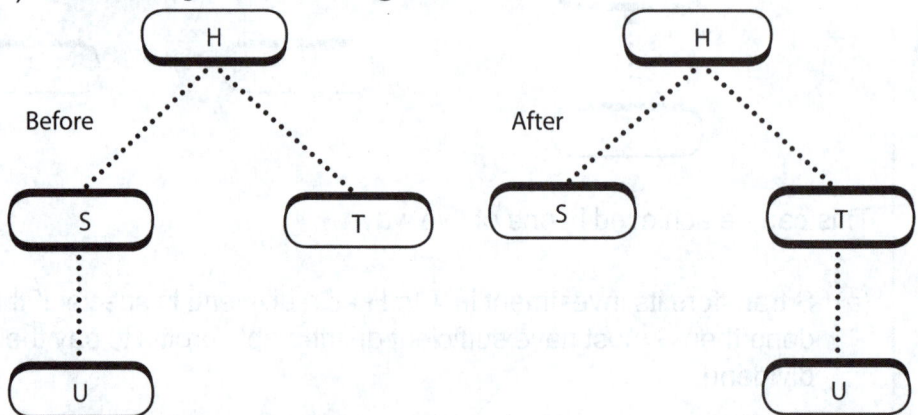

This is carried out by T paying cash (or other assets) to S. The consideration would not normally be in the form of shares because a typical reason for such a reconstruction would be to allow S to be managed as a separate part of the group or even disposed of completely. This could not be achieved effectively were S to have a shareholding in T.

If the purpose of the reorganisation is to allow S to leave the group, the purchase price paid by T should not be less than the fair value of the investment in U, otherwise S may be deemed to be receiving financial assistance for the purchase of its own shares, which is illegal in many jurisdictions.

Expandable text - Reverse acquisitions

Definition

A **reverse acquisition** occurs when an entity obtains ownership of the shares of another entity, which in turn issues sufficient shares so that the acquired entity has control of the combined entity.

Reverse acquisitions are a method of allowing unlisted companies to obtain a stock exchange quotation by taking over a smaller listed company.

For example, a private company arranges to be acquired by a listed company. This is effected by the public entity issuing shares to the private company so that the private company's shareholders end up controlling the listed entity. Legally, the public entity is the parent, but the substance of the transaction is that the private entity has acquired the listed entity.

Expandable text - Assessment of group reorganisations

Previous examination questions testing group reorganisations have provided a scenario with a group considering a number of reorganisation options. The questions have then asked for an evaluation and recommendation of a particular proposal.

In order to do this, you will need to consider the following:

*   the impact of the proposal on the individual accounts of the group entities

*   the impact of the proposal on the group accounts

*   the purpose of the reorganisation

*   whether there is any impairment of any of the group's assets

*   whether any impairment loss should be recognised in relation to the investment in subsidiaries in the parent company accounts.

Chapter summary

> **Reasons for group reorganisations**
> - Transfer of shares in a subsidiary from one group entity to another
> - Addition of a new parent entity to a group
> - Transfer of shares in one or more subsidiaries of a group to a new entity that is not a group entity, but whose shareholders are the same as those of the group's parent
> - Combination into a group of two or more companies that before the combination had the same shareholders

> **Types of group reorganisations**
> - New holding company
> - Change of ownership of an entity within the group
> - Reverse acquisition

> **Assessment of group reorganisations**
> - Look for the effect on the group and individual financial statements
> - Look for any impairment of assets in the group
> - Look for any impairment of investments in the parent company

Group accounting – foreign currency

Chapter learning objectives

Upon completion of this chapter you will be able to:

- outline the principles for translating foreign currency amounts, including translations into the functional currency and presentation currency
- apply these principles
- account for the consolidation of foreign operations and their disposal.

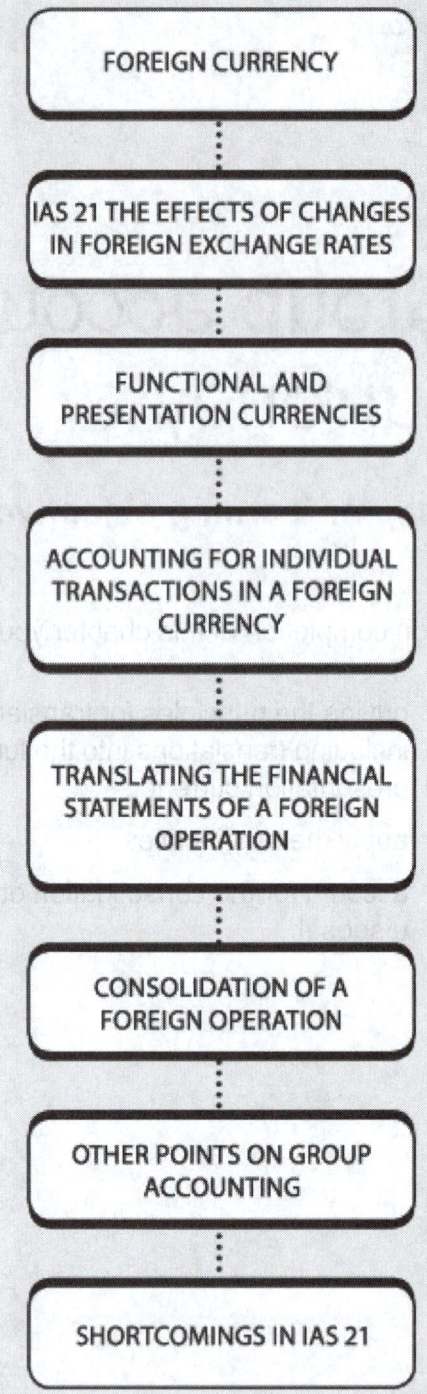

1 IAS 21 The effects of changes in foreign exchange rates

IAS 21 deals with:

- the definition of functional and presentation currencies
- accounting for individual transactions in a foreign currency
- translating the financial statements of a foreign operation.

Functional and presentation currencies

The **functional currency** is the currency of the primary economic environment where the entity operates. In most cases this will be the local currency.

An entity should consider the following when determining its functional currency.

- The currency that mainly influences sales prices for goods and services.

- The currency of the country whose competitive forces and regulations mainly determine the sales price of goods and services.

- The currency that mainly influences labour, material and other costs of providing goods and services.

The entity maintains its day-to-day financial records in its functional currency.

The **presentation currency** is the currency in which the entity presents its financial statements. This can be different from the functional currency, particularly if the entity in question is a foreign- owned subsidiary. It may have to present its financial statements in the currency of its parent, even though that is different from its own functional currency.

Expandable text - Functional and presentation currencies

The **functional currency** is the currency an entity will use in its day-to-day transactions. In addition to the points noted previously, IAS 21 also identifies that that an entity should consider the following factors in determining its functional currency:

- The currency in which funding from issuing debt and equity is generated.

- The currency in which receipts from operating activities are usually retained.

Let us consider an example to illustrate this point. Entity A operates in the UK. It sells goods throughout the UK and Europe with all transactions denominated in sterling. Cash is received from sales in sterling. It raises finance locally from UK banks with all loans denominated in sterling.

Looking at the factors listed above it is apparent that the functional currency for Entity A is sterling. It trades in this currency and raises finance in this currency.

Therefore Entity A would record its accounting transactions in sterling as its functional currency.

One complication in determining functional currency arises if an entity is a foreign operation. For example, if Entity A (from above) has a subsidiary Entity B located in Europe, Entity B will also have to determine its functional currency. The question arises as to whether this will be the same as the parent or will be the local currency where Entity B is located.

The factors that must be considered are:

- whether the activities of the foreign operation are carried out as an extension of the parent, rather than with a significant degree of autonomy

- whether transactions with the parent are a high or low proportion of the foreign operation's activities

- whether cash flows from the foreign operation directly affect the cash flows of the parent and are readily available for remittance to it

- whether cash flows from the activities of the foreign operation are sufficient to service existing debt obligations without funds being made available by the parent.

So, continuing with the example above, if Entity B operates as an independent operation, generating income and expenses in its local currency and raising finance in its local currency, then its functional currency would be its local currency and not that of Entity A. However, if Entity B was merely an extension of Entity A, only selling goods imported from Entity A and remitting all profits back to Entity A, then the functional currency should be the same as the parent. In this case Entity B would record its transactions in sterling and not its local currency.

Once a functional currency is determined it is not changed unless there is a change in the underlying circumstances that were relevant when determining the original functional currency.

IAS 21 states that whereas an entity is constrained by the factors listed above in determining its functional currency, it has a completely free choice as to the currency in which it presents its financial statements. If the **presentation currency** is different from the functional currency, then the financial statements must be translated into the presentation currency. For example, a group may have subsidiaries whose functional currencies are different to that of the parent. These must be translated into the presentation currency so that the consolidation procedure can take place.

Accounting for individual transactions in a foreign currency

Where an entity enters into a transaction denominated in a currency other than its functional currency, that transaction must be translated into the functional currency before it is recorded.

Expandable text - Examples of foreign currency transactions

Whenever a business enters into a contract where the consideration is expressed in a foreign currency, it will be necessary to translate that foreign currency amount at some stage into the functional currency for inclusion into its own accounts. Examples include:

- imports of raw materials

- exports of finished goods

- importation of foreign-manufactured non-current assets

- investments in foreign securities

- raising an overseas loan.

The exchange rate used should be:

- the spot exchange rate on the date the transaction occurred

- an average rate over a period of time, providing the exchange rate has not fluctuated significantly.

Cash settlement

When cash settlement occurs, for example payment by a receivable, the settled amount should be translated using the spot exchange rate on the settlement date. If this amount differs from that used when the transaction occurred, there will be an exchange difference.

Exchange differences on settlement

These must be recognised in profit or loss in the period in which they arise.

Expandable text - Illustration: exchange differences on settlement

On 7 May 20X6 a dollar-based entity sells goods to a German entity for € 48,000 when the rate of exchange was $1 = € 3.2.

To record the sale:

	$
Dr Customer € 48,000 @ 3.2	15,000
Cr Sales	15,000

On 20 July 20X6 the customer remitted a draft for € 48,000 when the rate of exchange was $1 = €3.17.

	$
Dr Bank € 48,000 @ 3.17	15,142
Cr Customer	15,000
Cr Income statement (exchange gain)	142

The $142 exchange gain forms part of the profit for the year.

Test your understanding 1 - Butler, Waiter and Attendant

(a) An entity, Butler, has a reporting date of 31 December. On 27 November 20X6 Butler plc buys goods from a Swedish supplier for SwK 324,000.

On 19 December 20X6 Butler plc pays the Swedish supplier in full.

Exchange rates were as follows:

27 November 20X6 $1 = SwK 11.15

19 December 20X6 $1 = SwK 10.93

Required:

Show how the expense and liability, together with the exchange difference arising, should be accounted for in the financial statements.

(b) An entity, Waiter, which has a reporting date of 31 December and the dollar ($) as its functional currency borrows in the foreign currency of the Kram (K). The loan of K120,000 was taken out on 1 January 20X7. A repayment of K40,000 was made on 1 March 20X7.

The following rates of exchange are relevant:

	K1 to $
1 January 20X7	K1: $2
1 March 20X7	K1: $3
31 December 20X7	K1: $3.5

Required:

Show how the liability and the exchange difference will be represented in the year end financial statements.

(c) An entity, Attendant, which has a reporting date of 31 December, has the dollar ($) as its functional currency purchased a plot of land overseas on 1 March 20X0. The entity paid for the land in the currency of the Rylands (R). The purchase cost of the land at was R60,000. The value of the land at the reporting date was R80,000.

Rates of exchange were as follows:
1 March 20X0   R8 : $1
31 December 20X0 R10 :$1

Required:

Show how this transaction should be accounted for in the financial statements for the year ended 31 December 20X0:

- **if the land is carried at cost**
- **if the land is carried at valuation**

Treatment of year-end balances

The treatment of any 'foreign' items remaining in the statement of financial position at the yearend will depend on whether they are classified as monetary or non-monetary:

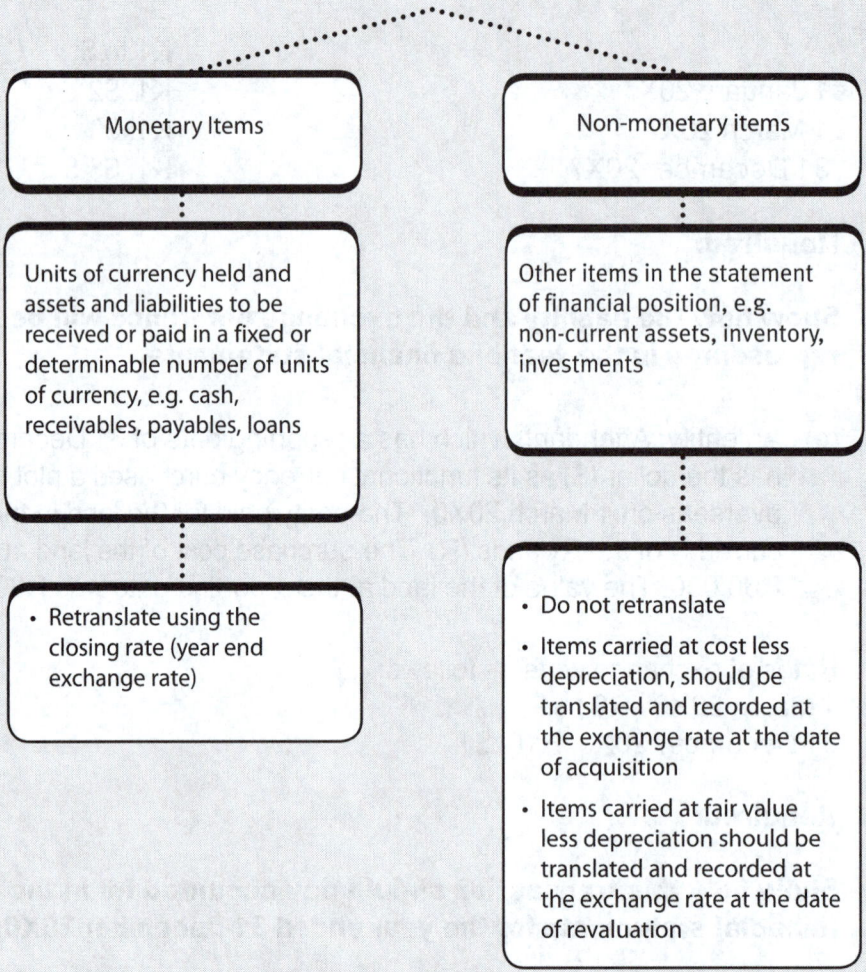

Monetary Items	Non-monetary items
Units of currency held and assets and liabilities to be received or paid in a fixed or determinable number of units of currency, e.g. cash, receivables, payables, loans	Other items in the statement of financial position, e.g. non-current assets, inventory, investments
• Retranslate using the closing rate (year end exchange rate)	• Do not retranslate • Items carried at cost less depreciation, should be translated and recorded at the exchange rate at the date of acquisition • Items carried at fair value less depreciation should be translated and recorded at the exchange rate at the date of revaluation

Exchange differences on retranslation of monetary items

These must be recognised in profit or loss in the period in which they arise.

Expandable text - Illustration: Non-monetary items

An entity purchases plant, for its own use, from a foreign supplier on 30 June 20X7 for cash of FC90,000 when the rate of exchange was $1 = FC1.80.

The asset is recorded at $50,000 (FC90,000 @ 1.80):

Dr Non-current asset	$50,000
Cr Cash	$50,000

No further translation will occur. All depreciation charged on this asset will be based on $50,000.

Test your understanding 2 - Carter & Jeyes

(a) On 15 March an entity, Carter, purchased a non-current asset on one month's credit for KR20,000.

Exchange rates

15 March   KR5 : $1
31 March   KR4 : $1

Required:

Explain and illustrate how the transaction is recorded and dealt with if the reporting date is 31 March

(b) The following transactions were undertaken by Jeyes plc in the accounting year ended 31 December 20X1.

Date	Narrative	Amount KR
1 January 20X1	Purchase of a non-current asset on credit	100,000
31 March 20X1	Payment for the non-current asset	100,000
	Purchases on credit	50,000
30 June 20X1	Sales on credit	95,000
30 September 20X1	Payment for purchases	50,000
30 November 20X1	Long-term loan taken out	200,000

Exchange rates	KR : $
1 January 20X1	2.0 : 1
31 March 20X1	2.3 : 1
30 June 20X1	2.1 : 1
30 September 20X1	2.0 : 1
30 November 20X1	1.8 : 1
31 December 20X1	1.9 : 1

Required:

Prepare journal entries to record the above transactions.

Translating the financial statements of a foreign operation

Where a subsidiary entity's functional currency is different from the presentation currency of its parent, its financial statements must be translated into the parent's presentation currency prior to consolidation.

The following exchange rates should be used in the translation:

Income statement/statement of comprehensive income

Income	) At the rate for each transaction or, as an approximation, the
Expenses	) average rate for the year

Statement of financial position

Assets and liabilities	)
Share capital	) At the closing rate
Pre-acquisition reserves	) (i.e. rate on reporting date)
Post-acquisition reserves	)

The balancing figure that makes up the post-acquisition reserves includes the exchange difference for the year and prior post-acquisition years. This amount should be disclosed as a component of other comprehensive income and, strictly speaking, accumulated in a separate component of equity. The following section deals with its calculation.

Exchange difference arising on translation of accounts

Exchange differences arise because items are translated at different points in time at different rates of exchange.

The exchange difference arising on translation of foreign currency accounts arises as follows:

Opening net assets	+ Profit	= Closing net assets
These were translated at last year's closing rate (CR) for the purpose of last year's accounts. For the purpose of this year's accounts they are included within closing net assets at this year's closing rate.	Revenue and expenses are translated within the income statement at the average rate. The profit is, however, included within this year's closing net assets at the closing rate.	

Consolidation of a foreign operation

In principle, the same workings and adjustments required in any consolidation question will be required. You should prepare a group structure, and workings for net assets, goodwill, non-controlling interest and retained earnings will typically be required. However, IAS 21 requires that goodwill is calculated using the functional currency of the subsidiary and then subject to annual retranslation at the closing rate at each reporting date. It follows that the cost of investment and NCI should be calculated using the same closing exchange rate.

Where goodwill is calculated on a "full" or "fair value" basis, it should be calculated using a two-stage approach. This will determine the respective group and NCI share of goodwill. This ratio will then be used to allocate exchange gains or losses arising on retranslation of goodwill each year between the group and NCI.

Goodwill on consolidation
Goodwill is calculated as follows:

	$
Cost to group of gaining control	X
Less: group share of net assets at acquisition	(X)
	—
Proportionate goodwill	X
	—
NCI at fair value	X
Less: NCI share of net assets at acquisition	(X)
NCI goodwill	X
	—
Goodwill at fair value	X
	—

IAS 21 states that the fair value of net assets acquired should be restated at each year end using the closing exchange rate. This annual restatement will result in an exchange difference, calculated as:

Goodwill (in foreign currency) at this year's closing rate	X
Goodwill (in foreign currency) at last year's closing rate	X
	—
Exchange gain(loss) on retranslation	X

In the consolidated accounts this exchange difference will form part of the total exchange difference disclosed as other comprehensive income and accumulated in other components of equity.

The exchange difference arising on goodwill will be allocated as follows:

- to the group only if goodwill is accounted for on a proportionate basis.
- between group and NCI if goodwill is accounted for on a full (fair value) basis. Note that the allocation is made based upon their respective share of total goodwill. This will therefore require goodwill to be calculated in a two-stage process as identified earlier within this section..

In order to calculate the foreign exchange differences arising on the net investment in a foreign operation, calculate the following:

Illustration 1 - Calculation of exchange differences

The three elements of foreign exchange differences are as follows:

- opening net assets of subsidiary
- profit for the year of subsidiary
- goodwill - whether calculated on a fair value or proportionate basis

			Parent	NCI
Opening net assets of subsidiary				
(= equity brought forward)	@ closing rate	X		
	@ opening rate	(X)		
		—		
Gain/(loss)		X/(X)	x parent% X/(X)	
			x NCI%	X/(X)

Profit of subsidiary for year	@ closing rate	X			
	@ average rate	(X)			
		───			
Gain/(loss)		X/(X)	x parent%	X/(X)	
			x NCI%		X/(X)
Opening goodwill – P's share	@ closing rate	X			
	@ opening rate	(X)			
		───			
Gain/(loss)		X/(X)	x 100%	X/(X)	
Opening goodwill – NCI's share					
Note: full goodwill method only	@ closing rate	X			
	@ opening rate	(X)			
		───			
Gain/(loss)		X/(X)	x 100%	–	X/(X)
				───	───
Gain/(loss) for year				X/(X)	X/(X)
				───	───

Expandable text - Illustration: Translation of Goodwill

Siren, whose currency is the Dracma (DR), acquired 75% of Flash on 1 June 20X5 for cash consideration of $250,000. The equity and liabilities of Flash at 31 May 20X6 are as follows:

		$
Equity capital		100,000
Retained earnings	– at 1 June 20X5	125,000
	– profit for the year	75,000
		───────
		300,000
		───────

The Siren Group values the non-controlling interest using the proportion of net assets method

Required:

At what value should the goodwill be shown in the consolidated financial statements of Siren for the year ended 31 May 20X6?

Exchange rates were as follows:

	$ to DR
1 June 20X5	2.5
31 May 20X6	2.0

Expandable text - Solution

Step 1

The net assets of Flash must be translated into DR at the closing rate on 31 May 20X6:

	$	Rate	DR
Equity capital	100,000	2.0	50,000
Retained earnings – at 1 June 20X5	125,000	2.0	62,500
– profit for the year	75,000	2.0	37,500
	300,000		150,000

This also gives us the net assets at acquisition translated at this year's closing rate, being the total of the equity capital and the pre-acquisition retained earnings, i.e. DR50,000 + DR62,500 = DR112,500.

Step 2

The cost of investment must be calculated. When Siren bought the shares in Flash, $250,000 cash was paid and the exchange rate at that date was $2.5 : DR1. The investment would have been recorded in the individual accounts of Siren as follows:

Dr Cost of investment ($250,000/2.5)	DR100,000
Cr Cash	DR100,000

If we are to calculate goodwill at the year end, the cost of investment needs to be retranslated to the closing rate. As seen in Step 1, the net assets at acquisition have been translated at the closing rate, so the cost of investment must be on the same basis.

Therefore, the cost of investment will become:

$250,000/2.0 = DR125,000

Siren has a gain on the cost of investment of DR25,000. This must be credited to group reserves. The other side of the entry is in goodwill, as the cost of investment that has been retranslated is the one used to calculate goodwill at the closing rate.

Step 3

Now we have both components of goodwill and can calculate the goodwill at 31 May 20X6.

	DR
Cost of investment (step 2)	125,000
Non-controlling interest	
(25% x (50,000 + 62,500))	28,125
	153,125
Net assets of Flash at acq'n	(112,500)
	40,625

Cost of investment – parent's books

Since IAS 21 requires the cost of investment within the goodwill calculation to be based on the closing rate, an extra adjustment is required as part of the consolidation process.

The cost of investment in the parent's accounts must be retranslated to the closing rate. An exchange gain or loss is recorded as a component of other comprehensive income in the group accounts, and so accumulated as a component of equity.

Expandable text - Goodwill retranslation journals

- As part of the consolidation process, the investment in the parent entity's accounts is replaced with the group share of the subsidiary's net assets and goodwill arising on acquisition.

- Although the journal is embedded within the consolidation workings, this is in part achieved by:

Dr Goodwill calculation   cost of investment
Cr Investment in Parent's account   cost of investment

- In the parent's own accounts, the cost of investment is treated as a non-monetary asset and so held at the historic rate of exchange.

- The IAS 21 rules on the calculation of goodwill, as seen above, require the cost of investment to be retranslated prior to calculating goodwill, based on the closing rate.

- These rules mean that the above journal does not involve equal amounts.

- Therefore, as part of the consolidation process, the investment held in the parent's accounts must be retranslated using the closing rate.

- The resulting exchange gain or loss is disclosed as an element of other comprehensive income and recorded within other components of equity

Non-controlling interests

Income statement
: The non-controlling interest is the share of the subsidiary's profit after tax for the year as translated for consolidation purposes.

Statement of financial position
: The non-controlling interest is computed by reference to either fair value at acquisition plus share of post acquisition retained earnings or the net assets of the subsidiary, in either case translated at the closing rate at the reporting date.

KAPLAN PUBLISHING

Illustration 2 – IAS 21 Changes in foreign exchange rates

On 1 July 20X1 H acquired 80% of ABC Inc, whose functional currency is KRs. The cost of gaining control was KR7,500. Their financial statements at 30 June 20X2 were as follows.

Statement of financial position

	H	ABC
Assets	$	KR
Investment in ABC	5,000	–
Non-current assets	10,000	3,000
Current assets	5,000	2,000
	20,000	5,000

	H	ABC
Equity and liabilities	$	KR
Equity capital	6,000	1,500
Retained earnings	4,000	2,500
Liabilities	10,000	1,000
	20,000	5,000

Income statement

	H	ABC
	$	KR
Revenue	25,000	35,000
Operating costs	(15,000)	(26,250)
Profit before tax	10,000	8,750
Tax	(8,000)	(7,450)
Profit for the year	2,000	1,300

Neither entity recognised any components of other comprehensive income in their individual accounts in the period.

The following information is applicable.

(i) At the date of acquisition the fair value of the net assets of ABC were KR6,000. The increase in the fair value is attributable to land that remains carried by ABC at its historical cost.

(ii) During the year H sold goods on cash terms for $1,000 to ABC.

(iii) On 1 June 20X2 H made a short-term loan to ABC of $400. The liability is recorded by ABC at the historic rate. The loan is recorded within current assets and liabilities as appropriate

(iv) The non-controlling interest is valued using the proportion of net assets method.

Exchange rates to $1.

	KR
1 July 20X1	1.50
Average rate	1.75
1 June 20X2	1.90
30 June 20X2	2

Required:

Prepare the group statement of financial position, income statement and statement of other comprehensive income.

Expandable text - Solution

H & ABC Group statement of financial position

Assets:	$
Non-current assets	
Intangible – goodwill **(W3)**	1,350
Tangible (10,000 + (KR3,000 + KR3,300) /2.0	13,150
	——
	14,500
Current assets (5,000 + KR2,000 /2.0 – inter-co 400)	5,600
	——
	20,100
	——

Equity and liabilities	$
Share capital	6,000
Retained earnings **(W5)**	4,576
Group exchange differences **(W8)**	(1,322)
	——
	9,254
Non-controlling interest **(W4)**	726
	——
Equity	9,980
Liabilities (10,000 + (KR1.000 + 40(W1)) /2.0 - inter-co 400)	10,120
	——
	20,100
	——

	$
Revenue (25,000 + (35,000/1.75) – interco 1,000)	44,000
Operating costs (15,000 + (26,250 + 40(W1) /1.75) – interco 1,000)	(29,023)
	——
Profit before tax	14,977
Tax (8,000 + (7,450 /1.75))	(12,257)
	——

Profit attributable to:

Owners of parent (β)	2,576
Non-controlling interest (20% × ((1,260 (**W2**)) /1.75))	144

$

Comprehensive income:

Profit for the year	2,720
Exchange differences on translation of foreign operations (**W8**)	(1,540)
Total comprehensive income for the year	1,180
Total comprehensive income attributable to:	
Owners of parent (2,576 – 1322 (**W8**))	1,254
Non-controlling interest (144 – 218 (**W8**))	(74)
	1,180

(W1) Group structure

H

|80%

NCI = 20% for full year

ABC

Note (iii) error to correct before translation

H has made a loan to ABC. ABC therefore has a liability outstanding at the reporting date of a monetary item denominated in foreign currency - this needs to be restated at the closing rate prior to translation at the year-end. Any gain or loss on translation is part of the operating results of ABC for the year.

1 June ABC received loan of $400 @ 1.9 = KR760

30 June restate loan at closing rate $400 @ 2.0 = KR800

i.e. increased liability and exchange loss of KR40 for ABC

(W2) Net assets of subsidiary in own functional currency

	KR	KR	
Equity capital	1,500	1,500	
Retained earnings	1,200	2,500	
FVA - land	3,300	3,300	to SOFP
Exchange loss (W1)		(40)	
	_____	_____	
Movement in post acq'n retained earnings	6,000	7,260	1,260
	_____	_____	_____

(W3) Goodwill in ABC functional currency - proportionate basis

	KR
Investment in ABC $5,000 @ 1.5	7,500
80%(W1) x 6,000(W2)	4,800
	_____
Prop goodwill to SOFP	2,700
- no impairment to date - @ CR 2.0 = $1,350	_____

	$
Exchange loss by parent company on retranslation of cost of investment	
At acq'n KR 7,500 @ 1.5	5,000
At cl rate KR 7,500 @ 2.0	3,750
	_____
Exchange loss on retranslation of cost of investment (W6)	1,250
	_____

(W4) NCI - need to translate sub NA at closing rate

	$
20%(W1) x KR7,260(W2) / 2.0 =	726
	_____

(W5) Retained earnings

	$
Parent	4,000
80%(W1) x (W2)KR1,260/1.75	576
i.e. post-acquisition retained earnings of sub @ average rate	_____
	4,576
	_____

(W6) Group retained earnings including other equity components

	$
Parent	4,000
Less exchange loss on cost of investment by parent **(W3)**	(1,250)
Less goodwill impaired	Nil
Plus group % of post-acquisition (80% × (KR1,260**(W2)** / 2.0))	504
	3,254

(W7) Proof of group retained earnings including other equity components

	$
Opening group retained earnings (parent only (4,000 – 2,000))	2,000
Group income for the year – per SOCI	2,576
Group exchange difference **(W8)**	(1,322)
Closing group retained earnings	3,254

These group reserves comprise both realised profit and unrealised group exchange differences; strictly, they should be separated out.

(W8) Exchange difference

On opening net assets	$	$	Group	NCI
KR6,000(W2) @ 2.0 cl rate	3,000		80%	20%
KR6,000(W2) @ 1.5 acq'n rate	(4,000)			
		(1,000)		
On income				
KR1,260 (W2) @ 2.0 cl rate	630			
KR 1,260 (W2) @ 1.75 ave rate	(720)			
		(90)		
		(1,090)	(872)	(218)
On goodwill - prop basis				
KR2,700 @ 2.0 cl rate	1,350			
KR2,700 @ 1.5 acq'n rate	1,800			
		(450)	(450)	
Summary of total exchange gains and losses		(1,540)	(1,322)	(218)

Test your understanding 3 - Parent & Overseas

Parent is an entity that owns 80% of the ordinary shares of its foreign subsidiary that has the Shilling as its the functional currency. The subsidiary was acquired at the start of the current accounting period on 1 January 20X7 when its reported reserves were 6,000 Shillings.

At that date the fair value of the net assets of the subsidiary was 20,000 Shillings. This included a fair value adjustment in respect of land of 4,000 Shillings that the subsidiary has not incorporated into its accounting records and still owns.

Parent wishes the presentation currency of the group accounts to be $. Goodwill is to be accounted for on a fair value basis, which is unimpaired at the reporting date. At the date of acquisition, the non-controlling interest in Overseas had a fair value of 5,000 Shillings.

Statements of financial position	Parent	Overseas
	$	Shillings
Investment (21,000 shillings)	3,818	
Assets	9,500	40,000
	13,318	40,000

Equity and liabilities	$	Shillings
Equity capital	5,000	10,000
Retained earnings	6,000	8,200
Liabilities	2,318	21,800
	13,318	40,000

Statement of comprehensive income	Parent	Overseas
	$	Shillings
Revenue	8,000	5,200
Costs	(2,500)	(2,600)
Profit before tax	5,500	2,600
Tax	(2,000)	(400)
Profit for the year	3,500	2,200

Neither entity recognised any other comprehensive income in their individual accounts in the period.

Relevant exchange rates (Shillings to $1) are:

Date	Exchange rate (Shillings to $1)
1 January 20X7	5.5
31 December 20X7	5.0
Weighted average for year	5.2

Required:

Prepare the consolidated statement of financial position at 31 December 20X7, together with a consolidated income statement for the year ended 31 December 20X7, a statement showing other comprehensive income and a schedule of the movement over the year on retained earnings and other components of equity.

Test your understanding 4 - Saint & Albans

On the 1 July 20X1 Saint acquired 60% of Albans Inc, whose functional currency is D's. The financial statements of both entities as at 30 June 20X2 were as follows.

	Saint	Albans
Assets:	$	D
Investment in Albans	5,000	–
Loan to Alban	1,400	–
Tangible assets	10,000	15,400
Inventory	5,000	4,000
Receivables	4,000	500
Cash at bank	1,600	560
	27,000	20,460

Equity and liabilities	$	D
Equity capital ($1 / D1)	10,000	1,000
Share Premium	3,000	500
Reserves	4,000	12,500
Non Current Liabilities	5,000	5,460
Current Liabilities	5,000	1,000
	27,000	20,460

	Saint	Albans
	$	D
Revenue	50,000	60,000
Cost of sales	(20,000)	(30,000)
Gross profit	30,000	30,000
Distribution and Administration expenses	(20,000)	(12,000)
Profit before tax	10,000	18,000
Tax	(8,000)	(6,000)
Income for Year	2,000	12,000

The following information is applicable.

(i) Saint purchased the shares in Albans for D10,000 on the first day of the accounting period. At the date of acquisition the retained earnings of Albans were D500 and there was an upward fair value adjustment of D1,000. The fair value adjustment is attributable to plant with a remaining five-year life as at the date of acquisition. This plant remains held by Albans and has not been revalued. No shares have issued since the date of acquisition.

(ii) Just before the year-end Saint acquired some goods from a third party at a cost of $800, which it sold to Albans for cash at a mark up of 50%. At the reporting date all the goods remain unsold.

(iii) On 1 June X2 Saint lent Albans $1,400. The liability is recorded at the historic rate within the non-current liabilities of Albans.

(iv) No dividends have been paid. Neither company has recognised any gain or loss in reserves.

(v) Goodwill is to be accounted for on a "full" fair value basis. No goodwill has been impaired. The fair value of the non-controlling interest at the date of acquisition was D5,000. The presentational currency of the group is to be the $.

Exchange rates to $1.	D
1 July 20X1	2.00
Average rate	3.00
1 June 20X2	3.90
30 June 20X2	4.00

Required:

(1) Prepare the group statement of financial position at 30 June 20X2

(2) Prepare the group income statement for the year ended 30 June 20X2

(3) Prepare the group statement of other comprehensive income for the period showing the group exchange difference arising in the year.

Other points on group accounting

Disposal of a foreign entity

On the disposal of a foreign subsidiary, the cumulative exchange difference recognised as other comprehensive income and accumulated in a separate component of equity (because it was unrealised) becomes realised. The standard requires the exchange reserve to be reclassified on the disposal of the subsidiary as part of the gain/loss on disposal.

Test your understanding 5 - LUMS Group

The LUMS group has sold its entire 100% holding in an overseas subsidiary for proceeds of $50,000. The net assets at the date of disposal were $20,000 and the carrying value of goodwill at that date was $10,000. The cumulative balance on the group foreign currency reserve is a gain of $5,000. Tax can be ignored.

Calculate the exceptional gain arising to the group on the disposal of the foreign subsidiary.

Equity accounting

The principles to be used in translating a subsidiary's financial statements also apply to the translation of an associate's.

Once the results are translated, the carrying amount of the associate (cost (at the closing rate) plus the share of post-acquisition retained earnings) can be calculated together with the group's share of the profits for the period and included in the group financial statements.

Expandable text - Shortcomings in IAS 21

There are a number of issues on which IAS 21 is either silent or fails to give adequate guidance.

(a) Under IAS 21 transactions should be recorded at the rate ruling at the date the transaction occurs (i.e. the date when the transaction qualifies for recognition in the accounts), but in some cases this date is difficult to establish. For example, it could be the order date, the date of invoice or the date on which the goods were received.

(b) IAS 21 states that average rates can be used if these do not fluctuate significantly, but what period should be used to calculate average rates? Should the average rate be adjusted to take account of material transactions?

(c) IAS 21 provides only limited guidance where there are two or more exchange rates for a particular currency or where an exchange rate is suspended. It has been suggested that companies should use whichever rate seems appropriate given the nature of the transaction and have regard to prudence if necessary.

(d) IAS 21 makes a distinction between the translation of monetary and non-monetary items, but in practice some items (such as progress payments paid against non-current assets or inventories, and debt securities held as investments) may have characteristics of both.

(e) Retranslating the opening reserves at the closing rate gives a difference that goes direct to reserves under the closing rate method. The reasoning behind this is that these exchange differences do not result from the operations of the group. To include them in profit or loss would be to distort the results of the group's trading operations. However, some commentators consider that all such gains and losses are part of a group's profit and should be recorded in profit or loss.

Illustration 3 - Large and Little

Question 1

Little was incorporated over 20 years ago, operating as an independent entity for 15 years until 1 April 20X0 when it was taken over by Large. Large's directors decided that the local expertise of Little's management should be utilised as far as possible, and since the takeover they have allowed the subsidiary to operate independently, maintaining its existing supplier and customer bases. Large exercises 'arms' length' strategic control, but takes no part in day-to-day operational decisions.

The statements of financial position of Large and Little at 31 March 20X4 are given below. The statement of financial position of Little is prepared in francos (F), its functional currency.

	$000	Large $000	F000	Little F000
Non-current assets:				
Property, plant and equipment	63,000		80,000	
Investments	12,000		–	
		75,000		80,000
Current assets:				
Inventories	25,000		30,000	
Trade receivables	20,000		28,000	
Cash	6,000		5,000	
		51,000		63,000
		126,000		143,000
Equity:				
Equity capital (50 cents/1 Franco shares)		30,000		40,000
Revaluation reserve		–		6,000
Retained earnings		35,000		34,000
		65,000		80,000
Non-current liabilities:				
Long-term borrowings	20,000		25,000	
Deferred tax	6,000		10,000	
		26,000		35,000
Current liabilities:				
Trade payables	25,000		20,000	
Tax	7,000		8,000	
Bank overdraft	3,000		–	
		35,000		28,000
		126,000		143,000

Notes to the SFPs

Note 1 – Investment by Large in Little

On 1 April 20X0 Large purchased 36 million shares in Little for 72 million francos. The retained earnings of Little at that date were 26 million francos. It is group accounting policy to account for goodwill on a proportionate basis. At 1 April 20X3 goodwill had been fully written off as a result of impairment losses.

Note 2 – Intra-group trading

Little sells goods to Large, charging a mark-up of one-third on production cost. At 31 March 20X4, Large held $1 million (at cost to Large) of goods purchased from Little in its inventories. The goods were purchased during March 20X4 and were recorded by Large using an exchange rate of $1 = 5 francos. (There were minimal fluctuations between the two currencies during March 20X4). At 31 March 20X4, Large's inventories included no goods purchased from Little. On 29 March 20X4, Large sent Little a cheque for $1 million to clear the intra-group payable. Little received and recorded this cheque on 3 April 20X4.

Note 3 – Accounting policies

The accounting policies of the two entities are the same, except that the directors of Little have decided to adopt a policy of revaluation of property, whereas Large includes all property in its statement of financial position at depreciated historical cost. Until 1 April 20X3, Little operated from rented warehouse premises. On that date, the entity purchased a leasehold building for 25 million francos, taking out a long-term loan to finance the purchase. The building's estimated useful life at 1 April 20X3 was 25 years, with an estimated residual value of nil, and the directors decided to adopt a policy of straight line depreciation. The building was professionally revalued at 30 million francos on 31 March 20X4, and the directors have included the revalued amount in the statement of financial position. No other property was owned by Little during the year.

Note 4 – Exchange rates

Date	Exchange rate (francos to $1)
1 April 20X0	6.0
31 March 20X3	5.5
31 March 20X4	5.0
Weighted average for the year to 31 March 20X4	5.2
Weighted average for the dates of acquisition of closing inventory	5.1

Required:

(a) Explain (with reference to relevant accounting standards to support your argument) how the financial statements (statement of financial position, income statement, and statement of other comprehensive income) of Little should be translated into $s for the consolidation of Large and Little.

(5 marks)

(b) Translate the statement of financial position of Little at 31 March 20X4 into $s and prepare the consolidated statement of financial position of the Large group at 31 March 20X4.

(20 marks)

Note: Ignore any deferred tax implications of the property revaluation and the intra-group trading. and assume that the Large Group uses the proportion of net assets method to value the non-controlling interest.

(Total: 25 marks)

Expandable text - Solution

Group accounting – foreign currency Large and Little

Answer 1

(1) It is clear from the information contained in the question that, on a day-to-day basis, Little operates as a relatively independent entity, with its own supplier and customer bases. Therefore, the cash flows of Little do not have a day-to-day impact on the cash flows of Large. The functional currency of Little is the Franco, rather than the dollar. For consolidation purposes, the financial statements of Little must be translated into a presentation currency: the dollar (the functional currency of Large, in which the consolidated financial statements of Large are presented). In these circumstances, IAS 21 The effects of changes in foreign exchange rates requires that the financial statements be translated using the closing rate (or net investment) method (the presentation currency method). This involves translating the net assets in the statement of financial position at the spot rate of exchange at the reporting date and income and expenses in the income statement and statement of other comprehensive income at the rate on the date of the transactions, or as an approximation, a weighted average rate for the year.

Exchange differences are reported as other comprehensive income as they do not impact on the cash flows of the group until the relevant investment is disposed of.

(b) Group statement of financial position - Large Group

		$000
Non-current assets	63,000 + ((80,000 - 6,000) / 5)	77,800
Current assets		
Inventories	25,000 + ((30,000) / 5) - 250 (URPS)	30,750
Trade receivables	20,000 + (28,000 / 5) - 1,000 (CIT)	24,600
Cash	6,000 + (5,000 / 5) + 1.000 (CIT)	8,000
		141,150
Equity share capital		30,000
Revaluation reserve	(6,000 – 6,000)	–
Retained earnings:	(W5)	36,095
Non-controlling interest	(W4)	1,455
Total equity		67,550
Non-current liabilities	20,000 + (25,000 / 5)	25,000
Deferred tax	6,000 + (10,000 / 5)	8,000
Current liabilities		
Payables	25,000 + (20,000 / 5)	29,000
Tax	7,000 + (8,000 / 5)	8,600
Overdraft	3,000 + 0	3,000
		141,150

Workings

(W1) Group structure

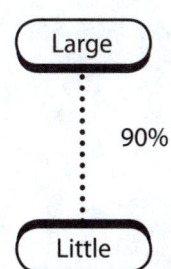

Large

90%

Little

(W2) Net assets of subsidiary in functional currency

	Acquisition Date F000	Reporting date F000
Equity capital	40,000	40,000
Retained earnings	26,000	34,000
Revaluation reserve		6,000
Accounting policy adjustment		(6,000)
	66,000	74,000

(W3) Goodwill on proportionate basis in subsidiary functional currency

	F000
Cost	72,000
90% x 66,000(W2)	59,400
	12,600
Translated at closing rate @ 5 - fully impaired (W5)	$2,520

Gain or loss on retranslation of cost of investment:	
Cost at acquisition F72,000 @ 6	$12,000
Cost retranslated at closing rate F72,000 @ 5	$14,400
Gain to parent (W5)	2,400

(W4) Non-controlling interest on proportionate basis

	$000
F74,000 (W2) @ 5 x 10%	1,480
NCI share of URPS $1,000 x 25% x 10%	(25)
	1,455

(W5) Group retained earnings

		$000
Large		35,000
Little	F8,000 @ 5 x 90%	1,440
Goodwill impaired (W3)		(2,520)
Gain on retranslation of cost of investment (W3)		2,400
Group share of URPS	$1,000 x 25% x 90%	(225)
		———
		36,095
		———

2 Chapter summary

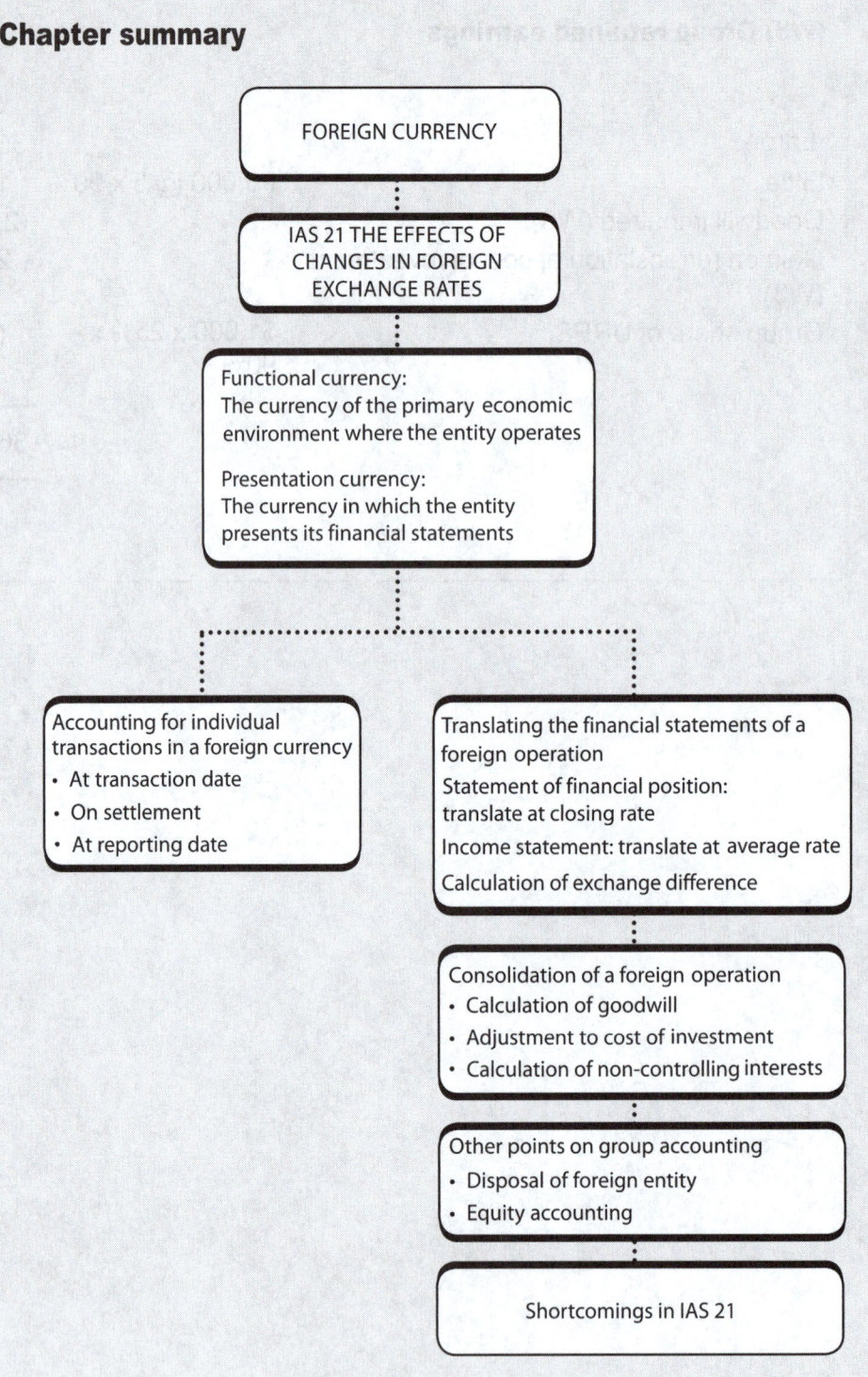

FOREIGN CURRENCY

IAS 21 THE EFFECTS OF CHANGES IN FOREIGN EXCHANGE RATES

Functional currency:
The currency of the primary economic environment where the entity operates

Presentation currency:
The currency in which the entity presents its financial statements

Accounting for individual transactions in a foreign currency
- At transaction date
- On settlement
- At reporting date

Translating the financial statements of a foreign operation
Statement of financial position: translate at closing rate
Income statement: translate at average rate
Calculation of exchange difference

Consolidation of a foreign operation
- Calculation of goodwill
- Adjustment to cost of investment
- Calculation of non-controlling interests

Other points on group accounting
- Disposal of foreign entity
- Equity accounting

Shortcomings in IAS 21

Test your understanding answers

Test your understanding 1 - Butler, Waiter and Attendant

(a) Butler - Solution

	Translate transaction prior to recording:	324,000 / 11.15 = $29,058

27 November 20X6

Dr Purchases	$29,058
Cr Payables	$29,058

19 December 20X6

	SwK 324,000 is paid. At 19 December rate this is:	324,000 / 10.93 = $29,643
Dr Payables	$29,058 (being the payable created on 27 November)	
Dr Income statement	$585 i.e. exchange loss	
Cr Cash	$29,643	

$585 is an exchange loss arising because the functional currency ($) has weakened against the transaction currency (SwK) since the transaction occurred.

(b) Waiter - Solution

	Z	Rate	$
1 January 20X7 record liability	120,000	2.0	240,000
1 March 20X7 repay part of liability	(40,000)	3.0	(120,000)
Exchange loss - balancing figure - taken to income			(160,000)
31 December 20X7	80,000	3.5	280,000

The $160,000 is the loss that will be reported in income for the year. The liability as a monetary item has been retranslated at the closing rate will be reported on the statement of financial position as $280,000.

(c) Attendant

As the asset is a non-monetary item, it will not be subject to retranslation at the reporting date. If the land is carried at cost, the asset remains stated at $ cost translated at the rate ruling at the date of purchase as follows:

R60,000 divided by 8 = $7,500

Assuming that the asset is revalued then the revalued amount will be translated to create a gain or loss that is taken directly to equity / reserves.

	R	Rate	$
1 March 20X0 purchase land	60,000	8.0	7,500
Gain to equity			500
31 December 20X0	80,000	10.0	8,000

Test your understanding 2 - Carter & Jeyes

Carter

On 15 March the purchase is recorded using the exchange rate on that date.

Dr Non-current asset	(KR20,000/5)	$4,000
Cr Payable		$4,000

- At the year end the non-current asset, being a non-monetary item, is not retranslated but remains measured at $4,000.

- The payable remains outstanding at the year-end. This is a monetary item and must be retranslated using the closing rate: KR20,000 / 4 = $5,000

- The payable must be increased by $1,000, giving rise to an unrealised exchange loss:

Dr Income statement (exchange loss)	$1,000
Cr Payable	$1,000

Jeyes

1 January 20X1	KR100,000 / 2.0	= $50,000	Dr Non-current assets	$50,000
			Cr Payable	$50,000
31 March 20X1	KR100,000 / 2.3	= $43,478	Dr Payable	$50,000
			Cr Cash	$43,478
			Cr Income statement	$6,522
	KR 50,000 / 2.3	= $21,739	Dr Purchases	$21,739
			Cr Payables	$21,739
30 June 20X1	KR 95,000 / 2.1	= $45,238	Dr Receivables	$45,238
			Cr Sales revenue	$45,238
30 September 20X1		= $25,000	Dr Payables	$21,739
			Dr Income statement	$3,261
			Cr Cash	$25,000
30 November 20X1		= $111,111	Dr Cash	$111,111
			Cr Loan	$111,111
31 December 20X1		= $50,000	Dr Receivables	$4,762
			Cr Income statement	$4,762
		= $105,263	Dr Loan	$5,848
			Cr Income statement	$5,848

Group statement of financial position

Note: the assets and liabilities of Overseas have been translated at the closing rate of 5 Shillings - $1.

		$
Goodwill	(W3)	1,200
Assets 9,500 + ((40,000 + 4000) / 5.0)		18,300
		19,500

		$
Equity and liabilities		
Equity capital		5,000
Retained earnings and other components of equity	(W5)	6,734
		11,734
Non-controlling interest	(W4)	1,088
		12,822
Total equity of the group		
Liabilities (2,318 + (21,800 / 5.0)		6,678
		19,500

Group income statement

Note: the income and expenses for Overseas have been translated at the average rate of 5.2 Shillings = $1

	$
Revenue (8,000 + (5,200 / 5.2)	9,000
Costs (2,500 + (2,600 / 5.2)	(3,000)
Profit before tax	6,000
Tax (2,000 + (400 / 5.2)	(2,077)
Profit for the year	3,923
Other comprehensive income	
Exchange gains on net investment of foreign subsidiary	490
Total comprehensive income for the year	4,413
Profit for the year attributable to:	
Owners of Parent (β)	3,838
Non-controlling interest (20% × (2,200 / 5.2))	85
	3,923
Total comprehensive income attributable to:	
Owners of Parent (β)	4,234
Non-controlling interest 85 (per IS) + 94 (W6)	179
Total comprehensive income	4,413

Workings

(W1) Group structure

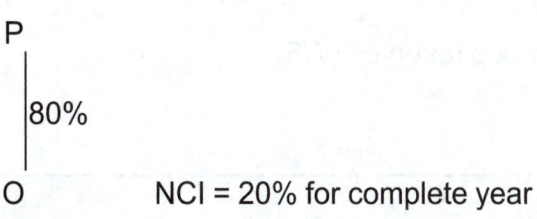

P

80%

O   NCI = 20% for complete year

(W2) Net assets of subsidiary in functional currency

	Acq'n date Shillings	Rep date Shillings	Shillings
Share capital	10,000	10,000	
Retained earnings	6,000	8,200	
Fair value adjustment - land	4,000	4,000	
Post-acquisition movement	20,000	22,200	2,200

(W3) Goodwill at fair value in subsidiary functional currency

Calculate both elements of goodwill for parent and NCI separately as this will help to calculate exchange differences correctly

		Shillings
Parent share of goodwill		
Cost of investment $3,818 @ 5.5		20,999
80% x 20,000(W2)		(16,000)
Proportionate goodwill		4,999
NCI at fair value	5,000	
20% x 20,000(W2)	4,000	1.000
		5,999
Translate at closing rate @ 5.0		$1,200

Gain or loss to Parent on retranslation of cost of investment:

Cost of investment in Overseas 20,999 Shillings @ 5.5 acquisition rate = $3,818

Cost of investment in Overseas 20,000 Shillings @ 5.0 closing rate = $4,200

Exchange gain $382 to group reserves (W5)

(W4) Non-controlling interest at fair value

	Shillings	$
Fair value at acquisition	5,000	
NCI share of post-acquisition profit (20% x 2,200 (W2))	440	
	─────	
Translated at closing rate @ 5.0	5,440	1,088

(W5) Group reserves

	Shillings	$
Parent		6,000
Group share of post-acquisition profit (80% x 2,200 (W2))	1,760	
Translated at closing rate @ 5.0		352
Gain on retranslation of cost of investment (W3)		382
		6,734

Comprising group retained earnings of $6,338 and exchange gains on net investment in foreign subsidiary $396 - see below:

Group retained earnings	$
Parent	6,000
Group share of post-acquisition profit (80% x 2,200 (W2))	
Translated at average rate @ 5.2	338
	6,338

(W7) Group exchange difference

The group exchange difference is dealt with as other comprehensive income and it arises on the retranslation of three elements: the opening net assets, the subsidiary profit for the year and goodwill as follows.

Opening net assets		$	$ Group	NCI
20,000 Shillings	@ 5.5 opening (or acq'n) rate	3,636		
20,000 Shillings	@ 5.0 closing rate	4,000		
Exchange gain	split (80:20)		364 291	73
Profit for the year				
2,200 Shillings	@ 5.2 average rate	423		
2,200 Shillings	@ 5.0 closing rate	440		
Exchange gain	split (80:20)		17 14	3
Goodwill at fair value				
5,999 Shillings	@ 5.5 opening (or acq'n) rate	1,091		
5,999 Shillings	@ 5.0 closing rate	1,200		
Exchange gain	split in proportion per W3 (5:1)		109 91	18
			490 396	94

Test your understanding 4 - Saint & Albans

Saint Albans Group

Note: Assets and liabilities of Albans translated at the closing rate of D4 = $1

Statement of financial position				$
Goodwill (W3)				3,000
Loan to Alban	1,400		Interco (1,400)	Nil
Tangible assets	10,000	+ 4,050		14,050
Inventory	5,000	+ 1,000	purp (W5) (400)	5,600
Receivables	4,000	+ 125		4,125
Cash at bank	1,600	+ 140		1,740
				28,515

				$
Equity capital				10,000
Share premium				3,000
Group reserves (W5)				2,849
(profit 5,932(W6) + foreign currency loss (3,083)(W7))				
Non-controlling interest (W4)				2,416
Non-current liabilities	5,000	+ 1,400	Interco (1,400)	5,000
Current liabilities	5,000	+ 250		5,250
				28,515

Note: income and expenses of Albans translated at the average rate for the year of D3 = $1.

Income statement			$
Revenue	50,000 + 20,000	Less Interco ($1,200)	68,800
Cost of sales	20,000 + 10,000	Less Interco ($1,200)	(29,314)
		purp $400	
		depr on FV D200 @ 3 = $67	
		correction D140 @ 3 = $47	
Gross profit			39,486
Admin exps	20,000 + 4,000		(24,000)
Profit before tax			15,486
Tax	8,000 + 2,000		(10,000)
Profit for Year			5,486

Statement of other Comprehensive Income

Profit for the Year		5,486
Total exchange differences translating foreign operations W7		(4,722)
Total Comprehensive income for the year		764

Profit for the year

Attributable to Group	Bal fig	3,931
Attributable to NCI (D11,660(W2) @ 3 x 40%)		1,555
		5,486

Total comprehensive income

Attributable to Group	Bal fig	848
Attributable to NCI (1,555 – 1,639)(W7)	W8	(84)
		764

W1 Group Structure

Saint

60 % acquired one year ago - NCI = 40%

Albans

W2 Net assets of subsidiary in own functional currency

	At acquisition	Rep date	
	D	D	D
Equity capital	1,000	1,000	
Share premium	500	500	
Retained earnings	500	12,500	
Fair value adjustment - plant	1,000	1,000	
FVA - dep'n on plant (1/5)		(200)	
Exchange loss on loan		(140)	
Post acquisition movement	3,000	14,660	11,660

Exchange loss on loan received by Albans

Received 1 June X2 $1,400 @ 3.9 = D5,460

Non-current liability 30 June X2 $1,400 @ 4.0 = D5,600

Exchange loss Albans = D140 and increased non-current liability

W3 Goodwill at fair value in functional currency of subsidiary

In order to correctly calculate exchange differences on the net investment in a foreign subsidiary, goodwill needs to be calculated seperately for the group and non-controlling interests elements as folllows:

		D
Cost to parent $5,000 @2		10,000
Groiup share of NA acquired (60% × 3,000)		1,800
Proportionate goodwill - parent share		8,200
NCI @ FV	5,200	
NCI share of NA at acquisition (40% × 3,000)	1,200	3,800
Fair value goodwill - not impaired		12,000
Translate at closing rate @ 4 for SOFP		3,000

There is also an exchange gain or loss to the parent entity due to the annual retranslation of the cost of investment calculated as follows:

Cost of investment to parent D10,000 at acq'n rate @ 2 = $5,000

Cost of investment to parent D10,000 at closing rate @ 4 = $2,500

Exchange loss to parent on retranslation of cost of investment = $2,500

W4 Non-controlling interest at fair value

	D	$
FV at acquisition per question	5,000	
NCI share of post acquisition profit (40% x D11,660)	4,664	
Translate at closing rate @ 4 to SOFP	9,664	2,416

W5 Group reserves

	$
Parent retained earnings	4,000
Exchange loss to parent on cost of investment (W3)	(2,500)
Group share of post-acq'n profit 60% x (D11,660 / 4) cl rate	1,749
URPS on inventory (800 x 1.5 = 1,200 - 800 = 400)	(400)
	2,849

Alternatively:

	$
Group b'fwd: (only Saint)	2,000
Group income after tax per IS	3,932
Group exchange gains and losses on net investment in foreign subsidiary (W7)	(3,083)
	2,849

Comprising:

	$
Group retained earnings (W6)	5,932
Group exchange gains and losses on net investment in foreign subsidiary (W7)	(3,083)
	2,849

KAPLAN PUBLISHING

W6 Group retained earnings

	$
Parent retained earnings	4,000
Group share of post-acq'n profit 60% x (D11,660 / 3) ave rate	2,332
URPS on inventory (800 x 1.5 = 1,200 - 800 = 400)	(400)
	─────
	5,932
	─────

W7 Exchange differences on net investment in foreign subsidiary

On fair value goodwill	D	Rate	$	Group	NCI
at acq'n rate	12,000	2.0	6,000		
at rep date	12,000	4.0	3,000		
			─────		
Exchange loss (split per respective share of total goodwill per W3 (8,200:3,800)			3,000	(2,050)	(950)
			─────		

On opening net assets					
at opening date	3,000	2.0	1,500		
at rep date	3,000	4.0	750		
			─────		
Exchange loss split per respective shareholdings (60:40)			(750)	(450)	(300)
			─────		

On subsidiary profit for the year					
ave rate of year	11,660	3.0	3,887		
at rep date	11,660	4.0	2,915		
			─────		
Exchange loss split per respective shareholdings (60:40)			(972)	(583)	(389)
			─────		

				─────	─────
Summary of total exchange gains and losses on net investment			**(4,722)**	**(3083)**	**(1,639)**
				─────	─────

Test your understanding 5 - LUMS Group

		$
Proceeds		50,000
Net assets recorded prior to disposal:		
Net assets	20,000	
Goodwill	10,000	
	———	
		(30,000)
Realisation of the group exchange		5,000
difference, reclassified to profit as part of the gain		———
		25,000

6

Group statement of cash flows

Chapter learning objectives

Upon completion of this chapter you will be able to:

*   prepare and discuss the group statement of cash flows.

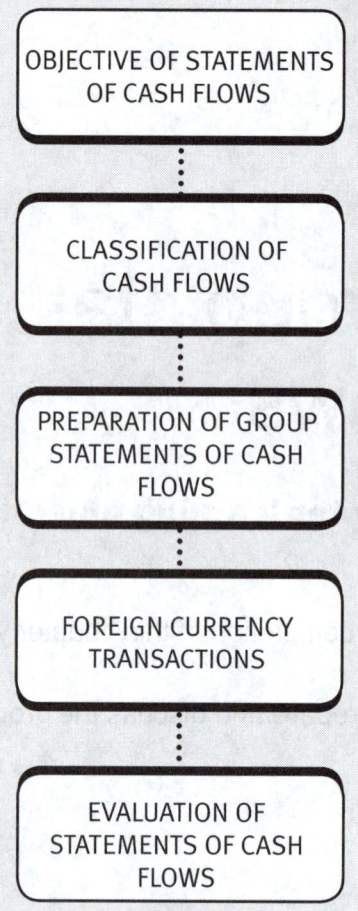

OBJECTIVE OF STATEMENTS OF CASH FLOWS

CLASSIFICATION OF CASH FLOWS

PREPARATION OF GROUP STATEMENTS OF CASH FLOWS

FOREIGN CURRENCY TRANSACTIONS

EVALUATION OF STATEMENTS OF CASH FLOWS

1 Objective of statements of cash flows

- IAS 7 **Statement of cash flows** provides guidance on the preparation of a statement of cash flow.

- The objective of a statement of cash flows is to provide information on an entity's changes in cash and cash equivalents during the period.

- The statement of financial position and income statement (SCI) are prepared on an accruals basis and do not show how the business has generated and used cash in the accounting period.

- The income statement (SCI) may show profits on an accruals basis even if the company is suffering severe cash flow problems.

- Statements of cash flows enable users of the financial statements to assess the **liquidity, solvency** and **financial adaptability** of a business.

Definitions:

- **Cash** consists of cash in hand and deposits repayable upon demand, less overdrafts. This includes cash held in a foreign currency.

- **Cash equivalents** are short-term, highly liquid investments that are readily convertible to known amounts of cash and are subject to an insignificant risk of changes in value.

- **Cash flows** are inflows and outflows of cash and cash equivalents.

2 Classification of cash flows

IAS 7 does not prescribe a specific format for the statement of cash flows, although it requires that cash flows are classified under three headings:

- cash flows from operating activities, defined as the entity's principal revenue earning activities and other activities that do not fall under the next two headings
- cash flows from investing activities, defined as the acquisition and disposal of long-term assets and other investments (excluding cash equivalents)
- cash flows from financing activities, defined as activities that change the size and composition of the entity's equity and borrowings.

Proforma statement of cash flow per IAS 7

	$	$
Operating activities		
Profit before tax		X
Add: interest payable		X
Less: Income from associate		
Adjust for non-cash items dealt with in arriving at operating profit:		
Add: depreciation		X
Add: loss on impairment		X
Add: loss on disposal of non-current assets		X
Add: increase in provisions		X
		X
Changes in working capital:		
Increase in inventory		(X)
Increase in receivables		(X)
Decrease in payables		(X)
Cash generated		X
Interest paid		(X)
Taxation paid		(X)

Investing activities

Payments to purchase NCA	(X)
Receipts from NCA disposals	X
Cash paid to acquire subsidiary (net of cash balances acquired)	(X)
Cash proceeds from subsidiary disposal (net of cash balances disposed)	X
Dividend received from associate	X
Interest received	X
	───── X(X)

Financing activities

Proceeds from share issue	X
Proceeds from loan or debenture issue	X
Cash repayment of loans or debentures	(X)
Finance lease repayments	(X)
Equity dividend paid	(X)
Dividend paid to NCI	(X)
	───── X(X)

Change in cash and equivalents	X(X)
Cash and equivalents brought forward	X(X)
	─────
Cash and equivalents carried forward	X(X)
	─────

Expandable text - Classification of cash flows

Cash flows from operating activities

There are two methods of calculating the cash from operations.

- The **direct method** shows operating cash receipts and payments. This includes cash receipts from customers, cash payments to suppliers and cash payments to and on behalf of employees. The Examiner has indicated that the direct method will not be examined and is not considered further within this text.

- The **indirect method** starts with profit before tax and adjusts it for non-cash charges and credits, to reconcile it to the net cash flow from operating activities.

IAS 7 permits either method.

Under the **indirect method** adjustments are needed for a number of items, the most frequently occurring of which are:

*   depreciation
*   amortisation
*   profit or loss on disposal of non current assets
*   change in inventory
*   change in receivables
*   change in payables.

Cash flows from investing activities

Cash flows to appear under this heading include:

*   cash paid for property, plant and equipment and other non-current assets
*   cash received on the sale of property, plant and equipment and other non-current assets
*   cash paid for investments in or loans to other entities (excluding movements on loans from financial institutions, which are shown under financing)
*   cash received for the sale of investments or the repayment of loans to other entities (again excluding loans from financial institutions).

Cash flows from financing activities

Financing cash flows mainly comprise receipts or repayments of principal from or to external providers of finance.

Financing **cash inflows** include:

*   receipts from issuing shares or other equity instruments
*   receipts from issuing debentures, loans, notes and bonds and from other long-term and short-term borrowings (other than overdrafts, which are normally included in cash and cash equivalents).

Financing **cash outflows** include:

*   repayments of amounts borrowed (other than overdrafts)
*   the capital element of finance lease rental payments
*   payments to reacquire or redeem the entity's shares.

Interest and dividends

There are divergent and strongly held views about how interest and dividends cash flows should be classified. Some regard them as part of operating activities, because they are as much part of the day to day activities as receipts from customers, payments to suppliers and payments to staff. Others regard them as part of financing activities, the heading under which the instruments giving rise to the payments and receipts are classified. Still others believe they are part of investing activities, because this is what the long-term finance raised in this way is used for.

IAS 7 allows interest and dividends, whether received or paid, to be classified under any of the three headings, provided the classification is consistent from period to period.

The practice adopted in this workbook is to classify:

- interest received as a cash flow from investing activities

- interest paid as a cash flow from operating activities

- dividends received as a cash flow from investing activities

- dividends paid as a cash flow from financing activities.

Expandable text - Cash flows from operating activities

A comparison of the direct and indirect methods is shown below. The methods differ only as regards the derivation of the item 'net cash inflow from operating activities'. Subsequent inflows and outflows for investing and financing are the same.

Indirect method

	$000
Profit before tax	6,022
Depreciation charges	899
Increase in inventory	(194)
Increase in receivables	(72)
Increase in payables	234
behalf of employees	(2,200)
Other cash payments	(511)
Net cash inflow from operating activities	6,889

The principal advantage of the indirect method is that it highlights the differences between reported profit and net cash flow from operating activities. Many users of financial statements believe that such a reconciliation is essential to give an indication of the quality of the reporting entity's earnings. Some investors and lenders assess future cash flows by estimating future income and then allowing for accruals adjustments; information about past accruals adjustments may be useful to them to help estimate future adjustments.

Calculation of net cash flow from operating activities

Profit before tax is computed on the accruals basis, whereas net cash flow from operating activities only records the cash inflows and outflows arising out of trading.

The main categories of items in the income statement /statement of comprehensive income and on the statement of financial position that form part of the reconciliation between profit before tax and net cash flow from operating activities are:

- **Depreciation**.

   Depreciation is a non-cash cost, being a book write-off of capital expenditure. Capital expenditure will be recorded under 'investing activities' at the time of the cash outflow. Depreciation therefore represents an **addition** to reported profit in deriving cash inflow.

- **Profit/loss on disposal of non-current assets**.

   The cash inflow from such a disposal needs to be recorded under 'investing activities'. If the profit or loss on the sale has been included in profit before tax, an adjustment is necessary in computing operating cash flow. A loss on disposal is added to reported profit, while a profit on disposal is deducted from reported profit.

- **Statement of financial position change in inventories**

   Inventory at the reporting date represents a purchase that has not actually been charged against current profits. However, as cash was spent on its purchase or a payable incurred, it does represent an actual or potential cash outflow. The effect on the statement of cash flows of a change in inventories is:

   - an increase in inventory is a deduction from reported profit, because it requires financing

   - a decrease in inventory is an addition to reported profit, because the amount of financing required has fallen.

- **Statement of financial position change in receivables**

  A sale once made creates income irrespective of the date of cash receipt. If the cash has not been received by the reporting date, there is no cash inflow from operating activities for the current accounting period. Similarly, opening receivables represent sales of a previous accounting period, most of which will be cash receipts in the current period.

  The change between opening and closing receivables will thus represent the adjustment required to move from profit to net cash inflow. The reasoning is the same as for inventories.

  - An increase in receivables is a deduction from reported profit.
  - A decrease in receivables is an addition to reported profit.

- **Statement of financial position change in payables**

  A purchase represents the incurring of expenditure and a charge or potential charge to the income statement (SCI). It does not represent a cash outflow until paid. To the extent that a purchase results in a charge to the income statement (SCI):

  - an increase in payables between two reporting dates is an addition to reported profit
  - a decrease in payables is a deduction from reported profit.

  If the purchase does not result in a charge to the income statement in the current year, the corresponding payable is not included in the reconciliation of profit to net cash inflow. For example, a payable in respect of a non-current asset is not included.

Income taxes

Cash flows arising from taxes on income should be separately disclosed as part of operating activities unless they can be specifically identified with financing or investing activities. It is reasonable to include income taxes as part of operating activities unless a question gives a clear indication to the contrary.

If income tax payments are allocated over more than one class of activity, the total should be disclosed by note.

The computation of income taxes paid may present a practical problem.

It is often convenient to arrive at the figure by means of a single tax working account into which all tax balances, whether current or deferred, are entered.

Sales tax

The existence of sales tax raises the question of whether the relevant cash flows should be reported gross or net of the tax element and how the balance of tax paid to, or repaid by, the taxing authorities should be reported.

The cash flows of an entity include sales tax where appropriate and thus strictly the various elements of the statement of cash flows should include sales tax. However, this treatment does not take into account the fact that normally sales tax is a short-term timing difference as far as the entity's overall cash flows are concerned and the inclusion of sales tax in the cash flows may distort the allocation of cash flows to standard headings.

In order to avoid this distortion and to show cash flows attributable to the reporting entity's activities, it is usual for amounts to be shown net of sales taxes and the net movement on the amount payable to, or receivable from, the taxing authority should be allocated to cash flows from operating activities unless a different treatment is more appropriate in the particular circumstances concerned.

Expandable text - Unusual items and non-cash transactions

Unusual cash flows

Where cash flows are unusual because of their size or incidence, sufficient disclosure should be given to explain their cause and nature.

For a cash flow to be unusual on the grounds of its size alone, it must be unusual in relation to cash flows of a similar nature.

Discontinued activities

Cash flows relating to discontinued activities are required by IFRS 5 to be shown separately, either on the face of the statement of cash flows or by note.

Major non-cash transactions

Material transactions not resulting in movements of cash should be disclosed in the notes to the statement of cash flows if disclosure is necessary for an understanding of the underlying transactions.

Consideration for transactions may be in a form other than cash. The purpose of a statement of cash flows is to report cash flows, and non-cash transactions should therefore not be reported in a statement of cash flows. However, to obtain a full picture of the alterations in financial position caused by the transactions for the period, separate disclosure of material non-cash transactions is also necessary.

Examples of non-cash transactions are:

- **the acquisition of assets by finance leases**

Finance leases are accounted for by the lessee capitalising the present value of the minimum lease payments (see later chapter). A liability and a corresponding asset are produced, which do not reflect cash flows in the accounting period. The statement of cash flows records the cash flow, i.e. the rentals paid, with the reduction in liability shown under financing. The interest element of the payment may be included in operating activities with only the portion of the payment which reduces the lease liability shown under financing activities.

- **the conversion of debt to equity**

If debt is issued with conversion rights attached it will be cancelled using an issue of shares and no cash flow will arise. The statement of cash flows is not affected.

- **the acquisition of a subsidiary by issue of shares**.

If the purchase consideration on acquisition of a subsidiary is settled using a share for share exchange no cash flow will arise and the statement of cash flows is not affected.

3 Preparation of group statements of cash flows

So far in this chapter, we have revised the basics on statements of cash flows. You should be familiar with this from previous studies.

Group statements of cash flows add three extra elements:

- cash paid to non-controlling interests
- cash received from associates
- acquisition and disposal of subsidiaries.

Expandable text - Cash paid to non-controlling interests

- When a subsidiary that is not wholly owned pays a dividend, some of that dividend is paid outside of the group to the non-controlling interest.

- Such dividends paid to non-controlling interests should be disclosed separately in the statement of cash flows.

- To calculate the amount paid, reconcile the non-controlling interest in the statement of financial position from the opening to the closing balance. You can use a T-account to do this. This working remains the same whichever method is used to value the non-controlling interest.

Expandable text - Illustration: Non-controlling interest

The following information has been extracted from the consolidated financial statements of WG for the years ended 31 December:

	20X7	20X6
	$000	$000
NCI in consolidated net assets	780	690
NCI in consolidated profit after tax	120	230

What is the dividend paid to non-controlling interests in the year 20X6?

Expandable text - Solution

Steps:

(1) Set up a T account for the NCI interest balance.

(2) Insert the opening and closing balances for net assets and the NCI share of profit after tax.

(3) Balance the account.

(4) The balancing figure is the cash paid to the NCI.

Non-controlling interests

	$000		$000
Dividends paid (bal fig)	30	Balance b/d NCI	690
Balance c/d NCI	780	Share of profits in year	120
	810		810

Watch out for an acquisition or disposal of a subsidiary in the year. This will affect the NCI and will need to be taken account of in the T-account, showing the NCI that has been acquired or disposed of in the period.

Expandable text - Associates

Associates

Associates generate cash flows into or out of the group to the extent that:

- dividends are received out of the profits of the associate
- trading occurs between the group and associate
- further investment is made in the associate.

Associates are usually dealt with under the equity method of accounting and this terminology is used below. (This also applies to jointly controlled entities as defined un IAS 31 **Interests in joint ventures**).

Standard accounting practice

- The cash flows of any equity accounted entity should be included in the group statement of cash flows only to the extent of the actual cash flows between the group and the entity concerned, for example dividends received in cash and loans made or repaid.

Dividends

- Only dividends received represent a cash inflow. Dividends declared but unpaid represent an increase in group receivables.

- When reconciling group net cash inflow to group reported profit, the movement between opening and closing receivables must exclude dividends receivable from the associate so that dividends received can be shown in the statement of cash flows.

- Dividends received from associates should be included as a separate item in the group statement of cash flows.

Trading between group and associate

- Trading between the group and an associate will give rise to inter-entity balances in the group statement of financial position at the year end.

- The balances will be treated in the same way as any other trading receivables and payables, i.e. the movement between opening and closing balances forms part of the reconciliation between group profit and group net cash inflow from operating activities.

Change in investment in associate

A change in investment in the associate can arise when:

- an additional shareholding is purchased or part of the shareholding is sold

- loans are made to/from the associate or amounts previously loaned are repaid.

Expandable text - Illustration: associate

The following information has been extracted from the consolidated financial statements of H for the year ended 31 December 20X1:

Group income statement

	$000
Operating profit	734
Income from associate	68
Profit before tax	802
Tax on profit (including 20 in respect of associate)	(324)
Profit after tax	478

Show the relevant figures to be included in the group statement of cash flows for the year ended 31 December 20X1.

Group statement of financial position

	20X1	20X0
	$000	$000
Investments in associates		
Share of net assets	466	456
Loan to associate	380	300
Current assets		
Receivables	260	190
Included within group receivables is the following amount:		
Current account with associate	40	70

Show the relevant figures to be included in the group statement of cash flows for the year ended 31 December 20X1.

Expandable text

When dealing with the dividend from the associate, the process is the same as we have already seen with the non-controlling interest.

Set up a T account and bring in all the balances that relate to the associate. When you balance the account, the balancing figure will be the cash received from the associate.

W1 Dividend received from associate

Associate

	$000		$000
Balance b/d		Dividend received	
Share of net assets	456	(bal fig)	38
		Share of net assets	466
Share of profit after tax (68-20)	48		
	504		504

Note that the current account with the associate remains within receivables.

Extracts from statement of cash flows

	$000
Cash flows from operating activities	
Profit before tax	802
Share of profit of associate	(68)
Investing activities	
Dividend received from associate (W1)	58
Loan to associate (380 – 300)	(80)

Expandable text - Acquisition and disposal of subsidiaries

Standard accounting practice

- If a subsidiary joins or leaves a group during a financial year, the cash flows of the group should include the cash flows of that subsidiary for the same period that the results of the subsidiary are included in the income statement / SCI.

- Cash payments to acquire subsidiaries and receipts from disposals of subsidiaries must be reported separately in the statement of cash flows under investing activities. The cash and cash equivalents acquired or disposed of should be shown separately.

- A note to the statement of cash flows should show a summary of the effects of acquisitions and disposals of subsidiaries, indicating how much of the consideration comprised cash and cash equivalents, and the assets and liabilities acquired or disposed of.

Acquisitions

- In the statement of cash flows we must record the actual cash flow for the purchase, not the net assets acquired.

- The assets and liabilities purchased will not be shown with the cash outflow in the statement of cash flows.

- All assets and liabilities acquired must be included in any workings to calculate the cash movement for an item during the year. If they are not included in deriving the balancing figure, the incorrect cash flow figure will be calculated. This applies to all assets and liabilities acquired including the non-controlling interest.

Disposals

- The statement of cash flows will show the cash received from the sale of the subsidiary, net of any cash balances that were transferred out with the sale.

- The assets and liabilities disposed of are not shown in the cash flow. When calculating the movement between the opening and closing balance of an item, the assets and liabilities that have been disposed of must be taken into account in order to calculate the correct cash figure. As with acquisitions, this applies to all assets and liabilities and the non-controlling interest.

Expandable text - Illustration: Acquisition / disposal of subsidiary

The extracts of a company's statement of financial position is shown below:

	20X8	20X7
	$	$
Inventory	74,666	53,019

During the year, a subsidiary was acquired. At the date of acquisition, the subsidiary had an inventory balance of $9,384.

Calculate the movement on inventory for the statement of cash flows.

Expandable text

At the beginning of the year, the inventory balance of $53,019 **does not** include the inventory of the subsidiary.

At the end of the year, the inventory balance of $74,666 **does** include the inventory of the newly acquired subsidiary.

In order to calculate the correct cash movement, the acquired inventory must be excluded as it is dealt with in the cash paid to acquire the subsidiary. The comparison of the opening and closing inventory figures is then calculated on the same basis.

The movement on inventory is: (74,666 – 9,384) – 53,019 = $12,263 increase. This is shown as a negative cash flow.

KAPLAN PUBLISHING

Disposals

The same principle applies if there is a disposal in the period.

For example, the year end receivables balance was as follows:

	20X8	20X7
	$	$
Receivables	52,335	48,991

During the year, a subsidiary was disposed of. At the date of disposal the subsidiary had a receivables balance of $6,543.

Calculate the movement on receivables for the statement of cash flows.

Solution

At the beginning of the year, the receivables balance of $48,911 **does** include the receivables of the subsidiary.

At the end of the year, the receivables balance of $52,335 **does not** include the receivables of the disposed subsidiary.

In order to calculate the correct cash movement, the receivables of the disposed subsidiary must be excluded.

The movement on receivables is:

52,335 – (48,911 – 6,543) = $9,967 increase, which is shown as a negative cash flow.

Test your understanding 1 - Extracts

CASH FLOW EXERCISES

Calculate the cash flows given the following extracts from statements of financial position drawn up at the year ended 31 December 20X0 and 20X1.

(1)	20X0	20X1
	$	$
Non-current assets (CV)	100	250

During the year depreciation charged was $20, a revaluation surplus of $60 was recorded, non-current assets with a CV of $15 were disposed of and non-current assets acquired subject to finance leases had a CV of $30.

Required:

How much cash was spent on non-current assets in the period?

(2)	20X0	20X1
	$	$
Deferred tax	50	100
Income tax liability	100	120

The income tax charge was $180.

Required:

How much tax was paid in the period?

(3)	20X0	20X1
	$	$
Non-controlling interest	440	840

The group income statement reported a non-controlling interest of $500.

Required:

How much was the cash dividend paid to the non-controlling interest?

(4)	20X0	20X1
	$	$
Non-controlling interest	500	850

The group income statement reported a non-controlling interest of $600.

Required:

How much was the cash dividend paid to the non-controlling interest?

KAPLAN PUBLISHING

(5)

	20X0	20X1
	$	$
Investment in associate undertaking	200	500

The group income statement reported 'Income from Associate Undertakings' of $750.

Required:

How much was the cash dividend received by the group?

(6)

	20X0	20X1
	$	$
Investment in associate undertaking	600	3200

The group income statement reported 'Income from Associate Undertakings' of $4,000

In addition, during the period the associate revalued its non-current assets, the group share of which is $500.

Required:

How much was the cash dividend received by the group?

(7)

	20X0	20X1
	$	$
Non-current asset (CV)	150	500

During the year depreciation charged was $50, and the group acquired a subsidiary with non-current assets of $200.

Required:

How much cash was spent on non-current assets in the period?

(8)

	20X0	20X1
	$	$
Loan	2,500	1,000

The loan is denominated in an overseas currency, and a loss of $200 has been recorded on the retranslation.

Required:

How much cash was paid?

The group had the following working capital:

(9)	20X0	20X1
	$	$
Inventory	200	100
Receivables	200	300
Trade payables	200	500

During the period the group acquired a subsidiary with the following working capital.

Inventory	50
Receivables	200
Trade Payables	40

During the period the group disposed of a subsidiary with the following working capital.

Inventory	25
Receivables	45
Trade Payables	20

During the period the group experienced the following exchange rate differences.

Inventory	11	Gain
Receivables	21	Gain
Trade payables	31	Loss

Required:

Calculate the extract from the statement of cash flows for working capital.

Test your understanding 2 - AH Group

Extracts from the consolidated financial statements of the AH Group for the year ended 30 June 20X5 are given below:

AH Group: Consolidated income statement for the year ended 30 June 20X5

	20X5
	$000
Revenue	85,000
Cost of sales	(60,750)
	———
Gross profit	24,250
Operating expenses	(5,650)
	———
Operating Profit	18,600
Finance cost	(1,400)
	———
Profit before disposal of property	17,200
Disposal of property (note 2)	1,250
	———
Profit before tax	18,450
Tax	(6,250)
	———
Profit for the period	12,200
	———
Attributable to:	
Non-controlling interest	405
Owners of the parent	11,795
	———
	12,200
	———

AH Group: Statement of financial position, with comparatives, at 30 June 20X5

	20X5		20X4	
ASSETS	$000	$000	$000	$000
Non-current assets				
Property, plant and equipment	50,600		44,050	
Goodwill (note 3)	5,910		4,160	
		56,510		48,210
Current assets				
Inventories	33,500		28,750	
Trade receivables	27,130		26,300	
Cash	1,870		3,900	
		62,500		58,950
		119,010		107,160

EQUITY AND LIABILITIES				
	$000	$000	$000	$000
Equity shares @ $1 each	20,000		18,000	
Share premium	12,000		10,000	
Retained earnings	24,135		18,340	
		56,135		46,340
Non-controlling interest		3,875		1,920
Total equity		60,010		48,260
Non-current liabilities				
Interest-bearing borrowings		18,200		19,200
Current liabilities				
Trade payables	33,340		32,810	
Interest payables	1,360		1,440	
Tax	6,100		5,450	
		40,800		39,700
		119,010		107,160

Notes:

(1) Several years ago, AH acquired 80% of the issued equity shares of its subsidiary, BI. On 1 January 20X5, AH acquired 75% of the issued equity shares of CJ in exchange for a fresh issue of 2 million of its own $1 equity shares (issued at a premium of $1 each) and $2 million in cash. The net assets of CJ at the date of acquisition were assessed as having the following fair values:

	$000
Property, plant and equipment	4,200
Inventories	1,650
Receivables	1,300
Cash	50
Trade payables	(1,950)
Tax	(250)
	5,000

(2) During the year, AH disposed of a non-current asset of property for proceeds of $2,250,000. The carrying value of the asset at the date of disposal was $1,000,000. There were no other disposals of non-current assets. Depreciation of $7,950,000 was charged against consolidated profits for the year.

(3) Goodwill on acquisition relates to the acquisition of two subsidiaries. Entity BI was acquired many years ago, and goodwill relating to this acquisition was calculated on a proportion of net assets basis. Goodwill relating to the acquisition of entity CJ during the year was calculated on the full goodwill basis. On 1 January 20X5 when CJ was acquired, the fair value of the non-controlling interest was $1,750,000. Any impairment of goodwill during the year was accounted for within cost of sales.

Required:

Prepare the consolidated statement of cash flows of the AH Group for the financial year ended 30 June 20X5 in the form required by IAS 7 Statements of Cash Flows, and using the indirect method. Notes to the statement of cash flows are NOT required, but full workings should be shown.

Test your understanding 3 - Kelly

Extracts from the consolidated financial statements of Kelly are given below:

Consolidated statements of financial position as at 31 March

	20X5		20X4	
	$000	$000	$000	$000
Non-current assets				
Property, plant and eqipment	5,900		4,400	
Goodwill	85		130	
Investment in associate	170		140	
		6,155		4,670
Current assets				
Inventories	1,000		930	
Receivables	1,340		1,140	
Short-term deposits	35		20	
Cash at bank	180		120	
		2,555		2,210
		8,710		6,880
Equity and liabilities				
Equity capital	2,000		1,500	
Share premium	300		–	
Other components of equity	50		–	
Retained earnings	3,400		3,320	
		5,750		4,820
Non-controlling interests		75		175
Total equity		5,825		4,995
Non-current liabilities				
Interest-bearing borrowings	1,400		1,000	
Obligations under finance leases	210		45	
Deferred tax	340		305	
		1,950		1,350

Current liabilities		
Trade payables	885	495
Accrued interest	7	9
Income tax	28	21
Obligations under finance leases	15	10
	935	535
	8,710	6,880

Consolidated statement of comprehensive income for the year ended 31 March 20X5

	$000
Revenue	875
Cost of sales	(440)
Gross profit	435
Other operating expenses	(210)
Profit from operations	225
Finance cost	(100)
Gain on sale of subsidiary	30
Share of associate's profit	38
Profit before tax	193
Tax	(48)
Profit for the year	145
Other comprehensive income	
Gains on land revaluation	50
Total comprehensive income for the year	195
Profit attributable to:	
Equity holders of the parent	120
Non-controlling interests	25
	145

Group statement of cash flows

Total comprehensive income attributable to:

Equity holders of the parent	170
Non-controlling interests	25
	195

Notes:

Dividends

Kelly paid a dividend of $40,000 during the year.

Property, plant and equipment

The following transactions took place during the year:

- Land was revalued upwards by $50,000 on 1st April 20X4.
- During the year, depreciation of $80,000 was charged in the income statement.
- Additions include $300,000 acquired under finance leases.
- A property was disposed of during the year for $250,000 cash. Its carrying amount was $295,000 at the date of disposal. The loss on disposal has been included within cost of sales.

Gain on sale of subsidiary

On 1 January 20X5, Kelly disposed of a 80% owned subsidiary for $390,000 in cash. The subsidiary had the following net assets at the date of disposal:

	$000
Property, plant and equipment	635
Inventory	20
Receivables	45
Cash	35
Payables	(130)
Income tax	(5)
Interest-bearing borrowings	(200)
	400

This subsidiary had been acquired on 1 January 20X1 for a cash payment of $220,000 when its net assets had a fair value of $225,000 and the non-controlling interest had a fair value of $50,000.

242

KAPLAN PUBLISHING

Goodwill

The Kelly Group uses the full goodwill method to calculate goodwill. No impairments have arisen during the year.

Required:

Prepare the consolidated statement of cash flows of the Kelly group for the year ended 31 March 20X5 in the form required by IAS 7 Statement of cash flows. Show your workings clearly.

Expandable text - Foreign currency transactions

It is likely that any statement of cash flows question will require you to deal with exchange gains and losses.

Individual entity stage

- Exchange differences arising at the individual entity stage are in most instances reported as part of operating profit. If the foreign currency transaction has been settled in the year, the cash flows will reflect the reporting currency cash receipt or payment and thus no problem arises.

- An unsettled foreign currency transaction will, however, give rise to an exchange difference for which there is no cash flow effect in the current year. Such exchange differences therefore need to be eliminated in computing net cash flows from operating activities.

- Fortunately this will not require much work if the unsettled foreign currency transaction is in working capital. Adjusting profit by movements in working capital will automatically adjust correctly for the non-cash flow exchange gains and losses.

Expandable text - Illustration: Foreign currency transactions

The financial statements of A are as follows:

Statements of financial position at 31 December

	20X3	20X4
	$	$
Non-current assets	–	–
Current assets		
Inventory	300,000	300,000
Cash	335,000	595,000
	635,000	895,000
Capital and reserves	100,000	190,000
Foreign currency loan	235,000	245,000
Trade payables	300,000	460,000
	635,000	895,000
Capital and reserves	100,000	190,000
Foreign currency loan	235,000	245,000
Trade payables	300,000	460,000
	635,000	895,000

Income statement for the year ended 31 December 20X4

	$	$
Revenue – all cash sales		1,003,000
Cost of sales		(910,000)
Operating profit before exchange differences		93,000
Exchange differences		
Trading (2 + 5)	7,000	
Loan (245 – 235)	(10,000)	
		(3,000)
Profit before tax		90,000
Tax		–
Profit for the period		90,000

During the year, A purchased raw materials for Z200,000, recorded in its books as $100,000. By the year end A had settled half the debt for $48,000 and the remaining payable is retranslated at closing rate at $45,000.

These transactions are included in the purchase ledger control account, which is as follows:

Purchase ledger control

	$		$
Cash	743,000	Balance b/d	300,000
Exchange gains		Purchases	910,000
On settled transaction			
(50,000 – 48,000)	2,000		
On unsettled transaction			
(50,000 – 45,000)	5,000		
Balance c/d			
Foreign currency			
payable	45,000		
Other	415,000		
	1,210,000		1,210,000

Show the gross cash flows (i.e. cash flows under the direct method) from operating activities, together with a reconciliation of profit before tax to net cash flow from operating activities.

Expandable text: Solution

Statement of cash flows for the year

	$	$
Cash received from customers	1,003,000	
Cash payments to suppliers	743,000	
Net cash inflow from operations		260,000
Increase in cash		260,000

Note that because there is no change in inventory, cost of sales is the same as purchases.

Reconciliation of profit before tax to net cash inflow from operating activities

	$
Profit before tax	90,000
Exchange loss on foreign currency loan	10,000
Increase in payables	160,000
Net cash inflow from operations	260,000

KAPLAN PUBLISHING

Expandable text - Consolidated statements of cash flow

- The key to the preparation of a group statement of cash flows involving a foreign subsidiary is an understanding of the make-up of the foreign exchange differences themselves.

- None of the differences reflects a cash inflow/outflow to the group. The main concern, therefore, is to determine the real cash flows, particularly if they have to be derived as balancing figures from the opening and closing statements of financial position.

- If cash balances are partly denominated in a foreign currency, the effect of exchange rate movements on cash is reported in the statement of cash flows in order to reconcile the cash balances at the beginning and end of the period. This amount is presented separately from cash flows from operating, investing and financing activities.

Closing rate/net investment method

- Using the closing rate/net investment method, the exchange difference on translating the statements of the foreign entity will relate to the opening net assets of that entity (i.e. non-current assets, inventories, receivables, cash, payables and loans) and also to the difference between the average and the closing rates of exchange on translation of the result for the period.

- Under the closing rate/net investment method, translation exchange differences are disclosed as other comprehensive income and taken to other components of equity in the statement of financial position.

Care needs to be taken in two areas:

- **Analysis of non-current assets**

  Non-current assets may require analysis in order to determine cash expenditure. Part of the movement in non-current assets may reflect an exchange gain/loss.

- **Analysis of non-controlling interests**

  If non-controlling interests require analysis to determine the dividend paid to them, it must be remembered that they have a share in the exchange gain/loss arising from the translation of the subsidiary's accounts.

Group statement of cash flows

Expandable text - Illustration: Foreign currency transactions

B Group recognised a gain of $160,000 on the translation of the financial statements of a 75% owned foreign subsidiary for the year ended 31 December 20X7. This gain is found to be made up as follows

	$
Gain on opening net assets:	
Non-current assets	90,000
Inventories	30,000
Receivables	50,000
Payables	(40,000)
Cash	30,000
	160,000

B Group recognised a loss of $70,000 on retranslating the parent entity's foreign currency loan. This loss has been disclosed as other comprehensive income and charged to reserves in the draft financial statements.

KAPLAN PUBLISHING

Consolidated statements of financial position as at 31 December

	20X7	20X6
	$000	$000
Non-current assets	2,100	1,700
Inventories	650	480
Receivables	990	800
Cash	500	160
	4,240	3,140
Share capital	1,000	1,000
Consolidated reserves	1,600	770
	2,600	1,770
Non-controlling interest	520	370
Equity	3,120	2,140
Long-term loan	250	180
Payables	870	820
	4,240	3,140

There were no non-current asset disposals during the year.

Consolidated income statement for the year ended 31 December 20X7

	$000
Profit before tax (after depreciation of $220,000)	2,170
Tax	(650)
Group profit for the year	1,520
Profit attributable to:	
Owners of the parent	1,260
Non-controlling interest	260
Net profit for the period	1,520

Note:

The dividend paid during the year was $480,000.

Prepare a statement of cash flows for the year ended 31 December 20X7.

Expandable text - Solution

The first stage is to produce a statement of reserves so as to analyse the movements during the year.

Statement of reserves

	$000
Reserves brought forward	770
Retained profit (1,260 – 480)	780
Exchange gain	
(160,000 × 75%) – 70,000	50
	———
Reserves carried forward	1,600
	———

Statement of cash flows for the year ended 31 December 20X7

Cash flows from operating activities	$000
Profit before tax	2,170
Depreciation charges	220
Increase in inventory (650 – 480 – 30)	(140)
Increase in receivables (990 – 800 – 50)	(140)
Increase in payables (870 – 820 – 40)	10
	———
Cash generated from operations	2,120
Income taxes paid	(650)
	———
Net cash from operating activities	1,470

Cash flows from investing activities

Purchase of non-current assets (W2)   (530)

                                                                        (530)

Cash flows from financing activities

Dividends paid to non-controlling interests (W1)   (150)
Dividends paid   (480)

                                                                        (630)
Exchange gain on cash   30

Increase in cash   340
Cash at 1 Jan 20X7   160

Cash at 31 Dec 20X7   500

Workings (WI) Non-controlling interest

	$000		$000
Dividend paid (bal fig)	150	Balance b/d	370
Balance c/d	520	Total comprehensive income (Note)	300
	670		670

Note: i.e. NCI share of tax 260 + (25% x $160,000 exchange gain) = 300

(W2) Non-current assets

	$000		$000
Balance b/d	1,700	Depreciation	220
Exchange gain	90	Balance c/d	2,100
Additions (bal fig)	530	Exchange gain	
	2,320		2,320

Illustration 1 foreign exchange

The following are excerpts from a group's financial statements

	Opening balance $000	Closing balance $000
Group statement of financial position extracts		
Non-current assets	400	500
Loans	600	300
Tax	300	200
Income statement extracts		
Depreciation	50	
Loss on disposal of non-current asset (sold for $30,000)	10	
Tax charge	200	

During the accounting period, one subsidiary was sold, and another acquired. Extracts from the statements of financial position are as follows:

	Sold $000	Acquired $000
Non-current assets	60	70
Loans	110	80
Tax	45	65

During the accounting period, the following net exchange gain arose in respect of overseas net assets:

	$000
Non-current assets	40
Loans	(5)
Tax	(5)

Required:

Calculate the group cash flows for non-current assets, loans and tax.

Expandable text - solution

Non-current assets	$000
Opening balance	400
Depreciation	(50)
Disposal (30 + 10)	(40)
Disposal of subsidiary	(60)
Acquisition of subsidiary	70
Exchange gain	40
	——
	360
Cash acquisitions (bal figure)	140
	——
Closing balance	500
	——

Loans	
Opening balance	600
Disposal of subsidiary	(110)
Acquisition of subsidiary	80
Exchange loss	5
	——
	575
Therefore redemption	(275)
	——
Closing balance	300
	——

Tax	
Opening balance	300
Charge for the year	200
Disposal of subsidiary	(45)
Acquisition of subsidiary	65
Exchange loss	5
	——
	525
Therefore cash paid	(325)
	——
Closing balance	200
	——

Test your understanding 4 - Boardres

Set out below is a summary of the accounts of Boardres, a public limited company, for the year ended 31 December 20X7.

Consolidated income statement for the year ended 31 December 20X7

	$000
Revenue	44,754
Cost of sales and other expenses	(39,613)
Income from associates	30
Finance cost	(305)
Profit before tax	4,866
Tax:	(2,038)
Net profit for the period	2,828
Attributable to:	
Owners of the parent	2,805
Non-controlling interests	23
	2,828

Statement of other comprehensive income	$000
Profit for the year	2,828
Exchange difference on translation of foreign operations (note 5)	302
Total comprehensive income	3,130

	$000
Changes in capital and reserves of equity holders of the parent	
Equity capital and reserves b/f	14,164
Profit for year	2,805
Dividends paid	(445)
Exchange differences	302
Equity capital and reserves c/f	16,826

Consolidated statements of financial position at 31 December

	Note	20X7 $000	20X7 $000	20X6 $000	20X6 $000
Non-current assets					
Intangible assets - goodwill			500		–
Tangible assets	(1)		11,157		8,985
Investment in associate			300		280
			11,957		9,265
Current assets					
Inventories		9,749		7,624	
Receivables		5,354		4,420	
Short-term investments		1,543		741	
Cash at bank and in hand		1,013	17,659	394	13,179
			29,616		22,444
Equity and liabilities					
			$000		$000
Equity share capital @ $1			1,997		1,997
Share premium			5,808		5,808
Retained earnings			9,021		6,359
			16,826		14,164
Non-controlling interest			170		17
Total equity			16,996		14,181
Non-current liabilities:					
Loans			2,102		1,682
Provisions	(3)		1,290		935
Current liabilities:	(2)		9,228		5,646
			29,616		22,444

Notes to the accounts

(1) Tangible assets

Non-current asset movements included the following:

	$000
Disposals at carrying amount	305
Proceeds from asset sales	854
Depreciation provided for the year	907

(2) Current liabilities

	20X7	20X6
	$000	'000
Bank overdrafts	1,228	91
Trade payables	4,278	2,989
Tax	3,722	2,566
	9,228	5,646

(3) Provisions

	Pensions	Deferred taxation	Total
	$000	$000	$000
At 31 December 20X6	246	689	935
Exchange rate adjustment	29	–	29
Increase in provision	460	–	460
Decrease in provision	–	(134)	(134)
At 31 December 20X7	735	555	1,290

(4) Liberated

During the year, the company acquired 82% of the issued equity capital of Liberated for a cash consideration of $1,268,000. The fair values of the assets of Liberated were as follows:

	$000
Non-current assets	208
Inventories	612
Trade receivables	500
Cash in hand	232
Trade payables	(407)
Debenture loans	(312)
	833

(5) Exchange gains

Exchange gains on translating the financial statements of a wholly-owned subsidiary have been taken to equity and comprise differences on the retranslation of the following:

	$000
Non-current assets	138
Pensions	(29)
Inventories	116
Trade receivables	286
Trade payables	(209)
	302

(6) Non-controlling interest

The non-controlling interest is valued using the proportion of net assets method.

Required:

Prepare a statement of cash flows for the year ended 31 December 20X7.

4 Evaluation of statements of cash flows

Usefulness of the statement of cash flows

A statement of cash flows can provide information that is not available from statements of financial position and statements of comprehensive income.

(a) It may assist users of financial statements in making judgements on the amount, timing and degree of certainty of future cash flows.

(b) It gives an indication of the relationship between profitability and cash generating ability, and thus of the quality of the profit earned.

(c) Analysts and other users of financial information often, formally or informally, develop models to assess and compare the present value of the future cash flow of entities. Historical cash flow information could be useful to check the accuracy of past assessments.

(d) A statement of cash flow in conjunction with a statement of financial position provides information on liquidity, solvency and adaptability. The statement of financial position is often used to obtain information on liquidity, but the information is incomplete for this purpose as the statement of financial position is drawn up at a particular point in time.

(e) Cash flow cannot easily be manipulated and is not affected by judgement or by accounting policies.

Limitations of the statement of cash flows

Statements of cash flows should normally be used in conjunction with income statements/statements of comprehensive income and statements of financial position when making an assessment of future cash flows.

(a) Statements of cash flows are based on historical information and therefore do not provide complete information for assessing future cash flows.

(b) There is some scope for manipulation of cash flows. For example, a business may delay paying suppliers until after the year-end, or it may structure transactions so that the cash balance is favourably affected. It can be argued that cash management is an important aspect of stewardship and therefore desirable. However, more deliberate manipulation is possible (e.g. assets may be sold and then immediately repurchased). Application of the substance over form principle should alert users of the financial statements to the true nature of such arrangements.

(c) Cash flow is necessary for survival in the short term, but in order to survive in the long term a business must be profitable. It is often necessary to sacrifice cash flow in the short term in order to generate profits in the long term (e.g. by investment in non-current assets). A substantial cash balance is not a sign of good management if the cash could be invested elsewhere to generate profit.

Neither cash flow nor profit provides a complete picture of an entity's performance when looked at in isolation.

Expandable text - UK syllabus focus

The ACCA UK syllabus contains a requirement that UK variant candidates should be able to discuss and apply the key differences between UK GAAP and IFRS GAAP. As with other areas of group accounts, the accounting requirements of UK GAAP and IFRS GAAP are very similar in this area; the basic mechanics of the workings required are the same. The only real distinctions relate to the flow-through of workings relating to goodwill and minority interest on a proportionate basis, together with the slightly different format under FRS 1.

Both of these points are illustrated in the question and answer which follow this narrative.

Under FRS 1, the starting point of the cash flow statement is operating profit for the year. This must be adjusted for items affecting operating profit, but for which there is not a matching cash flow, to arrive at cash flow on operating activities.

Extracts from the consolidated financial statements of the AH Group for the year ended 30 June 20X5 are given below:

AH Group: Consolidated income statement for the year ended 30 June 20X5

	20X5
	£000
Turnover	85,000
Cost of sales	(59,750)
Gross profit	25,250
Operating expenses	(5,650)
Operating Profit	19,600
Finance cost	(1,400)
Profit before disposal of property	18,200
Disposal of property (note 2)	1,250
Profit before tax	19,450
Tax	(6,250)
Profit for the period	13,200
Attributable to:	
Minority interest	655
Owners of the parent	12,545
	13,200

AH Group: Balance sheet, with comparatives, at 30 June 20X5

	20X5			20X4
	£000	£000	$000	£000
Fixed assets				
Property, plant and equipment	50,600		44,050	
Goodwill (note 3)	6,410		4,160	
		57,010		48,210
Current assets:				
Stock	33,500		28,750	
Debtors	27,130		26,300	
Cash	1,870		3,900	
	62,500		58,950	
Current liabilities:				
Trade creditors	(33,340)		(32,810)	
Interest payable	(1,360)		(1,440)	
Tax	(6,100)		(5,450)	
		21,700		19,250
Long term liabilities:				
Loans		(18,200)		(19,200)
		60,510		48,260

Share capital and reserves				
	£000	£000	£000	£000
Share capital @ £1 each	20,000		18,000	
Share premium	12,000		10,000	
P&L reserve	24,885		18,340	
		56,885		46,340
Minority interest		3,625		1,920
		60,510		48,260

Notes:

(1) Several years ago, AH acquired 80% of the issued ordinary shares of its subsidiary, BI. On 1 January 20X5, AH acquired 75% of the issued ordinary shares of CJ in exchange for a fresh issue of 2 million of its own £1 ordinary shares (issued at a premium of £1 each) and £2 million in cash. The net assets of CJ at the date of acquisition were assessed as having the following fair values:

	£000
Property, plant and equipment	4,200
Stock	1,650
Trade debtors	1,300
Cash	50
Trade creditors	(1,950)
Tax	(250)
	5,000

(2) During the year, AH disposed of a property for proceeds of £2,250,000. The carrying value of the asset at the date of disposal was £1,000,000. There were no other disposals of fixed assets. Depreciation of £7,950,000 was charged against consolidated profits for the year.

(3) Intangible assets comprise goodwill on acquisition of BI and CJ. Entity BI was acquired many years ago.Goodwill is accounted for as a permanent asset, and is unimpaired since acquisition.

Required:

Prepare the consolidated cash flow statement of the AH Group for the financial year ended 30 June 20X5 in the form required by FRS 1 using the indirect method. Notes to the statement of cash flows are NOT required, but full workings should be shown.

Expandable text - UK GAAP answer

Consolidated cash flow statement for the year ended 30 June 20X5

	£000	£000
Reconciliation of operating profit to net cash flow from operating activities:		
Operatiing profit		19,600
Adjustment for non-cash items dealt with in arriving at operating profit:		
Depreciation		7,950
Decrease in trade debtors (27,130 – 26,300 – 1,300)		470
Increase in stocks (33,500 – 28,750 – 1,650)		(3,100)
Decrease in trade creditors (33,340 – 32,810 – 1,950)		(1,420)
Cash generated from operations		23,500
Dividends from associates		nil
Returns on investments and servicing of finance:		
Interest paid (W1)	(1,480)	
Dividend paid to minority interest (W4)	(200)	(1,680)
Taxation paid (W2)		(5,850)
Capital expenditure		
Purchase of property, plant, and equipment (W3)	(11,300)	
Proceeds from sale of property	2,250	(9,050)
Acquisition/disposal of subsidiaries:		
Net cash impact of subsidiary acquired ((2,000 - 50)		(1,950)

Equity dividend paid (W5)		(6,000)
Financing activities:		
Repayment of l0o		(1,000)
.ng term loan (18,200 - 19,200)		
Net decrease in cash for the year (3,900 - 1,870)		(2,030)

Workings

(W1)

Interest paid

	£000		£000
Cash paid (balancing figure)	1,480	Balance b/d	1,440
Balance c/d	1,360	P&L a/c	1,400
	2,840		2,840

(W2)

Tax paid

	£000		£000
Cash paid (balancing figure)	5,850	Balance b/d	5,450
		P&L a/c	6,250
Balance c/d	6,100	New subsidiary	250
	11,950		11,950

(W3)

Property, plant and equipment

	£000		£000
Balance b/d	44,050	Depreciation	7,950
New subsidiary	4,200	Disposals	1,000
Additions (balancing figure)	11,300	Balance c/d	50,600
	59,550		59,550

(W4)

Minority interest

	£000		£000
Dividend paid (balancing figure)	200	Balance b/d	1,920
		MI re CJ acquired (25% x 5,000)	1,250
Balance c/d	3,625	P&L a/c	655
	_____		_____
	3,825		3,825
	_____		_____

(W5)

Retained profits

	£000		£000
Dividend paid (balancing figure)	6,000	Balance b/d	18,340
Balance c/d	24,885	P&L a/c	12,545
	_____		_____
	30,885		30,885
	_____		_____

5 Chapter summary

Objective of statements of cash flows

- To provide information on changes in cash and cash equivalents
- To enable users to assess the liquidity, solvency and financial adaptability of a business

Classifications of cash flows

- No specific format for the cash flow in IAS 7
- IAS 7 only requires 3 headings:
  - Operating
  - Investing
  - Financing

Preparation of group statements of cash flows

- Three additional elements:
  - Cash paid to non-controlling interest
  - Cash received from associates
  - Acquisition and disposal of subsidiaries/ associates

Foreign currency transactions

- Individual company transactions are likely to have been settled in the year and no adjustment will be required
- Foreign subsidiary – exchange gains must be taken out of the statement of financial position movements as they are not cash

Evaluation of statements of cash flows

- Proivdes information not available in the statement of financial position and income statement
- Shows relationship between profitability and cash generating ability

Test your understanding answers

Test your understanding 1 - Extracts

(1)

Non-current assets (CV)

	$		$
Balance b/f	100	Depreciation	20
Revaluation	60	Disposals	15
Additions (bal fig)	125	Balance c/f	250
	285		285

Cash additions = 125 – finance lease additions of 30 = 95

(2)

Tax

	$		$
Tax paid (bal fig)	110	Balances b/fwd	
		DT	50
		CT	100
Balances c/fwd			
DT	100		
CT	120	Income statement	180
	330		330

(3)

Non-controlling interest

	$		$
		Balance b/f	440
Cash dividend paid (bal fig)	100	Income statement	500
Balance c/f	840		
	940		940

(4)

Non-controlling interest

	$		$
		Balance b/f	500
Cash dividend paid (bal fig)	250	Income statement	600
Balance c/f	850		
	1,100		1,100

(5)

Associate

	$		$
Balance b/f	200	Cash received (bal fig)	450
Income statement	750	Balance c/f	500
	950		950

(6)

Associate

	$		$
Balance b/f	600		
Income statement	4,000	Cash received (bal fig)	1,900
Revaluation	500	Balance c/f	3,200
	5,100		5,100

(7)

Non-current assets (CV)

	$		$
Balance b/f	150	Depreciation	50
New subsidiary	200		
Cash additions (bal fig)	200	Balance c/f	500
	550		550

KAPLAN PUBLISHING

(8)

Loan

	$		$
		Balance b/f	2,500
Cash paid (bal fig)	1,700	Exchange loss	200
Balance c/f	1,000		
	———		———
	2,700		2,700
	———		———

(9)

	$
Movement in inventory (W1)	136
Movement in receivables (W2)	76
Movement in payables (W3)	249

(W1) Movement in inventory

	$		$
B/f balance	200	C/f balance	100
Disposal	(25)	Acquisition	(50)
		Exchange gain	(11)
	———		———
Revised b/f	175	Revised c/f	39
	———		———

Movement therefore a decrease of 136

(W2) Movement of receivables

	$		$
B/f balance	200	C/f balance	300
Disposal	(45)	Acquisition	(200)
		Exchange gain	(21)
	———		———
Revised b/f	155	Revised c/f	79
	———		———

Movement therefore a decrease of 76

(W3) Movement of payables

	$		$
B/f balance	200	C/f balance	500
Disposal	(20)	Acquisition	(40)
		Exchange loss	(31)
Revised b/f	180	Revised c/f	429

Movement therefore an increase of 249

Test your understanding 2 - AH Group

Consolidated statement of cash flows for the year ended 30 June 20X5

	$000	$000
Operating activities		
Profit before tax		18,450
Adjustment		
Less: gain on disposal of property		(1,250)
Add: finance cost		1,400
Adjustment for non-cash items dealt with in arriving at operating profit:		
Depreciation		7,950
Decrease in trade and other receivables (27,130 – 26,300 – 1,300)		470
Increase in inventories (33,500 – 28,750 – 1,650)		(3,100)
Decrease in trade payables (33,340 – 32,810 – 1,950)		(1,420)
Goodwill impaired (W4)		1,000
Cash generated from operations		23,500
Interest paid (W1)		(1,480)
Income taxes paid (W2)		(5,850)
Net cash from operating activities		16,170

Investing activities

Acquisition of subsidiary net of cash acquired (2,000 – 50)	(1,950)	
Purchase of property, plant, and equipment (W3)	(11,300)	
Proceeds from sale of property	2,250	
Net cash used in investing activities		(11,000)

Financing activities

Repayment of long-term borrowings (18,200 – 19,200)	(1,000)	
Dividend paid by parent (W7)	(6,000)	
Dividends paid to NCI (W6)	(200)	
Net cash used in financing activies		(7,200)
Net decrease in cash and cash equivalents		(2,030)
Cash and cash equivalents at 1 July 20X4		3,900
Cash and cash equivalents at 30 June 20X5		1,870

Workings

(W1)

Interest paid

	$000		$000
Cash paid (balancing figure)	1,480	Balance b/d	1,440
Balance c/d	1,360	Income statement	1,400
	2,840		2,840

(W2)

Income taxes paid

	$000		$000
Cash paid (balancing figure)	5,850	Balance b/d	5,450
		Income statement	6,250
Balance c/d	6,100	New subsidiary	250
	11,950		11,950

(W3)

Property, plant and equipment

	$000		$000
Balance b/d	44,050	Depreciation	7,950
New subsidiary	4,200	Disposals	1,000
Additions (balancing figure)	11,300	Balance c/d	50,600
	59,550		59,550

(W4) Goodwill re acquisition during year

		$000
Fair value of shares issued	Equity capital - nominal value	2,000
	Share premium	2,000
Cash paid		2,000
		6,000
Fair value of NCI	per question	1,750
		7,750
Fair value of net assets at acquisition	per question	5,000
Full goodwill at acquisition		2,750

(W5)

Goodwill

	$000		$000
Balance b/d	4,160	Impaired in year (bal fig)	1,000
Full goodwill on subsidiary acquired (W4)	2,750	Balance c/d	5,910
	6,910		6,910

(W6)

Non-controlling interest

	$000		$000
Dividend paid (balancing figure)	200	Balance b/d	1,920
		NCI at fair value re CJ acquired	1,750
Balance c/d	3,875	Income statement	405
	4,075		4,075

(W7)

Retained earnings

	$000		$000
Dividend paid (balancing figure)	6,000	Balance b/d	18,340
Balance c/d	24,135	Income statement	11,795
	30,135		30,135

Test your understanding 3 - Kelly

Consolidated statement of cash flows for the year ended 31 March 20X5

	$000	$000
Cash flows from operating activities		
Profit before tax	193	
Gain on sale of subsidiary	(30)	
Share of associate's profit	(38)	
Finance costs	100	
Adjust for non-cash items dealt with in arriving at operating profit:		
Depreciation	80	
Loss on disposal of property (250 - 295)	45	
	———	
Operating profit before working capital changes	350	
Increase in inventory (1,000 – (930 – 20))	(90)	
Increase in receivables		
(1,340 – (1,140 – 45))	(245)	
Increase in payables (885 – (495 – 130))	520	
	———	
	535	
Finance costs paid (W2)	(102)	
Tax paid (W3)	(1)	
	———	
		432
Cash flows from investing activities		
Sale of property	250	
Purchases of property, plant and equipment (W4)	(2,160)	
Dividends received from associate (W5)	8	
Proceeds from sale of subsidiary, net of cash balances (390 – 35)	355	
	———	
		(1,547)

Cash flows from financing activities

Repayments of finance leases (W6)	(130)
Cash raised from interest-bearing borrowings (W7)	600
Issue of shares (500 + 300)	800
Dividends paid to equity shareholders of parent	(40)
Dividends paid to non-controlling interests (W8)	(40)

	1,190
Increase in cash and cash equivalents	75
Opening cash and cash equivalents (120 + 20)	140
Closing cash and cash equivalents (180 + 35)	215

(1) Goodwill

	$000
Goodwill on acquisition of subsidiary disposed of during the year	
Fair value of consideration paid	220
Fair value of NCI	50
	270
Less: Fair value of net assets at acquisition	(225)
Full goodwill at acquisition	45

Goodwill

	$000		$000
Bal b/d	130	Disposal of sub (as above)	45
		Bal c/d	85
	130		130

(2) Finance

Finance

	$000		$000
Cash (bal fig)	102	Bal b/d	9
Bal b/d	7	SCI	100
	___		___
	109		109
	___		___

(3) Tax paid

Tax

		Bal b/d – IT	21
		Bal b/d – DT	305
Disposal of sub	5		
		SCI – group	48
Tax paid (bal fig)	1		
Bal c/d – IT	28		
Bal c/d – DT	340		
	___		___
	374		374
	___		___

(4) Purchase of non-current assets

Property, plant and equipment

Bal b/d	4,400		
Revaluation	50	Depreciation	80
Finance leases (W6)	300	Disposal –property	295
Cash (bal fig)	2,160	Disposal – sub	635
		Bal c/d	5,900
	_____		_____
	6,910		6,910
	_____		_____

(5) Dividend from associate

Associates

Bal b/d	140		
Share of profit for the year	38	Dividend received (bal fig)	8
		Bal c/d	170
	_____		_____
	178		178
	_____		_____

(6) Repayment of finance leases

Finance leases

		Bal b/d (10 + 45)	55
		New leases (W4)	300
Repayments (bal fig)	130		
Bal c/d (15 + 210)	225		
	_____		_____
	355		355
	_____		_____

(7) Cash raised from borrowings

Interest-bearing borrowings

		Bal b/d	1,000
Disposal of sub	200		
		Cash (bal fig)	600
Bal b/d	1,400		
	_____		_____
	1,600		1,600
	_____		_____

(8) Dividend paid to non-controlling interests

Non-controlling interests

		Bal b/d	175
Disposal of sub		Share of profits	25
Share of net assets + NCI goodwill (20% x 400 + (50 – (20% x 225))	85		
Dividends paid (bal fig)	40		
Bal c/d	75		
	——		——
	200		200
	——		——

Test your understanding 4 - Boardres

Statement of cash flows for the year ended 31 December 20X7

	$000	$000
Operating activities		
Profit before tax	4,866	
Interest payable	305	
Income from associate	(30)	
	─────	
Operating profit	5,141	
Non-cash items		
Depreciation	907	
Goodwill (W7)	85	
Gain on disposal of assets (W1)	(549)	
Increase in pension provision	460	
	─────	
	6,044	
Change in working capital		
Increase in inventory		
(9,749 – 7,624 – 612 acq – 116 ex diff)	(1,397)	
Increase in receivables		
(5,354 – 4,420 – 500 acq – 286 ex diff)	(148)	
Increase in payables		
(4,278 – 2,989 – 407 acq – 209 ex diff)	673	
	─────	
	5,172	
Interest paid	(305)	
Tax paid (W2)	(1,016)	
	─────	
		3,851
Investing activities		
Purchase of non-current assets (W3)	(3,038)	
Proceeds on disposal	854	
Cash consideration paid on acquisition		
of subsidiary, net of cash acquired		
(1,268 – 232)	(1,036)	
Dividend received from associate (W4)	10	
	─────	
		(3,210)

Financing activities

Dividends paid	(445)
Dividends paid to NCI (W6)	(20)
Proceeds from debt issue (W5)	108
	(357)
Change in cash and cash equivalents	284
Opening cash and cash equivalents	
(394 + 741 – 91)	1,044
Closing cash and cash equivalents	
(1,013 + 1,543 – 1,228)	1,328

Workings

(W1) Proceeds of disposal of NCA

	$
Sales proceeds	854
CV	(305)
Profit on disposal	549

(W2) Tax

	$		$
Cash	1,016	Balance b/f–CT	2,566
Balance c/f-CT	3,722	Balance b/f–DT	689
Balance c/f-DT	555	I/S	2,038
	5,293		5,293

(W3) Non-current assets

	$		$
Balance b/f	8,985	Depreciation	907
Exchange gain	138	Disposal	305
Acquisition	208	Balance c/f	11,157
Cash	3,038		
	─────		─────
	12,369		12,369
	─────		─────

(W4) Dividends from associates

	$		$
Balance b/f	280	Cash	10
Profit	30	Balance c/f	300
	─────		─────
	310		310
	─────		─────

(W5) Debentures

	$		$
Balance c/f	2,102	Balance b/f	1,682
		Acquisition	312
		Cash	108
	─────		─────
	2,102		2,102
	─────		─────

(W6) Non-controlling interest

	$		$
Cash	20	Balance b/f	17
Balance c/f	170	I/S	23
		Acquisition (18% × 833)	150
	190		190

(W7) Goodwill

	$
Cost of investment	1,268
Less net assets acquired 82% x 833	(683)
Goodwill arising	585
Amount written off (BF)	85
Remaining in statement of financial position	500

The professional and ethical duty of the accountant

Chapter learning objectives

Upon completion of this chapter you will be able to:

- appraise the ethical and professional issues in advising on corporate reporting

- assess the relevance and importance of ethical and professional issues in complying with accounting standards

- appraise the potential ethical implications of professional and managerial decisions in the preparation of corporate reports

- assess the consequences of not upholding ethical principles in the preparation of corporate reports.

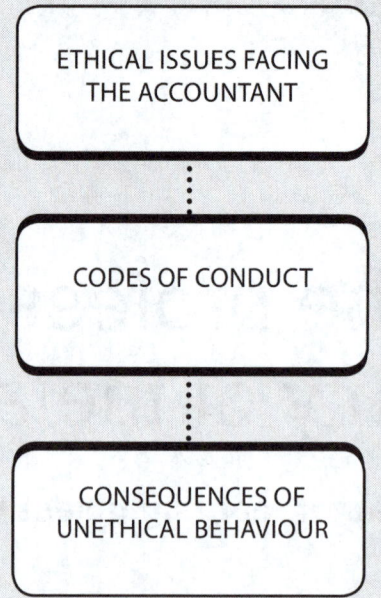

Expandable text - The ethical issues facing the accountant

Definition: Professional ethics are the principles and standards that underlie the responsibilities and conduct of a person in performing his/her function in a particular field of expertise.

Introduction

- Ethical principles are important in a business organisation as they set the tone for the culture and behaviour of employees and management.

- For example, a business's ethical aim may be to treat employees fairly and to be honest in all business transactions.

- The application of ethics can sometimes be intangible. Ethics is often described as 'doing the right thing' but this can mean different things to different individuals.

- After the accounting scandals in Enron, Worldcom, Parmalat and others, business ethics has become more prominent in the accounting world.

- As a result, many companies have an ethical code that sets out their ethical objectives. This can be a huge benefit for businesses, as employees tend to prefer to work for a company with good guidelines of moral behaviour, and customers and suppliers will prefer to deal with such a business.

Issues in advising on corporate reporting

- An audit is an independent examination of, and report on, the financial statements and therefore it is expected that the auditors are independent.

- However, there has always been an area of contention in the accountancy profession as to whether auditors can actually be independent when their clients pay for their services.

- Many audit fees are very high, for example, in 2000 Enron Corp paid Arthur Andersen US$25 million for the audit. It becomes very difficult for the auditor to say no to a client when such great sums of money are involved.

- There is a balance between agreeing with the client's accounting practices in order to keep the client, and allowing them to get away with dubious accounting practices and potentially being fined, not allowed to practise or even ending up in prison.

- Another independence issue is that accountancy firms complete non-audit work for their clients in addition to the audit. This work is often of a higher value than the audit and, again, makes it difficult for the auditor to be completely independent as they potentially could lose a great deal of fee income.

- Accountancy bodies such as the ACCA, the Institute of Chartered Accountants in England and Wales (ICAEW) and the Chartered Institute of Management Accountants (CIMA) are aware of this and issue codes of conduct and ethical guidelines that they require their members to comply with.

The preparation of accounting information

- Ethics in the preparation of business information starts in the individual entity with those responsible for preparing the entity's financial statements.

- A key role for professional accountants is to drive the ethics process from the bottom up, ensuring that the financial statements have been prepared in accordance with accounting standards and present a true and fair view.

- One of the issues in preparing financial information is the pressure that may be put on individuals by officers of the organisation who are acting unethically. If an individual's senior is asking him or her to prepare financial information in a misleading way, then it can be very difficult to speak up and refuse to do what is being asked for.

- In many cases, accountants know what they should do, but often there are adverse consequences for them if they take a stand. It takes a great deal of courage to speak out and potentially lose one's job for doing so.

- Ethical codes of conduct take into account the accountant and business and offer guidance on how to deal with ethical issues.

- Some accountancy bodies, such as the ICAEW and the CIMA, operate ethics helplines where members can phone for advice on ethical issues facing them.

Ethical conflicts of interest

Situations may arise in which an accountant might be asked to behave (or might be tempted to behave) in a way that conflicts with ethical standards and guidelines.

Conflicts of interest could relate to unimportant matters, but they might also involve fraud or some other illegal activity. Examples of such ethical conflicts of interest are as follows:

- There could be pressure from an overbearing supervisor, manager or director, adversely affecting the accountant's integrity.

- An accountant might mislead his or her employer as to the amount of experience or expertise they have, when in reality the expert advice of someone else should be sought.

- An accountant might be asked to act contrary to a technical or professional standard. Divided loyalty between the accountant's superior and the required professional standards of conduct could arise.

- A conflict of interest could arise when the employer publishes (or proposes to publish) misleading information that will benefit the employer, and may or may not benefit the accountant personally as well.

Resolution of ethical conflicts of interest

Conflicts of interest can arise in so many different ways that it would be difficult to provide a detailed set of guidelines for their resolution.

Accountants faced with conflicts should evaluate their significance. Unless they are so insignificant that they can be ignored, the accountant should consider the safeguards that are available for their elimination or reduction.

For example, it may be possible to:

- obtain advice from within the employing organisation, an independent professional adviser or a relevant professional body

- invoke a formal dispute resolution process within the employing organisation

- seek legal advice.

Ethical implications of preparing corporate reports

- Preparers of financial information must prepare that information honestly and fairly. Financial information may be relied upon by users of the financial statements, investors and potential investors, banks, suppliers, etc.

- Such information must be prepared in accordance with accounting standards so that it complies with current practice and presents a true and fair view.

- If financial information is not prepared in this manner, the risk is that is does not show a true and fair view of the performance and position of the entity and is misleading.

- Users who make decisions based on the information reported stand to lose out if it subsequently turns out that the entity is not what it seems.

- This was certainly the case in Enron who misstated five years of financial statements, reporting profits rather than losses. Shares in Enron became worthless and many investors and employees lost a lot of money.

Expandable text - Sarbanes-Oxley

Sarbanes-Oxley

The Sarbanes-Oxley Act 2002 was introduced in the US after a series of corporate accounting scandals. Public trust in accounting and financial reporting practices was declining due to the number of scandals uncovered, such as those at– Enron, Worldcom and Tyco.

It has been described as 'corporate accountability legislation'. Unlike the UK, the US has taken a strong legislative and regulatory route for the achievement of good corporate governance.

The Act itself contains various specific requirements:

- The Act places personal responsibility for the accuracy of a company's financial statements on its chief executive officer (CEO) and the chief financial officer (CFO, the equivalent of the finance director in the UK).

- All companies with a US listing must provide a signed certificate to the Securities and Exchange Commission vouching for the accuracy of the company's financial statements, signed by the CEO and CFO. There must be such a certificate for each report containing financial information that is filed with the SEC by the company.

- The CEO and CFO are therefore required to take direct responsibility for the accuracy of their company's financial statements. (This requirement is more specific than the provisions in the UK Combined Code, under which the responsibility for preparing the financial statements and a going concern statement lies with the board as a whole.)

- This requirement applies to foreign companies with a US listing, as well as to US companies.

- The SEC also requires the CEO and CFO to certify in each quarterly and annual report:
  - the accuracy of the information in the report
  - the fairness of the financial information.

- The report should contain information about the effectiveness of the company's 'disclosure controls and procedures' and its internal controls over financial reporting. This should be covered by the certifications.

- The CEO and CFO must return bonuses to the company, including equity or incentive compensation awards, awarded to them in the preceding twelve months, if their company's financial statements are re-stated due to material non-compliance with accounting rules and standards.

Increased financial disclosures

The Act includes a number of provisions for greater or more rapid disclosure of financial information.

- In its financial reports, the company must disclose details about its off-balance sheet transactions and their material effects.

- Material changes should be disclosed on a 'rapid and current basis'. The Act gave responsibility to the SEC for making the detailed regulations. Material changes should include matters such as creating a new off-balance sheet transaction, a decision to make a one-off writing down charge, or the loss of a contract with a major customer.

Internal control report

Companies should include a report on 'internal control over financial reporting' in their annual report. This internal control report must:

- include a statement of management's responsibility for an adequate internal control system

- identify the framework used to evaluate internal control

- provide an assessment by management of the effectiveness of internal control and any material weakness.

In addition, there must be an annual evaluation of the internal controls by the company's external auditors, who must provide an 'attestation' about them.

In other words, the external auditors must provide a statement confirming that the internal controls are sufficiently effective.

Amendments

In 2007 the SEC amended the requirements of Sarbanes-Oxley in relation to the assessment of internal control as the current compliance was costly and time consuming.

The changes are principles-based and require management to design controls to prevent financial misstatement and assess their effectiveness according to a risk based review.

Audit committee

Stock exchanges are prohibited from listing the securities of any company that does not comply with certain audit committee requirements. These include the following:

- Every member of the audit committee should be independent.
- The audit committee must have responsibility for the appointment and compensation of the external auditors.
- The audit committee must have responsibility for the oversight of the work of the external auditors.
- The committee must establish procedures for whistleblowers who raise concerns about questionable accounting or auditing matters.

Auditors and the audit

Restrictions have been placed on the types of non-audit work that can be carried out by the audit firm for a client company. Prohibited services include:

- book-keeping services and other services related to the accounting records or financial statements of the company
- the design and implementation of financial information systems
- actuarial services
- valuation services
- internal auditing (outsourced)

- legal services

- management functions

- broker/dealer or investment advice services.

Tax services are specifically permitted by the Act, unless they come within a prohibited category of non-audit services.

There is a compulsory five-year rotation of both the lead audit partner and the concurring partner working on the audit of a corporate client.

It is illegal for the directors and officers of a company to coerce, manipulate, mislead or fraudulently influence an auditor, in the knowledge that such action, if successful, could make the financial statements materially misleading.

US stock exchange rules

Following the Sarbanes-Oxley Act and regulations by the SEC, the national securities exchanges in the US were required to develop corporate governance rules for companies whose shares are listed on the exchange. The rules drawn up by the New York Stock Exchange can be compared directly with a number of the principles and provisions in the UK Combined Code.

The majority of the board of directors should be independent directors. 'We believe requiring a majority of independent directors will increase the quality of board oversight and lessen the possibility of damaging conflicts of interest.' The definition of 'independent' is quite strict.

Example

The chief financial officer of Cardinal Bankshares, a Virginia company, raised concerns with his superiors about insider trading, faulty internal controls and irregularities in financial reporting. The company initiated an investigation into his whistle blowing allegations, but he became sufficiently concerned to call in a lawyer to give him legal representation.

The company sacked the individual, alleging that he had failed to comply in an internal audit, and he took his case to court under the Sarbanes-Oxley legislation.

The court ruled (March 2004) that the individual had been sacked because of his whistle blowing. It ordered the company to re-employ him with back-pay, to reimburse his legal fees and to pay damages.

This was the first reported case of the use in a court of the Sarbanes-Oxley legislation.

Expandable text - Codes of ethics

Professional accountants are expected to act with honesty and integrity and the accounting bodies to which they belong provide a code of ethics by which they require their members to abide.

Expandable text - Consequences of unethical behaviour

The consequences of unethical behaviour in deliberately presenting incorrect financial information, or failing to audit such information properly, are severe. Many accountants have been fined or jailed for not fulfilling their professional duties.

Consequences for preparers of financial statements

As can be seen from the review of the Enron fraud in section 1, the consequences for deliberately preparing false accounting information and lying to the stock market brings severe penalties. The senior management at Enron were given long prison sentences and the fraud brought about the downfall of the company.

The consequences for individuals include:

- prison sentence
- fines or repayments of amounts fraudulently taken
- loss of professional reputation
- being prevented from acting as a director or officer of a public company in the future
- possibility of being expelled by professional accountancy body, if membership held.

It can be difficult to pluck up the courage to report fraudulent behaviour as the consequences for the individuals concerned can be frightening. These can include losing their job, losing their professional reputation in the firm, and being prevented from testifying in legal cases in the future.

Consequences for auditors of financial statements

The consequences for auditors can be as severe as those for the preparers of financial statements. They include:

- the audit firm being taken to court and charged with a criminal offence
- individual partners of the audit firm being banned from audit work
- loss of reputation leading to the loss of clients and income

- fines or compensation payable
- investigation by accounting body, such as ACCA or ICAEW.

Arthur Andersen, the Enron auditor, ceased operating because of the effect of the scandal. Clients moved to other audit firms and Arthur Andersen was prosecuted for obstructing the course of justice.

Expandable text - Ethical & professional issue

Question:

An entity is considering entering into a number of leasing agreements. It is aware of the required accounting treatment of leases based upon IAS 17, including how to distinguish between finance and operating leases.

The nature of the lease agreements is that the entity would take on substantially the risks and rewards associated with owning the assets concerned. However, the finance director of the entity is in discussion with the leasing company to establish whether, having agreed the terms and conditions of the leasing agreements, they would be willing to refer to the agreements as operating leases. If this was done, the entity would then regard the agreements as operating leases and would account for the leases on that basis. One possibility would be to have an initial lease period which would indicate that it was an operating lease, with a secondary lease period on advantageous terms so that it would be taken up by the entity.

Additionally, the finance director has heard that reporting standards dealing with leases may be revised, such that all leases will be accounted for in the same way. The finance director has therefore come to the conclusion that the current reporting standard need not be followed if it is expected to be replaced at some later date.

Required:

Discuss why an entity may seek to do this, explain the accounting treatment for leases and evaluate the ethical and professional issues arising from this situation.

Answer - Ethical and professional issue

An entity may seek to exclude liabilities from its statement of financial position in order to improve the view presented by the statement of financial position. Additionally, the annual depreciation charge on such assets, (which should be capitalised) and finance costs associated with the lease obligation will also be excluded from the statement of comprehensive income. There would also be operating lease rentals wrongly included within expenses.

If liabilities are excluded from the statement of financial position, accounting ratios such as measures of gearing will be misstated. This may be particularly important for current or potential providers of loan finance who may rely upon this financial information as a basis for their decision-making.

Similarly, performance and investment appraisal measures, such as return on capital employed and earnings per share may also be distorted, leading to inappropriate decisions being made by users of that financial information.

If the finance director is successful in achieving a misrepresentation of the leases, the financial statements may not show a true and fair view. The reliability of the financial statements would have been undermined. It would also result in a lack of comparability with financial information from other companies who have correctly applied the relevant reporting standard.

The requirements of IAS 17 are that leases which transfer substantially all of the risks and rewards of ownership are regarded as finance leases. Such leases should be capitalised as assets, and depreciated over their expected useful life to the business. The loan obligation should also be capitalised, with loan repayments and finance costs recognised over the lease term.

Any lease not meeting the definition of a finance lease is regarded as being an operating lease. The accounting treatment for operating leases is to regard them as rental agreements and spread the total payments associated with such leases over the lease period on a straight-line basis. There may be an accrual for amounts paid in advance or arrears at the reporting date.

The terms of the lease should be evaluated using the expected lease term, including any secondary term which is expected to taken up. Therefore, if the lease is classified and treated as an operating lease, it would be an inappropriate accounting treatment.

The finance director is likely to be a professionally qualified accountant. If this is the case, he or she will be bound by a professional and ethical code by virtue of their membership of a professional accountancy institute, such as ACCA. Failure to uphold the ethical and professional standards expected of a professional accountant may leave the individual concerned liable to criminal penalties if they have committed an offence or liable to civil action for damages if others suffered financial loss as a result of their action. In the content of being an employee, the finance director may face the possibility of disciplinary action, which could result in dismissal from their post.

In principle, reporting standards should be complied with if financial statements are to give a true and fair view. If departure from a reporting standard is done in order for the financial statements to show a true and fair view, this would be an unusual situation, and would need to be explained and justified in the supporting notes. The potential replacement of a reporting standard is not, in itself, a good enough reason not to apply the current standard, unless it has been formally withdrawn..

If the ACCA ethical guide is used as a basis for evaluating the actions of the finance director, issues of professional competence should be considered. It would be expected that the finance director is aware of, and understands the requirements of, IAS 17. Competence may be developed from a combination of practical work experience, technical expertise and professional qualification. Where an individual has achieved competence, this should be maintained by practical experience and Continuing Professional Development (CPD) which is mandatory for professionally qualified accountants.

Associated with competence is due care and skill in the performance of work or discharge of responsibilities. Application of due care and skill may be regarded as the application f competence. If the finance director did not perform his or her work with the required degree of care, they would be negligent in the performance of their duties.

A more insidious interpretation could be that the finance director is seeking to deliberately distort the financial information presented to others. This may be due to seeking personal gain, such as achieving a performance indicator used to determine eligibility for bonus payments. Such behaviour will call into question the professional integrity of the finance director if they knowingly misrepresent financial information they are responsible for.

Professional accountants should also be objective in performance of their work. This means that they should be free from bias and act in an open and honest manner in the performance of their work. Clearly, if integrity can be questioned, it is likely that objectivity will also be compromised and undermined.

A further issue is the perception of poor professional behaviour by the finance director. This will adversely affect the professional reputation of the individual concerned. Furthermore, it will undermine the professional reputation of qualified accountants generally in the eyes of the general public. By falling short of the high standards expected from a professionally qualified accountant, they leave themselves exposed to the possibility of disciplinary action by their institute.

If such an action is pursued and proven, the finance director may be liable to a range of disciplinary sanctions as follows:

- Warning or admonishment
- Fine
- Suspension o membership
- Exclusion from membership

Chapter summary

Ethical issues facing the accountant

- An accountant must be independent and must speak out if a client is following irregular accounting practices
- Accountants must follow the Codes of Ethics for the professional body of which they are a member
- Financial information must be prepared so that it meets accounting standards and shows a true and fair view/fair presentation of the financial position of the entity
- An employer may ask an accountant to act unethically by preparing the financial statements in a way that does not show the true picture

Codes of ethics

The principles in the ACCA Code of Ethics and Conduct are:

- Integrity
- Objectivity
- Professional competence and due care
- Confidentiality
- Professional behaviour

Consequences of unethical behaviour

The consequences of failing to act ethically are many and can be severe. They include:

- Prison sentence
- Fines or repayments of amounts taken fraudulently
- Loss of professional reputation
- Being prevented from acting in the same capacity in the future
- Investigation by professional accountancy body

8

The financial reporting framework

Chapter learning objectives

Upon completion of this chapter you will be able to:

- evaluate the consistency and clarity of corporate reports

- assess the insight into financial and operational risks provided by corporate reports

- discuss the usefulness of corporate reports in making investment decisions

- evaluate models adopted by standards setters

- discuss the use of the Framework for the preparation and presentation of financial statements (Framework) in the production of accounting standards

- assess the success of the Framework in introducing rigorous and consistent accounting standards

- identify the relationship between accounting theory and practice

- critically evaluate accounting principles and practices used in corporate reporting.

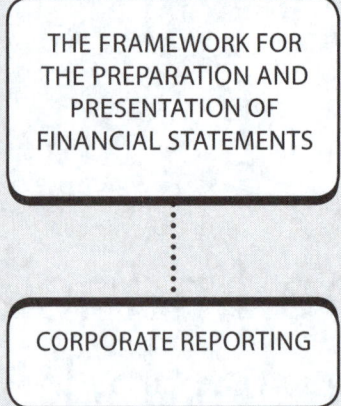

THE FRAMEWORK FOR
THE PREPARATION AND
PRESENTATION OF
FINANCIAL STATEMENTS

CORPORATE REPORTING

Expandable text - Framework document

This section briefly recaps the IASB's Framework. This has been examinable in previous papers and should be familiar to you.

The purpose of the Framework

The purpose of the Framework is to:

(a) assist in the development of future accounting standards and in the review of existing standards

(b) provide a basis for reducing the number of alternative accounting treatments permitted by international standards

(c) assist national standard setters in developing national standards

(d) assist preparers of financial statements in applying international standards and in dealing with issues not covered by international standards

(e) assist auditors in forming an opinion whether financial statements conform to international standards

(f) assist users of financial statements in interpreting the information contained in financial statements complying with international standards

(g) provide information about the IASB's approach to setting international standards.

The content of the Framework

Key points

- The objective of financial statements is to provide useful information to users.

- Financial statements complying with international standards should meet the common needs of most users. However, financial statements do not provide all the information that users may need because they concentrate on the financial effects of past events.

- The user groups of financial statements vary, including equity investors, employees, lenders, suppliers, customers, government and the public.

- The underlying assumptions of financial statements are the accrual basis and going concern.

Underlying assumptions

The underlying assumptions governing the financial statements are:

The accruals basis

The accruals basis of accounting means that the effects of transactions and other events are recognised as they occur and not as cash or its equivalent is received or paid.

Going concern

The going concern basis assumes that the entity has neither the need nor the intention to liquidate or curtail materially the scale of its operations.

Expandable text - Qualitative characteristics

The qualitative characteristics of financial statements

The Framework states that there are four qualitative characteristics that make information in financial statements useful to users:

- relevance - predictive and confirmatory value to users

- reliability - users are able to base their decisions upon the information

- comparability - of entity financial statements over time, and also between entities. This requires disclosure and application of consistent accounting policies, together with disclosure of comparative amounts.

- understandability - this assumes that the user has a reasonable knowledge of business and accounting to understand the technical content of financial statements.

There is also the threshold quality of materiality - misstatement or omission of an item in the financial statements is regarded as material if it affects the decisions of users of those financial statements. In addition, relevance may be lost if there is undue delay in the reporting of financial information. The qualitative characteristics noted above are also subject to costs of providing the information should be outweighed by the benefits to users of having access to that information.

Fair presentation

- Financial statements are frequently described as giving a true and fair view of, or presenting fairly, the position and performance of an entity.

- The Framework does not define these ideas, but compliance with international standards and the Framework will help to achieve them.

The elements of financial statements

The Framework identifies five elements of financial statements:

An **asset** is a resource controlled by the entity as a result of past events and from which future economic benefits are expected to flow to the entity.

A **liability** is a present obligation of the entity arising from past events, the settlement of which is expected to result in an outflow from the entity of resources embodying economic benefits.

Equity is the residual interest in an entity's assets after deducting all its liabilities.

Income is the increase in economic benefits during an accounting period.

Expenses are decreases in economic benefits during an accounting period.

Recognition of the elements of financial statements

An item should be recognised in the financial statements if:

- it meets one of the definitions of an **element**

- it is probable that any future economic benefit associated with the item will flow to or from the entity

- the item can be measured at a monetary amount (cost or value) with sufficient reliability.

The recognition of assets and liabilities falls into three stages:

- initial recognition (e.g. the purchase of a non-current asset)

- subsequent remeasurement (e.g. revaluation of the above asset)

- derecognition (e.g. sale of the asset).

Derecognition

Derecognition occurs when:

- an event occurs that eliminates a previously recognised asset or liability (e.g. a trade receivable is irrecoverable)

- there is no longer sufficient evidence to support continued recognition. For example, a reorganisation provision may no longer be needed.

Measurement of the elements of financial statements

The Framework identifies four possible measurement base, with no particular measurement basis stated as being preferred as follows:

Historical cost

Assets are recorded at the amount of cash or cash equivalents paid to acquire them.

Liabilities are recorded at the proceeds received in exchange for the obligation, or at the amounts expected to be paid to satisfy the liability.

Current cost

Assets are carried at their current purchase price.

Liabilities are carried at the undiscounted amount currently required to settle them.

Realisable value

Assets are carried at the amount that could currently be obtained by an orderly disposal. Liabilities are carried at their settlement values – the amount to be paid to satisfy them in the normal course of business.

Although historical cost is the most common basis, the others are often used to modify historical cost. For example, inventories are usually carried at the lower of cost and net realisable value, investments may be carried at market value and pension liabilities are carried at their present value.

Present value

Assets are carried at the present discounted value of the future net cash inflows that the item is expected to generate in the normal course of business. Liabilities are carried at the present discounted value of the expected cash outflows necessary to settle them.

Assessment of the Framework

- The Framework provides a conceptual underpinning for IFRS.

- One of the objectives of the Framework is to provide a basis for the formulation of IFRS.

- By providing definitions of assets, liabilities, etc. and guidance on recognition and measurement, the Framework forms a basis for dealing with any accounting issues that arise which are not covered by accounting standards.

- The Framework's approach builds corporate reporting around the definitions of assets and liabilities and the criteria for recognising and measuring them in the statement of financial position.

- This approach views accounting from the perspective of the statement of financial position ('a balance sheet perspective'), whereas most companies would not consider the measurement and recognition of assets and liabilities as the starting point for the determination of profit.

- In many jurisdictions, the financial statements form the basis of dividend payments, the starting point for the assessment of taxation, and often the basis for executive remuneration. A balance sheet fair value system, which the IASB seems to favour, would have a major impact on the above elements.

Expandable text - Current developments

Current developments - Conceptual Framework for Financial Reporting 2010

This is a long-term joint project between IFRS and the US FASB, which was first agreed in 2004. The end point of the eight-stage project will be approval of a single, self-contained document which will create a foundation for the development of future accounting standards that are principles based, internally consistent and internationally converged. Ultimately, it will replace the Framework for the Preparation and Presentation of Financial Statements which was first published in 1989.

As this project progresses and individual chapters are approved, the new Conceptual Framework for Financial Reporting 2010 will be updated and the superseded provisions of the original Framework document, currently included as chapter 4, will be deleted.

The Conceptual Framework for Financial Reporting 2010 project has the following phases:

Phase A – objectives and qualitative characteristics

In September 2010, the IASB and FASB approved the following chapters of the updated 2010 Conceptual Framework:

- Chapter 1 The objective of general purpose financial reporting
- Chapter 3 Qualitative characteristics of useful financial information.

There is no significant change to the underlying purpose and objectives of the Framework as established in the 1989 document and considered earlier within this chapter of the text. The underlying assumptions of accruals and going concern are currently retained within chapter 1 para 17 and chapter 4 para 1 respectively of the 2010 document.

However, there is a change within chapter 3 of the 2010 document dealing with qualitative characteristics of useful financial information. There are two fundamental qualitative characteristics of relevance and faithful representation, and each is considered in turn:

Relevance:
Relevant financial information is regarded as information which is capable of making a difference in decisions made by users of that information. It will be regarded as being relevant if it has either predictive value and/or confirmatory value to a user.

Relevance is supported by materiality considerations. Information is regarded as material if its omission or misstatement could influence the decisions made by users of that information.

Faithful representation:

For financial information to be faithfully presented, it must be complete, neutral and free from error. Therefore, it must comprise information necessary for a proper understanding, it must be without bias or manipulation and clearly described.

In addition to the two fundamental qualitative characteristics, there are four enhancing characteristics which enhance the usefulness of information which is regarded as relevant and faithfully represented as follows:

Comparability:

Information is more useful if it can be compared with similar information about other entities, or even the same entity over different time periods. Consistency of methodology, approach or presentation helps to achieve comparability of financial information. Permitting different accounting treatments for similar items is likely to reduce comparability.

Verifiability:

Verifiability of financial information provides assurance to users regarding its credibility and reliability. It means that different, knowledgeable and independent observers could reach consensus, although not necessarily complete agreement, that a particular presentation of an item or items is a faithful representation.

Timeliness:

This means uses should have information within a timescale which is likely to influence their decisions.

Understandability:

Appropriate classification, characterisation and presentation of information will help to make it understandable. For example, standard formats of information and standard accounting treatments help users to understand the information presented.

Notwithstanding the fundamental qualitative and enhancing qualitative characteristics of financial reporting information, it is important that costs incurred in reporting that information are outweighed by the benefits of providing that information. Ultimately, information which is relevant and faithfully represented leads to improved confidence in decisions made by users of that information and results in the more efficient working of the capital markets.

Phase B – elements and recognition

The objectives of this phase of the project are to refine and converge the IASB and FASB frameworks as follows:

- Revise and clarify the definitions of asset and liability.
- Resolve differences regarding other elements and their definitions.
- Revise the recognition criteria concepts to eliminate differences and provide a basis for resolving issues such as derecognition and unit of account.

Based upon progress to September 2010, draft definitions are as follows:

- An asset of an entity is a present economic resource to which the entity has either a right or other access that others do not have
- A liability of an entity is a present economic obligation for which the entity is the obligor

The principal reasons for reviewing and potentially changing these definitions are as follows:

(1) The definitions place too much emphasis on identifying the future inflow or outflow of economic benefits, instead of focusing on the item that presently exists, an economic resource or economic obligation.

(2) The definitions place undue emphasis on identifying the past transactions or events that gave rise to the asset or the liability, instead of focusing on whether the entity has an economic resource or obligation at the reporting date.

(3) It is unclear how the definitions apply to contractual obligations.

Phase C – measurement

In July 2010 the IASB reached the following tentative decisions relating to the development of preliminary views for the measurement chapter of the Conceptual Framework:

- Implications of the objective of financial reporting for measurement - The best way to satisfy the objective of financial reporting through measurement is to consider the effect of a particular measurement selection on all of the financial statements, instead of emphasising the statement of financial position over the statement of comprehensive income or vice versa.

- General implications of the fundamental qualitative characteristics for measurement - Selection of bases of measurement should be related to the qualitative requirements that financial information should be relevant and faithfully presented.

- Specific implications of the fundamental qualitative characteristics for historical cost and fair value - The objective of selecting a measurement for a particular item is to maximise the information about the reporting entity's prospects for future cash flows subject to the ability to faithfully represent it at a cost that is justified by the benefits.

- What should the measurement chapter accomplish - The measurement chapter should list and describe possible measurements, arrange or classify the measurements in a manner that facilitates standard-setting decisions, describe the advantages and disadvantages of each measurement in terms of the qualitative characteristics of useful financial information, and discuss at a conceptual level how the qualitative characteristics and cost constraint should be considered together in identifying an appropriate measurement. Without prescribing specific measurements for particular assets and liabilities, the measurement chapter should discuss how its concepts might be applied to individual classes of assets and liabilities.

Phase D – the reporting entity

An ED was issued in July 2010 dealing with this topic which will comprise chapter 2 of the 2010 Conceptual Framework. Typically, this is likely to be either an individual entity or a combined group of entities under common control.

The following phases of the project are not yet active at September 2010:

- Phase E – presentation and disclosure
- Phase F – purpose and status
- Phase G – application to not-for-profit entities
- Phase H – remaining issues

Current developments - Fair value measurements

The problems with historical cost

There are a number of shortcomings of the historical cost (HC) basis of accounting.

- The HC method ignores the current value of assets; the amounts reported in the statement of financial position are out of date and do not give a true picture of the resources employed by the entity.

- As no account is made of the changing value of money over time, the trends reported may be difficult to interpret.

- Current revenues are matched with historical costs. If an item of inventory is purchased at the beginning of the year and not sold for six months, the cost of that inventory may have increased and the profit reported is based on an out-of-date asset value.

Fair value measurement - recent developments

The FASB and the IASB are both involved in a project on fair value measurement with the following objectives:

- to establish a single source of guidance for all fair value measurements;

- to clarify the definition of fair value and related guidance;

- to enhance disclosures about fair value measurements; and

- to increase the convergence of IFRS and US GAAP.

The expectation is that a reporting standard will be issued in the third quarter of 2010; however, as at early September 2010, it had not been published.

To ensure consistency between IFRSs and US generally accepted accounting principles (GAAP), the proposals incorporate recent guidance on fair value measurement published by FASB and are consistent with a report of the IASB's Expert Advisory Panel published in October 2008 on fair value measurement in illiquid markets. This project forms part of a long-term programme by the IASB and the FASB to achieve convergence of IFRSs and US GAAP. The IASB's starting point in developing the ED was the equivalent US standard, SFAS 157 Fair Value Measurements as amended. The proposed definition of fair value is identical to the definition in SFAS 157 and the supporting guidance is largely consistent with US GAAP.

In the ED, fair value is defined as the price that would be received to sell an asset or paid to transfer a liability in an orderly transaction between market participants at the measurement date.

Current developments - Credit Risk in Liability Management (DP/2009/2)

Arguably, questions about the role of credit risk in liability measurement have generated more comment and controversy than any other aspect of fair value measurement. For example; should current measurements of liabilities (including fair value) incorporate the chance that an entity will fail to perform as required? If not, what are the alternatives?

An entity's credit standing affects the credit risk of its liabilities, but the effect may be different from one liability to another. For example, a liability which is secured against assets of the business has less credit risk than an entity's other liabilities. For those other liabilities, the credit risk of the entity translates directly to the credit risk of those liabilities. The IASB has stressed that it is the particular liability that is being measured, and the relevant credit risk is the risk associated with that liability, rather than all liabilities collectively.

The DP outlines the three most often-cited arguments in favour of including credit risk and the three most often-cited arguments against. This paper includes within its scope all current measurements of liabilities. Standard-setters have concluded that the fair value of a liability is a price and, thus, necessarily includes the credit standing of that liability. It does not follow that other current measurements of the liability should do so. Alternative current measurements of liabilities might include, for example:

- fulfilment value, as it is being developed in the IASBs joint project with FASB on insurance contracts;

- the value at which the liability could be settled with the counterparty;

- fair value, but excluding the effects of credit risk, and

- the value at which the liability could be transferred in a transaction permitted by industry regulators.

Just as there are several alternative current measures of a liability, there are several reasons why the reported amount of a liability might change. Some of those changes do not involve changes in credit risk, for example, changes in expected cash flows or currency exchange rates.

Some liability measurements have always included the effects of credit risk. Explicit consideration of the idea in standards and concepts is relatively recent.

In 2000 the FASB published Concepts Statement No 7 Using Cash Flow Information and Present Value in Accounting Measurements. That Statement described the role of present value in 'fresh start' measurements of the fair value of assets and liabilities. In doing so, it could not avoid the question of the entity's credit standing. Within that document, the FASB said 'The most relevant measure of a liability always reflects the credit standing of the entity obligated to pay'.

Expandable text - Corporate reporting

Definition

Corporate reports aim to provide information about the resources and performance of the reporting entity to users of such reports.

Reporting corporate performance

- Traditional corporate reports include historical financial information regarding the operating and financial performance of the entity.

- Financial information and ratios can be supplemented by commentary on the performance and strategy of the company, such as the chairman's report.

- In recent years, non-financial information has become more prevalent. More and more users of financial information require information on an entity's policies towards the environment, employees and society.

- IFRSs do not require these non-financial reports, but many companies produce them voluntarily.

- Investors require up-to-date information and in this sense financial reports do not meet this need. By the time the information is published, it is already several months out of date.

- Up-to-date financial information is freely available to investors from online news and market-information companies, databases and financial statements.

Usefulness of corporate reporting

- Financial reports will always need to be produced to satisfy statutory requirements, such as filing accounts or for the preparation of tax returns.

- As the harmonisation of accounting standards takes place on a global scale, corporate reports become more comparable. This is particularly useful for investors who should be able to compare financial information from different entities that are located in different countries.

- The number of disclosures in financial statements is increasing and companies have to be more transparent in their reporting. Recent developments have continued this trend. For example, IFRS 8 **Segment reporting** requires segment information to be reported on the basis that information is reported to the management of an entity, thus showing how the company is structured and assessed internally.

- The IASB's discussion paper **Management commentary** (see chapter 20) is concerned with the adoption of a formal process of commentary on the performance of the business. Entities should disclose the nature of the business as well as its objectives, strategies results, prospects and performance measures.

- It is in the interests of an entity to make its information as accessible to users as possible and many corporate reports include a great deal of information on strategy and activities of entities.

- Increased disclosure of non-financial information such as environmental and social reports is also a positive move for users of financial statements, who can see the progress the entity is making in certain areas.

Compliance with accounting standards

- Despite the number of accounting standards in issue and the requirement for accounts to present a true and fair view, there are still a number of companies that fail to comply with requirements of the standards.

- The Financial Reporting Review Panel (FRRP) in the UK has the aim of ensuring that both public and private companies comply with the Companies Act and accounting standards. It has expanded its role to assess financial statements prepared under IFRS in the UK.

- It has the authority to require the directors of a company to amend their financial statements to remove any departures from requirements.

- There is no equivalent under IFRS; individual countries are each responsible for policing compliance.

Expandable text - Question and answer

Question:

Although it may come as a surprise to many non-accountants, the accounting profession internationally has encountered a great deal of problems in arriving at robust definitions for the 'elements' of financial statements. Defining assets, liabilities, and gains and losses (income and expenditure) has been particularly problematical. These definitions form the core of any conceptual Framework that is to be used as a basis for preparing financial statements. It is also in this area that the International Accounting Standards Committee's Framework for the Preparation and Presentation of Financial Statements (Framework) has come in for some criticism.

It seems that the current accounting treatment of certain items does not (fully) agree with definitions in the Framework. A major objective of the Framework is to exclude from the statement of financial position items that are neither assets nor liabilities; and to make 'off balance sheet' assets and liabilities more visible by putting them on the statement of financial position whenever practicable.

(a) **Critically discuss the definition of assets and liabilities contained in the Framework**.

Your answer should explain the importance of the definitions and the relevance of each component of the definitions.

(b) Below is a series of transactions or events that have arisen in relation to Worthright. The company's year end is 31 March 20X1.

   (i) Worthright has entered into two contracts. The first contract entails Worthright installing and maintaining a telephone system in a building owned by Cranbourne. The installation will be completed by June 20X1 and the contract will run for ten years. Worthright will receive a payment of $200,000 per annum. Worthright has installed many similar systems and it can reliably estimate that the annual cost of the contract will amount to $150,000 per annum.

In order to secure supplies, Worthright entered into a second contract agreeing to purchase 50,000 units of gas heating fuel per annum for the next five years at a price of $20 per unit. The contract, which is non-cancellable, was signed on 20 February 20X1. The supply of gas will commence on 1 September 20X1.

Since the contract was signed there have been several large discoveries of this type of gas field and as a consequence the market price of the gas has fallen to $14 per unit. This market price is expected to prevail for the whole of the period of Worthright's contract.

(ii) On 1 April 20X0 Worthright purchased a new office building at a cost of $1 million. The building has an estimated life of 50 years, but it contains a sophisticated air conditioning and heating system (included in the price of the building), which will require replacement every ten years at a cost of $100,000. Worthright intends to depreciate the building at $20,000 per annum and provide a further $10,000 each year to facilitate the replacement of the heating system

(iii) Worthright is approximately half way through a three-year contract to build a sugar refinery for Sweetness. The contract contains a severe penalty clause that would require Worthright to pay Sweetness $1.5 million if the contract is not completed by its due date of 30 September 20X2. Although the contract is currently on schedule, Worthright is not entirely confident that the penalty will be avoided. It therefore considers it prudent to provide for the penalty as a liability.

The refinery is being constructed under local building regulations, which require the builder of new properties to give a five-year warranty against defective materials and defective construction techniques. Worthright's past experience is that there are usually some warranty claims, but they are seldom of high value and in the past have been charged to the period in which they have arisen

(iv) Worthright undertakes a considerable amount of research and development work. Most of this work is done on its own behalf, but occasionally it undertakes this type of work for other companies. Before any of its own projects progress to the development stage, they are assessed by an internal committee, which carefully analyses all information relating to the project. This process has led to a very good record of development projects delivering profitable results. Despite this, Worthright deems it prudent to write off immediately all research and development work, including that which it does for other companies.

For the items (i) to (iv) above, discuss whether the transactions or events give rise to assets or liabilities; and describe how they should be recognised and measured under current International Accounting Standards and conventionally accepted practice.

Answer:

(a) **Importance of the definitions**:

The definitions of assets and liabilities are fundamental to the IASB's Framework. Apart from forming the obvious basis for the preparation of a statement of financial position, they are also the two elements of financial statements that are used to derive the other elements. Equity (ownership) interest is the residue of assets less liabilities. Gains and losses are changes in ownership interests, other than contributions from, and distributions to, the owners. In effect, a gain is an increase in an asset or a reduction of a liability whereas a loss is the reverse of this. Transactions with owners are defined in a straightforward manner in order to exclude them from the definitions of gains and losses.

Assets:

The IASB's Framework defines assets as 'a resource controlled by an entity as a result of past events and from which future economic benefits are expected to flow to the entity'. This definition is similar to equivalent definitions in the USA and UK. The first part of the definition 'a resource controlled by an entity' is a refinement of the principle that an asset must be owned by the entity. This refinement allows assets that are not legally owned by an entity, but over which the entity has the rights that are normally conveyed by ownership, such as the right to use or occupy an asset, to be recognised as an asset of the entity.

The essence of this approach is that an asset is not the physical item that one might expect it to be, such as a machine or a building, but it is the right to enjoy the future economic benefits that the asset will produce (normally future cash flows). Perhaps the best known example of this type of arrangement is a finance lease. Control not only allows the entity to obtain the economic benefits of assets but also to restrict the access of others to them. Where an entity develops an alternative manufacturing process that reduces future cash outflows in terms of lower cost of production, this too can be an asset. Assets can also arise where there is no legal control. The Framework cites the example of 'know-how' derived from a development activity. Where an entity has the capacity to keep this a secret, the entity controls the benefits that are expected to flow from it.

Notably, other versions of the definition of an asset (e.g. in the USA) refer to future economic benefits being probable. This wording recognises that all future economic benefits are subject to some degree of risk or uncertainty. The IASB deals with the 'probable' issue by saying that future economic benefits are only 'expected' and therefore need not be certain.

The reference to past events makes it clear that transactions arising after the reporting date that may lead to economic benefits cannot be treated as assets. The use of the word 'events' in this part of the definition recognises that it is not only transactions that can create assets or liabilities (see below), but other events such as 'legal wrongs' that may lead to damages claims. This aspect of the definition does cause some problems. For example, it could be argued that signing a profitable contract before the reporting date is an 'event' that gives rise to a future economic benefit. It is widely held that the justification for not recognising future profitable contracts as assets is that the rights and obligations under these contracts are equal (which is unlikely to be true) and also that the historical cost of 'signing' them is zero.

Liabilities:

The IASB defines liabilities as 'a present obligation of the entity arising from past events which is expected to result in an outflow from the entity of resources embodying economic benefits'. The IASB stress that the essential characteristic is the 'present obligation'. Although the definition is complementary to that of assets, it is perceived as less controversial. Most other parts of the definition have the same meaning as in the definition of assets, e.g. the terms 'economic benefits' and 'past events'.

Most liabilities are legal or contractual obligations to transfer known amounts of cash, e.g. trade payables and loans. Occasionally they may be settled other than for cash such as in a barter transaction, but this still constitutes transferring economic benefits. It is necessary to consider the principles and definitions in the Framework alongside those of the IASB's IAS 37 **Provisions, contingent liabilities and contingent assets**. Within the Framework the IASB introduces the concept of obligations arising from 'normal business practice' being liabilities. One such example is rectifying faults in goods sold even when the warranty period has expired. IAS 37 explores this principle more fully and refers to them as 'constructive' obligations. These occur where an entity creates a valid expectation that it will discharge responsibilities that it is not legally obliged to. This is usually as a result of past behaviour, or by commitments given in a published statement (e.g. voluntarily incurring environmental costs).

Where the exact amount of a liability is uncertain it is usually referred to as a provision.

Obligations may exist that are not expected to require 'transfers of economic benefits'. These again are described in IAS 37 and are more generally known as contingent liabilities. For example, where a holding company guarantees a subsidiary's loan.

Similar to assets, costs to be incurred in the future do not represent liabilities. This is because either the entity has the ability to avoid the costs, or if it cannot (e.g. where a contract exists), then incurring the cost would be matched by receiving an asset of equal value.

(b) (i) This example illustrates the asymmetry of accepted practice in accounting for profits and losses. Most people would consider the first contract, which is going to be profitable, to be an asset. It results from a past event (the signing of the contract) and in all probability will result in future economic benefits. Indeed, there have been examples of companies that were unsuccessful in bidding for a contract actually buying the company that was awarded the contract. This presumably occurs because the contract is seen to be a valuable asset.

Despite the nature of this contract appearing to be an asset, Worthright would not be able to recognise it as such in its statement of financial position. As noted in (a) the IASB consider that an uncompleted contra ct has both rights and obligations that are in balance, as well as the fact that the transaction has no historic cost. So despite an expected income stream of $200,000 with associated costs of the $150,000 per annum (which are clearly not in balance), this contract cannot be shown as an asset.

The second contract, by contrast, appears to represent an obligation. The company is committed to purchasing goods for the next five years at a price that is above current market prices. It is not immediately obvious that this contract will result in future losses, but if the gas is to be consumed by Worthright, then the losses are an opportunity cost of $6 per unit of fuel. If the gas is to be sold on by Worthright then, given the fall in market prices, it is unlikely that it will be sold at a profit. It is therefore highly likely that this represents an onerous contract for which a liability should be provided. More information and analysis would be needed to determine the amount of the liability.

(ii) On first impressions there may appear to be a liability for the replacement of the air conditioning and heating system. If the company wishes to use the property for the whole of its life then it will certainly have to replace the system several times. The past event is the purchase of the building and replacing the system will involve the future transfer of economic benefits. However, this analysis misses the important point that the company is not committed to using the building; it could choose to sell it. Even if it does not sell the building, it does not have to replace the system.

(1) The solution to the treatment of the building lies in IAS 16 **Property, plant and equipment**. Para 13 states that in certain circumstances it is appropriate to allocate the total expenditure on an asset to its component parts and to account for them separately. The building and the air conditioning system should be treated as separate assets and depreciated over their relative lives. The depreciation of the building will be $18,000 per annum ($1 million – $100,000/50 years) and the depreciation of the heating system will be $10,000 per annum ($100,000/10 years). When this approach is adopted, it becomes clear that if Worthright were to make a provision for the replacement of the system, as well as depreciating it, it would be 'double charging' for the asset.

(2) There are two aspects to consider here: whether (i) the penalty clause and (ii) the warranty represent liabilities. Arguably they are both contingent liabilities in that it will be future uncertain events that will determine whether an outflow of future economic benefits will arise. A careful consideration of the Framework's definition of a liability would result in the view that the penalty clause is not a liability. This is because there is no past event. One may consider the signing of the contract to be the past event, but this does not cause the liability. It would be finishing the contract late that would cause a liability, and this has not yet occurred. In effect, the penalty costs can be avoided by performing the contract as it was agreed, i.e. on time. Avoidable costs are not liabilities.

The warranty, on the other hand, should be considered as a liability under the requirements of IAS 37 **Provisions, contingent liabilities and contingent assets**. The signing of the contract gives rise to this potential liability. It is difficult to quantify (as it is in the future and it may not happen) and it may not be material. In principle the company's current policy of charging warranty costs to the period in which they arise is incorrect. These costs should be matched with the benefits from the contract, i.e. its revenues/profits. Although most warranty costs may be relatively small amounts, it is possible that a large claim could arise. Worthright should provide, as part of the contract costs, the best estimate of the cost of the warranty over the period of the contract.

(iv) For many years, research and development costs have represented the classic dilemma of whether they are an asset or an expense. If they result in future economic benefits, they are assets; if not, they are expenses. Unfortunately, the resolution to this question (at the time of preparing financial statements) lies in the future and is therefore unknown. Empirical research in the USA some time ago showed that less than 5% of all research resulted in profitable products, and perhaps, surprisingly, most projects that progressed through to development did not prove to be profitable either. From this evidence, based on probabilities, most research and development is not an asset.

In the case of the development expenditure of Worthright, it appears that it may satisfy the criteria in IAS 38 **Intangible assets** to be treated as an intangible asset, particularly in view of Worthright's impressive track record on development projects. More details would have to be obtained in order to determine whether the expenditure does qualify as an asset. If it does, the company's existing policy would not be permitted under IAS 38, as this says that if the recognition criteria are met, the expenditure should be capitalised. It does not offer a choice. Interestingly, under USA standards, development, expenditure is always written off, and other domestic standards (including the UK) allow a choice.

The above only applies to Worthright's own development costs. The company also performs research and development for clients and here the case is different. Although it is conducting research and development, it is in fact carrying out contract work. The costs of this research and development should be matched with the revenues it will bring. To the extent it has been invoiced to clients, it should be recognised as cost of sales in the income statement (not as research and development). Any unbilled costs should appear as a current asset under work in progress.

Expandable text - UK syllabus focus

The ACCA UK syllabus contains a requirement that candidates should be able to discuss and apply the key differences between UK GAAP and IFRS GAAP. The accounting requirements of UK GAAP anf IFRS GAAP are similar in this area; the key issues include the following:

The preparation of single company and group accounts in the UK is governed by the Companies Act 2006. The form and content of financial statements is specified in CA2006 and supplemented by IFRS or UK FRS (as applicable) to comply with the requirement that financial statements show a true and fair view.

KAPLAN PUBLISHING

Companies or groups must disclose the accounting framework used as the basis for the preparation of the financial statements. The normal expectation is that financial statements should comply with all relevant reporting standards to show a true and fair view. Where there has been departure from a reporting standard in order to give a true and fair view, this must be disclosed and explained within the financial statements.

For companies or groups listed on a stock exchange within the EU, they are obliged to prepare their annual financial statements in accordance with IFRS GAAP. Accounts for listed companies and groups should be filed at Companies House within six months of the annual reporting date. Typically, they will adopt a slightly different presentation style; the balance sheet is typically presented showing assets, together with equity and liabilities, rather than the net assets style of presentnation normally adopted under UK GAAP. There are also some differences in termonology bwteen the two frameworks as summarised below:

UK GAAP	IFRS GAAP
Balance sheet	Statement of financial position
Reserves	Equity
Profit and loss acount	Income statement
Statement of other recognised gains and losses	Other comprehensive income
Debtors	Receivables
Creditors	Payables
Corporation tax	Income tax
Turnover	Revenue
Minority interest	Non-controlling interest

Non-listed companies and groups can prepare and file their annual financial statements either in accordance with UK GAAP as regulated by the ASB, or in accordance with IFRS GAAP. For non-listed companies and groups, annual financial statements should be filed within nine months of the annual reporting date.

Chapter summary

The framework
- Underpins accounting standards
- Characteristics of useful information are:
  - relevant
  - reliable
  - understandable
  - comparable
- Defines assets, liabilities, gains and losses, ownership interest and contributions and distributions to owners

Corporate reporting
- Provide information about performance and resources of an entity to its users
- Financial information is historic, but there are many online companies providing up-to-date information
- Non-financial information is widely distributed with the annual report including environmental and social reports
- Future developments and strategies can be reported in the management commentary

9

Performance reporting

Chapter learning objectives

Upon completion of this chapter you will be able to:

- prepare reports relating to corporate performance for external stakeholders
- discuss the issues relating to the recognition of revenue
- evaluate proposed changes to reporting financial performance.

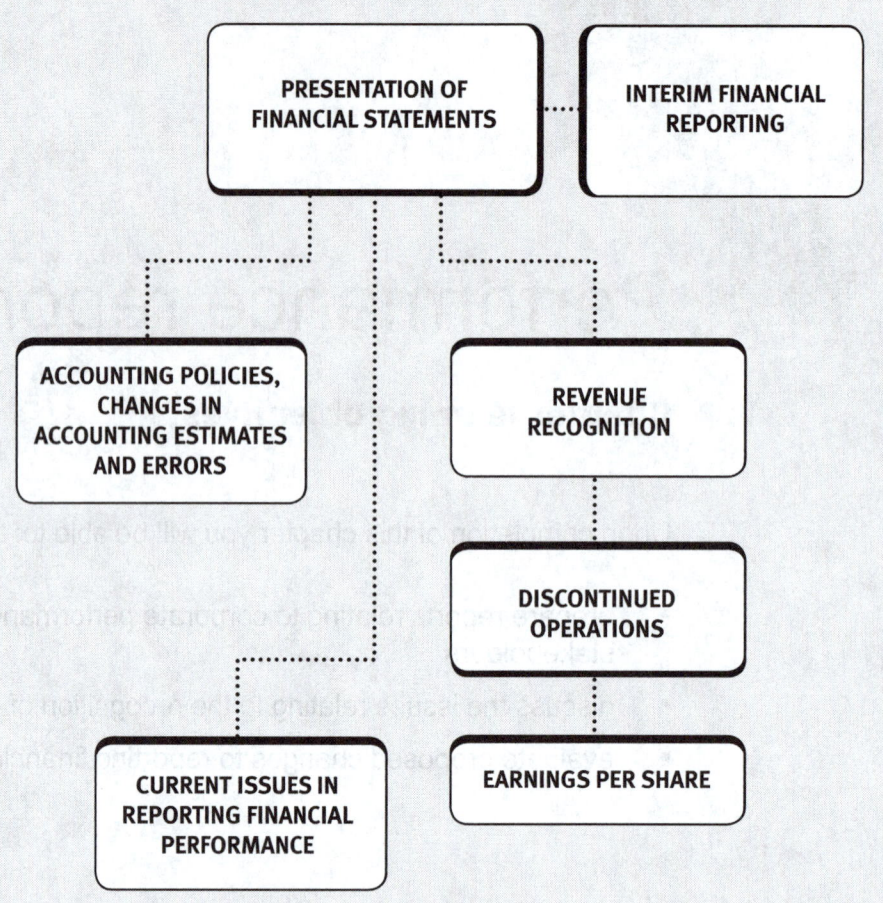

1 Presentation of financial statements (IAS 1 revised)

Expandable text - Components of financial statements

The IASB issued IAS 1 revised in September 2007. The intention of the revision was to aggregate information in the financial statements on the basis of shared characteristics and so improve the information provided to users.

Components of financial statements

A complete set of financial statements has the following components:

- a statement of financial position at the end of the reporting period

- a statement of comprehensive income for the period (or income statement and separate statement showing other comprehensive income)

- a statement of changes in equity for the period

- a statement of cash flows for the period

- accounting policies note and other explanatory notes.

- a statement of financial position at the beginning of the earliest comparative period when an entity applies an accounting policy retrospectively or corrects an error retrospectively

The titles used by IAS 1 are not mandatory. An entity may continue to use the previous title of balance sheet and cash flow statement.

Other reports and statements in the annual report, e.g. a financial review, an environmental report, a social report, etc, are outside the scope of this IFRS.

Statement of financial position

The statement of financial position is largely the same as the balance sheet presented in the previous version of IAS 1, with one exception:

- Reserves other than share capital and retained earnings are now referred to as 'other components of equity'.

Expandable text - Statement of comprehensive income

Statement of comprehensive income

Total comprehensive income is the realised profit or loss for the period plus other comprehensive income.

Other comprehensive income is income and expenses that are not recognised in profit or loss, but instead recognised directly in equity (reserves).

Other comprehensive income includes:

(a) changes in revaluation surplus

(b) actuarial gains and losses on defined benefit plans recognised in accordance with IAS 19 Employee Benefits

(c) gains and losses arising from translating the financial statements of a foreign operation

(d) gains and losses on remeasuring available-for-sale financial assets

(e) the effective portion of gains and losses on hedging instruments in a cash flow hedge

IAS 1 allows a choice of two presentations of comprehensive income:

(1) A statement of comprehensive income showing all non-owner changes in equity (total comprehensive income) , or

(2) An income statement showing the income and expenses recognised in profit or loss PLUS a statement showing income and expenses required to be recognised outside of profit or loss (other comprehensive income).

Format one: statement of comprehensive income

For illustration, one of the recommended formats is as follows (previous year comparative would normally be included):

XYZ Group – Statement of comprehensive income for the year ended 31 December 20X3

	$000
Revenue	X
Cost of sales	(X)
Gross profit	X
Other operating income	X
Distribution costs	(X)
Administrative expenses	(X)
Other operating expenses	(X)
Profit from operations	X
Finance costs	(X)
Share of profit of associates	X
Profit before tax	X
Income tax expense	(X)
Profit for the period	X

Other comprehensive income	
Exchange differences on translating foreign operations	X
Available-for-sale financial assets	(X)
Cash flow hedges	(X)
Gain on property revaluation	X
Actuarial gains (losses) on defined benefit pension plans	X
Share of other comprehensive income of associates	X
Income tax relating to components of other Comprehensive income	(X)
Other comprehensive income for the year net of tax	X
Total comprehensive income for the year	X

Profit attributable to:

	$000
Owners of the parent	X
Non-controlling interest	X
	X

Total comprehensive income attributable to:

Owners of the parent	X
Non-controlling interest	X
	X

Other comprehensive income and related tax

IAS 1 requires an entity to disclose income tax relating to each component of other comprehensive income.

This may be achieved by either

- Disclosing each component of other comprehensive income net of any related tax effect, or

- Disclosing other comprehensive income before related tax effects with one amount shown for tax (as shown in the above examples).

The purpose of this is to provide users with tax information relating to these components, as they often have tax rates different from those applied to profit or loss.

Expandable text - Statement of changes in equity

The previous version of IAS 1 required items of income or expense not recognised in profit or loss, such as revaluation gains, to be presented in the statement of changes in equity together with owner changes in equity.

IAS 1 now requires all changes in equity arising from transactions with owners in their capacity as owners to be presented separately from non-owner changes in equity.

The statement of changes in equity presents changes to equity arising from transactions with owners in their capacity as owners, in particular:

- Issues of shares

- Dividends.

Total comprehensive income is shown in aggregate only for the purposes of reconciling opening to closing equity.

XYZ Group – Statement of changes in equity for the year ended 31 December 20X3

	Equity capt'l	Ret'd earng's	Transl'n of for'gn operations	Financial assets thru' OCI	Cash flow hdg's	Reval'n surplus	Total
	$000	$000	$000	$000	$000	$000	$000
Balance at 1 Jan 20X3	X	X	(X)	X	X	–	X
Changes in accounting policy	–	X	–	–	–	–	X
Restated balance	X	X	X	X	X	X	X
Changes in equity for 20X3							
Dividends	–	(X)	–	–	–	–	(X)
Issue of equity capital	X	–	–	–	–	–	X
Total comprehensive income for year	–	X	X	X	X	X	X
Transfer to retained earnings	–	X	–	–	–	(X)	–
Balance at 31 December 20X3	X	X	X	X	X	X	X

In addition to these six columns, there should be columns headed:

(a) Non-controlling interest

(b) Total equity

A comparative statement for the prior period must also be published.

Expandable text - Overall considerations

Overall considerations

(a) Going concern

Once management's assessment is that there are no material uncertainties as to the ability of an entity to continue for the foreseeable future, financial statements should be prepared on the assumption that the entity will in fact continue, the going concern basis.

(b) Accruals basis of accounting

The accruals basis of accounting means that transactions and events are recognised when they occur, not when cash is received or paid for them. IFRS in general, and IAS 1 in particular, do not approach things from a matching viewpoint.

(c) Consistency of presentation

The presentation and classification of items in the financial statements should be retained from one period to the next unless:

* it is clear that a change will result in a more appropriate presentation
* a change is required by a Standard (IAS or IFRS) or an Interpretation (SIC or IFRIC).

(d) Materiality and aggregation

An item is material if its omission or misstatement could influence the economic decisions of users taken on the basis of the financial statements. Financial statements should therefore show material items separately, but immaterial items may be aggregated with amounts of a similar nature.

(e) Offsetting

Assets and liabilities, and income and expenses, should not be offset except when required or permitted by a Standard or an Interpretation.

(f) Comparative information

Comparative information for the previous period should be disclosed, unless a Standard or an Interpretation permits or requires otherwise.

(g) Compliance with IFRS

An entity whose financial statements comply with IFRS should make an explicit and unreserved statement of such compliance in the notes.

Accounting policies

The accounting policies note should describe:

- the measurement basis (or bases) used in preparing the financial statements (e.g. historical cost, fair value, etc)
- each significant accounting policy.

Sources of uncertainty

An entity should disclose information about the key sources of estimation uncertainty that may cause a material adjustment to assets and liabilities within the next year, e.g. key assumptions about the future.

Reclassification adjustments

Reclassification adjustments are amounts reclassified to profit or loss in the current period that were recognised in other comprehensive income in the current or previous periods. This is sometimes referred to as 'recycling'.

IAS 1 requires that reclassification adjustments should be disclosed, either on the face of the statement of comprehensive income or in the notes.

This is necessary to inform users of amounts that are included as other comprehensive income in previous periods and in profit or loss in the current period, so that they can assess the effect of such reclassifications on profit or loss.

Dividends

Unlike the previous version of the standard, IAS 1 revised does not permit the disclosure of dividends recognised as distributions to equity holders on the face of the income statement or statement of total comprehensive income.

Instead, these must be disclosed in the statement of changes in equity or in the notes.

This requirement is in line with separate disclosure of owner and non-owner changes in equity discussed earlier.

Expandable text - Accounting policies (IAS 8)

Where a Standard or Interpretation exists in respect of a transaction, the accounting policy is determined by applying the Standard or Interpretation.

- Where there is no applicable standard or interpretation, management must use its judgement to develop and apply an accounting policy. The accounting policy selected must result in information that is relevant and reliable.

- Management should refer to the following:
  - first, Standards and Interpretations dealing with similar and related issues; then
  - the Framework.

- Provided they do not conflict with the sources above, management may also consider:
  - the most recent pronouncements of other standard-setting bodies that use a similar conceptual framework (e.g. the UK ASB and the US FASB)
  - other accounting literature and accepted industry practices.

- An entity must select and apply its accounting policies consistently for similar transactions.

Changes in accounting policies

An entity should only change its accounting policies if the change is required by a Standard or Interpretation; or it results in reliable and more relevant information.

- New accounting standards normally explain how to deal with any resulting changes in accounting policy (through transitional requirements).

- Otherwise, the new policy should be applied retrospectively. The entity adjusts the opening balance of each affected component of equity, and the comparative figures are presented as if the new policy had always been applied.

- Where a change is applied retrospectively, IAS 1 revised requires an entity to include in its financial statements a statement of financial position at the beginning of the earliest comparative period. In practice this will result in 3 statements of financial position
  - at the reporting date
  - at the start of the current reporting period
  - at the start of the previous reporting period

Changes in accounting estimates

Making estimates is an essential part of the preparation of financial statements. For example, preparers may have to estimate allowances for receivables, inventory obsolescence or the useful lives of non-current assets.

- A change in an accounting estimate is not a change in accounting policy.

- The effect of a change in an accounting estimate must be recognised prospectively, by including it in the statement of comprehensive income/income statement for the current period and any future periods that are also affected.

Expandable text - Correction of prior period errors

Prior period errors are omissions from, and misstatements in, the entity's financial statements for one or more prior periods arising from a failure to use reliable information that was available when the financial statements were authorised for issue, and could reasonably be expected to have been taken into account.

- They include mistakes in applying accounting policies, oversights and the effects of fraud.

- Material prior period errors should be corrected retrospectively in the first set of financial statements authorised for issue after their discovery. Opening balances of equity, and the comparative figures, should be adjusted to correct the error.

- IAS 1 revised also requires that where a prior period error is corrected retrospectively, a statement of financial position is provided at the beginning of the earliest comparative period

2 Revenue recognition (IAS18)

Revenue

Revenue is the gross inflow of economic benefits during the period arising from the ordinary activities of the entity (IAS 18 Revenue).

- Revenue results from the sale of goods, the rendering of services and from the receipt of interest, royalties and dividends.

- 'Revenue' presented in the statement of comprehensive income/income statement should not include items such as proceeds from the sale of its non-current assets. Although IAS 18 does not specifically prohibit this, IAS 16 prohibits any gain on the disposal of property, plant and equipment from being classified as revenue. 'Ordinary activities' here means normal trading or operating activities.

- IAS 18 does not apply to rental and lease agreements (see IAS 17), associates (see IAS 28) or construction contracts (see IAS 11).

Measurement of revenue

Revenue should be measured at the fair value of the consideration received or receivable.

- For a cash sale, the revenue is the immediate proceeds of sale.
- For a credit sale, the revenue is the anticipated cash receivable.
- If the effect of the time value of money is material, the revenue should be discounted to present value.
- Revenue excludes sales taxes and similar items (these are not economic benefits for the reporting entity).

Expandable text - Further detail

Allowances for irrecoverable debts and returns are usually calculated and disclosed separately. Irrecoverable debts are charged as an expense, not as a reduction in revenue.

If the goods are sold on extended credit, then there may be two transactions: a sale and the provision of finance. The sale (and trade receivable) is then measured at the discounted present value of the future cash flows. Future cash receipts are split between the repayment of capital and interest income.

Revenue from the sale of goods

The following conditions must be satisfied before revenue from the sale of goods can be recognised:

- the seller transfers the significant risks and rewards of ownership to the buyer
- the seller does not retain management or control over the goods sold
- the amount of revenue can be measured reliably

- the transaction's economic benefits will probably flow to the seller

- the costs incurred or to be incurred can be measured reliably.

Revenue from services

Revenue from services is recognised according to the stage of completion. The following conditions must be met:

- the revenue can be measured reliably

- the transaction's economic benefits will probably flow to the provider

- the stage of completion at the reporting date can be measured reliably

- the costs incurred and the costs to complete can be measured reliably.

If these conditions are not met, then revenue should be restricted to any recoverable costs incurred.

Interest, royalties and dividends

Revenue from these sources should be recognised when the receipt is probable and the revenues are measurable. Revenue should be recognised as follows:

- interest is recognised on a time proportion basis, taking into account the effective yield on the asset

- royalties are accrued in accordance with the relevant contract

- dividends are recognised when the shareholder's right to receive payment is established.

Illustration 1 – Car dealer revenue recognition

A car dealer sells a car on credit terms. When should the revenue be recognised?

Expandable text - Solution

This transaction gives rise to two different types of revenue – the trading profit and the finance income from the sale on credit. If the credit agreement is such that the user of the car becomes the legal owner either immediately or at some time in the future, then the risks and rewards are transferred to the user and the trading profit can be regarded as earned when the credit agreement is signed. However the finance income must be spread over the time period of the credit agreement.

Problem areas

Area	Guidance
Long-term contractual performance	Recognise in accordance with the performance of contractual obligations.
Separation or linking of contractual arrangements (e.g. the sale of goods with a maintenance contract)	Where the two components operate independently of each other, then recognise as separate transactions. Otherwise recognise as a single transaction.
Bill and hold arrangements	Recognise revenue if the substance of the arrangement is that the goods represent an asset of the customer.
Sale with right of return	Exclude the sales value of estimated returns from revenue. Continue to monitor the accuracy of estimates with any changes reported within revenue.
Presentation of turnover as principal or agent	The issue is whether in a transaction on behalf of a third party a seller should record total turnover or merely the commission received from the third party (e.g. the on-line retailer of holidays through a website). The IAS states that the substance of the arrangement needs to be examined.

Expandable text - Specific situations

IAS 18 includes an Appendix which gives guidance on specific situations:

(a) **Bill and hold arrangements**

This is a contract for the supply of goods, where the buyer accepts title to the goods but does not take physical delivery of them until a later date. Provided the goods are available for delivery, the buyer gives explicit instructions to delay delivery and there are no alterations to the terms on which the seller normally trades with the buyer, revenue should recognise when the buyer accepts title.

(b) **Payments for goods in advance (e.g. deposits)**

Revenue should be recognised when delivery of the goods to the buyer takes place. Until then, any payments in advance should be treated as liabilities.

(c) **Payments for goods by instalments**

Revenue is recognised when the significant risks and rewards of ownership have been transferred, which is usually when delivery is made. If the effect of the time value of money is material, the sale price should be discounted to its present value.

(d) **Sale or return**

Sometimes goods are delivered to a customer but the customer can return them within a certain time period. Revenue is normally recognised when the goods are delivered.

Revenue should then be reduced by an estimate of the returns. In most cases, a seller can estimate returns from past experience. For example, a retailer would know on average what percentage of goods were returned after the year end and could adjust revenue by the amount of expected returns.

(e) **Presentation of revenue as a principal or as agent**

The principal supplies goods or services on its own account, whilst the agent receives a fee or commission for arranging provision of goods or services by the principal. The principal is exposed to the risks and rewards of the transaction and therefore records revenue as the gross amount receivable. The agent only records the commission receivable on the transaction as revenue. An example would be a cosmetics agent who earns commission on the number of cosmetics sold. The agent owns no inventory, so is not exposed to obsolescence and therefore could only record commission as its revenue. The cosmetics company is exposed to inventory obsolescence and selling price changes, so would record the gross amount of the sale as revenue.

(f) **Separation and linking of contractual arrangements**

Sometimes businesses provide a number of different goods or services to customers as a package. For example, a customer might purchase software together with regular upgrades for one year. The problem here is whether the sale is one transaction or two separate transactions.

A 'package' such as this can only be treated as more than one separate transaction if each product or service is capable of being sold independently and if a reliable fair value can be assigned to each separate component. Using the example above, if the support service is an optional extra and the software can be operated without it, the sale is two (or more) separate transactions. If the software cannot operate successfully without the upgrades, then the sale is one transaction and the amount of revenue recognised depends on the extent to which the seller has performed at the reporting date.

Disclosure requirements

An entity should disclose:

- It's accounting policies for revenue including the methods adopted to determine the stage of completion of service transactions

- the amount of each significant category of revenue recognised during the period

- the amount of revenue arising from exchanges of goods or services.

Aggressive earnings management

Since IAS 18 was originally issued, businesses and transactions have become much more complex. For example, computer companies frequently enter into barter transactions. Transactions may include options, for example, to buy shares or to return goods within a specified time.

Some entities have exploited the weaknesses in IAS 18 in order to artificially enhance revenue (a practice sometimes called **'aggressive earnings management'**). For example, some software companies recognise sales when orders are made, well before it is reasonably certain that cash will be received.

The main issue is one of timing. At what point in a transaction should an entity recognise revenue?

Three questions can be helpful in dealing with an unusual transaction or situation:

- When is the 'critical event'? This is the point at which most or all of the uncertainty surrounding a transaction is removed.

- Has the seller actually performed? Transactions that give rise to revenue are legally contractual arrangements, regardless of whether a formal contract exists. Revenue can only be recognised when an entity has performed its obligations under the contract. For example, an entity cannot recognise revenue at the time that it receives payment in advance.

- Has the transaction increased the entity's net assets/equity? For example, when an entity makes a sale, its assets increase, because it has receivables (access to future economic benefits in the form of cash). Therefore it recognises a gain. This is one of the main principles in the Framework.

Expandable text - Asset and liability model for revenue

The revenue recognition requirements in IAS 18 focus on the occurrence of critical events rather than changes in assets and liabilities. Some believe that this approach leads to debits and credits that do not meet the definition of assets and liabilities being recognised in the statement of financial position.

The Board has developed two approaches to implement the asset and liability model:

- The fair value (measurement) model, in which performance obligations are initially measured at fair value

- The customer consideration model, in which performance obligations are initially measured by allocating the customer consideration amount.

It is likely that neither of these will be the final model and the final standard is expected to be drawn from both of them.

Contracts providing more than one good or service

A practical weakness of IAS 18 is that it gives insufficient guidance on contracts that provide more than one good or service to the customer. It is unclear when contracts should be divided into components and how much revenue should be attributed to each component. The IFRIC receives frequent requests for guidance on the application of IAS 18.

Test your understanding 1 - Revenue recognition

Explain how much revenue should be recognised in each of the following situations.

(a) **Tuition provider**

A company trades as a tuition provider and charges a price of $5,000 for a course of tuition together with material. Fees are non refundable. An invoice is raised at the commencement of the course. The course length is 20 classes which are held weekly. At the commencement of the course each customer is also issued with course material which can be separately purchased for $1,000. At the current year end the company has ten customers enrolled on the course, six of whom have fully paid and four of whom have been credit checked and agreed credit terms. At the reporting date these customers have only paid $2,000 each and the yearend the company has delivered 5 of the 20 classes.

Magazine publisher

A company publishes a magazine and on 1 July, sold annual subscriptions totalling $200,000. The monies have been received and are non-refundable. The financial year-end of the company is 31 December.

(c) **Internet travel agent**

An internet travel agent receives $1,000 for arranging a hotel booking, and will pass on $900 in due course to the hotel.

(d) **Furniture retailer**

A furniture retailer offers two-year 0% finance on furniture offered for sale at $10,000.

Required:

Calculate the revenue that can be recognised in the current year for each of the situations outlined above.

Expandable text - Discontinued operations (IFRS 5)

Definition

A discontinued operation is a component of an entity that either has been disposed of, or is classified as held for sale, and:

- represents a separate major line of business or geographical area of operations

- is part of a single co-ordinated plan to dispose of a separate major line of business or geographical area of operations

- is a subsidiary acquired exclusively with a view to resale.

A component of an entity may be a business, geographical, or reportable segment, a cash-generating unit, or a subsidiary.

If the component/operation has not already been sold, then it will only be a discontinued operation if it is held for sale.

An operation is **held for sale** if its carrying amount will not be recovered principally by continuing use. To be classified as held for sale (and therefore to be a discontinued operation) at the reporting date, it must meet the following criteria.

- The operation is available for immediate sale in its present condition.

- The sale is highly probable and is expected to be completed within one year.

- Management is committed to the sale.

- The operation is being actively marketed.

- The operation is being offered for sale at a reasonable price in relation to its current fair value.

- It is unlikely that the plan will change or be withdrawn.

Expandable text - Presentation

Presentation

Users of the financial statements are more interested in future profits than past profits. They are able to make a better assessment of future profits if they are informed about operations that have been discontinued during the period.

IFRS 5 requires information about discontinued operations to be presented in the financial statements.

- **On the face of the statement of comprehensive income/income statement** a single amount comprising:
  - the total of the post-tax profit or loss of discontinued operations
  - the post-tax gain or loss on the measurement to fair value less costs to sell or on the disposal of the discontinued operation.

- **Either on the face of or in the notes to the statement of comprehensive income/income statement** an analysis of the single amount described above into:
  - the revenue, expenses and pre-tax profit or loss of discontinued operations
  - the related tax expense
  - the gain or loss recognised on the measurement to fair value less costs to sell or on the disposal of the discontinued operation
  - the related tax expense.

- **Either on the face of or in the notes to the statement of cash flows** the net cash flows attributable to the operating, investing and financing activities of discontinued operations.

- If a decision to sell an operation is taken after the year-end but before the accounts are approved, this is treated as a non-adjusting event after the reporting date and disclosed in the notes. The operation does **not** qualify as a discontinued operation at the reporting date and separate presentation is not appropriate.

- In the comparative figures the operations are also shown as discontinued (even though they were not classified as such at the end of the previous year).

Expandable text - Example presentation

Income statement (showing discontinued operations as a single amount, with analysis in the notes)

	20X2	20X1
	$m	$m
Revenue	100	90
Operating expenses	(60)	(65)
	———	———
Operating profit	40	25
Interest expense	(20)	(10)
	———	———
Profit before tax	20	15
Income tax expense	(6)	(7)
	———	———
Profit from continuing operations	14	8
Discontinued operations		
Loss from discontinued operations*	(25)	(1)
	———	———
Profit/(loss) for the year	(11)	7
	———	———

The entity did not recognise any components of other comprehensive income in the periods presented.

* The analysis of this loss would be given in a note to the accounts.

Expandable text - Discontinued operations illustration

During the year ended 30 June 20X5, Glendale, a company with a number of subsidiary companies, sold a subsidiary, Janus for $4.6 million.

The net assets of Janus totalled $5 million at the date of sale. During the year ended 30 June 20X5, Janus had sales revenue of $940,000, operating expenses of $580,000 and an expected tax charge of $100,000.

The draft consolidated income statement for the remainder of the Glendale group is as follows:

	$000
Revenue	3,240
Operating expenses	(2,057)
Profit from operations	1,183
Finance cost	(58)
Profit before tax	1,125
Income tax expense	(293)
Profit for the year	832

Show how the consolidated income statement would appear according to IFRS 5.

Expandable text - Solution

Consolidated income statement for the year ended 30 June 20X5

Continuing operations	$000
Revenue	3,240
Operating expenses	(2,057)
Operating profit	1,183
Interest expense	(58)
Profit before tax	1,125
Income tax expense	(293)
Profit for the year from continuing operations	832
Loss from discontinued operation (working)	(140)
Profit for the year	692

Working

	$000
Revenue	940
Operating expenses	(580)
Loss on disposal (4,600 – 5,000)	(400)
Income tax expense	(100)
Loss for the year	(140)

Expandable text - Example presentation 2

ABC Group – Statement of comprehensive income for the year ended 31 December 20X7

	$000 20X7	$000 20X6
Revenue	1,000,000	800,000
Cost of sales	(600,000)	(500,000)
Gross profit	400,000	300,000
Other income	10,000	10,000
Distribution costs	(100,000)	(80,000)
Administrative expenses	(200,000)	(160,000)
	110,000	70,000
Finance costs	(30,000)	(20,000)
Share of profits of associates	20,000	15,000
Share of profits of joint venture entities	10,000	8,000
Profit before tax	110,000	73,000
Income tax expense	(35,000)	(25,000)
Profit for the year from continuing operations	75,000	48,000
Loss for the year from discontinued operations	(15,000)	(10,000)
PROFIT FOR THE YEAR	(60,000)	38,000

Other comprehensive income:

Gains on property revaluation	40,000	10,000
Share of other comprehensive income of associates	4,000	–
Actuarial gains (losses) on defined benefit pension plans	(30,000)	(15,000)
Exchange differences on translating foreign operations	5,000	4,000
Available-for-sale financial assets	(4,000)	5,000
Cash flow hedges	(1,000)	2,000
Income tax relating to components of other comprehensive income	(5,000)	(2,000)
Other comprehensive income for the year, net of tax	9,000	4,000
TOTAL COMPREHENSIVE INCOME FOR THE YEAR	69,000	42,000

Profit for the period attributable to:		
Owners of the parent		
From continuing operations	57,000	40,000
From discontinued operations	(12,000)	(8,000)
	45,000	32,000
Non-controlling interest		
From continuing operations	18,000	8,000
From discontinued operations	(3,000)	(2,000)
	15,000	6,000
	60,000	38,000

Total comprehensive income attributable to:

Owners of the parent		
From continuing operations	62,000	43,000
From discontinued operations	(12,000)	(8,000)
	50,000	35,000
Non-controlling interest		
From continuing operations	22,000	9,000
From discontinued operations	(3,000)	(2,000)
	19,000	7,000
	69,000	42,000

Test your understanding 2 - Portugal group

The Portugal group of companies has a financial year-end of 30 June 20X4. The financial statements are signed off three months later. The group is disposing of many of its subsidiaries, each of which is a separate major line of business or geographical area.

- Subsidiary England was sold on 1 January 20X4.

- On 1 January 20X4, an announcement was made that there were advanced negotiations to sell subsidiary Switzerland, and subject to regulatory approval, this is expected to be completed by 31 October 20X4.

- The board has also decided to divest the independent cash-generating unit known as France. Agents have been appointed to find a suitable buyer but so far none has yet emerged. The agent's advice is that potential buyers are deterred by unquantified potential environmental damages and the expected price that Portugal hopes to achieve.

- On 10 July 20X4, an announcement was made that geographical segment Croatia was for sale and indeed it was sold by 10 September 20X4.

Explain whether these are discontinued operations as defined by IFRS 5.

3 Earnings per share (IAS 33)

Expandable text - Earnings per share (IAS 33)

Scope and definitions

IAS 33 applies to entities whose equity shares are publicly traded. Private entities must also follow IAS 33, if they disclose an earnings per share figure.

An **equity share** is an equity instrument that is subordinate to all other classes of equity instruments.

A potential equity share is a financial instrument or other contract that may entitle its holder to equity shares.

The basic calculation

The actual earnings per share (EPS) for the period is called the **basic EPS** and is calculated as:

$$\frac{\text{Profit or loss for the period attributable to equity shareholders}}{\text{Weighted average number of equity shares outstanding in the period}}$$

Basic earnings are profit after tax less NCI and preference dividends (if any). If an entity prepares consolidated financial statements, then EPS will be based on the consolidated results.

- The weighted average number of shares takes into account when shares were issued during the year.

Expandable text - Basic illustration

An entity issued 200,000 shares at full market price ($3.00) on 1 July 20X8.

Relevant information

	20X8	20X7
Profit attributable to the ordinary shareholders for the year ending 31 Dec	$550,000	$460,000
Number of ordinary shares in issue at 31 Dec	1,000,000	800,000

Calculation of earnings per share

20X7 = $460,000 / 800,000 = 57.50c

20X8 = $550,000 / 800,000 + (½ × 200,000) = 61.11c

Since the additional 200,000 shares were issued at full market price but have only contributed finance for half a year, then only half their number is used. The earnings figure is not adjusted.

Expandable text - Bonus issues

Bonus issues

If an entity makes a bonus issue, share capital increases, but no cash is received and there is no affect on earnings. Therefore, a bonus issue reduces EPS.

- The new shares are treated as if they have always been in issue. Comparative EPS is also adjusted

Expandable text - Bonus issue illustration

An entity made a bonus issue of one new share for every five existing shares held on 1 July 20X8.

Relevant information

	20X8	20X7
Profit attributable to the ordinary shareholders for the year ending 31 Dec	$550,000	$460,000
Number of ordinary shares in issue at 31 Dec	1,200,000	1,000,000

Calculation of earnings per share in 20X8 accounts

20X7 = $460,000 / 1,200,000 = 38.33c
(the comparative figure presented in the 20X8 accounts)

20X8 = $550,000 / 1,200,000 = 45.83c

In the 20X7 accounts, the EPS for the year would have appeared as 46c ($460,000 ÷ 1,000,000).

In 20X8, the EPS for 20X7 can be recalculated (as above), or the original EPS of 46c can be adjusted for the bonus issue as follows:

Original EPS of 46c × 1,000,000 / 1,200,000 = 38.33c

Expandable text - Rights issues

Rights issues

Because rights issues are normally made at less than the full market price, a rights issue combines the characteristics of an issue at full market price with those of a bonus issue.

The weighted average includes the bonus element for the full year plus the full price element on a time-apportioned basis.

Expandable text - Rights issue illustration

An entity issued one new share for every two existing shares held by way of rights at $1.50 per share on 1 July 20X8. The pre-issue market price was $3.00 per share.

Relevant information

	20X8	20X7
Profit attributable to the ordinary shareholders for the year ending 31 Dec	$550,000	$460,000
Number of ordinary shares in issue at 31 Dec	1,200,000	800,000

Expandable text - Solution

Step 1: Calculate the bonus element

This is done by multiplying the original number of shares by the following:

Actual cum rights price / Theoretical ex rights price

The actual cum rights price is the market value before the rights issue. The theoretical ex rights price is what each share should be worth immediately after the rights issue. It can be calculated as follows:

	Shares in issue	Price per Share	Market capitalisation $
Before the rights issue	800,000	300c	2,400,000
Rights issue	400,000	150c	600,000
After the rights issue	1,200,000	**250c**	3,000,000

The bonus adjustment can now be calculated:

800,000 shares × 300/250 = 960,000 shares

Step 2: Calculate the full-price element

The total number of shares after the rights issue is 1,200,000. We have just calculated that there were 960,000 shares after the bonus element adjustment. Therefore, there must have been 240,000 shares issued at full price (1,200,000 – 960,000).

Step 3: Calculate the weighted average number of shares

	Shares	Time	Average
Original shares	800,000	12/12	800,000
Bonus element of the rights issue	160,000	12/12	160,000
Full market price element of the rights issue	240,000	6/12	120,000
	1,200,000		1,080,000

Step 4: Calculate the earnings per share for the current year

$$\frac{\text{Earnings}}{\text{Equity shares in issue}} = \frac{\$550,000}{1,080,000 \text{ shares}} = 50.93 \text{ cents}$$

Step 5: Re-calculate or restate the EPS for the prior year.

Last year's earnings of $460,000 is divided by the number of shares in issue after the bonus element of this year's issue.

Earnings / Equity shares in issue = $460,000 / 960,000 shares = **47.92 cents**

or

$460,000 / 800,000 =

57.5 cents × Theoretical ex rights price/Actual cum rights price = 250c/300c = **47.92 cents**

Expandable text - Diluted earnings per share

Diluted earnings per share

Many companies issue convertible instruments, options and warrants that entitle their holders to purchase shares in the future at below the market price. When these shares are eventually issued, the interests of the original shareholders will be diluted. The dilution occurs because these shares will have been issued at below market price.

The Examiner has indicated that diluted earnings per share will not be examined in detail; however, students should have awareness of the topic as summarised below:

- Shares and other instruments that may dilute the interests of the existing shareholders are called potential ordinary shares.

- Examples of potential ordinary shares include:
  - debt and other instruments, including preference shares, that are convertible into ordinary shares. This includes partly-paid shares
  - share warrants and options (instruments that give the holder the right to purchase ordinary shares)
  - employee plans that allow employees to receive ordinary shares as part of their remuneration and other share purchase plans
  - contingently issuable shares (i.e. shares issuable if certain conditions are met).

- Where there are dilutive potential ordinary shares in issue, the diluted EPS must be disclosed as well as the basic EPS. This provides relevant information to current and potential investors.

- Diluted EPS is calculated using current earnings but assuming that the worst possible dilution has already happened.

- The profit used in the basic EPS calculation is adjusted for any expenses that would no longer be paid if the convertible instrument were converted into shares, e.g. preference dividends, loan interest.

- The weighted average number of shares used in the basic EPS calculation is adjusted for the conversion of the potential ordinary shares. This is deemed to occur at the beginning of the period or the date of issue, if they were not in existence at the beginning of the period.

Expandable text - Presentation

An entity should present basic and diluted earnings per share on the face of the statement of comprehensive income/income statement, for each class of ordinary shares that has a different right to share in the net profit for the period.

- An entity should present basic and diluted earnings per share with equal prominence for all periods presented.

- If an entity has discontuinued operations, it should also present basic and diluted EPS from continuing operations.

- An entity that reports a discontinued operation must disclose the basic and diluted EPS for the operation, either on the face of the statement of comprehensive income/income statement or in the notes.

- IAS 33 also requires basic and diluted losses per share to be disclosed.

- In most cases, if basic EPS is a loss, then the diluted EPS will be the same as the basic EPS. This is because the loss per share will be diluted, and therefore reduced. Diluted EPS only relates to factors that decrease a profit or increase a loss.

Expandable text - Disclosure

An entity should disclose the following.

- The earnings used for basic and diluted EPS. These earnings should be reconciled to the net profit or loss for the period.

- The weighted average number of ordinary shares used for basic and diluted EPS. The two averages should be reconciled to each other.

- An entity may disclose an alternative EPS in addition to the IAS 33 requirements provided that:
    - the earnings figure is reconciled back to the statement of comprehensive income/income statement
    - the same weighted average number of shares is used as for the IAS 33 calculations
    - basic and diluted EPS is disclosed
    - the alternative figure is shown in the notes, not on the face of the statement of comprehensive/income statement.

Expandable text - EPS as a performance measure

The EPS figure is used to compute the major stock market indicator of performance, the Price/Earnings ratio (P/E ratio). Rightly or wrongly, the stock market places great emphasis on the earnings per share figure and the P/E ratio. IAS 33 sets out a standard method of calculating EPS, which enhances the comparability of the figure.

However, EPS has limited usefulness as a performance measure.

- An entity's earnings are affected by its choice of accounting policies. Therefore, it may not always be appropriate to compare the EPS of different companies.

- EPS does not take account of inflation. Apparent growth in earnings may not be true growth.

- EPS does not provide predictive value. High earnings and growth in earnings may be achieved at the expense of investment, which would have generated increased earnings in the future.

- In theory, diluted EPS serves as a warning to equity shareholders that the return on their investment may fall in future periods. However, diluted EPS as currently required by IAS 33 is not intended to be forward-looking but is an additional past performance measure. Diluted EPS is based on current earnings, not forecast earnings. Therefore, diluted EPS is only of limited use as a prediction of future EPS.

- EPS is a measure of profitability. Profitability is only one aspect of performance. Concentration on earnings per share and 'the bottom line' arguably detracts from other important aspects of an entity's affairs, for example, cash flow and stewardship of assets.

Expandable text - Interim reporting (IAS 34)

- Condensed financial statements should include all of the headings and sub-totals used in the most recent annual financial statements.

- If an entity publishes a complete set of financial statements in its interim report, then they should comply with IAS 1 in full.

- Basic and diluted EPS should be presented on the face of interim statements of comprehensive income for those entities within the scope of IAS 33

Interim financial reports are prepared for a period shorter than a full financial year. Entities may be required to prepare interim financial reports under local law or listing regulations.

- IAS 34 does not require the preparation of interim reports, but sets out the principles that should be followed if they are prepared and specifies their minimum content.

- An interim financial report should include, as a minimum, the following components:
  - condensed statement of financial position as at the end of the current interim period, with a comparative statement of financial position as at the end of the previous financial year

  - condensed statement of comprehensive income for the current interim period and cumulatively for the current financial year to date (if, for example the entity reports quarterly), with comparatives for the interim periods (current and year to date) of the preceding financial year

  - condensed statement showing changes in equity. This statement should show changes in equity cumulatively for the current year with comparatives for the corresponding period of the preceding financial year

  - condensed statement of cash flows cumulatively for the year to date, with a comparative statement to the same date in the previous year

  - selected explanatory notes.

- Condensed financial statements should include all of the headings and sub-totals used in the most recent annual financial statements.

- If an entity publishes a complete set of financial statements in its interim report, then they should comply with IAS 1 in full.

- Basic and diluted EPS should be presented on the face of interim statements of comprehensive income for those entities within the scope of IAS 33.

Expandable text - Current issues in performance reporting

Revenue recognition

As part of a joint project (also part of the MoU) with FASB, the IASB issued a DP - Preliminary Views on Revenue Recognition in Contracts with Customers in December 2008.

Revenue is a crucial number to users of the financial statements in assessing a company's performance and prospects. The IASB and the FASB together initiated a joint project to clarify the principles for recognising revenue from contracts with customers. It applies to all contracts with customers except leases, financial instruments and insurance contracts. In June 2010, an ED was issued, with the target of issuing a reporting standard during 2011.

The main objectives of this project are as follows:

- To remove inconsistencies and weaknesses in existing revenue recognition standards by providing clear principles for revenue recognition in a robust framework

- To provide a single revenue recognition model which will improve comparability over a range of industries, companies and geographical boundaries

- To simplify the preparation of financial statements by reducing the number of requirements to which preparers must refer.

- US GAAP consists of broad revenue recognition concepts around which numerous industry- and transaction- specific requirements have evolved to deal with individual types of contracts. IFRSs contain fewer standards, but the two main standards can be difficult to apply to complex transaction.

The key principles on which the proposed model is based – revenue is recognised on transfer to the customer, measured at transaction price- are consistent with much of current practice. The boards believe the proposed standard will improve financial reporting by:

- providing a more robust framework for addressing issues as they arise

- increasing comparability across industries and capital markets

- providing enhanced disclosures

- clarifying accounting for contract costs

Earnings per share

The amendments to IAS 33 expected as a result of this project will change the existing treasury stock method of calculating the effects of dilutive options and warrants on EPS. The proposed amendments to IAS 33 are in line with those proposed to the equivalent US standard. The proposal would:

- Amend the treasury stock method to include as assumed proceeds the end-of-period carrying value of a liability that is assumed to be settled in shares and use the end-of-period market price in the computation of incremental shares.

- Adopt a new 'fair value method' for all instruments that can be settled in cash or shares, are classified as a liability and are measured at fair value (with changes to this shown in profit or loss.

- Include options and warrants with a nominal exercise price in the computation of basic EPS if
  - The instruments are currently exercisable or convertible into ordinary shares for little or no cost to the holder, or
  - The option or warrant currently participates in earnings with ordinary shareholders.

Current status of the project

As at August 2010, there has been no tangible progress since the issue of an ED in August 2008 due to changed priorities for other issues such as the global financial crisis. Any further decisions regarding progress of this project are to be confirmed at a later date.

Financial statements presentation project

In April 2004, the IASB and the FASB decided to combine their projects on the reporting and classification of revenue, expenses, gains and losses. The joint project was undertaken to establish a common, high quality standard for presentation of information in the financial statements.

The objective of the project is to present information in the financial statements that improves the ability of the users of the financial statement to understand the financial position, change in position and cash flows of an entity. Specifically, this means users will be able to:

- understand the entity's present and past financial position

- understand the past operating, financing and other activities that caused the financial position to change and

- use the financial statement information amongst other sources of information to assess an entity's future cash flows.

The standard that is developed from this project will initially only apply to business entities and not to not-for-profit entities.

Phases of the project

- Phase A deals with the question of what constitutes a complete set of financial statements and the requirement to present comparative information. This was completed with the issue of IAS 1 revised in September 2007.

- Phase B addresses the more fundamental issue of the presentation of information on the face of the financial statements.

- Phase C will address the reporting of interim financial information in US GAAP. This may lead to the IASB reviewing the content of IAS 34 Interim financial reporting.

The current status of the project can be considered by reviewing each of the separate components.

Replacement of IAS 1 and IAS 7

The IASB and the US FASB are undertaking a project to develop a joint standard for financial statement presentation.
In IFRSs, the new proposals will replace the existing standards on financial statement presentation, IAS 1 Presentation of Financial Statements and IAS 7 Statement of Cash Flows.

The objective of the financial statement presentation project is to establish a global standard that will guide the organisation and presentation of information in the financial statements. The standard would directly affect how the management of an entity communicates financial statement information to the users of its financial statements, such as existing and potential equity investors, lenders and other creditors. The boards' goal is to improve the usefulness of the information provided in an entity's financial statements to help those users in their decision-making.

The IASB and the US FASB initiated the joint project on financial statement presentation to address users' concerns that existing requirements permit too many alternative types of presentation, and that information in financial statements is highly aggregated and inconsistently presented, making it difficult to understand fully the relationship between an entity's financial statements and its financial results.

The project's main proposals are:

- cohesive financial statements that share a common structure, separately presenting operating, investing and financing activities as well as income tax and discontinued operations;

- disaggregation in each financial statement, considering its function, nature and measurement basis, with some disaggregation included in the notes

- more disaggregation of operating cash receipts and payments, and reconciliation of profit or loss from operating activities to cash flows from operating activities;

- analyses of changes in asset and liability line items (including net debt – IASB only);

- and disclosure of remeasurement information.

The proposals would improve the comparability and understandability of information presented in financial statements, by imposing some degree of standardisation in the way that information is presented in the financial statements, particularly regarding how information is classified, and the degree to which it is disaggregated.

As at August 2010, the target is to issue an ED in early 2011, with a new reporting standard by the end of that year.

Discontinued operations

There is a joint project between IASB and FASB develop a common definition of discontinued operations and require common disclosures related to disposals of components of an entity. The project commenced in 2008, with an ED issued in September of that year. There was no change to the definition and measurement of non-current assets held for sale.

The objective of this project is to develop, jointly with the FASB, a common definition of discontinued operations, and to require common disclosures related to disposals of components of an entity. As a result of this joint project, the IASB expects to amend IFRS 5 Non-current Assets Held for Sale and Discontinued Operations, and the FASB expects to amend its equivalent reporting requirements.

In their joint project on financial statement presentation, the IASB and the US FASB decided to develop a common definition of a discontinued operation, and to require common disclosures about components of an entity that have been (or will be) disposed of. The boards decided to address these issues separately from the main financial statement presentation project (the replacement of IAS 1 and IAS 7).

In May 2010, the boards decided to align the project timetable with the main financial statement presentation project. The boards now plan to publish an ED in early 2011 of a converged definition of a discontinued operation and related disclosures, with a reporting standard issued by the end of that year.

Other comprehensive income

The IASB is undertaking a project on the presentation of items of other comprehensive income (OCI). The presentation of items of OCI is becoming more important as the Board has decided in various projects that entities should present particular items of income and expense in OCI. The US FASB is also taking on a similar project.
The main issues that the IASB aims to address with the proposed amendments are the lack of distinction between different items in OCI and the lack of clarity in the presentation of items in OCI, including:

- Lack of distinction between different items in OCI. A range of very different items are presented in OCI without any distinctions. However, some of the items presented in OCI can have a considerable effect on the overall financial performance of an entity.

- Lack of consistency in presentation. Existing requirements give entities an option to present items of OCI. There are however substantially more options under US GAAP, than IFRS.

- Lack of comparability between IFRS and US GAAP. US GAAP and IFRSs currently differ on the presentation of OCI items.

Under the proposals, profit or loss and OCI will be displayed consecutively. The Board believes it is important that all income and expenses that are components of the total non-owner changes in equity should be presented together.

- The Board recognises the importance of profit or loss (the net income line) and is committed to maintaining this important number.

- There will be no changes to how earnings per share are calculated.

- The attribution of profit or loss between the parent shareholders of the entity and its non-controlling interest will also remain.

The Board is also proposing that items in OCI are grouped on the basis of whether they are reclassified from OCI to profit or loss. This will address the issue that some of the items that are presented within OCI, such as cash flow hedges, are eventually re-presented as part of the profit or loss section (IAS 1 calls this reclassification) whilst others, such as asset revaluations, are not.

In addition to that the IASB is proposing to use the title of 'statement of profit or loss and other comprehensive income' for the statement containing all items of income and expense. The proposals do not dictate how the statement of profit or loss and other comprehensive income would be presented. Apart from the proposed titles, totals and subtotals in this amendment, entities are still allowed to use other titles for the statement.

As at August 2010, the expectation is that a new reporting standard will be issued by the end of 2010.

KAPLAN PUBLISHING

4 Chapter summary

Presentation of financial statements
- Statement of financial position
- Statement of comprehensive income
- Statement of changes in equity

INTERIM FINANCIAL REPORTING

Accounting policies, changes in accounting estimates and errors
- Selection
- Changing policies and estimates
- Prior period errors

Revenue recognition
- Measurement
- Recognition/timing
- Sale of goods
- Rendering of services

Discontinued operations
- Definition
- Presentation

Earnings per share
- Basic
- Diluted
- Presentation

Current issues in reporting financial performance
- Financial statement presentation project
- Revenue recognition joint project
- EPS convergence project

Test your understanding answers

Test your understanding 1 - Revenue recognition

(a) **Tuition provider**

It is not relevant that the some customers have paid and others not in determining the revenue to be recognised, as it can be measured with reliability. Whilst invoices of 10 x $5,000 = $50,000 have been raised this is not the trigger for the recognition of revenue in the financial statements.

The company is selling both goods and services. All of the revenue from the sale of the goods (course materials) can be recognised as the goods have been delivered 10 x $1,000 = $10,000.
The services for tuition have a value of $4,000 ($5,000 - $1,000) and have only been partially delivered (5/20). Accordingly the revenue from tuition that can be recognised is 5/20 x $4,000 x 10 = $10,000.
The total revenue that can be recognised is therefore $10,000 + $10,000 = $20,000.

(b) **Magazine publisher**

Revenue earned is only $100,000, as this is recognised as each magazine is published. The balance is deferred income; there is an obligation to publish the remaining magazines, even if not to actually refund the subscriptions in advance.

(c) **Internet travel agent**

The travel agent is an agent, so it only recognises commission received for arranging the transaction on behalf of the hotel. Revenue is $100. The $900 would be recognised as a liability until such time as it is paid over to the hotel.

(d) **Furniture retailer**

The furniture dealer has sold furniture on credit to the customer. The total of $1,000 should be divided into two elements comprising the sale of furniture and also the present value of the receipt of interest at an appropriate rate of return over two years. The revenue on the sale of furniture can be recognised immediately, presumably on sale or delivery as the risks and rewards have been transferred to the customer at that point. The interest receivable for two years should be recognised at a constant rate over the two-year period.

Test your understanding 2 - Portugal group

The issue is whether or not these qualify as discontinued operations.

England has been sold during the year. It is a discontinued operation per IFRS 5. The results will be consolidated up to the date of disposal.

Switzerland is a discontinued operation per IFRS 5. There is clear intention to sell, and completion will occur within 12 months.

France is not a discontinued operation per IFRS 5. There are problems with the condition of the asset, the price being asked and there is no indication that it will be completed within 12 months.

Croatia is not a discontinued operation per IFRS 5 because it was after the year-end that it met the conditions for classification as held for sale.

Employee benefits

Chapter learning objectives

Upon completion of this chapter you will be able to:

- apply and discuss the accounting treatment of defined contribution and defined benefit plans

- account for gains and losses on settlements and curtailments

- account for the 'Asset Ceiling' test and the reporting of actuarial gains and losses.

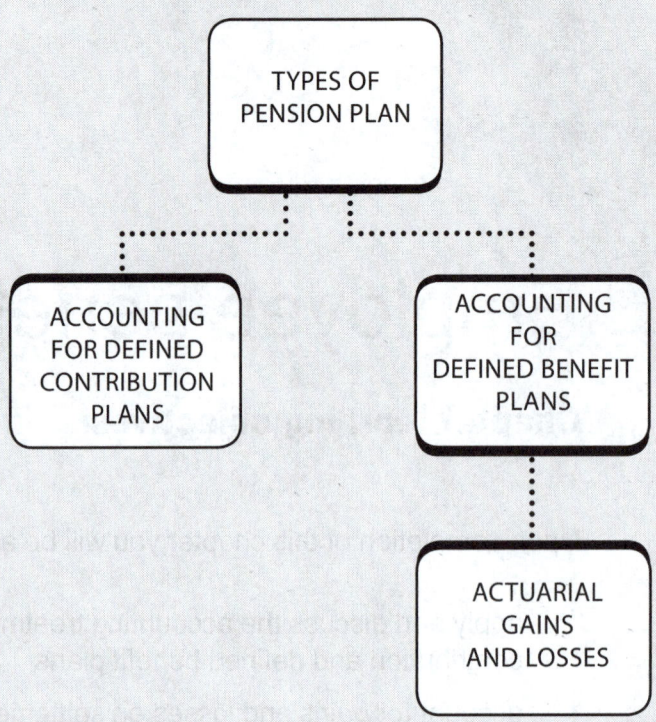

1 Types of pension plan

Introduction

A pension plan (sometimes called a post-employment benefit scheme) consists of a pool of assets and a liability for pensions owed to employees. Pension plan assets normally consist of investments, cash and (sometimes) properties. The return earned on the assets is used to pay pensions.

There are two main types of pension plan:

- defined contribution plans
- defined benefit plans.

Defined contribution plans

The pension payable on retirement depends on the contributions paid into the plan by the employee and the employer.

- The employer's contribution is usually a fixed percentage of the employee's salary. The employer has no further obligation after this amount is paid.
- Therefore, the annual cost to the employer is reasonably predictable.
- Defined contribution plans present few accounting problems.

Defined benefit plans

The pension payable on retirement normally depends on either the final salary or the average salary of the employee during their career.

- The employer undertakes to finance a pension income of a certain amount, e.g.

  2/3 × final salary × (years of service / 40 years)

- The employer has an ongoing obligation to make sufficient contributions to the plan to fund the pensions.

- An actuary calculates the amount that must be paid into the plan each year in order to provide the promised pension. The calculation is based on various estimates and assumptions including:
  - life expectancy
  - investment returns
  - wage inflation.

- Therefore, the cost of providing pensions is not certain and varies from year to year.

 The actual contribution paid in a period does not usually represent the true cost to the employer of providing pensions in that period. The financial statements must reflect the true cost of providing pensions.

Multi-employer plans

Often a small company does not have the resources to run a pension plan in-house, so it pays pension contributions over to an insurance company which runs a multi-employer plan. Such a plan can be either of a defined contribution nature or a defined benefit nature.

Alternatively, a group may operate a plan for the employees of all its subsidiaries.

2 Accounting for pension plans (IAS 19)

Defined contribution plans

The expense of providing pensions in the period is normally the same as the amount of contributions paid.

- The entity should charge the agreed pension contribution to profit or loss as an employment expense in each period.

- An asset or liability for pensions only arises if the cash paid does not equal the amount of contributions paid.

- IAS 19 requires disclosure of the amount recognised as an expense in the period.

Test your understanding 1

A company makes contributions to the pension fund of employees at a rate of 5% of gross salary. The contributions made are $10,000 per month for convenience with the balance being contributed in the first month of the following accounting year. The wages and salaries for 20X6 are $2.7m.

Calculate the pension expense for 20X6, and the accrual/prepayment at the end of the year.

Defined benefit plans: the basic principle

The entity recognises both the liability for future pension payments and the scheme assets.

- If the liability exceeds the assets, there is a deficit (the usual situation) and a liability is reported in the statement of financial position.

- If the scheme assets exceed the liability, there is a surplus and an asset is reported in the statement of financial position.

- In simple terms, the pension expense for the period is the difference between the deficit/surplus at the beginning of the period and the deficit/surplus at the end of the period.

Measuring the liability and the assets

In practice, the actuary measures the plan assets and liabilities using a number of estimates and assumptions.

- The plan liability is measured at the present value of the defined benefit obligation, using the Projected Unit Credit Method. This is an actuarial valuation method.

- Discounting is necessary because the liability will be settled many years in the future and therefore, the effect of the time value of money is material. The discount rate used should be determined by market yields on high quality corporate bonds at the reporting date.

- Plan assets are measured at fair value. This is normally market value. Where no market value is available, fair value is estimated (for example, by calculating the present value of expected future cash flows).

- Valuations should be carried out with sufficient regularity to ensure that the amounts recognised in the financial statements do not differ materially from actual fair values at the reporting date. In other words, IAS 19 does not prescribe a maximum time interval between valuations.

- Where there are unpaid contributions at the year-end, these are not included in the plan assets. Unpaid contributions are treated as an ordinary liability; they are owed by the entity/employer to the plan.

Recognising the amounts in the financial statements

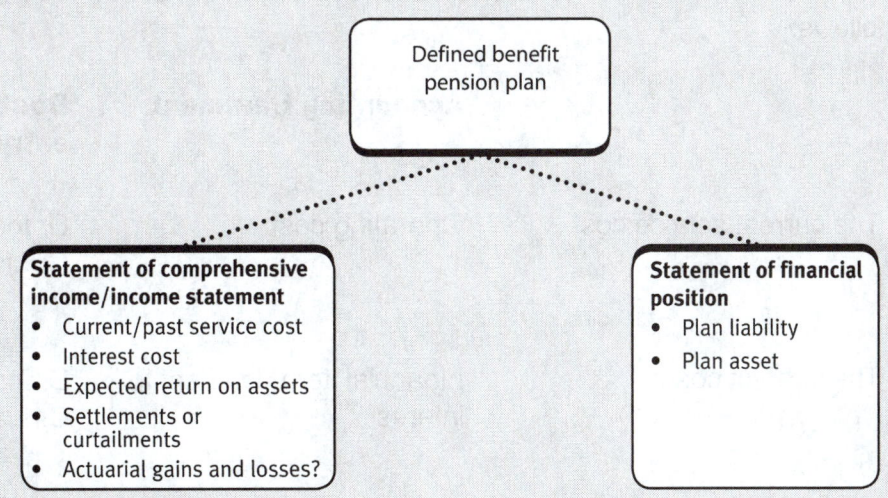

 Explanation of the terms used.

- **Current service cost** is the increase in the actuarial liability (present value of the defined benefit obligation) resulting from employee service in the current period.

- **Past service cost** is the increase in the actuarial liability relating to employee service in the previous period but only arising in the current period. Past service costs usually arise because there has been an improvement in the benefits being provided under the plan.

- **Interest cost** is the increase in the pension liability arising from the unwinding of the discount as the liability is one period nearer to being settled.

- **Expected return on assets** is the expected return earned from the pension scheme assets.

- In IAS 19, **Curtailments and settlements** are the gains and losses arising when major reductions are made to the number of employees in the plan or the benefits promised to them.

- **Actuarial gains and losses** are increases and decreases in the pension asset or liability that occur either because the actuarial assumptions have changed or because of differences between the previous actuarial assumptions and what has actually happened (experience adjustments). For example, the investment income from the assets may have been greater than expected.

Effect on profit or loss for the period

The changes in the defined benefit asset/liability in the period are treated as follows:

	Accounting treatment	Double entry
The current service cost	Operating cost	Dr Income Cr Liability
The interest cost	Financial item adjacent to interest	Dr Income Cr Liability
The expected return on assets	Financial item adjacent to interest	Dr Asset Cr Income
Past service costs (if any)	Operating cost	Dr Income Cr Liability
Curtailments and settlements (if any)	Operating cost	Dr Income Cr Liability

- IAS 19 does not specify in which line items should be reported, but this treatment is the logical one to adopt.
- Actuarial gains and losses may also be reported in profit or loss (this is covered in detail later in the chapter).

Expandable text - Illustration: Acc'tg for defined benefit plans

The following information is given about a defined benefit plan. All transactions are assumed to occur at the year-end. The present value of the obligation and the fair value of the plan assets were both $1,000 at 1 January 20X1.

	20X1	20X2	20X3
Discount rate at start of year	10.0%	9.0%	8.0%
Expected rate of return on plan assets at start of year	12.0%	11.1%	10.3%
Current service cost ($)	130	220	150
Benefits paid ($)	150	180	190
Contributions received ($)	90	100	110
Present value of obligation at 31 December ($)	1,141	1,197	1,295
Fair value of plan assets at 31 December ($)	1,092	1,109	1,093

All actuarial gains and losses are recognised immediately in profit or loss for the year.

Step 1: Determine the amount of the actuarial gains or losses for the period.

This is done by analysing the change in assets and in the pension obligation for the period. The actuarial gains or losses are balancing figures.

The calculations are made year by year because the closing figures for each year form the opening figures for the following year.

It may be difficult to understand which figures appear in the 'obligations' calculation and which in the 'assets' calculation.

- Actual cash receipts and payments appear in the plan assets calculation. Contributions received increase the plan assets and benefits paid reduce the plan assets.

- Benefits paid appear in both calculations because the payment reduces assets but also reduces the liability.

Liability

	20X1	20X2	20X3
	$	$	$
Present value of obligation, 1 January	1,000	1,141	1,197
Interest cost (at discount rate for each year)	100	103	96
Current service cost	130	220	150
Benefits paid	(150)	(180)	(190)
Actuarial (gain) loss on obligation (balancing figure)	61	(87)	42
Present value of obligation, 31 December	1,141	1,197	1,295
Contributions received	90	100	110
	32	(24)	(50)

Assets

	$	$	$
Fair value of plan assets, 1 January	1,000	1,092	1,109
Expected return on plan assets (at expected rate for each year)	120	121	114
Contributions received	90	100	110
Benefits paid	(150)	(180)	(190)
Actuarial gain (loss) on plan assets (balancing figure)	32	(24)	(50)
Fair value of plan assets, 31 December	1,092	1,109	1,093

Step 2: Calculate the liability

This is the difference between the plan obligations and the plan assets (net liability):

	20X1	20X2	20X3
Present value of the obligation	1,141	1,197	1,295
Fair value of plan assets	(1,092)	(1,109)	(1,093)
Liability recognised in statement of financial position	49	88	202

Step 3 : Calculate the charge to profits

This is the current service cost plus interest cost, minus the return on plan assets, adjusted for the actuarial gains and losses:

	20X1	20X2	20X3
Current service cost	130	220	150
Interest cost	100	103	96
Expected return on plan assets	(120)	(121)	(114)
Net actuarial loss (gain) recognised in year (61 – 32, (87) – (24), 42 – (50))	29	(63)	92
Expense recognised in the profit or loss	139	139	224

KAPLAN PUBLISHING

Movements in the net liability recognised in the statement of financial position (proof)

	20X1	20X2	20X3
Opening net liability	–	49	88
Expense as above	139	139	224
Contributions	(90)	(100)	(110)
Closing net liability	49	88	202

This statement reconciles the figures in the statement of financial position using the charges to profit or loss.

Test your understanding 2

The following information is given about a defined benefit plan. To keep the computations simple, all transactions are assumed to occur at the year-end. The present value of the obligation and the market value of the plan assets were both $1,000 at 1 January 20X1.

	20X1	20X2	20X3
Discount rate at start of year	10%	9%	8%
Expected rate of return on plan assets at start of year	12%	11%	10%
Current service cost	130	140	150
Benefits paid	150	180	190
Contributions paid	90	100	110
Present value of obligations at 31 December	1,100	1,380	1,408
Market value of plan assets at 31 December	1,190	1,372	1,188

Show how the pension scheme would be shown in the accounts for 20X1, 20X2 and 20X3, given the immediate recognition of the actuarial gain/loss arising in the year in income.

Expandable text - Problems with the IAS 19 approach

Retirement benefit accounting is a controversial area. Commentators have perceived the following problems with the IAS 19 approach.

- Fair values of plan assets may be volatile. Even though actuarial gains and losses may not all immediately recognised in the profit or loss, there may be significant fluctuations in the statement of financial position.

- IAS 19 requires plan assets to be valued at fair value (normally market value). Fair values of plan assets are not relevant to the economic reality of most pension schemes. Under the requirements of IAS 19, assets are valued at short-term amounts, but most pension scheme assets and liabilities are held for the long term. The actuarial basis of valuing plan assets would better reflect the long-term costs of funding a pension scheme.

- The treatment of pension costs in the income statement is complex and may not be easily understood by users of the financial statements. It has been argued that all the components of the pension cost are so interrelated that it does not make sense to present them separately.

- A pension plan surplus meets the IASB's definition of an asset and so IAS 19 treats it as if it 'belongs' to the employer. However, in practice the situation is that the surplus 'belongs' to the members of the plan and must be applied for their benefit. IAS 19 does not reflect the legal and economic reality of the situation.

Multi-employer plans

Multi-employer plans are classified as either defined contribution plans or defined benefit plans.

Defined contribution multi-employer plans do not pose a problem because the employer's cost is limited to the contributions payable.

Defined benefit multi-employer plans expose participating employers to the actuarial risks associated with the current and former employees of other entities. There are also potential problems because an employer may be unable to identify its share of the underlying assets and liabilities.

IAS 19 states that where a multi-employer plan is a defined benefit plan, the entity accounts for its proportionate share of the obligations, benefits and costs associated with the plan in the same way as usual.

KAPLAN PUBLISHING

Where sufficient information is not available to do this, the entity accounts for the plan as if it were a defined contribution plan and discloses:

- the fact that the plan is a defined benefit plan

- the reason why sufficient information is not available to account for the plan as a defined benefit plan.

Past service costs

Past service costs arise either where a new retirement benefit plan is introduced, or where the benefits under an existing plan are improved. Where a new plan is introduced, employees are often given benefit rights for their years of service before the introduction of the plan.

- If employees have the right to receive benefits under the plan immediately, the benefits are said to be 'vested' and the cost must be recognised immediately.

- If employees become entitled to benefits only at some later date, the benefits become vested at that later date, and the costs may be spread on a straight-line basis over the average period until the vesting date.

- Because recognised past service costs increase the plan liability, any that are unrecognised past service costs are deducted in arriving at the plan liability in the statement of financial position.

Illustration 1 – Accounting for pension plans

An entity operates a pension plan that provides a pension of 2% of final salary for each year of service. The benefits become vested after five years of service. On 1 January 20X5, the entity improves the pension to 2.5% of final salary, for each year of service starting from 1 January 20X1. At the date of the improvement, the present value of the additional benefits for service from 1 January 20X1 to 1 January 20X5, is as follows:

	$000
Employees with more than five years' service at 1.1.X5	150
Employees with less than five years' service at 1.1.X5	
(average period until vesting: three years)	120
	270

How are the additional benefits treated in the financial statements of the entity?

> **Expandable text - Solution**
>
> The entity recognises $150,000 immediately, because those benefits are already vested.
>
> The entity recognises $120,000 on a straight-line basis over three years from 1 January 20X5.

Curtailments and settlements

A **curtailment** occurs when an entity:

- is demonstrably committed to making a material reduction in the number of employees covered by a plan

- amends the terms of a plan such that a material element of future service by current employees will qualify for no or reduced benefits

- for example, an entity closes a plant and makes those employees redundant.

A **settlement** occurs when an entity enters into a transaction to eliminate the obligation for part or all of the benefits under a plan.

For example, an employee leaves the entity for a new job elsewhere, and is paid a cheque by the retirement benefit plan to transfer out of that plan.

The gain or loss arising on a curtailment or settlement should be recognised when the curtailment or settlement occurs.

The gain or loss comprises the difference between the fair value of the plan assets paid out and the reduction in the present value of the defined benefit obligation (together with the relevant proportion of any unrecognised actuarial gains and losses and past service costs in respect of the transaction).

Curtailments and settlements do not affect profit and loss if they have already been allowed for in the actuarial assumptions.

Liability in statement of financial position

Under IAS 19 the carrying amount of the defined benefit liability is the net total of:

- the present value of the defined benefit obligation at the reporting date

- plus any actuarial gains (less actuarial losses) not yet recognised (see later in this chapter for the rules for not recognising such gains/losses)

- minus any past service cost not yet recognised
- minus the fair value of the plan assets at the reporting date.

It may seem odd to **add** unrecognised gains (and **deduct** unrealised losses) in arriving at the net liability. The way to think of this is that if the gains were recognised, they would reduce the plan liability or increase the plan assets; either way, the net liability would be reduced. As they have not been recognised, they must increase the liability. (And vice versa for unrecognised losses.)

Illustration 2 – Accounting for pension plans

AB decides to close a business segment. The segment's employees are made redundant and will earn no further pension benefits. Their plan assets will remain in the scheme so that the employees will be paid a reduced pension when they reach pensionable age (i.e. this is a curtailment without a settlement).

Before the curtailment, the plan assets had a fair value of $500,000, the defined benefit obligation had a present value of $600,000 and there were net cumulative unrecognised actuarial gains of $30,000. The curtailment reduces the present value of the obligation by $60,000 (because the employees will not now receive the pay rises they would have been awarded).

What is the gain or loss arising on the curtailment?

Expandable text - Solution

60 / 600 = 10% of the obligation is eliminated on the curtailment, so we recognise 10% of the previously unrecognised actuarial gains (which are an additional liability of the plan).

	Before	On curtailment	After
	$000	$000	$000
Present value of obligation	600	(60)	540
Fair value of plan assets	(500)	–	(500)
Unrecognised actuarial gains	30	(3)	27
Net liability in SFP	130	(63)	67

The gain on curtailment is $63,000.

Expandable text - Additional illustration

T has a defined benefit pension plan and makes up financial statements to 31 March each year. The net pension liability (i.e. obligation less plan assets) at 31 March 20X3, was $40 million ($35 million at 31 March 20X2). The following additional information is relevant for the year ended 31 March 20X3:

- The net pension liability at 31 March 20X3, is stated before making any adjustment in respect of actuarial gains or losses arising in the year.

- No actuarial gains or losses were recognised in profit or loss for the year.

- The expected return on assets was $60 million.

- The unwinding of the discount on the pension liability was $30 million.

- The current service cost was $45 million.

- The company granted additional benefits to existing pensioners that vested immediately and that have a present value of $10 million. These were not allowed for in the original actuarial assumptions.

- The company paid pension contributions of $40 million.

What is the actuarial gain or loss arising in the year ended 31 March 20X3?

Solution

	$m
Liability b/f	(35)
Expected return on assets	60
Unwinding of discount (interest cost)	(30)
Current service cost	(45)
Additional benefits granted (past service costs)	(10)
Pension contributions paid	40
Actuarial loss (bal fig)	(20)
Liability c/f	(40)

KAPLAN PUBLISHING

3 Reporting actuarial gains and losses

Methods of recognising actuarial gains and losses

Actuarial valuations are based on assumptions. Actuarial gains and losses arise because the actual outturn does not match the original estimates and 'experience adjustments' are needed. Actuarial assumptions may also be changed in the light of events, such as increasing life expectancy.

IAS 19 allows several methods of dealing with actuarial gains and losses.

- They may be recognised immediately in profit or loss.

- They may be recognised immediately as other comprehensive income and recorded in equity.

- If they fall within certain size limits, they may be carried forward in the statement of financial position to be spread over future periods. An unrecognised actuarial gain is added to the plan liability; an unrecognised actuarial loss is deducted from the plan liability.

Expandable text

There are arguments for each of the methods of dealing with actuarial gains and losses. The basis chosen must be applied consistently for both gains and losses and from period to period.

Immediate recognition in profit or loss treats actuarial gains and losses in a similar way to long-term provisions for future losses. It can be argued that this method results in the recognition of the 'full' cost of providing a pension, but it can make reported results very unpredictable.

Recognition in other comprehensive income means that gains and losses are treated in a similar way to gains and losses when assets are revalued. They are included in an entity's total performance for the year, but their volatility does not have an impact on reported profits. This approach is consistent with the equivalent UK standard.

Carrying gains and losses forward in the statement of financial position treats them as actual assets and liabilities. Many argue that showing the unrecognised cumulative actuarial gains and losses in the statement of financial position is contrary to the IASB Framework, since they are not assets, liabilities or equity. The main argument for this approach is that because actuarial gains and losses may cancel out over a period of time, they should not be recognised until they become material.

It can also be argued that allowing such a wide range of possible treatments could enable preparers of financial statements to manipulate profits. The choice of method may make it difficult for users to understand the impact of the pension plan on the financial statements and to compare the financial statements of different entities.

The '10% corridor'

Where actuarial gains and losses are carried forward in the statement of financial position (not recognised in one of the performance statements), IAS 19 states that if the net cumulative unrecognised actuarial gains and losses at the end of the **previous** period, exceed the greater of:

- 10% of the present value of the plan obligation
- 10% of the fair value of plan assets

the excess must be recognised in profit or loss.

- The whole of the gain or loss need not be recognised immediately, it may be spread over the expected average remaining working lives of the employees.
- Other methods of spreading the gains and losses may be used provided that:
  - the alternative method results in a faster recognition of actuarial gains and losses
  - the same basis is applied to both gains and losses
  - the basis is applied consistently from period to period.

Illustration 3 – Reporting actuarial gains and losses

The following figures relate to a defined benefit pension plan for 20X7. Unrecognised actuarial gains were $40 million at the beginning of the year. The average remaining service lives of the employees is 8 years.

	$m
Plan assets	
Balance at 1 January 20X7	300
Expected return on plan assets	30
Contributions received	25
Benefits paid	(20)
Actuarial gain (balancing figure)	5
Balance at 31 December 20X7	340

Plan liabilities

Balance at 1 January 20X7	320
Interest cost	25
Current service cost	10
Benefits paid	(20)
Actuarial loss (balancing figure)	20
	___
Balance at 31 December 20X7	355
	___

Calculate the pension expense recognised in the profit or loss for the year ended 31 December 20X7 and the net liability in the statement of financial position at 31 December 20X7.

Expandable text - Solution

Calculate the limits of the 'corridor'. These are the greater of:

- 10% of the opening liabilities: 10% × 320 = $32 million
- 10% of the opening plan assets: 10% × 300 = $30 million.

Some of the actuarial gains must be recognised as the $40 million amount of the unrecognised gains brought forward is greater than $32 million.

The amount to be recognised is $8 million (40 – 32) divided by the average remaining service life of 8 years = $1 million.

Therefore, the expense recognised in profit or loss is:

	$m
Current service cost	10
Interest cost	25
Expected return on plan assets	(30)
Actuarial gain recognised	(1)
	___
	4
	___

Unrecognised actuarial gains at 31 December 20X7 are:

	$m
Balance at 1 January	40
Actuarial gain for the year – plan assets	5
Actuarial loss for the year – plan liabilities	(20)
Actuarial gain recognised in profit or loss	(1)
	___
Balance at 31 December	24
	___

The amount recognised in the statement of financial position is:

	$m
Plan liabilities	355
Plan assets	(340)
	___
	15
Unrecognised actuarial gains	24
	___
Net liability	39
	___

Test your understanding 3 - Jake

The 10% corridor approach - question

Jake is finalising its accounts for the year ended 30 June 20X8. Jake operates a defined benefit pension scheme for all its eligible employees. The current service cost of operating the scheme was $10.1 million for the year ended 30 June 20X8. At 30 June 20X7, the fair value of the pension scheme assets was $94.9 million and the present value of the pension scheme liabilities was $104.0 million. $12.5 million of unrecognised actuarial losses were brought forward at 1 July 20X7.

Jake made contributions to the scheme in the year of $11.4 million. The expected return on the pension scheme assets is 8.5% and the finance cost for the year is $13.2 million. The pension scheme paid out $5.2 million in benefits in the year to 30 June 20X8.
Jake adopts IAS 19 Employee Benefits and follows the corridor approach in recognising actuarial gains and losses. As at 30 June 20X8, the fair value of pension scheme assets was $109.0 million and the present value of pension scheme liabilities was $123.5 million. The average remaining service lives of employees who participate in the scheme is 7 years.

Required:

(a) **Calculate the expense, in respect of the pension scheme, that Jake will include in its income statement for the year ended 30 June 20X8.**

(b) **Calculate the net pension asset or liability that will appear in the statement of financial position of Jake as at 30 June 20X8.**

Expandable text - The 'Asset Ceiling'

Sometimes the deduction of plan assets from the pension obligation results in a negative amount: an asset. IAS 19 states that pension plan assets (surpluses) are measured at the **lower** of:

• the amount calculated above

• the total of:
  – any cumulative unrecognised net actuarial losses and past service costs
  – the present value of any economic benefits available in the form of refunds from the plan or reductions in future contributions to the plan.

Applying the 'asset ceiling' means that a surplus can only be recognised to the extent that it will be recoverable in the form of refunds or reduced contributions in future.

Expandable text illustration - The asset ceiling

The following information relates to a defined benefit plan:	$000
Fair value of plan assets	950
Present value of pension liability	800
Present value of future refunds and reductions in future contributions	70
Unrecognised actuarial losses	80
Unrecognised past service cost	50

What is the amount of the asset that is recognised in the financial statements?

Expandable text - Solution

The amount that can be recognised is the lower of:

	$000
Present value of pension liability	800
Fair value of plan assets	(950)
	(150)
Unrecognised actuarial losses	(80)
Unrecognised past service cost	(50)
Surplus (pension plan asset)	(280)

	$000
Unrecognised actuarial losses	80
Unrecognised past service cost	50
Present value of future refunds and reductions in future contributions	70
	200

Therefore the amount of the asset recognised is restricted to $200,000.

Expandable text – IFRIC 14

IFRIC 14 – IAS 19 – The limit on a defined benefit asset minimum funding requirements and their interaction

IFRIC 14 addresses areas of IAS 19 where detailed guidance is lacking, namely:

- How to determine the asset ceiling

- The effect of a minimum funding requirement (MFR) on that calculation.

- When an MFR creates an onerous obligation that should be recognised as a liability.

It therefore only applies to those entities which have a plan surplus or are subject to minimum funding requirements.

Entities with a plan surplus

IAS 19 states that pension plan surpluses are limited to the total of

- Cumulative unrecognised net actuarial losses and past service costs
- The present value of any economic benefits available in the form of refunds from the plan or reductions in future contributions to the plan.

IFRIC 14, together with a subsequent amendment dated 26 November 2009, clarifies several issues relating to IAS 19:

- **'Available'**

  An economic benefit, in the form of a refund or reduction in future is 'available' if the entity has an **unconditional** right to realise the benefit at some point during the life of the plan or when the plan is settled, even if the benefit is not realisable immediately at the reporting date.

  If such a right is conditional no asset in respect of refunds or reductions in contributions can be recognised.

- **Minimum funding requirements**

In many countries, laws or contractual terms require employers to make minimum funding payments (MFR) for their pension or other employee benefit plans. This enhances the security of the retirement benefit promise made to members of an employee benefit plan.

A liability is recognised for MFR contributions to cover existing plan shortfalls in respect of services already received if the contribution payable is not expected to be available after it is paid into a plan.

In the specific situation where there is a MFR in place, and there has been early payment of contributions to cover the MFR, the amendment to IFRIC 14 enables the benefits of that early payment to be recognised as an asset.

Expandable text - Disclosure requirements

IAS 19 has extensive disclosure requirements.

In summary, an entity should disclose the following information about defined benefit plans:

- the entity's accounting policy for recognising actuarial gains and losses

- a general description of the type of plan

- a reconciliation of the assets and liabilities recognised in the statement of financial position

- a reconciliation showing the movements during the period in the net liability (or asset) recognised in the statement of financial position

- the total expense recognised in profit or loss the actual return on plan assets

- the principal actuarial assumptions used as at the reporting date.

Expandable text - Question A

A

A, a public limited company, operates a defined benefit plan. A full actuarial valuation by an independent actuary revealed that the value of the liability at 31 May 20X0 was $1,500 million. This was updated to 31 May 20X1 by the actuary and the value of the liability at that date was $2,000 million. The scheme assets comprised mainly bonds and equities and the fair value of these assets was as follows:

	31 May 20X0	31 May 20X1
	$m	$m
Fixed interest and index linked bonds	380	600
Equities	1,300	1,900
Other investments	290	450
	_____	_____
	1,970	2,950
	_____	_____

KAPLAN PUBLISHING

The scheme had been altered during the year with improved benefits arising for the employees and this had been taken into account by the actuaries. The increase in the actuarial liability in respect of employee service in prior periods was $25 million (past service cost). The increase in the actuarial liability resulting from employee service in the current period was $70 million (current service cost). The company had not recognised any net actuarial gain or loss in the income statement to date.

The company had paid contributions of $60 million to the scheme during the period. The company expects its return on the scheme assets at 31 May 20X1 to be $295 million and the interest on pension liabilities to be $230 million.

The average expected remaining working lives of the employees is 10 years and the net cumulative unrecognized gains at 1 June 20X0 were $247 million.

Required:

(a) Explain the main accounting requirements of IAS 19 (Employee benefits) with respect to pensions and describe the particular problems which IAS 19 creates in respect of defined benefit schemes, such as the one operated by A.

(10 marks)

(b) Calculate the amount which will be shown as the net plan asset in the statement of financial position of A as at 31 May 20X1, showing a reconciliation of the movement in the plan surplus during the year and a statement of those amounts which would be charged to operating profit. (Candidates should utilise IAS 19 **Employee benefits** in answering the question.)

(15 marks)

(Total: 25 marks)

Expandable text - Solution

Answer A

(a) IAS 19 regards the cost of providing a pension as part of the cost of obtaining the services of its work force, even though that pension might not be paid until sometime in the relatively distant future.

IAS 19 requires that the cost of the pension should be recognised on a systematic and rational basis over the period during which the company benefits from the employee's services. Thus, the IAS requires the application of the matching concept so that the full cost of an employee's pension is charged to the profit and loss account during that person's period of service.

Under a defined benefit scheme, the employees are entitled to a pension which is likely to be based on their salary at the time of their retirement. A defined benefit scheme creates a potential liability which is related to a variety of unknown factors: salaries at time of retirement, life expectancy after retirement, probability of death in service, etc. This creates a potential liability which is extremely difficult to measure. Companies must normally seek advice from actuaries, experts in statistics and investment who specialise in this type of field.

Given this requirement, it is possible that the charge to the income statement will not be the same as the amount of the company's annual contribution. In particular, some basis has to be found for accounting for the effects of surpluses or deficits from investments or changes in the expected value of the future pension commitments.

(b) Net plan asset for inclusion on the statement of financial position:

	31 May 20X1	31 May 20X0
	$m	$m
Asset at fair value	(2,950)	(1,970)
Liability at present value	2,000	1,500
Unrecognised actuarial gains (Step 3 below)	692	247
Net plan asset	(258)	(223)

This requires application of the "10% corridor" approach to recognition of excess actuarial gains or losses as follows:

Step 1 - identify the 10% corridor limit:

10% of the greater of the PV of the liability brought forward or 10% of the FV of the asset brought forward - take 10% x 1970 = $197m

Step 2 - compare this with the cumulative unrecognised actuarial gains or losses brought forward = $247m - this gives excess actuarial gains of $50m which should be released to income on a systematic basis - normally the average working lives of employees - in this case 10 years.

The release of the excess unrecognised gains to income should therefore be at the annual rate of $5m over the next ten years.

Step 3 - reconcile the cumulative unrecognised gains or losses to carry forward to the next accounting period:

Unrecognised actuarial gains reconciliation	$m
Balance b'fwd	247
Actuarial gains on assets for the year (W1)	625
Actuarial loss on liabilities for the year (W1)	(175)
Excess transferred to income for the year (Step 2 above)	(5)
Cumulative unrecognised gains carried forward	692

(W1) Reconciliation of scheme assets and liabilities	Assets	Liabilities	IS charge
	$m	$m	$m
Bal b'fwd	1,970	1,500	
Expected return	295		(295)
Finance cost		230	230
Current service cost		70	70
Past service cost		25	25
Contributions into scheme	60		
Actuarial gain (bal fig)	625		
Actuarial loss (bal fig)		175	
Release of excess actuarial gains (W)			(5)
bal c'fwd	2,950	2,000	25

Workings

(W1)

	$m
Unrecognised actuarial gains at 1 June 20X0	247
Actuarial gain/(loss) – obligation (2,000 – 1,500)	(500)
Actuarial gain/(loss) – plan assets (2,950 – 1,970)	980
Actuarial gain recognised	(5)
Unrecognised actuarial gain 31 May 20X1	722

	Net contributions in year is:	
	Contributions	60
	Net charge to income	(25)
	Actuarial gain	(5)
		———
		30
		———

(W2)	The actuarial gain will be recognised as follows:		$m
	Net unrecognised gain		247
	Limits of 10% corridor (greater of 10% of 1,500 or 10% of 1,970)		(197)
			———
	Excess		50
			———
	Amortisation is therefore (50 ÷10 years)		5
			———

Charge to income statement

Current service cost	70
Past service cost	25
Interest on liabilities	230
Actuarial gain recognised	(5)
Return on scheme assets	(295)
	———
Net charge to income statement	25
	———

Movement in plan surplus

Opening surplus – asset	197	
– liability	(150)	
	———	470
Unrecognised actuarial gain		(247)
		———
Opening net surplus		223
Expense as above		(25)
Net contributions		30
		———
Closing net surplus in plan		228
		———

Note: As the benefits are vested immediately following an alteration to the plan, the past service cost is recognised immediately.

Expandable text - Current issues

In March 2008, the IASB published a discussion paper, **Preliminary views on amendments to IAS 19 Employee benefits.**
This is the first step in a comprehensive project to review all aspects of post –employment benefit accounting, and focuses on short-term improvements to IAS 19. In the longer term, the IASB and FASB intend to work towards a new common standard on the topic.

The scope of the DP was limited to:

*   The deferred recognition of some gains and losses arising from defined benefit plans

*   Presentation of defined benefit liabilities

*   Accounting for benefits that are based on contributions and a promised return

*   Accounting for benefit promises with a 'higher of' option.

The next step

Comments on the DP were invited by September 2008, following which the IASB Board decided to work towards three separate exposure drafts as follows:

*   An ED on the discount rate for measuring employee benefits. This was published in August 2009; however, at its October 2009 meeting, IASB decided not to proceed with an amendment to the discount rate for measuring employee benefits. The consequence of this decision is that entities will still need to refer to a government bond rate when there is no market in high quality corporate bonds.

*   An ED on the recognition and presentation of changes in the defined benefit obligation and in plan assets, disclosures, and other issues. This is expected to be issued in early 2010.

*   An ED on contribution-based promises, potentially as part of a comprehensive review of pension accounting. A date has still to be set for the issue of this ED.

The IASB aims to make fundamental improvements to the recognition, presentation and disclosures of defined benefit plans by mid-2011. These improvements will make it easier for users of financial statements to understand how defined benefit plans affect an entity's financial position, financial performance and cash flows. The project was added to the IASB's agenda in July 2006 and is part of the FASB and the IASB's work programme towards convergence.

Defined benefit plans

In April 2010, the IASB published an ED and plans to finalise amendments to IAS 19 in mid-2011.

Defined benefit plans give rise to large and highly uncertain costs for many companies and estimating those costs can be extremely complex. Investors, analysts and others need relevant information about those items that is easy to understand and permits comparison between companies. The ED proposes improvements in the following areas:

- Immediate recognition of defined benefit cost

- Presentation

- Disclosure

Termination Benefits

In June 2005, the IASB published an ED of Amendments to IAS 19, dealing with the accounting for termination benefits, together with proposed amendments to IAS 37 Provisions, Contingent Liabilities and Contingent Assets.

Proposals within the ED included change to the definition of what may constitute termination benefits. The definition of termination benefits in IAS 19 includes employee benefits that are payable as a result of an employee's decision to accept voluntary redundancy in exchange for those benefits. The proposal is that the amended definition should clarify that benefits that are payable in exchange for an employee's decision to accept voluntary redundancy are termination benefits only if they are offered for a short period.

In addition, IAS 19 states that termination benefits should be recognised when the entity is demonstrably committed either to terminating the employment of employees before the normal retirement date or to providing termination benefits as a result of an offer made in order to encourage voluntary redundancy.

It is proposed that:

- voluntary termination benefits should be recognised when employees accept the entity's offer of those benefits.

- involuntary termination benefits should be recognised when the entity has communicated its plan of termination to the affected employees and the plan meets specified criteria, unless the involuntary termination benefits are provided in exchange for employees' future services (ie in substance they are a 'stay bonus'). In such cases, the liability for those benefits should be recognised over the future service period.

The date of publication of the final amendment is yet to be confirmed.

Discount rate for Employee Benefits

IAS 19 requires an entity to determine the rate used to discount employee benefits by reference to market yields on high quality corporate bonds at the end of the reporting period. However, when there is no deep market in such bonds, IAS 19 requires an entity to use market yields on government bonds instead.

Some responses to the DP indicated that this requirement means that entities with similar employee benefit obligations can report them at very different amounts. This effect has been much greater as a result of the global financial crisis because of the significant widening of the spread between yields on corporate bonds and yields on government bonds. It has also been suggested that the issue could be resolved without pre-empting the IASB's plans for a more fundamental review of accounting for employee benefits.

The Board concluded that there would be benefit in improving the comparability of financial statements across entities and through time for the same entity in the current circumstances, and in August 2009 published the ED Discount Rate for Employee Benefits aimed at addressing the issue expeditiously.

The ED proposed to remove the requirement to use a government bond rate when there is no deep market in high quality corporate bonds. Instead, an entity would be required to estimate the rate for a high quality corporate bond using the guidance on determining fair value in IAS 39. Entities would apply the proposed amendment prospectively from the end of the accounting period in which the amendment is adopted, with any adjustment arising from the change in accounting policy going direct to retained earnings.

Responses to the ED indicated that the proposed amendment raised more complex issues than had been expected. It was therefore decided to adhere to the original plan to address measurement issues only in the context of a fundamental review. Consequently, a decision was made not to proceed with the amendment. This means that entities will still need to refer to a government bond rate when there is no deep market in high-quality corporate bonds.

In October 2009, the decision was made to not tp proceed with this amendment.

Expandable text - UK syllabus focus

The ACCA UK syllabus contains a requirement that candidates should be able to discuss and apply the key differences between UK GAAP and IFRS GAAP. The accounting requirements of UK GAAP and IFRS GAAP are very similar in this area; the key issues associated with UK reporting standard requirements are as follows:

- under UK FRS 17, the accounting treatment for actuarial gains and losses is that they are taken to STRGL (i.e. reserves). The rationale for this treatment is that any gains or losses are recognised as part of overall performance, but without distortion of reported profits. In addition, having only one accounting treatment improves comparability of reported results.

4 Chapter summary

Types of pension plan
- Defined contribution
- Defined benefit

ACCOUNTING FOR DEFINED CONTRIBUTION PLANS

Accounting for defined benefit plans
- Recognising plan assets and obligations
- Measuring plan assets and obligations
- Reporting in the statement of financial position
- Reporting in the income statement/statement of comprehensive income
- Past service costs
- Curtailments and settlements

Actuarial gains and losses
- Recognition methods
- 10% corridor
- Applying the asset ceiling

Test your understanding answers

Test your understanding 1

This appears to be a defined contribution scheme.

The charge to income should be:

$2.7m × 5% = $135,000

The statement of financial position will therefore show an accrual of $15,000, being the difference between the $135,000 and the $120,000 paid in the year.

Test your understanding 2

Step 1 - Calculate actuarial gains and losses

On obligations	20X1	20X2	20X3
Obligation at start of the year	1,000	1,100	1,380
Interest	100	99	110
Current service cost	130	140	150
Benefits paid	(50)	(180)	(190)
Actuarial (gain) loss - bal.fig	20	221	(42)
Obligation at end of the year	1,100	1,380	1,408

On assets	20X1	20X2	20X3
Market value at start of the year	1,000	1,190	1,372
Expected return on the assets	120	131	137
Contributions	90	100	110
Benefits paid	(150)	(180)	(190)
Actuarial gain (loss) - bal. fig	130	131	(241)
Market value at end of the year	1,190	1,372	1,188

Step 2 - The statement of financial position

Pension assets	1,190	1,372	1,188
Pension obligations	(1,100)	(1,380)	(1,408)
Pension asset (liability)	90	(8)	(220)

Step 3 - The income statement / statement of comprehensive income

	20X1	20X2	20X3
Operating expense			
Current service cost	130	140	150
Interest cost	100	99	110
Expected return on assets	(120)	(131)	(137)
	110	108	123
Actuarial (gain) loss on assets	(130)	(131)	241
Actuarial (gain) loss on obligation	20	221	(42)

Test your understanding 3 - Jake

The 10% corridor approach - answer

(a) Expense recognised in the income statement for the year ended 30 June 20X8:

	$m
Current service cost	10.1
Return on assets (8.5% × $94.9m)	(8.0)
Finance cost - given in question	13.2
Actuarial gain/(loss) to recognise(W1)	0.3
	———
	15.6
	———

(b) Net pension asset or liability recognised in the statement of financial position at 30 June 20X8:

	$m	$m
Closing pension liability	123.5	
Closing pension asset	(109.0)	
	———	14.5
Unrecognised actuarial losses carried forward (W2)		(13.7)
		———
		0.8
		———

W1 Actuarial gain or loss ro recognise in income statement for the year to 30 June 20X8:

	$m	$m
Unrecognised actuarial losses brought forward		12.5
10% corridor is the higher of:		
10% opening asset $94.9m = $9.5m		
10% opening liability $104.0 = $10.4m		(10.4)
		———
		2.1
Spread over remaining average service life of 7 years	0.3	———

W2 Unrecognised actuarial gains and losses in current year:

	$m
Unrecognised actuarial losses brought forward	12.5
Actuarial loss arising in the current year (W3)	1.5
Actuarial loss recognised in the current year	(0.3)
Unrecognised actuarial loss at 30 June 20X8 carried forward	13.7

W3 Actuarial gain or loss in the year to 30 June 20X8:

	$m	$m
Opening liability	104.0	
Opening asset	(94.9)	
		9.1
Current service cost		10.1
Contributions into scheme		(11.4)
Return on assets (8.5% × $94.9m)		(8.0)
Finance cost (given in question)		13.2
		13.0
Net actuarial loss (bal fig)		1.5
Closing liability	123.5	
Closing asset	(109.0)	14.5

Share-based payment

Chapter learning objectives

Upon completion of this chapter you will be able to:

- apply and discuss the recognition and measurement criteria for share-based payment transactions

- account for modifications, cancellations and settlements of share-based payment transactions.

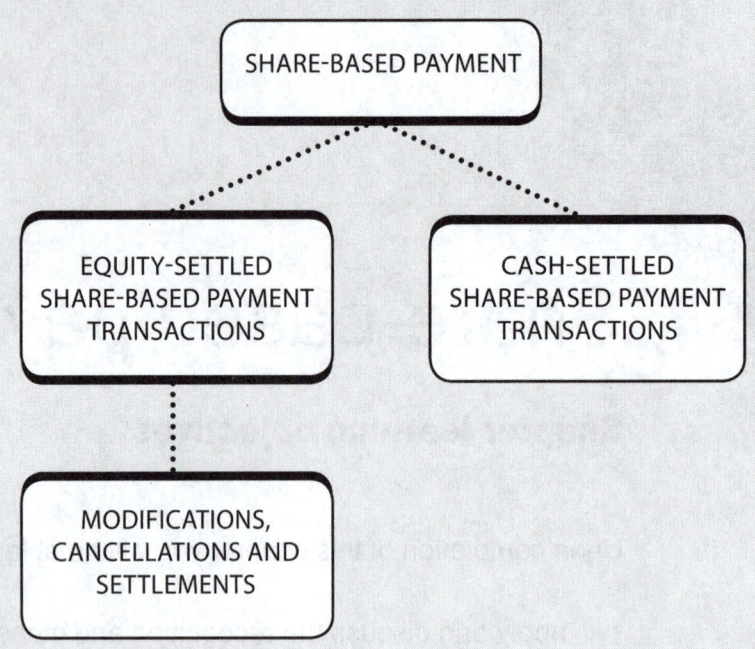

1 Share-based payment

Introduction

Share-based payment has become increasingly common. Share-based payment occurs when an entity buys goods or services from other parties (such as employees or suppliers), and settles the amounts payable by issuing shares or share options to them.

- Part of the remuneration of directors is often in the form of shares or options. Employees may also be granted share options.

- Many new 'e-businesses' do not expect to be profitable in their early years, so try to attract quality staff by offering to employees share schemes rather than high cash salaries.

The problem

If a company pays for goods or services in cash, an expense is recognised in profit or loss. If a company 'pays' for goods or services in share options, there is no cash outflow and under traditional accounting, no expense would be recognised.

- But when a company issues shares to acquire an investment in another entity, it is accepted that the acquirer has incurred a cost that should be recognised in the financial statements at fair value. Issuing shares to acquire goods or services is arguably no different.

- When a company issues shares to employees, a transaction has occurred; the employees have provided a valuable service to the entity, in exchange for the shares/options. It is illogical not to recognise this transaction in the financial statements.

- IFRS 2 **Share-based payment** was issued to deal with this accounting anomaly. IFRS 2 requires that all share-based payment transactions must be recognised in the financial statements.

Expandable text

There are a number of arguments for **not** recognising share-based payment. IFRS 2 rejects them all, arguing in favour of recognising share-based payment.

No cost therefore no charge

A charge for shares or options should not be recognised because the entity does not have to sacrifice cash or other assets. There is no cost to the entity.

This argument ignores the fact that a transaction has occurred. The employees have provided valuable services to the entity in return for valuable shares or options. If this argument were accepted, the financial statements would fail to reflect the economic transactions that had occurred.

Earnings per share would be hit twice

The charge to profit for the employee services consumed reduces the entity's earnings. At the same time there is an increase in the number of shares issued (or to be issued).

However, the double impact on earnings per share simply reflects the two economic events that have occurred: the entity has issued shares, thus increasing the denominator of the EPS calculation, and it has also consumed the resources it received for those shares, thus reducing the numerator. Issuing shares to employees, instead of paying them in cash, requires a greater increase in the entity's earnings in order to maintain its earnings per share. Recognising the transaction ensures that its economic consequences are reported.

Adverse economic consequences

Recognition of employee share-based payment might discourage entities from introducing or continuing employee share plans.

If this were the case, this might be because the requirement for entities to account properly for employee share plans had revealed the economic consequences of such plans. This would correct the economic distortion, whereby entities are able to obtain and consume resources by issuing valuable shares or options without having to account for such transactions.

Types of transaction

IFRS 2 applies to all types of share-based payment transaction. There are two main types:

- in an **equity-settled share-based payment transaction**, the entity receives goods or services in exchange for equity instruments of the entity (e.g. shares or share options)

- in a **cash-settled share-based payment transaction**, the entity acquires goods or services in exchange for amounts of cash measured by reference to the entity's share price.

The most common type of share-based payment transaction is where share options are granted to employees or directors as part of their remuneration.

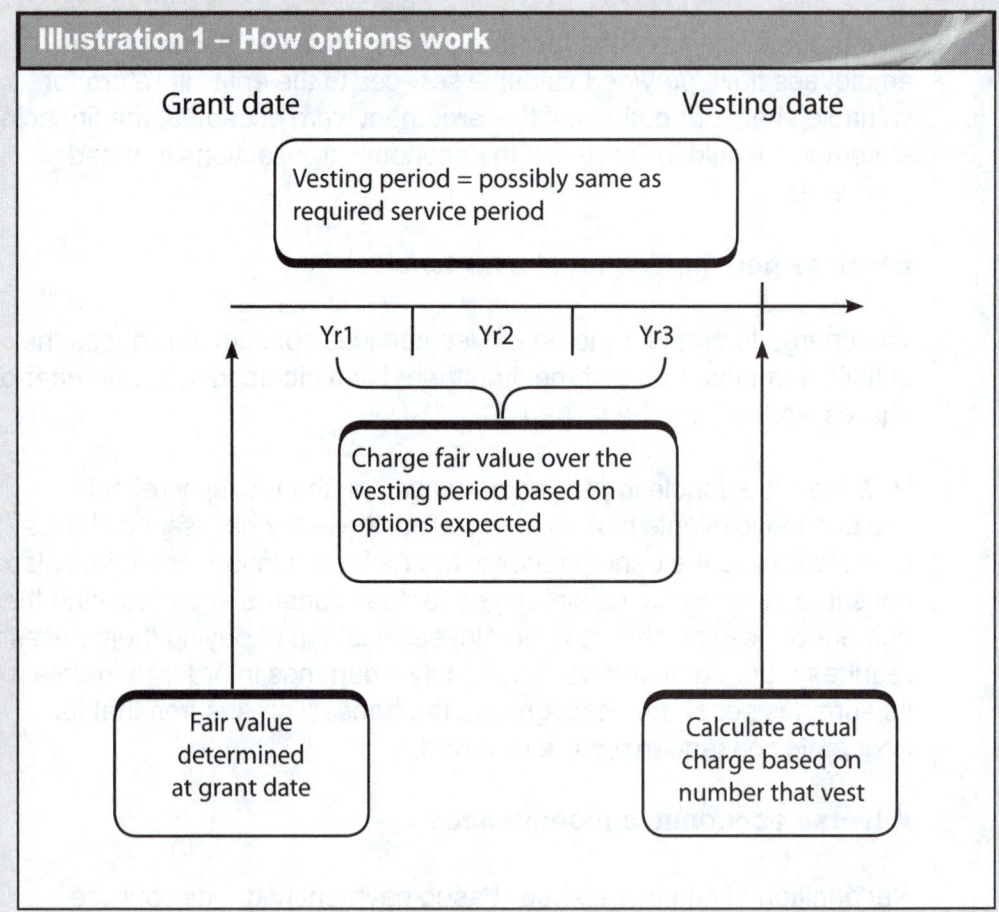

Illustration 1 – How options work

Grant date

Vesting date

Vesting period = possibly same as required service period

Yr1 Yr2 Yr3

Charge fair value over the vesting period based on options expected

Fair value determined at grant date

Calculate actual charge based on number that vest

The basic principles

When an entity receives goods or services as a result of a share-based payment transaction, it recognises either an expense or an asset.

- If the goods or services are received in exchange for equity (e.g., for share options), the entity recognises an increase in equity.
  - The double entry is: Dr Expense/Asset; Cr Equity (normally a special reserve).

- If the goods or services are received or acquired in a cash-settled share-based payment transaction, the entity recognises a liability.
  - The double entry is: Dr Expense/Asset; Cr Liability.

 All share-based payment transactions are measured at fair value.

2 Equity-settled share-based payment transactions
Measurement

The basic principle is that all transactions are measured at fair value.

 Fair value is the amount for which an asset could be exchanged, a liability settled, or an equity instrument granted could be exchanged, between knowledgeable, willing parties in an arm's length transaction.

How fair value is determined:

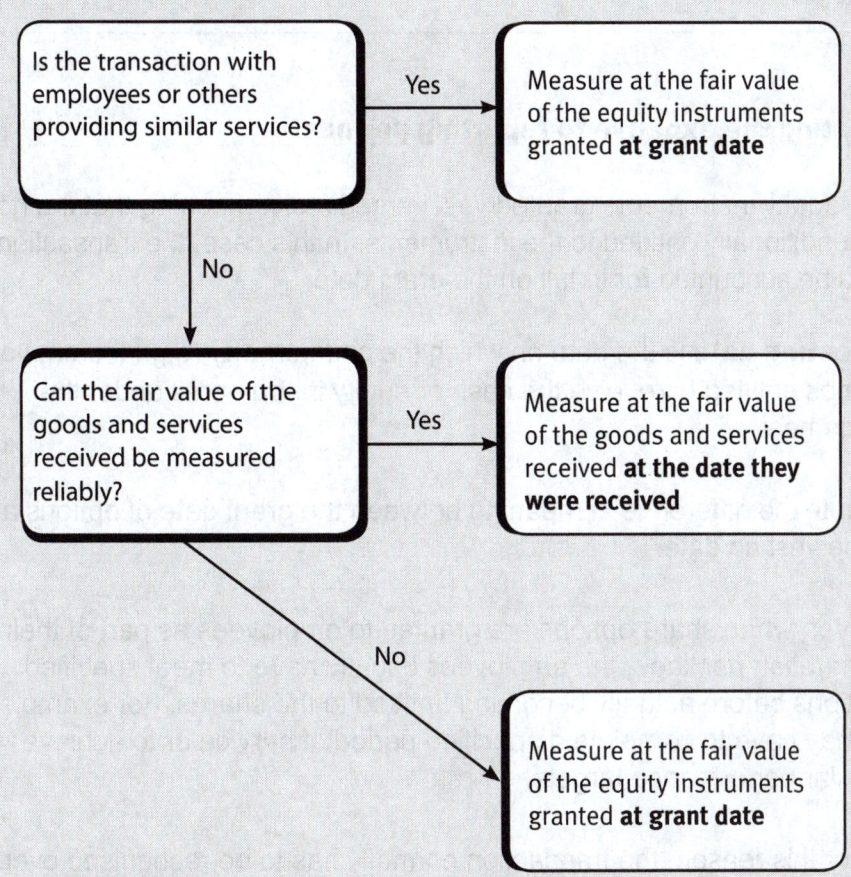

 The **grant date** is the date at which the entity and another party agree to the arrangement.

Expandable text - Determining fair value

Where a share-based payment transaction is with parties other than employees, it is assumed that the fair value of the goods and services received can be measured reliably, at their cash price for example.

Where shares or share options are granted to employees as part of their remuneration, it is not usually possible to arrive at a reliable value for the services received in return. For this reason, the entity measures the transaction by reference to the fair value of the equity instruments granted.

The fair value of equity instruments is market value, if this is available. Where no market price is available (for example, if the instruments are unquoted), a valuation technique is used.

The fair value of share options is harder to determine. In rare cases there may be publicly quoted traded options with similar terms, whose market value can be used as the fair value of the options we are considering. Otherwise, the fair value of options must be estimated using a recognised option-pricing model. IFRS 2 does not require any specific model to be used. The most commonly used is the Black-Scholes model.

Allocating the expense to reporting periods

Some equity instruments granted vest immediately, meaning that the holder is unconditionally entitled to the instruments. In this case, the transaction should be accounted for in full on the grant date.

The **vesting date** is the date on which the counterparty (e.g., the employee) becomes entitled to receive the cash or equity instruments under the arrangement.

*   Note the difference in meaning between the grant date of options and the vesting date.

However, when share options are granted to employees as part of their remuneration package, the employees usually have to meet specified conditions before actually becoming entitled to the shares. For example, they may have to complete a specified period of service or to achieve particular performance targets.

*   For this reason, the transaction normally has to be recognised over more than one accounting period.

KAPLAN PUBLISHING

IFRS 2 states that an entity should account for services as they are rendered during the vesting period.

- The vesting period is the period during which all the specified vesting conditions are satisfied.

Expandable text - Equity-settled share-based payment

On 1 January 20X1, A awards 1,000 share options to an employee, on condition that he is still working for the company in two years' time. The grant date is 1 January 20X1. The vesting period is from 1 January 20X1 to 31 December 20X2. The vesting date is 31 December 20X2.

The entity should recognise an amount for the goods or services received during the vesting period based on the best available estimate of the number of equity instruments expected to vest.

- Each year it should revise that estimate of the number of equity instruments expected to vest if subsequent information indicates that this number differs from previous estimates.

- On vesting date, the entity should revise the estimate to equal the number of equity instruments that actually vest.

- Sometimes one of the vesting conditions is a 'market condition', for example, where the share price must be above a certain amount on the vesting date. Market conditions are taken into account when estimating the fair value of the option at the grant date. Failure to satisfy a market condition is not taken into account when subsequently calculating the amounts recognised in profit and loss and equity over the vesting period.

Before the shares vest, the amount recognised in equity is normally credited to a special reserve called (for example) 'shares to be issued'.

- After the share options vest and the shares are issued, the relevant amount is usually transferred to share capital.

Expandable text - Illustration: Equity-settled share-based payment

On 1 January 20X1 an entity grants 100 share options to each of its 500 employees. Each grant is conditional upon the employee working for the entity until 31 December 20X3. At the grant date the fair value of each share option is $15.

During 20X1, 20 employees leave and the entity estimates that a total of 20% of the 500 employees will leave during the three-year period.

During 20X2, a further 20 employees leave and the entity now estimates that only a total of 15% of its 500 employees will leave during the three-year period.

During 20X3, a further 10 employees leave.

Calculate the remuneration expense that will be recognised in respect of the share-based payment transaction for each of the three years ended 31 December 20X3.

Expandable text - Solution

The entity recognises the remuneration expense as the employees' services are received during the three-year vesting period. The amount recognised is based on the fair value of the share options granted at the grant date (1 January 20X1).

Assuming that no employees left, the total expense would be $750,000 (100 × 500 × 15) and the expense charged to profit or loss for each of the three years would be $250,000 (750,000/3).

In practice, the entity estimates the number of options expected to vest by estimating the number of employees likely to leave. This estimate is revised at each year end. The expense recognised for the year is based on this re-estimate. On the vesting date (31 December 20X3), it recognises an amount based on the number of options that actually vest.

A total of 50 employees left during the three-year period and therefore 45,000 options (500 – 50 × 100) vested.

The amount recognised as an expense for each of the three years is calculated as follows:

	Expense for year (change in cumulative)	Cumulative expense at year-end
	$	$
20X1 100 × (500 × 80%) × 15 × 1/3	200,000	200,000
20X2 100 × (500 × 85%) × 15 × 2/3	225,000	425,000
20X3 45,000 × 15	250,000	675,000

The financial statements will include the following amounts:

Income statement	20X1	20X2	20X3
	$	$	$
Staff costs	200,000	225,000	250,000

Statement of financial position	Year 1	Year 2	Year 3
	$	$	$
Included with equity	200,000	425,000	675,000

Test your understanding 1

Beginner offered directors an option scheme based on a three-year period of service. The number of options granted to directors at the inception of the scheme was 10 million. The options were exercisable shortly after the end of the third year. The fair value of the options and the estimates of the number of options expected to vest were:

Year	Rights expected to vest	Fair value of the option
Start of Year One	8m	30c
End of Year One	7m	33c
End of Year Two	8m	37c
End of Year Three	9m	74c

Show how the option scheme will affect the financial statements for each of the three years.

Test your understanding 2

Asif has set up an employee option scheme to motivate its sales team of ten key sales people. Each sales person was offered 1 million options exercisable at 10c, conditional upon the employee remaining with the company during the vesting period of 5 years. The options are then exercisable three weeks after the end of the vesting period.

This is year two of the scheme. At the start of the year, two sales people suggested that they would be leaving the company during the second year. However, although one did leave, the other recommitted to the company and the scheme. The other employees have always been committed to the scheme and stated their intention to stay with the company during the 5 years. Relevant market values are as follows:

Date	Share price	Option price
Grant date	10c	20c
End of Year One	24c	38c
End of Year Two	21c	33c

The option price is the market price of an equivalent marketable option on the relevant date.

Show the effect of the scheme on the financial statements of Asif for Year Two.

Expandable text - Illustration: Equity-settled share-based payment

JJ grants 100 share options to each of its 20 employees providing they meet performance targets for each of the next two years. At the end of the first year, it was estimated that 80% of the employees would meet the targets over both years. Improved performance meant that at the end of the second year it turned out that 85% of employees had done so.

The fair value of the option at the grant date was $10.

Calculate the charge to profits for each year.

Expandable text - Solution

At the end of year 1, 16 employees are eligible for the shares (20 × 80%).

The fair value of the options is: 100 × 16 × $10 = $16,000

This is spread over the two-year vesting period, so the charge to profits $8,000 ($16,000/2).

Dr Staff costs (income statement)	$8,000
Cr Equity	$8,000

At the end of the second year, 17 employees are eligible for shares (20 × 85%). This is the vesting date, so these 17 employees will receive share options.

The fair value of the options is: 100 × 17 × $10 = $17,000

$8,000 has already been charged to profits in the previous year, so to increase the charge and the corresponding equity balance, the charge for the second year is $9,000.

Dr Staff costs	$9,000
Cr Equity	$9,000

Test your understanding 3

Bahzad has singled out the inventory control director for an employee option scheme. He has been offered 3 million options exercisable at 20c, conditional upon him remaining with the company for three years and improving inventory control by the end of that period. The proportion of the options that vest is dependent upon the inventory days on the last day of the three years. The schedule is as follows:

Inventory days	Proportion vesting
5	100%
6	90%
7	70%
8	40%
9	10%

The options also have a vesting criteria related to market value. They only vest if the share price is above 25c on the vesting day, i.e. at the end of the third year.

This is the second of the three years. At the start of the year it was estimated that the inventory days at the end of the third year would be 7. However, during the year inventory control improved and at the end of the year the estimate of inventory days at the end of the third year was 6. The relevant market data is as follows:

Date	Share price	Option price
Grant date	20c	10c
End of Year One	19c	6c
End of Year Two	37c	19c

The option price is the market price of an equivalent marketable option on the relevant date.

Show the effect of the scheme on the financial statements of Bahzad for Year Two.

Accounting after vesting date

IFRS 2 states that no further adjustments to total equity should be made after vesting date. This applies even if some of the equity instruments do not vest (for example, because some of the employees do not exercise their right to buy shares).

- But for those who do not vest, a transfer may be made from shares to be issued to retained earnings.

3 Cash-settled share-based payment transactions

Examples of cash-settled share-based payment transactions include:

- share appreciation rights (SARs), where employees become entitled to a future cash payment based on the increase in the entity's share price from a specified level over a specified period of time

- those where employees are granted a right to shares that are redeemable. This gives them a right to receive a future payment of cash.

The basic principle is that the entity measures the goods or services acquired and the liability incurred at the **fair value of the liability**.

- Until the liability is settled, the entity remeasures the fair value of the liability at each reporting date until the liability is settled and at the date of settlement. (Notice that this is different from accounting for equity share-based payments, where the fair value is fixed at the grant date.)

- Changes in fair value are recognised in profit or loss for the period.

- Where services are received, (for example in return for SARs) these are recognised over the period that the employees render the services. (This is the same principle as for equity-settled transactions).

- The expense recognised in each accounting period has a double entry to a provision/liability account. On the vesting date, the amount of the provision/liability should equal the cash paid.

Illustration 2 – Cash-settled share-based payment transactions

On 1 January 20X1 an entity grants 100 cash share appreciation rights (SAR) to each of its 300 employees, on condition that they continue to work for the entity until 31 December 20X3.

During 20X1, 20 employees leave. The entity estimates that a further 40 will leave during 20X2 and 20X3.

During 20X2, 10 employees leave. The entity estimates that a further 20 will leave during 20X3.

During 20X3, 10 employees leave.

The fair values of one SAR for each year are shown below.

	Fair value
	$
20X1	10.00
20X2	12.00
20X3	15.00

Calculate the amount to be recognised as an expense for each of the three years ended 31 December 20X3 and the liability to be recognised in the statement of financial position at 31 December for each of the three years.

Expandable text - Solution

Year	Liability at year-end	Expense for year
	$000	$000
20X1 ((300 – 20 – 40) × 100 × 10 × 1/3)	80	80
20X2 ((300 – 20 – 10 – 20) × 100 × 12 × 2/3)	200	120
20X3 ((300 – 20 – 10 – 10) × 100 × 15)	390	190

Test your understanding 4

On 1 January 20X4 Growler granted 200 cash share appreciation rights (SARs) to each of its 500 employees, on condition that they continue to work for the entity for four years. At 1 January 20X4, the entity expects that, based upon past experience, 5% of that number is expected to leave each year.

During 20X4, 20 employees leave, and the entity expects that this number will leave in each future year of the scheme.

During 20X5, 24 employees leave, and the entity expects that a total of 44 employees will leave over the remaining two-year period of the scheme.

During 20X6, eighteen employees leave, with a further 20 expected to leave in the final year. During 20X7, only 10 employees leave

The fair value of each SAR was as follows:

31 December 20X4 - $5
31 December 20X5 - $7
31 December 20X6 - $8
31 December 20X7 - $9

Required:

Calculate the amount to be recognised as a remuneration expense in the statement of comprehensive income, together with the liability to be recognised in the statement of financial position for each of the four years of the scheme, commencing with the reporting date 31 December 20X4.

Expandable text - Hybrid transactions

Some share-based payment transactions give either the reporting entity or the other party the choice of settling in cash or in equity instruments.

IFRS 2 states that if the entity has incurred a liability to settle in cash or other assets, the transaction should be accounted for as a cash-settled share-based payment transaction. Otherwise, it should be accounted for as an equity-settled share-based payment transaction.

Expandable text - Disclosures

Entities should disclose information that enables users of the financial statements to understand the nature and extent of share-based payment arrangements that existed during the period. The main disclosures are as follows:

- a description of each type of share-based payment arrangement that existed at any time during the period
- the number and weighted average exercise prices of share options:

(i) outstanding at the beginning of the period

(ii) granted during the period

(iii) forfeited during the period

(iv) exercised during the period

(v) expired during the period

(vi) outstanding at the end of the period

(vii) exercisable at the end of the period.

- for share options exercised during the period, the weighted average share price at the date of exercise

- for share options outstanding at the end of the period, the range of exercise prices and weighted average remaining contractual life.

IFRS 2 also requires disclosure of information that enables users of the financial statements to understand how the fair value of the goods or services received, or the fair value of the equity instruments granted, during the period was determined.

Entities should also disclose information that enables users of the financial statements to understand the effect of share-based payment transactions on the entity's profit or loss for the period and on its financial position, that is:

- the total expense recognised for the period arising from share-based payment transactions

- for liabilities arising from share-based payment transactions:
    - the total carrying amount at the end of the period
    - the total intrinsic value at the end of the period of liabilities for which the counterparty's right to cash or other assets had vested by the end of the period.

Expandable text - Modifications, cancellations and settlements

Modifications to the terms on which equity instruments are granted

An entity may alter the terms and conditions of share option schemes during the vesting period.

- For example, it might increase or reduce the exercise price of the options, which makes the scheme less favourable or more favourable to employees.

- It might also change the vesting conditions, to make it more likely or less likely that the options will vest.

The general rule is that, apart from dealing with reductions due to failure to satisfy vesting conditions, the entity must **always** recognise at least the amount that would have been recognised if the terms and conditions had not been modified (that is, if the original terms had remained in force).

- If the change reduces the amount that the employee will receive, there is no reduction in the expense recognised in profit or loss.

- If the change increases the amount that the employee will receive, the difference between the fair value of the new arrangement and the fair value of the original arrangement (the incremental fair value) must be recognised as a charge to profit. The extra cost is spread over the period from the date of the change to the vesting date.

Expandable text - Illustration: Modifications

An entity grants 100 share options to each of its 500 employees, provided that they remain in service over the next three years. The fair value of each option is $20.

During year one, 50 employees leave. The entity estimates that a further 60 employees will leave during years two and three.

At the end of year one the entity reprices its share options because the share price has fallen. The other vesting conditions remain unchanged. At the date of repricing, the fair value of each of the original share options granted (before taking the repricing into account) was $10. The fair value of each repriced share option is $15.

During year two, a further 30 employees leave. The entity estimates that a further 30 employees will leave during year three.

During year three, a further 30 employees leave.

Calculate the amounts to be recognised in the financial statements for each of the three years of the scheme.

Expandable text - Solution

The repricing means that the total fair value of the arrangement has increased and this will benefit the employees. This in turn means that the entity must account for an increased remuneration expense. The increased cost is based upon the difference in the fair value of the option, immediately before and after the repricing. Under the original arrangement, the fair value of the option at the date of repricing was $10, which increased to $15 following the repricing of the options, for each share estimated to vest. The additional cost is recognised over the remainder of the vesting period (years two and three).

The amounts recognised in the financial statements for each of the three years are as follows:

		Amount included in equity	Expense
		$	$
Year one Original	(500 – 50 – 60) × 100 × 20 × 1/3	260,000	260,000
Year two Original	(500 – 50 – 30 – 30) × 100 × 20 × 2/3	520,000	260,000
Incremental	(500 – 50 – 30 – 30) × 100 × 5 × 1/2	97,500	97,500
		617,500	357,500
Year three Original	(500 – 50 – 30 – 30) × 100 × 20	780,000	260,000
Incremental	(500 – 50 – 30 – 30) × 100 × 5	195,000	97,500
		975,000	357,500

Expandable text - Further illustration

An entity grants 100 share options to each of the 15 employees in its sales team, on condition that they remain in service over the next three years. There is also a performance condition: the team must sell more than 40,000 units of a particular product over the three-year period. At the grant date the fair value of each option is $20.

During Year 2, the entity increases the sales target to 70,000 units. By the end of Year 3, only 60,000 units have been sold and the share options do not vest.

All 15 employees remain with the entity for the full three years.

Calculate the amounts to be recognised in the financial statements for each of the three years of the scheme.

Solution

IFRS 2 states that when a share option scheme is modified, the entity must recognise, as a minimum, the services received, measured at the fair value at the grant date. The employees have not met the modified sales target, but **did** meet the original target set on grant date.

This means that the entity must recognise the expense that it would have incurred had the original scheme continued in force.

The total amount recognised in equity is $30,000 (15 × 100 × 20). The entity recognises an expense of $10,000 for each of the three years.

Expandable text - Cancellations and settlements

An entity may also cancel or settle a share option scheme before vesting date. In a settlement, the employees receive compensation because the scheme is cancelled.

- If the cancellation or settlement occurs during the vesting period, the entity immediately recognises the amount that would otherwise have been recognised for services received over the vesting period (an acceleration of vesting).
- Any payment made to employees up to the fair value of the equity instruments granted at cancellation or settlement date is accounted for as a deduction from equity (repurchase of an equity interest).
- Any payment made to employees in excess of the fair value of the equity instruments granted at cancellation or settlement date is accounted for as an expense.

Expandable text - Recent developments

Amendments to IFRS 2

Amendments to IFRS 2 – **Share-based payment** were – published in January 2008.

The amendments clarify the definition of vesting conditions and provide guidance on the accounting treatment of cancellations by parties other than the entity.

Vesting conditions

Vesting conditions are defined in IFRS 2 as:

'The conditions that must be satisfied for the counterparty to become entitled to receive cash, other assets or equity instruments of the entity under a share-based payment arrangement. Vesting conditions include service conditions, which require the other party to complete a specified period of service, and performance conditions, which require specific performance conditions to be met.'

Previously, IFRS 2 was silent on whether features of a share-based payment transaction other than service conditions and performance conditions were vesting conditions. In the 2008 amendment to the standard, the IASB has clarified that only service and performance conditions are vesting conditions. Other features of a share-based payment are not, but should be included in the grant date fair value of the share-based payment.

Cancellations

IFRS 2 specified the accounting treatment when an entity cancels a grant of equity instruments. However, it did not state how cancellations by a party other than the entity should be accounted for.

The amended standard clarifies that all cancellations, whether by the entity or by other parties, should receive the same accounting treatment.

The amendments above are effective for annual periods beginning on or after 1 January 2009, with earlier adoption permitted.

Amendments to IFRS 2 - dated June 2009

In June 2009, the IASB issued a clarification of accounting for group cash-settled share-based payment transactions. The amendments respond to requests the IASB received to clarify how an individual subsidiary in a group should account for some share-based payment arrangements in its own financial statements.

In these arrangements, the subsidiary receives goods or services from employees or suppliers but its parent or another entity in the group must pay those suppliers. The amendments issued today clarify:

- the scope of IFRS 2. An entity that receives goods or services in a share-based payment arrangement must account for those goods or services no matter which entity in the group settles the transaction, and no matter whether the transaction is settled in shares or cash.

- the interaction of IFRS 2 and other standards. The Board clarified that in IFRS 2 a 'group' has the same meaning as in IAS 27 Consolidated and Separate Financial Statements, that is, it includes only a parent and its subsidiaries.

The amendments to IFRS 2 also incorporate guidance previously included in IFRIC 8 Scope of IFRS 2 and IFRIC 11 IFRS 2—Group and Treasury Share Transactions. As a result, the IASB has withdrawn IFRIC 8 and IFRIC 11.

Expandable text - UK syllabus focus

The ACCA UK syllabus contains a requirement that candidates should be able to discuss and apply the key differences between UK GAAP and IFRS GAAP. UK FRS 20 and IFRS 2 essentially use the same definitions and apply the same accounting requirements.

4 Chapter summary

```
┌─────────────────────────────┐
│ Share-based payment          │
│ • What it is                 │
│ • Types of transaction       │
│ • Basic principles           │
└─────────────────────────────┘
```

```
┌─────────────────────────────┐     ┌─────────────────────────────┐
│ Equity-settled share-based   │     │ Cash-settled share-based     │
│ payment transactions         │     │ payment transactions         │
│ • Measurement                │     │ • Measurement                │
│ • Allocating the expense to  │     │ • Accounting treatment       │
│   reporting periods          │     │                              │
└─────────────────────────────┘     └─────────────────────────────┘
```

```
┌─────────────────────────────────┐
│ Modifications, cancellations and │
│ settlements                      │
│ • Accounting treatment of        │
│   modifications                  │
│ • Accounting treatment of        │
│   cancellations                  │
│   and settlements                │
└─────────────────────────────────┘
```

Test your understanding answers

Test your understanding 1

Year		Expense	Amount included in equity
		$000	$000
One	(7m × 30c × 1/3)	700	700
Two	(8m × 30c × 2/3)	900	1,600
Three	(9m × 30c)	1,100	2,700

Note: the expense is measured using the fair value of the option at the grant date, i.e. the start of year one.

Test your understanding 2

The expense is measured using the fair value of the option at the grant date, i.e. 20c.

At the end of year two the amount recognised in equity should be $720,000 (1m × (10 – 1) × 20c × 2/5).

At the beginning of year two the amount recognised in equity would have been $320,000 (1m × 8 × 20c × 1/5).

The charge to profit for Year Two is the difference between the two: $400,000 (720 – 320).

Test your understanding 3

One of the conditions of vesting is a 'market condition' (the share price must be above 25c on the vesting day). This should already have been taken into account when the option price was fixed and it does not affect the calculations below.

At the end of year two the amount recognised in equity is $180,000 (3m × 10c × 90% × 2/3).

At the beginning of year two the amount recognised in equity should have been $70,000 (3m × 10c × 70% × 1/3).

Therefore the charge to profit for year two is $110,000 (180,000 – 70,000).

Test your understanding 4

Answer:

The liability is remeasured at each reporting date, based upon the current information available relating to known and expected leavers, together with the fair value of the SAR at each date. The remuneration expense recognised is the movement in the liability from one reporting date to the next as summarised below:

Reporting date	Workings	SOFP - liability $	Change in liability $	SOCI - expense $
31/12/20X4	(500 - 20 - 20 - 20 - 20) = 420 × 200 × $5 × 1/4	105,000		105,000
31/12/20X5	(500 - 20 - 24 - 44) = 412 × 200 × $7 × 2/4	288,400	288,400 - 105,000	183,400
31/12/20X6	(500 - 20 - 24 - 18 - 20) = 418 × 200 × $8 × 3/4	501,600	501,600 - 288,400	213,200
31/12/20X7	(500 - 20 - 24 - 18 - 10) = 428 × 200 × $9 × 4/4	770,400	770,400 - 501,600	268,800

Related parties

Chapter learning objectives

Upon completion of this chapter you will be able to:

- determine the parties considered to be related to an entity
- identify the implications of related party relationships and the need for disclosure.

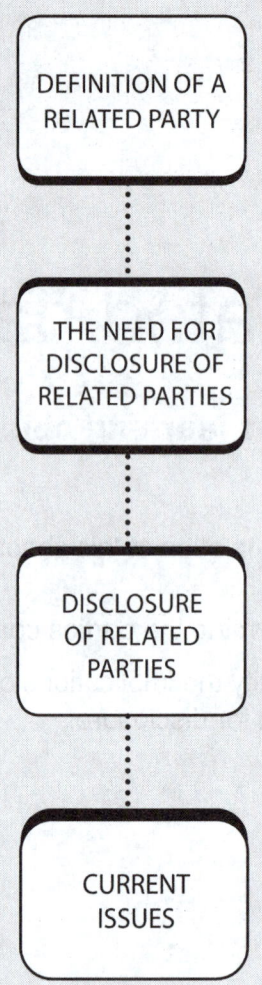

DEFINITION OF A RELATED PARTY

THE NEED FOR DISCLOSURE OF RELATED PARTIES

DISCLOSURE OF RELATED PARTIES

CURRENT ISSUES

1 Definition of a related party

IAS 24 **Related party disclosures**, as revised in November 2009, states that a party (an individual or an entity) is related to another entity if it:

- controls, is controlled by, or is under common control with the entity

- has significant influence over the entity

- has joint control over the entity

- is an associate of the entity

- is a joint venture of the entity

- is a member of the key management personnel of the entity or its parent

- is a close family member of anyone with control, joint control or significant influence over the entity or of any members of key management personnel

- is controlled, jointly controlled or significantly influenced by any individual referred to above

- is a post-employment benefit plan for the benefit of employees of the entity or any of its other related parties.

Previously, if a government controlled, or significantly influenced, an entity, the entity was required to disclose information about all transactions with other entities controlled, or significantly influenced by the same government. The revised standard still requires disclosures that are important to users of financial statements but eliminates requirements to disclose information that is costly to gather and of less value to users. It achieves this balance by requiring disclosure about these transactions only if they are individually or collectively significant.

Similarly, the revised definition introduces symmetry in the definition to either identify two entities as either being related or not related, from whichever perspective is considered. The main amendments to the definition are:

(1) The inclusion of:

– the relationship between a subsidiary and an associate of the same parent, in the individual financial statements of both the subsidiary and the associate.

– two entities where one is an investee of a member of key management personnel (KMP) and the other is the entity managed by the person that is a member of KMP.

(2) The removal of:

– situations in which two entities are related to each other because a person has significant influence over one entity and a close member of the family of that person has significant influence over the other entity.

The most common related party relationship occurs where one entity controls or has significant influence over the other.

Related parties

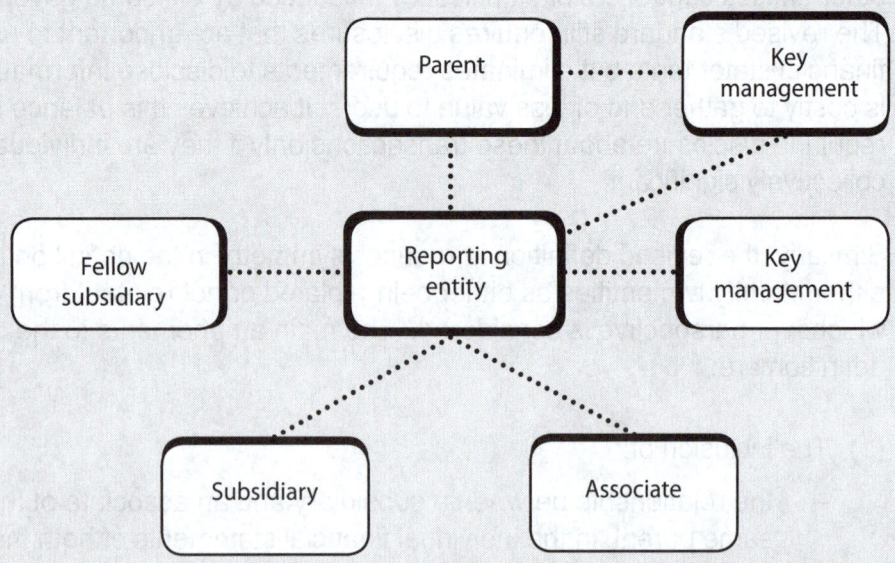

Expandable text - Further detail on definitions

Control is the power to govern the financial and operating policies of an entity so as to obtain benefits from its activities.

Significant influence is the power to participate in the financial and operating policy decisions of an entity, but is not control over those policies. An entity can gain significant influence over another by share ownership, statute or agreement.

Control and significant influence can be:

- direct. An example: parent owns more than half the shares in a subsidiary.

- indirect. An example: parent owns more than half the shares in subsidiary 1, which owns more than half the shares in subsidiary 2, Through its direct control of subsidiary 1, which itself has direct control over subsidiary 2, parent has 'indirect' control over subsidiary 2.

Key management personnel are those persons having authority and responsibility for planning, directing and controlling the activities of the entity. They include executive and non-executive **directors**.

In many situations it is easy to identify a related party relationship. For example, a subsidiary is clearly a related party of its parent. In more complicated situations it may be necessary to consider whether the parties are included in the list in the definition; and to consider the basic principle of control and influence.

What actually happens in practice within a relationship is often important. For example, two companies that have a single director in common are not necessarily related parties. A related party relationship only exists if it can be shown that the director is able to influence the policies of both companies in their mutual dealings.

Test your understanding 1 - X

X is an 80% owned subsidiary of T. The directors of X are A, B, C and D. Which of the following are related parties of X?

(a) V, which is not part of the T group, but of which A is a director.

(b) Y, who owns 20% of the shares in X.

(c) K, the financial controller of X (who is not a director).

(d) M, the wife of the chairman of Q, an entity in the T group.

2 The need for disclosure of related parties

A **related party transaction** is the transfer of resources, services or obligations between related parties, regardless of whether a price is charged.

- Transactions between related parties are a normal feature of business.
- But a related party relationship can affect the performance and financial position of an entity as shown by its financial statements.

Expandable text - Illustration

Company A owns 75% of the equity shares of B. B supplies goods to A at prices significantly below market rate. As a result, the profit of B is less than it would have been if it had been free to sell all its goods to a third party.

The performance of B is not comparable with that of a similar company which is not subject to the same restrictions.

- Users of the financial statements need to be made aware of any related party transactions that have occurred.
- They also need to be made aware of the existence of related party relationships even where there have been no transactions during the period.

Expandable text - Examples of related party transactions

Related party transactions could include:

- purchases or sales of goods

- purchases or sales of non-current assets

- giving or receiving of services e.g. accounting or management services

- leasing arrangements, e.g. allowing the use of an asset

- transfers of research and development

- financing arrangements (including loans)

- provision of guarantees or collateral

- settlement of liabilities on behalf of the entity.

Directors may not want to disclose related party relationships and transactions. Sometimes this is because they believe that disclosure will give users of the financial statements the impression of poor stewardship or wrong-doing The reason why transactions and relationships must be disclosed is that users need to be made aware of them. Otherwise they will assume that the entity has entered into all its transactions on the same terms that it could have obtained from a third party (on an arms' length basis) and that it has acted in its own interests throughout the period. They will then assess the entity's results and position on this basis and may be misled as a result.

A related party relationship can affect the financial position and operating results of an entity in a number of ways, particularly in a group situation.

- An entity may enter into transactions which may not have occurred if the relationship did not exist, e.g. a subsidiary may sell most of its production to its parent, where it might have found an alternative customer if the parent company had not purchased the goods.

- An entity may enter into transactions on different terms from those with an unrelated party, e.g. a subsidiary may lease equipment to another group company on terms imposed by the parent, possibly at a low rent or for no rent.

- Transactions with third parties may be affected by the existence of the relationship, e.g. a parent could instruct a subsidiary to sell goods to a particular customer or to close down a particular operation.

3 Disclosure of related parties

Disclosure of control

IAS 24 requires that relationships between parents and subsidiaries are disclosed including the:

- name of the parent
- name of the ultimate controlling party (if different)
- relationship, whether or not any transactions have taken place between the parties during the period.

Disclosure of management compensation

Any compensation granted to key management personnel should be disclosed in total and for each of the following categories:

- short-term employee benefits
- post-employment benefits
- other long-term benefits
- termination benefits
- share-based payment.

Disclosure of transactions and balances

If there have been transactions between related parties, the reporting entity should disclose:

- the nature of the related party relationship
- a description of the transactions
- the amounts of the transactions
- the amounts and details of any outstanding balances
- allowances for receivables in respect of the outstanding balances
- the irrecoverable debt expense in respect of outstanding balances.

Disclosure should be made whether or not a price is charged.

Expandable text - Further detail on disclosures

The existence of a parent/subsidiary relationship should be disclosed even where transactions have been entered into on normal commercial terms or where there have been no transactions at all. This information alerts users to the possibility that the entity's performance and position could be affected by related party transactions in future.

Further detail

All the disclosures required must be made separately for each of the following categories:

- the parent
- entities with joint control or significant influence over the entity
- subsidiaries
- associates
- joint ventures in which the entity is a venturer
- key management personnel
- other related parties.

Intra-group transactions

Transactions between a parent and a subsidiary are disclosed in their separate financial statements. Intra-group transactions are eliminated from the consolidated financial statements and therefore no disclosure is necessary in the group accounts.

IAS 24 is silent on what should happen where a related party relationship existed for only part of the year but transactions between the parties occurred throughout the year. For example, suppose that a group sells a subsidiary part way through the year. Transactions that take place after the sale are not eliminated on consolidation. Should they be disclosed?

The answer is probably yes. For ethical reasons it is advisable to disclose the information. This means that there is no possibility that users of the financial statements could be misled.

Arm's length transactions

IAS 24 states that related party transactions should be described as being made 'at arm's length' only if this can be substantiated, i.e. the transactions were carried out in all respects on the same terms as if they had been with independent third parties. By definition, related party transactions cannot be made at arm's length. Instead, the expressions 'at normal selling prices' or 'on normal commercial terms' should be used where appropriate.

Exemptions

Relationships and transactions with the following do not have to be disclosed since they are deemed not to be related parties in the course of their normal dealings with the entity:

- providers of finance

- trade unions

- utility companies

- government departments and agencies

- customers, suppliers, franchisers, distributors and general agents with whom the entity transacts a significant volume of business.

Test your understanding 2 - Ace

Ace

The objective of IAS 24 **Related party disclosures** is to ensure that an entity's financial statements contain the disclosures necessary to draw attention to the possibility that its financial position and profit or loss may have been affected by the existence of related parties and by transactions and outstanding balances with such parties

On 1 April 20X7, Ace owned 75% of the equity share capital of Deuce and 80% of the equity share capital of Trey. On 1 April 20X8, Ace purchased the remaining 25% of the equity shares of Deuce. In the two years ended 31 March 20X9, the following transactions occurred between the three companies:

(i) On 30 June 20X7 Ace manufactured a machine for use by Deuce. The cost of manufacture was $20,000. The machine was delivered to Deuce for an invoiced price of $25,000. Deuce paid the invoice on 31 August 20X7. Deuce depreciated the machine over its anticipated useful life of five years, charging a full year's depreciation in the year of purchase.

(ii) On 30 September 20X8, Deuce sold some goods to Trey at an invoiced price of $15,000. Trey paid the invoice on 30 November 20X8. The goods had cost Deuce $12,000 to manufacture. By 31 March 20X9, Trey had sold all the goods outside the group.

(iii) For each of the two years ended 31 March 20X9, Ace provided management services to Deuce and Trey. Ace did not charge for these services in the year ended 31 March 20X8 but in the year ended 31 March 20X9 decided to impose a charge of $10,000 per annum to each company. The amounts of $10,000 are due to be paid by each company on 31 May 20X9.

Required:

(a) **Explain why related party disclosures are needed.**

(6 marks)

(b) **Summarise the related-party disclosures which will be required in respect of transactions (i) to (iii) above for BOTH of the years ended 31 March 20X8 and 31 March 20X9 in the financial statements of Ace, Deuce and Trey.**

(14 marks)

You may assume that Ace presents consolidated financial statements for BOTH of the years dealt with in the question.

(Total: 20 marks)

Expandable text - UK syllabus focus

The ACCA UK syllabus contains a requirement that candidates should be able to discuss and apply the key differences between UK GAAP and IFRS GAAP. The accounting requirements of UK GAAP and IFRS GAAP are very similar in this area; the key issues associated with UK reporting standard requirements are as follows:

FRS 8 - Related party disclosures. The basic definition of a related party from FRS 8 – that being someone in a position to control or influence the terms on which transactions may be entered into is similar to that included within IAS 24. At some point, it is expected that the definition within FRS 8 will be expanded to encompass jointly controlled entities and post-employment benefit plans as they do under IFRS GAAP.

IFRS 8 requires disclosure of related parties, typically between group members. In addition, disclosure is required of **material transactions** - i.e. those which may be reasonably expected to influence decisions by the users of that information. Note that IAS 24 does not require any consideration of materiality when dealing with disclosure of related party transactions.

During 2008, amendments were made to IFRS 8 following the introduction of the Companies Act 2006. Key management personnel are defined as: "Those persons having authority and responsibility for planning, directing, and controlling the activities of the entity, directly or indirectly, including any director (whether executive or otherwise) of that entity.

Amendment to the definition of 'related parties – a party is related to an entity if:

- directly, or indirectly through one or more intermediaries, the party:
  (i) controls, is controlled by, or is under common control with, the entity (this includes parents,
  subsidiaries and fellow subsidiaries);
  (ii) has an interest in the entity that gives it significant influence over the entity; or
  (iii) has joint control over the entity;

- (b) the party is an associate (as defined in FRS 9, 'Associates and joint ventures') of the entity;

- (c) the party is a joint venture in which the entity is a venturer (as defined in FRS 9, 'Associates and joint ventures');

- (d) the party is a member of the key management personnel of the entity or its parent;

- (e) the party is a close member of the family of any individual referred to in subparagraph (a) or (d);

- (f) the party is an entity that is controlled, jointly controlled or significantly influenced by, or for
  which significant voting power in such entity resides with directly or indirectly, any individual referred to in (d) or (e); or

- (g) the party is a retirement benefit scheme for the benefit of employees of the entity, or of any entity that is a related party of the entity.

4 Chapter summary

> **Reporting not-for-profit entities**
> - These entities are in the public sector or are charities
> - The objectives of these entities is to achieve their aims, not to make a profit
> - Guidance is provided in SORP 2005 and the ASB's don't Statement of Principles for public benefit entities

> **The need for disclosure of related parties**
> - Users need to be aware of related party relationships
>   - Users need to know which transactions have not been made at arm's length

> **Disclosure of related parties**
> - Parent/subsidiary relationships
> - Disclosure of transactions and balances
> - Key management compensation

> **Current issues**
> Amended standard expected in 2008 which clarifies existing requirements

Test your understanding answers

Test your understanding 1 - X

(a) V and X are subject to common influence from A, but V is not a related party unless one or both companies have subordinated their own separate interests in entering into a transaction. (This assumes that A is the only director to serve on both boards; if there were a common nucleus of directors, a related party relationship would almost certainly exist.)

(b) Y is almost certainly not a related party. According to the definition Y might be presumed to be a related party, but the existence of a parent entity (T owns the other 80% of the shares) means that Y is unlikely to be able to exert significant influence over X in practice.

(c) K may be a related party, despite the fact that he or she is not a director. A financial controller would probably come within the definition of key management personnel (i.e. 'those persons having authority and responsibility for planning, directing and controlling the activities of the entity'). The issue would be decided by the extent to which K is able to control or influence the policies of the entity in practice.

(d) M may be a related party. Companies Q and X are under common control and M falls within the definition of close family of a related party of Q. M is not a related party if it can be demonstrated that she has not influenced the policies of X in such a way as to inhibit the pursuit of separate interests.

Test your understanding 2 - Ace

Answer - Ace

(a) The financial statements would be very difficult to understand if readers were not informed of any related party transactions. For example, cost or selling prices could be distorted by the fact that goods are being purchased from or sold to a related party. In extreme cases, this might be part of a deliberate strategy to manipulate the apparent profitability of one or other party. For example, one person might own two businesses and might have one sell to the other at a premium or a discount. This could make one business appear more profitable if our owner ever decides to sell it. There could also be tax advantages to making one generate a profit and the other a loss.

Related party disclosures may be enough to enable a reader to adjust for the effects of any mispricing or other concessions and thereby obtain a better insight into the true profitability of the company. Even if this is impossible, it is useful to know that such an adjustment might be necessary.

The fact that a business has a related party could be enough in itself to require some disclosure. For example, the fact that a business can be compelled to enter into an agreement that may be contrary to its interests is potentially relevant to a reader who wishes a true and fair view of its overall profitability.

Knowledge of the related parties could also be important from a stewardship perspective. Shareholders might want to raise questions about these transactions at the annual general meeting.

(b) **Disclosure of related party transactions**

The first step is to determine whether related party relationships existed between the three companies during each of the two accounting periods.

Year ended 31 March 20X8

Ace owns 75% of the equity share capital of Deuce and 80% of the equity share capital of Trey. This means that Ace is a related party of both subsidiaries, as it controls both of them. (An entity is presumed to be a related party of another entity if that entity owns more than 20% of its equity share capital.)

Deuce and Trey are related parties as they are under common control.

Year ended 31 March 20X9

Ace owns 100% of the equity share capital of Deuce and 80% of the equity share capital of Trey. Therefore all three companies are still related parties of each other. As Ace now owns over 90% of the equity shares in Deuce, Deuce need not disclose transactions with Ace.

Three sets of financial statements are relevant:

- the consolidated financial statements of Ace

- the individual financial statements of Deuce

- the individual financial statements of Trey.

Ace will not prepare individual company financial statements and so there is no distinction between the transactions of Ace and the transactions of the Ace Group.

Related party disclosures

The following details of each related party transaction are required:

- name of related party with which the transaction was made

- description of the relationship between the parties

- description of the transaction and the amounts involved (including the fair value of the transaction if this is different from the actual value)

- any amounts due to or from related parties at the year end (including any doubtful debts)

- any amounts written off related party receivables

- any other information necessary for an understanding of the transaction and its effect on the financial statements.

- It is assumed that all the related party transactions are material.

The transactions are summarised in the following table:

Year ended 31 March 20X8

		Ace: Consolidated financial statements	Deuce	Trey
(i)	Sale of machine by Ace to Deuce	Disclose intra-group profit on sale of $5,000. Otherwise sale eliminated on consolidation	Disclose purchase of machine from parent at $25,000 and depreciation charge of $5,000. No amounts outstanding at year end	
(ii)	Not applicable			
(iii)	Management charges made by Ace to both Deuce and Trey	No disclosure: eliminated on consolidation	Disclose purchase of management services from parent at no charge	Disclose purchase of management services from parent at no charge

Year ended 31 March 20X9

	Ace: Consolidated financial statements	Deuce	Trey
(i) Sale of machine by Ace to Deuce	No disclosure as transaction completed	Disclose depreciation charge of $5,000 on machine purchased from parent in previous year	
(ii) Sale of goods by Deuce to Trey		Disclose sale of goods to Trey for $15,000 and profit of $3,000. No debt written off or outstanding at year end	Disclose purchase of goods from Deuce for $15,000. No amounts outstanding at year end. All inventory sold at year end
(iii) Management charges made by Ace to both Deuce and Trey	No disclosure: eliminated on consolidation	No disclosure because more than 90% of equity share capital owned	Disclose purchase of management services from parent for $10,000. Disclose $10,000 due to parent at year end

Segment reporting

Chapter learning objectives

Upon completion of this chapter you will be able to:

- determine the nature and extent of reportable segments
- specify and discuss the nature of segment information to be disclosed.

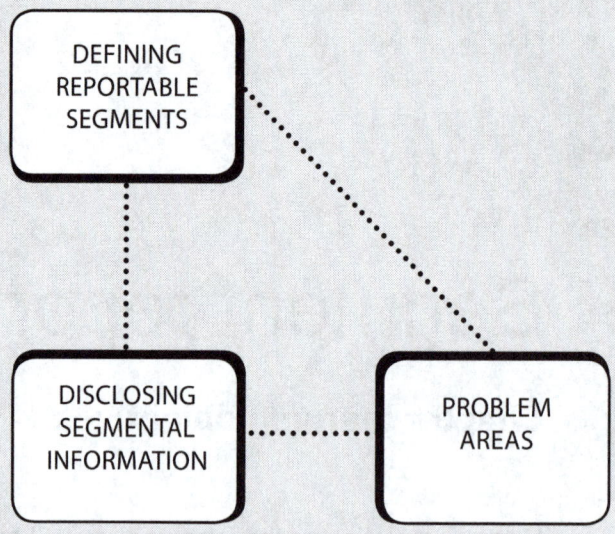

1 Defining reportable segments

Expandable text - Development of IFRS 8

- IFRS 8 was issued in November 2006 and forms part of the joint project between the IASB and the US standards setter, the FASB (Financial Accounting Standards Board).

- IFRS 8 largely adopts the US standard on segment reporting, FASB 131 **Disclosures about segments of an enterprise and related information**. The objective was to reduce differences in segment reporting between IFRS and US GAAP.

Introduction

IFRS 8 **Operating segments** requires an entity to disclose information about each of its operating segments.

- The purpose is to enable users of the financial statements to evaluate the nature and financial effects of the business activities in which it engages and the economic environments in which it operates.

IFRS 8 defines an **operating segment** as a component of an entity:

- that engages in business activities from which it may earn revenues and incur expenses

- whose operating results are regularly reviewed by the entity's chief operating decision maker to make decisions about resources to be allocated to the segment and assess its performance

- for which discrete financial information is available.

Segmental reports are designed to reveal significant information that might otherwise be hidden by the process of presenting a single statement of comprehensive income / income statement and statement of financial position for an entity.

How to define reportable segments

Under IFRS 8 segment information reflects the way that the entity is actually managed. An entity's reportable segments (its operating segments) are those that are used in its internal management reports. Therefore management identifies the operating segments.

- Start-up operations may be operating segments even before they begin to earn revenue.

- A part of an entity that only sells goods to other parts of the entity is a reportable segment if management treats it as one.

- Corporate headquarters and other similar departments do not earn revenue and are therefore not operating segments. An entity's pension plan is not an operating segment.

- Management may use more than one set of segment information. For example, an entity can analyse information by classes of business (different products or services) and by geographical areas.

- If management uses more than one set of segment information, it should identify a **single** set of components on which to base the segmental disclosures. The basis of reporting information should be the one that best enables users to understand the business and the environment in which it operates.

- Operating segments can be combined into one reportable segment provided that they have similar characteristics.

Quantitative thresholds

An entity must separately report information about an operating segment that meets any of the following quantitative thresholds:

- its reported revenue, including both sales to external customers and inter-segment sales, is ten per cent or more of the combined revenue of all operating segments

- its reported profit or loss is ten per cent or more of the greater, in absolute amount, of:
    - the combined reported profit of all operating segments that did not report a loss and
    - the combined reported loss of all operating segments that reported a loss.

- its assets are ten per cent or more of the combined assets of all operating segments.

At least 75% of the entity's external revenue should be included in reportable segments. So if the quantitative test results in segmental disclosure of less than this 75%, other segments should be identified as reportable segments until this 75% is reached.

Information about other business activities and operating segments that are not reportable are combined into an 'all other segments' category.

There is no precise limit to the number of segments that can be disclosed, but if there are more than ten, the resulting information may become too detailed.

Although IFRS 8 defines a reportable segment in terms of size, size is not the only criterion to be taken into account. There is some scope for subjectivity.

Expandable text - Illustration defining reportable segments

Diverse carries out a number of different business activities. Summarised information is given below.

	Revenue	Profit before tax	Total assets
	$m	$m	$m
Manufacture and sale of computer hardware	83	23	34
Development and supply of bespoke software:			
to users of the company's hardware products	22	12	6
to other users	5	3	1
Technical support and training	10	2	4
Contract work on information technology products	30	10	10
	150	50	55

Which of the company's activities should be identified as separate operating segments?

KAPLAN PUBLISHING

Expandable text - Illustration solution

Manufacture and sale of computer hardware and contract work on information technology products are clearly reportable segments by virtue of size. Each of these two operations exceeds all three 'ten per cent thresholds'.

On the face of it, it appears that development of bespoke software is a third segment. It would make logical sense for both parts of this operation to be reported together, as supply to users of other hardware forms only three per cent of total revenue and six per cent of total profit before tax.

Although technical support and training falls below all three 'ten per cent thresholds', it should be disclosed as a fourth reportable segment if (as seems likely) management treat it as a separate segment because it has different characteristics from the rest of the business.

Expandable text - Approaches to identify reportable segments

There are two main approaches to identifying reportable segments:

- the 'risks and returns' approach
- the 'managerial' approach.

The 'risks and returns' approach identifies segments on the basis of different risks and returns arising from different lines of business and geographical areas. Broadly speaking, this was the approach adopted by IAS 14 **Segment reporting**, which has been replaced by IFRS 8.

The 'managerial' approach identifies segments corresponding to the internal organisation structure of the entity. This is the approach adopted by IFRS 8.

The 'risks and returns' approach

The 'risks and returns' approach is believed to have the following advantages:

- it produces information that is more comparable between companies and consistent over time than the 'managerial' approach
- it assists in the assessment of profitability and the risks and returns of the component parts of the entity
- it reflects the approach taken in the financial statements for external reporting.

The main disadvantage of the approach is that defining segments can be difficult in practice and also subjective. This affects comparability.

The 'managerial' approach

The 'managerial' approach bases both the segments reported and the information reported about them on the information used internally for decision making. This means that management defines the reportable segments.

Arguments for the 'managerial approach' include the following.

- Segments based on an entity's internal structure are less subjective than those identified by the 'risks and returns' approach.

- It highlights the risks and opportunities that management believes are important.

- It provides information with predictive value because it enables users of the financial statements to see the entity through the eyes of management.

- The cost of providing the information is low (because it should already have been provided for management's use).

- It will produce segment information that is consistent with the way in which management discuss their business in other parts of the annual report (e.g. in the Chairman's Statement and the Operating and Financial Review).

Arguments against the 'managerial approach' include the following.

- Segments based on internal reporting structures are unlikely to be comparable between entities and may not be comparable from year to year for an individual entity. (For example, organisation structures, or the way in which they are perceived, may change as a result of new managers being appointed.)

- The information is likely to be commercially sensitive (because entities are organised strategically).

- In theory, segmental information could be given other than by products or services or geographically. This might be more difficult to analyse.

- Using the managerial approach could lead to segments with different risks and returns being combined.

- Analysts define their area of expertise by industry segment, usually based on product or service. The IAS 14 version of segmental reporting is more likely to reflect these.

However, it should be remembered that for many entities, the risks and returns approach and the managerial approach will probably identify exactly the same reportable segments.

2 Disclosing reportable segments

General information

IFRS 8 requires disclosure of the following.

- Factors used to identify the entity's reportable segments, including the basis of organisation (for example, whether segments are based on products and services, geographical areas or a combination of these).

- The types of products and services from which each reportable segment derives its revenues.

Information about profit or loss and other segment items

For each reportable segment an entity should report:

- a measure of profit or loss
- a measure of total assets
- a measure of total liabilities (if such an amount is regularly used in decision making).

IFRS 8 does not define segment revenue, segment result (profit or loss) or segment assets.

- Therefore, the following amounts must be disclosed if they are included in segment profit or loss:
    - revenues from external customers
    - revenues from inter-segment transactions
    - interest revenue
    - interest expense
    - depreciation and amortisation
    - material items of income and expense (exceptional items)
    - interests in the profit or loss of associates and joint ventures accounted for by the equity method
    - income tax expense
    - material non-cash items other than depreciation or amortisation.

- Interest revenue can be disclosed net of interest expense only if a majority of the segment's revenues are from interest and net interest revenue is used in decision making.

- The following amounts must be disclosed if they are included in segment assets:
  - investments in associates and joint ventures accounted for by the equity method
  - amounts of additions to non-current assets other than financial instruments.

- An entity must provide reconciliations of the totals disclosed in the segment report to the amounts reported in the financial statements as follows:
  - segment revenue
  - segment profit or loss (before tax and discontinued operations unless these items are allocated to segments)
  - segment assets
  - segment liabilities (if reported)
  - any other material item of segment information disclosed.

Entity wide disclosures

IFRS 8 also requires the following disclosures about the entity as a whole, even if it only has one reportable segment.

- The revenues from external customers for each product and service or each group of similar products and services.

- Revenues from external customers split between the entity's country of domicile and all foreign countries in total.

- Non-current assets split between those located in the entity's country of domicile and all foreign countries in total.

- Revenue from a single external customer which amounts to ten per cent or more of an entity's revenue. The identity of the customer does not need to be disclosed.

Measurement

IFRS 8 requires segmental reports to be based on the information reported to and used by management, even where this is prepared on a different basis from the rest of the financial statements.

Therefore, an entity must provide explanations of the measurement of segment profit or loss, segment assets and segment liabilities, including:

- the basis of accounting for any transactions between reportable segments

- the nature of differences between the measurement of segment profit or loss, assets and liabilities and the amounts reported in the financial statements. Differences could result from accounting policies and/or policies for the allocation of common costs and jointly used assets to segments

- the nature of any changes from prior periods in measurement methods

- the nature and effect of any asymmetrical allocations to segments (for example, where an entity allocates depreciation expense but not the related non-current assets).

Preparing segmental reports

The illustration provides a useful format to follow when preparing a segmental report.

Expandable text - Illustration

	Segment A	Segment B	Segment C	Segment D	All other	Totals
	$000	$000	$000	$000	$000	$'000
Revenues from external customers	5,000	9,500	12,000	5,000	1,000	32,500
Revenues from inter-segment transactions	–	3,000	1,500	–	–	4,500
Interest revenue	800	1,000	1,500	1,000	–	4,300
Interest expense	600	700	1,100	–	–	2,400
Depreciation and amortisation	100	50	1,500	900	–	2,550
Exceptional costs	–	–	–	200	–	200
Segment profit	70	900	2,300	500	100	3,870
Impairment of assets	200	–	–	–	–	200
Segment assets	5,000	3,000	12,000	57,000	2,000	79,000

Additions to non-current assets	700	500	800	600 –	2,600
Segment liabilities	3,000	1,800	8,000	30,000 –	42,800

Notes

(1) The 'all other' column shows amounts relating to segments that fall below the quantitative thresholds.

(2) Impairment of assets is disclosed as a material non-cash item.

(3) Comparatives should be provided. These should be restated if an entity changes the structure of its internal organisation so that its reportable segments change, unless the information is not available and the cost of preparing it would be excessive.

3 Problem areas in segmental reporting

Segmental reports can provide useful information, but they also have important limitations.

- IFRS 8 states that segments should reflect the way in which the entity is managed. This means that segments are defined by the directors. Arguably, this provides too much flexibility. It also means that segmental information is only useful for comparing the performance of the same entity over time, not for comparing the performance of different entities.

- Common costs may be allocated to different segments on whatever basis the directors believe is reasonable. This can lead to arbitrary allocation of these costs.

- A segment's operating results can be distorted by trading with other segments on non-commercial terms.

- These limitations have applied to most systems of segmental reporting, regardless of the accounting standard being applied. IFRS 8 requires disclosure of some information about the way in which common costs are allocated and the basis of accounting for inter-segment transactions.

Expandable text - Further problem areas

IFRS 8 was issued relatively recently (November 2006) and will only be fully effective from 2009. Presently, at January 2010, it is too early to say whether it will be more successful than its predecessor, IAS 14. There are some potential problem areas, which are briefly discussed below.

KAPLAN PUBLISHING

Determining reportable segments

IAS 14 required an entity to prepare two segmental reports: one based on business segments and one based on geographical segments. IFRS 8 only requires one segmental report. If management uses more than one set of segment information, it should identify a single set of components on which to base the segmental disclosures. In practice, this may be both difficult to do, and subjective. For example, some entities adopt a 'matrix' form of organisation in which some managers are responsible for different products worldwide, while others are responsible for particular geographical areas.

Disclosure of segment information

Some information (for example, segment liabilities) is only required if it is regularly provided to the chief operating decision maker. In theory, it would be possible to avoid disclosing 'bad news' or other sensitive information on the grounds that the information was not used in decision making.

Measurement of segment results and segment assets

IFRS 8 does not define segment results and segment assets. Although the standard requires disclosure of certain figures if these are included in the totals, the amounts will not necessarily be measured on the same basis as the amounts in the main financial statements. This may be a particular issue in countries such as the UK, where the consolidated financial statements are prepared using IFRSs but internal financial information may still follow local GAAP. Totals must be reconciled to the main financial statements, but users may still find it difficult to understand the disclosures.

IAS 14 required segmental information to conform with the accounting policies used in the main financial statements.

Changes to the way in which an entity is organised

One of the disadvantages of the IFRS 8 approach is that if a company changes the way in which it is organised, its reportable segments may also change. IFRS 8 requires an entity to restate its comparative information for earlier periods unless the information is not available and the cost of developing it would be excessive. If an entity does not restate its comparative figures, segment information for the current period must be disclosed both on the old basis and on the new basis. The disclosures should help users to understand the effect of the change, but some users may find it difficult to analyse the information, particularly where an entity undergoes frequent restructurings.

Test your understanding 1 - Segments

An entity has prepared the following segmental report:

Operating segments

	Fruit grow'g		Canning		Other		Group	
	20X2	20X1	20X2	20X1	20X2	20X1	20X2	20X1
	$000	$000	$000	$000	$000	$000	$000	$000
Total revenue.	13,635	15,188	20,520	16,200	5,400	4,050	39,555	35,438
Less inter-segment. revenue.	3,485	1,688	2,970	3,105			6,455	4,793
External. revenue.	10,150	13,500	17,550	13,095	5,400	4,050	33,100	30,645
Segment. profit	3,565	3,375	4,725	3,600	412	540	8,702	7,515
Seg. assets	33,750	32,400	40,500	33,750	18,765	17,563	93,015	83,713
Unallocated (common) assets							13,500	11,003
Total assets							106,515	94,716

Required:

Identify areas in which the segmental report provided below does not necessarily result in the disclosure of useful information.

Test your understanding 2 - Tab

Tab

Tab has recently acquired four large overseas subsidiaries. These subsidiaries manufacture products which are totally different from those of the holding company. The holding company manufactures paper and related products whereas the subsidiaries manufacture the following:

	Product	Location
Subsidiary 1	Car products	Spain
Subsidiary 2	Textiles	Korea
Subsidiary 3	Kitchen utensils	France
Subsidiary 4	Fashion garments	Thailand

The directors have purchased these subsidiaries in order to diversify their product base but do not have any knowledge on the information which is required in the financial statements, regarding these subsidiaries, other than the statutory requirements. The directors of the company realise that there is a need to disclose segmental information but do not understand what the term means or what the implications are for the published accounts.

Required:

(a) Explain to the directors the purpose of segmental reporting of financial information.

(4 marks)

(b) Explain to the directors the criteria which should be used to identify the separate reportable segments (you should illustrate your answer by reference to the above information).

(6 marks)

(c) Advise the directors on the information which should be disclosed in financial statements for each segment.

(7 marks)

(d) Critically evaluate IFRS 8 Operating segments, setting out the major problems with the standard.

(8 marks)

(Total: 25 marks)

Expandable text - UK syllabus focus

The ACCA UK syllabus contains a requirement that candidates should be able to discuss and apply the key differences between UK GAAP and IFRS GAAP. The accounting requirements of UK GAAP and IFRS GAAP are simil;ar in principle, but there are some differencesas follows:

SSAP 25 - Segment reporting. UK GAAP requires that reportable segments are identified using a "risks and rewards" approach, rather than the "managerial approach" adopted under the equivalent regulation of IFRS 8 under IFRS GAAP. In addition, SSAP 25 requires more extensive disclosure of information; typically between both different classes of business and also geographical analysis.

The main argument in favour of IFRS 8 is that identification of segments, together with supporting disclosures, is based upon the operational managerial structure of the business, thus making it relatively easy to prepare such information for the annual report and accounts. By comparison, UK GAAP disclosures based upon risks and rewards is unlikely to be on the same lines as managerial decision-making, therefore resulting in additional time and cost to contain the information to include in the financial statements. There is also the issue of whether or not this information is of any value to users of financial statements.

Both reporting standards use a "10% rule" as a rule of thumb for identification of segments, and have similar deficiencies regarding issues such as how to account for common costs, and intra-segment trading within the same reporting entity.

4 Chapter summary

```
┌─────────────────────────────┐
│ Defining reportable         │
│ segments                    │
│  • Managerial approach      │
│  • Ten per cent thresholds  │
└─────────────────────────────┘
```

```
┌─────────────────────────────┐      ┌──────────────────────────┐
│ Disclosing segmental        │      │ Problem areas            │
│ information                 │      │  • Subjectivity          │
│  • General information      │      │  • Common costs          │
│  • Information about profit │      │  • Inter-segment sales   │
│    or loss and other        │      └──────────────────────────┘
│    segment items            │
│  • Entity wide disclosures  │
│  • Measurement              │
│  • Reconciliations          │
└─────────────────────────────┘
```

Test your understanding answers

Test your understanding 1 - Segments

Your answer may have included some of the following.

(i) **Definition of segments:** It would be helpful to know whether there are any other classes of business included within the three operating segments supplied by the company which are material. This is particularly important when one looks at the Canning segment and notices that it comprises 50% of the total sales to customers outside the group.

(ii) **Inter-segment sales:** The inter-segment sales for fruit growing are a relatively high percentage (at around 25% ($3,485/13,635)) of its total revenue. In assessing the risk and economic trends it might well be that those of the receiving segment are more useful in predicting future prospects than those of the segment from which the sale originated.

(iii) **Analysis of assets:** Users often need to calculate a return on capital employed for each segment. Therefore, it is important to ensure that the segment profit and assets are appropriately defined, so that segment profit can be usefully related to the assets figure to produce a meaningful ratio. This means that both the operating profit and assets figure need to be precisely defined. If, for example, the assets are the gross assets, then the operating profits should be before deduction of interest. This means that the preparer of the segmental report needs to be aware of the reader's information needs.

(iv) **Unallocated items:** The information provided includes unallocated assets that represent around 12% of the total assets. It is not clear what these assets represent.

(v) **Treatment of interest:** It would be useful to know if there has been any interest charge incurred and to ascertain whether it is material and whether it can be reasonably identified as relating to any particular segment. As mentioned in (iii) above, it is not clear how segment profit is defined or how it has been derived.

Test your understanding 2 - Tab

(a) The purpose of segmental information is to provide users of financial statements with sufficient details for them to be able to appreciate the different rates of profitability, different opportunities for growth and different degrees of risk that apply to an entity's classes of business and various geographical locations.

The segmental information should enable users to:

(i) appreciate more thoroughly the results and financial position of the entity by permitting a better understanding of the entity's past performance and thus a better assessment of its future prospects

(ii) be aware of the impact that changes in significant components of a business may have on the business as a whole.

(b) IFRS 8 defines an operating segment as a component of an entity:

- that engages in business activities from which it may earn revenues and incur expenses (including revenues and expenses relating to transactions with other components of the same entity)

- whose operating results are regularly reviewed by the entity's chief operating decision-maker to make decisions about resources to be allocated to the segment and assess its performance

- for which discrete financial information is available.

These qualitative criteria are supplemented by quantitative:

- reported revenue, including both sales to external customers and intersegment sales or transfers, is 10% or more of the combined revenue, internal and external, of all operating segments

- the absolute amount of its reported profit or loss is 10% or more of the greater, in absolute amount, of (i) the combined reported profit of all operating segments that did not report a loss and (ii) the combined reported loss of all operating segments that reported a loss

- assets are 10% or more of the combined assets of all operating segments.

(c) An entity shall disclose the factors used to identify the entity's reportable segments and types of products and services from which each reportable segment derives its revenues.

The following information will be reported about profit or loss, assets and liabilities for each segment:

An entity shall report a measure of profit or loss and total assets for each reportable segment:

- a measure of liabilities for each reportable segment if such an amount is regularly provided to the chief operating decision-maker.

- An entity shall also disclose the following about each reportable segment if the specified amounts are included in the measure of segment profit or loss reviewed by the chief operating decision-maker, or are otherwise regularly provided to the chief operating decision-maker, even if not included in that measure of segment profit or loss:

  - revenues from external customers;

  - revenues from transactions with other operating segments of the same entity;

  - interest revenue;

  - interest expense;

  - depreciation and amortisation;

  - material items of income and expense disclosed in accordance with IAS 1 **Presentation of financial statements**;

  - the entity's interest in the profit or loss of associates and joint ventures accounted for by the equity method;

  - income tax expense or income and

  - material non-cash items other than depreciation and amortisation.

TAB could classify on a geographical basis under the headings 'Europe' and 'The Far East'.

TAB has five types of products and more information is really required on the commonality of any of these five. A product split could thus be for five segments.

Likely candidates for grouping together are textiles and fashion garments, perhaps under the heading 'textiles' or 'textiles and clothing'. In addition it may be reasonable to group car products and kitchen utensils under the heading 'domestic products'.

(d) IFRS 8 lays down some very broad and inclusive criteria for reporting segments. Unlike earlier attempts to define segments in more quantitative terms, segments are defined largely in terms of the breakdown and analysis used by management. This is, potentially, a very powerful method of ensuring that preparers provide useful segmental information.

There will still be problems in deciding which segments to report, if only because management may still attempt to reduce the amount of commercially sensitive information that they produce.

The growing use of executive information systems and data management within businesses makes it easier to generate reports on an ad hoc basis. It would be relatively easy to provide management with a very basic set of internal reports and analyses and leave individual managers to prepare their own more detailed information using the interrogation software provided by the system. If such analyses became routine then they would be reportable under IFRS 8, but that would be very difficult to check and audit.

There are problems in the measurement of segmental performance if the segments trade with each other. Disclosure of details of inter-segment pricing policy is often considered to be detrimental to the good of a company. There is little guidance on the policy for transfer pricing.

Differing internal reporting structures could lead to inconsistent and incompatible segmental reports, even from companies in the same industry.

Non-current assets and inventories

Chapter learning objectives

Upon completion of this chapter you will be able to:

- apply and discuss the timing of the recognition of non-current assets and the determination of their carrying amounts including impairment and revaluations

- apply and discuss the treatment of non-current assets held for sale

- apply and discuss the accounting treatment of investment properties including classification, recognition and measurement issues

- apply and discuss the accounting treatment of intangible assets including the criteria for recognition and measurement subsequent to acquisition and classification

- apply and discuss the accounting treatment of inventories.

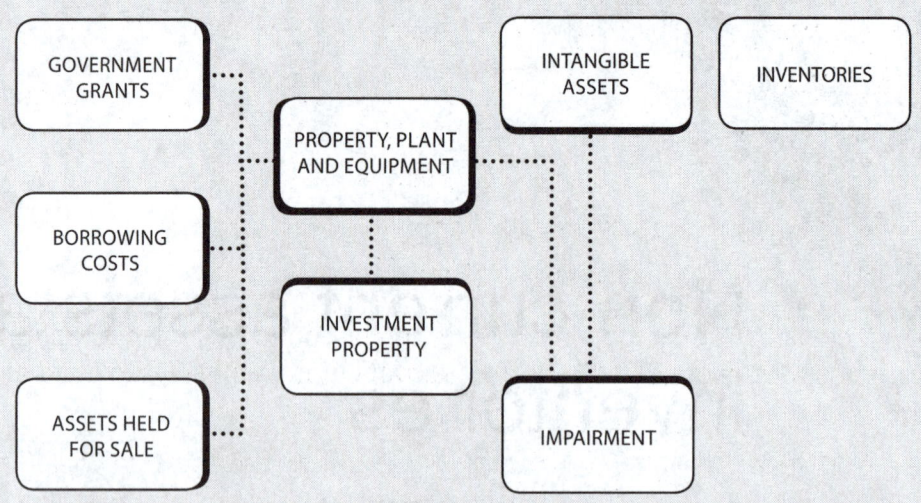

Expandable text - PP&E IAS 16 - recognition and measurement

Property, plant and equipment are tangible items that:

- are held for use in the production or supply of goods or services, for rental to others, or for administrative purposes
- are expected to be used during more than one period.

Tangible items have physical substance and can be touched.

- An item of property, plant and equipment should be recognised as an asset when:
  - it is probable that future economic benefits associated with the asset will flow to the entity
  - the cost of the asset can be measured reliably.

Measurement on initial recognition

A tangible non-current asset should initially be measured at its cost. Its cost comprises:

- its purchase price
- any costs directly attributable to bringing the asset to the location and condition necessary for it to be capable of operating in the manner intended by management, i.e. it is ready for use (whether or not it is actually in use)
- the initial estimate of the costs of dismantling and removing the item and restoring the site on which it is located. This might apply where, for example, an entity has to recognise a provision for the cost of decommissioning an oil rig or a nuclear power station.

Directly attributable costs include commissioning costs (e.g. sea trials for a ship, testing a computer system before it goes live).

The following costs, specifically identified, should never be capitalised:

- administration and general overheads

- abnormal costs (repairs, wastage, idle time)

- costs incurred after the asset is physically ready for use

- costs incurred in the initial operating period (e.g. initial operating losses and any further costs incurred before a machine is used at its full capacity)

- costs of opening a new facility, introducing a new product (including advertising and promotional costs) and conducting business in a new location or with a new class of customer (including training costs)

- costs of relocating/reorganising an entity's operations.

Expandable text - Subsequent cost

Where additional costs are incurred after the asset becomes operational, the entity applies the normal recognition principle for assets: is it probable that future economic benefits will flow to the entity?

The costs of day-to-day servicing (repairs and maintenance) should not be capitalised; rather than increasing economic benefits, they protect those expected at the time of the initial capitalisation. Instead, they should be recognised in profit or loss as they are incurred.

In contrast, the cost of replacing parts of items of property, plant and equipment is normally capitalised as it meets the recognition criteria. Examples:

- a furnace may require relining after a specified number of hours of use

- the interior walls of a building may need to be replaced.

Expandable text - Measurement after initial recognition

IAS 16 allows a choice between the cost model and the revaluation model.

- Under the **cost model**, property, plant and equipment is valued at cost less accumulated depreciation.

- Under the **revaluation model**, property, plant and equipment is carried at fair value less any subsequent accumulated depreciation.

- Fair value is normally open market value (not existing use value). Depreciated replacement cost may be used where there is no reliable market value (for example, because the asset is specialised or rare).

- Revaluations must be made with 'sufficient regularity' to ensure that the carrying amount does not differ materially from the fair value at each reporting date.

- If an item is revalued, the entire class of assets to which the item belongs must be revalued.

- If a revaluation increases the value of an asset, the increase is disclosed as other comprehensive income and credited to other components of equity under the heading 'revaluation surplus' unless it reverses a previous decrease in value of the same asset that has been recognised as an expense. It should then be recognised in profit or loss.

- If a revaluation decreases the value of the asset, the decrease should be recognised immediately in profit or loss, unless there is a revaluation reserve representing a surplus on the same asset.

Expandable text - Depreciation

All assets with a finite useful life must be depreciated.

Depreciation is the systematic allocation of the depreciable amount of an asset over its useful life.

The depreciable amount of an asset is its cost less its residual value.

The residual value is the amount that the entity would **currently** obtain from disposal, net of selling costs, if the asset were already of the age and in the condition expected at the end of its useful life.

- IAS 16 does not prescribe a depreciation method, but the method used must reflect the pattern in which the asset's future economic benefits are expected to be consumed.

- Depreciation begins when the asset is available for use and continues until the asset is derecognised, even if it is idle.

- If an asset is measured at historical cost, the depreciation charge is based on historical cost.

- If an asset has been revalued, then the depreciation charge is based on the revalued amount.

- The residual value and the useful life of an asset should be reviewed at least at each financial year-end and revised if necessary. Depreciation methods should also be reviewed at least annually.

- Any adjustments are accounted for as a change in accounting estimate under IAS 8 **Accounting policies, changes in accounting estimates and errors**, rather than as a change in accounting policy. This means that they are reflected in the current and future statements of comprehensive income / income statements.

Expandable text - Illustration: change in depreciation estimates

An asset was purchased for $100,000 on 1 January 20X5 and straight line depreciation of $20,000 per annum was charged (five year life, no residual value). A general review of asset lives is undertaken and for this particular asset, the remaining useful life as at 31 December 20X7 is seven years.

What should the annual depreciation charge be for 20X7 and subsequent years?

Solution

CV as at 31 December 20X6 (60% × $100,000)	$60,000
Remaining useful life as at 1 January 20X7	8 years
Annual depreciation charge	$7,500

Note that the estimated remaining life is seven years from 31 December 20X7, but this information is used to compute the current year's charge as well.

Expandable text - Depreciation of separate components

Certain large assets are in fact a collection of smaller assets, each with a different cost and useful life. For example, an aeroplane consists of an airframe (which may last for 40 years or so) plus engines, radar equipment, seats, etc. all of which have a relatively short life. Instead of calculating depreciation on the aeroplane as a whole, depreciation is charged on each component (airframe, engines, etc.) instead.

For example, an entity buys a ship for $12m. The ship as a whole should last for 25 years. The engines, however, will need replacing after 7 years. The cost price of $12m included about $1.4m in respect of the engines.

The annual depreciation charge will be $624,000 made up as follows:

engines: $1.4m over seven years = $200,000 pa, plus

the rest of the ship: $10.6m over 25 years = $424,000 pa.

Expandable text - Derecognition

Assets are derecognised either on disposal; or when no future economic benefits are expected from their use or disposal.

- The gain or loss on derecognition of an asset is the difference between the net disposal proceeds, if any, and the carrying amount of the item.

- When a revalued asset is disposed of, any revaluation surplus may be transferred directly to retained earnings, or it may be left in equity under the heading revaluation surplus. The transfer to retained earnings should not be made through the statement of comprehensive income.

Expandable text - Disclosures

The following should be disclosed for each class of property, plant and equipment:

- the measurement bases used for determining the gross carrying amount

- the depreciation methods used

- the useful lives or the depreciation rates used

- the gross carrying amount and the accumulated depreciation (aggregated with accumulated impairment losses) at the beginning and end of the period

- a reconciliation of the carrying amount at the beginning and end of the period showing: additions; disposals; increases or decreases resulting from revaluations and from impairment losses; depreciation; and other changes.

If items of property, plant and equipment are stated at revalued amounts, information about the revaluation should also be disclosed.

1 Impairment of assets (IAS 36)

When to carry out an impairment review

Definition

Impairment is a reduction in the recoverable amount of an asset or cash-generating unit below its carrying amount.

An entity should carry out an impairment review at least annually if:

- an intangible asset is not being amortised because it has an indefinite useful life

- goodwill has arisen on a business combination.

Otherwise, an impairment review is required only where there is evidence that an impairment may have occurred.

Indications of impairment

Indications that an impairment might have happened can come from external or internal sources.

- **External sources of information**:
    - unexpected decreases in an asset's market value
    - significant adverse changes have taken place, or are about to take place, in the technological, market, economic or legal environment
    - increased interest rates have decreased an asset's recoverable amount
    - the entity's net assets are measured at more than its market capitalisation.

- **Internal sources of information**:
    - evidence of obsolescence or damage
    - there is, or is about to be, a material reduction in usage of an asset
    - evidence that the economic performance of an asset has been, or will be, worse than expected.

Calculating an impairment loss

An impairment occurs if the carrying amount of an asset is greater than its recoverable amount.

The **recoverable amount** is the higher of fair value less costs to sell and value in use.

Fair value less costs to sell is the amount obtainable from the sale of an asset in an arm's length transaction between knowledgeable, willing parties, less the costs of disposal.

Value in use is the present value of future cash flows from using an asset, including its eventual disposal.

Carrying out an impairment test

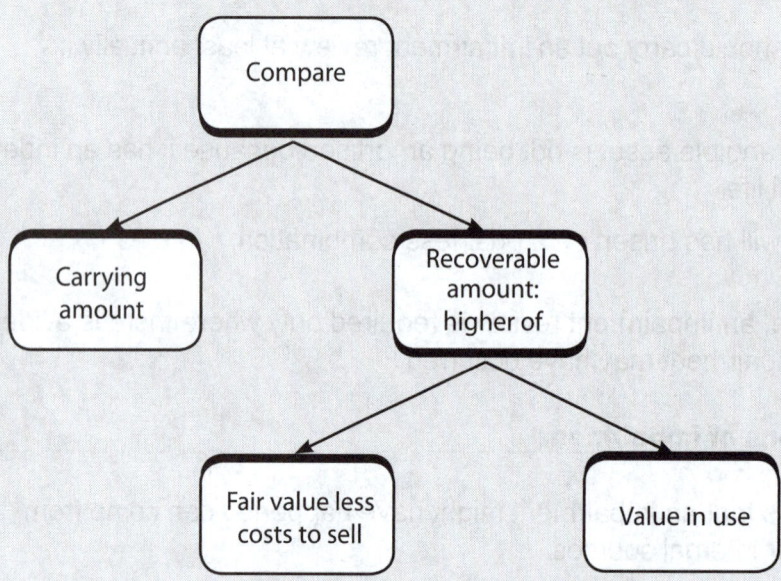

- If fair value less costs to sell is higher than the carrying amount, there is no impairment and no need to calculate value in use.

Illustration 1 – Impairment of assets (IAS 36)

An item of plant is included in the financial statements at a carrying amount of $350,000. The present value of the future cash flows from continuing to operate the plant is $320,000. Alternatively, the plant could be sold for net proceeds of $275,000.

What is the recoverable amount?

Is the plant impaired?

Expandable text - Solution

The recoverable amount is determined taking the greater of net selling costs and value in use. Net selling costs are $275,000 and value in use is $320,000 so the recoverable amount is $320,000.

To determine whether the plant is impaired, the carrying amount is compared to the recoverable amount. The carrying amount at $350,000 is greater than the recoverable amount, so the asset must be written down to its recoverable amount. Therefore, the impairment loss is $30,000.

Expandable text - Measurement of recoverable amount

(a) Measuring fair value less costs to sell

Possible indicators of fair value are:

- a binding sale agreement
- if an active market exists, the current market price less costs of disposal
- failing either of these indicators, the best information available must be relied on.

Direct selling costs might include:

- legal costs
- stamp duty
- costs relating to the removal of a sitting tenant (in the case of a building).

Redundancy and reorganisation costs (e.g. following the sale of a business) are not direct selling costs.

(b) Measuring value in use

Value in use is calculated by estimating future cash inflows and outflows from the use of the asset and its ultimate disposal, and applying a suitable discount rate to these cash flows.

Therefore, there are two steps to the calculation.

(1) Estimate future cash flows.

(2) Discount them to arrive at their present value.

Where possible, value in use should be estimated for individual assets. However, it may not always be possible to identify cash flows arising from individual assets. If this is the case, value in use is calculated for cash-generating units (groups of assets that produce independent income streams).

Test your understanding 1 - Impaired asset

Information about an asset is given below.

	$000
Carrying amount	500
Fair value less costs to sell	300
Future cash flows (per annum) for 2 years	200
Discount rate	10%

Determine the outcome of the impairment review.

Recognising impairment losses in the financial statements

An impairment loss is normally charged immediately in the statement of comprehensive income/income statement to the same heading as the related depreciation (e.g. cost of sales or administration).

- If the asset has previously been revalued upwards, the impairment is recognised as comprehensive income and is debited to the revaluation reserve until the surplus relating to that asset has been exhausted. The remainder of the impairment loss is recognised in the profit or loss.

- The recoverable (impaired) amount is then depreciated over its remaining useful life.

Illustration 2 – Impairment of assets (IAS 36)

At 1 January 20X7 a non-current asset had a carrying amount of $20,000, based on its revalued amount, and a depreciated historical cost of $10,000. An impairment loss of $12,000 arose in the year ended 31 December 20X7..

How should this loss be reported in the financial statements for the year ended 31 December 20X7?

Expandable text - Solution

A loss of $10,000 ($20,000 – $10,000) is recognised as other comprehensive income and debited to the revaluation surplus within other components of equity. The remaining loss of $2,000 is recognised as an expense in the period.

Cash-generating units

It is not usually possible to identify cash flows relating to particular assets. For example, a factory production line is made up of many individual machines, but the revenues are earned by the production line as a whole. This means that value in use must be calculated (and the impairment review performed) for groups of assets, rather than individual assets.

- These groups of assets are called cash-generating units (CGUs).

Cash-generating units are segments of the business whose income streams are largely independent of each other.

- In practice they are likely to mirror the strategic business units used for monitoring the performance of the business.

- It could also include a subsidiary or associate within a corporate group structure.

Test your understanding 2 - Cash generating units

An entity comprises three stages of production, A (growing and felling trees), B (creating parts of wooden furniture) and C (assembling the parts from B into finished goods). The output of A is timber that is partly transferred to B and partly sold in an external market. If A did not exist, B could buy its timber from the market. The output of B has no external market and is transferred to C at an internal transfer price. C sells the finished product in an external market and the sales revenue achieved by C is not affected by the fact that the three stages of production are all performed by the entity.

Identify the cash-generating unit(s).

Allocating assets to cash-generating units

The net assets of the business (including capitalised goodwill, but excluding tax balances and interest-bearing debt) are allocated to cash-generating units. There are two particular problem areas.

- Corporate assets: assets that are used by several cash-generating units (e.g. a head office building or a research centre). They do not generate their own cash inflows, so do not themselves qualify as cash-generating units.

- Goodwill, which does not generate cash flows independently of other assets and often relates to a whole business.

It may be possible to allocate corporate assets and/or goodwill over other cash-generating units on a reasonable basis.

A cash-generating unit to which goodwill has been allocated must be tested for impairment at least annually.

If no reasonable allocation of corporate assets or goodwill is possible, then a group of cash-generating units must be tested for impairment together in a two-stage process.

Illustration 3 – Impairment of assets (IAS 36)

An entity acquires a business comprising three cash-generating units, D, E and F, but there is no reasonable way of allocating goodwill to them. After three years, the carrying amount and the recoverable amount of the net assets in the cash-generating units and the purchased goodwill are as follows:

	D	E	F	Goodwill	Total
	$000	$000	$000	$000	$000
Carrying amount	240	360	420	150	1,170
Recoverable amount	300	420	360		1,080

Expandable text - Solution

Step 1: Review the individual units for impairment.

F is impaired. A loss of $60,000 is recognised and its carrying amount is reduced to $360,000.

Step 2: Compare the carrying amount of the business as a whole, including the goodwill, with its recoverable amount.

The total carrying amount of the business is now $1,110,000 (1,170,000 – 60,000). A further impairment loss of $30,000 must then be recognised in respect of the goodwill (1,110,000 – 1,080,000).

Allocation of an impairment to the unit's assets

If an impairment loss arises in respect of a cash-generating unit, it is allocated among the assets in the unit in the following order:

- any individual assets that are obviously impaired
- goodwill
- other assets pro rata to their carrying amount.

However, the carrying amount of an asset cannot be reduced below the highest of:

- its fair value less costs to sell (if determinable)
- its value in use (if determinable)
- zero.

Illustration 4 – Impairment of assets (IAS 36)

Tinud has identified an impairment loss of $41m for one of its cash-generating units. The carrying amount of the unit's net assets was $150m, whereas the unit's recoverable amount was only $109m.

The draft values of the net assets of the unit are as follows:

	$m
Goodwill	13
Property	20
Machinery	49
Vehicles	35
Patents	14
Net monetary assets	19
	150

The net selling price of the unit's assets were insignificant except for the property, which had a market value of $35m. The net monetary assets will be realised in full.

How is the impairment loss allocated to the assets?

Expandable text - Solution

Firstly, the goodwill is reduced to zero.

No impairment loss can be set against the property because its net selling price is greater than its carrying amount.

Likewise, no impairment loss can be set against the net monetary assets (receivables, cash, etc.) because they will be realised in full.

The balance of $28m ($41m – $13m) is apportioned between the remaining assets on a pro rata basis (so (49/(49 + 35 + 14)) × 28 to machinery, and so on).

The table below shows how the impairment will be allocated.

	Draft values	Impairment loss	Impaired value
	$m	$m	$m
Goodwill	13	(13)	–
Property	20	–	20
Machinery	49	(14)	35
Vehicles	35	(10)	25
Patents	14	(4)	10
Net monetary assets	19	–	19
	150	(41)	109

Test your understanding 3 - Factory explosion

There was an explosion in a factory. The carrying amounts of its assets were as follows:

	$000
Goodwill	100
Patents	200
Machines	300
Computers	500
Buildings	1,500
	2,600

The factory operates as a cash-generating unit. An impairment review reveals a net selling price of $1.2m for the factory and value in use of $1.95m. Half of the machines have been blown to pieces but the other half can be sold for at least their book value. The patents have been superseded and are now considered worthless.

Show the effect of the explosion on the asset values.

2 Impairment of goodwill

IAS 36 **Impairment of assets** requires that once recognised according to IFRS 3 revised, goodwill is tested for impairment annually or more frequently if circumstances indicate it might be impaired.

Goodwill must not be amortised.

Accounting for an impairment

An **impairment loss** is the amount by which the carrying amount of an asset or a cash generating unit exceeds its recoverable amount.

Recoverable amount is the higher of fair value less costs to sell and value in use.

Key points:

- As goodwill does not generate cash flows of its own, its impairment is tested within the cash-generating unit to which the goodwill belongs.

- The goodwill is allocated to a specific cash-generating unit (CGU), or multiple cash generating units where the goodwill cannot be allocated to a single CGU, and the impairment test is carried out on the group of assets including the goodwill.

- Any impairment loss is allocated in the following order:
  - to goodwill allocated to the CGU
  - to other assets in the CGU on a pro rata basis. No asset can be written down below its net realisable value.

- A reversal of an impairment loss can occur if the conditions that caused the original impairment have improved. This reversal is recognised as income in the income statement.

- If the reversal relates to a cash generating unit, the reversal is allocated to the assets of the unit on a pro rata basis according to their carrying value except goodwill which cannot be rewritten into the books.

- IFRIC 10, issued in 2006, confirms that, where impairment of goodwill has been recognised in interim financial statements, it cannot subsequently be written back or reversed in the next annual financial statements.

Test your understanding 4 - Cedar

The following information relates to a 60% subsidiary, Cedar:

Net assets at acquisition	Net assets at reporting date	Fair value of NCI at acquisition	Cost of investment at acquisition	Recoverable amount at reporting date
$m	$m	$m	$m	$m
500	600	250	800	1,000

Required:

Determine the outcome of the impairment review at the reporting date.

Test your understanding 5 - Homer

The following information relates to an 80% subsidiary, Homer.

Net assets at acquisition	Net assets at reporting date	Fair value of NCI at acquisition	Cost of investment at acquisition	Recoverable amount at reporting date
$m	$m	$m	$m	$m
100	150	25	200	255

Required

Determine the outcome of the impairment review at the reporting date.

KAPLAN PUBLISHING

Accounting for an impairment with a non-controlling interest

Full method of valuing NCI

- The accounting treatment above also applies where there is a non-controlling interest valued using the full method.

- In this case goodwill shown in the group statement of financial position represents full goodwill, and so together with the rest of the CGU it can be compared to recoverable amount of the CGU on a like for like basis.

- Any impairment of goodwill is therefore allocated between the group and the NCI based upon their respective shareholdings. Note - this could result in the NCI share of impairment exceeding their share of goodwill upon acquisition.

Proportion of net assets method of valuing NCI

- Where this method is adopted, the NCI share of goodwill is not reflected in the group accounts.

- Therefore any comparison between the carrying value of a CGU (including goodwill) and its recoverable amount will not be on a like for like basis.

- In order to address this problem, goodwill must be grossed up to include goodwill attributable to the NCI prior to conducting the impairment review.

- This grossed up goodwill is known as 'total notional goodwill'.

- Once any impairment loss is determined, it should be allocated firstly to the total notional goodwill and then to the CGU's assets on a pro rata basis.

- As only the parent's share of the goodwill is recognised in the group accounts, only the parent's share of the impairment loss should be recognised.

Illustration 5 - Impairment of full value goodwill

A owns 80% of B. At 31 October 20X6 the carrying amount of B's net assets is $60 million, excluding goodwill of $8 million that arose on the original acquisition. The non-controlling interest is valued using the fair value method.

Calculate the impairment loss if the recoverable amount of B is:

(a) $64 million

(b) $50 million

Expandable text - Solution

Solution (a)

	Goodwill	Net assets	Total
	$m	$m	$m
Carrying amount	8	60	68
Recoverable amount			64
Impairment	(4)		4

The impairment loss relates only to goodwill. This will be charged to income, with the effect that it will be borne by the group and the NCI based upon their respective shareholdings.

Solution (b)

	Goodwill	Net assets	Total
	$m	$m	$m
Carrying amount	8	60	68
Recoverable amount			50
Impairment	(8)	(10)	18

The impairment loss relates first to goodwill, with the remainder set against other assets on a pro-rata basis, unless there is further information available regarding the recoverable amount of other individual assets. The impairment of $18m is charged to income, with the effect that it will be borne by the group and NCI based upon their respective shareholdings.

Illustration 6

A owns 80% of B. At 31 October 20X6 the carrying amount of B's net assets is $60 million, excluding goodwill of $8 million that arose on the original acquisition. The non-controlling interest is valued using the proportion of net assets method.

Calculate the impairment loss if the recoverable amount is:

(a) $64 million

(b) $50 million

Expandable text - Solution

Solution (a)

	Goodwill	Net assets	Total
	$m	$m	$m
Carrying amount	8	60	68
Notional NCI (20/80)	2		2
Notionally adjusted carrying amount	10	60	70
Recoverable amount			64
Impairment			6

The impairment loss only relates to goodwill. Only the proportion relating to the recognised goodwill is recognised in the financial statements, so 80% of $6m, i.e. $4.8 million.

Solution (b)

	Goodwill	Net assets	Total
	$m	$m	$m
Carrying amount	8	60	68
Notional NCI (20/80)	2		2
Notionally adjusted carrying amount	10	60	70
Recoverable amount			50
Impairment			20

The impairment loss is allocated as follows: $8 million to recognised goodwill (as before) and the remaining $10 million (20 – 10) to other net assets.

Test your understanding 6 - Happy

On 1 January 20X5, Lucky group purchased 80% of Happy for $500,000. The net assets of Happy at the date of acquisition amounted to $560,000.

The carrying amount of Happy's assets at 31 December is $520,000. Happy is a cash-generating unit on its own.

At 31 December 20X5 the recoverable amount of Happy is $510,000.

Calculate the impairment loss in Happy and explain how this would be dealt with in the financial statements of the Lucky group. It is Lucky Group policy to value the non-controlling interest at its proportionate share of the fair value of the subsidiary's identifiable net assets.

Reversal of an impairment loss

The calculation of impairment losses is based on predictions of what may happen in the future. Sometimes, actual events turn out to be better than predicted. If this happens, the recoverable amount is re-calculated and the previous write-down is reversed.

- Impaired assets should be reviewed at each reporting date to see whether there are indications that the impairment has reversed.

- A reversal of an impairment loss is recognised immediately as income in profit or loss. If the original impairment was charged against the revaluation surplus, it is recognised as other comprehensive income and credited to the revaluation reserve.

- The reversal must not take the value of the asset above the amount it would have been if the original impairment had never been recorded. The depreciation that would have been charged in the meantime must be taken into account.

- The depreciation charge for future periods should be revised to reflect the changed carrying amount.

 An impairment loss recognised for goodwill cannot be reversed in a subsequent period.

Expandable text - Indications that an impairment has reversed

Indications of a reversal are the opposite of the indicators of impairment.

- External indicators

    (i) Increases in the asset's market value.

    (ii) Favourable changes in the technological, market, economic or legal environment.

    (iii) Decreases in interest rates.

- Internal indicators

(i)   Favourable changes in the use of the asset.

(ii) Improvements in the asset's economic performance.

Reversing the impairment of a cash-generating unit: If the reversal relates to a cash-generating unit, the reversal is allocated to assets other than goodwill on a pro rata basis. The carrying amount of an asset must not be increased above the lower of:

- its recoverable amount (if determinable)
- the carrying amount that would have been determined (net of amortisation or depreciation) had no impairment loss been recognised for the asset in prior periods.

The amount that would otherwise have been allocated to the asset is allocated pro rata to the other assets of the unit, except for goodwill.

Reversals and goodwill: Impairment losses relating to goodwill can never be reversed. The reason for this is that once purchased goodwill has become impaired, any subsequent increase in its recoverable amount is likely to be an increase in internally generated goodwill, rather than a reversal of the impairment loss recognised for the original purchased goodwill. Internally generated goodwill cannot be recognised.

Expandable text - IAS 36 disclosure requirements

IAS 36 requires extensive disclosures about impairments, but the main ones are:

- losses recognised during the period, and where charged in the statement of comprehensive/income statement
- reversals recognised during the period, and where credited in the statement of comprehensive income/income statement
- for each material loss or reversal:
    - the amount of loss or reversal and the events causing it
    - the nature of the asset (or cash-generating unit) and its reportable segment
    - whether the recoverable amount is the fair value less costs to sell or value in use
    - basis used to determine the fair value less costs to sell
    - the discount rate(s) used in estimating the value in use.

Technical article

Tom Clendon and Sally Baker of Kaplan Financial wrote an article discussing the issue of impairment of goodwill for the August 2009 edition of Student Accountant magazine. You can access this article from the ACCA website (www.accaglobal.com).

Expandable text - Government grants IAS 20 - definitions

Government grants are transfers of resources to an entity in return for past or future compliance with certain conditions. They exclude assistance that cannot be valued and normal trade with governments.

Government refers to government, government agencies and similar bodies whether local, national or international.

Government assistance is government action designed to provide an economic benefit to a specific entity. It does not include indirect help such as infrastructure development.

Expandable text - General principles

General principles

Grants should not be recognised until the conditions for receipt have been complied with and there is reasonable assurance that the grant will be received.

- Grants should be recognised in profit or loss so as to match them with the expenditure towards which they are intended to contribute.
- Income grants given to subsidise expenditure should be matched to the related costs.
- Income grants given to help achieve a non-financial goal (such as job creation) should be matched to the costs incurred to meet that goal.

Grants related to assets

Grants for purchases of non-current assets should be recognised over the expected useful lives of the related assets. There are two acceptable accounting policies for this:

- deduct the grant from the cost of the asset and depreciate the net cost

- treat the grant as deferred income. Release the grant to profit or loss over the life of the asset. This is the method most commonly used.

Expandable text - Other grants and repayment

Purpose of grant	Recognise in profit/loss
To give immediate financial support	When receivable
To reimburse previously incurred costs	When receivable
To finance general activities over a period	In relevant period
To compensate for a loss of income	In relevant period

Repayment of government grants

A government grant that becomes repayable is accounted for as a revision of an accounting estimate.

(a) Income-based grants

Firstly, debit the repayment to any liability for deferred income. Any excess repayment must be charged to profits immediately.

(b) Capital-based grants deducted from cost

Increase the cost of the asset with the repayment. This will also increase the amount of depreciation that should have been charged in the past. This should be recognised and charged immediately.

(c) Capital-based grants treated as deferred income

Firstly, debit the repayment to any liability for deferred income. Any excess repayment must be charged against profits immediately.

Government assistance

As implied in the definition set out above, government assistance helps businesses through loan guarantees, loans at a low rate of interest, advice, procurement policies and similar methods. It is not possible to place reliable values on these forms of assistance, so they are not recognised.

Disclosure

The disclosure requirements of IAS 20 are:

*   the accounting policy adopted for government grants, including the methods of presentation adopted in the financial statements
*   the nature and extent of government grants recognised in the financial statements and other forms of government assistance received
*   unfulfilled conditions and other contingencies attaching to government assistance that has been recognised.

Expandable text - Borrowing costs IAS 23 - general principle

As part of the short-term convergence project, the IASB issued IAS 23 revised in March 2007.

The revised standard removes the option to expense all borrowing costs as incurred (the benchmark treatment of the previous version of IAS 23).

Instead it requires that an entity capitalise borrowing costs directly attributable to the acquisition or construction of a qualifying asset as part of the cost of that asset. This was a permitted alternative treatment under the previous version of IAS 23.

Expandable text - Rules for capitalising interest

Accounting rules for capitalising interest

Interest should only be capitalised if it relates to the acquisition, construction or production of a qualifying asset, i.e. an asset that necessarily takes a substantial period of time to get ready for its intended use or sale.

*   The interest capitalised should relate to the costs incurred on the project and the cost of the entity's borrowings.
*   The total amount of finance costs capitalised during a period should not exceed the total amount of finance costs incurred during that period.

KAPLAN PUBLISHING

Capitalisation period

Interest should only be capitalised while construction is in progress.

- Capitalisation of borrowing costs should commence when:
    - expenditure for the asset is being incurred
    - borrowing costs are being incurred
    - activities that are necessary to get the asset ready for use are in progress.
- Capitalisation of finance costs should cease when substantially all the activities that are necessary to get the asset ready for use are complete.
- Capitalisation of borrowing costs should be suspended during extended periods in which active development is interrupted.
- When construction of a qualifying asset is completed in parts and each part is capable of being used while construction continues on other parts, capitalisation of finance costs relating to a part should cease when substantially all the activities that are necessary to get that part ready for use are completed.

Expandable text - How to calculate the interest cost

Where a loan is taken out specifically to finance the construction of an asset, the amount to be capitalised is the interest payable on that loan, less any investment income on the temporary investment of the borrowings.

Arriving at the interest cost is more complicated when the acquisition or construction of an asset is financed from an entity's general borrowings. In this situation it is necessary to calculate the finance cost by applying a notional rate of interest (the capitalisation rate) to the expenditure on the asset.

- The capitalisation rate is the weighted average of rates applicable to general borrowings outstanding in the period.
- General borrowings do not include loans for other specific purposes, such as constructing other qualifying assets.

IAS 23 is silent on how to arrive at the expenditure on the asset, but it would be reasonable to calculate it as the weighted average carrying amount of the asset during the period, including finance costs previously capitalised.

Disclosure requirements

The financial statements should disclose:

- the accounting policy adopted for borrowing costs
- the amount of borrowing costs capitalised during the period
- the capitalisation rate used.

3 Non-current assets held for sale (IFRS 5)
Classification as 'held for sale'

A non-current asset or disposal group should be classified as 'held for sale' if its carrying amount will be recovered principally through a sale transaction rather than through continuing use.

A **disposal group** is a group of assets (and possibly liabilities) that the entity intends to dispose of in a single transaction.

- IFRS 5 applies to disposal groups as well as to individual non-current assets that are held for sale.
- A disposal group may include goodwill acquired in a business combination if the group is a cash-generating unit to which goodwill has been allocated (IAS 36).
- Subsidiaries acquired exclusively with a view to resale are classified as disposal groups held for sale if they meet the conditions below.

IFRS 5 requires the following conditions to be met before an asset or disposal group can be classified as 'held for sale'.

- The item is available for immediate sale in its present condition.
- The sale is highly probable.
- Management is committed to a plan to sell the item.
- An active programme to locate a buyer has been initiated.
- The item is being actively marketed at a reasonable price in relation to its current fair value.
- The sale is expected to be completed within one year from the date of classification.
- It is unlikely that the plan will change significantly or be withdrawn.

Assets that are to be abandoned or wound down gradually cannot be classified as held for sale (although they may qualify as discontinued operations once they have been abandoned), because their carrying amounts will not be recovered principally through a sale transaction.

Measurement of assets and disposal groups held for sale

Items classified as held for sale should be measured at the lower of their carrying amount and fair value less costs to sell.

- Where fair value less costs to sell is lower than carrying amount, the item is written down and the write down is treated as an impairment loss.

- Where a non-current asset has been previously revalued and is now classified as being held for sale, it should be revalued to fair value immediately before it is classified as held for sale. It is then revalued again at the lower of the carrying amount and the fair value less costs to sell. The difference is the selling costs and these should be charged against profits in the period.

- When a disposal group is being written down to fair value less costs to sell, the impairment loss reduces the carrying amount of assets in the order prescribed by IAS 36 – that is write down goodwill first, then allocate the remaining loss to the assets pro rata based on their carrying amount.

- A gain can be recognised for any subsequent increase in fair value less costs to sell, but not in excess of the cumulative impairment loss that has already been recognised, either when the assets were written down to fair value less costs to sell or previously under IAS 36.

- An asset held for sale is not depreciated, even if it is still being used by the entity.

Illustration 7 – Non-current assets held for sale (IFRS 5)

On 1 January 20X1 AB acquires a building for $200,000 with an expected life of 50 years. On 31 December 20X4 AB puts the building up for immediate sale. On that date the building has a market value of $220,000 and expenses of $10,000 and tax of $5,000 will be payable on the sale. Describe the accounting for this building.

Expandable text - Solution

Until 31 December 20X4 the building is a normal non-current asset governed by IAS 16, being depreciated at $200,000 / 50 = $4,000 pa. The carrying amount at 31 December 20X4 is therefore $200,000 / (4 × $4,000) = $184,000.

On 31 December 20X4 the building is reclassified as a non-current asset held for sale. It is measured at the lower of carrying amount ($184,000) and fair value less costs to sell ($220,000 – $10,000 = $210,000). Note that any applicable tax expense is excluded from the determination of costs to sell.

The building will therefore be measured at 31 December 20X4 at $184,000.

Changes to a plan of sale

If a sale does not take place within one year, an asset (or disposal group) can still be classified as held for sale if:

- the delay has been caused by events or circumstances beyond the entity's control

- there is sufficient evidence that the entity is still committed to the sale.

If the criteria for 'held for sale' are no longer met, then the entity must cease to classify the assets or disposal group as held for sale. The assets or disposal group must be measured at the lower of:

- its carrying amount before it was classified as held for sale adjusted for any depreciation, amortisation or revaluations that would have been recognised had it not been classified as held for sale

- its recoverable amount at the date of the subsequent decision not to sell.

Any adjustment required is recognised in profit or loss as a gain or loss from continuing operations.

Presentation in the statement of financial position

IFRS 5 states that assets classified as held for sale should be presented separately from other assets in the statement of financial position. The liabilities of a disposal group classified as held for sale should be presented separately from other liabilities in the statement of financial position.

- Assets and liabilities held for sale should not be offset and presented as a single amount.

- The major classes of assets and liabilities classified as held for sale must be separately disclosed either on the face of the statement of financial position or in the notes.

- Where an asset or disposal group is classified as held for sale after the reporting date, but before the issue of the financial statements, details should be disclosed in the notes (this is a non-adjusting event after the reporting date).

Illustration 8 – Non-current assets held for sale (IFRS 5)

Statement of financial position (showing non-current assets held for sale)

	20X2	20X1
	$m	$m
ASSETS		
Non-current assets		
Property, plant and equipment	X	X
Goodwill	X	X
Financial assets	X	X
	X	X
Current assets		
Inventories	X	X
Trade receivables	X	X
Cash and cash equivalents	X	
Non-current assets classified as held for sale	X	X
	X	X
Total assets	X	X

Disclosures in notes to the accounts

In the period in which a non-current asset or disposal group has been either classified as held for sale, or sold, the notes to the accounts must include:

- a description of the non-current asset (or disposal group)

- a description of the facts and circumstances of the sale or expected sale

- any impairment losses or reversals recognised

- if applicable, the segment in which the non-current asset (or disposal group) is presented in accordance with IFRS 8 **Operating segments**.

Test your understanding 7 - Hyssop

Hyssop is preparing its financial statements for the year ended 31 December 20X7.

(a) On 1 December 20X7, the entity became committed to a plan to sell a surplus office property and has already found a potential buyer. On 15 December 20X7 a survey was carried out and it was discovered that the building had dry rot and substantial remedial work would be necessary. The buyer is prepared to wait for the work to be carried out, but the property will not be sold until the problem has been rectified. This is not expected to occur until summer 20X8.

Can the property be classified as 'held for sale'?

(b) A subsidiary entity, B, is for sale at a price of $3 million. There has been some interest by prospective buyers but no sale as of yet. One buyer has made an offer of $2 million but the Directors of Hyssop rejected the offer as they were hoping to achieve a price of $3 million. The Directors have just received advice from their accountants that the fair value of the business is $2.5 million. They have decided not to reduce the sale price of B at the moment.

Can the subsidiary be classified as 'held for sale'?

Expandable text - Investment property IAS 40 - definition

Definition of investment property

Investment property is property (land or a building – or part of a building – or both) held (by the owner or by the lessee under a finance lease) to earn rentals or for capital appreciation or both.

Examples of investment property are a:

*   land held for long-term capital appreciation
*   land held for undecided future use
*   building leased out under an operating lease
*   vacant building held to be leased out under an operating lease.

The following are **not** investment property:

*   property held for use in the production or supply of goods or services or for administrative purposes (IAS 16 **Property, plant and equipment** applies)

- property held for sale in the ordinary course of business or in the process of construction of development for such sale (IAS 2 **Inventories** applies)

- property being constructed or developed on behalf of third parties (IAS 11 **Construction contracts** applies)

- owner-occupied property (IAS 16 applies)

- property that is being constructed or developed for use as an investment property (IAS 16 currently applies until the property is ready for use, at which time IAS 40 starts to apply - see note below)

- property leased to another entity under a finance lease (IAS 17 **Leases** applies).

Expandable text - Measurement

On recognition, investment property shall be recognised at cost, measured along the lines of the principles in IAS 16.

After recognition an entity may choose either:

- the fair value model
- the cost model.

The policy chosen must be applied to all investment properties.

Change from one model to the other is permitted only if this results in a more appropriate presentation. IAS 40 notes that this is highly unlikely for a change from the fair value model to the cost model.

The cost model is the normal accounting treatment set out in IAS 16. Properties are held at historical cost less depreciation without any revaluation.

The fair value model

Under the fair value model, the entity remeasures its investment properties at fair value each year. There is no depreciation charge.

Fair value is defined as the amount for which the property could be exchanged between knowledgeable, willing parties in an arm's length transaction.

- Fair value is normally the active market price. There should be no deduction for transaction costs. Where there is no market for similar properties, the following values may be considered:
  - current prices in an active market for properties of a different nature, condition or location, adjusted to reflect those differences
  - recent prices in less active markets
  - discounted cash flow projections based on reliable estimates of future cash flows.

If in exceptional circumstances, it is impossible to measure the fair value of an individual investment property reliably, then the cost model should be adopted.

- All gains and losses on revaluation are reported in as part of the profit for the period.

- The profit or loss on disposal of an investment property is the difference between the net disposal proceeds and the then carrying amount in the statement of financial position.

Operating leases

A property interest that is held by a lessee under an operating lease may be classified as an investment property, if, and only if, the property would meet the definition if it were not held under an operating lease.

- This classification is available on a property-by-property basis.

- The lessee accounts for the property as if it were a finance lease.

- Once the classification has been made for such property interest, the fair value model must be used for all investment properties held by the entity.

Expandable text - Transfers

Transfers to or from investment property can only be made if there is a change of use. There are several possible situations in which this might occur and the accounting treatment for each is set out below.

Transfer from investment property to owner-occupied property

Use the fair value at the date of the change for subsequent accounting under IAS 16.

KAPLAN PUBLISHING

Transfer from investment property to inventory

Use the fair value at the date of the change for subsequent accounting under IAS 2 Inventories.

Transfer from owner-occupied property to investment property to be carried at fair value

Normal accounting under IAS 16 (cost less depreciation) will have been applied up to the date of the change. On adopting fair value, there is normally an increase in value. This is recognised as other comprehensive income and credited to the revaluation surplus in equity in accordance with IAS 16. If the fair valuation causes a decrease in value, then it should be charged to profits.

Transfer from inventories to investment property to be carried at fair value

Any change in the carrying amount caused by the transfer should be recognised in profit or loss.

Expandable text - Illustration:investment property

Lavender owns a property, which it rents out to some of its employees. The property was purchased for $40 million on 1 January 20X2 and had a useful life of 30 years at that date. On 1 January 20X7 it had a market value of $50 million and its remaining useful life remained unchanged. Management wish to measure properties at fair value where this is allowed by accounting standards.

How should the property be treated in the financial statements of Lavender for the year ended 31 December 20X7.

(a) Carrying amount $32 million (original cost less 6 years' depreciation).

(b) Carrying amount $48 million (revalued amount less 1 year's depreciation); gain on revaluation in other components of equity.

(c) Carrying amount $50 million (revalued amount); gain on revaluation in other components of equity.

(d) Carrying amount $50 million (revalued amount); gain on revaluation in profit or loss.

Solution

The answer is B. Because the property is rented out to employees, it is owner-occupied, and cannot be classified as an investment property.

Management wish to measure the property at fair value, so Lavender adopts the fair value model in IAS 16 **Property, plant and equipment**, depreciating the asset over its useful life and recognising the revaluation gain in other components of equity (revaluation surplus).

4 Intangible assets (IAS 38)

Expandable text - Intangible assets IAS-38 defnition

Definition and recognition criteria

An **intangible asset** is an identifiable non-monetary asset without physical substance.

An intangible asset should be recognised if all the following criteria are met.

- It is identifiable.
- It is controlled by the entity (the entity has the power to obtain economic benefits from it).
- It is expected to generate future economic benefits for the entity.
- It has a cost that can be measured reliably.

These recognition criteria apply whether an intangible asset is acquired externally or generated internally.

- An intangible asset is identifiable when it:
    - is separable (capable of being separated and sold, transferred, licensed, rented, or exchanged, either individually or as part of a package)
    - it arises from contractual or other legal rights, regardless of whether those rights are transferable or separable from the entity or from other rights and obligations.
- If an intangible asset does not meet the recognition criteria, then it should be charged to profits as it is incurred. Once the expenditure has been so charged, it cannot be capitalised at a later date.

Definition and recognition criteria

An **intangible asset** is an identifiable non-monetary asset without physical substance.

KAPLAN PUBLISHING

An intangible asset should be recognised if all the following criteria are met.

*   It is identifiable.

*   It is controlled by the entity (the entity has the power to obtain economic benefits from it).

*   It is expected to generate future economic benefits for the entity.

*   It has a cost that can be measured reliably.

These recognition criteria apply whether an intangible asset is acquired externally or generated internally.

*   An intangible asset is identifiable when it:
    *   is separable (capable of being separated and sold, transferred, licensed, rented, or exchanged, either individually or as part of a package)
    *   it arises from contractual or other legal rights, regardless of whether those rights are transferable or separable from the entity or from other rights and obligations.

*   If an intangible asset does not meet the recognition criteria, then it should be charged to profits as it is incurred. Once the expenditure has been so charged, it cannot be capitalised at a later date.

Expandable text - Examples of intangible assets

Examples of intangible assets

Examples of possible intangible assets include:

*   goodwill acquired in a business combination

*   computer software

*   patents

*   copyrights

*   motion picture films

*   customer list

*   mortgage servicing rights

*   licences

*   import quotas

*   franchises

*   customer and supplier relationships

*   marketing rights.

The following **internally generated intangible assets** are not capable of being recognised as assets and IAS 38 prohibits their recognition:

- start-up, pre-opening, and pre-operating costs
- training costs
- relocation costs
- advertising cost
- goodwill
- brands
- mastheads
- publishing titles
- customer lists and items similar in substance.

Expandable text - Meeting the recognition criteria

(a) Identifiability

Intangible assets such as customer relationships cannot be separated from goodwill unless they:

- arise as a result of a legal right, if there are ongoing supply contracts, for example
- are separable, i.e. can be sold separately. This is unlikely unless there are legal contracts in existence, in which case they fall under the previous bullet point.

If they cannot be separated, then in a business combination such assets would become part of goodwill.

(b) Control

The knowledge that the staff have is an asset. It can be possible for the entity to control this knowledge. Patents, copyrights and restraint-of-trade agreements will give the entity legal rights to the future economic benefits and prevent other people from obtaining them. Therefore copyrights and patents can be capitalised.

(c) Probable future economic benefits

An intangible asset can generate future economic benefits in two ways. Owning a brand name can boost revenues, while owning the patent for a production process may help to reduce production costs. Either way, the entity's profits will be increased.

When an entity assesses the probability of future economic benefits, the assessment must be based on reasonable and supportable assumptions about conditions that will exist over the life of the asset.

(d) Reliable measurement

If the asset is acquired separately then this is straightforward. For example, the purchase price of a franchise should be capitalised, along with all the related legal and professional costs.

If the asset is acquired as part of a business combination, then its cost will equal its fair value at the date of acquisition. The best measure of fair value is the quoted price of similar assets on an active market. In an active market, the items traded are homogenous, willing buyers and sellers can be found at any time, there are frequent transactions and prices are available to the public.

Expandable text - Measurement

When an intangible asset is initially recognised, it is measured at cost. After recognition, an entity must choose either the cost model or the revaluation model for each class of intangible asset.

- The cost model measures the asset at cost less accumulated amortisation and impairment.

- The revaluation model measures the asset at fair value less accumulated amortisation and impairment.

The revaluation model can only be adopted if fair value can be determined by reference to an **active market**. An active market is one where the products are homogenous, there are willing buyers and sellers to be found at all times, and prices are available to the public.

Active markets for intangible assets are rare. They may exist for assets such as:

- milk quotas
- European Union fishing quotas
- stock exchange seats.

Active markets are unlikely to exist for brands, newspaper mastheads, music and film publishing rights, patents or trademarks.

Revaluations should be made with sufficient regularity such that the carrying amount does not differ materially from actual fair value at the reporting date.

Revaluation gains and losses are accounted for in the same way as revaluation gains and losses of tangible assets under IAS 16.

Amortisation

An entity must assess whether the useful life of an intangible asset is finite or indefinite.

- An asset with a finite useful life must be amortised on a systematic basis over that life. Normally the straight-line method with a zero residual value should be used. Amortisation starts when the asset is available for use.

- An asset has an indefinite useful life when there is no foreseeable limit to the period over which the asset is expected to generate net cash inflows. It shouuld not be amortised, but be subject to an annual impariment review.

Expandable text - Research and development expenditure

Research is original and planned investigation undertaken with the prospect of gaining new scientific or technical knowledge and understanding.

Development is the application of research findings or other knowledge to a plan or design for the production of new or substantially improved materials, devices, products, processes, systems or services before the start of commercial production or use.

- Research expenditure cannot be recognised as an intangible asset. (Tangible assets used in research should be recognised as plant and equipment).

KAPLAN PUBLISHING

- Development expenditure should be recognised as an intangible asset if an entity can demonstrate that:
    - the project is technically feasible
    - the entity intends to complete the intangible asset, and then use it or sell it
    - it is able to use or sell the intangible asset
    - the intangible asset will generate future economic benefits. There must either be a market for the product or an internal use for it
    - the entity has adequate technical, financial and other resources to complete the project
    - it can reliably measure the attributable expenditure on the project.

Expandable text - Computer intangibles

Computer software

Some computer software is an integral part of the related hardware, for example the computer programme in a production-line robot or the operating system on a PC. The hardware will not work without the software, and so the software is capitalised as part of the hardware. This type of software is a tangible non-current asset subject to IAS 16.

Stand-alone computer software (for example an accounts package) is an intangible asset subject to IAS 38.

Expandable text - Illustration: intangible assets

Rue has developed a software programme during the year to 30 November 20X2. The cost of developing the software was $5 million. The software is used by the rest of the group and sold to third parties. Net revenue of $4 million is expected from sales of the software, which has quickly become a market leader in its field. The software is expected to generate revenue for four years, after which an upgraded version will be developed.

Should Rue recognise the software as an intangible asset?

Solution

IAS 38 **Intangible assets** prohibits the recognition of internally generated brands, mastheads, publishing titles, customer lists and similar items as intangible assets. It could be argued that the software is a similar asset.

However, IAS 38 also requires internally generated intangibles to be recognised, provided that they meet certain criteria. An entity must demonstrate the technical feasibility of the asset, the ability to complete and use or sell the asset, the probable future economic benefits of the asset and the availability of adequate technical, financial and other resources before it can be recognised. It must also be possible to measure the expenditure attributable to the asset reliably and it should be capable of generating cash inflows in excess of cash outflows.

Because the software is generating external revenue, these criteria appear to be met. It is not clear how the cost of $5 million is made up, but it is possible that it includes items such as staff training and overheads that may not be capitalised under IAS 38.

It is also not clear when the cost of $5 million was incurred, relative to the date when the development met the criteria set out above. Only expenditure incurred after that date should be capitalised.

More information is therefore required about the components of the cost and when it was incurred. Any asset that is recognised should be amortised over its expected useful life of four years.

Expandable text - Current issues

Rate-regulated activities

An ED was issued on this topic in July 2009 and seeks to clarify in what circumstances regulated entities should recognise assets or liabilities as a result of rate regulation. The proposed IFRS defines regulatory assets and regulatory liabilities, sets out criteria for their recognition, specifies how they should be measured and requires disclosures about their financial effects.

Rate regulation is a restriction in the setting of prices that can be charged to customers for services or products. Generally, it is imposed by regulatory bodies or governments when an entity has a monopoly or a dominant market position that gives it excessive market power. In the United Kingdom for example, this could apply to the provision of electricity and gas.

In December 2008, the IASB added a project on Rate-regulated Activities to its agenda. The project objective was to develop a standard on rate-regulated activities that clarifies whether regulated entities could or should recognise an asset or a liability as a result of rate regulation.

The proposed IFRS addresses only those rate-regulated activities that meet the following two criteria:

- an authorised body is empowered to establish rates that bind customers; and

- the price established by regulation(the rate) is designed to recover the specific costs the entity incurs in providing the regulated goods or services and to earn a specified return.

The following definition are applied within the ED:

- A regulatory asset exists because the entity obtains from the regulator the present right to set rates at a level that will ensure the entity recovers its previously incurred costs by receiving cash flows from its aggregate customer base.

- A regulatory liability arises from a present obligation enforced by the regulator to return previously collected amounts to the aggregate customer base by reducing rates.

This form of regulation is often referred to as 'cost-of-service' or 'return on rate base' regulation

Although a specific standard on accounting for the effects of rate regulation exists in the United States, it has no counterpart in IFRSs. However, rate regulation is widespread and significantly affects the economic environment of rate-regulated entities. Many billions of dollars of 'regulatory' assets and liabilities are currently recognised in jurisdictions that refer to US GAAP. Some of these jurisdictions are already converging to IFRSs. Clarifying whether assets and liabilities arise from rate regulation in IFRSs and if so, how to account for them is therefore important.

Following expiry of the comment period for the ED in February 2010, the IASB decided to continue research and analysis on this project and to focus on the key issue of whether regulatory assets and regulatory liabilities exist in accordance with the current Framework for the Preparation and Presentation of Financial Statements and whether they are consistent with other current IFRSs.

At August 2010, development work continues and focuses upon whether regulatory assets and liabilities exist, and whether they should be recognised in accordance with the Framework, and whether they are consistent with other reporting standards.

Emission Trading Schemes

The objective of the project is to develop comprehensive guidance on the accounting for emissions trading schemes, including (but not limited to) the following issues:

- Are emissions allowances assets? Is this conclusion affected by how the allowance is acquired? What is the nature of the allowance (e.g. licence to emit or form of emission currency)? If allowances are assets, should they be recognised and, if so, how should they be measured initially?

- What is the corresponding entry for an entity that receives allowances from government free of charge? Does a liability exist? If so, what is the nature of the liability and how should it be measured both initially and subsequently?

- How should allowances be accounted for subsequently? Is the existing model in IAS 38 Intangible Assets or IAS 39 Financial Instruments: Recognition and Measurement appropriate? If not, what is the appropriate accounting?

- When should an entity recognise its obligations in emissions trading schemes and how should they be measured? How does IAS 37 Provisions, Contingent Liabilities and Contingent Assets apply?

- What are the overall financial reporting effects of the above decisions?

Among the reasons for adding the topic to the agenda, the Board noted in particular the increasing international use (or planned use) of schemes designed to achieve reduction of greenhouse gases through the use of tradeable permits. It also noted that there was a risk of diverse accounting practices for such schemes following the withdrawal of IFRIC 3 Emission Rights and that this would impair the comparability and usefulness of financial statement information.

As at August 2010, development is still at the preliminary stage, with an ED not expected until late 2011, to be followed by a reporting standard by the end of 2012.

Expandable text - Inventories (IAS 2)

Inventories are measured at the lower of cost and net realisable value.

Cost includes all purchase costs, conversion costs and other costs incurred in bringing the inventories to their present condition and location.

- **Purchase costs** include the purchase price (less discounts and rebates), import duties, irrecoverable taxes, transport and handling costs and any other directly attributable costs.

- **Conversion costs** include all direct costs of conversion (materials, labour, expenses, etc), and a proportion of the fixed and variable production overheads. The allocation of production overheads must be based on the normal level of activity.

- Abnormal wastage, storage costs, administration costs and selling costs must be excluded from the valuation and charged as expenses in the period in which they are incurred.

Net realisable value is the expected selling price less the estimated costs of completion and sale.

- IAS 2 **Inventories** allows three methods of arriving at cost:
  - actual unit cost
  - first-in, first-out (FIFO)
  - weighted average cost (AVCO).

- Actual unit cost must be used where items of inventory are not ordinarily interchangeable.

- The same method of arriving at cost should be used for all inventories having similar nature and use to the entity. Different cost methods may be justified for inventories with different nature or use.

- Entities should disclose:
  - their accounting policy and cost formulas
  - total carrying amount of inventories by category
  - details of inventories carried at net realisable value.

Expandable text - Valuation of inventories

How should the following be valued?

(a) Materials costing $12,000 bought for processing and assembly for a profitable special order. Since buying these items, the cost price has fallen to $10,000.

(b) Equipment constructed for a customer for an agreed price of $18,000. This has recently been completed at a cost of $16,800. It has now been discovered that, in order to meet certain regulations, conversion with an extra cost of $4,200 will be required. The customer has accepted partial responsibility and agreed to meet half the extra cost.

Solution

(a) Value at $12,000. The $10,000 is irrelevant. The rule is lower of cost or net realisable value, not lower of cost or replacement cost. Since the materials will be processed before sale there is no reason to believe that net realisable value will be below cost.

(b) Value at net realisable value, i.e. $15,900 (contract price $18,000 − constructor's share of modification cost $2,100), because this is below cost.

Expandable text - UK syllabus focus

The ACCA UK syllabus contains a requirement that candidates should be able to discuss and apply the key differences between UK GAAP and IFRS GAAP. The accounting requirements of UK GAAP and IFRS GAAP are very similar in this area; the relevant UK reporting standards are as follows:

SSAP 4 - Government grants. There are no significant differences in accounting treatment in comparison with IAS 20.

SSAP 9 – Stock. There are no significant differences between SSAP 9 and IAS 2 under IFRS GAAP. Note that the P2 syllabus excludes accounting for construction or long-term contracts.

SSAP 13 – Research and development. There are no significant differences in accounting treatment in comparison with IAS 38. Note that development costs must be capitalised where they meet defined criteria under IFRS GAAP. Under UK GAAP, development costs can either be capitalised and amortised, or written off as incurred.

SSAP 19 – Investment property. The definition of an investment property is the same under both accounting frameworks. Under UK GAAP, investment property must be carried at market value, and not subject to depreciation, unless it is a leasehold property with twenty years or less remaining. Any change in carrying value is taken to reserves. In accordance with IAS 40, there is a choice of accounting treatment, based upon either cost or fair value. The cost model applies the accounting requirements equivalent to FRS 15 tangible fixed assets, with depreciation charged if the investment property has a finite useful life. If the fair value model is used, any change in carrying value is taken to profit or loss, rather than directly to equity.

FRS 10 - Goodwill and intangible assets. There are similar recognition criteria for intangible assets under both frameworks. Under IFRS GAAP, IFRS 3 permits a choice of accounting treatment for goodwill on an acquisition-by-acquisition basis. In effect, goodwill can be calculated either on a "full" or "gross" basis, or on a proportionate basis. The former recognises goodwill on acquisition for the subsidiary as a whole; the latter basis recognises goodwill only on the controlling company's interest in the subsidiary. Within this publication, any group accounts questions which require goodwill (or non-controlling interest) to be calculated on a proportionate basis are suitable for UK GAAP accounting.

However, under UK GAAP, FRS 10 requires goodwill on acquisition to be computed based upon the controlling company's holding only; this is essentially the proportionate basis under IFRS GAAP. Upon calculation of goodwill, FRS 10 requires that goodwill would normally be amortised on a systematic basis over its expected useful life, rather than accounted for as a permanent non-current intangible asset as required by IFRS 3.

FRS 11 – Impairment of fixed assets and goodwill. Impairment treatment of tangible assets and most intangible assets are similar under both frameworks. For impairment of goodwill, under UK GAAP, only impairment on the controlling company's investment is accounted for. Under IFRS GAAP, under the full goodwill basis, any impairment would be for the subsidiary as a whole, with any impairment borne by the group and non-controlling interest (i.e minority interest) based upon their respective shareholdings. Under IFRS GAAP, where goodwill has been calculated on a proportionate basis, accounting for impairment would be similar to accounting for impairment under UK GAAP.

FRS 15 - Tangible fixed assets. There are no significant differences in accounting for tangible fixed assets under UK GAAP and the equivalent requirements of IAS 16. Both frameworks permit accounting for fixed asset under the cost or fair value basis, provided they are appropriate and properly disclosed, for example in relation to land and buildings. One distinction is that under FRS 15, a company has the choice to either capitalise or write off finance costs in relation to acquisition of an asset; under IAS 23, it is compulsory to capitalise such costs if the criteria have been met.

5 Chapter summary

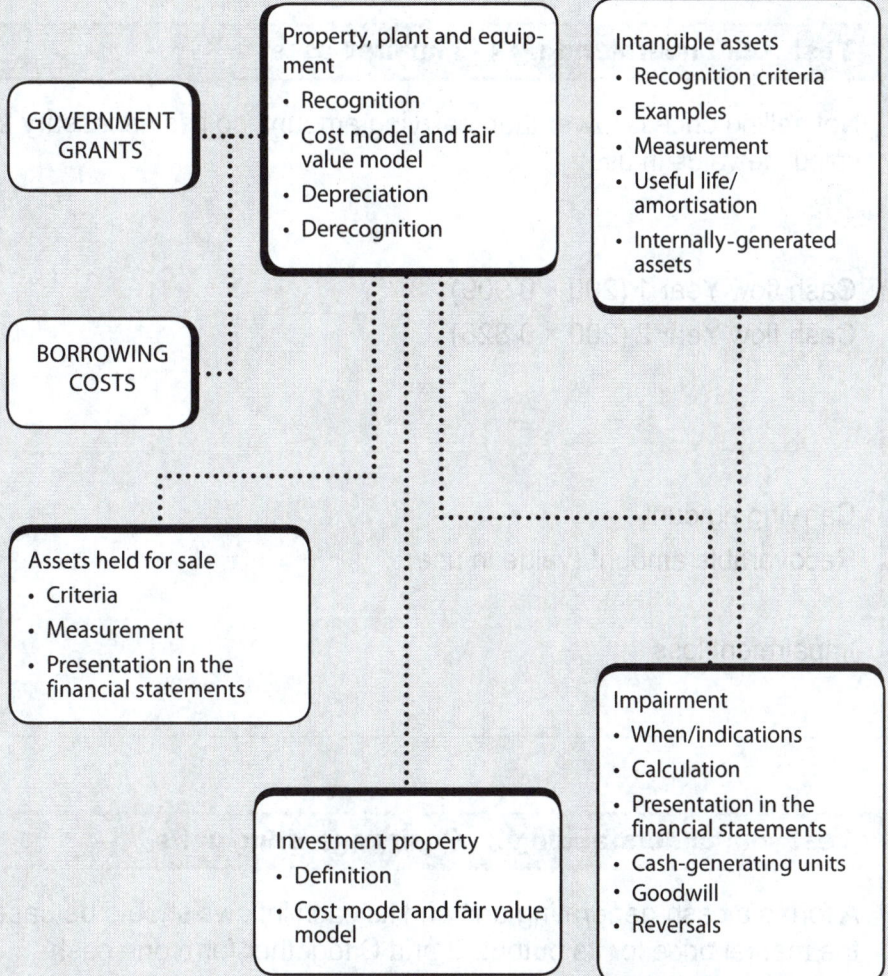

Test your understanding answers

Test your understanding 1 - Impaired asset

Net selling price is lower than carrying amount, so it is necessary to calculate value in use:

	$000
Cash flow Year 1 (200 × 0.909)	182
Cash flow Year 2 (200 × 0.826)	165
	347
Carrying amount	500
Recoverable amount (value in use)	347
Impairment loss	153

Test your understanding 2 - Cash generating units

A forms a cash-generating unit and its cash inflows should be based on the market price for its output. B and C together form one cash-generating unit because there is no market available for the output of B. In calculating the cash outflows of the cash-generating unit B + C, the timber received by B from A should be priced by reference to the market, not any internal transfer price.

Test your understanding 3 - Factory explosion

As the value in use is higher than the net selling price, the impairment loss is £650,000 (£2.6m – 1.95m). It is allocated:

- first to goodwill, leaving $550,000 to be dealt with

- then to patents (200) and half the machines (150), leaving $200,000 to be dealt with

- then pro rata to computers ((500/(500 + 1,500) × 200) and buildings (note that because they can be sold for at least their book value, the remaining machines are not included in this pro rata exercise).

	Opening	Impairment	Closing
	$000	$000	$000
Goodwill	100	(100)	Nil
Patents	200	(200)	Nil
Machines	300	(150)	150
Computers	500	(50)	450
Buildings	1,500	(150)	1,350
	2,600	(650)	1,950

Test your understanding 4 - Cedar

Impairment of gross goodwill - 60% subsidiary Cedar

The gross goodwill at acquisition is:

	$m
Parent investment	800
FV of NCI	250
	1,050
Less: FV of net assets at acquisition	(500)
Gross goodwill	550

Impairment review of gross goodwill at reporting date:

	$m
CV of net assets	600
CV of unimpaired goodwill	550
Recoverable amount	1,150
Impairment loss	1,000
	150

The impairment loss on the gross goodwill will be allocated between the parent and the NCI in the normal proportion that profits and losses are shared (i.e their respective shareholdings) - so 40% x 150 = $60m of the impairment loss will be charged against the NCI, and $16m will be charged against the retained earnings. The goodwill asset reported on the group statement of financial position will be $550m less $150m = $400m. Note that recoverable amount of a subsidiary is normally for the entity as a whole.

Test your understanding 5 - Homer

Impairment of gross goodwill - Homer 80% subsidiary

The gross goodwill at acquisition is:

	$m
Parent investment	200
FV of NCI	25
	___
	225
Less: FV of net assets at acquisition	(100)
	___
Gross goodwill at acquisition	125
	___

Impairment review of gross goodwill at reporting date:

	$m
CV of net assets	150
CV of unimpaired goodwill	125
	___
	275
Recoverable amount	255
	___
Impairment loss	20
	___

The impairment loss on the gross goodwill will be allocated between the parent and the NCI in the normal proportion that profits and losses are shared (i.e; based upon respective shareholdings in the subsidiary) - so 20% x 20 = $4m of the impairment loss will be charged against the NCI, and $16m will be charged against the retained earnings. The goodwill asset reported on the group statement of financial position will be $125m less $20m = $105m. Note that recoverable amount of a subsidiary is normally for the entity as a whole.

Test your understanding 6 - Happy

	$000
Consideration	500
Group share of net assets (80% x $560,000)	448
	———
Parent company goodwill	52
	———

Gross up goodwill:

Total notional goodwill 52 × 100/80 = $65,000

The carrying amount of Happy at 31 December 20X5 is:

	$000
Assets	520
Total notional goodwill	65
	———
	585
	———

The recoverable amount is $510,000, which means there is an impairment loss of $75,000.

This loss is allocated to total notional goodwill first, writing off the entire balance of $65,000. As $13,000 is attributable to the non-controlling interest, only $52,000 of the loss is charged to the income statement relating to the parent's goodwill.

The remaining $10,000 impairment loss is allocated to the other assets. They would be written down on a pro-rata basis according to their carrying values.

Test your understanding 7 - Hyssop

(a) IFRS 5 states that in order to be classified as 'held for sale' the property should be available for immediate sale in its present condition. The property will not be sold until the work has been carried out; this demonstrates that the facility is not available for immediate sale. Therefore the property cannot be classified as 'held for sale'.

(b) The subsidiary B does not meet the criteria for classification as 'held for sale', because while actions to locate a buyer are in place, the subsidiary is not for sale at a price that is reasonable compared with its fair value. The fair value of the subsidiary is $2.5 million, but it is up for sale for $3 million. It cannot be classified as held for sale' until the sale price is reduced.

15

Leases

Chapter learning objectives

Upon completion of this chapter you will be able to:

- apply and discuss the classification of leases and accounting by lessors and lessees

- account for and discuss the accounting for sale and leaseback transactions.

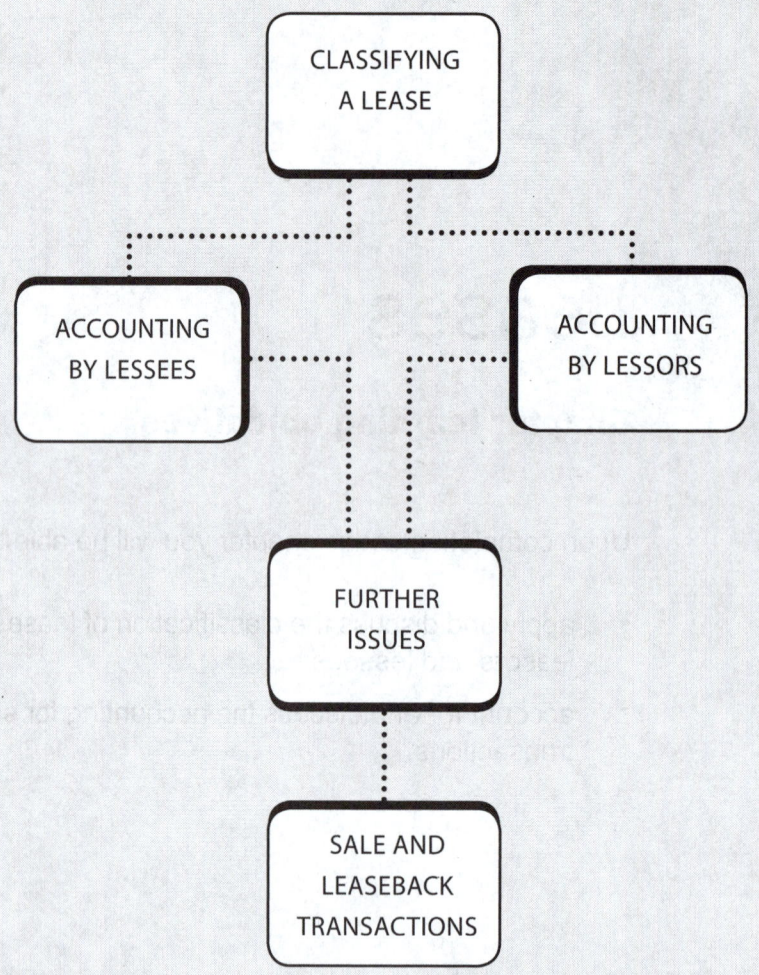

1 Classifying a lease

Definitions

Leases are classified as either finance leases or operating leases at inception (normally the date of the lease agreement).

A **finance lease** transfers substantially all the risks and rewards incident to ownership of an asset.

An **operating lease** is a lease other than a finance lease.

Whether a lease is a finance lease or an operating lease depends on the substance of the agreement.

- A finance lease (as its name suggests) is basically a way of financing the use of an asset (by spreading the payment over the life of the asset, instead of paying the full amount all at once).

- An operating lease is similar to a rental agreement. The entity normally rents the asset for only part of its useful life.

How to classify a lease

IAS 17 Leases explains that a lease is probably a finance lease if one or more of the following apply.

- Ownership is transferred to the lessee at the end of the lease (as in hire purchase agreements).

- The lessee has the option to purchase the asset for less than its expected fair value at the date the option becomes exercisable (so it is reasonably certain that the option will be exercised).

- The lease term is for the major part of the economic life of the asset, even if title is not transferred. The length of the lease includes any secondary period.

- At the inception of the lease, the present value of the minimum lease payments amounts to at least substantially all of the fair value of the leased asset.

- The leased assets are of a specialised nature so that only the lessee can use them without major modifications being made.

- The lessee will compensate the lessor if the lease is cancelled.

- Gains or losses from fluctuations in the fair value of the residual fall to the lessee (for example, by means of a rebate of lease payments).

- The lessee has the ability to continue the lease for a secondary period at a rent that is substantially lower than market rent.

Expandable text - How to classify a lease

In most cases, it should be fairly easy to tell whether or not any of the above situations apply. The exception is the fourth item, comparing the present value of the minimum lease payments with the fair value of the leased asset. The present value of the minimum lease payments normally has to be calculated, using an appropriate discount rate.

Illustration 1 – Classifying a lease

A company can buy an asset for cash at a cost of $5,800 or it can lease the asset on the following terms:

(1) the lease term is for four years from 1 January 20X2, with a rental of $2,000 pa payable on the 31 December each year

(2) the interest rate implicit in the lease is 15%.

Is the lease a finance lease?

Expandable text - Solution

The minimum lease payments are $8,000 (4 × 2,000)

Present value of minimum lease payments:

From discount tables, the present value at 15% of four annual sums first payable at the end of the first year is:

$2,000 × 2.855 = $5,710

The fair value of the asset is $5,800.

Therefore, the minimum lease payments are 98% of the fair value of the asset.

This strongly suggests that the lease is a finance lease.

Problem areas

IAS 17 does not define 'substantially all', but in practice this is often taken to mean 'more than 90%'.

IAS 17 defines minimum lease payments:

Minimum lease payments are the payments over the lease term that the lessee is, or can be required, to make (excluding contingent rent, costs for services and taxes to be paid by and reimbursed to the lessor), together with:

- in the case of the lessee, any amounts guaranteed by the lessee
- in the case of the lessor, any residual value guaranteed to the lessor by the lessee.

Contingent rent is that portion of the lease payments that is not fixed in amount but is based on a factor other than just the passage of time (for example, percentage of sales, amount of usage, price indices, market rates of interest).

Leases of land and buildings

Land and buildings are often leased together, but IAS 17 requires the land and buildings elements to be classified separately.

- The land element is normally classified as an operating lease unless title passes to the lessee at the end of the lease term.

- The buildings element may be classified as either a finance or an operating lease depending upon the nature of the lease contract.

- The minimum lease payments are allocated between the land and buildings elements in proportion to their relative fair values.

2 Accounting by lessees

Finance leases

IAS 17 requires the accounting treatment to report the substance of the transaction: the lessee controls an asset and has a liability for the outstanding rentals.

- At the beginning of the lease term, the lessee recognises the leased asset and the obligation to make lease payments as an asset and a liability in the statement of financial position.

- The asset and the liability are measured at the lower of:
  - the fair value of the asset
  - the present value of the minimum lease payments (discounted at the interest rate implicit in the lease, if practicable, or else at the entity's incremental borrowing rate).

- The lease payments are split between the finance charge and the repayment of the outstanding liability.

- The finance charge is allocated so as to produce a constant periodic rate of interest on the remaining balance of the liability. The actuarial method gives the most accurate charge, but the sum of the digits is normally a reasonable approximation.

- The leased asset is depreciated over the shorter of:
  - its useful life
  - the lease term (including secondary period).

Illustrtaion 2 - Lease classification

Wrighty acquired use of plant over three years by way of a lease. Instalments of $700,000, are paid six monthly in arrears on 30 June and 31 December. Delivery of the plant was on 1 January 20X0 so the first payment of $700,000 was on 30 June 20X0. The present value of minimum lease payment is $3,000,000. Interest implicit in the above is 10% per six months. The Plant would normally be expected to last three years. Wrighty is required to insure the plant and cannot return it to the lessor without severe penalties.

(a) **Describe whether the above lease should be classified as an operating or finance lease.**

> (b) **Calculate the effect of the above on the income statement and statement of financial position for the year ended 31 December 20X0.**

Expandable text - Solution

(a) Risks and rewards of ownership of the machine are with Wrighty; so this is a finance lease.

(b) **Income statement (extract)**

	$
Depreciation (3000 / 3 years)	1,000
Interest (W1) (300 + 260)	560

Statement of financial position (extract)

Long-term liabilities (W1)	1,144
Current liabilities (W1) (2160 – 1144)	1,016

(W1) Leasing table

Period	Opening loan	Interest (10%)	Instalment	Closing loan
	$000	$000	$000	$000
1	3,000	300	(700)	2,600
2	2,600	260	(700)	2,160
3	2,160	216	(700)	1,676
4	1,676	168	(700)	1,144

Operating leases

The substance of the transaction is that the lessee uses an asset, but does not own or control it.

- The lessee does not recognise the leased asset in its statement of financial position.

- Rentals are charged as an expense on a straight line basis over the term of the lease unless another systematic and rational basis is more appropriate.

- Any difference between amounts charged and amounts paid should be adjusted to prepayments or accruals.

Expandable text - Leases: off-balance sheet finance

If an entity leases a lot of its assets, accounting for them as finance leases can have a significant impact on the financial statements.

- Return on capital employed decreases, because of the additional assets.

- Earnings (and earnings per share) may decrease, because of the additional depreciation.

- Gearing increases, because of the additional liabilities (obligations to pay future rentals).

Therefore, management may have incentives to try to keep lease assets and liabilities out of the statement of financial position ('off balance sheet'). For example, the entity may already have a high level of long-term debt, or need to raise additional finance, or may be in danger of breaching loan covenants (agreements). Loan covenants often include a clause stating that the gearing ratio or the ratio of assets to liabilities must not exceed a certain figure.

However, the classification of leases is subjective. It is possible to structure a lease agreement so that technically the lease appears to be an operating lease when it is actually a finance lease.

This is a form of 'creative accounting'. IAS 17 requires that the classification of a lease should always reflect the **substance** of the agreement.

3 Accounting by lessors
Finance leases

Here, the lessee, not the lessor, has control of the asset.

- The lessor recognises the lease as a receivable. The carrying value is the lessor's net investment in the lease.

- The net investment in the lease equals:
  - the present value of the minimum lease payments receivable; plus
  - the present value of any unguaranteed residual value accruing to the lessor (e.g. the residual value of the leased asset when it is repossessed at the end of the lease).

- In practice, the lessor's net investment in the lease is the same as the lessee's lease liability.

- The lease receipts are split between finance income and a repayment of the principal. The finance income is calculated using a constant periodic rate of interest.

Expandable text - Accounting by lessors illustration

Vache leases machinery to Toro. The lease is for four years at an annual cost of $2,000 payable annually in arrears. The normal cash price (and fair value) of the asset is $5,900. The present value of the minimum lease payments is $5,710. The implicit rate of interest is 15%.

Show how the net investment in the lease is presented in Vache's statement of financial position at the end of Year 1.

Expandable text - Solution

Vache recognises the net investment in the lease as a receivable. This is the present value of the minimum lease payments: $5,710.

Vache receives lease rentals each year. These are split between finance income and a repayment of the principal.

Total finance income is $2,290 ($8,000 – $5,710). This is allocated as follows:

Year	Opening balance	Finance income @ 15%	Cash received	Closing balance
	$	$	$	$
1	5,710	856	(2,000)	4,566
2	4,566	685	(2,000)	3,251
3	3,251	488	(2,000)	1,739
4	1,739	261	(2,000)	–
		2,290		

Extract from the statement of financial position at the end of Year 1

	$
Current assets:	
Net investment in finance leases (see note)	1,315
Non-current assets:	
Net investment in finance leases	3,251

Note: the current asset is the next instalment less next year's interest, so $2,000 – 685 = $1,315. The non-current asset is the remainder, so $4,566 – 1,315 = $3,251.

Operating leases

If a lessor has an operating lease, it continues to recognise the leased asset.

- Assets held under operating leases are recognised in the statement of financial position as non-current assets. They should be presented according to the nature of the asset and depreciated in the normal way.

- Rental income from operating leases is recognised in profit or loss on a straight-line basis over the term of the lease, unless another systematic and rational basis is more appropriate.

- Any difference between amounts charged and amounts paid should be adjusted to receivables or deferred income.

Expandable text - Accounting by lessors illustration

Oroc hires out industrial plant on long-term operating leases. On 1 January 20X1, it entered into a seven-year lease on a mobile crane. The terms of the lease are $175,000 payable on 1 January 20X1, followed by six rentals of $70,000 payable on1 January 20X2 – 20X7. The crane will be returned to Oroc on 31 December 20X7. The crane cost $880,000 and has a 25-year useful life with no residual value.

(a) **Calculate the annual rental income that will be recognised by Oroc.**

(b) **Prepare extracts from the income statement and statement of financial position of Oroc for 20X1 and 20X2.**

Expandable text - Solution

(a) Rental income must be recognised on a straight line basis. Therefore annual rental income is $85,000 (595,000 ÷ 7).

(b) Oroc recognises the crane in its statement of financial position and depreciates it over its useful life. The annual depreciation charge is $35,200 (880,000 ÷ 25).

The statement of financial position also includes a liability for deferred income (allocated between current liabilities and non-current liabilities). This is the difference between rental income received and rental income recognised in the income statement.

Working for deferred income

Year	Cash Received	Income claimed	Difference	Cumulative difference
	$	$	$	$
20X1	175,000	85,000	90,000	90,000
20X2	70,000	85,000	(15,000)	75,000
				Deferred income

Extracts from the income statement and statement of financial position for 20X1 and 20X2

	20X1	20X2
Income statement	$	$
Operating income: Rentals receivable	85,000	85,000
Operating expenses: Depreciation	(35,200)	(35,200)
	49,800	49,800
Statement of financial position		
Non-current assets		
Equipment held for use in operating leases	$	$
Cost	880,000	880,000
Depreciation	(35,200)	(70,400)
Carrying amount	844,800	809,600
Non-current liabilities Deferred income	75,000	60,000
Current liabilities Deferred income	15,000	15,000

Summary

Finance lease	Operating lease
• Substance = lessee has the asset	• Substance = lessor has the asset
• Substance = financing agreement	• Substance = rental agreement
• Lessee recognises asset in SFP	• Lessor recognises asset in SFP
• Lessee recognises liability for future rentals	• Lessor recognises lease rentals as income
• Lessor recognises net investment in lease (a receivable)	• Lessee recognises lease rentals as an expense
• Interest accrues on outstanding amount and is paid by lessee/received by lessor	
• Lease receivable/liability is reduced by lease rentals over the term of the lease	

Expandable text - Further issues in accounting for leases

Initial direct costs

Initial direct costs are costs that are directly attributable to negotiating and arranging a lease, for example, commissions, legal fees and premiums. Both lessees and lessors may incur these costs. The treatment is summarised below.

	Costs incurred by lessee	Costs incurred by lessor
Finance lease	Add to amount recognised as an asset; depreciate over asset's useful life	Include in initial measurement of receivable; reduce income receivable over lease term
Operating lease	Treat as part of lease rentals; expense over lease term on straight line basis	Add to carrying amount of leased asset; expense over lease term on same basis as lease income

- Exclude general overheads (these are not directly attributable to arranging the lease).

- Special rules apply to manufacturer or dealer lessors.

Operating leases: incentives

An operating lease agreement may include incentives for the lessee to sign the lease. Typical incentives include an up-front cash payment to the lessee (a reverse premium), rent-free periods, or contributions by the lessor to the lessee's relocation costs.

- Any incentives given by the lessor should be recognised over the life of the lease on a straight line basis. (SIC 15 Operating Leases – Incentives).

- This applies in the accounts of both the lessee and the lessor.

Depreciation of leased assets

Leased assets should be depreciated on the same basis as similar assets that the entity owns. This applies in the accounts of both the lessee (under a finance lease) and the lessor (under an operating lease).

Expandable text - Manufacturer or dealer lessors

Finance leases can be arranged with a third party, such as a bank, or they can be provided by the manufacturer or dealer of the goods. A manufacturer or dealer may offer customers the option to lease an asset as a way of encouraging sales.

A finance lease results in two transactions:

- a sale on normal terms (see below) giving rise to sales income and a profit or loss

- the provision of finance, giving rise to finance income.

The sales proceeds are measured at the lower of:

- fair value (i.e. the normal sales price)

- the present value of the minimum lease payments discounted at a commercial rate of interest (regardless of the rate of interest quoted to the customer). The requirement to use a commercial rate of interest prevents companies inflating the value of their sales and their profits by claiming to offer low rates of finance.

KAPLAN PUBLISHING

The cost of sales is the cost (or carrying amount) of the asset sold, less the present value of any unguaranteed residual value. All initial direct costs are charged when the sale is made.

Determining whether an arrangement contains a lease

Sometimes transactions or arrangements do not take the legal form of a lease but convey rights to use assets in return for a payment or series of payments. Examples of such arrangements include:

- outsourcing arrangements
- telecommunication contracts that provide rights to capacity
- take-or-pay contracts, in which purchasers must make specified payments whether or not they take delivery of the contracted products or services.

4 Sale and leaseback transactions
Introduction

Under a sale and leaseback transaction an entity sells one of its own assets and immediately leases the asset back.

- This is a common way of raising finance whilst retaining the use of the related assets. The buyer and lessor is normally a bank.
- There are two key questions to ask when assessing the substance of these transactions:
  - is the new lease a finance lease or an operating lease
  - if the new lease is an operating lease, was the original sale at fair value or not?
- The leaseback is classified in accordance with the usual criteria set out in IAS 17.

Sale and leaseback under a finance lease

A sale and finance leaseback is a loan to the lessee, secured on the asset. No actual sale has taken place.

- The lessee continues to recognise the original asset at its original cost (less depreciation).

- The sales proceeds are credited to a finance lease liability account.

- The subsequent lease payments are then treated in the normal way, split between principal and interest.

Expandable text - Sale and finance leaseback illustration

Lash sold an item of machinery and leased it back on a five-year finance lease. The sale took place on 1 January 20X4, and the company has a 31 December year-end. The details of the scheme are as follows:

	$
Proceeds of sale	1,000,000
	————
Fair value at the time of sale	1,000,000
	————
Carrying amount at the time of sale:	
Cost	1,500,000
Depreciation	(750,000)
	————
	750,000
	————

The remaining useful life of the machine at the time of sale is five years.

There are five annual lease payments of $277,409 each, commencing on 31 December 20X4. The implicit rate of interest is 12%.

(a) **Prepare relevant extracts from Lash's statement of financial position immediately after the sale on 1 January 20X4.**

(b) **Prepare relevant extracts from Lash's income statement and statement of financial position for the year ended 31 December 20X4.**

Expandable text - Solution

The statement of financial position on 1 January 20X4, shows the original asset at its carrying amount. There will also be the asset of $1m cash and its related liability.

Statement of financial position as at 1 January 20X4

		$
Machinery	Cost	1,500,000
	Depreciation	(750,000)
	Carrying value	750,000
Current assets	Cash	1,000,000
Liabilities: obligations under finance leases	Current (W1)	157,409
	Non-current (W2)	842,591
		1,000,000

Workings

(1) Lease payments $277,409 – Finance charge 12% × $1m.

(2) Total liability $1m – Current liability $157,409.

The income statement shows the annual depreciation charge based upon original cost and the finance charge on the lease. There will be no recognition of the sale or of its related profit.

Income statement for the year ended 31 December 20X4

		$
Depreciation charge	$1,500,000 / 10 years	150,000
Finance charge	$1,000,000 @ 12%	120,000

Statement of financial position as at 31 December 20X4

		$
Machinery	Cost	1,500,000
	Depreciation	(900,000)
	Carrying Value	600,000
Liabilities: obligations under finance leases	Current (W1)	176,298
	Non-current (W2)	666,293
		842,591

Workings

(1) Lease payments $277,409 – Finance charge 12% × $842,591

(2) Total liability $842,591 – Current liability $176,298

Expandable text - Value of sales proceeds

The accounting treatment of a sale and finance leaseback is not affected if the sales proceeds are above or below the carrying value of the asset. The asset is only being used as security for the loan, and so it is up to the lender as to whether they are prepared to lend more or less than the value of the security.

However, if the sales proceeds are significantly lower than the asset's carrying amount, this suggests that the entity needs to carry out an impairment review. Alternatively, if sales proceeds are significantly higher than carrying amount, the entity may consider revaluing the asset. These adjustments are dealt with in the normal way and they do not affect the substance of the sale and leaseback transaction itself.

Sale and leaseback under an operating lease

A sale and operating leaseback transfers the risks and rewards incident to ownership to the buyer/lessor. Therefore it is treated as a sale.

- The asset is removed from the seller's statement of financial position.
- Operating lease rentals are recognised as an expense in profit or loss.

Summary

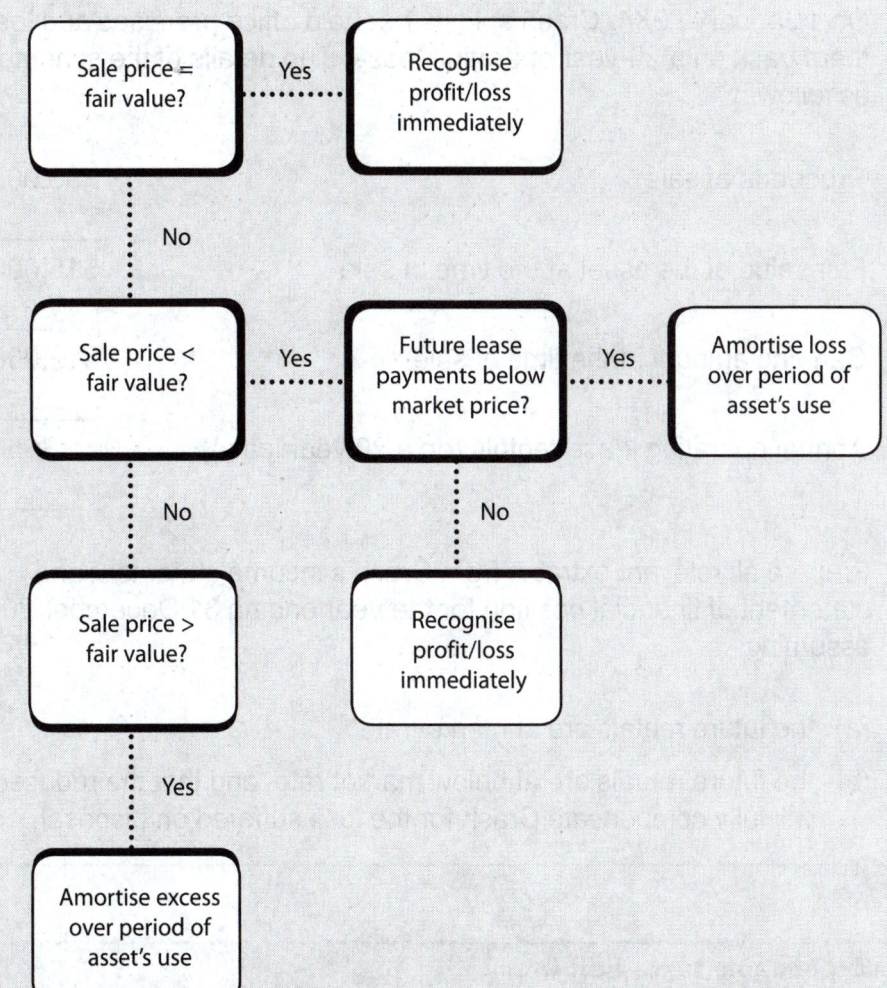

Expandable text - Sale and operating leaseback illustration

On 1 January 20X4, Crash sold its freehold office premises and leased them back on a 20-year operating lease. The details of the scheme are as follows:

Proceeds of sale	$8,000,000
Fair value of the asset at the time of sale	$15,000,000
Carrying amount at the time of sale	$12,000,000
Annual operating lease rentals (on a 20 year lease)	$650,000

Prepare all relevant extracts from Crash's income statement and statement of financial position for the year ending 31 December 2004, assuming:

(a) the future rentals are at market rate

(b) the future rentals are at below market rate, and that the reduced rate will fully compensate Crash for the loss suffered on disposal.

Expandable text - Solution

(a) **Future rentals at market rate**

If the rentals are at market rate (or above), then the loss must be recognised immediately and no asset is carried forward in the statement of financial position.

Income statement for the year ended 31 December 20X4

		$
Loss on disposal	$8m proceeds less $12m CV	4,000,000 Dr
Operating lease rentals	Amount paid	650,000 Dr

KAPLAN PUBLISHING

(b) Future rentals at below market rate

If the rentals are below market rate, the loss is deferred and amortised over the life of the lease.

Income statement for the year ended 31 December 20X4

	$	$
Loss on disposal		Nil
Operating lease rentals		
Amount paid	650,000	
Plus: amortisation of deferred		
loss $4m / 20 years	200,000	
	————	
Amount charged to the income statement		850,000

Statement of financial position as at 31 December 20X4

Assets	$
Deferred loss on disposal	
Brought forward	—
Arising during the year	4,000,000
Amortised	(200,000)
	————
Carried down	3,800,000
	————

$3,600,000 of this loss would be separately disclosed as being recoverable after more than 12 months.

Expandable text - Sale price less than fair value

If a loss on disposal arises because the proceeds are less than the fair value of the asset, then the loss can only be deferred if the future operating lease rentals are also at below the market rate. This is because deferring a loss gives rise to an asset in the statement of financial position, and assets can only be recognised if there are future economic benefits. The economic benefits that will justify deferring this loss are reduced rentals.

If a loss is deferred.

- The loss should be amortised over the period the asset is expected to be used.

- It would be wise to conduct regular impairment reviews on such assets, because changes in market rentals and/or interest rates could easily impair the benefit of the reduced rent. For instance, if the lease rentals were $650,000 per year and the market rate for a property fell to $600,000 per year, then there would no longer be any benefit to be had from an agreed rent of $650,000. If there are no future benefits, then there is no asset to recognise.

If the sale proceeds are less than the fair value, and the fair value is less than the carrying value of the asset, then only the difference between the proceeds and the fair value can be deferred. The difference between the fair value and the carrying value must be recognised as a loss immediately.

For example, if a building with a carrying value of $9m and a fair value of $7m was sold for $4m, then a loss of $2m would be recognised on disposal, and the $3m difference between the proceeds and the fair value would be deferred.

Expandable text - Sale and operating leaseback illustration

Ash sells its freehold office premises and leases them back on a 20-year operating lease. The sale took place on 1 January 20X4, and the company has a 31 December year-end.

The details of the scheme are as follows:

Proceeds of sale	$10,000,000
Fair value of the asset at the time of sale	$9,000,000
Carrying amount at the time of sale	$3,500,000
Lease payments (annual rental)	$480,000
Market rate for similar premises (annual rental)	$410,000

(a) **Calculate the profit on disposal that Ash should claim in 20X4.**

(b) **Calculate the annual rental that Ash will charge in its income statement.**

(c) **Prepare all relevant extracts from Ash's income statement and statement of financial position for the year ending 31 December 20X4.**

Expandable text - Solution

(a) Ash can only claim a profit on disposal based upon the fair value of the asset. This will give a profit on disposal of $5,500,000 ($9,000,000 fair value less $3,500,000 CV).

(b) The $1m difference between the proceeds and the fair value is credited to deferred income and released over the life of the lease on a straight line basis. The annual release will be $50,000 ($1m / 20 years). This reduces the rent charged to $430,000.

(c) **Income statement for the year ended 31 December 20X4**

	$	$
Profit on disposal at fair value		5,500,000 Cr
Operating lease rentals	480,000 Dr	
Less: release of deferred income	50,000 Cr	
		430,000 Dr

Statement of financial position as at 31 December 20X4

		$
Deferred income	Brought forward	–
	Arising during the year	1,000,000
	Released to the income statement	(50,000)
	Carried down	950,000

$900,000 of this liability is non-current.

Expandable text - Sale price more than fair value

Where the proceeds of a sale and operating leaseback are greater than the fair value of the asset, it is usual for the lessor to recoup the excess proceeds by charging an above market rent. IAS 17 states that the excess profit should be spread forward over the period of the lease to match the additional rentals.

However, it is possible to view the agreement as two transactions: a sale of the asset at its fair value and the receipt of a loan. The logical accounting treatment would then be to recognise the liability to repay the loan immediately. The lease rentals would be treated as partly an operating expense (the rental of the asset), partly the capital repayment of the loan and partly the finance charge on the loan.

Many would argue for this accounting treatment because it recognises the substance of the transaction, whereas the treatment required by IAS 17 does not.

SIC 27 Evaluating the substance of transactions involving the legal form of a lease

This SIC refers to situations where an entity (A) leases an asset to another entity (B), and then immediately leases it back again on the same terms and conditions. Sometimes the leaseback is shorter than the original lease, but A will then have an option to repurchase the asset at the end of the lease. These transactions are designed to minimise tax liabilities or to obtain cheaper sources of finance.

When all the transactions are considered (the lease and the leaseback), there has obviously been no change to the risks and rewards that A is exposed to. Therefore, the legal form of the lease is ignored, and A continues to recognise the asset in the same way as before the leases were entered into.

Test your understanding 1 - Sale and leaseback

Details of several sale and leaseback transactions are shown below.

Description	Sale proceeds	Fair value	Carrying amount
	$000	$000	$000
(i) Sale and finance lease back	10,000	10,000	8,000
(ii) Sale at fair value with an operating lease back	10,000	10,000	8,000
(iii) Sale at under value and operating lease back	10,000	15,000	12,000
(iv) Sale in excess of fair value and operating lease back	15,000	10,000	8,000

Required:

Explain how the seller accounts for each sale and lease back transaction.

Expandable text - Current issue

There is a joint project between IASB and FASB work towards convergence of accounting treatment for leasing. The aim of the project is to develop a new common approach to lease accounting that would ensure that all assets and liabilities arising under lease contracts are recognised in the statement of financial position. if this was to happen, operating leases would no longer be recognised and accounted for. The IASB and FASB published a DP on leases in March 2009, followed by the publication of an ED in August 2010 setting out a proposed new reporting standard.

The problem is that IAS 17 Leases (and under US GAAP) have two lease categories: finance leases and operating leases. Categorisation is based on various factors. If a lease is classified as a finance lease, assets and liabilities are shown on the lessee's statement of financial position. However, for an operating lease the lessee does not show any assets or liabilities on the statement of financial position. The lessee simply accounts for the lease payments as an expense over the lease term. Hence, investors have to estimate the effect of operating leases on financial leverage and earnings. If lessees recorded the assets and liabilities that arise from all lease contracts, investors would better understand leasing activity.

There are greater deficiencies in the quality of information in relation to lessees than lessors. However, many believe that it is important to have consistent accounting for lessees and lessors. Consequently, the ED proposes a consistent accounting model for both lessees and lessors.

What is being proposed?
A lessee has acquired a right to use the underlying asset, and it pays for that right with the lease payments. A lessee would record:

- an asset for its right to use the underlying asset (the right-of-use asset), and

- a liability to pay rentals (liability for lease payments).

The right-of-use asset would originally be recorded at the present value of the lease payments. It would then be amortised over the life of the lease and tested for impairment. A lessee (under IFRSs) could revalue its right-of-use assets. The right-of-use asset would be presented within the property, plant and equipment category on the statement of financial position but separately from assets that the lessee owns.

As at August 2010, the expectation is that a new resporting standard will be issued in mid-2011.

The ACCA UK syllabus contains a requirement that candidates should be able to discuss and apply the key differences between UK GAAP and IFRS GAAP. The accounting requirements of UK GAAP and IFRS GAAP are very similar in this area; the relevant UK reporting standard requirements are as follows:

SSAP 21 – Leases. The accounting treatment is essentially the same under UK GAAP and IAS 17. There is distinction between finance leases and operating leases under both accounting frameworks; finance leases are capitalised and operating leases are recognised as an expense spread over the lease term.

One distinction is in the criteria used to determine whether or not a lease is a finance lease. UK GAAP includes a "90% test", when comparing the present value of the minimum lease payments with the fair value of the leased asset. If this is 90% or more then, unless there is clear evidence to the contrary, it is assumed that substantially the risks and rewards have been transferred – i.e. it is a finance lease. Even if the "90% test" is failed, it could still be classified as a finance lease if substantially the risks and rewards have been transferred. There is no "90%" test under IFRS GAAP; lease classification is determined based upon an assessment of whether substantially the risks and rewards have been transferred under the lease.

5 Chapter summary

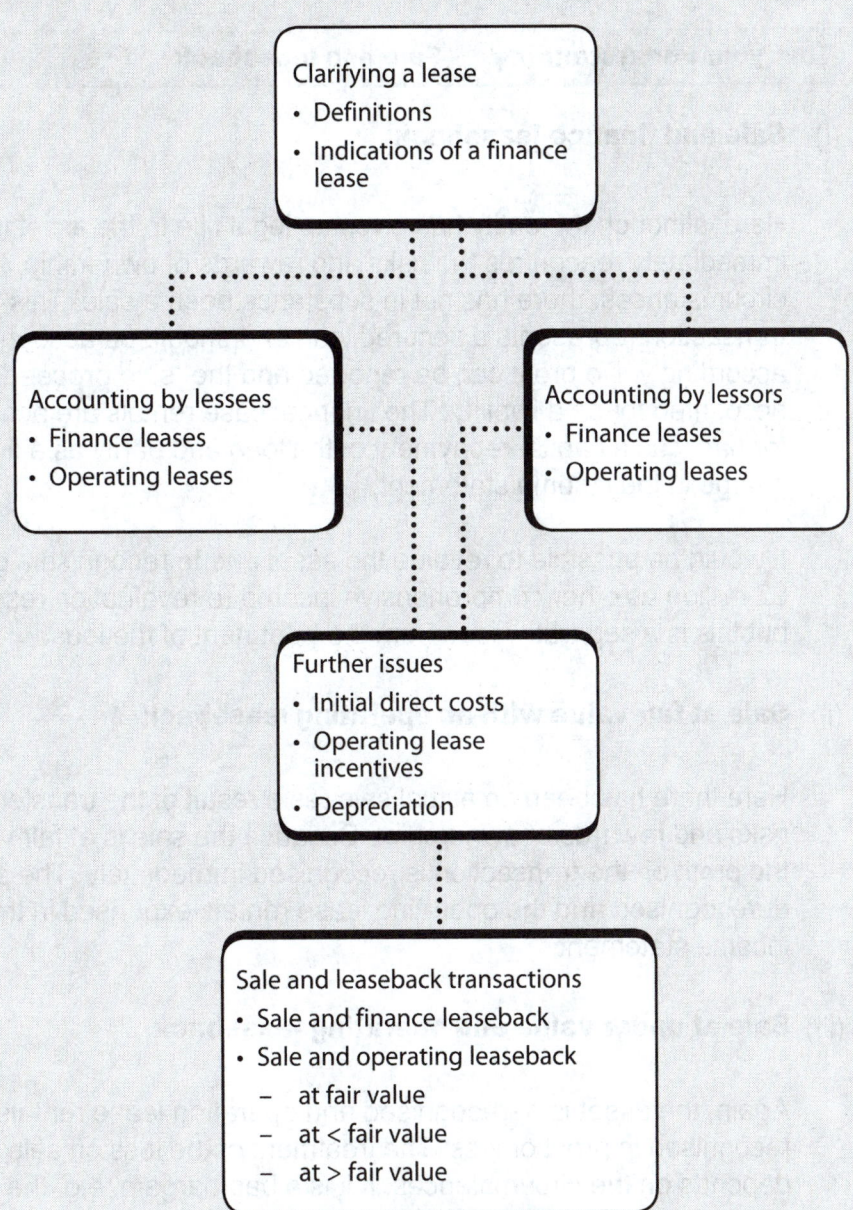

Clarifying a lease
- Definitions
- Indications of a finance lease

Accounting by lessees
- Finance leases
- Operating leases

Accounting by lessors
- Finance leases
- Operating leases

Further issues
- Initial direct costs
- Operating lease incentives
- Depreciation

Sale and leaseback transactions
- Sale and finance leaseback
- Sale and operating leaseback
  - at fair value
  - at < fair value
  - at > fair value

Test your understanding answers

(i) Sale and finance leaseback

Here, although the entity has given up legal title to the asset it immediately reacquires the risks and rewards of ownership. In such circumstances, there has not in substance been a sale. This transaction represents a secured loan and should be accounted for accordingly. No profit can be reported and the 'sale proceeds' are accounted for as a liability. The finance lease rentals are accounted for partly as a capital repayment of the loan and partly as a finance charge in the income statement.

It would be possible to revalue the asset and to recognise a gain of $2 million as other comprehensive income (a revaluation reserve) but this is a separate issue from the treatment of the lease.

(ii) Sale at fair value with an operating leaseback

Here there has been an actual sale (as a result of the transfer of the risks and rewards of ownership). Because the sale is at fair value, the profit on the transaction is recognised immediately. The asset is derecognised and the operating lease rentals expensed in the income statement.

(iii) Sale at under value and operating leaseback

Again, the asset is derecognised and operating lease rentals recognised in profit or loss. The treatment of the loss on sale depends on the circumstances. If it is a bad bargain, e.g. the sale was made in desperation for the cash, then the loss is recognised immediately. If, however, the lease payments are also at undervalue, then the loss is deferred and amortised over the period until the end of the lease.

(iv) **Sale in excess of fair value and operating leaseback**

Again, there really has been a sale and the asset is derecognised. The profit on the disposal of the asset must be restricted to the difference between the fair value of the asset and its carrying amount ($2 million). IAS 17 requires that the excess profit ($5 million) is deferred and amortised over the period of the lease. This treatment assumes that the buyer/lessor will charge lease rentals above the market rate to compensate for the loss.

Financial instruments

Chapter learning objectives

Upon completion of this chapter you will be able to:

- apply and discuss the recognition and derecognition of a financial asset or financial liability

- apply and discuss the classification of a financial asset or financial liability and their measurement

- apply and discuss the treatment of gains and losses arising on financial assets and financial liabilities

- apply and discuss the treatment of impairment of financial assets

- record the accounting for derivative financial instruments, and simple embedded derivatives

- outline the principle of hedge accounting, and account for fair value hedges and cash flow hedges including hedge effectiveness.

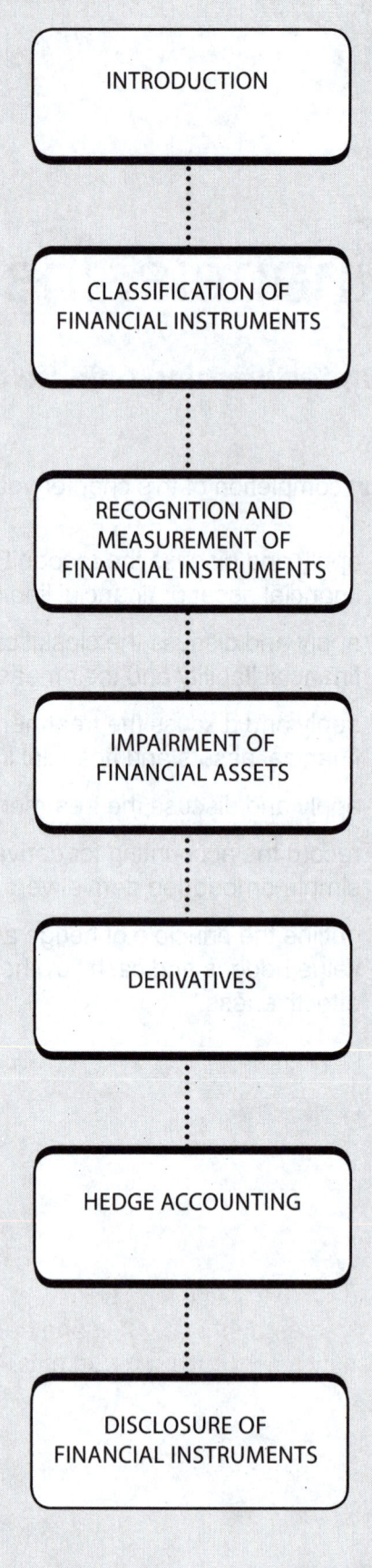

INTRODUCTION

CLASSIFICATION OF
FINANCIAL INSTRUMENTS

RECOGNITION AND
MEASUREMENT OF
FINANCIAL INSTRUMENTS

IMPAIRMENT OF
FINANCIAL ASSETS

DERIVATIVES

HEDGE ACCOUNTING

DISCLOSURE OF
FINANCIAL INSTRUMENTS

1 Introduction

Definitions

 A **financial instrument** is any contract that gives rise to a financial asset of one entity and a financial liability or equity instrument of another entity.

 A **financial asset** is any asset that is:

- cash
- an equity instrument of another entity
- a contractual right to receive cash or another financial asset from another entity
- a contractual right to exchange financial instruments with another entity under conditions that are potentially favourable
- a contract that will or may be settled in the entity's own equity instruments, and is a non-derivative for which the entity is or may be obliged to receive a variable number of the entity's own equity instruments
- a contract that will or may be settled in the entity's own equity instruments, and is a derivative that will or may be settled other than by the exchange of a fixed amount of cash or another financial asset for a fixed number of the entity's own equity instruments.

 A **financial liability** is any liability that is a contractual obligation:

- to deliver cash or another financial asset to another entity
- to exchange financial instruments with another entity under conditions that are potentially unfavourable
- a contract that will or may be settled in the entity's own equity instruments, and is a non-derivative for which the entity is or may be obliged to deliver a variable number of the entity's own equity instruments
- a contract that will or may be settled in the entity's own equity instruments, and is a derivative that will or may be settled other than by exchange of a fixed amount of cash or another financial asset for a fixed number of the entity's own equity instruments.

 An **equity instrument** is any contract that evidences a residual interest in the assets of an entity after deducting all of its liabilities.

Accounting standards

There are four reporting standards that deal with financial instruments:

*   IAS 32 **Financial instruments: presentation**
*   IAS 39 **Financial instruments: recognition and measurement**
*   IFRS 7 **Financial instruments: disclosures**
*   IFRS 9 **Financial instruments**

IAS 32 deals with the classification of financial instruments and their presentation in financial statements.

IAS 39 deals with how financial instruments are measured and when they should be recognised in financial statements.

IFRS 7 deals with the disclosure of financial instruments in financial statements.

 IFRS 9 was issued on 12 November 2009 and will eventually replace IAS 39. IFRS 9 is effective for accounting periods commencing from 1 January 2013, although earlier adoption is permitted. Where early adoption is taken up, to the extent that IFRS 9 has not yet been fully updated and effective, the provisions of the earlier standards continue to apply. As at August 2010, only provisions relating to classification and measurement of financial assets are contained within IFRS 9. The current expectation is that IAS 39 will be replaced by mid-2011.

2 Classification of financial instruments

IAS 32 **Financial instruments: presentation** provides the rules on classifying financial instruments as liabilities or equity. These are detailed below.

Presentation of liabilities and equity

The issuer of a financial instrument must classify it as a financial liability, financial asset or equity instrument on initial recognition according to its substance.

Financial liabilities

The instrument will be classified as a liability if the issuer has a contractual obligation:

*   to deliver cash (or another financial asset) to the holder
*   to exchange financial instruments on potentially unfavourable terms.

A redeemable preference share will be classified as a liability, because the issuer has the contractual obligation to deliver cash to the holders on the redemption date.

Equity instruments

A financial instrument is only an equity instrument if both of the following conditions are met:

(a) The instrument includes no contractual obligation to deliver cash or another financial asset to another entity; or to exchange financial assets or liabilities with another under conditions that are potentially unfavourable to the issuer.

(b) If the instrument will or may be settled in the issuer's own equity instruments, it is a non-derivative that includes no contractual obligation for the issuer to deliver a variable number of its own equity instruments; or it is a derivative that will be settled only by the issuer exchanging a fixed amount of cash or another financial asset for a fixed number of its own equity shares.

Interest, dividends, losses and gains

- The accounting treatment of interest, dividends, losses and gains relating to a financial instrument follows the treatment of the instrument itself.

- For example, dividends paid in respect of preference shares classified as a liability will be charged as a finance expense through profit or loss.

- Dividends paid on shares classified as equity will be reported in the statement of changes in equity.

Offsetting a financial asset and a financial liability

IAS 32 states that a financial asset and a financial liability may only be offset in very limited circumstances. The net amount may only be reported when the entity:

- has a legally enforceable right to set off the amounts

- intends either to settle on a net basis, or to realise the asset and settle the liability simultaneously.

3 Recognition and measurement of financial assets

Initial recognition of financial assets

IFRS 9 deals with recognition and measurement of financial assets. An entity should recognise a financial asset on its statement of financial position when, and only when, the entity becomes party to the contractual provisions of the instrument.

Examples of this principle are as follows:

- Unconditional receivables are recognised when the entity becomes a party to the contract. At that point the entity has a legal right to receive cash.

- Commitments to sell goods etc are not recognised until one party has fulfilled its part of the contract. For example, a sales order will not be recognised as revenue and a receivable until the goods have been delivered.

- Forward contracts are recognised as assets on the commitment date, not on the date when the item under contract is transferred from seller to buyer. (A forward contract is a commitment to buy or sell a financial instrument or a commodity.)

The four classifications of financial assets previously recognised under IAS 39 no longer apply.

Initial measurement of financial assets

At initial recognition, all financial assets are measured at fair value. This is likely to be purchase consideration paid to acquire the financial asset and will normally exclude transactions costs.

Subsequent measurement of financial assets

Subsequent measurement then depends upon whether the financial asset is a debt instrument or an equity instrument as follows:

Debt instruments:

Debt instruments would normally be measured at fair value through profit or loss (FVTPL), but could be measured at amortised cost if the entity chooses to do so, provided the following two tests are passed:

- the business model test, and
- the contractual cash flow characteristics test.

The **business model test** establishes whether the entity holds the financial asset to collect the contractual cash flows or whether the objective is to sell the financial asset prior to maturity to realise changes in fair value. If it is the former, it implies that there will be no or few sales of such financial assets from a portfolio prior to their maturity date. If this is the case, the test is passed. Where this is not the case, it would suggest that the assets are not being held with the objective to collect contractual cashflows, but perhaps may be disposed of to respond to changes in fair value. In this situation, the test is failed and the financial asset cannot be measured at amortised cost.

Where an entity changes its business model, it may be required to reclassify its financial assets as a consequence, but this is expected to be infrequent occurrence. If reclassification does occur, it is accounted for from the first day of the accounting period in which reclassification takes place.

The **contractual cash flow characteristics test** determines whether the contractual terms of the financial asset give rise to cash flows on specified dates that are **solely** of principal and interest based upon the principal amount outstanding. If this is not the case, the test is failed and the financial asset cannot be measured at amortised cost. For example, convertible bonds contain rights in addition to the repayment of interest and principal (the right to convert the bond to equity) and therefore would fail the test and must be accounted for as fair value through profit or loss.

In summary, for a debt instrument to be measured at amortised cost, it will therefore require that:

- the asset is held within a business model whose objective is to hold the assets to collect the contractual cashflows, and

- the contractual terms of the financial asset give rise, on specified dates, to cash flows that are solely payments of principal and interest on the principal outstanding.

Even if a financial instrument passes both tests, it is still possible to designate a debt instrument as FVTPL if doing so eliminates or significantly reduces a measurement or recognition inconsistency (i.e. accounting mismatch) that would otherwise arise from measuring assets or liabilities or from recognising the gains or losses on them on different bases. Therefore, it is now possible to have financial assets that meet the criteria above and which will now be measured at amortised cost, even if they are quoted in an active market.

Equity instruments

Equity instruments are measured at either:

- fair value either through profit or loss, or
- fair value through other comprehensive income.

The normal expectation is that equity instruments will have the designation of **fair value through profit or loss**, with the price paid to acquire the financial asset initially regarded as fair value. This could include unquoted equity investments, which may present problems in arriving at a reliable fair value at each reporting date. However, IFRS 9 does not include a general exception for unquoted equity investments to be measured at cost; rather it provides guidance on when cost may, or may not, be regarded as a reliable indicator of fair value.

It is possible to designate an equity instrument as **fair value through other comprehensive income**, provided specified conditions have been complied with as follows:

- the equity instrument cannot be held for trading, and
- there must be an irrevocable choice for this designation upon initial recognition.

In this situation, initial recognition will also include directly attributable transactions costs. This may apply, for example, to strategic investments to be held on a continuing basis which are not held to take advantage of changes in fair value. Equity derivatives are excluded from adopting this designation.

Dividends on financial assets through other comprehensive income must be taken to profit or loss, unless they represent a recovery of part of the investment. Changes in fair value will be recognised in other comprehensive income.

If an equity instrument has been designated as fair value through other comprehensive income, the requirements in IAS 39 to undertake an assessment of impairment no longer apply as all fair value movements now remain in equity. It would appear from IFRS 9 that there is no recycling of gains and losses through profit or loss upon derecognition, although there may be a transfer within equity.

Overview of recognition and measurement of financial assets

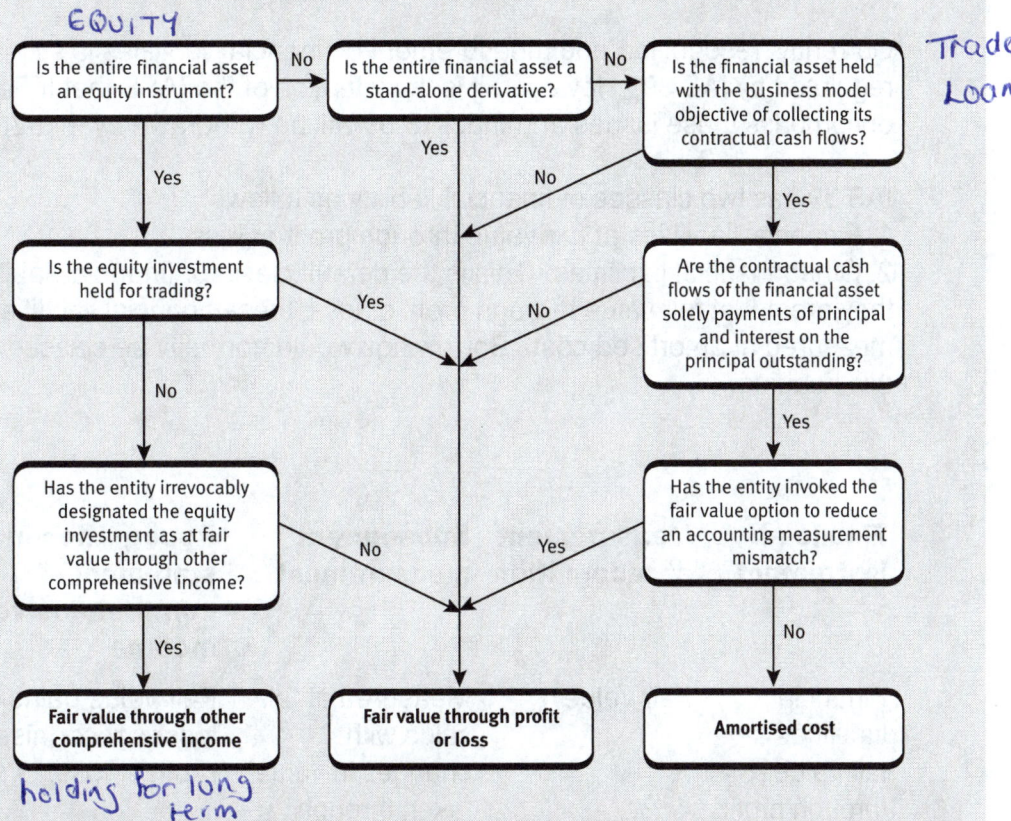

EQUITY

Trade Recewables
Loans

holding for long term

Test your understanding 1 - Ashes

Ashes has the following financial assets:

(1) Investments held for trading purposes.

(2) Interest-bearing debt instruments that will be redeemed in five years; Ashes intends to collect the contractual cash flows which consist solely of repayments of interest and capital.

(3) A trade receivable.

(4) Derivatives held for speculation purposes.

(5) Equity shares that Ashes has no intention of selling.

(6) A convertible bond which is due to be converted into equity shares in three years time.

Required:

How should Ashes classify its financial assets?

4 Recognition and measurement of financial liabilities

Currently, recognition and measurement of financial liabilities is still regulated by IAS 39. However, it is the intention of the IASB that IFRS 9 will encompass these issues and that IAS 39 will be withdrawn by mid-2011.

IAS 39 has two classes of financial liability as follows:
1. Financial liabilities at fair value through profit or loss
2. Other financial liabilities. This is the default class for financial liabilities if they are not at fair value through profit or loss; these financial liabilities are measured at amortised cost. Borrowings would normally be classed under this heading.

Financial instrument	Measurement at recognition	Subsequent measurement	Recognition in statement of comprehensive income
Financial liabilities at fair value through profit or loss	Fair value	Measured at fair value with changes in value taken through profit or loss	Fair value gains and losses recognised in profit or loss.
Other financial liabilities	Amortised cost	Measured at amortised cost using the effective interest rate	The interest calculated using the effective rate is charged to profit or loss within the income statement as a finance cost

Two forms of financial instrument which need to be considered are deep discounted bonds and compound instruments.

Deep discounted bonds measured at amortised cost

- One common form of financial instrument for many entities will be loans payable. These will be measured at amortised cost. The amortised cost of a liability equals: initial cost plus interest less repayments. (We will also use this method with compound instruments.)

- The interest will be charged at the effective rate or level yield. This is the internal rate of return of the instrument.

An example of a loan that uses an effective rate of interest is a deep discount bond.

It has the following features.

- This instrument is issued at a significant discount to its par value.

- Typically it has a coupon rate much lower than market rates of interest, e.g. a 2% bond when market interest is 10% pa.

- The initial carrying amount of the bond will be the net proceeds of issue.

- The full finance cost will be charged over the life of the instrument so as to give a constant periodic rate of interest.

- The full cost will include:
  - issue costs
  - deep discount on issue
  - annual interest payments
  - premium on redemption.

The constant periodic rate of interest (sometimes called the effective rate) can be calculated in the same way that the internal rate of return is calculated. In questions, the effective rate of interest will normally be given.

Illustration 1 – Deep discount bond

On 1 January 20X1 James issued a deep discount bond with a $50,000 nominal value.

The discount was 16% of nominal value, and the costs of issue were $2,000.

Interest of 5% of nominal value is payable annually in arrears.

The bond must be redeemed on 1 January 20X6 (after 5 years) at a premium of $4,611.

The effective rate of interest is 12% p.a.

Required

How will this be reported in the financial statements of James over the period to redemption?

Expandable text - Solution

Firstly, we must establish at what amount the bond will be initially recognised in the statement of financial position. The calculation set out below also works out the total finance cost to be charged to profits.

	$	$
Net proceeds		
Face value	50,000	
Less: 16% discount	(8,000)	
Less: Issue costs	(2,000)	
		40,000
Initial recognition of liability		
Repayments		
Capital	50,000	
Premium on redemption	4,611	
Principal to be redeemed	54,611	
Interest paid: $50,000 × 5% × 5 years	12,500	
		67,111
Total finance cost		27,111

Secondly, we set up a table (similar to that used for compound instruments) to work out the balance of the loan at the end of each period.

Year	Opening balance	Effective interest rate 12%	Payments 5%	Closing balance
	$	$	$	$
1	40,000	4,800	(2,500)	42,300
2	42,300	5,076	(2,500)	44,876
3	44,876	5,385	(2,500)	47,761
4	47,761	5,731	(2,500)	50,992
5	50,992	6,119	(2,500)	54,611
		27,111	(12,500)	
		To: Income statement	To: Statement of cash flows	To: Statement of financial position

The finance charge taken to the income statement is greater than the actual interest paid, and so the balance shown as a liability increases over the life of the instrument until it equals the redemption value at the end of its term.

In Years 1 to 4 the balance shown as a liability is less than the amount that will be payable on redemption. Therefore the full amount payable must be disclosed in the notes to the accounts.

Test your understanding 2 - Giles

Giles issues three debt instruments, each with a nominal value of $10,000 and redeemable in two years. The effective interest rate for all three is 10%.

D1 has a coupon rate of 0%, is issued at par and is redeemed at a premium of $2,100.

D2 has a coupon rate of 0%, is issued at a discount of $1,736 and is redeemed at par.

D3 has a coupon rate of 2%, is issued at a discount of $500 and is redeemed at a premium of $1,075.

Required:

How should these debt instruments be accounted for?

Presentation of compound instruments

The issuer of a financial instrument must classify it as a financial liability or equity instrument on initial recognition according to its substance.

- A **compound instrument** is a financial instrument that has characteristics of both equity and liabilities, for example debt that can be converted into shares.

- The bondholder has the prospect of acquiring cheap shares in an entity, because the terms of conversion are normally quite generous. Even if the bondholder wants cash rather than shares, the deal may still be good. On maturity the cash-hungry bondholder will accept the conversion, and then sell the shares on the market for a tidy profit.

- In exchange though, the bondholders normally have to accept a below-market rate of interest, and will have to wait some time before they get the shares that form a large part of their return. There is also the risk that the entity's shares will under-perform, making the conversion unattractive.

- IAS 32 requires compound financial instruments be split into their component parts:
  - a financial liability (the debt)
  - an equity instrument (the option to convert into shares).

- These must be shown separately in the financial statements.

Illustration 2 – Compound instruments

On 1 January 20X1 Daniels issued a $50m three-year convertible bond at par.

- There were no issue costs.

- The coupon rate is 10%, payable annually in arrears on 31 December.

- The bond is redeemable at par on 1 January 20X4.

- Bondholders may opt for conversion. The terms of conversion are two 25-cent equity shares for every $1 owed to each bondholder on 1 January 20X4.

- Bonds issued by similar entities without any conversion rights currently bear interest at 15%.

- Assume that all bondholders opt for conversion in full.

How will this be accounted for by Daniels?

Expandable text - Solution

On initial recognition, the method of splitting the bond between equity and liabilities is as follows.

- Calculate the present value of the debt component by discounting the cash flows at the market rate of interest for an instrument similar in all respects, except that it does not have conversion rights.

- Deduct the present value of the debt from the proceeds of the issue. The difference is the equity component.

(1) Splitting the proceeds

The cash payments on the bond should be discounted to their present value using the interest rate for a bond without the conversion rights, i.e. 15%.

Date		Cash flow	Discount factor @ 15%	Present value
		$000		$000
31-Dec-X1	Interest	5,000	$1/1.15$	4,347.8
31-Dec-X2	Interest	5,000	$1/1.15^2$	3,780.7
31-Dec-X3	Interest	5,000	$1/1.15^3$	3,287.6
1-Jan-X4	Principal	50,000	$1/1.15^3$	32,875.8
Present value (the liability component)	A			44,291.9
As the net proceeds of issue were	B			50,000.0
So the equity component is	B – A			5,708.1

(2) The annual finance costs and year end carrying amounts

	Opening balance	Effective interest rate 15%	Payments	Closing balance
	$000	$000	$000	$000
20X1	44,291.9	6,643.8	(5,000)	45,935.7
20X2	45,935.7	6,890.4	(5,000)	47,826.1
20X3	47,826.1	7,173.9	(5,000)	50,000.0

(3) **The conversion of the bond**

The carrying amounts at 1 January 20X4 are:

	$000
Equity	5,708.1
Liability – bond	50,000.0
	55,708.1

The conversion terms are two 25-cent equity shares for every $1, so $50m × 2 = 100m shares, which have a nominal value of $25m. The remaining $30,708,100 should be classified as the share premium, also within equity. There is no remaining liability, because conversion has extinguished it.

Test your understanding 3 - Craig

Craig issues a $100,000 4% three-year convertible loan on 1 January 20X6. The market rate of interest for a similar loan without conversion rights is 8%. The conversion terms are one equity share ($1 nominal value)for every $2 of debt. Conversion or redemption at par takes place on 31 December 20X8.

Required:

How should this be accounted for:

(a) **if all holders elect for the conversion**

(b) **no holders elect for the conversion?**

5 Derecognition of financial instruments

Derecognition is currently part of the IASB work plan for the development of reporting standards. As at August 2010, a standard had still to be finalised. Current developments relating to derecognition are considered later within this chapter. Until the new standard is approved, the derecognition criteria, currently included in IAS 39, continue to apply.

A **financial asset** should be derecognised if one of the following criteria occur:

- the contractual rights to the cash flows of the financial asset have expired, e.g. when an option held by the entity has expired worthless

- the financial asset has been sold and the transfer qualifies for derecognition because substantially all the risks and rewards of ownership have been transferred from the seller to the buyer.

The analysis of where the risks and rewards of ownership lie after the transaction is critical. For example if an entity sells an investment in shares and enters into a total return swap with the buyer, the buyer will return any increases in value to the entity or the entity will pay the buyer for any decrease in value. In this case the entity has retained substantially all of the risks and rewards of the investment, which therefore should not be derecognised.

A financial liability should be derecognised when, and only when, the obligation specified in the contract is discharged, cancelled or expires.

On derecognition, the difference between the carrying amount of the asset or liability and the amount received or paid for it should be recognised in the profit or loss for the period.

Test your understanding 4 - Ming

Ming has two receivables that it has factored to a bank in return for immediate cash proceeds of less than the face value of the invoices. Both receivables are due from long standing customers who are expected to pay in full and on time. Ming has agreed a three-month credit period with both customers.

The first receivable is for $200,000 and in return for assigning the receivable Ming has just received from the factor $180,000. Under the terms of the factoring arrangement this the only money that Ming will receive regardless of when or even if the customer settles the debt, i.e. the factoring arrangement is said to be "without recourse ".

The second receivable is for $100,000 and in return for assigning the receivable Ming has just received $70,000. Under the terms of this factoring arrangement if the customer settles the account on time then a further $5,000 will be paid by the factoring bank to Ming, but if the customer does not settle the account in accordance with the agreed terms then the receivable will be reassigned back to Ming who will then be obliged to refund the factor the original $70,000 plus a further $10,000. This factoring arrangement is said to be "with recourse".

Required:

Discuss Ming's accounting treatment of the monies received under the terms of the two factoring arrangements.

Test your understanding 5 - Jones

Jones bought an investment for $40 million plus associated transaction costs of $1 million. The asset was designated upon initial recognition as fair value through other comprehensive income. At the reporting date the fair value of the financial asset had risen to $60 million. Shortly after the reporting date the financial asset was sold for $70 million.

Required:

(1) **How should this be accounted for?**

(2) **How would the answer have been different if the investment had been classified as at fair value through profit and loss?**

6 Impairment of financial assets

Impairment of financial assets will, in due course, be included within updated requirements of IFRS 9. Until that occurs, impairment requirements are as specified in IAS 39, subject to minor amendment following the publication of IFRS 9 containing revised classification of financial assets. Current developments relating to impairment of financial assets are considered elsewhere in this chapter.

The present situation as at August 2010 is as follows:

- Financial assets that are measured at fair value through profit or loss are not subject to an impairment review. Remeasurement of fair value at each reporting date will automatically take account of any impairment.

- Similarly, financial assets measured at fair value through other comprehensive income are not subject to an impairment review. Any changes in fair value, including those which may relate to impairment, are recognised in other comprehensive income. There is no recognition or recycling of impairment to profit or loss.

- For financial assets measured at amortised cost, IAS 39 requires that that an assessment be made, at every reporting date, as to whether there is any objective evidence that a financial asset is impaired, i.e. whether an event has occurred that has had a negative impact on the expected future cash flows of the asset.

- The event causing the negative impact must have already happened. An event causing an impairment in the future shall not be anticipated.

  - For example, on the last day of its financial year a bank lends a customer $100,000. The bank has consistently experienced a default rate of 5% across all its loans. The bank is **not** permitted immediately to write this loan down to $95,000 based on its past experience, because no default has occurred at the reporting date.

Impairment review of financial assets measured at amortised cost

Examples of objective evidence of impairment at the reporting date include: significant financial difficulty of the borrower, and the failure of the borrower to make interest payments on the due date.

An impairment loss on financial assets measured at amortised cost is determined as follows:

	$
Carrying value of the asset per the financial statements	X
Less:	
PV of the estimated future cash flows discounted at the original effective interest rate	(X)
Impairment loss	X

Any impairment loss is recognised as an expense in profit or loss.

If recoverable amount exceeds carrying value, the asset is not impaired.

Illustration 3 - Impairment of financial assets

On 1 February 20X6, Eve makes a four-year loan of $10,000 to Fern. The coupon rate on the loan is 6%, the same as the effective rate of interest. Interest is received at the end of each year.

During February 20X9, it becomes clear that Fern is in financial difficulties. This is the necessary objective evidence of impairment. At this time the current market interest rate is 8%.

It is estimated that the future remaining cash flows from the loan will be only $6,000, instead of $10,600 (the $10,000 principal plus interest for the fourth year of $600).

Expandable text - Solution

Because the coupon and the effective interest rate are the same, the carrying amount of the principal will remain constant at $10,000.

On 1 February 20X9, the carrying amount of the loan should be restated to the present value of the estimated cash flows of $6,000, discounted at the original effective interest rate of 6% for one year.

6,000 × 1/1.06 = $5,660

The result is an impairment loss of $4,340 ($10,000 – $5,660).

The impairment loss is recognised as an expense in profit or loss.

The asset will continue to be accounted for using amortised cost, based on the revised carrying amount of the loan. In the last year of the loan, the interest income of $340 (5,660 × 6%) will be recognised in profit or loss.

Test your understanding 6 - Harmison

On 1 January 20X2, Harmison makes a five-year loan of $10,000 with an interest rate of 10% (the same as the effective rate of interest), with the principal being repaid at the end of five years.

During January 20X6, the borrower is in financial difficulty and it is estimated that the future cash flows will be $4,000 rather than $11,000 ($10,000 principal plus $1,000 interest). At this date the current market interest rate is 9%.

Required:

How should this be accounted for?

Reversals of impairment losses

Reversal of an impairment loss is only permitted as a result of an event occurring after the impairment loss has been recognised. An example would be the credit rating of a customer being revised upwards by a credit rating agency.

Reversal of impairment losses in respect of financial assets measured at amortised cost are recognised in profit or loss.

7 Derivatives

Definitions

A derivative is a financial instrument with the following characteristics:

(a) Its value changes in response to the change in a specified interest rate, security price, commodity price, foreign exchange rate, index of prices or rates, a credit rating or credit index or similar variable (called the 'underlying').

(b) It requires little or no initial net investment relative to other types of contract that have a similar response to changes in market conditions.

(c) It is settled at a future date.

Expandable text - The problems of derivatives

- Derivatives were originally designed to hedge against fluctuations in agricultural commodity prices on the Chicago Stock Exchange. A speculator would pay a small amount (say $100) now for the contractual obligation to buy a thousand units of wheat in three months' time for $10,000. If in three months time one thousand units of wheat costs $11,000, then the speculator would make a profit of $900 (11,000 – 100 – 10,000). This would be a 900% return on the original investment over 3 months, which is one of the attractions of derivatives to speculators. But if the price had dropped to $9,000, then the trader would have made a loss of $1,100 (100 + 1,000) despite the initial investment only having been $100.

- This shows that losses on derivatives can be far greater than the historical cost-carrying amount of the related asset. Therefore, shareholders need to be given additional information about derivatives in order to assess the entity's exposure to loss.

- In most cases, entering into a derivative is at a low or no cost. Therefore it is important that derivatives are recognised and disclosed in the financial statements as they have very little initial outlay but can expose the entity to significant gains and losses.

Expandable text - Typical derivatives

Typical derivatives

Derivatives include the following types of contracts:

Forward contracts

- The holder of a forward contract is obliged to buy or sell a defined amount of a specific underlying asset, at a specified price at a specified future date.

- For example, a forward contract for foreign currency might require £100,000 to be exchanged for $150,000 in three months time. Both parties to the contract have both a financial asset and a financial liability. For example, one party has the right to receive $150,000 and the obligation to pay £100,000.

- Forward currency contracts may be used to minimise the risk on amounts receivable or payable in foreign currencies.

Forward rate agreements

- Forward rate agreements can be used to fix the interest charge on a floating rate loan.

- For example, an entity has a $1m floating rate loan, and the current rate of interest is 7%. The rates are reset to the market rate every six months, and the entity cannot afford to pay more than 9% interest. The entity enters into a six-month forward rate agreement (with, say, a bank) at 9% on $1m. If the market rates go up to 10%, then the bank will pay them $50,000 (1% of $1m for 6 months) which in effect reduces their finance cost to 9%. If the rates only go up to 8% then the entity pays the bank $50,000. The forward rate agreement effectively sets the interest rate payable at 9% for the period.

Futures contracts

- Futures contracts oblige the holder to buy or sell a standard quantity of a specific underlying item at a specified future date.

- Futures contracts are very similar to forward contracts. The difference is that futures contracts have standard terms and are traded on a financial exchange, whereas forward contracts are tailor-made and are not traded on a financial exchange. Also, whereas forward contracts will always be settled, a futures contract will rarely be held to maturity.

Swaps

- Two parties agree to exchange periodic payments at specified intervals over a specified time period.

- For example, in an interest rate swap, the parties may agree to exchange fixed and floating rate interest payments calculated by reference to a notional principal amount.

- This enables companies to keep a balance between their fixed and floating rate interest payments without having to change the underlying loans.

Options

- These give the holder the right, but not the obligation, to buy or sell a specific underlying asset on or before a specified future date.

Measurement of derivatives

- On recognition, derivatives should initially be measured at fair value. Transaction costs may not be included.

- Subsequent measurement depends on how the derivative is categorised. In many cases, this will involve the derivative being measured at fair value with changes in the fair value recognised in profit or loss. However if the derivative is used as a hedge (see later in this chapter), then the changes in fair value should be recognised in equity.

Illustration 4 – Derivatives

Entity A enters into a call option on 1 June 20X5, to purchase 10,000 shares in another entity on 1 November 20X5 at a price of $10 per share. The cost of each option is $1. A has a year end of 30 September.

By 30 September the fair value of each option has increased to $1.30 and by 1 November to $1.50, with the share price on the same date being $11. A exercises the option on 1 November and the shares are classified as at fair value through profit or loss.

Expandable text - Solution

On 1 June 20X5 the cost of the option is recognised:

Debit	Call option (10,000 × $1)	$10,000
Credit	Cash	$10,000

On 30 September the increase in fair value is recorded:

Debit	Call option (10,000 × ($1.30 – 1))	$3,000
Credit	Profit or loss	$3,000

On 1 November the option is exercised, the shares recognised and the call option derecognised. As the shares are financial assets at fair value through profit or loss, they are recognised at $110,000 (10,000 × the current market price of $11)

Debit	Investment in shares at fair value	$110,000
Debit	Expense – loss on call option	$3,000
	((10,000 + 3,000 + 100,000) – 110, 000)	
Credit	Cash (10,000 × $10)	$100,000
Credit	Call option (10,000 + 3,000 carrying amount)	$13,000

Test your understanding 7 - Hoggard

Hoggard buys a call option on 1 January 20X6 for $5 per option that gives the right to buy 100 shares in Rowling on 31 December at a price of $10 per share.

Required:

How should this be accounted for, given the following outcomes?

(a) **The options are sold on 1 July 20X6 for $15 each.**

(b) **On 31 December 20X6, Rowling's share price is $8 and Hoggard lets the option lapse unexercised.**

(c) **The option is exercised on 31 December when Rowling's share price is $25. The shares are classified as held for trading.**

KAPLAN PUBLISHING

Expandable text - Further points

Embedded derivatives

IAS 39 required separation of certain embedded derivates. IFRS 9 removes this requirement when the host contract is a financial asset within the scope of IAS 39.

As a result, embedded derivatives that would have been separately accounted for at fair value through profit or loss under IAS 39 because they were not closely related to the financial asset host will no longer be separated. Instead, the contractual cash flows of the financial asset are assessed as a whole and the asset is measured as fair value through profit or loss if any of its cash flows do not represent payments of principal and interest as outlined in IFRS 9.

Remember that, so far, IFRS 9 applies only to financial assets, the requirement to assess contractual arrangements for non-closely related embedded derivatives still applies to all hybrid contracts with a financial liability host and non-financial host contacts that are outside the scope of IAS 39.

For example:

An entity has an investment in a convertible bond, which can be converted into a fixed number of equity shares at a specified future date. Normally, under IAS 39, the convertible bond is bifurcated (i.e. separated) into the host debt instrument and the conversion option which is the embedded derivative. This was required as risks attaching to conversion option were not closely matched to those of the debt instrument. They were also measured differently as the debt instrument under IAS 39 would normally be measured at amortised cost with the conversion option measured at fair value through profit or loss.

IFRS 9 now requires that embedded derivatives, such as the the convertible, bond are evaluated for correct classification in their entirety due to the presence of the conversion option. In practical terms it would mean that the bond would fail the contractual cash flow characteristics test and would therefore be measured at fair value through profit or loss.

The need for a financial reporting standard

Derivatives can be easily acquired, often for little or no cost, but their values can change very rapidly, exposing holders to the risk of large profits or losses. Because many derivatives have no cost, they may not appear in a traditional historical cost statement of financial position, even if they represent substantial assets or liabilities of the entity. Gains and losses have traditionally not been recorded until cash is exchanged. Gains and losses can be easily realised, often simply by making a telephone call. If gains and losses are recognised on a cash basis, then management can choose when to report these gains and losses.

Derivatives can rapidly transform the position, performance and risk profile of an entity. Consequently, there is great debate regarding the accounting for derivatives, together with ensuring that there are adequate disclosures for users to fully understand and appreciate their impact upon the reported financial performance and postion of an entity. Current developments relating to financial instruments are dealt with elsewhere in this chapter.

Measurement of derivatives

Under IAS 39, derivatives should initially be measured at fair value in the statement of financial position (usually cost); and subsequent measurement depends will involve the derivative being measured at fair through profit or loss. However if the derivative is used as a hedge (see later) then the changes in fair value should be recognised as other comprehensive income.

The arguments for using fair value for these items rather than historical cost are as follows.

(a) Sometimes these items have no historical cost, and so they are ignored by conventional accounting.

(b) Fair valuation reports gains and losses as they arise, not just when they are realised in cash. This gives a better and more objective indication of a entity's performance.

(c) Fair valuation reports the way in which risks are being managed.

(d) Fair valuation promotes comparability. All derivatives will be carried at their fair value at the reporting date, rather than at out-of-date historical costs. Different entities will also be using the same up-to-date fair values.

(e) Fair values have more predictive value.

(f) It is practical, because many derivatives are traded on active markets and are therefore easy to value.

KAPLAN PUBLISHING

However, some people still disagree with using fair values. Some of the arguments against fair values are as follows.

(a) Reporting changes in fair value will result in volatile profits. (However, as these profits reflect real changes in value, some would say that they must be reported.)

(b) Some of the changes in fair value might never be realised. Therefore, the profit or loss will include losses that never arise and profits that are never realised.

(c) It may not always be possible to value all derivatives reliably.

8 Hedge accounting

Definitions

Hedging is a method of managing risk by designating one or more hedging instruments so that their change in fair value is offset, in whole or in part, to the change in fair value or cash flows of a hedged item.

A **hedged item** is an asset or liability that exposes the entity to risks of changes in fair value or future cash flows (and is designated as being hedged).

A **hedging instrument** is a designated derivative whose fair value or cash flows are expected to offset changes in fair value or future cash flows of the hedged item.

So the **item** generates the risk and the **instrument** modifies it.

Introduction

As at August 2010, IFRS 9 does not contain any specific requirements relating to hedge accounting; this constitutes the third phase of the project to replace IAS 39 with IFRS 9. Accordingly, the requirements specified in IAS 39 continue to apply until withdrawn.

- Hedging is a means of reducing risk.

- One simple hedge is where an entity takes out a foreign currency loan to finance a foreign currency investment. If the foreign currency strengthens, then the value of the asset and the burden of the liability will increase by the same amount. Any gains or losses will be cancelled out.

- Hedge accounting recognises symmetrically the offsetting effects, on net profit or loss, of changes in the fair values of the hedging instrument and the related item being hedged.

- The hedging instrument will often be a derivative.

- Hedge accounting is allowed under IAS 39 provided that the hedging relationship is clearly defined, measurable, and actually effective.

IAS 39 identifies three types of hedge, two of which are within the P2 syllabus:

(1) Fair value hedge –This hedges against the risk of changes in the fair value of a recognised asset or liability. For example, the fair value of fixed rate debt will change as a result of changes in interest rates.

(2) Cash flow hedge – This hedges against the risk of changes in expected cash flows. For example, a UK entity may have an unrecognised contractual commitment to purchase goods in a year's time for a fixed amount of US dollars.

Accounting for a fair value hedge

Under IAS 39 hedge accounting rules can only be applied to a fair value hedge if the hedging relationship meets four criteria.

(1) At the inception of the hedge there must be formal documentation identifying the hedged item and the hedging instrument.

(2) The hedge is expected to be highly effective.

(3) The effectiveness of the hedge can be measured reliably (i.e. the fair value/cash flows of the item and the instrument can be measured reliably).

(4) The hedge has been assessed on an on-going basis and is determined to have been effective.

Accounting treatment

- The hedging instrument will be remeasured at fair value, with all gains and losses being reported in profit or loss for the year.

- The hedged portion of the hedged item will be remeasured at fair value, with all gains and losses being reported in profit or loss for the year.

One consequence of introducing redefined classifications of financial assets under IFRS 9 is that some financial assets, previously measured at amortised cost, would now be measured at fair value through profit or loss under IFRS 9. If this is the case, both the hedged item and the hedging instrument would fall to be measured at fair value through profit or loss. Any change in fair value would therefore be matched in profit or loss and hedge accounting would be discontinued.

It is possible for a financial asset measured at amortised cost to be part of a fair value hedge. If this is the case, it would be measured at fair value, with any change in fair value taken to profit or loss as part of the hedge arrangement as identified above.

A further issue arises with the designation of items as fair value through other comprehensive income under IFRS 9. This designation must be made at initial recognition and is irrevocable. Similarly, any hedging arrangement must also be clearly designated at the point of inception. One reason for designation as fair value through other comprehensive income is to eliminate an accounting mismatch, where assets and liabilities are recognised or measured on different bases. It would appear possible that a fair value hedge arrangement could include a financial asset at fair value through other comprehensive income, with the remeasurement of both the hedged item and the hedging instrument both reported in either profit or loss (the current situation uner IAS 39) or in other comprehensive income. This may arise following the elimination of the available-for-sale category of financial asset identified under IAS 39.

It is expected that eligibility conditions for the fair value option will be reconsidered again as the hedge accounting phase of the project to replace IAS 39 is progressed.

Expandable text - Illustration: Hedge accounting

An entity purchases a debt instrument with a principal amount and fair value of $500,000 and fixed interest of 5% per annum. This is classified as fair value through other comprehensive income.

The exposure here is that if interest rates increase, the value of the debt instrument will fall. Therefore the entity enters into an interest rate swap, exchanging the fixed interest it is receiving on the debt instrument for floating interest rate payments in order to offset the risk of this exposure. The swap is designated and documented as a hedging instrument for the debt instrument.

Interest rates do in fact increase to 6%.

Expandable text - Solution

As the market interest rate has increased to 6% the value of the debt instrument will fall to $416,667 ($(500,000 × 5%)/0.06) giving a loss of $83,333. As the instrument is classified as fair value through other comprehensive income, this decrease in fair value would be normally be recorded in other comprehensive income. However as this is a hedged item in a fair value hedge, the change in fair value would be recognised in profit or loss:

Debit	Profit or loss	$83,333
Credit	Financial asset	$83,333

Suppose also that the fair value of the swap has increased by $83,333. As the swap is a derivative, it is measured at fair value with changes recognised in profit or loss.

Debit	Swap asset	$83,333
Credit	Profit or loss	$83,333

As the hedge was 100% effective (in that the loss was precisely offset by the gain), there is no net effect on profit or loss.

Test your understanding 8 - Strauss

Strauss buys an 8% $10-million fixed rate debenture when interest rates are 8% for the fair value of $10 million. The asset is classified as fair value through other comprehensive income.

Strauss is risk averse and wishes to enter into a derivative to protect it against a fall in the value of the asset if interest rates should rise. As a result it enters into an interest rate swap, which is designated as a hedging instrument for the debenture.

Interest rates increase to 9%.

Required:

How should this be accounted for?

Expandable text - Accounting for a cash flow hedge

Before the IAS 39 hedge accounting rules can be applied to a cash flow hedge, the hedging relationship must meet five criteria. These are the four listed for a fair value hedge, plus:

• the transaction giving rise to the cash flow risk is highly probable and will ultimately affect profitability.

Accounting treatment

• The hedging instrument will be remeasured at fair value. The gain (or loss) on the portion of the instrument that is deemed to be an effective hedge will be taken to equity and recognised in the statement of changes in equity.

• The ineffective portion of the gain or loss will be reported immediately in the income statement.

• If the hedged item eventually results in the recognition of a non-financial asset or liability, the gain or loss held in equity must be recycled in one of the two following ways

    – the gain / loss goes to adjust the carrying amount of the non-financial assets/liability.

    – the gain / loss is transferred to profit and loss in line with the consumption of the non-financial assets / liability.

Test your understanding 9 - Brit

Brit has contracted to buy one hundred tonnes of raw materials from a German entity. The materials will cost €500,000, and will be delivered and paid for in Euros on 30 June 20X5. Brit takes out a forward contract to buy €500,000 on 30 June 20X5 at a cost of $320,000. At the year end of 30 April 20X5, the Euro has appreciated and the value of €500,000 is now $325,000.

Required:

How should this be accounted for?

Test your understanding 10 - Grayton

Grayton (whose functional currency is the $) decided in January that it will need to buy an item of plant in one year's time for KR 200,000. As a result of being risk averse, it wishes to hedge the risk that the cost of buying KRs will rise and so enters into a forward rate agreement to buy KR 200,000 in one year's time for the fixed sum of $100,000. The fair value of this contract at inception is zero and is designated as a hedging instrument.

At Grayton's reporting date on 31 July, the KR has depreciated and the value of KR 200,000 is $90,000. It remains at that value until the plant is bought.

Required:

How should this be accounted for?

Hedge effectiveness

One of the requirements of IAS 39 is that to use hedge accounting, the hedge must be effective. IAS 39 describes this as the degree to which the changes in fair value or cash flows of the hedged item are offset by changes in the fair value or cash flows of the hedging instrument.

A hedge is viewed as being highly effective if actual results are within a range of 80% to 125%.

Illustration 5 – Hedge accounting

Joseph uses hedging transaction to minimise the risk of exposure to foreign exchange fluctuations. He buys goods from overseas and takes out forward contracts to fix the price of his inputs.

The gain on his forward contract for November was $570. The loss on a foreign currency creditor was $600.

The effectiveness of the hedge is determined by dividing 570 by 600 or 600 by 570.

This gives an effectiveness percentage of 95% and 105% respectively. The hedge meets the criteria of 80–125% and is effective.

9 Disclosure of financial instruments

IFRS 7 **Financial instruments: disclosures** provides the disclosure requirements for financial instruments. A summary of the requirements is detailed below.

The two main categories of disclosures required are:

(1) Information about the significance of financial instruments.

(2) Information about the nature and extent of risks arising from financial instruments.

The disclosures made should be made by each class of financial instrument.

Significance of financial instruments

- An entity must disclose the **significance** of financial instruments for their financial position and performance. The disclosures must be made for each class of financial instruments.

- An entity must disclose items of income, expense, gains, and losses, with separate disclosure of gains and losses from each class of financial instrument.

Nature and extent of risks arising from financial instruments

Qualitative disclosures

The qualitative disclosures describe:

- risk exposures for each type of financial instrument

- management's objectives, policies, and processes for managing those risks

- changes from the prior period.

Quantitative disclosures

The quantitative disclosures provide information about the extent to which the entity is exposed to risk, based on information provided internally to the entity's key management personnel. These disclosures include:

- summary quantitative data about exposure to each risk at the reporting date

- disclosures about credit risk, liquidity risk, and market risk as further described below

- concentrations of risk.

Expandable text - IFRS 7 Disclosures

Introduction

IFRS 7 was issued in August 2005 and replaced the disclosure elements of IAS 32. The presentation elements of IAS 32 remain the same. It adds to the disclosures that were required by IAS 32 and includes both quantitative and qualitative disclosures.

Additionally, some of the disclosure requirements have been amended following the introduction of IFRS 9. In principle, there should be sufficient information to enable users of financial statements to fully understand:

- how financial assets and liabilities have been designated

- the date, reason and effect of any reclassification of financial assets

The two main categories of disclosures required are:

(1) Accounting policies applied in respect of accounting for financial instruments

(2) Information about the significance of financial instruments upon the financial erformance and position of the entity.

(3) Information about the nature and extent of risks arising from financial instruments.

(4) Detailed disclosures relating the the nature and extent of accounting for fair value and cash flow hedging arrangements.

Types of risk

There are four types of financial risk:

(1) **Market risk** – This refers to the possibility that the value of an asset (or burden of a liability) might go up or down. Market risk includes three types of risk: currency risk, interest rate risk and price risk.

    (a) **Currency risk** is the risk that the value of a financial instrument will fluctuate because of changes in foreign exchange rates.

    (b) Fair value **interest rate risk** is the risk that the value of a financial instrument will fluctuate due to changes in market interest rates. This is a common problem with fixed interest rate bonds. The price of these bonds goes up and down as interest rates go down and up.

(c) Price risk refers to other factors affecting price changes. These can be specific to the enterprise (bad financial results will cause a share price to fall), relate to the sector as a whole (all Tech-Stocks boomed in the late nineties, and crashed in the new century) or relate to the type of security (bonds do well when shares are doing badly, and vice versa).

Market risk embodies not only the potential for a loss to be made but also a gain to be made.

(2) **Credit risk** – The risk that one party to a financial instrument fails to discharge its obligations, causing a financial loss to the other party. For example, a bank is exposed to credit risk on its loans, because a borrower might default on its loan.

(3) **Liquidity risk** – This is also referred to as funding risk. This is the risk that an enterprise will be unable to meet its commitments on its financial instruments. For example, a business may be unable to repay its loans when they fall due.

(4) **Cash flow interest rate risk** – This is the risk that future cash flows associated with a monetary financial instrument will fluctuate in amount due to changes in market interest rates. For example, the cash paid (or received) on floating rate loans will fluctuate in line with market interest rates.

Expandable text - Current issues

Impairment

In November 2009, the IASB published an ED/2009/12 on the subject of impairment. Following changes introduced by IFRS 9, this ED is now required to deal only with financial assets measured at amortised cost.

The current methodology of accounting for impairment of financial assets - an 'incurred loss model' is to recognise impairment only when there is evidence to the contrary at the reporting date.

The model proposed in the ED is an 'expected loss model'. Under this model, expected losses are recognised throughout the life of a loan or other financial asset measured at amortised cost, not just after a loss event has been identified (as is currently the case). This avoids a possible mismatch under the incurred loss model – front-loading of interest revenue (which includes an amount to cover the lender's expected loan loss) while the impairment loss is recognised only after a loss event occurs. Supporters of this model believe it gives a better reflection of the lending decision. .

Under the IASB's proposed expected loss model:

- Initial measurement. An entity determines the amortised cost carrying amount of a financial asset or portfolio of financial assets at initial recognition on the basis of the present value of future expected cash flows in considering expectations about future credit losses.

- Subsequent measurement. Subsequent to initial recognition the entity re-estimates the future expected cash flows and determines the present value. An impairment loss is therefore recognised only if there is an adverse change in expected cash flows, and a reversal of impairment losses is recognised if there is a favourable change in expected cash flows with any adjustment recognised in profit or loss. All measurements are made on the basis of present values, not market values. Extensive disclosure requirements would provide investors with an understanding of the loss estimates that an entity judges necessary.

Amortised cost is calculated based on the effective interest rate method as present value of the expected cash flows over the remaining life of the financial instrument discounted at that rate. Expected cash flows are estimates based on probability-weighted possible outcomes (that is, even if the most likely outcome is full repayment, the likelihood of the debtor not repaying all contractual principal and interest is also factored into the estimate).

For a fixed rate financial instrument, the effective interest rate is held constant over the life of the financial asset and does not change as market interest rates change. For a floating-rate financial instrument (such as a financial asset that pays LIBOR plus a fixed credit spread), the effective interest rate not a single, constant interest rate. Instead it is proposed that the effective interest rate be determined by combining the spot interest rate curve for the benchmark interest rate (for example, LIBOR) and a derived initial effective spread.

This expected loss approach will result in earlier loss recognition than the incurred loss model by taking into account future credit losses expected over the life of loans or other financial assets. Under this approach, an allowance for expected future losses is gradually built over the life of a financial asset by deducting a margin for future credit losses from gross interest revenue even if no losses have yet been incurred. This approach is based on the principle on which a lender would price a loan; that is, based on net yield after deducting a margin for expected credit losses.

The ED also proposes comprehensive presentation and disclosure requirements intended to enable users of the financial statements to evaluate the financial effects of interest revenues and expense and the quality of financial assets including credit risk. This is expected to provide significant challenges in terms of drafting and the final standard, together with practical difficulties regarding its application upon publication

Hedging

An ED is scheduled for the third quarter of 2010 – as at late August 2010, this has not been published. It would appear that there has been considerable debate during the development of the ED regarding how both fair value hedges and cash flow hedges should be recognised and accounted for.

Previously the IASB decided tentatively to improve hedge accounting requirements by replacing the mechanics used for fair value hedge accounting with an approach that is similar to cash flow hedge accounting. Arguably, this approach would provide consistenct in reporting the consequences of hedging arrangements. However, due to feedback received, this was changed to an approach for fair value hedge accounting that presents the cumulative gain or loss on the hedged item attributable to the hedged risk as a separate line item in the statement of financial position. Fair value changes of both the hedging instrument and the hedged item attributable to the hedged risk are recognised in other comprehensive income, and any ineffectiveness is recognised immediately in profit or loss.

Linked presentation of the hedged item and the hedging instrument has also been considered. However, the current view would appear not to allow the presentation of gross assets and gross liabilities that are related because of the application of fair value hedge accounting in proximity to one another on the face of the statement of financial position. The many different types of relationships that can exist between assets and liabilities make it too difficult to establish an appropriate basis for determining when this linked presentation would be required.

Derecognition

This project encompasses the requirements in IAS 39 Financial Instruments: Recognition and Measurement (IAS 39) for when a financial asset or financial liability must be removed from an entity's statement of financial position and the related derecognition disclosure requirements in IFRS 7 Financial Instruments: Disclosures. The objectives of the project are:

- To improve the derecognition requirements for financial assets in IAS 39, which have been perceived to be complex to understand and apply in practice.

- To provide users with more information about an entity's exposure to the risks of transferred financial assets,

- To facilitate convergence between the derecognition requirements in IAS 39 and those in US GAAP

In March 2009, the IASB published an ED Derecognition - Proposed amendments to IAS 39 and IFRS 7. During early 2010, IASB developed more fully the alternative model described in the ED. The IASB and the FASB discussed that model during several joint meetings. In May 2010, the boards reconsidered their strategies and plans for derecognition in light of:

- their joint discussions of the alternative derecognition model developed by the IASB

- the recent FASB amendments that reduce the differences between IFRSs and US GAAP

- the guidance the IASB received from National Standards-Setters on the largely favourable effects of the IFRS derecognition requirements during the financial crisis.

The boards agreed that their short-term priority should be on increasing the transparency and comparability of their standards by improving and converging US GAAP and IFRS disclosure requirements for financial assets transferred to another entity. They also decided to conduct additional research and analysis, including a post-implementation review of the FASB's recently amended requirements, as a basis for assessing the nature and direction of any further efforts to improve or converge IFRSs and US GAAP.

As a result of the above, the IASB plans to finalise the disclosure requirements that were included in the exposure draft Derecognition - Proposed amendments to IAS 39 and IFRS 7 with the view of converging the disclosure requirements in IFRS to the US GAAP requirements for transfers of financial assets. The target date for publication of the final standard is before the end of 2010. As at August 2010, this has still to happen.

Classification of rights issues: amendment to IAS 32

The amendment addresses the accounting for rights issues (rights, options or warrants) that are denominated in a currency other than the functional currency of the issuer. Previously such rights issues were accounted for as derivative liabilities. However, the amendment issued today requires that, provided certain conditions are met, such rights issues are classified as equity regardless of the currency in which the exercise price is denominated.

The global financial crisis has led to an increase in the number of such rights issues as entities seek to raise additional capital. The IASB has therefore moved swiftly to address this issue.

Entities are required to apply the amendment for annual periods beginning on or after 1 February 2010, but earlier application is permitted.

Fair value option for financial liabilities

This ED was published in May 2010, and it proposes a two-step approach to deal with own credit for most issued debt that is measured at fair value. Accounting for derivatives and trading liabilities would not be affected by these proposals, so would remain unchanged). The two-step approach would address volatility in profit or loss arising from own credit as follows:

(1) The total fair value change for issued debt measured at fair value would be reported in P&L, then

(2) The portion of the fair value change due to own credit would be reversed out of P&L and reported in other comprehensive income

This own credit effect is currently required to be disclosed in the notes to the financial statements. However, the proposal would elevate this figure to the face of the P&L statement, but would subsequently exclude this amount from the calculation of profit or loss. All issued debt measured at fair value would continue to be measured at full fair value on the statement of financial position. No other changes are proposed to the accounting for financial liabilities.

Asset and liability offsetting

In response to stakeholders' concerns the IASB and FASB decided to jointly issue an ED proposing changes to address differences in their standards on balance sheet netting of derivative contracts and other financial instruments that can result in material differences in financial reporting by financial institutions. The boards understand the importance of this issue, which is one of the more significant financial instrument presentation differences between IFRSs and US GAAP. The ED is expected to be published by the end of 2010.

Fair value option for financial liabilities

Following publication of IFRS 9 in November 2009, the IASB has now turned to consideration of the classification and measurement of financial liabilities. In May 2010, the IASB published an ED, Fair Value Option for Financial Liabilities.

The ED proposes a two-step approach to deal with own credit for most issued debt that is measured at fair value. (The accounting for derivatives and trading liabilities would not be affected by these proposals, so would be unchanged). The two-step approach would address the P&L volatility arising from own credit as follows:

(1) the total fair value change for issued debt measured at fair value would be reported in P&L, followed by

(2) the portion of the fair value change due to own credit would be reversed out of P&L and reported in other comprehensive income

This own credit effect is currently required to be disclosed in the notes to the financial statements. However, the proposal would elevate this figure to the face of the income statement, but would subsequently exclude this amount from the calculation of profit or loss. All issued debt measured at fair value would continue to be measured at full fair value on the statement of financial position. No other changes are proposed to the accounting for financial liabilities.

Financial instruments with the characteristics of equity

IAS 32 provides the relevant guidance for distinguishing between asset and liability instruments (non-equity instruments) and equity instruments. The IASB is reviewing this guidance to address some practice issues, including eliminating current rules-based approaches, and to achieve convergence with US GAAP.

Following publication of a DP in February 2008 the IASB and US FASB decided to begin future deliberations using the principles underlying the perpetual and basic ownership approaches. They have developed a model where classification is based on the form of an instrument's settlement, assets (eg cash) or its own equity instruments (eg shares) as follows:

Test your understanding answers

Test your understanding 1 - Ashes

Financial asset	Classification
(1) Investments held for trading purposes	Financial assets at fair value through profit or loss
(2) Interest-bearing debt instruments that will be redeemed in five years; Ashes intends to collect the contractual cash flows which consist solely of repayments of interest and capital.	Debt instrument which passes both the business model test and the contractual cash flow characteristics test. It can be measured at amortised cost.
(3) A trade receivable	Debt instrument presumably held to collect cash flows due. This should pass both the business model test and the contractual cash flow characteristics test; it can be measured at amortised cost.
(4) Derivatives held for speculation purposes	Financial assets at fair value through profit or loss
(5) Equity shares that Ashes has no intention of selling	Financial assets at fair value through profit or loss, although it can be designated upon initial recognition to be be fair value through other comprehensive income.
(6) A convertible bond which is due to be converted into equity shares in three years time.	As the bond contains rights in addition to the repayment of interest and principal, the contractual cash flow characteristics test is failed; it cannot be measured at amortised cost. The financial asset as a whole must be measured at fair value through profit or loss.

These are financial liabilities to be measured at amortised cost.

Each financial liability is initially recorded at the fair value of the consideration received, i.e. the cash received. This amount is then increased each year to redemption by interest added at the effective rate and reduced by the interest actually paid, with the result that the carrying amount at the end of the first year is at amortised cost.

	Opening balance	Effective interest rate 10%	Payments	Closing balance
	$	$	$	$
D1 Year 1	10,000	1,000	Nil	11,000
Year 2	11,000	1,100	(12,100) (including $2,100 premium)	Nil
D2 Year 1	8,264 (10,000 – 1,736)	826	Nil	9,090
Year 2	9,090	910	(10,000) (no premium)	Nil
D3 Year 1	9,500 (10,000 – 500)	950	(200)	10,250
Year 2	10,250	1,025	(11,275) (including $200 interest and $1,075 premium)	Nil

Test your understanding 3 - Craig

Up to 31 December 20X8, the accounting entries are the same under both scenarios.

(1) Splitting the proceeds

The cash payments on the bond should be discounted to their present value using the interest rate for a bond without the conversion rights, i.e. 8%.

Date		Cash flow	Discount factor @ 15%	Present value
		$		$
31-Dec-X6	Interest	4,000	$1/1.08$	3,704
31-Dec-X7	Interest	4,000	$1/1.08^2$	3,429
31-Dec-X8	Interest and principal	104,000	$1/1.08^3$	82,559

Present value (the liability component)	A	89,692
As the net proceeds of issue were	B	100,000
So the equity component is	B – A	10,308

(2) The annual finance costs and year end carrying amounts

	Opening balance	Effective interest rate 8%	Payments 4%	Closing balance
	$	$	$	$
20X6	89,692	7,175	(4,000)	92,867
20X7	92,867	7,429	(4,000)	96,296
20X8	96,296	7,704	(4,000)	100,000

3a. **Conversion**

The carrying amounts at 31 December 20X8 are:

	$
Equity	10,308
Liability – bond	100,000
	———
	110,308
	———

If the conversion rights are exercised, then 50,000 ($100,000 ÷ 2) equity shares of $1 are issued and $60,308 is classified as share premium.

3b. **Redemption**

The carrying amounts at 31 December 20X8 are the same as under 3a. On redemption, the $100,000 liability is extinguished by cash payments. The equity component remains within equity, probably as a non-distributable reserve.

Test your understanding 4 - Ming

The principle at stake with derecognition or otherwise of receivables is whether, under the factoring arrangement, the risks and rewards of ownership pass from the trading company ie Ming. The principal risk with regard to receivables is the risk of bad debt.

In the first arrangement the $180,000 has been received as a one-off, non refundable sum. This is factoring without recourse for bad debts. The risk of bad debt has clearly passed from Ming to the factoring bank. Accordingly Ming should derecognise the receivable and there will be an expense of $20,000 recognised. No liability will be recognised.

In the second arrangement the $70,000 is simply a payment on account. More may be received by Ming implying that Ming retains an element of reward. The monies received are refundable in the event of default and as such represent an obligation. This means that the risk of slow payment and bad debt remains with Ming who is liable to repay the monies so far received. As such despite the passage of legal title the asset of receivable should remain recognised in the accounts of Ming. In substance Ming has borrowed $70,000 and this loan should be recognised immediately. This will increase the gearing of Ming.

Test your understanding 5 - Jones

(1) On purchase the investment is recorded at the consideration paid including, as the asset is classified as fair value through other comprehensive income, the associated transaction costs:

		$m
Dr	Asset	41
Cr	Cash	41

At the reporting date the asset is remeasured and the gain is recognised in other comprehensive income and taken to equity:

Dr	Asset	19
Cr	Other components of equity	19

On disposal, the asset is derecognised, the gain or loss on disposal is determined by comparing disposal proceeds and carrying value, with the result taken to profit or loss.

Dr	Cash	70
Cr	Asset	60
Cr	Profit	10

Note that the any gains or losses previously taken to equity are **not** recycled upon derecognition, although they may be reclassified within equity.

(2) If Jones had designated the investment as fair value through profit and loss, the transaction costs would have been recognised as an expense in profit or loss. So on purchase:

Dr	Asset	40m
Cr	Cash	40m
Dr	Expense	1m
Cr	Cash	1m

Subsequent measurement - at fair value through profit or loss:

Dr	Asset	20m
Cr	Profit	20m

On disposal the asset is derecognised with the gain taken to income

Dr	Cash	70
Cr	Asset	60
Cr	Profit	10

Note that the reported profit on derecognition of $10 million is the same, whether designated as fair value through profit or loss or fair value through other comprehensive income. This is one change brought about by IFRS 9 as recycling of gains and losses previously recognised in other comprehensive income is no longer done.

Test your understanding 6 - Harmison

Because the coupon and the effective interest rate are the same, the carrying amount of the principal will remain constant at $10,000.

On 1 January 20X6 the impairment loss is calculated as:

	$
Carrying amount	10,000
Recoverable amount (being the present value of the future cash flows discounted at the original effective interest rate:	
i.e. 4,000× 1/1.1)	3,636
	─────
Impairment loss	6,364
	─────

The impairment loss is recognised as an expense in profit or loss.

The asset will continue to be accounted for using amortised cost, based on the revised carrying amount of the loan. In the last year of the loan, the interest income of $364 (3,636 × 10%) will be recognised in profit or loss.

Test your understanding 7 - Hoggard

In all scenarios the cost of the derivative on 1 January 20X6 is $500 ($5 × 100) and an asset is recognised in the statement of financial position.

Dr	Asset - option	$500
Cr	Cash	$500

Outcome A

If the option is sold for $1,500 (100 × $15) before the exercise date, it is derecognised at a profit of $1,000.

Dr	Cash	$1,500
Cr	Asset - option	$500
Cr	Profit	$1,000

Outcome B

If the option lapses unexercised, then it is derecognised and there is a loss to be taken to profit or loss:

Dr	Expense	$500
Cr	Asset - option	$500

Outcome C

If the option is exercised, the option is derecognised, cash paid upon exercise and the investment in shares is recognised at fair value. An immediate profit is recognised:

Dr	Asset - investment (100 × $25)	$2,500
Cr	Cash 100 × $10)	$1,000
Cr	Asset - option	$500
Cr	Profit	$1,000

Test your understanding 8 - Strauss

This is a fair value hedge.

Normally the change in the value of an asset classified as fair value through other comprehensive income would be recognised as other comprehensive income, but because the asset is subject to a fair value hedge, it is recognised in profit or loss.

This is then matched with change in the value of the hedging instrument, which should have the opposite effect.

As the interest rate has increased to 9%, the value of the debt instrument will fall.

Its fair value will be (10m × 0.08) / 0.09 = $8.9m.

This gives a loss of $1.1m and is recognised in profit or loss:

Debit	Expense	$1.1m
Credit	Financial asset	$1.1m

Suppose that the fair value of the interest rate swap has increased by $1.1m.

As the swap is a derivative, it is measured at fair value with changes recognised in profit or loss.

Debit	Swap asset	$1.1m
Credit	Profit	$1.1m

The gains on the swap exactly offsets the loss on the debenture.

Test your understanding 9 - Brit

This is an example of a cash flow hedge. At its inception the forward contract has a cost, and fair value, of zero.

The cost of the materials is still €500,000 at the reporting date but this is now equivalent to $325,000, whereas the forward contract ensures that it will only cost the entity $320,000. Therefore the hedge has been completely effective. And therefore the entire change in the fair value of the hedging instrument, the forward contract, is recognised as other comprehensive income and recorded in a cash flow hedge reserve within other components of equity.

Debit	Forward contract	$5,000
Credit	Cash flow hedge reserve	$5,000

If the forward contract is then settled with no further changes in exchange rates, the forward contract will be settled for $320,000 cash and the materials valued at cost of $325,000.

The materials are purchased for €500,000 with a value of $325,000 and are recorded as:

Debit	Materials	$325,000
Credit	Cash	$320,000
Credit	Forward contract	$5,000

Because the cash flow hedge resulted in the recognition of materials (a non-financial asset), the gain of $5,000 held in the cash flow hedge reserve is dealt with as follows.

- It is immediately deducted from the $325,000 cost of the materials, to bring the carrying amount back to $320,000.

- It is recognised in profit or loss as the materials are charged to cost of sales.

Either way, the net cost of the materials in profit or loss over time is $320,000.

Test your understanding 10 - Grayton

This is a cash flow hedge.

Because the forward rate agreement has no fair value at its inception, the need to account for the derivative really first arises at the reporting date, when it has a value and the change in value has to be recorded.

Because it has been designated a cash flow hedge, the change in value is recognised as other comprehensive income and taken to a cash flow hedge reserve, to be carried forward to be matched against the future cash flow. The agreement is showing a loss of $10,000 at the reporting date because Grayton is locked into buying KR 200,000 for $100,000 when everyone else can buy them for $90,000.

In hindsight there was no need to have hedged, because the price of buying the foreign currency has come down, not gone up.

On 31 July, the derivative is recognised in the financial statements:

Dr Cash flow hedge reserve (other components of equity) $10,000
Cr Liability – derivative $10,000

(Had this not been designated a hedging instrument, the loss would have been recognised immediately in profit or loss.)

The forward contract will be settled and closed when the asset is purchased.

Although the loss on the derivative could be recognised in profit or loss as the plant is depreciated (effectively becoming additional depreciation), it will be more sensible for Grayton to use it to adjust the plant's carrying amount upwards on initial recognition (this has the same net effect over time).

This will result in the non-current asset being recognised at $100,000, which is what the hedging transaction was seeking to ensure.

Dr	Liability – derivative	$10,000
Dr	Plant	$90,000
Cr	Cash	$100,000
Dr	Plant	$10,000
Cr	Other components of equity	$10,000

Provisions

Chapter learning objectives

Upon completion of this chapter you will be able to:

- apply and discuss the recognition, derecognition and measurement of provisions, contingent liabilities and contingent assets including environmental provisions

- calculate and discuss the accrual of restructuring provisions

- apply and discuss accounting for events after the reporting date

- determine and report going concern issues arising after the reporting date

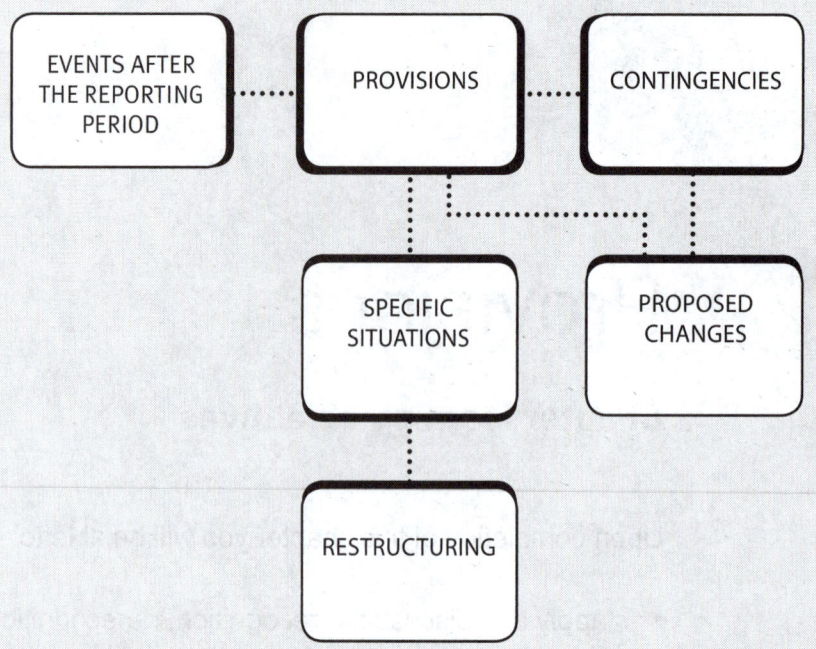

1 Provisions
Recognition

A **provision** is a liability of uncertain timing or amount.

A **liability** is a present obligation arising from past events, the settlement of which is expected to result in an outflow of economic benefits.

A provision can only be recognised if it meets the definition of a liability.

IAS 37 **Provisions, contingent liabilities and contingent assets** requires that a provision should be recognised when and only when:

* an entity has a present obligation (legal or constructive) as a result of a past event

* it is probable that a outflow of resources embodying economic benefits will be required to settle the obligation

* a reliable estimate can be made of the amount of the obligation.

An obligation is something that **cannot be avoided.**

* An entity has a **constructive obligation** if, by an established pattern of past practice, published policies or a sufficiently specific current statement, it has indicated to other parties that it will accept certain responsibilities; and as a result, it has created a valid expectation on the part of those other parties that it will discharge those responsibilities.

- A provision cannot be recognised unless there has been a past event, which is an **obligating event**. This is an event, which creates a legal, or constructive obligation and that results in an entity having no realistic alternative to settling that obligation. The obligating event is the past event that leads to the present obligation.

- An outflow of economic benefits is regarded as probable if it is **more likely than not** to occur.

- Where there are a number of similar obligations (for example product warranties), it is necessary to consider the class of obligations as a whole.

- Only in extremely rare cases is it impossible to make a reliable estimate of the amount of the obligation.

Derecognition

Provisions should be reviewed at the end of each reporting period.

- They should be reversed if it is no longer probable that an outflow of economic benefits will be required to settle the obligation.

- Provisions should be used only for expenditure that relates to the matter for which the provision was originally recognised.

Measurement

The amount recognised as a provision should be the best estimate of the expenditure required to settle the obligation that existed at the reporting date.

- The estimate should take into account:
    - risks and uncertainties associated with the cash flows
    - expected future events (for example, new technology or new legislation)
    - the time value of money, if it has a material effect.

- If the effect of the time value of money is material, then the provision should be discounted. The discount rate should be pre-tax and risk-specific.

- The unwinding of the discount is a finance cost, and it should be disclosed separately on the face of the statement of comprehensive income/income statement.

- Provisions should be reviewed at each reporting date and adjusted to reflect the current best estimate.

Expandable text - Provisions and 'creative accounting'

Before IAS 37 was issued, provisions were recognised on the basis of prudence. Little guidance was given as to when a provision should be recognised and how it should be measured. This gave rise to inconsistencies, and also allowed profits to be manipulated.

In particular, provisions could be created when profits were high and released when profits were low, in order to smooth reported results. This was common where an entity made an acquisition. The acquirer would create excessive provisions for the cost of integrating a new subsidiary's operations into the group. When the provisions were released, the profits reported by the group as a whole would be artificially inflated.

As well as disguising poor performance in a particular year, profit smoothing can also create an impression that profits are less volatile (and therefore less risky), than they really are. This tends to boost share prices.

IAS 37 prevents entities from recognising excessive provisions by focusing on the statement of financial position and applying the definitions and recognition criteria in the Framework for the preparation and presentation of financial statements. A provision cannot be recognised unless it represents a genuine liability.

Offset

Sometimes an entity may be able to recover the costs required to settle a provision. For example, it may have an insurance policy to cover the costs of a law suit. In general, the liability and the recovery should be treated as a separate liability and a separate asset. This is because the entity remains liable for the full amount, regardless of whether it can recover expenditure from a third party.

Amounts should only be offset where the reporting entity no longer has an obligation for that part of the expenditure to be met by the third party.

Expandable text - Contingent liabilities and contingent assets

Contingent liabilities

A **contingent liability** is

- a possible obligation that arises from past events and whose existence will be confirmed only by the outcome of one or more uncertain future events not wholly within the control of the entity

KAPLAN PUBLISHING

- a present obligation that arises from past events, but does not meet the criteria for recognition as a provision. This is either because an outflow of economic benefits is not probable; or (more rarely) because it is not possible to make a reliable estimate of the obligation.

A contingent liability should not be recognised.

- Instead, it should be disclosed, unless the possibility of a future outflow of economic benefits is remote.

- Contingent liabilities should be reviewed regularly. If an outflow of economic benefits becomes probable, then they must be reclassified as provisions.

Contingent assets

A **contingent asset** is a possible asset that arises from past events and whose existence will be confirmed only by the outcome of one or more uncertain future events, not wholly within the control of the entity.

A contingent asset should not be recognised.

- A contingent asset should be disclosed if the future inflow of economic benefits is probable.

- If the future inflow of benefits is virtually certain, then it ceases to be a contingent asset and should be recognised as a normal asset.

Summary

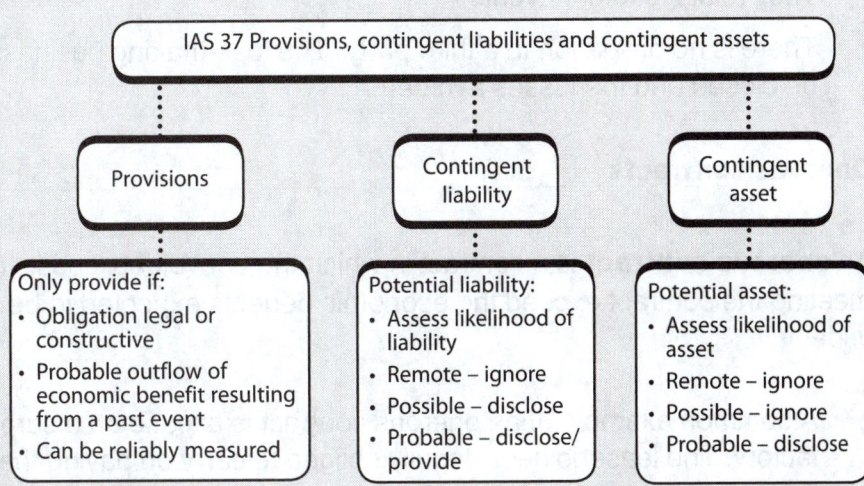

Expandable text - Problems in applying IAS 37

(a) Definition of contingent liability

The definition of a contingent liability gives particular problems, because 'possible' is not defined. However, IAS 37 says that 'probable' means 'more likely than not'. Because probable means 'more than 50% likely' it is reasonable to assume that 'possible' means 'less than 50% likely'.

Therefore, a contingent liability is often taken to be a liability whose existence is less than 50% likely or where the probability of an outflow of economic benefits is less than 50%.

(b) 'Virtually certain' and 'remote'

Contingent assets should be recognised if they are virtually certain and contingent liabilities should not be disclosed if they are remote. There is no definition of 'virtually certain' or 'remote'.

However, it is usually assumed that 'virtually certain' means more than 95% probable and 'remote' means less than 5% probable.

2 Specific situations

Future operating losses

In the past, provisions were recognised for future operating losses on the grounds of prudence. However, these should not be provided for the following reasons.

- They relate to future events.
- There is no obligation to a third party. The loss-making business could be closed and the losses avoided.

Onerous contracts

An **onerous contract** is a contract in which the unavoidable costs of meeting the contract exceed the economic benefits expected to be received under it.

- A common example of an onerous contract is a lease on a surplus factory. The leaseholder is legally obliged to carry on paying the rent on the factory, but they will not get any benefit from using the factory.

- If an entity has an onerous contract, a provision should be recognised for the present obligation under the contract. (The signing of the contract was the past event giving rise to the present obligation.)

- The provision is measured at the least net cost: the lower of the cost of fulfilling the contract or of terminating it and suffering any penalty payments.

- Some assets may have been bought specifically for use in fulfilling the onerous contract. These should be reviewed for impairment before any separate provision is made for the contract itself.

Expandable text - Illustration - specific situation

Droopers has recently bought all of the trade, assets and liabilities of Dolittle, an unincorporated business. As part of the takeover, all of the combined business's activities have been relocated to Droopers' main site. As a result Dolittle's premises are now empty and surplus to requirements.

Just before the acquisition, Dolittle had signed a three-year lease for its premises at $6,000 per month. At 31 December 20X3, this lease had 32 months left to run and the landlord had refused to terminate the lease. A sub-tenant has taken over part of the premises for the rest of the lease at a rent of $2,500 per month.

(a) Should Droopers recognise a provision for an onerous contract in respect of this lease?

(b) Show how this information will be presented in the financial statements for 20X3 and 20X4. Ignore the time value of money.

Expandable text - Solution

Despite not making any use of the premises, Droopers has a legal obligation to pay a further $192,000 ($6,000 × 32), to the landlord, as a result of a lease signed before the year-end (the obligating event). Therefore, an onerous contract exists and a provision must be recognised.

There is also an amount recoverable from the sub-tenant of $80,000 ($2,500 × 32). This is shown separately in the statement of financial position as an asset.

The $192,000 payable and the $80,000 recoverable can be netted off in the income statement.

Income statements	20X3	20X4
	$	$
Provision for onerous lease contract (net)	112,000 Dr	–
Statements of financial position		
Receivables		
Amounts recoverable from sub-tenants	80,000 Dr	50,000 Dr
Liabilities		
Amounts payable on onerous contracts	192,000 Cr	120,000 Cr

Future repairs to assets

Some assets need to be repaired or to have parts replaced every few years. For example, an airline may be required by law to overhaul all its aircraft every three years.

- Provisions cannot normally be recognised for the cost of future repairs or replacement parts.

- This is because the obligating event is the repair or purchase of the replacement part, which has not yet occurred.

- Even if the future expenditure is required by law, the entity has an alternative to incurring it; it could sell the asset.

- Instead, the expenditure should be capitalised and depreciated over its useful life (for example, the period until the next major overhaul is required).

Environmental provisions

Environmental provisions are often referred to as clean-up costs because they usually relate to the cost of decontaminating and restoring an industrial site, when production has ceased. The normal rules in IAS 37 apply.

- A provision is recognised if there is an obligation (legal or constructive) to repair environmental damage.

- Merely causing damage or intending to clean-up a site does not create an obligation.

- An entity may have a constructive obligation to repair environmental damage. This will be the case if (for example), an entity publicises policies that include environmental awareness or explicitly undertakes to clean up the damage caused by its operations.

There must have been a past obligating event. A provision can only be set up to rectify environmental damage that has **already happened.**

The **full cost** of an environmental provision should be recognised as soon as the obligation arises.

- Because it may be many years before the costs relating to the provision are paid out, the effect of the time value of money is usually material. Therefore, an environmental provision is normally discounted to its present value.

- If the expenditure results in future economic benefits an equivalent asset can be recognised. This is depreciated over its useful life, which is the same as the 'life' of the provision. (Note that IAS 37 is silent on whether an asset should be recognised at the same time as a provision. But IAS 16 **Property, plant and equipment** requires capitalisation of the provision if it relates to an item of property, etc.)

Expandable text - Illustration - specific situation

On 1 January 20X6, Scrubber paid the Government of Metallica $5m for a three-year licence to quarry gravel. At the end of the licence, Scrubber must restore the quarry to its natural state. This will cost a further $3m. These costs will be incurred on 1 January 20X9. Scrubber's cost of capital is 10%.

Explain how this expenditure is treated in the financial statements of Scrubber.

Expandable text - Solution

Scrubber has a legal obligation (the obligating event is the taking out of the licence). Therefore, it recognises a provision for $3m at 1 January 20X6. This provision is discounted to its present value.

Each year, the discount unwinds and the provision increases. The unwinding of the discount is charged to profit as a finance cost.

Movement on provision	20X6	20X7	20X8	20X9
	$000	$000	$000	$000
Opening balance	2,253	2,478	2,727	3,000
Finance cost at 10%	225	249	273	–
Release to profit	–	–	–	(3,000)
Closing balance	2,478	2,727	3,000	–

Scrubber could not carry out its quarrying operation without incurring the clean-up costs. Therefore, incurring the costs gives it access to future economic benefits. It includes the additional expenditure in the cost of the licence and recognises this as an asset. The licence is depreciated over the three years.

Cost of licence	$000
Cash paid 1 January 20X6	5,000
Present value of clean-up costs 1 January 20X9	2,253
Total	7,253

The effect on the financial statements is shown below:

Income statement	20X6	20X7	20X8	20X9
	$000	$000	$000	$000
Operating costs				
Depreciation (over 3 years)	2,418	2,418	2,417	–
Finance costs				
Unwinding of discount	225	249	273	–

Statement of financial position	$000	$000	$000	$000
	20X6	20X7	20X8	20X9
Non-current assets				
Licence: Cost	7,253	7,253	7,253	–
Depreciation	(2,418)	(4,836)	(7,253)	–
Carrying value	4,835	2,417	–	–
Liabilities				
Clean-up provision	2,478	2,727	3,000	–

Test your understanding 1 - Situations

For each of the situations below, state whether a provision should be recognised.

(a) An entity has a policy of only carrying out work to rectify damage cause to the environment when it is required by local law so to do. For several years the entity has been operating an oil rig which causes such damage, in a country that did not have legislation in place, that required such rectification.

A new government has been elected in that country and at the reporting date, it is virtually certain the legislation will be enacted, that will require damage rectification; this legislation will have retrospective effect.

(b) Under a licence granted by a local government, an entity has constructed a rock-crushing plant to process material mined from the surrounding area. Mining activities have already started. Under the terms of the licence, the entity must remove the rock-crushing plant when mining activities have been completed and must landscape the mined area, so as to create a national park.

3 Restructuring provisions
Definition

A **restructuring** is a programme that is planned and controlled by management and has a material effect on:

- the scope of a business undertaken by the reporting entity in terms of the products or services it provides
- the manner in which a business undertaken by the reporting entity is conducted.

A restructuring could include:

- sale or termination of a line of business
- the closure of business locations in a country or region or the relocation of business activities from one country or region to another
- changes in management structure, for example, eliminating a layer of management
- fundamental reorganisations that have a material effect on the nature and focus of the entity's operations.

When can a provision be recognised?

Before IAS 37 was issued, entities would often set up unnecessary 'restructuring provisions' that could then be used for profit smoothing in later periods. IAS 37 has prohibited this.

A restructuring provision can only be recognised where an entity has a **constructive obligation** to carry out the restructuring.

A constructive obligation exists **only** if:

- there is a detailed formal plan for restructuring. This must identify the businesses, locations and employees affected

- those affected have a valid expectation that the restructuring will be carried out. For example, the plan is already being implemented or it has been announced to those affected by it

- the constructive obligation must exist at the year-end. (An obligation arising after the year-end may require disclosure under IAS 10 **Events after the reporting period** as a non-adjusting event after the reporting date.)

- a board decision alone does not create a constructive obligation unless:
  - the plan is already being implemented. For example, assets are being sold, redundancy negotiations have begun
  - the plan has been announced to those affected by it. The plan must have a strict timeframe without unreasonable delays
  - the board itself contains representatives of employees or other groups affected by the decision. (This is common in mainland Europe.)

- an announcement to sell an operation does not create a constructive obligation. An obligation only exists when a purchaser is found and there is a binding sale agreement.

Accruing a provision

A restructuring provision should only include the direct costs of restructuring. These must be both:

- necessarily entailed by the restructuring
- not associated with the ongoing activities of the entity.

The following costs relate to future events and therefore, must **not** be included:

- retraining or relocating staff
- marketing
- investment in new systems and distribution networks
- future operating losses (unless these arise from an onerous contract)
- profits on disposal of assets (but losses on disposal may need to be included as a restructuring may trigger an impairment review under IAS 36)

The amount recognised should be the best estimate of the expenditure required and it should take into account expected future events. This means that expenses should be measured at their actual cost, where this is known, even if this was only discovered after the reporting date (this is an adjusting event after the reporting date per IAS 10).

Illustration 1 – Restructuring provisions

On 15 January 20X5, the Board of Directors of Shane voted to proceed with two reorganisation schemes involving the closure of two factories. Shane's financial year-end is 31 March, and the financial statements will be finalised and published on 30 June.

Scheme 1

The closure costs will amount to $125,000. The factory is rented on a short-term lease, and there will be no gains or losses arising on this property. The closure will be announced in June, and will commence in August.

Scheme 2

The costs will amount to $45,000 (after crediting $105,000 profit on disposal of certain machines). The closure will take place in July, but redundancy negotiations began with the staff in March.

For each of the two schemes:

(a) Should a provision be recognised?

(b) If so, what is the amount of the provision?

Expandable text - Solution

Scheme 1. The obligating event is the announcement of the plan, which occurs in June. This is after the year-end, so there can be no provision. However, the announcement in June should be disclosed as a non-adjusting event after the reporting date.

Scheme 2. Although the closure will not begin until July, the employees will have had a valid expectation that it would happen when the redundancy negotiations began in March. Therefore, a provision should be recognised. The provision will be for $150,000 because the expected profit on disposal cannot be netted off against the expected costs.

Test your understanding 2 - Delta

On 30 June 20X2, the directors of Delta decided to close down a division. This decision was announced to the employees affected on 15 July 20X2 and the actual closure occurred on 31 August 20X2, prior to the 20X2 financial statements being authorised for issue.

Expenses and other items connected with the closure were as follows:

	$m
Redundancy costs (estimated)	22
Staff retraining (actual)	10
Operating loss for the 2 months to 31 August 20X2 (estimated at 30 June)	12
Profit on sale of property	5

The actual redundancy costs were $20 million and the actual operating loss for the two months to 31 August 20X2, was $15 million.

What is the amount of the restructuring provision to be recognised in the financial statements of Delta plc, for the year ended 31 July 20X2?

Test your understanding 3 - Repairs

A company has a year end of 31 December 20X7 and intends to repair an item of plant next year. The cost has been reliably estimated at the year-end as $10,000. The repair is made in February 20X8 in the period after the reporting date at a cost $12,000.

What provision (if any) should be recognised in the statement of financial position in the year ended 20X7?

Test your understanding 4 - Smoke filters

Under new legislation, an entity is required to fit smoke filters to its factories by 31 December 20X7. The entity has not fitted the smoke filters. The balance sheet date is 30 June 20X7.

Should a provision be made at the yearend for the estimated cost of fitting the filter?

Test your understanding 5 - Guarantee

An entity sells domestic appliances such as washing machines. These goods retail at $500 each and are sold with a one year guarantee. Under the terms of the guarantee if the machine needs to be repaired then the company will do so at no charge to the customer. In the company's experience 20% of machines sold do require some form of repair at an average cost of $50. The company has sold 200 machines. You may assume that the repairs are performed one year after the sale and that the relevant discount rate is 10%.

Required:
Calculate any provision required that arises under the guarantee.

Test your understanding 6 - Oil rig

An oil company has erected an oil rig in the North Sea. The installation costs are $50 million and the cost of construction $400 million. It is also estimated that it will cost $200 million to dismantle in twenty years time

When (if ever) should a provision be made for the decommissioning costs and what would any relevant accounting entries be?

Expandable text - Current issues: provisions & contingencies

Liabilities - amendments to IAS 37

IAS 37 addresses liabilities of uncertain timing or amount that are not within the scope of another standard. The objective of this project is to develop a new IFRS to replace IAS 37.

The proposed new IFRS would:

* align of the requirements for recording costs of restructuring activities with those in US GAAP

* align the criteria for recording liabilities with the criteria in other IFRSs

* provide more specific requirements on measuring the liabilities within its scope.

In June 2005, the Board published an ED of the proposed amendments to IAS 37, and in January 2010 a second ED was published, setting out proposed new measurement guidance.

The revised ED proposes that the measurement should be the amount that the entity would rationally pay at the measurement date to be relieved of the liability. Normally, this amount would be an estimate of the present value of the resources required to fulfil the liability. The estimate would take into account the expected outflows of resources, the time value of money and the risk that the actual outflows might ultimately differ from the expected outflows. For example:

* If the liability is to pay cash to a counterparty (for example to settle a legal dispute), the outflows would be the expected cash payments plus any associated costs, such as legal fees.

* If the liability is to undertake a service—for example to decommission plant—at a future date, the outflows would be the amounts that the entity estimates it would pay a contractor at the future date to undertake the service on its behalf.

As at August 2010, the expectation is that a new reporting standard will be issued in 2011.

Expandable text - Events after the reporting date IAS 10 -

Definition

Events after the reporting period are those events, both favourable and unfavourable, that occur between the reporting date and the date on which the financial statements are authorised for issue.

There are two types of event:

- adjusting events
- non-adjusting events.

Financial statements are prepared on the basis of conditions existing at the reporting date.

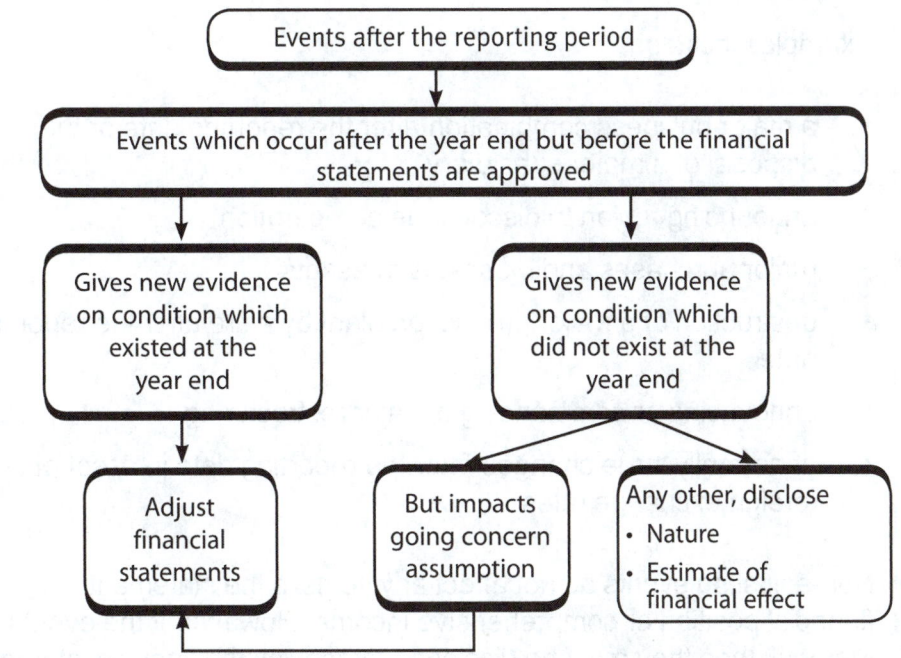

Expandable text - Further detail

Adjusting events

Adjusting events provide evidence of conditions that existed at the reporting date.

Examples include:

- the sale of inventory after the reporting date which gives evidence about its net realisable value at the reporting date

- the bankruptcy of a customer after the reporting date that confirms that an allowance is required against an outstanding balance at the reporting date
- the discovery of fraud or errors that show that the financial statements are incorrect
- the settlement after the reporting period of a court case that confirms that the entity had a present obligation at the reporting date. This would require a provision to be recognised in the financial statements (or an existing provision to be adjusted).

Adjusting events result in changes to the figures recognised in the financial statements.

Non-adjusting events

Non-adjusting events are those that are indicative of conditions that arose after the reporting period.

Examples include:

- a major business combination after the reporting date or the disposal of a major subsidiary
- announcing a plan to discontinue an operation
- major purchases and disposals of assets
- destruction of a major production plant by a fire after the reporting date
- announcing or commencing a major restructuring
- abnormally large changes after the reporting date in asset prices or foreign exchange rates.

Non-adjusting events do not affect any items in the statements of financial position or comprehensive income. However, if the events are material, then they must be disclosed, otherwise the financial statements could be misleading.

- The following should be disclosed for material non-adjusting events:
  - the nature of the event
  - an estimate of the financial effect, or a statement that such an estimate cannot be made.

- Equity dividends declared or proposed after the year-end are not a liability at the year-end (because no obligation to pay a dividend exists at that time). They should be disclosed in a note to the financial statements. This is a non-adjusting event.

KAPLAN PUBLISHING

Date of authorisation for issue

The date when the financial statements were authorised for issue, and who gave that authorisation, should be disclosed in the financial statements.

- If the entity's owners or others have the power to amend the financial statements after issue, this must also be disclosed.

- It is important that the authorisation date is disclosed as the financial statements do not reflect events occurring after this date.

Expandable text - Problems with events after the reporting date

(a) 'Window dressing'

Window dressing is the practice of entering into certain transactions before the year-end and reversing those transactions after the year-end. The objective of window dressing a set of accounts is to artificially improve the view given by the accounts. Management may have a particular incentive to enter into window dressing transactions, where there is a need to boost year-end profitability and liquidity (for example, where loan agreements specify that the current ratio should not fall below a certain level, or where directors' remuneration depends upon meeting certain targets).

Typical examples include.

- Obtaining a long-term loan before the year-end on the understanding that it will be repaid soon after the year-end. This will boost the current ratio at the year-end.
- Selling goods before the year-end on the understanding that they will be returned (and a credit note raised) after the year-end. This will boost the profits for the year.

IAS 10 does not refer to window dressing. Some have argued that disclosure of window dressing should be explicitly required. If IAS 10 is applied correctly, users of the financial statements should be made aware of any unusual transactions that reverse after the year-end. In addition, IAS 1 and the Framework require that entities report the substance of their transactions, rather than the strict legal form.

(b) Adjusting or non-adjusting?

Sometimes it can be difficult to determine whether an event took place before the reporting date or whether or not it provides evidence of conditions existing at the reporting date.

For example, suppose that a non-current asset is valued shortly after the year-end and this valuation reveals a significant fall in value. It is probably reasonable to assume that the fall in value occurred over a period of several months beforehand. The loss would then be an adjusting event. However, there may be evidence that the fall in value occurred after the year-end (perhaps as a result of a particular event). It is important to look at all the circumstances surrounding an event after the reporting period.

Expandable text - IAS 10 question

The following events have occurred after the reporting period.

	Adjusting	Non-adjusting

(i) Insolvency of a customer at the year-end.

(ii) Uninsured loss of inventory in a fire.

(iii) Detailed public announcement of any redundancies that had been decided by the board prior to the year-end.

(iv) Proposal of a final equity dividend.

(v) Change in foreign exchange rates.

Identify whether they are adjusting or non-adjusting.

Expandable text - IAS 10 solution

(i) Adjusting.

(ii) Non-adjusting.

(iii) Non-adjusting.

(iv) Non-adjusting.

(v) Non-adjusting.

Going concern issues arising after the reporting date

There is one important exception to the normal rule that the financial statements reflect conditions at the reporting date. If, after the reporting date, management decides to liquidate the entity or cease trading (or decides that it has no realistic alternative to these actions), the financial statements cannot be prepared on a going concern basis.

- If operating results and financial position have deteriorated since the reporting date, management may need to assess whether the going concern assumption is still appropriate.

- If the going concern assumption is no longer appropriate, the effect is so pervasive that there must be a fundamental change in the basis of accounting.

- If the financial statements are not prepared on a going concern basis, that fact must be disclosed (IAS 1).

- Management must also disclose any material uncertainties relating to events or conditions that cast significant doubt upon an entity's ability to continue trading. This applies if the events have arisen since the reporting period (IAS 1).

Expandable text - Going concern considerations

IAS 1 states that management should assess whether the going concern assumption is appropriate. In many cases, it will be obvious that the entity is a going concern and no detailed analysis is necessary.

Where there is uncertainty, management should consider all available information about the future, including current and expected profitability, debt repayment finance and potential sources of alternative finance. If there is greater doubt or uncertainty, then more work will be required to evaluate whether or not the entity can be regarded as a going concern. Here, 'the future' means at least twelve months from the reporting date.

Expandable text - Current issues

Replacement of IAS 37

IAS 37 addresses liabilities of uncertain timing or amount that are not within the scope of another standard. The objective of this project is to develop a new IFRS to replace IAS 37.

The proposed new IFRS would:

* align of the requirements for recording costs of restructuring activities with those in US GAAP
  align the criteria for recording liabilities with the criteria in other IFRSs
  provide more specific requirements on measuring the liabilities within its scope

In June 2005, the IASB published an ED of the proposed amendments to IAS 37 and. following feedback on the proposals, has tentatively decided to change some of the proposals in the light of comments received. Specifically, the IASB has decided to provide more guidance on applying the proposed measurement requirements. In January 2010 it published a second ED, setting out the proposed new measurement guidance. Work to date has consisted of focussing upon the following issues:

* how the criteria for recording liabilities proposed in the working draft IFRS differ from those in the existing IAS 37

* how the new criteria would apply to liabilities arising from lawsuits, and

* why the IASB is changing the criteria

Expandable text - UK syllabus focus

The ACCA UK syllabus contains a requirement that candidates should be able to discuss and apply the key differences between UK GAAP and IFRS GAAP. The accounting requirements of UK GAAP and IFRS GAAP are very similar in this area; the key issues associated with UK reporting standard requirements are as follows:

UK reporting standards FRS 12 and FRS 21 deal with accounting for provisions and post-balance sheet events respectively. There are no significant differences in the definitions and accounting treatments identified within the UK reporting standards and their international equivalents, IAS 37 and IAS 10 respectively.

4 Chapter summary

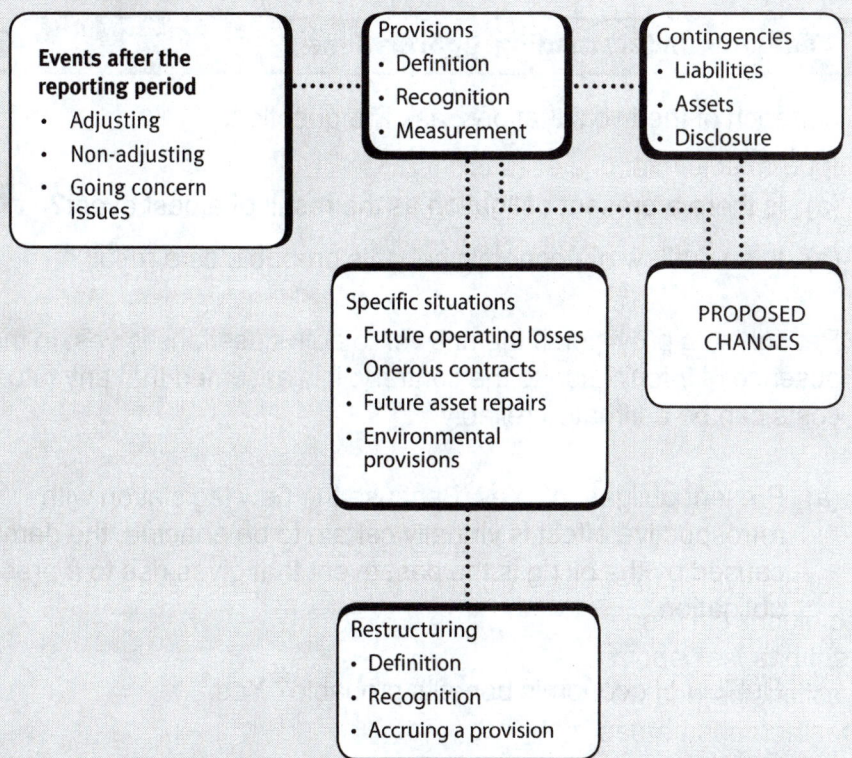

Test your understanding answers

Test your understanding 1 - Situations

For each of the two situations, ask two questions.

(a) Is there a present obligation as the result of a past event?

(b) Is an outflow of economic benefits probable as a result?

Recognise a provision if the answer to both questions is yes. In the absence of information to the contrary, it is assumed that any future costs can be estimated reliably.

(a) Present obligation? Yes. Because the new legislation with retrospective effect is virtually certain to be enacted, the damage caused by the oil rig is the past event that gives rise to a present obligation.

Outflow of economic benefits probable? Yes.

Conclusion – Recognise a provision.

(b) Present obligation? Yes. There is a legal obligation under the licence to remove the rock-crushing plant and to make good damage caused by the mining activities to date (but not any that may be caused by these activities in the future, because mining activities could be stopped and no such damage caused).

Outflow of economic benefits probable? Yes.

Conclusion – Recognise a provision for the best estimate of the eventual costs of rectifying the damage caused up to the reporting date.

Test your understanding 2 - Delta

The only item which can be included in the provision is the redundancy costs, measured at their actual amount of $20 million.

IAS 37 prohibits the recognition of future operating losses, staff retraining and profits on disposals of assets.

Test your understanding 3 - Repairs

The standard clearly states that no provision should be made for future repairs despite it being probable and capable of being reliably measured. There has been no relevant past event and there is no obligation at the yearend. Repair expenditure has to be expensed as incurred.

Test your understanding 4 - Smoke filters

No provision should be made for this future expenditure despite it being probable and capable of being reliably measured. There has been no relevant past event and there is no obligation at the year end.

Test your understanding 5 - Guarantee

A provision is required. The relevant past event creating the present obligation to repair the machines is the sale. The liability can be measured with reliability, using expected values and discounting as follows.

$50 repair cost x 200 machines x 20% expected value x 0.909 discount factor = $1,818

Test your understanding 6 - Oil rig

A provision is only required if either there is a legal obligation (e.g. the licences granting permission to drill contains a requirement to dismantle the rig) or a constructive obligation (e.g. the company has published suitable and detailed environmental policies). The decommissioning costs should be provided for in full and measured at present value to reflect the time value of money. The provision is capitalised as an asset and then subject to amortisation.

Tax

Chapter learning objectives

Upon completion of this chapter you will be able to:

- apply and discuss the recognition and measurement of deferred tax liabilities and deferred tax assets including the exceptions to recognition

- determine the recognition of tax expense or income and its inclusion in the financial statements.

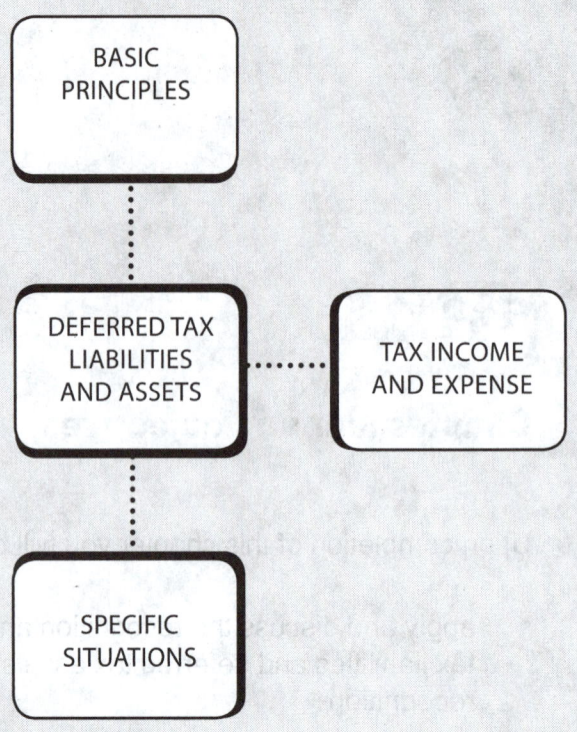

1 Basic principles of deferred tax

The need to provide for deferred tax

Taxable profits are nearly always different from accounting profits. Some differences are permanent; for example, fines, political donations and entertainment are normally disallowed for tax purposes. These items do not give rise to deferred tax. Some differences are temporary; for example, interest received and paid is normally taxed on a cash basis, whereas it is accounted for on an accruals basis.

- Temporary differences often mean that there is a delay between profits being reported for accounting purposes and tax being charged on those profits.

- They may also mean that tax is payable before profits are reported for accounting purposes.

- The tax effects of transactions should be reported in the same accounting period as the transactions themselves.

- As a result, there is a need to recognise a deferred tax liability or a deferred tax asset.

A **temporary difference** is the difference between the carrying amount of an asset or liability and its tax base.

The **tax base** is the amount attributed to an asset or liability for tax purposes.

- The most common example of a temporary difference relates to non-current assets. These attract tax relief (capital allowances or tax depreciation) at a different rate from the rate at which depreciation is charged to profits.

- Where there have been accelerated capital allowances, the carrying amount of the asset exceeds the tax base. This difference is the temporary difference on which deferred tax is provided.

Deferred tax is provided for on temporary differences in full, i.e. without any discounting.

Calculating a deferred tax liability

If tax allowances exceed the financial statements deductions, the net temporary differences at the yearend are multiplied by the current rate of tax. The result is the liability for deferred tax that is recognised in the statement of financial position.

The charge (or credit) to income is the difference between the deferred tax liability at the beginning of the year and the deferred tax liability at the end of the year.

Illustration 1 – Basic principles of deferred tax

Prudent prepares financial statements to 31 December each year. On 1 January 20X0, the entity purchased a non-current asset for $1.6 million that had an anticipated useful life of four years. This asset qualified for immediate tax relief of 100% of the cost of the asset.

For the year ending 31 December 20X0, the draft accounts showed a profit before tax of $2 million. The directors anticipate that this level of profit will be maintained for the foreseeable future.

Prudent pays tax at a rate of 30%. Apart from the differences caused by the purchase of the non-current asset in 20X0, there are no other differences between accounting profit and taxable profit or the tax base and carrying amount of net assets.

You are required to compute the pre, and post-tax profits for Prudent for each of the four years ending 31 December 20X0–20X3 inclusive and for the period as a whole assuming:

(a) that no deferred tax is recognised

(b) that deferred tax is recognised.

Expandable text - Solution

No deferred tax

First of all, it is necessary to compute the taxable profits of Prudent for each period and the current tax payable:

	Year ended 31 December				Total
	20X0	20X1	20X2	20X3	
	$000	$000	$000	$000	$000
Accounting profit	2,000	2,000	2,000	2,000	8,000
Add back Depreciation	400	400	400	400	1,600
Deduct Capital allowances	(1,600)	–	–	–	(1,600)
Taxable profits	800	2,400	2,400	2,400	8,000
Current tax at 30%	240	720	720	720	2,400

The differences between the accounting profit and the taxable profit that occur from one year to another, cancel out over the four years as a whole.

The income statements for each period and for the four years as a whole, are given below:

	Year ended 31 December				Total
	20X0	20X1	20X2	20X3	
	$000	$000	$000	$000	$000
Profit before tax	2,000	2,000	2,000	2,000	8,000
Current tax at 30%	(240)	(720)	(720)	(720)	(2,400)
Profit after tax	1,760	1,280	1,280	1,280	5,600

Ignoring deferred tax produces a performance profile that suggests a declining performance between 20X0 and 20X1.

In fact the decline in profits is caused by the timing of the current tax charge on them.

In 20X0, some of the accounting profit escapes tax, but the tax is only postponed until 20X1, 20X2 and 20X3, when the taxable profit is more than the accounting profit.

Deferred tax is recognised

The deferred tax figures that are required in the statement of financial position are given below:

	Year ended 31 December			
	20X0	20X1	20X2	20X3
	$000	$000	$000	$000
Carrying amount	1,200	800	400	Nil
Tax base	Nil	Nil	Nil	Nil
Temporary difference at year end	1,200	800	400	Nil
Closing deferred tax liability (30%)	360	240	120	Nil
Opening deferred tax liability	Nil	(360)	(240)	(120)
So charge/(credit) to income	360	(120)	(120)	(120)

The income statements for the four year period including deferred tax are shown below:

	Year ended 31 December				Total
	20X0	20X1	20X2	20X3	
	$000	$000	$000	$000	$000
Profit before tax	2,000	2,000	2,000	2,000	8,000
Current tax	(240)	(720)	(720)	(720)	(2,400)
Deferred tax	(360)	120	120	120	Nil
Profit after tax	1,400	1,400	1,400	1,400	5,600

A more meaningful performance profile is presented.

Expandable text - Reasons for recognising deferred tax

If a deferred tax liability is ignored, profits are inflated and the obligation to pay an increased amount of tax in the future is also ignored. The arguments for recognising deferred tax are summarised below.

- The accruals concept requires tax to be matched to profits as they are earned.
- The deferred tax will eventually become an actual tax liability.
- Ignoring deferred tax overstates profits, which may result in:
  - over-optimistic dividend payments based on inflated profits
  - distortion of earnings per share and of the price/earnings ratio, both important indicators of an entity's performance
  - shareholders being misled.

Methods of accounting for deferred tax

There are two main methods of accounting for deferred tax – the deferral method and the liability method. The liability method may be subdivided into two – the income statement liability method and the balance sheet liability method.

(a) The deferral method

Under the deferral method, the original amount set aside for deferred tax is retained without alteration for subsequent changes in tax rate.

The deferral method does not keep the deferred tax amount up to date as tax rates change, and is thus generally held to be inferior to the liability method.

(b) The liability method

Using the liability method, the deferred tax balance is adjusted as tax rates change, thus maintaining the amount at the actual liability expected to arise.

(c) **The income statement liability method and the balance sheet liability method**

The difference between these two methods is largely conceptual. The deferred tax figure will be the same. The income statement liability method focuses on the differences between taxable profit and accounting profit (timing differences), while under the balance sheet method the calculation is made by reference to differences between statement of financial position (balance sheet) values and tax values of assets and liabilities (temporary differences).

IAS 12 requires the use of the balance sheet liability method.

Examples of temporary differences

Examples of temporary differences include (but are not restricted to).

- Tax deductions for the cost of non-current assets that have a different pattern to the write-off of the asset in the financial statements, i.e. accelerated capital allowances.

- Pension liabilities that are accrued in the financial statements, but are allowed for tax only when the contributions are made to the pension fund at a later date.

- Intra-group profits in inventory that are unrealised for consolidation purposes yet taxable in the computation of the group entity that made the unrealised profit.

- A loss is reported in the financial statements and the related tax relief is only available by carry forward against future taxable profits.

- Assets are revalued upwards in the financial statements, but no adjustment is made for tax purposes.

- Development costs are capitalised and amortised to profit or loss in future periods, but were deducted for tax purposes as incurred.

- The cost of granting share options to employees is recognised in profit or loss, but no tax deduction is obtained until the options are exercised.

Calculating temporary differences

Deferred tax is calculated by reference to the tax base of an asset or liability. The tax base is the amount attributed to the asset or liability for tax purposes.

If the carrying amount of an asset exceeds the tax base, deferred tax must be provided for, and the temporary difference is said to be a **taxable** temporary difference (a liability).

If the tax base of an asset exceeds the carrying amount, the temporary difference is a **deductible** temporary difference (an asset).

Test your understanding 1 - Dive

An entity, Dive, provides the following information regarding its assets and liabilities.

ASSETS	Carrying amount	Tax base	Temporary difference
Machine cost $100,000 with depreciation to date $18,000 and capital allowances of $30,000			
Interest receivable in the statement of financial position is $1,000. The interest will be taxed when received.			
Trade receivables have a carrying amount of $10,000. The revenue has already been included in taxable profit.			
An entity writes down its inventory by $500 to a net realisable value of $4,500. The reduction is ignored for tax purposes until the inventory is sold.			
LIABILITIES			
Current liabilities include accrued expenses of $1,000. This is deductible for tax on a cash paid basis.			
Accrued expenses have a carrying amount of $5,000. The related expense has been deducted for tax purposes.			

Required:

Complete the following table to identify carrying amount, tax base and temporary difference for each of the assets and liabilities.

2 Deferred tax liabilities and assets
Recognition

IAS 12 Income taxes states that deferred tax liabilities should be provided on all taxable temporary differences, unless the deferred tax liability arises from:

- goodwill, for which amortisation is not tax deductible

- the initial recognition of an asset or liability in a transaction, which is not a business combination, and at the time of the transaction affects neither accounting profit nor taxable profit. An example is expenditure on a finite life intangible asset, which attracts no tax allowances. Accounting profit is only affected after the transaction (by subsequent amortisation), while taxable profit is never affected.

Deferred tax assets should be recognised on all deductible temporary differences unless the exceptions above also apply, provided that taxable profit will be available against which the deductible temporary difference can be utilised.

- It is appropriate to offset deferred tax assets and liabilities when presenting them in the statement of financial position as long as:
    - the entity has a legally enforceable right to set off **current** tax assets and **current** tax liabilities

    - the deferred tax assets and liabilities relate to tax levied by the same tax authority on either, the same taxable entity or different taxable entities, which settle **current** tax balances on a net basis.

Expandable text - Conceptual basis for recognition of deferred tax

The central principle behind accounting for deferred tax is that financial statements for a period should recognise the tax effects, whether current or deferred, of all transactions occurring in that period.

IAS 12 adopts the 'temporary difference' approach. Temporary differences are the differences between the carrying amounts of the assets and liabilities in the statement of financial position at the end of the period and the amounts that will actually be taxable or recoverable in respect of these assets and liabilities in the future. The temporary difference approach looks at the tax that would be payable, if the assets and liabilities were realised for the amounts at which they are stated in the statement of financial position. The reasoning behind this is that assets eventually generate cash flows at least equal to their carrying amount. The tax payable/receivable on these cash flows is a liability/asset of the entity and should be recognised.

The temporary difference approach focuses on the statement of financial position. The deferred tax charge (or credit) for the period, is the movement between the tax liability at the beginning of the period and the tax liability at the end of the period.

Temporary differences are similar to valuation adjustments, even though they may not be liabilities in their own right. A deferred tax liability is recognised in respect of accelerated capital allowances on a non-current asset, because that asset is carried at less than an otherwise equivalent asset that is still fully tax-deductible.

Problems with the temporary differences approach

Identifying and measuring temporary differences can be difficult in practice. For example, differences can arise where the financial statements of an overseas subsidiary are consolidated. These can be difficult to quantify, because some assets are eliminated on consolidation and others may or may not be taxable.

A more important disadvantage is that many believe that the 'temporary difference' approach is conceptually wrong. The framework for the preparation and presentation of financial statements defines a liability as an obligation to transfer economic benefits, as the result of a past event. In practice, a liability for deferred tax is often recognised before the entity actually has an obligation to pay the tax.

For example, suppose that an entity revalues a non-current asset and recognises a gain. It will not be liable for tax on the gain until the asset is sold. However, IAS 12 requires that deferred tax is recognised immediately on the revaluation gain, even if the entity has no intention of selling the asset (and realising the gain) for several years.

As a result, the IAS 12 approach could lead to the build-up of liabilities that may only crystallise in the distant future, if ever.

An important exception to the normal rule

In theory, a temporary difference arises as soon as an asset or a liability is recognised.

For example, say an entity acquires an asset for $100. This asset is subject to tax at 30%, but depreciation will not be allowable for tax. The asset's carrying amount is $100 and its tax base is nil and therefore, a deferred tax liability of $30 should be recognised.

However, this would effectively reduce the carrying amount of the asset in the financial statements. This is misleading. The entity would not have acquired the asset if its value had been less than its cost. To make the financial statements meaningful, the asset should still be recognised at its cost of $100.

For this reason, IAS 12 states that deferred tax liabilities and assets are not recognised if they result from the initial recognition of an asset or liability, which at the time of the transaction affects neither taxable nor accounting profit.

Timing differences: the alternative

An alternative approach to recognising deferred tax, focuses on timing differences rather than temporary differences.

Timing differences arise because some gains and losses are recognised in the financial statements in different accounting periods, from those in which they are assessed to tax. This results in differences between an entity's reported profit in the financial statements and its taxable profit. Timing differences originate in one period and may reverse in one or more subsequent periods.

The timing differences approach, focuses on profit and loss for the period and on the actual tax expense. It is normally simpler to apply than the temporary differences approach, as it is usually easy to identify timing differences from tax computations.

It is possible to argue that, like temporary differences, timing differences are a form of valuation adjustment. However, it is much more usual to think of timing differences as **incremental liabilities**.

Under the incremental liability approach, timing differences are recognised only if they represent rights or obligations at the reporting date, that is, only if the critical events that will cause their future reversal, have occurred by the reporting date. In other words, deferred tax is only recognised where it represents an asset or a liability in its own right.

For example, if an entity has capital allowances in excess of depreciation, it has an obligation to pay more tax in future. It cannot avoid this obligation. Therefore, it has a liability. In contrast, if an entity revalues a non-current asset, it will not have an obligation to pay more tax unless it enters into a binding agreement to sell the asset. Therefore, it does not have a liability and deferred tax is not provided.

Measurement

The tax rate in force (or expected to be in force) when the asset is realised or the liability is settled, should be used to calculated deferred tax.

- This rate must be based on tax rates and legislation that has been enacted or substantively enacted by the reporting date.

- Deferred tax assets and liabilities should not be discounted to present value.

Test your understanding 2 - Drown

An entity, Drown, has the following temporary differences:

	Start of year $000	End of year $000
Accelerated capital allowances	400	900
General provisions (disallowed for tax)	Nil	50
Accrued pension liabilities (tax relief is given on a cash basis)	60	40
Provision for unrealised profits	Nil	10
Loss relief being carried forward	Nil	100

Required:

Calculate the deferred tax charge for the year given a tax rate of 30%.

3 Specific situations

Revaluations

Deferred tax should be recognised on revaluation gains even if:

- there is no intention to sell the asset

- any tax due on the gain made on any sale of the asset can be deferred by being 'rolled over' against the cost of a replacement asset.

Test your understanding 3 - Dodge

An entity, Dodge, owns a non-current asset which cost $100,000 when purchased and depreciation totalling $40,000, has been charged up to the reporting date – 31 March 20X1. The entity has claimed total tax allowances on the asset of $50,000. On 31 March 20X1, the asset is revalued to $90,000. Assume that the tax rate is 30%.

Required:

Explain the deferred tax implications of this situation.

Share option schemes

Accounting for share option schemes involves recognising a remuneration expense in the income statement throughout the vesting period. However, tax relief is normally granted at a later date when the options are actually exercised, giving rise to a deferred tax asset until tax relief is obtained. IFRS 2 requires that, at each reporting date, an estimate of the future tax relief available should be based upon the intrinsic value of the option, which is the difference between the fair value of the share and the exercise price of the option. Where the amount of the estimated future tax deduction exceeds the accumulated remuneration expense, this indicates that the tax deduction relates partly to the remuneration expense and partly to equity.

Test your understanding 4 - Splash

An entity, Splash, has established a share option scheme for its four directors, commencing 1 July 2008. Each director will be entitled to 25,000 share options on condition that they remain with Splash for four years, from the date the scheme was introduced.
Information regarding the share options are as follows:

Fair value of option at grant date	$10
Fair value of option at 30 June 2009	$12
Exercise price of option	$5

The market value (i.e. fair value) of the shares at 30 June 2009 was $17 per share.

Tax allowances on any expense recognised for share options are only granted at the date when the options are exercised and will be based upon the intrinsic value of the options. Assume a tax rate of 30%.

Required:

Calculate and explain the amounts to be included in the financial statements of Splash for the year ended 30 June 2009, including explanation and calculation of any deferred tax implications.

Business combinations

A business combination can have several deferred tax consequences.

- The assets and liabilities of the acquired business are revalued to fair value. The revaluation to fair value of the assets does not always alter the tax base, and if this is the case, a temporary difference will arise.

- The deferred tax recognised on this difference is deducted in measuring the net assets acquired and, as a result, it increases the amount of goodwill.

- The goodwill itself does not give rise to deferred tax as IAS 12 specifically excludes it.

- The acquirer may be able to utilise the benefit of its own unused tax losses against the future taxable profit of the acquiree. In such cases, the acquirer recognises a deferred tax asset, but does not take it into account in determining the goodwill arising on the acquisition.

Test your understanding 5 - Complex

On 30 June 20X1, the Complex group acquired a new subsidiary. At the date of acquisition the subsidiary had inventory that was shown in its financial statements at a carrying amount of $50,000. The group assessed the fair amount of the inventory at $55,000. Assume the tax rate is 30%.

Required:

Explain the deferred tax implications.

Unremitted earnings

A temporary difference arises when the carrying amount of investments in subsidiaries, branches, associates or joint ventures is different from the tax base.

- The carrying amount in consolidated financial statements is the investor's share of the net assets of the investee, plus purchased goodwill, but the tax base is usually the cost of the investment. Unremitted earnings (i.e. undistributed profits) in the accounts of subsidiaries, branches, associates or joint ventures, will lead to a temporary difference.

- Deferred tax should be recognised on these temporary differences except when:
  - the parent, investor or venturer is able to control the timing of the reversal of the temporary difference and
  - it is probable that the temporary difference will not reverse in the foreseeable future.
- An investor can control the dividend policy of a subsidiary, but not always that of other types of investment. This means that deferred tax does not arise on investments in subsidiaries, but may on investments in associates and joint ventures. Trade investments will not usually give rise to deferred tax unless they are revalued.

Test your understanding 6 - Domestic

An entity, Domestic, has a subsidiary located overseas in Taxland. Domestic's share of the retained earnings of the subsidiary is $40,000. If the retained earnings were remitted to the entity as a dividend, then under tax legislation in Taxland, the subsidiary would need to deduct withholding tax equivalent to $4,000, from the payment. It is likely that these profits will be remitted as a dividend in the next couple of years.

Required:

Explain the deferred tax implications.

Unused tax losses

Where an entity has unused tax losses, IAS 12 allows a deferred tax asset to be recognised only to the extent that it is probable that future taxable profits will be available against which the unused tax losses can be utilised.

IAS 12 advises that the deferred tax asset should only be recognised after considering:

- whether an entity has sufficient taxable temporary differences against which the unused tax losses can be offset.
- whether it is probable the entity will have taxable profits before the unused tax losses expire.
- whether the tax losses result from identifiable causes which are unlikely to recur (otherwise, the existence of unused tax losses is strong evidence that future taxable profits may not be available).
- whether tax planning opportunities are available to the entity that will create taxable profit in the period that the tax losses can be utilised.

IAS 12 contains the following requirements relating to current tax.

- Unpaid tax for current and prior periods should be recognised as a liability. Overpaid current tax is recognised as an asset.

- Current tax should be accounted for in the income statement unless the tax relates to an item that has been accounted for in equity.

- If the item was disclosed as other comprehensive income and accounted for in equity, then the tax should be disclosed as relating to other comprehensive income and allocated to the equity.

- Tax is measured at the amount expected to be paid. Tax rates used should be those that have been enacted or substantively enacted by the reporting date.

Deferred tax

The deferred tax expense (or income) is the difference between the net liability at the beginning of the year and the net liability at the end of the year.

- If the item giving rise to the deferred tax is dealt with in the income statement, the related deferred tax should also be presented in the income statement.

- If the item giving rise to the deferred tax is dealt with on other comprehensive income, the related deferred tax should be disclosed as relating to other comprehensive income and recorded in equity.

Expandable text - Illustration

During 20X3, Upward revalued some land from $50m to $100m. Its profit before tax for the year ended 31 December 20X3, was $40m, on which it pays tax at 30%.

The opening balance on the retained earnings reserve was $220m, and there were no deferred tax balances brought forward.

Prepare all relevant extracts from Upwards' financial statements for the year ended 31 December 20X3.

Expandable text - Solution

Income statement for the year ended 31 December 20X3

	$000
Profit before tax	40,000
Income tax expense (at 30%)	(12,000)
Profit for the period	28,000

Statement of other comprehensive income

	$000
Profit for the period	28,000
Gain on revaluation	50,000
Tax relating to revaluation	(15,000)
Other comprehensive income net of tax	35,000
Total comprehensive income	63,000

Statement of financial position at 31 December 20X3

			$000
Non-current assets	Property	Cost	50,000
		Revaluation	50,000
		Revalued amount	100,000
Non-current liabilities	Deferred tax		15,000
Current liabilities	Current tax		12,000

Expandable text - Current issues

The IASB is currently undertaking a joint project with the US FASB to reduce the differences between IAS 12 and its US counterpart.

Although both standards take a balance sheet liability approach to deferred tax, differences arise because both standards have a number of exceptions to the basic principle. The approach to convergence in this project is not to reconsider the underlying approach, but rather to eliminate exceptions to the basic principle. The project is part of the short-term convergence project.

As at August 2010, the IASB redefined the project to include uncertain tax positions and deferred tax on property remeasurement at fair value. Consequently, an updated ED is expected in the latter part of 2010, wth a revised reporting standard expected by the end of 2011.

Technical article

Sally Baker and Tom Clendon of Kaplan Financial wrote an article discussing deferred tax for the August 2009 edition of Student Accountant magazine. You can access this article from the ACCA website (www.accaglobal.com).

Expandable text - UK syllabus focus

The ACCA UK syllabus contains a requirement that candidates should be able to discuss and apply the key differences between UK GAAP and IFRS GAAP. The accounting requirements of UK GAAP and IFRS GAAP are very similar in this area; the key issues associated with UK reporting standard requirements are as follows:

FRS 16 Current tax and FRS 19 Deferred tax. UK GAAP has two reporting standards dealing with accounting for current tax and deferred tax respectively; IFRS GAAP has one reporting standard, IAS 12, which deals with the issues covered by both of the UK standards.

One difference is that of terminology; UK GAAP refers to current or corporation tax; IAS 12 refers to income tax charged against the profits of entities. UK GAAP refers to the tax written down value of an asset or liability; IFRS GAAP refers to the tax base of the asset or liability.

For deferred tax, UK GAAP adopts a profit and loss perspective to identification of timing differences upon which deferred tax is calculated. IAS 12 adopts a temporary difference approach which focuses upon a balance sheet approach to identification of temporary differences upon which deferred tax is calculated. Essentially, both approaches will provide a similar outcome in accounting for deferred tax.

Two details on which accounting for deferred tax differs are as follows:

- in respect of revalued assets, under UK GAAP, revaluation gains on land and buildings are excluded from deferred tax calculations, whereas they are included within deferred tax calculations under IAS12.

- in respect of fair value adjustments, deferred tax is not recognised on fair value adjustmentswhen a subsidiary is consolidated for the first time, whereas they are included under IAS 12.

SSAP 5 accounting for value added tax confirms the basic principle that sales revenue should be accounted for excluding tax charged to customers (on outputs) and that expenses should be accounted for excluding such tax charged by suppliers (on inputs).

4 Chapter summary

Basic principles
- Temporary differences
- Examples
- Calculations

Deferred tax liabilities and assets
- Recognition
- Measurement

Tax income andexpense
- Current tax
- Deferred tax

Specific situations
- Revaluations
- Business combinations
- Unremitted earnings
- Losses

Test your understanding answers

Test your understanding 1 - Dive

	Carrying value	Tax base	Temp. difference	
	$	$	$	
Non-current asset	82,000	70,000	12,000	L
Interest receivable	1,000	Nil	1,000	L
Receivables	10,000	10,000	Nil	
Inventory	4,500	5,000	(500)	A
Accrual (cash basis for tax)	(1,000)	Nil	(1,000)	A
Accrual (already tax relief)	(5,000)	(5,000)	Nil	

Test your understanding 2 - Drown

	Start of year	End of year	
Temporary differences	$000	$000	
Accelerated capital allowances	400	900	L
General provision	Nil	(50)	A
Accrued pension liabilities	(60)	(40)	A
Provision for unrealised profits – provided tax on profit	Nil	(10)	A
Loss relief	Nil	(100)	a
	340	700	

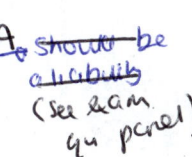 A should be allocated (see exam qu panel).

Deferred tax liability		
30% × 700 =		210
Less B/f 30% × 340 =		(102)
Therefore Charge to profits		108

Test your understanding 3 - Dodge

- The carrying amount of the asset before revaluation is $60,000 ($100,000 – $40,000) and its tax base is $50,000($100,000 – $50,000). The difference between the carrying amount and its tax base is $10,000 and this difference is referred to in IAS 12 as a temporary difference. Under IAS 12 deferred tax is recognised on most temporary differences, so the liability will be $3,000 ($10,000 × 30%).

- Revaluing the asset increases its carrying amount without altering its tax base (since revaluations have no immediate tax consequences). Therefore, the revaluation creates an additional temporary difference of $30,000 ($90,000 – $60,000) and so additional deferred tax of $9,000 ($30,000 × 30%), would be recognised.

- The revaluation gain is disclosed as other comprehensive income and credited to the revaluation reserve (within other components of equity). In line with this treatment, the deferred tax expense must be disclosed as tax relating to other comprehensive income and debited to the revaluation reserve.

Test your understanding 4 - Splash

Share options should be recognised as a remuneration expense as they are part of the work and service provided by the directors throughout the four-year vesting period to earn entitlement to exercise the options at the vesting date. The entity should also recognise an equity reserve as this represents part of the consideration towards payment for the shares. This is calculated based upon the fair value of the option at the grant date at the start of the vesting period for each year of the share option scheme.

As this is the first year of the scheme, calculate the equity reserve required, and this will also provide the expense required to be recognised for the year as follows:

Year-ended 30 June 2009
4 x 25,000 x $10 x 1/4 years $250,000

For each subsequent year, calculate the cumulative equity reserve required at that year-end; any increase in the equity reserve from the previous year will be the charge to recognise in the income statement as follows:

Year-ended 30 June 2010 Equity reserve
4 x 25,000 x $10 x 2/4 years $500,000

Remuneration expense for the year will be the movement in the equity reserve:

$500,000 - $250,000 = $250,000

Notice that the entity uses the fair value of the option at the grant date throughout the vesting period.

For tax purposes, tax relief is allowed only at the time the options are exercised, which will be at the end of the vesting period. Until then, the entity will have recognised an expense, on which tax relief will be obtained at a later date. This is a temporary difference for the purposes of accounting for deferred tax, giving rise to a deferred tax asset. The intrinsic value of the option is the difference between the market value of the shares at the reporting date and the option exercise price, and this should also be spread over the vesting period as follows:

Year ended 30 June 2009   Temporary difference
4 x 25,000 x ($17 - $5) x 1/4 $300,000

The temporary difference is then multiplied by the tax rate to determine the deferred tax asset:

$300,000 x 30% = $90,000

If the deferred tax asset is to be recognised, it must be capable of reliable measurement and also be regarded as recoverable.

Test your understanding 5 - Complex

The carrying amount of the inventory in the consolidated accounts is $55,000, while its tax base is $50,000. Deferred tax is recognised on the temporary difference of $5,000. Since the tax rate is 30%, then the deferred tax liability is $1,500.

Test your understanding 6 - Domestic

The existence of a potential tax charge on the payment of a dividend, affects the tax base of the net assets of the subsidiary in the consolidated accounts. Deferred tax is recognised for the $4,000 potentially payable, because the earnings are likely to be remitted by way of dividend.

Non-financial reporting

Chapter learning objectives

Upon completion of this chapter you will be able to:

- discuss the increased demand for transparency in corporate reports, and the emergence of non-financial reporting standards

- discuss the progress towards a framework for environmental and sustainability reporting

- appraise the impact of environmental, social and ethical factors on performance measurement

- evaluate current reporting requirements in the area

- discuss why entities might include disclosures relating to the environment and society.

Expandable text - Non-financial reporting

Non-financial reporting

Non-financial information, in the form of additional information provided alongside the financial information in the annual report, has become more important in recent years.

While financial information remains important, stakeholders are interested in other aspects of an entity's performance.

For example:

- how the business is managed
- its future prospects
- the entity's policy on the environment
- its attitude towards social responsibility, and so on.

All of this information is reported in a number of ways.

- An operating and financial review will assess the results of the period and discuss the future prospects of the business.
- A report on corporate governance will report on how the entity is directed.

- An environmental and social report will discuss responsibilities towards the environment and society, or both of these issues could be combined in a report on sustainability.

Expandable text - Management commentary

Management commentary

Management commentary is information that accompanies financial statements as part of an entity's financial reporting. It explains the main trends and factors underlying the development, performance and position of the entity's business during the period covered by the financial statements. It also explains the main trends and factors that are likely to affect the entity's future development, performance and position.

IASB Exposure Draft - Management Commentary

The IASB published a DP 'Management Commentary' in October 2005, which was followed by ED 2009/6 in June 2009. The objective was to propose a framework for the preparation of a decision-useful management commentary to accompany financial statements produced in accordance with IAS/IFRS. To fulfil that objective, management should not only report on what has happened during the reporting period, but should also include an explanation as to why it has happened and the potential future impact. In addition to reporting on the past and the current position of the entity, the ED proposes that management should communicate information about an entity's resources, the claims thereon, and transactions, events and other circumstances that may affect those resources and claims. When finalised, the commentary would be regarded as non-binding guidance.

Content of the ED

Key principles of management commentary

In the ED, the IASB identifies three key characteristics that distinguish decision-useful management commentary. Such decision-useful commentary:

- discusses and analyses the entity's performance, position and development through the eyes of management – disclosing information that is important for management in steering the entity;

- supplements and complements information contained in the financial statements – providing additional explanations of amounts presented in the financial statements and including information that is not presented in the financial statements; and

- has an orientation to the future – to communicate, from management's perspective, the direction the entity is taking. Management should include forward-looking information if it is aware of any factors that could impact the entity's financial position or performance, and should discuss the extent to which forward-looking disclosures made in prior periods have been borne out.

Presentation and content of management commentary

The form and content of management commentary should reflect the nature of the business, the strategies employed, and the legal and regulatory environment in which an entity operates. For this reason, the IASB does not propose a specific format or content for management commentary, but rather provides some general guidelines.

The ED proposes that if the financial statements include segment information, the information provided in management commentary should reflect that segmentation.

To assist users in identifying and understanding matters that are significant, the ED suggests that management should avoid duplicating in its management commentary the disclosures made in the notes to the financial statements. In addition, generic ('boilerplate') disclosures should be avoided because they do not contribute to an understanding of the specific entity. Regarding the content of management commentary, the IASB suggests that the information provided should enable users to understand:

- the nature of the business, which usually includes a macro- (e.g. industry, socio-economic and legal environment) as well as a micro-level discussion (business model, product portfolio, etc.);

- management's objectives and strategies for meeting those objectives, including priorities for action and addressing threats and opportunities of market trends;

- the entity's most significant financial and non-financial resources (e.g. personnel); its principal strategic, commercial, operational and financial risks and uncertainties; and those relationships that are likely to have an impact on the entity's performance and value (e.g. a discussion of the structure of its customer base);

- the results of operations, the extent to which those results may be indicative of future performance, and management's assessment of the entity's prospects (including targets for financial and non-financial measures and, if quantified, the risks and assumptions used); and

- the critical performance measures and indicators used by management to steer the entity and assess its performance against stated objectives.

As at August 2010, since the comment period for the ED expired in March 2010, there has been no further progress. It is expected that any best practice guidance on the form and content of a management commentary will be published before the end of 2010. Note that any such guidance will not be mandatory.

Expandable text - Sustainability

Definition

Sustainability is the process of conducting business in such a way that it enables an entity to meet its present needs without compromising the ability of future generations to meet their needs.

Introduction

In a corporate context, sustainability means that a business entity must attempt to reduce its environmental impact through more efficient use of natural resources and improving environmental practices.

More and more business entities are reporting their approach to sustainability in addition to the financial information reported in the annual report. There are increased public expectations for business entities and industries to take responsibility for the impact their activities have on the environment and society.

Reporting sustainability

- Currently, sustainability reporting is voluntary, although its use is increasing.

- Reports include highlights of non-financial performance such as environmental, social and economic reports during the accounting period.

- The report may be included in the annual report or published as a stand alone document, possibly on the entity's website.

- The increase in popularity of such reports highlights the growing trend that business entities are taking sustainability seriously and are attempting to be open about the impact of their activities.

- Reporting sustainability is sometimes called reporting the 'triple bottom line' covering environment, social and economic reporting.

Framework for sustainability reporting

- There is no framework for sustainability reporting in IFRS, so this reporting is voluntary.

- This lack of regulation leads to several potential problems:

  (a) Because disclosure is largely voluntary, not all businesses disclose information. Those that do tend to do so either because they are under particular pressure to prove their 'green' credentials (for example, large public utility companies whose operations directly affect the environment) or because they have deliberately built their reputation on environmental friendliness or social responsibility.

  (b) The information disclosed may not be complete or reliable. Many businesses see environmental reporting largely as a public relations exercise and therefore only provide information that shows them in a positive light.

  (c) The information may not be disclosed consistently from year to year.

  (d) Some businesses, particularly small and medium sized entities, may believe that the costs of preparing and circulating additional information outweigh the benefits of doing so.

- The most accepted framework for reporting sustainability is the Global Reporting Initiative's Sustainability Reporting Guidelines, the latest of which 'G3' – the third version of the guidelines - was issued in October 2006. As at August 2010, this is still the most recent version of the guidelines.

- The G3 Guidelines provide universal guidance for reporting on sustainability performance. They are applicable to all entities including SMEs and not-for-profit entities worldwide. The G3 consist of principles and disclosure items .The principles help to define report content, quality of the report, and give guidance on how to set the report boundary. Disclosure items include disclosures on management of issues, as well as performance indicators themselves.

The best way to understand sustainability is to look at some examples of sustainability reports in financial statements.

ACCA - ACCA hold annual awards for sustainability reporting. You can review sustainability reports of those companies commended by ACCA, and it will also provide you with an idea of the information typically used in these reports via the acca web site at: www.accaglobal.com.

Global Reporting Initiative

- You can also look at the Global Reporting Initiative website (www.globalreporting.org)

- The financial statements of companies that have applied the GRI guidelines are listed with a link to their reports.

Expandable text – The Global Reporting Initiative

Principles and guidance

This section of the G3 provides:

- Guidance for **defining report content**, by applying the principles of materiality, stakeholder inclusiveness, sustainability context and completeness.

- Principles for **ensuring report quality**, these being balance, comparability , accuracy, timeliness, reliability and clarity.

- Guidance for **report boundary setting** in terms of determining the range of entities to be included in the report.

Standard disclosures

There are three different types of measures that can be used to express strategic approach, management goals, and performance results:

- **Profile disclosures** set the overall context for understanding performance. This section of the report should include consideration of:

  Strategy and analysis:

  - statement from CEO explaining the relevance of sustainability to organisational strategy in the short, medium and long terms.

  - Description of organisation's key impacts on sustainability and impact of sustainability trends, risks and opportunities on the organisation.

  Organisational profile:

  - overview of the reporting entity in terms of products, organisational structure, location of operations and markets etc.

  Report parameters:

  - boundary of report

  - specific exclusions

  - basis for reporting on subsidiaries etc

  - location of standard disclosures in the report

Governance

– committees and responsibilities

– mechanisms for stakeholders to provide recommendations to governance bodies

– internal codes of conduct and their application

Commitments to external initiatives

– external initiatives to which the entity subscribes

– strategic memberships, funding and participation in industry associations

Stakeholder engagement

– list of stakeholder groups engaged by entity

– approach to stakeholder engagement

– key topics and concerns of stakeholders

- **Management Approach disclosures** are intended to address the entity's approach to managing the sustainability topics associated with risks and opportunities. Disclosures may include:
  – Goals and performance

  – Policy

  – Organisational responsibility

  – Training and awareness

  – Monitoring and follow up

  – Additional contextual information

- **Performance Indicator disclosures** elicit comparable information on a number of areas, including:
  – Environmental, for example, level of materials, energy and water used, biodiversity, level of emissions and waste, impact of products and services and transport.

  – Human rights, for example number of suppliers who have undergone human rights screening, number of discrimination actions, measures taken to contribute to the elimination of child and forced and compulsory labour.

- Labour practices, for example employment turnover, percentage of employees covered by collective bargaining agreements, rates of injury and occupational diseases, average hours training per employee per year, indicators of diversity.

- Society, for example impact of operations on communities, number of corruption investigations, number of legal actions for anti-competitive behaviour, level of fines for non-compliance with legal requirements.

- Product responsibility, for example results of customer satisfaction surveys, number of breaches of customer confidentiality and losses of personal data.

- Economic, for example level of spending on local suppliers, number of senior management hired from local community.

Expandable text - International Integrated Reporting Committee

What is the purpose of the IIRC?

The IIRC is being created to respond to this need for a concise, clear, comprehensive and comparable integrated reporting framework structured around the organization's strategic objectives, its governance and business model and integrating both material financial and non-financial information. The objectives for an integrated reporting framework are to:

- support the information needs of long-term investors, by showing the broader and longer-term consequences of decision-making;

- reflect the interconnections between environmental, social, governance and financial factors in decisions that affect long-term performance and condition, making clear the link between sustainability and economic value;

- provide the necessary framework for environmental and social factors to be taken into account systematically in reporting and decision-making;

- rebalance performance metrics away from an undue emphasis on short-term financial performance; and

- bring reporting closer to the information used by management to run the business on a day-to-day basis.

What is the role of the IIRC?

At present a range of standard-setters and regulatory bodies are responsible for individual elements of reporting. No single body has the oversight or authority to bring together these different elements that are essential to the presentation of an integrated picture of an organization and the impact of environmental and social factors on its performance. In addition, globalisation means that an accounting and reporting framework needs to be developed on an international basis. At present, there is a risk that, as individual regulators responds to the risks faced, multiple standards will emerge.

The role of the IIRC is to:

- raise awareness of this issue and develop a consensus among governments, listing authorities, business, investors, accounting bodies and standard setters for the best way to address it;

- develop an overarching integrated reporting framework setting out the scope of integrated reporting and its key components;

- identify priority areas where additional work is needed and provide a plan for development;

- consider whether standards in this area should be voluntary or mandatory and facilitate collaboration between standard-setters and convergence in the standards needed to underpin integrated reporting; and

- promote the adoption of integrated reporting by relevant regulators and report preparers.

Who is behind this?

In December 2009, His Royal Highness The Prince of Wales convened a high level meeting of investors, standard setters, companies, accounting bodies and UN representatives. At the meeting it was agreed that the Prince's Accounting for Sustainability and the Global Reporting Initiative should work together with other organizations to establish an international body to oversee the creation of a generally accepted integrated reporting framework that would connect financial and sustainability reporting.
Who are the members?

The IIRC brings together a powerful cross section of representatives from the corporate, accounting, securities, regulatory, and standard-setting sectors. Membership will comprise international representation from the following stakeholder groups: companies, investors, regulators, standard-setters, intergovernmental organizations, non-governmental organizations, the accounting profession, civil society and academia.

Further information on the IIRC can be found at
www.integratedreporting.org

Expandable text - Other issues in sustainability reporting

The World Business Council for Sustainable Development (WBCSD)

The WBCSD was formed in 1991 in Norway and now consists of over 180 international companies in a shared commitment to sustainable development through economic growth, ecological balance and social progress.

Its members come from more than 30 countries and 20 major industrial sectors.

It aims to get businesses involved in the issue of sustainability and to promote sustainable development through economic growth, ecological balance and social progress.

Legal requirements

- Legal requirements for sustainability reporting are the responsibility of the governments of individual countries.

- In 2006, for the first time, the UK government passed legislation requiring mandatory reporting on business' social and environmental performance. This is the seen as a very positive step by the corporate social responsibility community.

- The revised Companies Act requires directors to report on what they are doing and, therefore, they will have to consider how it affects the community and environment. The Act makes it mandatory for business to report anything concerning the welfare of the employees, community, environment, suppliers and the company itself. It will also allow shareholders and the general public to judge companies' performances.

- The law will not make companies report on anything that is considered commercially sensitive or confidential.

Expandable text - Environmental accounting

Definition

Environmental reporting is the disclosure of information in the published annual report or elsewhere, of the effect that the operations of the business have on the natural environment.

As detailed in section 2, the sustainability report combines environmental, social and economic reporting in one report. Environmental reports were the first step in reporting an entity's impact on its environment.

This section details the contents of an environment report together with any accounting issues.

Environmental reporting in practice

There are two main vehicles that companies use to publish information about the ways in which they interact with the natural environment:

(a) The published annual report (which includes the financial statements)

(b) A separate environment report (either as a paper document or simply posted on the company website.

The IASB encourages the presentation of environmental reports if management believe that they will assist users in making economic decisions, but they are not mandatory.

IAS 1 points out that any statement or report presented outside financial statements is outside the scope of IFRSs, so there are no mandatory IFRS requirements on separate environmental reports.

Expandable text - Separate environmental reports

Many large public companies publish environmental reports that are completely separate from the annual report and financial statements. The environmental report is often combined in a sustainability report.

Most environmental reports take the form of a combined statement of policy and review of activity. They cover issues such as:

*   waste management

*   pollution

- intrusion into the landscape
- the effect of an entity's activities upon wildlife
- use of energy
- the benefits to the environment of the entity's products and services.

Generally, the reports disclose the entity's targets and/or achievements, with direct comparison between the two in some cases. They may also disclose financial information, such as the amount invested in preserving the environment.

Public and media interest has tended to focus on the environmental report rather than on the disclosures in the published annual report and financial statements. This separation reflects the fact that the two reports are aimed at different audiences.

Shareholders are the main users of the annual report, while the environmental report is designed to be read by the general public. Many companies publish their environmental and social reports on their websites, which encourages access to a wide audience.

The content of environment reports

The content of an environment report may cover the following areas.

(a) **Environmental issues pertinent to the entity and industry**

- The entity's policy towards the environment and any improvements made since first adopting the policy.
- Whether the entity has a formal system for managing environmental risks.
- The identity of the director(s) responsible for environmental issues.
- The entity's perception of the risks to the environment from its operations.
- The extent to which the entity would be capable of responding to a major environmental disaster and an estimate of the full economic consequences of such a future major disaster.
- The effects of, and the entity's response to, any government legislation on environmental matters.
- Details of any significant infringement of environmental legislation or regulations.
- Material environmental legal issues in which the entity is involved.
- Details of any significant initiatives taken, if possible linked to amounts in financial statements.

- Details of key indicators (if any) used by the entity to measure environmental performance. Actual performance should be compared with targets and with performance in prior periods.

(b) **Financial information**

- The entity's accounting policies relating to environmental costs, provisions and contingencies.

- The amount charged to the income statement or statement of comprehensive income during the accounting period in respect of expenditure to prevent or rectify damage to the environment caused by the entity's operations. This could be analysed between expenditure that the entity was legally obliged to incur and other expenditure.

- The amount charged to the income statement or statement of comprehensive income during the accounting period in respect of expenditure to protect employees and society in general from the consequences of damage to the environment caused by the entity's operations. Again, this could be analysed between compulsory and voluntary expenditure.

- Details (including amounts) of any provisions or contingent liabilities relating to environmental matters.

- The amount of environmental expenditure capitalised during the year.

- Details of fines, penalties and compensation paid during the accounting period in respect of non-compliance with environmental regulations.

Expandable text - Accounting for environmental costs

Accounting for environment costs

Definitions

Environmental costs	include environmental measures and environmental losses.
Environmental measures	are the costs of preventing, reducing or repairing damage to the environment and the costs of conserving resources.
Environmental losses	are costs that bring no benefit to the business.

Environmental measures can include:

- capital expenditure
- closure or decommissioning costs
- clean-up costs
- development expenditure
- costs of recycling or conserving energy.

Environmental losses can include:

- fines, penalties and compensation
- impairment or disposal losses relating to assets that have to be scrapped or abandoned because they damage the environment.

Expandable text - Accounting treatment

Environmental costs are treated in accordance with the requirements of current accounting standards.

(a) Most expenditure is charged in the income statement or statement of comprehensive income in the period in which it is incurred. Material items may need to be disclosed separately in the notes to the accounts or on the face of the income statement/statement of comprehensive income as required by IAS 1.

(b) Entities may have to undertake fundamental reorganisations or restructuring or to discontinue particular activities in order to protect the environment. If a sale or termination meets the definition of a discontinued operation, its results must be separately disclosed in accordance with the requirements of IFRS 5. Material restructuring costs may need to be separately disclosed on the face of the income statement/statement of comprehensive income.

(c) Fines and penalties for non-compliance with regulations are charged to the income statement or statement of comprehensive income in the period in which they are incurred. This applies even if the activities that resulted in the penalties took place in an earlier accounting period, as they cannot be treated retrospectively as prior period adjustments.

(d) Expenditure on non-current assets is capitalised and depreciated in the usual way as per IAS 16 **Property, plant and equipment**. Any government grants received for expenditure that protects the environment are treated in accordance with IAS 20 **Accounting for government grants and disclosure of government assistance**.

(e) Non-current assets (including goodwill) may become impaired as a result of environmental legislation or new regulations. IAS 36 **Impairment of assets** lists events that could trigger an impairment review, one of which is a significant adverse change in the legal environment in which the business operates.

(f) Research and development expenditure in respect of environmentally friendly products, processes or services is covered by IAS 38 **Intangible assets**.

Expandable text - Provisions for environmental liabilities

IAS 37 **Provisions, contingent liabilities and contingent assets** states that three conditions must be met before a provision may be recognised:

(a) the entity has a present **obligation** as a result of a past event

(b) it is **probable** that a transfer of economic benefits will be required to settle the obligation

(c) a **reliable estimate** can be made of the amount of the obligation.

IAS 37 is covered in detail in a later chapter, but some points are particularly relevant to provisions for environmental costs.

(a) The fact that the entity's activities have caused environmental contamination does not in itself give rise to an obligation to rectify the damage. However, even if there is no legal obligation, there may be a constructive obligation. An entity almost certainly has a constructive obligation to rectify environmental damage if it has a policy of acting in an environmentally responsible way and this policy is well publicised.

(b) The obligation must arise from a past event. This means that a provision can only be set up to rectify environmental damage that has already happened. If an entity needs to incur expenditure to reduce pollution in the future, it should not set up a provision. This is because in theory it can avoid the expenditure by its future actions, for example by discontinuing the particular activity that causes the pollution.

Capitalisation of environmental expenditure

If environmental expenditure provides access to future economic benefits, it meets the IASB's definition of an asset. It would normally be capitalised and depreciated over the useful life of the asset.

An asset may also arise as the result of recognising a provision. In principle, when a provision or change in a provision is recognised, an asset should also be recognised when, and only when, the incurring of the present obligation gives access to future economic benefits. Otherwise the setting up of the provision should be charged immediately to the income statement or statement of comprehensive income.

Expandable text - Question

You are the chief accountant of Redstart and you are currently finalising the financial statements for the year ended 31 December 20X1. Your assistant (who has prepared the draft accounts) is unsure about the treatment of two transactions that have taken place during the year. She has written you a memorandum that explains the key principles of each transaction and also the treatment adopted in the draft accounts.

Transaction one

One of the corporate objectives of the enterprise is to ensure that its activities are conducted in such a way as to minimise any damage to the natural environment. It is committed in principle to spending extra money in pursuit of this objective but has not yet made any firm proposals. The directors believe that this objective will prove very popular with customers and are anxious to emphasise their environmentally friendly policies in the annual report.

Your assistant suggests that a sum should be set aside from profits each year to create a provision in the financial statements against the possible future costs of environmental protection. Accordingly, she has charged the income statement for the year ended 31 December 20X1 with a sum of $100,000 and proposes to disclose this fact in a note to the accounts.

Transaction two

A new law has recently been enacted that will require Redstart to change one of its production processes in order to reduce the amount of carbon dioxide that is emitted. This will involve purchasing and installing some new plant that is more efficient than the equipment currently in use. To comply with the law, the new plant must be operational by 31 December 20X2. The new plant has not yet been purchased.

In the draft financial statements for the year ended 31 December 20X1, your assistant has recognised a provision for $5 million (the cost of the new plant). This has been disclosed as a separate item in the notes to the income statement.

The memorandum from your assistant also expresses concern about the fact that there was no reference to environmental matters anywhere in the published financial statements for the year ended 31 December 20X0. As a result, she believes that the financial statements did not comply with the requirements of International Financial Reporting Standards and therefore must have been wrong.

Draft a reply to your assistant that:

(a) **reviews the treatment suggested by your assistant and recommends changes where relevant. In each case your reply should refer to relevant International Accounting Standards**

(b) **replies to her suggestion that the financial statements for the year ended 31 December 20X0 were wrong because they made no reference to environmental matters.**

Expandable text - Solution

MEMORANDUM

To: Assistant Accountant

From: Chief Accountant

Subject: Accounting treatment of two transactions and disclosure of environmental matters in the financial statements

Date: 25 March 20X2

(a) **Accounting treatment of two transactions**

Transaction one

IAS 37 **Provisions, contingent liabilities and contingent assets** states that provisions should only be recognised in the financial statements if:

- there is a present obligation as a result of a past event

- it is probable that a transfer of economic benefits will be required to settle the obligation

- a reliable estimate can be made of the amount of the obligation.

In this case, there is no obligation to incur expenditure. There may be a constructive obligation to do so in future, if the board creates a valid expectation that it will protect the environment, but a board decision alone does not create an obligation.

There is also some doubt as to whether the expenditure can be reliably quantified. The sum of $100,000 could be appropriated from retained earnings and transferred to an environmental protection reserve within other components of equity, subject to formal approval by the board. A note to the financial statements should explain the transfer.

Transaction two

Again, IAS 37 states that a provision cannot be recognised if there is no obligation to incur expenditure. At first sight it appears that there is an obligation to purchase the new equipment, because the new law has been enacted. However, the obligation must arise as the result of a past event. At 31 December 20X1, no such event had occurred as the new plant had not yet been purchased and the new law had not yet come into effect. In theory, the company does not have to purchase the new plant. It could completely discontinue the activities that cause pollution or it could continue to operate the old equipment and risk prosecution under the new law. Therefore no provision can be recognised for the cost of new equipment.

It is likely that another effect of the new law is that the company will have to dispose of the old plant before it would normally have expected to do so. IAS 36 **Impairment of assets** requires that the old plant must be reviewed for impairment. If its carrying value is greater than its recoverable amount, it must be written down and an impairment loss must be charged against profits. This should be disclosed separately in the notes to the income statement/statement of comprehensive income if it is material.

(b) **Reference to environmental matters in the financial statements**

At present, companies are not obliged to make any reference to environmental matters within their financial statements. Current international financial reporting practice is more designed to meet the needs of investors and potential investors, rather than the general public. Some companies choose to disclose information about the ways in which they attempt to safeguard the environment, something that is often carried out as a public relations exercise. Disclosures are often framed in very general terms and appear outside the financial statements proper. This means that they do not have to be audited.

Several companies publish fairly detailed 'environmental reports'. It could be argued that as Redstart's operations affect the wider community, it has a moral responsibility to disclose details of its activities and its environmental policies. However, at present it is not required to do so by IFRSs.

If a company has, or may have, an obligation to make good any environmental damage that it has caused, it is obliged to disclose information about this commitment in its financial statements (unless the likelihood of this is remote).

If it is probable (more likely than not) that the company will have to incur expenditure to meet its obligation, then it is also required to set up a provision in the financial statements.

In practice, these requirements are unlikely to apply unless a company is actually obliged by law to rectify environmental damage or unless it has made a firm commitment to the public to do so (for example, by promoting itself as an organisation that cares for the environment, as the directors propose that Redstart should do in future).

Expandable text - Social reporting

Definition

Corporate social reporting is the process of communicating the social and environmental effects of organisations' economic actions to particular interest groups within society and to society at large.

It involves extending the accountability of organisations (particularly companies) beyond the traditional role of providing a financial account to the owners of capital. Social and ethical reporting would seem to be at variance with the prevailing business. However, there are a number of reasons why entities publish social reports.

(a) They may have deliberately built their reputation on social responsibility (e.g. Body Shop, Traidcraft) in order to attract a particular customer base.

(b) They may perceive themselves as being under particular pressure to prove that their activities do not exploit society as a whole or certain sections of it (e.g. Shell International and large utility companies).

(c) They may be genuinely convinced that it is in their long-term interests to balance the needs of the various stakeholder groups.

(d) They may fear that the government will eventually require them to publish socially oriented information if they do not do so voluntarily.

Social responsibility

A business interacts with society in several different ways as follows.

- It employs human resources in the form of management and other employees.
- Its activities affect society as a whole, for example, it may:
  - be the reason for a particular community's existence
  - produce goods that are helpful or harmful to particular members of society
  - damage the environment in ways that harm society as a whole
  - undertake charitable works in the community or promote particular values.

If a business interacts with society in a responsible manner, the needs of other stakeholders should be taken into account and performance may encompass:

- providing fair remuneration and an acceptable working environment
- paying suppliers promptly
- minimising the damage to the environment caused by the entity's activities
- contributing to the community by providing employment or by other means.

Social reporting in practice

Social reporting in the financial statements

- Disclosures of social reporting matters in financial statements tend to be required by national legislation and by the stock exchange on which an entity is quoted. There is little mention of social matters in international accounting standards.
- IAS 1 requires disclosure of the total cost of employee benefits for the period. If the 'nature of expense' method is chosen for the income statement/statement of comprehensive income, then the total charge for employee costs will be shown on the face of the income statement/statement of comprehensive income. If the 'function of expense' method is chosen, then IAS 1 requires disclosure of the total employee costs in a note to the financial statements.
- IAS 24 **Related party disclosures** requires the benefits paid to key management personnel to be disclosed in total and analysed into the categories of benefits.

- Other possible disclosures (e.g. details of directors and corporate governance matters, employee policies, supplier payment policies, charitable contributions, etc.) are normally dealt with by local legislation and would only be required by IFRSs when such disclosure is necessary to present fairly the entity's financial performance.

Expandable text - Separate social reports

- Stand alone social and ethical reports do not have to be audited and there are no international regulations prescribing their content.

- There are some sets of non-mandatory guidelines and codes of best practice, for example, the standard AA1000, which has been issued by the Institute of Social and Ethical Accountability (ISEA).

- Some organisations have the data in their reports independently verified and include the auditor's report in their published document. The social report may or may not be combined with the environmental report.

It has been suggested that there should be three main types of information in the social report.

(a) **Information about relationships with stakeholders**, e.g. employee numbers, wages and salaries, provision of facilities for customers and information about involvement with local charities.

(b) **Information about the accountability of the entity**, e.g. sickness leave, accident rates, noise levels, numbers of disabled employees, compliance with current legal, ethical and industry standards.

(c) **Information about dialogue with stakeholders**, e.g. the way in which the entity consults with all stakeholders and provides public feedback on the stakeholders' perceptions of the entity's responsibilities to the community and its performance in meeting stakeholder needs.

Expandable text - Human capital management reporting

Human capital management reporting

Definition

Human Capital Management relates to the management of the recruitment, retention, training and development of employees. It views employees as a business asset, rather than just a cost.

HCM is a key source of competitive advantage and, ultimately, profitability. Any business needs to ensure that its workforce has the right mix of people, with appropriate skills and experiences, allowing the business to compete effectively.

Accounting for People Task Force

In January 2003, the Accounting for People Task Force was set up by the UK government to look at ways in which organisations can measure the quality and effectiveness of their HCM.

The Task Force recommended that reports on HCM should have a strategic focus and should include information on:

- the size and composition of the workforce
- retention and motivation of employees
- the skills and competences necessary for success, and training to achieve these
- remuneration and fair employment practices
- leadership and succession planning
- being balanced and objective, following a process that is susceptible to review by auditors
- providing information in a form that enables comparisons over time.

To take this further, the Task Force recommended that the UK's Accounting Standards Board develop guidelines on HCM reporting.

Expandable text - Question

(a) **Explain why companies may wish to make social and environmental disclosures in their annual report. Discuss how this content should be determined.**

(b) Company B owns a chemical plant, producing paint. The plant uses a great deal of energy and releases emissions into the environment. Its by-product is harmful and is treated before being safely disposed of. The company has been fined for damaging the environment following a spillage of the toxic waste product. Due to stricter monitoring routines set up by the company, the fines have reduced and in the current year they have not been in breach of any local environment laws.

The company, is aware that emissions are high and has been steadily reducing them. They purchase electricity from renewable sources and in the current year have employed a temporary consultant to calculate their carbon footprint so they can take steps to reduce it.

Discuss the information that could be included in Company B's environmental report.

Expandable text - Answer

(a) The way in which companies manage their social and environmental responsibilities is a high level strategic issue for management. Companies that actively manage these responsibilities can help create long-term sustainable performance in an increasingly competitive business environment.

Reports that disclose transparent information will benefit organisations and their stakeholders. These stakeholders will have an interest in knowing that the company is attempting to adopt best practice in the area. Institutional investors will see value in the 'responsible ownership' principle adopted by the company.

Although there is no universal 'best practice', there seems to be growing consensus that high performance is linked with high quality practice in such areas as recruitment, organisational culture, training and reduction of environmental risks and impact. Companies that actively reduce environmental risks and promote social disclosures could be considered to be potentially more sustainable, profitable, valuable and competitive. Many companies build their reputation on the basis of social and environmental responsibility and go to substantial lengths to prove that their activities do not exploit their workforce or any other section of society.

Governments are encouraging disclosure by passing legislation, for example in the area of anti-discrimination and by their own example in terms of the depth and breadth of reporting (also by requiring companies who provide services to the government to disclose such information). External awards and endorsements, such as environmental league tables and employer awards, encourage companies to adopt a more strategic approach to these issues. Finally, local cultural and social pressures are causing greater demands for transparency of reporting.

There is no IFRS that determines the content of an environmental and social report. While companies are allowed to include the information they wish to disclose, there is a lack of comparability and the potential that only the positive actions will be shown.

A common framework that provided guidelines on sustainability reporting would be useful for both companies and stakeholders.

The Global Reporting Initiative (GRI) provides guidelines on the content of a sustainability report, but these are not mandatory. However, a number of companies prepare their reports in accordance with the guidelines and the GRI is becoming the unofficial best practice guide in this area.

(b) Company B's environmental report should include the following information.

  (i)   A statement of the environmental policy covering all aspects of business activity. This can include their aim of using renewable electricity and reducing their carbon footprint – the amount of carbon dioxide released into the environment as a result of their activities.

  (ii) The management systems that reduce and minimise environmental risks.

  (iii) Details of environmental training and expertise.

  (iv) A report on their environmental performance including verified emissions to air/land and water, and how they are seeking to reduce these and other environmental impacts. Operating site reports for local communities for businesses with high environmental impacts. Company B's activities have a significant impact so it is important to show how this is dealt with. The emissions data could be graphed to show it is reducing. If they have the data, they could compare their carbon dioxide emissions or their electricity usage over previous periods. Presenting this information graphically helps stakeholders see how the business is performing in the areas it is targeting.

> (v) Details of any environmental offence that resulted in enforcement action, fine, etc. and any serious pollution incident. They can disclose how fines have been reducing and state that there have not been any pollution incidents in the current period.
>
> (vi) A report on historical trends for key indicators and a comparison with the corporate targets.

Expandable text - Social and HCM reporting

The social contract

The social contract is an expressed or implicit contract between individual entities and society as a whole.

Some academics believe that social and environmental accounting should develop in such a way that it reflects the existence of the 'social contract'.

Proponents of the social contract argue that every business is a social institution whose existence can only be justified in so far as it serves society in general and the particular groups from which it derives its power. Businesses are accountable to the communities in which they operate and to grow and survive they must demonstrate:

(a) that society requires their services

(b) that the groups benefiting from its rewards (e.g. earnings) have society's approval.

Corporate social reporting is one means by which an entity demonstrates its accountability.

The legitimacy of an organisation

Academics have developed theories to explain corporate social reporting practices.

Stakeholder theory views social reporting as a means by which organisations attempt to manage and negotiate their relationships with their stakeholders. The nature of the reporting reflects the importance that an organisation attaches to the various stakeholder groups.

Legitimacy theory views social reporting as a means by which organisations attempt to demonstrate that they reflect the same social value system as the society in which they operate.

Legitimacy theory is a development of stakeholder theory. It argues that organisations cannot continue to exist unless the society in which they are based perceives them as operating to the same values as that society. If an organisation feels that it is under threat (e.g. because there has been a financial scandal or a serious accident causing major pollution) it may adopt one or more legitimation strategies by attempting to:

(a) 'educate' stakeholders about its intentions to improve its performance

(b) change stakeholders' perceptions of the event (without changing its actual performance)

(c) distract attention away from the issue (by concentrating on positive actions not necessarily related to the event)

(d) manage expectations about its performance (e.g. by explaining that certain events are beyond its control).

Legitimacy theory can explain several aspects of social and environmental reporting as it exists in practice. For example, entities tend to report positive aspects of their behaviour and not to report negative ones.

Human capital management (HCM)

Accounting for People Task Force

In January 2003, the Accounting for People Task Force was set up by the UK government to look at ways in which organisations can measure the quality and effectiveness of their human capital management. Its brief was to:

• look at the performance measures currently used to assess investment in HCM

• consider best practice in human capital reporting, and the performance measures that are most valuable to stakeholders

• establish and champion the business case for producing such reports

• produce a final advisory report.

The Task Force believes that effective people policies and practices will benefit organisations and their stakeholders. Managers, investors, workers, consumers and clients all have an interest in knowing that an organisation is aiming for high performance by investing in their people.

The Task Force recommends that reports on HCM should have a strategic focus. They should communicate clearly, fairly and unambiguously the board's current understanding of the links between the HCM policies and practices, its business strategy and its performance.

They should include information on:

- the size and composition of the workforce
- retention and motivation of employees
- the skills and competences necessary for success, and training to achieve these
- remuneration and fair employment practices
- leadership and succession planning
- being balanced and objective, following a process that is susceptible to review by auditors
- providing information in a form that enables comparisons over time.

To take this further, the Task Force recommended that the UK's Accounting Standards Board develop guidelines on HCM reporting. They should undergo a consultation process with leading employers, investors, professional organisations and other relevant stakeholders. The ASB would then monitor the extent and depth of HCM reporting.

The response from the UK government was to agree that HCM reports should be included in the UK's Operating and Financial Review (the equivalent to the IASB's Management Commentary) and to review the area within a five year period.

In summary, this will become another area of corporate reporting alongside environmental and social reports that companies will be expected to produce. Already there is some guidance from the findings of the Task Force as to what should be included in such a report. It remains to be seen whether this requirement will become mandatory in the future. There is no doubt that by requiring companies to consider this area, the link between investment in employees and improved business performance will be made.

Expandable text - Impact on performance measures

The developments outlined above in the reporting of the environmental and social consequences of an entity's activities have identified a wide array of areas, over and above financial performance, in which management performance should be evaluated, such as:

- Environmental
- Social
- Management of customers
- Management of employees
- Ethics

(a) environmental:

- use of energy, including proportion from renewable sources
- efficiency of energy creation (for power generators)
- CO_2 emissions
- waste management
- accidents affecting environment
- transport.

(b) social:

- investment in local community initiatives
- time off for employees involved in charitable work
- matching money raised by employees for charitable work
- employment opportunities for the disadvantaged
- ethnic balance in workforce
- equality, e.g. women in senior management positions
- accidents affecting the community.

To these can be added other headings, such as:

(c) customers:

- failures to supply on time and in good condition
- customer complaints, e.g. about direct selling techniques
- fair pricing
- help for the disadvantaged through special pricing schemes.

(d) employees:

- absenteeism rates

- sickness leave

- diversity

- equal opportunities

- investment in training

- number of industrial relations tribunals in respect of the entity.

(e) ethics:

- number and cost of incidents leading to fines and/or penalties

- number and cost of incidents leading to compensation:
    - to customers
    - to employees
    - to others

- non-penalisation of whistle blowers.

But for performance measurement in these areas to be useful, the result must be information which is helpful in the making of economic decisions, whether they relate to the choice of investment, employment or suppliers. The IASB Framework's characteristics for useful financial information are that it should be relevant, reliable and comparable. These characteristics can be applied to environmental, social and ethical areas as follows.

- **Relevance**: how much weight do/will investors, employees and consumers give to these factors, compared with that given to financial factors (so return on investment, employee benefits and price, respectively)?

- **Reliability**: how much can the performance measured in these areas be relied on? How sure can users of this information be that it is a faithful representation of what has occurred, as opposed to a selective view, focusing on the successes? Are there external assurance processes that can validate the information, perhaps using the GRI guidelines?

- **Comparability**: is the information produced by different entities pulled together on a comparable basis, using similar measurement policies, so that the users can make informed choices between entities? If not, all that can be measured is an entity's performance compared with its own performance in previous periods.

Even if the information is reliable and comparable, is it useful, i.e. will it changes the behaviour of investors, employees and consumers?

The answers to these questions will determine whether entities take such reporting seriously or merely treat it as part of their promotional activities. And the answers in ten years' time will almost certainly be different from those of today.

Chapter summary

Non-financial reporting
- Important additional information provided by management
- Management commentary – assesses results of the period

Sustainability
- Method of conducting business to enable future generations to be able to meet their needs
- Organisations often produce a sustainability report which details their actions and policies towards the environment and society

Environmental reporting
- Details the effect of the business on the environment
- It is reported separately or as part of a sustainability report
- No mandatory guidelines, so Global Reporting Initiative guidelines tend to be used
- The effect of environmental provisions is reflected in the financial statements

Social reporting
- Details the organisation's approach to society
- This includes employees, local community, suppliers and customers
- It can be reported on a stand-alone basis or as part of a sustainability report

Impact on performance measures
- Can performance measures provide reliable and comparable information?
- Is this information relevant to needs of
  - investors?
  - employees
  - consumers?

chapter

20

Specialised entities and specialised transactions

Chapter learning objectives

Upon completion of this chapter you will be able to:

- account for transactions and events occurring in not- for-profit and public sector entities

- outline the principal considerations in developing a set of accounting standards for SMEs

- discuss solutions to the problem of differential financial reporting

- identify when an entity may no longer be viewed as a a going concern and outline circumstances when a reconstruction may be an alternative to corporate liquidation

- outline the appropriate accounting treatment required relating to reconstructions.

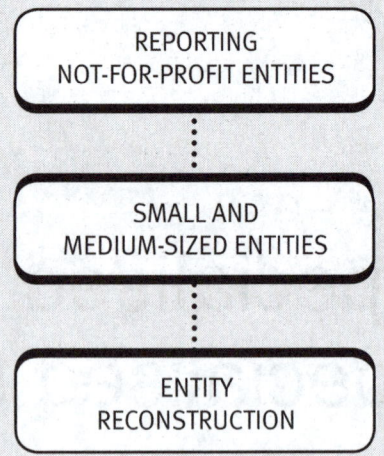

Expandable text - Reporting not-for-profit entities

Definition

A **not-for-profit entity** is one that does not carry on its activities for the purposes of profit or gain to particular persons, including its owners or members; and does not distribute its profits or assets to particular persons, including its owners or members.

The main types of not-for-profit entity are:

- clubs and societies

- charities

- public sector organisations (including central government, local government and National Health Service bodies).

The objectives of a not-for-profit entity

Key points

- The main objective of public sector organisations is to provide services to the general public. Their long-term aim is normally to break even, rather than to generate a surplus.

- Most public sector organisations aim to provide value for money, which is usually analysed into the three Es – economy, efficiency and effectiveness.

- Other not-for-profit entities include charities, clubs and societies whose objective is to carry out the activities for which they were created.

Assessing performance in a not-for-profit entity

- It can be difficult to monitor and evaluate the success of a not-for-profit organisation as the focus is not on a resultant profit as with a traditional business entity.

- The success of the organisation should be measured against the key indicators that reflect the visions and values of the organisation. The strategic plan will identify the goals and the strategies that the organisation needs to adopt to achieve these goals.

- The focus should be the measures of output, outcomes and their impact on what the charity is trying to achieve.

Accounting in a not-for-profit entity

The financial statements of a public sector entity or a charity are set out differently from those of a profit making entity, because their purpose is different. A public sector organisation is not reporting a profit; it is reporting on its income and how it has spent that income in achieving its aims.

The financial statements include a statement of financial position or balance sheet, but the income statement/statement of comprehensive income is usually replaced with a statement of financial activities or an income and expenditure account showing incoming resources and resources expended.

Expandable text - Example of not-for-profit accounts

An example of a statement of financial activities for a charity is shown below.

The Toytown Charity, Statement of Financial Activities for the year ended 31 March 20X7

	$
Incoming resources	
Resources from generated funds	
Grants	10,541,000
Legacies	5,165,232
Donations	1,598,700
Activities for generating funds	
Charity shop sales	10,052,693
Investment income	3,948,511
Total incoming resources	31,306,136

Resources expended

Cost of generating funds

Fund raising	(1,129,843)
Publicity	(819,828)
Charity shop operating costs	(6,168,923)

Charitable activities

Supporting local communities	(18,263,712)
Elderly care at home	(4,389,122)
Pride in Toytown campaign	(462,159)
Total resources expended	(31,233,587)
Net incoming resources for the year	72,549
Funds brought forward at 1 March 20X6	21,102
Funds carried forward at 31 March 20X7	93,651

The statement of financial position or balance sheet of a not-for-profit entity only differs from that of a profit making entity in the reserves section, where there will usually be an analysis of the different types of reserve, as shown below.

Toytown Charity, Balance sheet as at 31 March 20X7

	$
Non-current assets	
Tangible assets	80,500
Investments	12,468
	92,968
Current assets	
Inventory	2,168
Receivables	10,513
Cash	3,958
	16,639
Total assets	109,607

Reserves	
Restricted fund	20,200
Unrestricted funds	73,451
	———
	93,651
Non-current liabilities	
Pension liability	9,705
Current liabilities	
Payables	6,251
	———
Total funds	109,607
	———

The reserves are separated into restricted and unrestricted funds.

- Unrestricted funds are funds available for general purposes.

- Restricted funds are those that have been set aside for a specific purpose or in a situation where an individual has made a donation to the charity for a specific purpose, perhaps to replace some equipment, so these funds must be kept separate.

Expandable text - Accounting guidance

There is no specific reporting standard accounting for non-profit making entities within IFRS GAAP. However, there is guidance in the U.K. where four Statements of Recommended Practice (SORPs) relevant to public benefit activities have been issued. SORPs are issued by an industry or sponsoring body, recognised by the UK Accounting Standards Board (ASB) as being an appropriate body for that purpose. The nature of the transactions, together with organisational, legal and other factors require that SORPs are individual in nature, to meet specific accounting and reporting requirements. A summary of the relevant SORPs is as follows:

(1) Accounting and Reporting by Charities –(2nd edition – May 2008)

(2) Accounting for Further and Higher Education (Issued July 2007)

(3) Accounting by Registered Social Landlords (Revised 2007)

(4) Code of Practice on Local Authority Accounting in the UK 2009 (May 2009)

In June 2007, the ASB published an Interpretation for Public Benefit Entities of the Statement of Principles for Financial Reporting. The Interpretation explains how the principles in the Statement apply for public benefit entities. The Interpretation will support the work of those bodies within the public benefit sector that are recognised by the ASB for the purpose of issuing SORPs. It will also be of interest to international work, including the conceptual framework project that is being taken forward by the International Public Sector Accounting Standards Board. It comprises eight chapters as follows:

(1)   The objective of financial statements

(2)   The reporting entity

(3)   The qualitative characteristics of financial information

(4)   The elements of the financial statements

(5)   Recognition in the financial statements

(6)   Measurement in the financial statements

(7)   Presentation of financial statements

(8)   Accounting for interests in other entities

These chapter headings, together with much of the detail within, will be familiar to those who have knowledge of the UK ASB Statement of Principles or the IASB Framework document.

As an additional issue, the new IFRS-based Code of Practice on Local Authority Accounting will apply to local authority accounts from 1 April 2010.

1 Small and medium sized entities

Definition:

A SME may be defined or characterised as follows:

- they are usually owner-managed by a relatively small number of individuals such as a family group, rather than having an extensive ownership base,

- they are usually smaller entities in financial terms such as revenues generated and assets and liabilities under the control of the entity,

- they usually have a relatively small number of employees, and

- they usually undertake less complex or difficult transactions which are normally the focus of a financial reporting standard.

By contrast, listed companies have an extended base of ownership, principally financial institutions and professional investors. They invariably enter into a broader range of transactions and arrangements in their business dealings, which may be complex and which may require direction to ensure they are accounted for in an objective and consistent manner. Consequently, there is a need for specific and detailed reporting standards to direct entities to provide financial information to users which is relevant, reliable and comparable with other entities.

If SMEs can be identified as distinct from other entities, then it may be worth evaluating whether the financial reporting requirements of such entities should also be distinct or different from other entities. After all, one of the underlying requirements for financial reporting is that the cost and burden of producing financial reporting information for shareholders and other stakeholders is that it the benefits should outweigh the costs of making that information available.

There is no definitive definition of a SME. However a SME may be defined, it would appear clear that that its shares will not be listed on a public exchange. There is still the issue of making a judgement, based upon a range of size or other criteria, as to what may be regarded as a SME. It is also possible to identify particular classes of business activity which could be excluded from the definition of a SME if considered desirable. If monetary values are used to determine SME status, there may be problems of comparability on an international basis.

The problem of accounting for SMEs

One possible source of confusion in developing a reporting standard for SME is that the European Union (EU) has passed Directives defining small and medium-sized companies (and groups). In the UK, as well as other countries, it is now possible to identify three distinct financial reporting groups:

- Listed entities, with an extensive ownership and which generate significant revenues and control assets and liabilities with monetary carrying values in the financial statements in the millions. They will also be major employers. Full IFRS GAAP compliance is required from these companies.

- Small and medium-size companies as defined by European Union (EU) law to reduce filing and publicity requirements for such companies. For example, implementation of relevant the EU Directive in the UK by the 2006 Companies Act defines a company as small or medium-sized if it meets any two out of three specified criteria based upon annual sales revenue, assets total from the statement of financial position and the total number of employees.

If an entity meets the definition of either a small or medium-sized company, it is eligible to file abbreviated or reduced financial reporting information at Companies House. Additionally, small companies can choose to exempt themselves from the requirement for an annual audit. However, in principle, they would still need to comply fully with relevant reporting standards unless specifically exempt from doing so. Some companies are excluded from taking advantage of the audit exemption and reduced filing and disclosure requirements if they are banks, building societies or others operating in the financial services industry. In the UK, the Financial Reporting Standard for Smaller Entities (FRSSE) identifies which UK Financial Reporting Standards are applicable to entities which meet the definition of a small company based upon UK company law.

EU member states may need to consider whether to eliminate the law-based definition of a small company and use a definition for SME which can then apply to all non-publicly listed entities. If this is done, it will have a two-tier financial reporting system, rather than a three-tier system which may result in confusion.

- SME's which are non-listed and which are non-publicly accountable; they may or may not also meet the definition of a small or medium-sized company based upon EU or other national law. There is now an IFRS for SMEs which identifies the extent to which IFRS should be applied by SMEs, together with underlying concepts and principles to apply if a topic is not covered within the IFRS for SME. In the UK, and probably throughout the EU, the potential application of IFRS for SME is greater than the FRSSE (or national equivalent) as the latter only applies to companies meeting the statutory definition of a small company, whereas potentially IFRS for SME may be applied by any non-publicly accountable entity, irrespective of any size criteria.

Another possible problem is the reporting and compliance burden placed upon SME when full compliance with IFRS GAAP is required, particularly when they may have relatively few transactions covered by an applicable reporting standard. For example, ensuring compliance with IFRS 5 (assets held for sale) or IFRS 8 (segmental reporting) may result in benefits of providing that information to users of financial statements not being exceeded by the costs of making that information available.

It could also be argued that there may be a comparability problem if some entities comply with IFRS GAAP in full, whilst others comply with IFRS for SME.

How are reporting requirement for SMEs to be identified and communicated?

Having considered whether there is a need for a different financial reporting regime for SME, it is then worth considering how the financial reporting requirements for SME should be identified and reported. One possible approach could be to include specific references within each reporting standard whether it was to be applied by SMEs, or the extent to which it was relevant or exempt. This would be quite a cumbersome method to introduce and would require detailed consideration each time a reporting standard was to be revised or replaced. An alternative approach would be to produce a self-contained, stand-alone, reporting standard applicable only to SMEs.

The approach used in the UK and some other countries was to produce a stand-alone reporting standard, the Financial Reporting Standard for Smaller Entities (FRSSE)., the first of which was issued in 1997. The idea was to have was a one-stop shop for financial reporting requirements for those entities eligible to apply it. If a particular issue or transaction entered into was not covered within the requirements of the FRSSE, preparers of financial statements should refer to other reporting standards for guidance as to what may be regarded as current practice.

The IFRS for SME was issued in July 2009 and has adopted a similar approach to the UK. It is effective immediately, but note that it has been left for each country to determine which entities will be eligible to apply the IFRS for SME. Although the IASB regards this standard as relevant and applicable to all non-publicly accountable entities, national governments may permit or restrict its application as they see fit.

What is the effect of introducing the IFRS for SME?

Instead of complying fully with IFRS, consisting of approximately 3,000 disclosure points within approximately 37 reporting standards (and additional IFRICs or UITF announcements as appropriate), compliance with IFRS for SME will comprise approximately 300 disclosure points all contained within the one document. This significantly reduces the burden and associated time and cost of producing financial statements. Similarly, the IFRS for SME will be updated approximately every three years, rather than having to manage the ever-present risk of reporting standards being amended, revised or withdrawn and replaced altogether. On 13 August 2009, South Africa became the first country to adopt IFRS for SME. The UK will apply IFRS for SME for accounting periods commencing from 1 January 2013 onwards, with comparatives required for the preceding year. Initially, it had been expected to have application commencing from 1 January 2012; however, this was deferred twelve months to give entities who may want to apply the IFRS for SME time to change their accounting and information systems, and to permit legislators time to change relevant law and regulation.

The subject matter of several reporting standards has been omitted from the IFRS for SME as follows:

- Earnings per share (IAS 33)
- Interim reporting (IAS 34)
- Segmental reporting (IFRS 8)
- Assets held for sale (IFRS 5)

The subject matter of other reporting standards has been simplified for inclusion within the IFRS for SME. In principle, many of the recognition and measurement principles have been simplified, resulting in the elimination of choice where that was possible within IFRS, to apply the most straight-forward treatment such as:

- R & D always expensed
- Goodwill amortised (10 years)
- No revaluation of property, plant and equipment
- No available-for-sale financial instruments (note that this category of financial asset has been discarded by IFRS 9)
- Finance costs never capitalised

In countries where there is currently a Financial Reporting Standard for Smaller Entities (FRSSE) or equivalent, there may be differences between that national standard and the IFRS for SME. For example, one matter in which the IFRS for SME currently differs from the UK FRSSE is that the latter does not require a cash flow statement to be included as part of the annual financial statements.

Benefits expected to accrue following adoption of IFRS for SMEs

Expected benefits may include the following:

- Provide improved comparability for users of accounts with other entities who also use IFRS
- Enhance the overall confidence in the accounts of SMEs if they are seen to be applying reporting requirements which have some degree of comparability with compliance with IFRS in full.
- Reduce the significant costs involved in maintaining standards on a national basis. Potentially, this may lead to the demise of national standard setters as listed entities in many countries have adopted IFRS. If SME move towards adoption of IFRS for SME, there may be little left for national standard setters to regulate.
- Facilitate subsequent adoption of full IFRS, for example, if a SME intends to seek a stock exchange listing at a later date.

Technical Article

The P2 Examiner, Graham Holt, wrote an article discussing the issue of IFRS for SME in the March 2010 Student Accountant magazine. You can access this article from the ACCA website (www.accaglobal.com).

> ### Test your understanding 1 - SME
>
> (1) **Describe the reasons a standard for SMEs is required.**
> (2) **Describe the potential solutions to accounting for SMEs.**
> (3) **What is the IASB's method of reporting for SMEs?**

2 Entity reconstruction schemes

Key reason for an entity reconstruction

Financial difficulties

If an entity is in financial difficulty it may have no recourse but to accept liquidation as the final outcome. However it may be in a position to survive, and indeed flourish, by taking up some future contract or opportunities. The only hindrance to this may be that any future operations may need a prior cash injection. This cash injection cannot be raised because the present structure and status of the entity may not be attractive to current and outside investors.

A typical corporate profile of an entity in this situation could be as follows:

- Accumulated trading losses
- Arrears of unpaid debenture and loan interest
- No payment of equity dividends for several years
- Market value of equity shares below their nominal value
- Lack of investor and market confidence in the entity

To get a cash injection the entity will need to undergo a reorganisation or reconstruction.

To consider how a reconstruction may help the entity to survive, the rights and interests of the various stakeholders need to be considered.

Entity stakeholders

The capital structure of a corporate entity is designed to protect its principal stakeholders - normally identified as equity holders and providers of finance. Any changes to this structure are therefore restricted by corporate law in most countries to protect these stakeholders. Some of the ways in which this is achieved are explained below.

An entity with accumulated losses is normally prevented from paying equity dividends, usually until the accumulated losses have been recovered by trading profitably, which could take several years, because of corporate law restrictions on distributions to shareholders. This situation will not make the entity an attractive proposition for prospective equity investors.

Non-payment of equity dividends add to the problem for the following reasons:

- Current equity holders will find it difficult to sell their shares for what they may consider to be a satisfactory price; any potential purchase of their shares is likely to be at a low value.

- Potential investors will not be attracted by the poor dividend payment history, and the fact that this situation is unlikely to improve in the forseeable future.

- If the market price of equity shares is below their nominal value, a new issue of equity shares is unlikely to be successful as potential investors will seek to pay only market value for the shares. Many countries have corporate law which prevent equity capital being issued at less than its nominal value.

In summary, there is likely to be a lack of confidence in the entity to attract new investors, or to encourage existing investors to retain or increase their investment.

Providers of loan finance are primarliy concerned with recovery of their capital and interest. The operational performance and profitability is of secondary importance provided that they can recoup their capital and interest. Existing or threatened arrears of debenture or bank interest are a negative factor when trying to raise finance for the following reasons:

- They tie up any future resources for interest and capital payments which could otherwise be used for expansion.

- They tie up any future profits which could be used for distribution in the form of a dividend.

- They make it difficult to obtain new loan finance as past arrears will make any attempt to raise new finance unattractive to the market.

- Existing providers of loan finance may also have the right to enforce recovery of funds from the entity, perhaps by having secuity (i.e collateral) for their loans.

- There may be few, if any, assets available within the entity for use as security (i.e collateral) to support any future raising of finance.

A reconstruction of the entity's capital may help to alleviate these problems and may involve one or more of the following procedures:

- Write off the accumulated losses.

- Write off arrears of repayment of loan finance

- Write down the nominal value of the equity capital.

How is this achieved?

To do this the entity must ask all or some of its existing stakeholders to surrender existing rights and amounts owing in exchange for new rights under a new or reformed entity.

Why would stakeholders be willing to do this?

The main reason is that a reconstruction may result in an outcome preferable to any other alternative as follows:

- Providers of loan finance and other creditors may be left with little of no prospect of repayment.

- Providers of equity finance may be left with little of no prospect of a return (dividends and capital growth) on their investment.

- Corporate liquidation may provide some return to providers of loan finance, but is unlikely to provide any return to equity holders, depending upon the financial position of the entity.

How could this be agreed between the various stakeholders?

It may be helpful to review the situation faced by each group of stakeholders as follows:

Equity shareholders This is the last group to be allocated funds in a corporate liquidation, and therefore have a high chance of receiving no return at all. It would therefore seem appropriate that they should bear most of the losses from the present situation, in exchange for potential future benefits if the entity is profitable following reconstruction.

Trade creditors and payables may have some prospect of recovery of at least part of the amounts due to them as they rank ahead of equity holders for repayment upon corporate liquidation. Some trade creditors may also protect themselves from the risk of non-recovery by including the right to retain legal title or ownership of goods delivered to customers until they are paid for. In the event of non-recovery of amounts due to them, they will have the right to take repossession of their inventory.

Debenture holders often have a better chance of recovery of capital under liquidation than other stakeholders because such loans are often secured against entity assets. However, even in this situation, the full amount outstanding of such loans may not be recovered. In this case, any amount not recovered from the assets used as security (or collateral) would then normally be regarded as an unsecured creditor in the same way as trade payables.

There may be a situation where there is more than one debenture loan secured against entity assets. in this situation, the respective rights of each debenture holder would need to be examined to determine who would be paid off first in the event of there being insufficient assets to meet the claims of all secured loans. It could be, for example, that secured loans are paid off or settled in the order in which they were created; i.e. the oldest loans would be paid off first from available assets, then more recent loans would be paid off out of any available surplus.

It may therefore be in the best interests of all stakeholders to agree to a scheme of reconstruction. In effect, they give up existing rights and amounts owing (which are unlikely to be recovered) for the opportunity to share in the future profitability which may arise from the extra cash which can be generated as a consequence of their actions. This can only be achieved if all stakeholders are willing to compromise by waiving some or all of their existing rights, and if they can be convinced that there is an improved prospect of future returns as a result of a reconstruction scheme.

In examination questions, be alert to identify any information relating to the order in which liabilities are to be settled or paid off, and what happens to any amounts not paid due to inadequate security or collateral. This information should then be applied to ensure that liabilities are paid off in the correct order, having identified those liabilities secured by assets or collateral.

One additional factor is that there may be **professional fees** incurred as part of any reconstruction scheme. Carefully review the information in the question to determine whether:

- such creditors rank ahead of unsecured creditors for payment
- whether their fees are paid by any particular stakeholder group, depending upon who initiates the reconstruction scheme.

Capital reduction scheme

Using this scheme, an entity may:

- write off unpaid equity capital - this situation may arise, for example, if there are partly-paid shares in issue. The entity is effectively reducing the nominal value of its equity share capital by the amount not yet called up and paid by the equity holders. For example, partly paid equity shares with a nominal value of $1, may be reduced to the amount currently paid up, say, $0.75; in doing so, the equity holders will no longer be required to pay the amount still outstanding.

- write off any equity capital which is lost or not represented by available assets - in this situation, the entity has a deficit on retained earnings due to accumulated losses. This prevents payment of an equity dividend and also depresses the share price. In effect, the entity will write off this deficit against any other available components of equity to clear all or part of the deficit on retained earnings.

- write off any paid up equity capital which is in excess of requirements - in this situation, the entity uses surplus cash to repay its equity holders.

This scheme does not really affect creditors as the equity holders have reduced their capital stake in the entity, either by reducing the nominal value of the shares in issue, or by reducing the total number of shares in issue, or a combination of both.

This scheme is normally regulated by formalised procedures detailed in law, such as the Companies Act 2006 s641 in the United Kingdom, which may differ in other countries. **In examination questions**, it is unlikely that there will be questions set which require a specific and detailed knowledge of law from any particular jurisdiction; however, it is likely that students wil be expected to have an understanding of the principles of when such a scheme may be appropriate and how it may be applied. It is also possible that a question could be set which provided the rules to apply in a given scenario.

Illustration 1 - Struggler

Struggler has the following statement of financial position at 30 June 20X8:

	$000
Assets	500
	———
	500
	———

	$000
Equity and liabilities:	
Issued equity shares @ $1 each	600
Share premium	100
Retained earnings/(deficit)	(300)
Liabilities	100
	———
	500
	———

Struggler has the following problems:

- Accumulated losses which prevent payment of a dividend should the entity become profitable at some future date.

- Issued equity capital of $600,000 which is only backed by assets to the extent of $500,000.

- Difficulty in attracting new sources of equity and/or loan finance.

Required:

Apply a capital reduction scheme and restate the statement of financial position at 30 June 20X8.

Expandable text - Solution

Using the reduction of capital scheme, the deficit on retained earnings could be cleared by reducing both the share premium and issued equity capital accounts. Any balance on share premium account should be utilised first to minimise the reduction of equity capital as follows:

	$000	$000
Dr Share premium	100	
Dr Equity share capital	200	
Cr Retained earnings		300

The resulting statement of financial position would be:

	$000
Assets	500
	___
	500
	___

Equity and liabilities:	$000
Issued equity shares	400
Share premium	nil
Retained earnings/(deficit)	nil
Liabilities	100
	___
	500
	___

The equity holders have effectively recognised the financial reality of their situation by reducing the nominal value of the issued share capital. If the entity begins to make profits following the reconstruction, there is no longer a deficit on retained earnings to clear before a dividend can be paid. Potential equity and/or loan finance providers may also be encouraged by this situation.

The reduction in equity capital could be reflected by either a reduction in the nominal value per share (from $1 down to approximately (400/600) $0.67, or by converting and reducing shareholdings on a pro-rata basis. For example, if a person previously owned thirty shares with a nominal value of $1 each, following conversion and reduction, they would now own only twenty shares with a nominal value of $1 each. In either situation, the total equity share capital would be $400,000.

3 Reconstruction schemes

Reconstruction schemes extend the principles of the capital reduction schemes by including the various creditors within the scheme. In addition to reducing equity share capital, reconstruction schemes may also include:

- writing off debenture loan interest arrears

- replacement of debenture loans with new loans having different interest and capital repayment terms

- write off amounts owing to unsecured or trade payables.

Equity holders and creditors may be willing to do this if the entity is considered likely to survive and return to profitable trading in the future. They are effectively sacrificing their current legal and commercial rights for future legal and commercial rights which will hopefully bring them better financial returns than under their current position. Such reconstruction schemes may be subject to court or law-based formal approval procedures before they can be implemented.

In practical terms, this can only be achieved if all stakeholders agree to forego some of their current legal and commercial rights. For those in the weakest position, usually the equity holders, they would be expected to sacrifice more than others, such as secured debenture loan providers. Secured debenture loan providers could act in their own interest and enforce possession of the assets provided as security (i.e collateral), but this would often be to the detriment of other stakeholders and could lead to the liquidation of the entity if it can no longer operate. Consequently, due to their stonger position, secured loan providers will be reluctant to sacrifice as much as the equity holders in any reconstruction scheme.

In the United Kigdom, these schemes are governed by the Companies Act 2006 s895. As with the capital reduction scheme considered earlier, it is unlikely that an examination question will be set which requires a detailed knowledge of specific law from any one jurisdiction. However, questions may be set on the application of the principles, possibly including rules to apply in a given situation.

Illustration 2 - Machin

Consider the statement of financial position of Machin at 30 June 20X9:

	$000
Non-current assets:	
Intangible - brand	50,000
Tangible	220,000
	270,000
Current assets:	
Inventory	20,000
Receivables	30,000
	320,000

	$000
Equity and liabilities:	
Equity share capital @ $1 shares	100,000
Share premium	75,000
Retained earnings	(100,000)
	75,000
Non-current liabilities: Debenture loan	125,000
Current liabilities:	
Bank overdraft	20,000
Trade payables	100,000
	320,000

The following reconstruction scheme is to be applied:

(1) The equity shares of $1 nominal value currently in issue will be written off and will be replaced on a one-for-one basis by new equity shares with a nominal value of $0.25.

(2) The debenture loan will be replaced by the issue of new equity shares - four new equity shares with a nominal value of $0.25 each for every $1 of debenture loan converted.

(3) Existing equity holders will be offered the opportunity to subscribe for three new equity shares with a nominal value of $0.25 each for every one equity share currently held. The shares are to be issued at nominal value. It is expected that all current equity holders will take up this opportunity.

(4) The share premium account is to be eliminated.

(5) The brand is considered to be impaired and must be written off.

(6) Retained earnings deficit is to be eliminated

Required:

Prepare the statement of financial position of Machin immediately after the scheme has been put into effect. Show any workings required to arrive at the solution.

Expandable text - Solution

Begin by opening a reconstruction account:

All adjustments to the statement of financial position as a result of the reconstruction scheme must be accounted for within this account. Any balance remaining on this account will be used to either write down assets or create a capital reserve.

Reconstruction account

	$000		$000
New equity shares (100,000 x $0.25) (Note 1)	25,000	Equity shares @ $1 (Note 1)	100,000
New equity shares (125,000 x 4 x $0.25) (Note 2)	125,000	Debenture loan (Note 2)	125,000
Brand impaired (Note 5)	50,000	Share premium (Note 4)	75,000
Retained earnings (Note 6)	100,000		
	300,000		300,000

The note references refer to the details of the reconstruction scheme.

The debenture holders may be prepared to sacrifice their rights as a creditor if they believe that Machin will trade profitably following the reconstruction scheme. They will forego the rights of a creditor in exchange for the rights of an equity holder - i.e. future dividends plus growth in the capital value of their equity shares.

The resulting statement of financial position for Machin will be:

	$000
Non-current assets:	
Intangible - brand	nil
Tangible	220,000
	———
Current assets:	
Inventory	20,000
Receivables	30,000
Bank ((20,000) + 75,000) (Note 3)	55,000
	———
	325,000
Share premium	nil
Retained earnings	nil
	———
	225,000
Non-current liabilities: Debenture loan	nil
Current liabilities:	
Bank overdraft (eliminated by cash receipt from share issue)	nil
Trade payables	100,000
	———
	325,000
	———

(W1) confirmation of equity share capital following reorganisation:

		No
Note 1	Issue of one new equity share for one old equity share	100,000
Note 2	Convert debenture loan into new equity shares: 125,000 x 4	500,000
Note 3	Issue of new equity shares for cash	300,000
		———
		900,00
		———

Illustration 3 - Bentham

Bentham has been making losses for several years, principally due to severe competition, which has put downward pressure on revenues whilst costs have increased.

The statement of financial position for Bentham at 30 June 20X1 is as follows:

	$000
Non-current assets	7,200
Current assets	10,550
	17,750

	$000
Equity and liabilities	
Equity share capital @$1 shares	20,000
Retained earnings (deficit)	(17,250)
	2,750
Non-current liabilities:	
11 % debentures 20X3 (secured)	7,000
8% debentures 20X4 (secured)	5,000
Current liabilities	3,000
	17,750

The entity has changed its marketing strategy and, as a result, it is expected that annual profit before interest and tax will be $3,000,000 for the next five years. Bentham incurs tax at 25% on profit before tax.

The directors are proposing to reconstruct Bentham and have produced the following proposal for discussion:

(1) The existing $1 equity shares are to be cancelled and replaced by equity shares of $0.25.

(2) The 8% debentures are to be replaced by 8,000,000 equity shares of $0.25 each, regarded as fully paid up, plus $3,000,000 6% debentures 20X9.

(3) Existing shareholders will have their $1 equity shares replaced by 11,000,000 $0.25 equity shares, regarded as fully paid up.

4   The 11% debentures are to be redeemed in exchange for:

  –   for:$6,000,000 6% debentures 20X9, and

  –   4,000,000 equity shares of $0.25, regarded as fully paid up.

In the event of a liquidation, it is estimated that the net realisable value of the assets would be $6,200,000 for the non-current assets and $10,000,000 for the current assets.

Required:

- **Prepare a statement of financial position for Bentham at 1 July 20X1, immediately after the reconstruction scheme has been implemented.**

- **Prepare computations to show the effect of the proposed reconstruction scheme on each of the equity shareholders, 11% debenture holders and 8% debenture holders.**

- **Comment on the potential outcome of the scheme from the perspective of a shareholder who currently owns 10% of the equity share capital on whether to agree to the reconstruction scheme as proposed.**

Expandable text - Solution

Bentham - the revised statement of financial position at 1 July 20X1 following reconstruction would be:

	$000
Non-current assets	7,200
Current assets	10,550
	17,750

	$000
Equity and liabilities:	
Equity share capital (23 million shares @ $0.25)(W1)	5,750
Retained earnings (deficit)	nil
	5,750
Non-current liabilities:	
6% debentures 20X9 (W1)	9,000
Current liabilities	3,000
	17,750

(W1) The reconstruction account would be as follows:

Reconstruction account

	$000		$000
New 6% debentures	6,000	11% Debentures redeemed	7,000
New equity shares: 4m @ $0.25	1,000	8% Debenture redeemed	5,000
New equity shares: 11m @ $0.25	2,750	Equity cancelled	20,000
New equity shares: 8m @ $0.25	2,000		
New 6% debentures	3,000		
Deficit on retained earnings	17,250		
	32,000		32,000

KAPLAN PUBLISHING

If Bentham was to be put into liquidation, rather than undergo the reconstruction, the following could be the consequence:

	$000
Net realisable value of non-current assets	6,200
Net realisable value of current assets	10,000
	16,200
Repayment of 11% secured debenture loan	(7,000)
Repayment of 8% secured debenture loan	(5,000)
Available for unsecured creditors	4,200
Unsecured creditors	(3,000)
Available for equity holders	1,200

It can be seen that, whilst secured creditors will be paid off, and there should then be sufficient assets available for payment of unsecured creditors, equity shareholders would not fully recover the nominal value of their shareholding. The equity holders would receive only (1,200 / 20,000) $0.06 for each $1 equity share held. Note that this does not include any legal and professional fees that may be payable to implement such a scheme.

If the scheme is implemented, the debenture holders would forego part of their prior claim for repayment in exchange for equity shares. If they are to agree to this, they must be satisfied regarding the reliability of the profit forecast for future trading, so that they can receive future dividends and enjoy capital growth on the value of their shares. Additionally, they will have a significant equity holding of 12 million out of 23 million equity shares. This is just enough to give them a majority of the equity capital; they could then use their voting power to appoint or remove directors as they see appropriate.

If the reconstruction scheme is implemented, the revised capital structure results in significanly more equity shares in issue, with reduced long term liabilities in the form of secured debenture loans. It can be seen that the current debenture loan holders have deferred the repayment date of their loans from 20X3 and 20X4 respectively to 20X9, and accepted a reduced rate of interest on their loans. In addition, they have received some equity shares which will give them the opportunity to share in the future prosperity of Bentham if it becomes profitable following the reconstruction.

From the perspective of someone who holds 10% of the equity before the reconstruction takes place, the following comments can be made:

*   The gearing ratio ratio has reduced as follows:

Before:	$000	After:	$000
Gearing ratio	$\dfrac{12{,}000}{14{,}750} = 81.3\%$		$\dfrac{9{,}000}{14{,}750} = 61.0\%$

    The reduction in gearing will be regarded as a decrease in financial risk for the equity holders.

*   If the forecast regarding expected profit before interest and tax is reliable, then the following will result:

		$000
Profit before interest and tax		3,000
Less: debenture interest	9,000 x 6%	540
		___
Profit before tax		2,460
Tax @ 25%		(615)
		___
Profit after tax available to equity holders		1,845

    Potentially, there are retained profits available for payment of an equity dividend. Whilst it may not be advisable to distribute all profit after tax in the form of a dividend, it is a positive step to have retained earnings within the entity. Additionally, interest cover of (3,000 / 540) 5.5 may be regarded as reasonable in the circumstances.

*   One further factor is the change in proportionate voting power if the reconstruction scheme is implemented. Previously, someone who owned 10% of the equity share capital would have 10% x 11 million = 1.1 million equity shares in the restructured entity out of 23 million equity shares - i.e 4.7% of the equity shares. This is a significant dilution of voting power, but it may be a reasonable thing to give up in exchange for the future prospect of the continuation of Bentham, together with the potential receipt of a dividend if the forecast is realistic.

Test your understanding 2 - Wire

Wire has suffered from poor trading conditions over the last three years. Its statement of financial position at 30 June 20X1 is as follows:

	$	$
Non-current assets:		
Land and buildings		193,246
Plant and equipment		60,754
Investment in Cord		27,000
		_____
		281,000
Current assets:		
Inventory	120,247	
Receivables	70,692	
	_____	
		190,939
		_____
		471,939
		_____

		$
Equity and liabilities:		
Equity shares @$1		200,000
Retained earnings (deficit)		(39,821)
		_____
		160,179
Non-current liabilities:		
8% debenture 20X4	80,000	
5% debenture 20X5	70,000	
	_____	
		150,000
Current liabilities:		
Trade payables	112,247	
Interest payable	12,800	
Overdraft	36,713	
	_____	
		161,760
		_____
		471,939
		_____

It has been difficult to generate revenues and profits in the current year and inventory levels are very high. Interest has not beeen paid to the debenture holders for two years. Although the debentures are secured against the land and buildings, the debenture holders have demanded a scheme of reconstruction or the liquidation of Wire.

During a meeting of directors and representatives of the shareholders and debenture holders, it was decided to implement a scheme of reconstruction.

The following scheme has been agreed in principle:

(1) Each $1 equity share is to be redesignated as an equity share of $0.25.

(2) The existing 5% debenture is to be exchanged for a new issue of $35,000 9.5% loan stock, repayable in 20X9, plus 140,000 equity shares of $0.25 each. In addition, they will subscribe for $9,000 debenure stock, repayable 20X9, at par value. The rate of interest on this new debenture is 9.5%.

(3) The equity shareholders are to accept a reduction in the nominal value of their shares from $1 to $0.25 per share, and subscribe for a new issue on the basis of one-for-one at a price of $0.30 per share.

(4) The 8% debenture holders, who have received no interest for two years, are to receive 20,000 equity shares of $0.25 each in lieu of the interest payable. It is agreed that the value of the interest liability is equivalent to the fair value of the shares to be issued. In addition, they have agreed to defer repayment of their loan until 20X9, subject to an increased rate of interest of 9.5%.

(5) The deficit on retained earnings is to be written off.

(6) The investment in Cord has been subject to much speculation as Cord has just obtained the legal rights to a new production process. As a result, the value of the investment has increased to $60,000. This investment is to be sold as part of the reconstruction scheme.

(7) The bank overdraft is to be repaid.

(8) 10% of the receivables are regarded as non-recoverable and are to be written off.

(9) The remaining assets were independently valued, and should now be recognised at the following amounts:

	$
Land	80,000
Buildings	80,000
Equipment	30,000
Inventory	50,000

If the reconstruction goes ahead, the following is expected to happen:

(1) It is expected that, due to the refinancing, operating profits will be earned at the rate of $50,000 after depreciation, but before interest and tax.

(2) Wire will be subject to tax on its profit before tax at 25%.

Required:

- **Prepare the statement of financial position of Wire immediately after the reconstruction**

- **Advise the equity holders and debenture holders whether or not they should support the reconstruction scheme.**

4 External reconstructions

Such schemes normally involve the assets and liabilities of the current entity being transferred to a new entity on an agreed basis. Typically, this will require information regarding the following:

- details of purchase consideration to acquire the business as a whole, or specified assets and liabilities - this may give rise to goodwill for the purchaser.

- details of what will happen to assets and liabilities currently belonging to the entity which are to be sold, transferred, written off or realised as appropriate - this will lead to a profit or loss on realisation for the vendor.

- how repayment or settlement of capital of the selling entity is to be arranged.

Test your understanding 3 - Smith and Thompson

Smith has agreed to acquire the net assets, excluding the bank balance, and the debenture liability which is to be paid off in cash, of Thompson. The purchase consideration comprises the following:

	$000
50,000 equity shares @ $1 at a fair value of $1.10	52,000
$30,000 debenture loan issued at $0.90 per $1	30,000
Cash	18,000
	100,000

When determining the consideration to be paid, the directors of Smith valued the the land and buildings of Thompson at $40,000, inventory at $15,000 and receivables at carrying value, subject to a 3% write off for bad debts.

After the sale, Thompson is liquidated.

The statement of financial position of Thompson immediately before the acquisition is as follows:

	$
Non-current assets:	
Land and buildings	24,000
Plant and machinery	22,000
	46,000
Current assets:	
Inventory	19,000
Receivables	20,000
Bank	5,000
	90,000

	$
Equity and liabilities:	
Equity shares @ $1	30,000
Share premium	10,000
Retained earnings	16,000
	56,000
Non-current liabilities:	
6% debentures	20,000
Current liabilities:	
Trade payables	14,000
	90,000

Required:

- **Prepare the closing entries for Thompson**
- **Prepare the opening entries for Smith**

Expandable text - UK syllabus focus

UK GAAP has had a reporting standard for smaller companies, the Financial Reporting Standard for Smaller Entities "FRSSE" since 1997. More recently, the IASB has developed an equivalent reporting framework for smaller entities, IFRS for SME which was published in July 2009. The content of this chapter includes comparison between the FRSSE and IFRS for SME. The UK has approved IFRS for SME and initially set the effective date as 1 January 2012, with comparatives required from 2011; however, application has now been deferred twelve months to allow time for appropriate legal and regulatory issues to be dealt with, and to allow time for those companies who want to adopt the IFRS for SME to arrange compliance with its requirements.

The UK also has financial reporting and filing requirements based upon size criteria specified in the CA2006 as follows:

	Small--sized	Medium-sized
Turnover max. (£m)	6.5	25.9
Balance sheet total max. (£m)	3.2	12.9
Number of employees max.	50	250

The size criteria exclude banks, building societies, insurance and financial services companies, regardless of their size. This also applies to members of a group containing any of these companies. The UK FRSSE applies to individual companies and groups who meet the definition of being small.

In practical terms, small companies are required only to publish a balance sheet and limited supporting disclosure notes. Medium-sized companies can exclude disclosure of information prior to gross profit, but there is very little further exemption from accounting and disclosure requirements.

5 Chapter summary

Reporting not-for-profit entities
- These entities are in the public sector or are charities
- The objective of these entities is to achieve their aims, not to make a profit
- Guidance is provided in SORP 2005 and the ASB's Statement of Principles for public benefit entities

Small and medium-sized entities
- These entities need exemptions from some of the requirements of IFRSs
- Two possible solutions: exemption or differential reporting

Entity reconstruction
- Going concern issues
- Possible alternative to liquidation
- Accounting treatment

Test your understanding answers

Test your understanding 1 - SME

(1) SMEs are very different entities from the large listed companies that typically apply IFRS. The content of many IFRSs is not relevant to the needs of these smaller unlisted entities and many of them would be put off adopting IFRS due to the large reporting burden.

Primarily, the users of the financial statements of smaller entities are often banking institutions who have loaned money to the business. In many cases, small businesses are owner-managed and their focus is on the profitability and cash generation of the business. It makes sense that these entities should have their own reporting requirements more attuned to the needs of their businesses.

(2) There are two potential solutions to reporting for SMEs.
 (a) Exemptions from IFRS. A case can be made for requiring a lower level of disclosure from small and medium-sized entities, and in some countries this already happens.

 (b) Differential reporting. This is where a completely new set of standards is developed for small companies.

The first option is better, because it does not require completely new standards to be written and keeps both large and small companies applying the same standards even though the smaller companies are applying abbreviated versions. this is the approach used uin the UK with the issue of the Financial Reporting Standard for Smaller Entities ("FRSSE") which has then been updated periodically since it was first introduced in 1997.

(3) The IASB's method is a stand-alone standard for SMEs. The content of this will be a full IFRS that address transactions, events, or conditions commonly encountered by SMEs. It will provide a framework for the preparation of financial statements by a SME.

Those accounting requirements covered by reporting standards relating to transactions, events or conditions not generally encountered by SMEs are not included in the IFRS for SMEs. The goal is to minimise the circumstances in which an SME would need to fall back to full IFRS for guidance on how to account for a particular transaction or situation.

Test your understanding 2 - Wire

Wire - statement of financial position at 30 June 20X1

(after reconstruction)

	$
Non-current assets:	
Land and buildings at valuation	160,000
Equipment	30,000
Financial asset - investment in Cord	nil
	190,000
Current assets:	
Inventory	50,000
Receivables (70,692 x 90%)	63,623
Bank (W2)	92,287
	395,910

	$
Equity and liabilities:	
Equity shares @ $0.25 (W3)	140,000
Share premium (W3)	17,800
Retained earnings	nil
Capital reserve (W1)	1,863
	159,663
Non-current liabilities:	
9.5% debentures (W4)	124,000
Current liabilities:	
Trade payables	112,247
	395,910

Wire - workings:

(W1) Reconstruction account

	$	$
Carrying values:		
Land and buldings	193,246	
Equipment	60,754	
Investment in Cord	27,000	
Inventory	120,247	
Receivables written off (70,962 x 10%)	7,069	
Deficit on retained earnings written off	39,821	
Revised valuations:		
Land and buildings		160,000
Equipment		30,000
Investment in Cord		60,000
Inventory		50,000
Share capital reduced (200,000 @ $0.75)		150,000
Capital reserve (bal fig)	1,863	
	450,000	450,000

(W2) Bank account

		$
Overdraft		(36,713)
New equity share issue	200,000 @ $0.30	60,000
New debenure issue	9,000 at par value	9,000
Sale of investment - Cord		60,000
		92,287

(W3) Shareholdings

	Equity shares Number	$	Share premium $
Redesignated existing shares @ $0.25 each	200,000	50,000	
New issue @ $0.30 each	200,000	50,000	10,000
Part-exchange of 5% debenture	140,000	35,000	
Debenture interest (12,800 - 5,000) **	20,000	5.000	7,800
	560,000	140,000	17,800

**8% deb interest on $80,000 p.a for 2 years = $12,800 - $5,000 (20,000 @ $0.25) = $7,800 share premium.

(W4) Debenture loan	$
8% debenture 20X4 deferred to 20X9 with with 9.5% interest rate	80,000
New 9.5% debentures 20X9 - nominal value	9,000
New 9.5% debentures 20X9 - part conversion of 5% debenture	35,000
	124,000

Advice to equity and debt holders:

Based upon the situation at 30 June 20X1 before the reconstruction scheme was devised, the following can be ascertained:

(1) There are sufficient assets to repay the secured debentures and perhaps most of the arrears of interest.

(2) Unsecured creditors would be unlikely to receive payment in full for amounts owed.

(3) Equity shareholders are unlikely to receive anything upon liquidation.

If a reconstruction scheme is to be agreed between the various parties, those who are in the strongest position (secured creditors) would expect to give up the least. Those in the weakest postion (unsecured creditors and equity holders), would be expected to sacrifice more of their current entitlement to have any chance of recovery in the future.

The position of Wire if it was to go into liquidation is as follows:

	$
Land and buldings	160,000
Plant and equipment	30,000
Investment	60,000
Inventory	50,000
Receivables (70,962 x 90%)	63,623
Assets available	363,263
Secured liabilities (80,000 + 70,000)	(150,000)
	213,623

KAPLAN PUBLISHING

Current liabilities:		
Overdraft	36,713	
Interest	12,800	
Trade payables	112,247	
	————	(161,760)
		————
Available to equity holders		51,863
		————

The above summary identifies the position of the various stakeholders if there was no reconstruction scheme and Wire was liquidated. The debenture holders would be sure to receive their loan repayment, together with probably all of the arrears of interest, depending upon realised values of the assets and no other significant liabilities being uncovered.

The equity holders would not receive a full return of the nominal value of their capital, receiving only approximately (51,863 / 200,000) $0.26 per share.

Consequently, if the reconstruction scheme is implemented:

(1) The debenture holders are to be offered an increased rate of interest, but must also accept extension of the lending period to 20X9. It continues to be secured against land and buildings. Their position is relatively strong and safe.

(2) Some of the debenture holders have exchanged some of their legal rights as creditors for rights as equity holders. They must hope that Wire becomes profitable so that they can receive dividends in future years and that the share price increases. In addition, they must hope that, even if Wire gets into financial difficulties at a later date, there are still sufficient assets available to repay them, after the secured creditors have been repaid.

(3) It would appear that Wire will make profit after tax if the reconstruction goes ahead and if the profit forecast is reliable as follows:

	$
Profit before tax and interest	50,000
Less: debenture interest (9.5% x $124,000)	11,780
	————
Profit before tax	38,220
Tax @ 25%	(9,555)
	————
Profit available to equity holders	28,665
	————

Earnings per share would therefore be: $28,665 / 560,000 = 5.1 cents per share (i.e $0.051 per share)

Test your understanding 3 - Smith and Thompson

Closing accounting for Thompson:

(W1) Realisation account

	$	$
Carrying values:		
Land and buldings	24,000	
Plant and equipment	22,000	
Inventory	19,000	
Receivables	20,000	
Creditors		14,000
Purchase consideration		100,000
Profit on realisation (bal fig)	29,000	
	114,000	114,000

(W2) Bank and cash

	$	$
Balance b/fwd	5,000	
Cash received for sale of business	18,000	
Debenture stock paid off		20,000
Cash to shareholders via realisation a/c		3,000
	23,000	23,000

(W3) Capital settlement on winding up

	$	$
Equity shares	52,000	
Receivables	30,000	
Cash return to equity holders	3,000	
Debenture stock		30,000
Share premium		10,000
Retained earnings		16,000
Profit on realisation		29,000
	85,000	85,000

KAPLAN PUBLISHING

(W4)	Receivable Account - Smith	$	$
	Realisation account		
	Equity shares	100,000	
	Shares at FV		52,000
	Debenture loan		30,000
	Cash		18,000
		100,000	100,000

(W5)	Purchase of business account	$	$
	Equity shares issued - NV		50,000
	Share premium (less discount)**		2,000
	Debentures		30,000
	Cash		18,000
	Land and buldings	40,000	
	Plant and equipment	22,000	
	Inventory	15,000	
	Receivables	19,400	
	Trade payables	(14,000)	
	Goodwill - (bal fig)	17,600	
		114,600	100,000

** The fair value of equity shares issued = 50,000 @ $1.1 = $55,000

Of this: NV = $50,000, with share premium of $5,000.

Adoption of IFRS

Chapter learning objectives

Upon completion of this chapter you will be able to:

- apply and discuss the accounting implications of the first time adoption of a body of new accounting standards

- outline the issues in implementing a change to new accounting standards including organisational, behavioural and procedural changes within the entity

- evaluate the implications of worldwide convergence with International Financial Reporting Standards

- discuss the implementation issues arising from the convergence process

- identify the reasons for major differences in accounting practices, including culture

- discuss the influence of national regulators on international financial reporting.

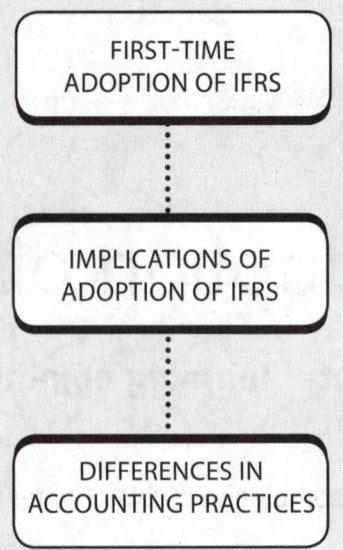

FIRST-TIME
ADOPTION OF IFRS

IMPLICATIONS OF
ADOPTION OF IFRS

DIFFERENCES IN
ACCOUNTING PRACTICES

Expandable text - IFRS 1 First time adoption of IFRS

Due to the drive towards convergence of reporting standards between
IAS/IFRS and US GAAP, and also national moves to harmonise national
standards with IAS/IFRS, many of the historical differences between the
different GAAPs have been reduced or eliminated. Where differences
remain between IAS/ IFRS and a particular set of national reporting
standards, they are not as significant as they may have been, say, 20
years ago. Consequently, the importance of first-time adoption of IFRS,
and the application of IFRS 1, may be perceived to be less important
than it has been in the past. However, it is still of importance for several
reasons:

- Entities who expect to seek a listing for the first time still need
  guidance on how the adoption process should be managed,
  accounted for, and disclosed in the financial statements.

- Entities who have no expectation of seeking a listing may choose to
  adopt IFRS if they perceive that IFRS is more relevant to their
  situation.

- Unlisted multinational corporate groups may choose to adopt
  IAS/IFRS as the basis for financial reporting throughout the group.
  This may save time and resources in the preparation of
  management information throughout the group, and streamline
  group annual financial reporting requirements.

- Entities may believe that adoption of IFRS could assist in their
  efforts to raise capital; if potential capital providers are familiar with
  IFRS, it may ease their evaluation of any capital investment
  opportunity.

- Entities may believe that they are 'doing the right thing' by adopting IFRS as it is already used by other, usually listed and often larger entities.

The above commentary demonstrates the significant progress to date made by the IASB and FASB towards achieve their desired outcome of producing high quality, compatible accounting standards that are suitable for both domestic and cross-border financial reporting. While there is still some way to go, and numerous obstacles to be negotiated, there appears to be a momentum which will ensure that progress continues in the coming

Introduction

- IFRS 1 First-time adoption of international financial reporting standards sets out the procedures to follow when an entity adopts IFRS in its published financial statements for the first time.

- Before adopting IFRS it will have applied its own national standards. This is called previous GAAP.

Definition

A **first-time adopter** is an entity that, for the first time, makes an explicit and unreserved statement that its annual financial statements comply with IFRS.

There are five issues that need to be addressed when adopting IFRS.

(1) The date of transition to IFRSs.

(2) Which IFRSs should be adopted.

(3) How gains or losses arising on adopting IFRS should be accounted for.

(4) The explanations and disclosures to be made in the year of transition.

(5) What exemptions are available.

Date of transition

Definition

The **date of transition** is the beginning of the earliest period for which an entity presents full comparative information under IFRS in its first IFRS financial statements.

- IFRS should be applied from the first day of the first set of financial statements published in compliance with IFRS. This is called the opening IFRS statement of financial position.

- Because IFRS require comparative statements to be published, the opening IFRS statement of financial position for an entity adopting IFRS for the first time in its 31 December 2008 financial statements and presenting one year of comparative information will be1 January 2007. This is the transition date – the first day of the comparative period.

- The opening IFRS statement of financial position itself need not be published, but it will provide the opening balances for the comparative period.

- If full comparative financial statements for preceding periods are published, then these too must comply with IFRS.

- If only selected information is disclosed about preceding periods, then these need not comply with IFRS. However, this non-compliance must be disclosed.

Which IFRS?

- The entity should use the same accounting policies for all the periods presented; these policies should be based solely on IFRS in force at the reporting date. (The term IFRS includes any IAS and Interpretations still in force.)

- A major problem for entities preparing for the change-over is that IFRSs themselves keep changing.

- Entities will have to collect information enabling them to prepare statements under previous GAAP, current IFRS and any proposed new standards or amendments.

- IFRS 1 states that the opening IFRS statement of financial position must:

  - recognise all assets and liabilities required by IFRS

  - not recognise assets and liabilities not permitted by IFRS

  - reclassify all assets, liabilities and equity components in accordance with IFRS

  - measure all assets and liabilities in accordance with IFRS.

Expandable text - Further points

Reporting gains and losses

Any gains or losses arising on the adoption of IFRS should be recognised directly in retained earnings, i.e. not recognised.

Explanations and disclosures

- Entities must explain how the transition to IFRS affects their reported financial performance, financial position and cash flows. Two main disclosures are required, which reconcile equity and profits.

    - The entity's equity as reported under previous GAAP must be reconciled to the equity reported under IFRS at two dates.

        - The date of transition. This is the opening reporting date.

        - The last statement of financial position prepared under previous GAAP.

    - The last annual reported under previous GAAP must be reconciled to the same year's total comprehensive income prepared under IFRS.

- Any material differences between the previous GAAP and the IFRS cash flows must also be explained.

- When preparing its first IFRS statements, an entity may identify errors made in previous years, or make or reverse impairments of assets. These adjustments must be disclosed separately.

Exemptions

IFRS 1 grants limited exemptions in situations where the cost of compliance would outweigh the benefits to the user. For example:

- Previous business combinations do not have to be restated in accordance with IFRS. In particular, mergers (pooling of interests) do not have to be reaccounted for as acquisitions, previously written off goodwill does not have to be reinstated and the fair values of assets and liabilities may be retained. However, an impairment test for any remaining goodwill must be made in the opening statement of financial position.

- ED 2009/11 Improvements to IFRS issued in August 2009 identifies that, if there are any changes to accounting policies in the first year of adoption of IFRS, but after the issue of the first interim statements, the changes need to be explained and reconciliations required should also be updated.

- ED 2009/11 also confirms that revaluations used as a basis for deemed cost may arise during the period covered by the first IFRS financial statements, rather than having been done in the period prior to this. Normally, deemed cost would be either fair value, determined in accordance with IAS 39, or the carrying value under previous national standards.

- An entity may elect to use fair values for property, plant and equipment, investment properties and intangibles as the deemed cost under IFRS. This fair value may have been a market-based revaluation or an indexed amount. This means that even if the cost model is used for these assets under IFRS, this valuation can be used to replace cost initially. Therefore, the entity can use fair value as the deemed cost but then not have to revalue the assets each year.

- Some actuarial gains and losses on pension schemes are left unrecognised under IAS 19 **Employee benefits**. A first-time adopter may find it easier to recognise all gains and losses at the date of transition and this option is given in IFRS 1.

- Past currency translation gains and losses included in revenue reserves need not be separated out into the currency translation reserve.

- Under IAS 32 **Financial instruments: presentation part of the proceeds of convertible debt** is classified as equity. If the debt had been repaid by the date of transition, no adjustment is needed for the equity component.

- If a subsidiary adopts IFRS later than its parent, then the subsidiary may value its assets and liabilities either at its own transition date or its parent's transition date (which would normally be easier).

There are also three situations where retrospective application of IFRS is prohibited. These relate to derecognition of financial assets and liabilities, hedging and estimates.

The IASB thought that it would be impractical to obtain the information necessary to restate past financial statements, and that restating past fair values and estimates was open to manipulation.

Implications of adoption of IFRS

There are a number of considerations to be made when adopting IFRS for the first time. The key factors on converting from local GAAP to IFRS are discussed below.

Factors to consider in implementing IFRS

Initial evaluation

The transition to IFRS requires careful and timely planning. Initially there are a number of questions that must be asked to assess the current position within the entity.

(a) Is there knowledge of IFRS within the entity?

(b) Are there any agreements (such as bank covenants) that are dependent on local GAAP?

(c) Will there be a need to change the information systems?

(d) Which IFRSs will affect the entity?

(e) Is this an opportunity to improve the accounting systems?

Once the initial evaluation of the current position has been made, the entity can determine the nature of any assistance required.

They may need to:

- engage IFRS experts for assistance. Such experts can provide staff training and assistance on the preparation of the opening statement of financial position and first set of accounts. They can inform the entity of the information that will be needed to ensure a smooth transition to IFRS. It is essential that the entity personnel understand the key differences between local GAAP and IFRS and in particular the IFRS that will most affect the entity

- inform key stakeholders of the impact that IFRS could have on reported performance. This includes analysts, bankers, loan creditors and employees. Head office personnel will not be the only staff to require training; managers of subsidiaries will need to know the impact on their finance functions as there will be budgeting and risk management issues

- produce a project plan that incorporates the resource requirements, training needs, management teams and timetable with a timescale that ensures there is enough time to produce the first IFRS financial statements

- investigate the effect of the change on the computer systems. Establish if the current system can easily be changed and, if not, what the alternatives will be. Potentially the IT cost could be significant if changes need to be made.

Other considerations

Aside from the practical aspect of implementing the move to IFRS, there are a number of other factors to consider:

(i) **Debt covenants**

- The entity will have to consider the impact of the adoption of IFRS on debt covenants and other legal contracts.

- Covenants based on financial position ratios (for example the gearing ratio) and income statement measures such as interest cover will probably be affected significantly by the adoption of IFRS.

- Debt covenants may need to be renegotiated and rewritten, as it would not seem to be sensible to retain covenants based on a local GAAP if this is no longer to be used.

(ii) **Performance related pay**

- There is a potential impact on income of moving to IFRS, which causes a problem in designing an appropriate means of determining executive bonuses, employee performance related pay and long-term incentive plans.

- With the increase in the use of fair values and the potential recycling of gains and losses under IFRS (e.g. IAS 21 **The effects of changes in foreign exchange rates**), the identification of relevant measures of performance will be quite difficult.

- If there are unrealised profits reported in the income statement/statement of comprehensive income, the entity will not wish to pay bonuses on the basis of profits that may never be realised in cash.

- There may be volatility in the reported figures, which will have little to do with financial performance but could result in major differences in the pay awarded to a director from one year to another.

(iii) **Views of financial analysts**

- It is important that the entity looks at the way it is to communicate the effects of a move to IFRS with the markets and the analysts.

- The focus of the communication should be to provide assurance about the process and to quantify the changes expected. Unexpected changes in ratios and profits could adversely affect share prices.

- Presentations can be made to interested parties of the potential impact of IFRS. Analysts should have more transparent and comparable data about multinational entities once IFRS has been adopted.

- Consistency over account classifications, formats, disclosures and measurement will assist the analyst's interpretation.

- Analysts will be particularly concerned about earnings volatility that may affect how they discount future profits to arrive at a present fair value for the business.

Expandable text - Benefits of harmonisation

Benefits of harmonisation

There are a number of reasons why the harmonisation of accounting standards would be beneficial. Businesses operate on a global scale and investors make investment decisions on a worldwide basis. There is thus a need for financial information to be presented on a consistent basis. The advantages are as follows.

(1) **Multi-national entities**

Multi-national entities would benefit from closer harmonisation for the following reasons.

(a) Access to international finance would be easier as financial information is more understandable if it is prepared on a consistent basis.

(b) In a business that operates in several countries, the preparation of financial information would be easier as it would all be prepared on the same basis.

(c) There would be greater efficiency in accounting departments.

(d) Consolidation of financial statements would be easier.

(2) **Investors**

If investors wish to make decisions based on the worldwide availability of investments, then better comparisons between entities are required. Harmonisation assists this process, as financial information would be consistent between different entities from different regions.

(3) **International economic groupings**

International economic groupings, e.g. the EU, could work more effectively if there were international harmonisation of accounting practices. Part of the function of international economic groupings is to make cross-border trade easier. Similar accounting regulations would improve access to capital markets and therefore help this process.

Expandable text - Reasons for differences in accounting practices

The reasons for differences in accounting practice

The reasons why, failing the introduction of a common set of international reporting standards, accounting practices may differ from one country to another, include the following.

- **Legal systems**. In some countries, financial statements are prepared according to a strict code imposed by the government. This is often because the accounts are being prepared primarily for tax purposes rather than for investment.

- **Professional traditions**. In contrast to countries where accounting standards are embedded in legislation, other countries have a strong and influential accounting profession and can rely on the profession to draft relevant standards.

- **User groups**. As mentioned above, in some countries the tax authorities are the main users of accounts, and so a standardised, rule-based approach to accounting emerges. Quite often, depreciation rates will be set by law rather than being based upon useful lives. In countries where businesses are generally financed by loans (rather than by equity) then financial statements will focus on a business' ability to service and pay back its debts. In the UK and the US, businesses are generally financed through equity. In these countries, the shareholders share the risks of profits and losses, and so they demand full disclosure of a business' financial affairs.

- **Nationalism**. Individual countries believe that their own standards are the best.

- **Culture**. Differences in culture can lead to differences in the objective and method of accounting.

Culture and local custom

Financial reporting practice may be influenced by cultural factors in a number of ways.

- Some nationalities are naturally conservative and this may affect their attitude to accounting estimates, particularly when it comes to providing for liabilities.

- Religion may affect accounting practices; for example, Islamic law forbids the charging or accepting of interest.

- Different nationalities have different attitudes to risk. For example, in Japan high gearing is usual and is a sign of confidence in an entity.

- Attitudes to disclosure also vary. Some cultures value openness while others have a strong tradition of confidentiality.

- In the UK and the USA, the main objective of management and shareholders is generally to maximise profit in the short term. However, in other countries, investors and management may have different or wider objectives, such as long-term growth, stability, benefiting the community and safeguarding the interests of employees.

Expandable text - Convergence with US GAAP

Convergence with US GAAP

In October 2002, the IASB and the US standard setter the Financial Accounting Standards Board (FASB) announced the issuance of a memorandum of understanding ('Norwalk Agreement'), marking a step towards formalising their commitment to the convergence of international accounting standards. This agreement was updated in February 2006 and is often referred to as the Roadmap.

Currently, the IASB and FASB have completed work on the **short-term convergence project.** The scope of the short-term convergence project was limited to those differences between US GAAP and IFRS in which convergence around a high-quality solution appears achievable in the short term (by 2008). Because of the nature of the differences, it was expected that a solution could be achieved by choosing between existing US GAAP and IFRS. Topics covered by the short-term convergence project included:

- IAS 23 permitted borrowing costs on the construction of an asset to be either capitalised or written off, whereas US GAAP required such costs to be capitalised. IAS 23 was amended in March 2007 and is now in line with US GAAP; from 1 January 2009, entities have been required to capitalise borrowing costs where specified criteria are met.

- IAS 14 has been superseded by IFRS 8, which deals with segmental reporting. IFRS 8 identifies reportable segments based on a 'managerial approach', which is consistent with the approach adopted under US GAAP, rather than the 'risk and returns' approach adopted by IAS 14.

- IAS 1 was revised in September 2007, with the balance sheet renamed as the 'statement of financial position'. The income statement was renamed as the 'statement of comprehensive income', and now includes items of income and expense that are not recognised in profit or loss but were directly recognised in equity, such as revaluation gains.

- IAS 27 and IFRS 3 were amended in January 2008. The new standards change the calculation of goodwill and also the treatment of piecemeal acquisitions. Along with changes to US GAAP, these amendments bring the accounting treatment for goodwill into line, although some differences still exist, such as the definition of control and fair value. A review is scheduled for 2012, by which date the revised standards would have been applied for two years.

Additionally, the IASB and FASB are also undertaking joint projects. **Joint projects** are those that the standard setters have agreed to conduct simultaneously in a co-ordinated manner. Joint projects involve the sharing of staff resources, and every effort is made to keep joint projects on a similar time schedule at each board.

There are also a number of longer-term projects to continue the harmonisation process between IFRS/US GAAP, including the following:

- Fair value measurement –the objective is to clarify the definition of fair value and to establish a single source of guidance for fair value measurement.

- Post-employment benefits – IASB and FASB intend to move to a common standard on this topic, but there are currently significant differences between their respective positions.

- Revenue recognition – the objective is to develop a single model for the recognition of revenue which can be applied across industries and geographical regions. This would improve comparability and understanding of financial reporting information.

- Leases – a new standard may result in operating leases being regarded as an asset for the right to use an item, while also recognising the liability to make rental payments. A standard on this topic is not expected until 2011.

- Earnings per share – this has involved both IASB and FASB reviewing proposed amendments to the calculation of diluted earnings per share.

- Conceptual framework – to date, this has focused on the objectives of financial reporting and the qualitative characteristics of financial reporting information.

Roadmap 2008

A **second Roadmap** towards convergence was agreed in November 2008. The objective of this Roadmap was to enable companies to file annual financial statements, prepared in accordance with IFRS GAAP, to be accepted by the Securities and Exchange Commission (SEC) in the US.

This followed on from an announcement in 2007 that the SEC would no longer require IFRS-compliant financial statements filed with the SEC to also include a reconciliation to US GAAP. Based on the 2008 Roadmap, a small group of companies will begin to prepare their financial statements using IFRS with effect from years starting 15 December 2009 onwards. Companies eligible must be one of the 20 largest in that industry (measured by market capitalisation), and financial reporting by those 20 major companies must have IFRS GAAP as the major basis for financial reporting.

This announcement was followed, in January 2009, by an SEC statement that a mandatory two-year dual-reporting period would begin for most companies in 2012, with IFRS only required by 2014. The SEC's decision reflects the increasing acceptance of IFRS as a widely used and high-quality financial reporting language.

A further driver towards convergence in recent months has been the global financial crisis. Whilst there were already proposals to harmonise accounting for financial instruments, this issue took on greater significance and priority. IFRS 9 Financial Instruments deals with derecognition of financial instruments and related disclosures and updates the provisions of IAS 39 and IFRS 7. The new standard was approved in November 2009 and becomes effective from 1 January 2013, with earlier adoption permitted.

Technical article

Tony Sweetman of Kaplan Publishing wrote an article discussing convergence between IFRS and US GAAP in the November 2009 issue of Student Accountant magazine. You can access this article from the ACCA website (www.accaglobal.com).

Expandable text - Differences in accounting treatment

Major differences between financial accounting practices in different countries

Introduction

In recent years, more and more countries are harmonising their accounting standards with IFRS. At the present time, the US standard setter, the Financial Accounting Standards Board (FASB), and the IASB are involved in a joint project to harmonise their accounting standards. The ASB in the UK has also adopted a number of international standards. However, some differences remain.

Goodwill	IASB	US GAAP	UK GAAP
Preferred treatment	Capitalise but do not amortise, subject to annual impairment review	Capitalise but do not amortise, subject to annual impairment review	Capitalise and amortise over economic useful life
Allowed alternative treatment	–	–	No need to amortise if life is indefinite and impairment is tested annually

Deferred tax	IASB	US GAAP	UK GAAP
Preferred treatment	Liability method, full provision based on temporary differences	Liability method, full provision based on temporary differences	Liability method, full provision based on timing differences

Valuation of property	IASB	US GAAP	UK GAAP
Preferred treatment	No preferred treatment	Cost	No preferred treatment
Allowed alternative	Cost or valuation	–	Cost or valuation
Not allowed	–	Valuation	–

Capitalisation of development costs	IASB	US GAAP	UK GAAP
Preferred treatment	Recognise such costs as assets when specified criteria are met and write off as expense when the criteria are not met	Write off as incurred	May recognise as assets when specific criteria are met; choice of immediate write off also permitted

Profits on long-term contracts	IASB	US GAAP	UK GAAP
Preferred treatment	Percentage of completion method	Percentage of completion or completed contract method	Percentage of completion method
Not allowed	Completed contract method	–	Completed contract method

Borrowing costs	IASB	US GAAP	UK GAAP
Preferred treatment	Capitalisation compulsory for certain assets	Capitalisation compulsory for certain assets	No preferred treatment
Allowed alternative treatment	–	–	Capitalise or write off immediately
Not allowed	Immediate write-off	Immediate write off for certain assets	–

Reconciliation statements

In some cases, an entity with a listing on more than one stock exchange may still be required to produce financial information that is expressed in terms of its domestic accounting policies.

A reconciliation statement reconciles the accounts prepared under domestic accounting policies with another GAAP, such as US GAAP or IFRS.

Expandable text - The role of national standard setters

The role of national standard setters

- The harmonisation process has gathered pace in the last few years. From 2005 all European listed entities were required to adopt IFRS in their group financial statements. Many other countries including Australia, Canada and New Zealand decided to follow a similar process. National standard setters are committed to a framework of accounting standards based on IFRS.

- Additionally, the US are committed to harmonise with IFRS and the FASB and the IASB are aiming for convergence over the next few years.

- In Europe, the EU has adopted IFRS for use in member countries, with the exception of part of IAS 39 Financial Instruments: recognition and measurement.

- In Japan, until the 1990s, financial reporting was not transparent and while the economy prospered, there was little pressure for change. However, the Asian economic crisis changed the situation, and Japan has committed itself to developing new accounting standards more in line with the IASC model.

- In Russia, large-scale adoption of IFRS has been planned since 1998. It is expected that this will be achieved by 2010.

- India announced in 2007 that it has decided to fully converge with IFRS for accounting periods commencing on or after April 1 2011. In line with other countries, this decision will initially be applied to listed companies and public service entities.

- The overall impact of the above is that the trend towards closer international harmonisation of accounting practices is now set. Currently, 102 countries require or permit use of IFRS in the preparation of financial statements in their countries. By 2011, this figure is expected to reach 150. It will become increasingly difficult for domestic standard setters to justify domestic standards at odds with IFRSs.

The role of accounting standard setters and the IASB

- In February 2005, the IASB issued a memorandum setting out the responsibilities of the IASB and national standard setters. It is most relevant to those who have adopted or converged with IFRSs'. It deals with the responsibilities of national standard setters to facilitate adoption or convergence with IFRS.

- It includes the responsibilities of the IASB to ensure that it makes information available on a timely basis so that national standard setters can be informed of the IASB's plans. Sufficient time should be allowed in relation to consultative documents so that national standard setters have sufficient time to prepare the information in their own context and to receive comments from their own users.

- The national standard setters should deal with domestic barriers to adopting or converging with IFRS. They should avoid amending an IFRS when adopting it in their own jurisdiction, so that the issue of non-compliance with the IFRS does not arise. They should encourage their own constituents to communicate their technical views to the IASB and they themselves should respond with comments on a timely basis. They should also make known any differences of opinion that they have with a project as early as possible in the process.

Expandable text - Question

Pailing

Pailing, a public limited entity, is registered in Erehwon. Under the local legislation, it is allowed to prepare its financial statements using IFRS or local GAAP and it uses local GAAP.

Klese, a UK registered entity who has adopted IFRS, is considering buying the entity but wishes to restate Pailing's group financial statements so that they are consistent with IFRS before any decision is made.

The Pailing group's net profit for the period drawn up utilising local GAAP is $89 million for the year ending 31 March 20X1 and its group net assets under local GAAP is $225 million as at 31 March 20X1.

The following accounting practices under local GAAP have been determined.

(a) A change in accounting policies has been dealt with by a cumulative catch up adjustment that is included in the current year's income. During the year, the accounting policy for the capitalisation of interest was changed from capitalising into non-current assets to charging directly to profits.

   The total interest included in non-current assets was $30 million, of which only $3m relates to the current year.

(b) Pailing had acquired 100% of a subsidiary entity, Odd, on 31 March 20X1. The assets stated in the statement of financial position were based on the carrying value of the net assets of the subsidiary before any fair value adjustments. The fair value and the carrying value of the net assets of Odd at the date of acquisition were $28 million and $24 million respectively.

(c) Pailing had paid $32 million for the subsidiary, Odd, on 31 March 20X1. There is an agreement to pay contingent consideration of $2 million in a year's time if Odd makes a net profit of $1 million. In the current year, Odd has made losses of $2 million. Pailing has made a provision in the financial statements for this amount, charging it to the profits.

(d) Pailing had spent $6 million during the period on development expenditure on a project that started commercial production on 28 February 20X1. So far, sales have been in excess of the forecast. Pailing writes off development expenditure as an expense in the period the amount arises.

> **Restate the Pailing group's net profit for the year ending 31 March 20X1 and net assets as at 31 March 20X1 in accordance with IFRS, commenting on your adjustments.**

Expandable text - Solution

Restatement

	Net profit	Capital and reserves
	$	$
Per local GAAP	**89**	**225**
(a) Under IFRS, qualifying borrowing costs should be capitalised into the cost of non-current assets. The $27m adjustment and $3m current year cost should be added back to profit and will increase non-current assets in the SFP.	30	30
(b) The assets should be stated at fair value so the carrying amount of the assets will increase by $4m and goodwill will decrease by $4m. Profit is unaffected. There is no effect on net assets.	–	–
(c) It is unlikely that Odd will make a profit given the large losses in the current year so there is no need to make a provision at the year end. In any event, it should not have been charged against profit but added on to the cost of investment. The provision must be reversed.	2	2
(d) Under IFRS, development expenditure on a feasible project must be capitalised. This project appears feasible given the strong sales so the expenditure must be removed from the income statement and capitalised as a non-current asset.	6	6
	127	263

Expandable text - Current issues

Current Issues - Amendments to IFRS 1

The objective of this project is to amend IFRS 1 First-time Adoption of International Financial Reporting Standards to address potential challenges for jurisdictions adopting IFRSs in the near future. Two separate amendments to IFRS 1 have been considered;

- Additional Exemptions for First-time Adopters: Amendments to IFRS 1 The IASB has completed its work on this amendment, and on 23 July 2009 it issued Additional Exemptions for First-time Adopters (Amendments to IFRS 1).

- Limited Exemption from Comparative IFRS 7 Disclosures for First-time Adopters (proposed amendment to IFRS 1) The IASB has completed its work on this amendment, and on 28 January 2010 it issued Limited Exemption from Comparative IFRS 7 Disclosures for First-time Adopters (Amendment to IFRS 1).

Proposed amendments to IFRS 1 were included in the Improvements to IFRSs ED published in August 2009 as part of the Annual Improvements project. The amendments are mainly minor technical issues, rather than significant changes in principles.

Chapter summary

First time adoption of IFRS

- Five points to consider are:
    - the date of transition to IFRS
    - which IFRS should be adopted
    - how gains or losses arising on adopting IFRS should be accounted for
    - the explanations and disclosures to be made in the year of transition
    - what exemptions are available

Implications of adoption of IFRS

- Consider practical implications – training, IT systems, planning project
- Also consider terms in debt covenants, calculation of performance-related pay and anything that is based on the profit figure
- Communicate with analysts on the expected changes to the financial statements

Differences in accounting practices

- There are historical reasons for differences in accounting systems such as legal, professional, culture
- Some accounting differences remain, but the harmonisation process is taking place
  Many countries are adopting IFRS
- The IASB is aiming to converge with the US standard-setter the FASB to harmonise IFRS with US GAAP

Current issues

Chapter learning objectives

Upon completion of this chapter you will be able to:

- discuss current issues in corporate reporting

- identify the issues and deficiencies that have led to a proposed change to an accounting standard

- apply and discuss the implications of a proposed change to an accounting standard on the performance and statement of financial position of an entity

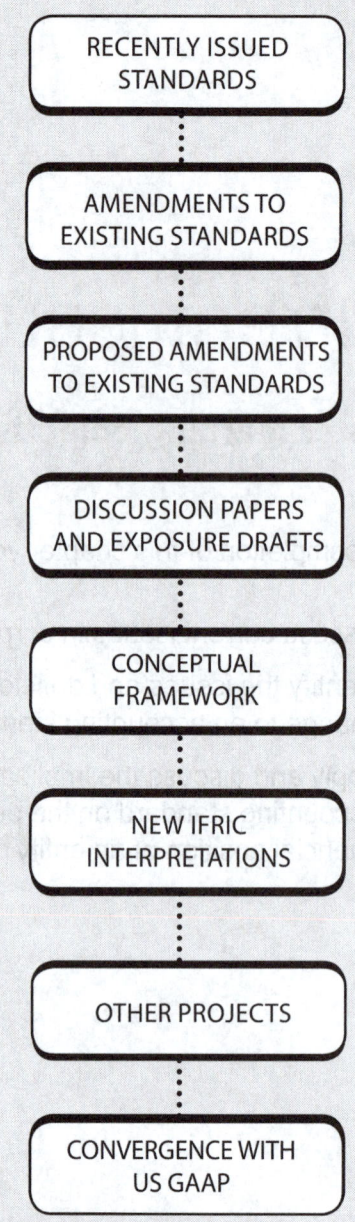

Expandable text - Introduction

The IASB is continually engaged in projects to update and improve existing standards and introduce new ones.

At any time there are a number of discussion papers (DPs) and exposure drafts (EDs) in issue as part of these projects.

In addition, the IFRIC continues to issue interpretations addressing newly identified reporting issues not covered in standards and issues where conflicting interpretations have arisen.

A good source of up to date information is the current projects page of the IASB website at www.iasb.org.

Expandable text - Recently issued standards

The most recent reporting standard issued which is examinable in 2011 examinations is IFRS 9 Financial Instruments, which was issued in November 2009. This standard is dealt with in chapter 16 of this text. Be aware that there is continuing development regarding the replacement of IAS 39 with IFRS 9 which is also covered in chapter 16 of this text.

Revisions and amendments have taken place to a number of existing standards, and they are also dealt with in the appropriate chapters dealing with those reporting standards.

Expandable text - Recently revised standards

From time-to-time, current reporting standards are revised or amended without formal withdrawal and introduction of a replacement standard. Where appropriate, this information is included within the appropriate chapter of this text; for example, a revised definition of what constitutes a related party is included within chapter 13.

Expandable text - Proposed amendments to existing standards

You should refer to the current issues section within each chapter as appropriate to identify current developments in the form of published Discussion Papers (DP) and Exposure Drafts (ED) and other documents. Examples (not an exhaustive list) of current developments included within this publication are:

Topic	Chapter
Conceptual Framework for Financial Reporting 2010	8
Credit risk in liability management (DP)	8
Fair value measurements	8
Revenue recognition in contracts with customers (ED)	9
Preliminary views on financial statement presentation - other comprehensive income	9
Preliminary views on financial statement presentation - replacement of IAS 1 and IAS 7	9
Preliminary views on financial statement presentation - discontinued operations	9
Defined benefit plans (ED)	10
Termination benefits (ED)	10
Rate regulated activities (ED)	14
Leases (ED)	15
Financial instruments - impairment (ED)	16

Annual improvements process

- The IASB has adopted an annual process to deal with non-urgent minor amendments to existing standards. These amendments tend to focus on areas of inconsistency in IFRSs or where clarification of wording is required. It is not part of the convergence project with FASB, but may include elements of harmonisation with US GAAP.

- Each year the IASB discusses and decides on proposed improvements to IFRSs as they arise throughout the year. In the third quarter of the year, an omnibus ED of the collected proposals is published for public comment, with a comment period of 90 days. After the IASB has considered the comments received, it aims to issue the amendments in final form in the following second quarter, with an effective date of 1 January of the subsequent year.

- In October 2007 the first 'omnibus' ED was issued, proposing minor improvements to 25 IFRSs.

- ED 2009/11 was issued in August 2009 and proposed amendment to 10 reporting standards. plus clarification of the definition of fair value to be applied per IFRIC 13. The final amendments were published in May 2010.

- The next cycle of improvements to be dealt with by this process are expected to have an ED published in October 2010, with the comment period open to 31 December 2010, with final amendments to the proposed standard in May 2011; it would then be effective from 1 January 2012.

Improvements to IFRS

The most recently issued Improvements to IFRSs was published in May 2010 and made relatively minor technical amendments to seven IFRS as follows:

IFRS	Subject of amendment
IFRS 1 First-time Adoption of IFRSs	Accounting policy changes in the year of adoption Revaluation basis as deemed cost Use of deemed cost for operations subject to rate regulation
IFRS 3 Business Combinations	Transition requirements for contingent consideration from a business combination that occurred before the effective date of the revised IFRS Measurement of non-controlling interests Un-replaced and voluntarily replaced share-based payment awards
IFRS 7 Financial Instruments: Disclosures	Clarification of disclosures
IAS 1 Presentation of Financial Statements	Clarification of statement of changes in equity
IAS 27 Consolidated and Separate Financial Statements	Transition requirements for amendments arising as a result of IAS 27
IAS 34 Interim Financial Reporting	Significant events and transactions
IFRIC 13 Customer Loyalty Programmes	Fair value of award credits

Most of the amendments are effective for annual periods beginning on or after 1 January 2011, although early adoption is usually permitted.

Expandable text - New IFRIC interpretations

IFRIC 18 Transfers of Assets from Customers

This IFRIC is based upon IFRIC D24 Customer Contributions . It is likely to be particularly relevant for the utility sector as it clarifies the requirements of IFRSs for agreements in which an entity receives from a customer an item of property, plant and equipment that the entity must then use either to connect the customer to a network or to provide the customer with ongoing access to a supply of goods or services (such as a supply of electricity, gas or water) or to do both. In some cases, the entity receives cash from a customer that must be used only to acquire or construct the item of property, plant and equipment in order to connect the customer to a network or provide the customer with ongoing access to a supply of goods or services (or to do both).

IFRSs, in particular the principles in IAS 18 Revenue, have been interpreted differently and the IFRIC provides additional guidance on the accounting for transfers of assets from customers. The interpretation clarifies:

- the circumstances in which the definition of an asset is met;

- the recognition of the asset and its measurement on initial recognition;

- the identification of the separately identifiable services (one or more services in exchange for the transferred asset),

- the recognition of revenue;

- the accounting for transfers of cash from customers.

The IASB issued IFRIC 18 Transfers of Assets from Customers on 29 January 2009. IFRIC 18 requires entities to apply the Interpretation prospectively to transfers of assets from customers received on or after 1 July 2009.

IFRIC 19 - Extinguishing Financial Liabilities with Equity Instruments

In the current environment, some entities are renegotiating the terms of financial liabilities with their creditors. In some circumstances, the creditor agrees to accept an entity's shares or other equity instruments to settle the financial liability fully or partially (sometimes referred to as a "debt for equity swap"). IFRIC 19 provides guidance on how an entity should account for such transactions in accordance with IAS 39 Financial Instruments: Recognition and Measurement and IAS 32 Financial Instruments: Presentation.

There has been diversity in practice in how entities measure the equity instruments issued in a debt for equity swap. Some recognise the equity instruments at the carrying amount of the financial liability and do not recognise any gain or loss in profit or loss. Others recognise the equity instruments at the fair value of either the equity instruments issued or the financial liability extinguished and recognise a difference between that amount and the carrying amount of the financial liability in profit or loss.

IFRIC 19 addresses the accounting by an entity when the terms of a financial liability are renegotiated and result in the entity issuing equity instruments to a creditor to extinguish all or part of the financial liability. It does not address the accounting by the creditor. IFRIC 19 does not apply to transactions when:

- the creditor is also a direct or indirect shareholder, and is acting in its capacity as a direct or indirect existing shareholder, or

- the creditor and the entity are controlled by the same party or parties before and after the transaction and the substance of the transaction includes an equity distribution by or contribution to the entity, or

- the extinguishment of the financial liability by issuing equity shares is in accordance with the original terms of the liability.

IFRIC 19 will standardise practice among debtors applying IFRSs to a debt for equity swap. It clarifies that the entity's equity instruments issued to a creditor are part of the consideration paid to extinguish the financial liability. IFRIC 19 requires that the equity instruments issued are measured at their fair value. If their fair value cannot be reliably measured, the equity instruments should be measured to reflect the fair value of the financial liability extinguished. IFRIC 19 states that any difference between the carrying amount of the financial liability extinguished and the initial measurement amount of the equity instruments issued is included in the entity's profit or loss for the period. As a result, IFRIC 19 will impact entities that have previously recognised the equity instruments issued in a debt for equity swap at the carrying amount of the financial liability.

IFRIC 19 also applies to partial extinguishments of the financial liability by the issue of equity instruments to the creditor and the modification of the terms of the financial liability that remains outstanding.

IFRIC 19 Extinguishing Financial Liabilities with Equity was issued on 26 November 2009. IFRIC 19 is effective for annual periods beginning on or after 1 July 2010 with earlier application permitted. Recognising that entities would face practical difficulties in determining the fair value of the equity instruments previously issued, retrospective application is required only from the beginning of the earliest comparative period presented.

Expandable text - Convergence with UK GAAP

This is a continuing process, and has resulted in co-operation between the IASB and US FASB to converge reporting standards. There is more specific information regarding this process within chapter 21 of this publication.

The Future of UK or national GAAP

In August 2009, the UK ASB issued a Consultation Paper 'Policy Proposal: the future of UK GAAP', which sets out its proposals for the future reporting requirements of UK and Irish entities. The issue of the proposals had been deferred pending the publication of IFRS for SME by the IASB, which the UK ASB believes can play a significant role in the future of UK GAAP.

The UK ASB proposals envisage a differential reporting system based upon public accountability, broadly in line with the IASB's definition of IFRS for SMEs, which state that entities have public accountability if:

- they trade their debt or equity instruments on a public market, or

- hold assets in a fiduciary capacity for a broad group of outsiders as one of their primary businesses.

The Consultation Paper explores whether interested parties would prefer to retain the current legal definition of public accountability. Based upon responses received, the UK ASB will work with the government to develop more fully the mechanisms required to implement a differential reporting regime based upon public accountability.

As at August 2010, responses received to the consultation paper are under consideration by the UK ASB.

Although this has a UK focus, other counrties who have their own national GAAP are likely to be going through a similar process. They will be considering to what extent they want to converge with IFRS, and how this should be managed, including national circumstances which may not well-suited to application of IFRS.

Expandable text - UK syllabus focus

Most current developments in financial reporting are based upon international issues which are dealt with throughout this publication in the relevant chapters. You should be aware that there are on-going developments to converge IFRS GAAP and US GAAP. Additionally, many other national GAAP have converged to a limited extent with IFRS, even if it is not the intention to achieve full convergence due to national law and business practice.

In August 2009, the ASB issued a consultation paper, **'Policy Proposal: the future of UK GAAP"** which sets out its proposals for the future reporting requirements for UK and Irish entities. The ASB proposals envisage a differential reporting system based on public accountability, broadly i line with the IASBs definition of IFRS for SME, which states that entities do have public accountability if:

- they trade their debt or equity instruments in a public market, or

- they hold assets in a fiduciary capacity for a broad range of outsiders as one of their primary businesses.

The ASB is proposing a three-tier approach to developing UK GAAP converged with IFRS GAAP as follows:

- Tier 1 – publicly accountable entities would apply IFRS GAAP as adopted by the EU

- Tier 2 – all other UK entities other than those who can apply the Financial Reporting Standard for Smaller Entities ("FRSSE") would could now apply the IFRS for SME

- Tier 3 – Small entities could choose to continue to apply the FRSSE.

Entities within Tiers 2 and 3 would have the option of using EU-adopted IFRS GAAP if they wished, and those within Tier 3 would have the option of using the IFRS for SME.

Current thinking is that there is no longer a case for retaining two sets of GAAP in the UK, with a two-tier or three-tier system of reporting in its place. Possible route forward include:

- All UK listed and publicly accountable entities would be required to apply full IFRS, irrespective of turnover and whether or not they present group accounts.

- The use of the ASBs FRSSE, which enables small entities to take advantage of simplified requirements, would be extended beyond small companies to include medium-sized entities.

- UK subsidiaries of group companies that apply IFRS GAAP would also be required to apply IFRS GAAP in respect of measurement and recognition, but with reduced disclosure requirements.

- There has not yet been a final decision on entities that do not fall into any of the above three categories; for these entities, he alternative would appear to be:
  a) extend the application of FRSSE
  b) apply IFRS GAAP to more entities
  c) retain UK GAAP
  d) some combination of the above three approaches

Chapter summary

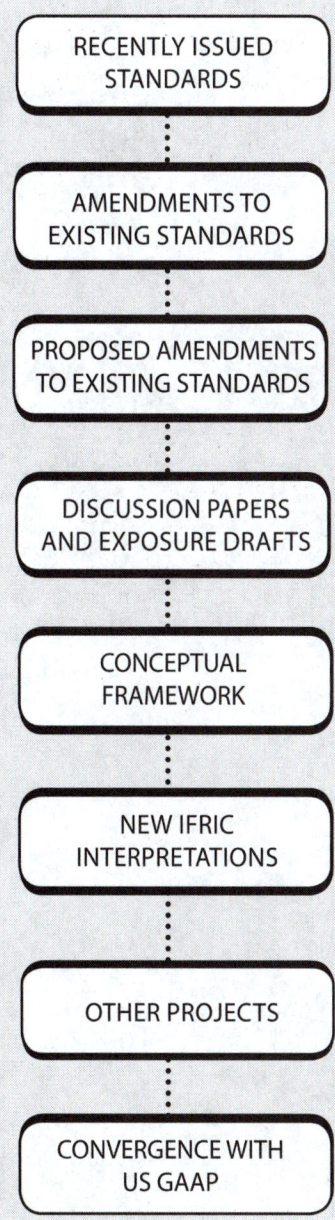

Assessing financial performance and position

Chapter learning objectives

Upon completion of this chapter you will be able to:

- develop accounting policies for an entity that meet the entity's reporting requirements

- identify accounting treatments adopted in financial statements and assess their suitability and acceptability

- select and calculate relevant indicators of financial and non-financial performance

- identify and evaluate significant features and issues in financial statements

- highlight inconsistencies in financial information through analysis and application of knowledge

- make inferences from the analysis of information taking into account the limitation of the information, the analytical methods used and the business environment in which the entity operates.

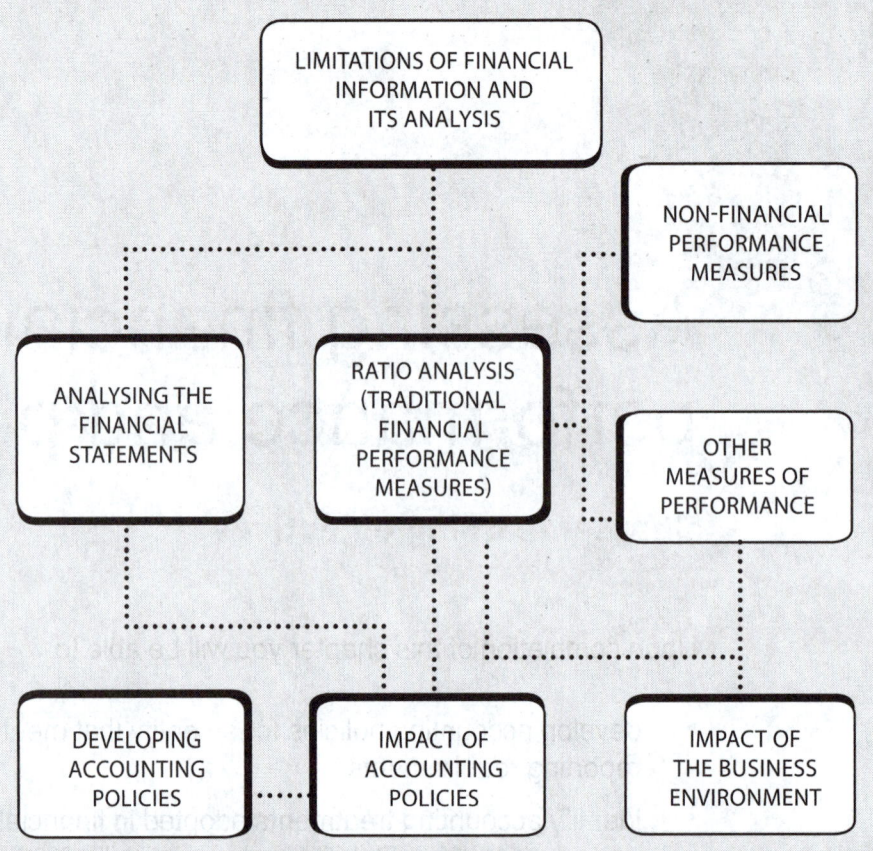

Expandable text - IAS 8

IAS 8 **Accounting policies, changes in accounting estimates and errors** states that where a Standard or Interpretation exists in respect of a transaction, the accounting policy is determined by applying the Standard or Interpretation.

- Where there is no applicable Standard or Interpretation, management must use its judgement to develop and apply an accounting policy.

- The accounting policy selected must result in information that is both relevant to the needs of users and reliable, in that the financial statements:

  - represent faithfully the financial position, financial performance and cash flows of the entity

  - reflects the economic substance of transactions, other events and conditions, and not merely the legal form

  - are neutral, i.e. free from bias

  - are prepared on a prudent basis

  - are complete in all material respects.

IAS 8 provides a 'hierarchy' of sources that the management should use to develop an appropriate accounting policy in the absence of a Standard or Interpretation that specifically applies. These sources should be used in the following order:

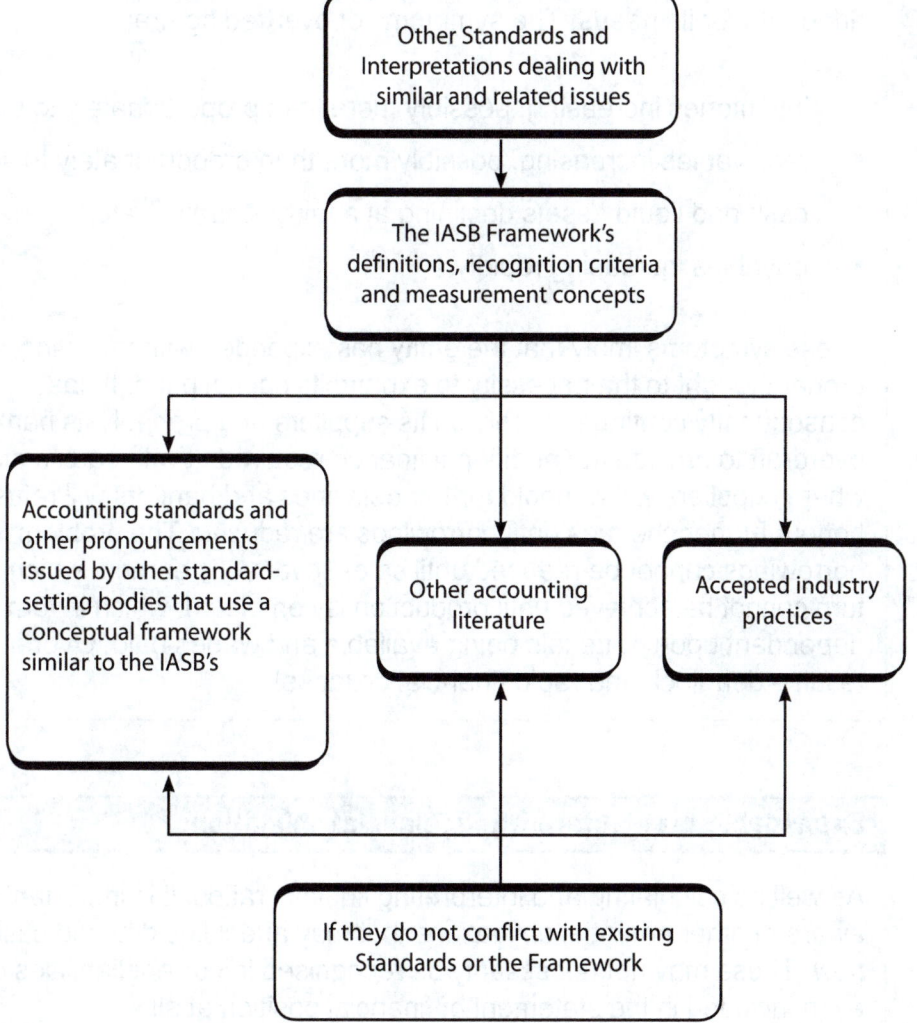

An entity must select and apply accounting policies consistently for similar transactions.

An entity should only change its accounting policies if the change:

- is required by a Standard or Interpretation
- results in reliable and more relevant information.

Expandable text - Overtrading

Overtrading is the term used to describe the situation where an entity expands its sales rapidly without securing additional long-term capital adequate for its needs. The symptoms of overtrading are:

- inventories increasing, possibly more than proportionately to sales

- receivables increasing, possibly more than proportionately to sales

- cash and liquid assets declining at a fairly alarming rate

- payables increasing rapidly.

These symptoms imply that the entity has expanded without giving proper thought to the necessity to expand its capital base. It has consequently continued to rely on its suppliers and probably its bank overdraft to provide the additional finance required. It will reach a stage where suppliers will withhold further deliveries and bankers will refuse to honour further cheques until borrowings are reduced. The problem is that borrowings cannot be reduced until sales revenue is earned, which in turn cannot be achieved until production is completed, which in turn is dependent upon materials being available and wages paid. Overall result – deadlock and rapid financial collapse!

Expandable text - Interpreting financial obligations

As well as calculating and interpreting liquidity ratios, it is important to be aware of other potential obligations that may affect liquidity and cash flow. These may not necessarily be recognised in current liabilities or even included in the statement of financial position at all.

(a) Earn out arrangements

Where one company acquires another, part of the consideration may be deferred to a later date because it is dependent (contingent) on the performance of the acquired entity. If this deferred consideration is recognised in the financial statements, the amount is likely to be based on an estimate. Alternatively, the acquirer's management may not have provided for the obligation because they believe that it is unlikely to become payable.

(b) Redeemable debt

A company may have raised finance by issuing loan notes that it is committed to redeem or repurchase, possibly at a premium.

(c) **Contingent liabilities**

Contingent liabilities are not recognised in the financial statements but must normally be disclosed in the notes.

(d) **Interpretation**

In all cases such as these, the obligation may involve a material cash outflow in the near future.

Where there are either provisions based on estimates or contingent liabilities, it is possible that the situation may have changed since the reporting date (for example, a contingent liability could have become an actual liability). It is necessary to use whatever information is available (e.g. selected notes to the financial statements, details of events since the publication of the latest financial statements) to determine the likelihood of the cash outflow occurring, its timing and whether the entity is likely to be able to meet the obligation in practice.

Expandable text - Non-financial performance measures

Non-financial performance measures are measures of performance based on non-financial information. They are becoming increasingly important both to management and to shareholders and other interested parties external to an entity.

Ratio analysis and other interpretation techniques based on the financial statements cannot measure all aspects of performance. For example, the effect of a business on the environment cannot be measured using financial criteria, but is increasingly regarded as an important aspect of performance.

- Where an entity presents an Operating and Financial Review or a Management Discussion and Analysis it may include Key Performance Indicators (KPIs) based on non-financial information.

- KPIs may also be included in an environmental or social report. Reports prepared in accordance with the Global Reporting Initiative (GRI) Sustainability Guidelines should contain economic indicators, environmental indicators and social indicators.

- Examples of non-financial performance measures are:
  - trend in market share
  - number of customers at the year end
  - sales per square foot of floor space (for a retailer)
  - percentage of revenue from new products
  - number of new products being developed at the year end
  - number of instances of environmental spillage per year
  - reduction in CO_2 emissions during the year
  - amount of waste (kg) arising from packaging on each $1,000 of products
  - employee turnover
  - training time per employee
  - lost time injury frequency rate (relating to employees).

- Non-financial performance measures are likely to be particularly relevant to 'not for profit' organisations, because these organisations need to measure the effectiveness with which services have been provided. Examples of non-financial performance indicators for public sector bodies could include:
  - pupil-teacher ratios
  - population per police officer
  - serious offences per 1,000 of the population
  - proportion of trains arriving on time
  - number of patients who wait more than one year for treatment.

- Where an entity presents non-financial measures:
  - the definition and calculation method should be explained
  - the purpose of the measure should be explained
  - the source of the data on which the measure is based should be disclosed
  - the measure should be presented and calculated consistently over time (and ideally, there should be comparative figures for the previous year)
  - any changes in the measures or in the way they are calculated should be disclosed and explained.

Expandable text - Illustration: non-financial measures

Verdant is an entity that manufactures hazardous substances. There have been several escapes of toxic gases from its plant over the last few years and the directors are concerned that this will damage the entity's reputation.

The directors decide to publish a key performance indicator to assess the effectiveness of the management of hazardous substances (and to demonstrate that the entity is taking steps to reduce the problem).

The measure is the number of significant incidents during the year. Significant incidents are defined as escapes of gas exceeding 10,000 cubic feet.

The data is taken from all Verdant's manufacturing plants.

In 20X6 there were 15 significant incidents compared with 21 gas escapes in 20X5.

Expandable text - Other measures of performance

In recent years, investment analysts have developed a number of new financial performance measures. These attempt to overcome the limitations of traditional ratios, such as earnings per share and return on capital employed.

- Earnings before interest, tax, depreciation and amortisation (EBITDA) is an approximation to operating cash flow and is therefore believed to be a better point of comparison between entities than earnings per share.

- Free cash flow is calculated as cash revenues less cash expenses, taxes paid, cash needed for working capital and cash required for routine capital expenditure. Analysts attach importance to this measure because cash is essential for an entity's survival and it is also less easy to manipulate than profit.

Shareholder value is created by generating future returns for equity investors that exceed the returns that those investors could expect to earn elsewhere.

- Many entities are adopting the enhancement of shareholder value, rather than the generation of profit, as their primary objective.

- A number of ways to measure shareholder value have been developed. The most important of these is probably Economic Value Added (EVA).

- EVA = adjusted net operating profit after tax – (weighted average cost of capital × adjusted invested capital). It is a variation on return on capital employed that adjusts the numerator and the denominator to remove the effects of accruals accounting and some of the effects of the entity's choice of accounting policies.

Expandable text - Alternative measures of performance

A number of ways of measuring shareholder value have been developed as follows. Measures of shareholder value have a number of common features.

- They focus on cash flow rather than on profit.

- They emphasise the 'whole' business. The idea behind the concept of shareholder value is that there are several 'drivers' within a business that can be managed to create value, e.g. growth in sales, increase in the operating profit margin, reduction in the cash tax rate. These are summarised into a single performance measure.

- They are essentially forward looking. In particular, calculating SVA involves estimating future performance.

(a) **Shareholder value analysis (SVA)**

SVA calculates a value for the entity that is based on projected future cash flows, discounted to their present value at the entity's cost of capital. The market value of debt is deducted from this figure to give shareholder value.

(b) **Market value added (MVA)**

MVA is the additional value that is added to an entity by its management in excess of the actual value of the funds invested by the shareholders.

MVA = Market value of entity – capital employed

The market value of the entity is the market share price multiplied by the number of shares in issue. Performance can be measured by calculating the yearly change in MVA.

(c) Economic value added (EVA)

EVA is calculated as follows:

EVA = adjusted net operating profit after tax − (WACC × adjusted invested capital)

EVA was developed as a sophisticated version of return on capital employed and similar methods of measuring the return on an investment. It can be argued that the normal calculation is distorted by the following factors:

- the effect of accruals based bookkeeping, which tends to hide the true 'cash' profitability of a business

- the effect of prudence, which often leads to a conservative bias and affects the relevance of reported figures (although this is less of a problem following the issue of IAS 37 **Provisions, contingent liabilities and contingent assets**)

- the effect of 'successful efforts accounting' whereby entities write off costs associated with unsuccessful investments. This tends to understate the 'true' capital of a business and subject the income statement to 'one off' gains and losses.

Therefore adjustments are made to operating profit and asset values. These can include the following:

- removing non-recurring gains and losses such as restructuring costs

- capitalising intangible assets such as research and development expenditure

- adding back 'unnecessary' provisions (such as deferred tax)

- capitalising the net present value of future operating lease payments.

A positive EVA for a single year does not necessarily mean that value has been created and a negative EVA for a single year does not necessarily mean that value has been destroyed. EVA is probably most helpful when it is used to interpret an entity's performance over a period of several years.

Expandable text - Analysing the financial statements

The best way to start to analyse the financial statements is by observation. This can often tell a reader more, more quickly, than calculating ratios (and it does not depend on selecting the correct ratios).

Analysis should take into account:

- the nature of the entity's business
- any particular concerns of the users of the information (for example, a shareholder may suspect that the financial statements have been manipulated)
- any important issues facing the business
- the accounting policies adopted by management (if these are known).

The statement of financial position

The main areas of interest in the statement of financial position are set out below.

Non-current assets	• Significant additions/disposals ?
	• Evidence of business expanding ?
	• Any unusual items (e.g. intangibles) ?
	• Revaluations ?
	• How are assets valued ?
	• Depreciation/amortisation/useful lives?
	• Any associates or joint ventures (equity accounting)?
Current assets/current liabilities	• Significant movements?
	• In line with revenue and cost of sales?
	• Any unusual items?
	• Cash position?
	• Financial instruments: accounting policy?
Equity	• Share issues in the year?
	• Reason (e.g. to finance asset purchases/ acquisitions)?
	• Any significant/unusual movements on reserves?
	• Increases/decreases in minority interest?

| Non-current liabilities | • | Increase/decrease in year? |
| | • | When do loans fall due? |

The statement of comprehensive income and statement of changes in equity

The main areas of interest in the statement of comprehensive income and statement of changes in equity are set out below.

Revenue	•	Increase/decrease? How significant?
Cost of sales/ Gross profit	•	Movement in line with revenue?
	•	Sales growth v profit growth?
Operating expenses/ Operating profit	•	In line with revenue (especially selling costs)?
	•	Any unusual items?
Finance costs	•	Reasonable given level of loans/overdraft? Movement? Interest cover?
Profit before tax	•	Any investment income, interests in associates, joint ventures?
Income tax expense/ Profit for the period	•	Effective rate of tax? (This should be reasonably constant from year to year).
Dividends	•	Trend, level, cover? A fall is usually a very bad sign.
Other comprehensive income	•	revaluations?

Operating expenses may include various items that affect the analysis, for example:

- one-off unusual items

- depreciation and profits or losses on disposal of non-current assets

- research and development expenditure

- advertising expenditure

- staff costs that may have risen in line with inflation (rather than sales)

- pension costs including any surpluses or deficiencies (dealt with according to IAS 19 **Employee benefits**)

- **amortisation of intangibles**
- **impairment losses (including goodwill)**
- **directors' emoluments (including share-based payment).**

Trend analysis

Comparative figures for one or more years provide information about the way in which the performance and financial position of a business has changed over a period. Published accounts give comparative information in two main areas:

- the corresponding amounts for items shown in the statements of financial position, comprehensive income, cash flows and changes in equity and notes. Such amounts are required by IAS 1 **Presentation of financial statements** for virtually all items disclosed in the accounts

- historical summaries of information covering several years.

It may be possible to predict future performance from trend information, particularly if the figures are very stable.

- The extent to which amounts and ratios are stable or volatile can reveal a great deal. Figures that are very volatile, or sudden changes in trends, may indicate that the company will experience problems in the future, even if performance is apparently improving.

- Trend information should be interpreted with caution because it does not take account of the effect of inflation.

Expandable text - Impact of accounting policies and choices

Introduction

Accounting policies can significantly affect the view presented by financial statements, and the ratios computed by reference to them, without affecting a business's core ability to generate profits and cash.

The potential impact of accounting policies is especially important where:

- accounting standards permit a choice (e.g. cost v fair value)

- judgement is needed in making accounting estimates (e.g. inventory valuation, depreciation, doubtful receivables, provisions)

- there is no accounting standard (e.g. some forms of revenue recognition).

Asset valuation

A key area is the measurement of non-current assets. Measuring assets at fair value rather than historic cost has the following effects (assuming fair value is increasing each year):

- earnings reduce (profits decrease due to the additional depreciation)

- return on capital employed reduces (capital employed increases while profits decrease)

- gearing reduces (capital employed /equity increases, while debt remains the same)

- another effect of fair value accounting is that profits and trends in ratios may become more volatile and therefore harder to interpret.

Expandable text - Illustration: impact of accounting policies

Three entities are identical in all respects, except for the way they finance the major productive capacity they need. The following information has been extracted from the financial statements of the three entities for the year ended 30 September 20X4:

	A	B	C
Income statement	$000	$000	$000
Revenue	200	200	200
Operating costs	(160)	(190)	(170)
Profit from operations	40	10	30
Statement of financial position			
Share capital	50	50	50
Retained earnings	90	60	50
Revaluation reserve	–	210	–
Capital employed	140	320	100
Operating profit margin	20%	5%	15%
Asset utilisation	1.43	0.63	2
Return on capital employed	28.6%	3.1%	30%

Entity A

A obtained the capacity needed by purchasing a non-current asset costing $200,000 four years ago. The asset is being depreciated on the straight-line basis over 10 years. Therefore, $20,000 of depreciation has been charged to this year's profit and the asset has a carrying value of $120,000 in the statement of financial position.

Entity B

B also purchased a non-current asset four years ago for the same price but revalued it to its fair value of $350,000 at the start of the current year. As a result, a revaluation gain of $210,000 has been recognised within other comprehensive income. With seven years, life remaining, the depreciation charge has been increased to $50,000 per annum.

The revaluation has caused the operating profit margin to fall due to the extra depreciation. Asset utilisation has also fallen due to the revaluation reserve being included in capital employed.

Hence the entity appears to be generating a lower return.

Entity C

C has obtained the capacity needed under an operating lease agreement, paying an annual rental of $30,000, which has been charged to operating expenses.

This causes its operating profit margin to be lower than A's, because the lease payments are higher than A's depreciation charges. However, the asset utilisation is higher than A's since the non-current asset is not recognised in the statement of financial position.

Expandable text - Recognition of assets and liabilities

Another key area is the recognition (or non-recognition) of assets and liabilities. IAS 1, IAS 8 and the IASB's Framework set out the general principle that an entity should report the substance of a transaction rather than its strict legal form.

- There is no accounting standard that specifically deals either with specific types of transaction (e.g. sale and repurchase agreements, debt factoring) or with substance in general.

- It is still possible for a company to account for complex transactions so that significant assets and liabilities are not recognised on in the statement of financial position.

- Non-recognition of assets normally improves ROCE while non-recognition of liabilities normally improves gearing. For example, leasing obligations increase debt and therefore increase gearing.

- Management may seek to keep liabilities off the balance sheet in order to manipulate the gearing ratio.

Expandable text - Illustration: impact of accounting policies

The following ratios have been calculated for Laxton, based on its financial statements for the year ended 31 December 20X4:

Return on capital employed	$45m/$160m	= 28%
Gearing	$80m/$160m	= 50%

During the year, Laxton sold a property with a carrying value of $40 million to a bank for $50 million. Laxton has treated this transaction as a sale, even though it continues to occupy the property and has agreed to repurchase it for $55 million on 31 December 20X9.

The substance of the transaction is that it is not a sale, but a secured loan. The difference between the sale proceeds and the amount at which the property will eventually be repurchased represents interest.

If the agreement is treated correctly, the effect is:

- profit before interest and tax is reduced by $10m (the profit on disposal)

- capital employed increases by $40m (the property continues to be recognised at its carrying value)

- debt increases by $50m (the amount received from the bank).

(Depreciation is ignored).

The ratios now become:

Return on capital employed	$35m/$200m = 17.5%
Gearing	$130m/$200m = 65%

Expandable text - Illustration: choice of accounting treatment

Below is an example of a situation in which a standard allows a choice of accounting treatment.

Joint ventures

IAS 31 **Interests in joint ventures** allows either proportional consolidation or equity accounting for jointly controlled entities.

Briefly explain how choices may affect the financial statements and the main performance measures: earnings per share, ROCE and gearing.

Expandable text - Solution

Earnings per share is not affected by the choice of accounting treatment. The venturer's share of profit recognised in the income statement is the same whichever method is used.

If the equity method is used, the interest in the joint venture appears as one line under non-current assets. Both ROCE and gearing will probably be lower than under proportionate consolidation, because this recognises the venturer's share of individual assets and liabilities.

One of the limitations of the equity method is that it allows the venturer's share of any significant liabilities to be 'hidden', so that the venturer's financial position can appear better than it actually is.

Expandable text - Intangible assets and intellectual property

A traditional manufacturing business generates profits mainly from the use of property, plant and equipment. Its financial statements can be interpreted fairly easily because there is a clear relationship between the plant and equipment and working capital in the statement of financial position and the profit or loss in the income statement.

Business practice has changed very significantly over the last 20 years. Many businesses now depend on assets such as copyrights, patents, customer databases and the technical or interpersonal skills of their staff.

KAPLAN PUBLISHING

These assets are not normally recognised in the statement of financial position, and there are important implications for analysis of the financial statements. Key ratios, such as ROCE and gearing may be virtually meaningless. Interpretations of performance have to be based on profit margins and sales growth. It can be much harder to predict future performance because this is more likely to be significantly affected by unpredictable events than in a business such as manufacturing or retailing. For example, in some situations it could be disastrous if several key members of staff left the company.

Expandable text - Creative accounting

Creative accounting is a form of accounting which, while complying with all regulations, nevertheless gives a biased impression (usually favourable) of the company's performance.

Management may have strong incentives to present the financial statements in the best possible light. For example:

- the directors want to sell the company in the near future

- the company is going through a difficult period (e.g. falling profits, lack of shareholder confidence, a possible takeover)

- directors' remuneration is strongly linked to performance (e.g. bonuses if earnings per share exceeds a certain amount or share based payment that depends on the entity's share price)

- the company is in danger of breaching loan covenants (for example, if the current/quick ratio or the gearing ratio falls below or above a certain figure).

There are a number of ways in which creative accounting can take place.

- **Off balance sheet finance**: transactions are deliberately constructed to allow the non-recognition of assets and (particularly) liabilities for loans. Examples include sale and repurchase agreements and the use of special-purpose entities (quasi-subsidiaries).

- **Aggressive earnings management**: recognising revenue before it has been earned.

- **Unusual assets**: an attempt to recognise an asset which, strictly speaking, is not an asset but an expense. Examples include marketing or advertising costs and recruitment costs (particularly where these have been incurred to recruit staff with essential skills or technical knowledge).

- **Unjustified changes to accounting policies or accounting estimates**: for example, extending the useful lives of assets with the object of reducing the depreciation expense and increasing earnings.
- **Profit smoothing:** manipulating the profit figure by setting up assets or liabilities in the statement of financial position and releasing these amounts to profit over time.

Expandable text - Question

Egremont, a mining company, has been fined for environmental pollution of the area in which it operates. The fine has been treated as an intangible asset and is being amortised over 15 years, the estimated remaining useful life of the quarry in which the pollution incident took place. The directors argue that this treatment is logical because operating the quarry brings them economic benefits in the form of revenues.

Required:

Comment on this accounting treatment.

Expandable text - Solution

An intangible asset is a resource controlled by the company as a result of past events and from which future economic benefits are expected to flow (IAS 38 **Intangible assets**).

The directors seem to be trying to argue that the fine is an unavoidable cost of operating the quarry and that economic benefits result from it. But the fine is avoidable and therefore it is an expense and not an asset.

The fine should be recognised in the profit or loss in the current year and possibly disclosed as a material item under IAS 1 **Presentation of financial statements**.

Expandable text - Limitations of financial information and its

Limitations of financial information

During the last few years, users of traditional financial statements have become increasingly aware of their limitations.

- Preparing financial statements involves a substantial degree of classification and aggregation. There is always a risk that essential information will either not be given sufficient prominence or will be lost completely.

- Financial statements focus on the financial effects of transactions and other events and do not focus to any significant extent on their non-financial effects or on non-financial information in general.

- They provide information that is largely historical. They do not reflect future events or transactions, nor do they anticipate the impact of potential changes to an entity. This means that it is not always possible to use them to predict future performance.

- There is often a time interval of several months between the year-end and the publication of the financial statements. Most financial information is out of date by the time it is actually published.

Limitations of financial analysis

Ratio analysis and other types of analysis such as trend analysis are a useful means of identifying significant relationships between different figures, but they have many limitations, including the following.

- Profit and capital employed are arbitrary figures. They depend on the accounting policies adopted by an entity.

- Many businesses produce accounts to a date on which there are relatively low amounts of trading activity. As a result the items on a statement of financial position are not typical of the items throughout the accounting period.

- Ratios based on historical cost accounts do not give a true picture of trends from year to year. An apparent increase in profit may not be a 'true' increase, because of the effects of inflation.

- Comparing the financial statements of similar businesses can be misleading for a number of reasons, including the effect of size differences and of operating in different markets.

- There are particular problems in comparing the financial statements of similar businesses that operate in different countries. There can be significant differences in accounting policies, terminology and presentation.

Expandable text - Impact of the environment

The type of business

It can often be helpful to consider whether the income statements/statements of comprehensive income and statements of financial position appear as they should for a particular type of business.

For example:

- Manufacturing industries are capital intensive, therefore they have relatively low asset turnover.

- Service industries depend mainly on people rather than capital assets, therefore asset turnover should be relatively high.

- A builder should have high inventories and work in progress, therefore inventory turnover is usually relatively low.

- A supermarket has perishable inventories, therefore inventory turnover should normally be high.

Expandable text - Question

Given below is information from the statements of financial position of five companies expressed as percentages of total assets less current liabilities.

The respective areas of activity of the companies are:

(a) Manufacturing

(b) Insurance brokers

(c) Housebuilding

(d) Retail stores

(e) Investment in properties for rental

The assets and liabilities shown as a percentage of total assets

	1	2	3	4	5
	%	%	%	%	%
Land and property	16	32	83	96	72
Other non-current assets	7	42	14	1	23
Inventory and work in progress	148	47	13	–	–
Trade receivables	31	41	4	1	436
Cash/short-term investments	1	11	6	4	91
	203	173	120	102	622
Trade payables	(36)	(60)	(11)	(2)	(509)
Bank overdraft	(67)	(13)	(9)	–	(13)
Total assets less current liabilities	100	100	100	100	100

Required:

State which statement of financial position belongs to each of the companies. giving your reasons for your opinion.

Expandable text - Solution

Company A (Manufacturing) - Statement of financial position No 2

Higher than average investment in other non-current assets (plant and equipment) together with relatively high inventories and work in progress and trade payables.

Company B (Insurance) - Statement of financial position No 5

No inventories and work in progress and comparatively small investment in other non-current assets, but very high proportions of receivables and payables.

Company C (Housebuilding) - Statement of financial position No 1

High investment in inventories and work in progress and relatively high payables.

Company D (Retail stores) - Statement of financial position No 3

High investment in land and property (shops). Low trade receivables. High cash.

Company E (Properties) - Statement of financial position No 4

High investment in land and property. Low other non-current assets and receivables. No inventories.

Expandable text - Groups and individual companies

Being part of a group can have quite a significant effect on the financial statements of an individual company. Intra-group transactions often take place on terms that are different (so more favourable to one of the entities, less favourable to the other) than between two independent companies trading at arms' length:

- Profit margins in the seller may be unusually high.

- The rate of Interest payable on intra-group loans may be unusually low.

- A group company may exist (for example) only to supply essential goods or services to another, so that it has a guaranteed market for its output.

- Services (e.g. administration) may be supplied free of charge.

Events taking place during the period

A significant event during the year often distorts the financial statements and accounting ratios for that year, particularly if it takes place near the year-end. This can make it harder for a user to predict future performance.

Expandable text - Illustration - events in the period

An entity increases its long-term borrowings from $40 million to $100 million just before the year end. Operating profit for the year is $25 million, interest for the year is $5 million and profit after tax for the year is $15 million. The average rate of interest on long-term borrowings is 10%.

Interest cover can be calculated as five times. However, the accounts do not include a full year's interest charge on the new borrowings.

Assuming that operating profit, tax charge and total long-term borrowings remain at the same level, interest cover for the next year will fall to approximately 2.5 times (25 ÷ (100 × 10%)) and profit after tax will fall to approximately $10 million (25 – ((100 × 10%) – 5 charged in current year)).

Significant events may include:

- acquisition or disposal of a subsidiary during the year

- management actions (e.g. price discounting to increase market share) or changes in the nature of the business (e.g. diversification or divestment)

- raising finance just before the year end

- significant asset sales or purchases just before the year end.

It can be useful to ask the following questions:

- What effect do these events have on performance (including cash flow) and key ratios for the current year?

- What effect might they be expected to have on performance and key ratios in the next period and in the longer term?

- What is the apparent or possible reason for the event? Has it taken place for a legitimate business reason, or is it a deliberate attempt to improve the appearance of the financial statements in the short term?

Expandable text - Other business factors

These may include the nature of the business, for example, whether it is highly seasonal or vulnerable to changes in fashion or the market. Other factors to consider are the quality of management and the state of the economy and market conditions.

- Better managed businesses are likely to be more profitable and have better working capital management than businesses where management is weak.

- If the market or the economy in general is depressed, this is likely to affect companies adversely and make most or all of their ratios appear worse. The impact may differ between market sectors.

Expandable text - Preparing a report

Preparing a report

An exam question may ask for a report.

REPORT

To

- The report should be focused on the reader(s) and their information needs.

From

Date

Subject

Introduction

- **Brief** introductory paragraph setting out the purpose of the report/terms of reference.

Discussion

This should:

- be structured with headings (usually the specific issues highlighted in the scenario)
- refer to calculations (including ratios) in an appendix (unless the question requires otherwise)
- (if required) interpret the information and any performance measures calculated (for example, possible reasons for a feature or a change)
- make connections between different areas, if the question asks for interpretation/analysis
- state what other information might be needed/would be useful (if appropriate or required by the question).

Conclusion

- Summarise findings and make a recommendation (if required).

Expandable text - Illustration: analysis of financial statements

The consolidated financial statements of TW for the year ended 30 April 20X4 are due to be published in June 20X4. The first draft of the 20X4 financial statements has just been prepared. Extracts from these statements are set out below:

Statement of comprehensive income – year ended 30 April:

	20X4 (draft)	20X3 (final)
	$ million	$ million
Revenue	3,600	3,400
Cost of sales	(2,300)	(2,250)
Gross profit	1,300	1,150
Other operating expenses	(700)	(600)
Profit from operations	600	550
Profit on sale of subsidiaries	350	Nil
Finance cost	(250)	(120)
Profit before tax	700	430
Income tax expense	(200)	(140)
Profit after tax	500	290
Other comprehensive income		
Gain on property revaluation	800	–
Total comprehensive income	1,300	290
Profit attributable to:		
Owners of the parent	440	235
Non-controlling interest	60	55
	500	290

	20X4 (draft) $ million	20X3 (final) $ million
Total comprehensive income attributable to		
Owners of the parent	1,200	235
Non-controlling interest	100	55
	1,300	290
Earnings per equity share	176 cents	94 cents

Statement of financial position at 30 April:

	20X4 (draft) $ million	$ million	20X3 (final) $ million	$ million
ASSETS				
Non-current assets:				
Property, plant and equipment	2,400		1,350	
Financial assets	180		250	
		2,580		1,600
Current assets:				
Inventories	430		400	
Trade receivables	600		550	
Deferred marketing costs	100		Nil	
Cash and cash equivalents	940		Nil	
		2,070		950
		4,650		2,550
EQUITY AND LIABILITIES				
Equity:				
Share capital ($1 equity shares)	250		250	
Share premium	150		150	
Revaluation reserve	800		Nil	
Retained earnings	1,050		610	
		2,250		1,010
Non-current liabilities:				
Long-term borrowings	2,000		1,000	
Deferred tax	180		100	
		2,180		1,100

Current liabilities:

Trade payables	220		200
Short-term borrowings	Nil		240
		220	440
		4,650	2,550

Notes to the draft financial statements

(i) During the financial year, the group decided to change the nature and focus of its operations. Consequently, on 31 March 20X4, the group disposed of two subsidiaries for total cash proceeds of $1,000 million. In the year to 30 April 20X4, the two subsidiaries that were disposed of contributed $800 million to group revenue, $320 million to group gross profit and $175 million to group profit from operations.

(ii) During the last few months of the year ended 30 April 20X4 the group embarked on an extensive marketing campaign to underpin the new operational focus. Marketing costs are normally charged to cost of sales but, in the draft financial statements, the directors of TW have included them in the statement of financial position on the basis that the new operational focus is likely to generate future economic benefits for the group.

(iii) The revaluation reserve is caused by a group-wide revaluation of property, plant and equipment on 31 March 20X4, immediately after the disposal of the two subsidiaries. Depreciation was charged on the revalued amounts from 1 April 20X4. The average remaining useful lives of the revalued assets at 1 April 20X4 was eight years.

Ms A is a newly-appointed non-executive director of TW. She wishes to seek your advice prior to the board meeting and her request is set out below.

'The papers contain an assertion from the Chief Executive that the financial statements show a very pleasing financial performance and position. The Chief Executive highlights the increase in revenue, profits, earnings per share and cash balances as evidence to support this assertion. I would like you to evaluate this assertion and to highlight any relevant issues.'

Prepare a reply to the question Ms A has raised.

Solution

Financial performance and position of TW

It is true that the draft financial statements show that revenue, profits, earnings per share and cash balances have all increased. However, the notes to the financial statements reveal a number of issues that should be taken into account when interpreting the figures. The potential effect of these issues on the gross profit margin and the operating profit margin are illustrated in the Appendix.

Disposal of subsidiaries

The group has disposed of two subsidiaries during the year, but their results have not been separately presented within the statement of comprehensive income. In fact the two subsidiaries contributed 22% of total revenue (800 as a percentage of 3,600); 25% of total gross profit (320 as a percentage of 1,300); and nearly 30% of total profit from operations (175 as a percentage of 600). In other words, the discontinued operations appear to be more profitable than the rest of the group. This suggests that the group may be less profitable in future years.

Profit before tax has increased by nearly two-thirds in the year, but this includes the exceptional profit on disposal of $350 million. This profit will not recur and without it profit before tax would have fallen, due to the fact that finance costs have doubled as the group has also doubled its long-term borrowings.

The group has experienced a total cash net inflow of $1,180 million (940 + 240) for the year. However, most of this increase results from the sale proceeds of $1,000 million. The group's cash flow position does not appear to be as healthy as the Chairman suggests.

Marketing costs

The treatment of the marketing costs of $100 million is not justified. An asset can only be recognised if it is probable that the group will obtain future economic benefits from the expenditure as a result of past events or transactions and if these benefits can be measured reliably. It is impossible to measure the economic benefits attributable to specific marketing costs (rather than to other factors, such as the reputation built up over many years), so IAS 38 **Intangible assets** prohibits the capitalisation of marketing costs. Profits are overstated by $100 million.

Revaluation

When non-current assets are revalued, the depreciation charge must be calculated on the revalued amount. This means that depreciation charges increase and profits are reduced. Because the revaluation took place on 1 April 20X4, the financial statements show the increase in property, plant and equipment, but only reflect one month's additional depreciation. However, the full depreciation charge will be reflected in the statement of comprehensive income for the year to 30 April 20X5. The effect of this can be estimated from the increase in the revaluation reserve: there will be a reduction in profit of approximately $92 million (800 ÷ 8 × 11/12).

Conclusion

The potential impact of all these issues is significant, particularly in relation to reported profit. On the face of it, the group's results for the current year may be good, but this trend is unlikely to continue into the future. The financial statements should be interpreted with caution.

Appendix

	Gross profit margin	Operating profit margin
20X4 as reported	1,300/3,600 =36.1%	600/3,600 =16.7%
20X4 adjusted:		
Removal of discontinued operations	980/2,800 =35%	425/2,80 =15.2%
As above less marketing costs now charged to income	880/2,800 =31.4%	325/2,800 =11.6%
As above less additional depreciation now charged to cost of sales	788/2,800 =28.1%	233/2,800 = 8.3%

Chapter summary

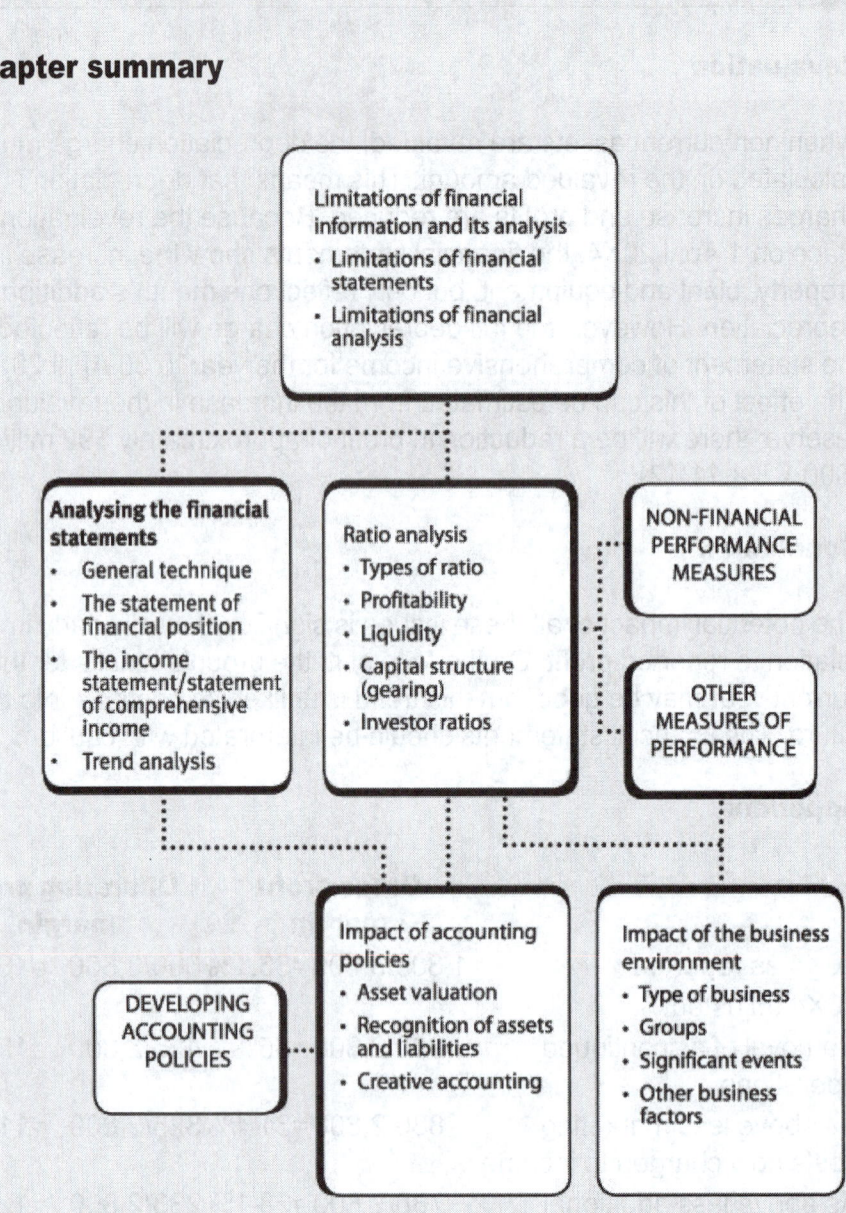

Questions & Answers

1 Pre-tuition and fixed tests

Pre-tuition Tests

Pre-tuition Test 1 - Hanford and Stopple

Pre-tuition Test 2 - Hepburn and Salter

These questions are **PRE-TUITION TESTS**. Please answer each Pre-tuition Test question in full, without reference to an answer.

Then log-in to en-gage and answer each Pre-tuition Test based on your full long-form answer.

......or alternatively register using the information at the back of your Complete Text and then go to www.en-gage.co.uk

Fixed Tests

Fixed Test 1 - Bacup

Fixed Test 2 - Hop,Skip and Jump

Fixed Test 3 - Holmes

Fixed Test 4 - Viper

Fixed Test 5 - Rowsley

These questions are **FIXED TESTS**. Please answer each Fixed Test question in full, without reference to an answer.

Then log-in to en-gage and answer each Fixed Test based on your full long-form answer

......or alternatively register using the information at the back of your Complete Text and then go to www.en-gage.co.uk

Hanford and Stopple – PRE-TUITION TEST 1

Question 1

Hanford acquired six million of Stopple's ordinary shares on 1 April 2001 for an agreed consideration of $24.85 million.

The consideration was settled by a share exchange of five new shares in Hanford for every three shares acquired in Stopple, and a cash payment of $4.85 million. The cash transaction has been recorded, but the share exchange has not.

KAPLAN PUBLISHING

The draft statements of financial position of the two companies at 30 September 2001 are:

	Hanford		Stopple	
	$000	$000	$000	$000
Assets				
Non-current assets				
Property, plant and equipment		78,690		27,180
Investment in Stopple		4,850		nil
		83,540		27,180
Current assets				
Inventory	7,450		4,310	
Accounts receivable	12,960		4,330	
Cash and bank	nil	20,410	520	9,160
Total assets		103,950		36,340
Equity and liabilities				
Equity				
Equity shares of $1 each		20,000		8,000
Reserves				
Share premium	10,000		2,000	
Retained earnings:				
At 1 October 2000	51,260		6,000	
For the year to 30 September 2001	12,000	73,260	8,000	16,000
		93,260		24,000
Non-current liabilities				
8% Loan notes 2004		nil		6,000
Current liabilities				
Accounts payable and accruals	5,920		4,160	
Bank overdraft	1,700		nil	
Provision for taxation	3,070		2,180	
		10,690		6,340
Total equity and liabilities		103,950		36,340

The following information is relevant:

(i)   The fair value of Stopple's land at the date of acquisition was $4 million in excess of its carrying value. The fair value of Stopple's other net assets approximated to their carrying values.

(ii) At the date of acquisition Hanford sold an item of plant that had cost $2 million to Stopple for $2.4 million. Stopple has charged depreciation of $240,000 on this plant since it was acquired.

(iii) Hanford's current account debit balance of $820,000 with Stopple does not agree with the corresponding balance in Stopple's books. Investigations revealed that on 26 September 2001 Hanford billed Stopple $200,000 for its share of central administration costs. Stopple has not yet recorded this invoice. Intercompany current accounts are included in accounts receivable or payable as appropriate.

(iv) It is group policy to value goodwill on a full "fair value" basis. At the date of acquisition, the fair value of the non-controlling interest was $7.0 million.

Required:

Prepare the consolidated statement of financial position of Hanford at 30 September 2001.

(Total: 20 marks)

Hepburn and Salter – PRE-TUITION TEST 2

Question 2

On 1 October 19X9 Hepburn acquired 80% of the equity share capital of Salter by way of a share exchange. Hepburn issued five of its own shares for every two shares it acquired in Salter. The market value of Hepburn's shares on 1 October 19X9 was $3 each. The share issue has not yet been recorded in Hepburn's books. The summarised financial statements of both companies are:

Income statements: Year to 31 March 20X0

	Hepburn	Salter
	$000	$000
Sales revenues	1,200	1,000
Cost of sales	(650)	(660)
Gross profit	550	340
Operating expenses	(120)	(88)
Debenture interest	nil	(12)
Profit before tax	430	240
Income tax expense	(100)	(40)
Profit for the year	330	200

Statements of financial position: as at 31 March 20X0

	Hepburn		Salter	
	$000	$000	$000	$000
Non-current assets				
Property, plant and equipment		620		660
Investments		20		10
		640		670
Current assets				
Inventory	240		280	
Accounts receivable	170		210	
Bank	20	430	40	530
Total assets		1,070		1,200
Equity and liabilities				
Equity shares of $1 each		400		150
Retained earnings		410		700
		810		850

Non-current liabilities		
8% Debentures	nil	150
Current liabilities		
Trade accounts payable	210	155
Taxation	50	45
	260	200
Total equity and liabilities	1,070	1,200

The following information is relevant:

(i)   The fair values of Salter's assets were equal to their book values with the exception of its land, which had a fair value of $125,000 in excess of its book value at the date of acquisition.

(ii) In the post acquisition period Hepburn sold goods to Salter at a price of $100,000, this was calculated to give a mark-up on cost of 25% to Hepburn. Salter had half of these goods in inventory at the year end.

(iii) The current accounts of the two companies disagreed due to a cash remittance of $20,000 to Hepburn on 26 March 20X0 not being received until after the year end. Before adjusting for this, Salter's debit balance in Hepburn's books was $56,000. Salter's current account balance with Hepburn has a credit balance of $36,000,

(iv) It is group policy to value the non-controlling interest using the full method. The fair value of the non-controlling interest in Salter on 1 October 19X9 was $230,000.

Required:

Prepare a consolidated income statement and statement of financial position for Hepburn for the year to 31 March 20X0.

(20 marks)

Bacup, Townley and Rishworth - FIXED TEST 1

Question 4

The summarised statements of financial position of Bacup, Townley and Rishworth as at 31 March 2007 are as follows:

	Bacup	Townley	Rishworth
	$000	$000	$000
Non-current assets:			
Tangible assets	3,820	4,425	500
Intangible asset - workforce	–	200	–
Investments	1,600	–	–
	5,420	4,625	500
Current assets:			
Inventory	2,740	1,280	250
Receivables	1,960	980	164
Cash at bank	1,260	–	86
	5,960	2,260	500
Total assets	11,380	6,885	1,000
Equity:			
Equity shares of 25 cents each	4,000	500	200
Reserves:			
Share premium	800	125	
Retained earnings at 31 March 20X6	2,300	380	450
Retained for year	1,760	400	150
	8,860	1,405	800

Current liabilities:			
Trade payables	2,120	3,070	142
Bank overdraft	–	2,260	–
Taxation	400	150	58
	2,520	5,480	200
Total equity and liabilities	11,380	6,885	1,000

The following information is relevant:

(i) **Investments**

Bacup acquired 1.6 million shares in Townley on 1 April 2006 paying 75 cents per share. On 1 October 2006 Bacup acquired 40% of the share capital of Rishworth for $400,000.

(ii) **Group accounting policies**

Human capital

The directors of Townley have always believed that their workforce is a significant asset which should be recognised in the financial statements. Consequently, they valued their workforce at $80,000 at the date of acquisition by Bacup and that this had increased to $200,000 at the reporting date. The increase in value was due to the relative scarcity of a particular type of skilled employee.

(iii) **Intra-group trading**

The inventory of Bacup includes goods at a transfer price of $200,000 purchased from Townley after the acquisition. The inventory of Rishworth includes goods at a transfer price of $125,000 purchased from Bacup. All transfers were at cost plus 25%.

The receivables of Bacup include an amount owing from Townley of $250,000. This does not agree with the corresponding amount in the books of Townley due to a cash payment of $50,000 made on 29 March 2007, which had not been received by Bacup at the year end.

(iv) **Share premium**

The share premium account of Townley arose prior to the acquisition by Bacup.

(v) It is group policy to value the non-controlling interest at fair value. At the date of acquisition, the fair value of the non-controlling interest in Townley was $200,000. Goodwill has been subject to an impairment review and is not impaired.

Required:

(a) A consolidated statement of financial position of the Bacup group as at 31 March 2007.

(18 marks)

(b) Norden Manufacturing has been approached by Mr Long, a representative of Townley. Mr Long is negotiating for Norden to supply Townley with goods on six-month credit. Mr Long has pointed out that Townley is part of the Bacup group and provides the consolidated statement of financial position to support the credit request.

Required:

Briefly discuss the usefulness of the group statement of financial position for assessing the creditworthiness of Townley and describe the further investigations you would advise Norden Manufacturing to make.

(7 marks)

(Total: 25 marks)

Hop, Skip and Jump - FIXED TEST 2

Question 1

The statements of comprehensive income of Hop, Skip and Jump for the year ended 30 September 2007 are given below:

	Hop	Skip	Jump
	$m	$m	$m
Revenue (Note 1)	500	400	300
Cost of sales	(200)	(150)	(120)
Gross profit	300	250	180
Other operating expenses	(150)	(130)	(90)
Profit from operations	150	120	90
Investment income (Notes 2 and 3)	24	–	–
Finance costs	(60)	(40)	(30)
Profit before tax	114	80	60
Income tax expense	(40)	(28)	(15)
Profit for the period	74	52	45
Retained earnings – 1 October 2006	250	160	165
Profit for the period	74	52	45
Dividends paid 30 September 2007	(50)	(32)	(25)
Retained earnings – 30 September 2007	274	180	185

Notes:

(1) Hop supplies a product used by Skip (but not by Jump). During the year ended 30 September 2007, sales of the product by Hop to Skip (all at cost to Hop plus a mark up of 25%) totalled $48 million. At 30 September 2007, the inventories of Skip included $18 million ($9 million as at 30 September 2006) in respect of goods supplied by Hop.

(2) Investments made by Hop in Skip and Jump were as follows:

(i) On 1 October 1997, Hop purchased 75% of the equity shares of Skip for $100 million. The statement of financial position of Skip at that date showed the following:

	$m
Equity share capital ($1 shares)	60
Retained earnings	60
	120

The fair values of the net assets of Skip on 1 October 1997 were the same as their book values.

(ii) On 1 October 1998, Hop purchased 80% of the equity shares of Jump for $120 million. The statement of financial position of Jump at that date showed the following:

	$m
Equity share capital ($1 shares)	50
Retained earnings	75
	125

The fair values of the net assets of Jump on 1 October 1998 were the same as their book values.

The policy of Hop is to value goodwill using the proportion of net assets method.

(3) On 31 May 2007, Hop disposed of the whole of its investment in Jump for $245 million. The taxation payable by Hop in connection with this disposal was estimated at $20 million. The effects of this disposal have NOT been incorporated into the income statement of Hop which appears above. The business of Jump is very similar to the business of Hop and the directors of Hop are reasonably confident that the revenue of Hop will increase following the disposal to the extent that the revenue of the Group as a whole will not be materially affected.

Required:
Prepare the consolidated statement of comprehensive income for the Hop Group for the year ended 30 September 2007 and include a statement of reserves.

(25 marks)

Holmes - FIXED TEST 3

Question 1

The following extracts have been taken from the consolidated financial statements of the Holmes group:

Consolidated income statement for the year ended

	30 September 2009	30 September 2008
	$m	$m
Revenue	600	500
Cost of sales	(305)	(240)
Gross profit	295	260
Other operating expenses (Note 1)	(140)	(130)
Profit from operations	155	130
Finance costs	(50)	(45)
Exceptional item (Note 2)	10	
Share of profit of associates	17	17
Profit before tax	132	102
Income tax expense	(35)	(25)
Profit for the period	97	77
Attributable to:		
Equity holders of the parent	87	71
Non-controlling interests	10	6
	97	77

There were no items of other comprehensive income in either year.

Consolidated statement of financial position at:

	30 September 2009		30 September 2008	
	$m	$m	$m	$m
Non-current assets:				
Tangible assets (Note 3)	240		280	
Intangible assets (Note 4)	33		19	
Investments in associates	80		70	
		353		369
Current assets:				
Inventories	105		90	
Receivables	120		100	
Investments	20		70	
Cash in hand	10		5	
		255		265
		608		634
Equity attributable to equity holders of the parent				
Equity share capital		100		100
Revaluation reserve		–		20
Retained earnings		229		147
		329		267
Non-controlling interests		74		45
		403		312

Non-current liabilities:

Obligations under finance leases	80		70	
12% loan notes	–		90	
Deferred taxation	30		24	
		110		184

Current liabilities:

Trade payables (Note 5)	40		30	
Taxation	10		8	
Obligations under finance leases	25		20	
Bank overdraft	20		80	
		95		138
		608		634

Notes to the financial statements

(1) Other operating expenses

	2009	2008
	$m	$m
Distribution costs	81	75
Administrative expenses	65	70
Investment income	(6)	(15)
	140	130

From time to time, the group invests short-term cash surpluses in highly liquid investments which are shown as current asset investments in the consolidated statement of financial position.

(2) Exceptional item

This represents the gain on sale of a large freehold property sold by Holmes on 1 October 2008 and leased back on an operating lease in line with the practice adopted by the rest of the group. The property was not depreciated in the current year. The property had been revalued in 2000 and the revaluation surplus credited to a revaluation reserve. No other entries had been made in the revaluation reserve prior to the sale of the property.

(3) Tangible non-current assets

	30 September 2009	30 September 2008
	$m	$m
Freehold land and buildings	–	90
Plant and machinery – owned	130	100
Plant and machinery – leased	90	70
Fixtures and fittings – owned	20	20
	240	280

During the year the group entered into new finance lease agreements in respect of some items of plant and machinery. The amounts debited to non-current assets in respect of such agreements during the year totalled $40 million. No disposals of plant and machinery (owned or leased) or fixtures and fittings took place during the year. Depreciation of tangible non-current assets for the year totalled $58 million.

(4) Intangible non-current assets

This comprises goodwill on acquisition of subsidiaries. During the year ended 30 September 2009, Holmes acquired 80% of the issued equity share capital of Watson for $100 million payable in cash. The net assets of Watson at the date of acquisition were assessed as having fair values as follows:

	$m
Plant and machinery – owned	50
Fixture and fittings – owned	10
Inventories	30
Receivables	25
Cash at bank and in hand	10
Trade payables	(15)
Taxation	(5)
	105

At that date, the fair value of the non-controlling interest in Watson was $24 million. It is group policy to value non-controlling interest on this acquisition at fair value. Apart from this acquisition of Watson, there were no other changes to the group structure in the year.

(5) Trade payables

Trade payables at 30 September 2009 and 30 September 2008 do not include any accrued interest.

Required:

Prepare the consolidated statement of cash flow of the Holmes group for the year ended 30 September 2009 in the form required by IAS 7 statements of cash flow. Show your workings clearly.

Do NOT prepare notes to the statement of cash flow.

(25 marks)

Viper - FIXED TEST 4

Question 1

The directors of Viper, a public limited company, are reviewing the impact of IFRS 2 **Share-based payment** on the financial statements for the year ended 31 May 20X5.

The following share option schemes were in existence at 31 May 20X5:

Dir's name	Grant date	Options granted	Fair value of options at grant date	Exer- cise price	Perf. conds.	Vest- ing date	Exer- cise date
			$	$			
J. Van Heflin	1 June 20X3	20,000	5	4.50	A	6/20X5	6/20X6
R. Ashworth	1 June 20X4	50,000	6	6	B	6/20X7	6/20X8

The price of the company's shares at 31 May 20X5 is $12 per share and at 31 May 20X4 was $12.50 per share.

The performance conditions which apply to the exercise of executive share options are as follows:

Performance Condition A

The share options do not vest if the growth in the company's earnings per share (EPS) for the year is less than 4%. The rate of growth of EPS was 4.5% (20X3), 4.1% (20X4), 4.2% (20X5). The directors must still work for the company on the vesting date.

Performance Condition B

The share options do not vest until the share price has increased from its value of $12.50 at the grant date (1 June 20X4) to above $13.50. The director must still work for the company on the vesting date.

No directors have left the company since the issue of the share options and none are expected to leave before June 20X7. The shares vest and can be exercised on the first day of the due month.

Required:

(a) Discuss the agency issues created by paying the directors with share options rather than by a more conventional salary scheme.

(10 marks)

(b) Explain (with suitable calculations) how the directors' share options should be accounted for in the financial statements for the year ended 31 May 20X5 including the adjustment to opening balances.

(10 marks)

(Total: 20 marks)

Rowsley - FIXED TEST 5

Question 1

Rowsley is a diverse group with many subsidiaries. The group is proud of its reputation as a 'caring' organisation and has adopted various ethical policies towards its employees and the wider community in which it operates. As part of its Annual Report, the group publishes details of its environmental policies, which include setting performance targets for activities such as recycling, controlling emissions of noxious substances and limiting use of non-renewable resources.

The finance director is reviewing the accounting treatment of various items prior to the signing of the accounts for the year ended 31 March 20X5. All four items are material in the context of the accounts as a whole. The accounts are to be approved by the directors on 30 June 20X5.

(1) On 15 February 20X5 the board of Rowsley decided to close down a large factory. The board is trying to draw up a plan to manage the effects of the reorganisation, and it is envisaged that production will be transferred to other factories, all of which are some distance away. The factory will be closed on 31 August 20X5, but at 31 March this decision had not yet been announced to the employees or to any other interested parties. Costs of the reorganisation have been estimated at $45 million.

(6 marks)

(2) During December 20X4 one of the subsidiary companies moved from Aytoun to Beetown in order to take advantage of regional development grants. It holds its main premises in Aytoun under an operating lease, which runs until 31 March 20X7. Annual rentals under the lease are $10 million. The company is unable to cancel the lease, but it has let some of the premises to a charitable organisation at a nominal rent. The company is attempting to rent the remainder of the premises at a commercial rent, but the directors have been advised that the chances of achieving this are less than 50%.

(6 marks)

(3) During the year to 31 March 20X5, a customer started legal proceedings against the group, claiming that one of the food products that it manufactures had caused several members of his family to become seriously ill. The group's lawyers have advised that this action will probably not succeed.

(3 marks)

(4) The group has an overseas subsidiary that is involved in mining precious metals. These activities cause significant damage to the environment, including deforestation. The company expects to abandon the mine in eight years time. The mine is situated in a country where there is no environmental legislation obliging companies to rectify environmental damage and it is very unlikely that any such legislation will be enacted within the next eight years. It has been estimated that the cost of cleaning the site and re-planting the trees will be $25 million if the re-planting were successful at the first attempt, but it will probably be necessary to make a further attempt, which will increase the cost by a further $5 million.

(5 marks)

Required:

Explain how each of the items (1) to (4) above should be treated in the consolidated accounts for the year ended 31 March 20X5.

(Total: 20 marks)

Expandable text - Answers

Pre-tuition tests

Pre-tuition test 1 - Hanford and Stopple

Pre-tuition test 2 - Hepburn and Salter

These questions are **PRE-TUITION TESTS**

They are set at F7 standard. Please answer each question in full, without reference to an answer.

Then log-in to en-gage and answer Pre-tuition test 1 and 2 respectively based on your full long form answers.

.....or alternatively register using the information at the back of your Complete Text and then go to www.en-gage.co.uk

When you have answered each of the questions, a full pdf version of the answers is available for printing - follow the link 'click here for full workings'.

Fixed Tests

Fixed Test 1 - Bacup

Fixed Test 2 - Hop,Skip and Jump

Fixed Test 3 - Holmes

Fixed Test 4 - Viper

Fixed Test 5 - Rowsley

These questions are **FIXED TESTS**. Please answer each Fixed Test question in full, without reference to an answer.

Then log-in to en-gage and answer each Fixed Test based on your full long-form answer

......or alternatively register using the information at the back of your Complete Text and then go to www.en-gage.co.uk

KAPLAN PUBLISHING

Index

Index

Index

Index

Index